Lecture Notes in Computer Science

Lecture Notes in Artificial Intelligence   14930

Founding Editor

Jörg Siekmann

AF173726

Series Editors

Randy Goebel, *University of Alberta, Edmonton, Canada*
Wolfgang Wahlster, *DFKI, Berlin, Germany*
Zhi-Hua Zhou, *Nanjing University, Nanjing, China*

The series Lecture Notes in Artificial Intelligence (LNAI) was established in 1988 as a topical subseries of LNCS devoted to artificial intelligence.

The series publishes state-of-the-art research results at a high level. As with the LNCS mother series, the mission of the series is to serve the international R & D community by providing an invaluable service, mainly focused on the publication of conference and workshop proceedings and postproceedings.

Nicholas S. Szczecinski ·
Victoria Webster-Wood · Matthew Tresch ·
William R. P. Nourse · Anna Mura ·
Roger D. Quinn
Editors

Biomimetic and Biohybrid Systems

13th International Conference, Living Machines 2024
Chicago, IL, USA, July 8–11, 2024
Proceedings

 Springer

Editors

Nicholas S. Szczecinski ⓘ
West Virginia University
Morgantown, WV, USA

Victoria Webster-Wood ⓘ
Carnegie Mellon University
Pittsburgh, USA

Matthew Tresch ⓘ
Northwestern University
Evanston, IL, USA

William R. P. Nourse ⓘ
Case Western Reserve University
Cleveland, OH, USA

Anna Mura ⓘ
Radboud University
Nijmegen, Gelderland, The Netherlands

Roger D. Quinn ⓘ
Case Western Reserve University
Cleveland, OH, USA

ISSN 0302-9743   ISSN 1611-3349 (electronic)
Lecture Notes in Artificial Intelligence
ISBN 978-3-031-72596-8   ISBN 978-3-031-72597-5 (eBook)
https://doi.org/10.1007/978-3-031-72597-5

LNCS Sublibrary: SL7 – Artificial Intelligence

Preface

This book constitutes the proceedings of the 13th International Conference on Biomimetic and Biohybrid Systems, Living Machines 2024, in Chicago, IL, USA, held July 8–11, 2024. The 27 full papers and 4 short papers presented were carefully reviewed and selected from 35 submissions. In addition, 21 late-breaking abstracts were submitted for poster presentations. These works present research on novel life-like technologies inspired by the scientific investigation of biological systems, biomimetics, and research that seeks to interface biological and artificial systems to create biohybrid systems. The conference aims to highlight the most exciting research in these fields, united by the theme of "Living Machines."

How do biological organisms achieve the adaptability, resilience, creativity, and robustness seen all around us in the natural world? And how can technology harness or advance our understanding of these capabilities? These questions strike at the heart of research in bioinspired, biomimetic, and biohybrid systems. Bioinspiration allows researchers to abstract principles from the natural world to create ever more capable robots, architectural elements, assistive devices, and much more. Biomimetics seeks to capture the dynamics, structures, and mechanics of living organisms to create physical models, thereby allowing us to better understand the associated organisms through controlled experimentation. Biohybrid systems combine both biological and synthetic elements to harness the capabilities of biological organisms directly and create more sustainable and adaptable robots, artificial organs, and medical devices. These thrusts exist along a research continuum requiring highly interdisciplinary and often collaborative research from experts in biology, neuroscience, engineering, robotics, materials science, computer science, philosophy, social sciences, machine learning, botany, and so many more.

The Living Machine conference brings together experts from across this multidisciplinary research space to foster interdisciplinary communication, seed future collaborations, and provide a forum for bringing new researchers into the field. Since the first instantiation of the Living Machines conference in 2011, this community has brought together researchers for the presentation and discussion of state-of-the-art advances in bioinspired, biomimetic, and biohybrid systems. The single-track format promotes truly interdisciplinary audiences and has historically seeded invigorating discussions. Furthermore, Living Machines has a history of providing a training environment for junior researchers where they are able to interact with and get feedback on their work from eminent senior researchers in the field. Through this forum, our community nurtures and recognizes the next generation of researchers in bioinspired, biohybrid, and biomimetic systems.

In these proceedings, you will find the accepted papers presented at Living Machines 2024 through podium and poster presentations. All long- and short-format articles underwent a rigorous single-blind review process, including required revisions in response to reviewer concerns. Additionally, Late-Breaking Abstracts were accepted for the first time to allow researchers from disciplines where conference papers are not standard to participate more readily. Abstracts were screened by the program chairs for relevance and format. A total of 35 paper submissions were received, with an acceptance rate of 88%. Furthermore, 21 Late-breaking Abstracts were received. Overall, 84 reviews were received, with an average of 2.4 reviews per paper. These reviews included detailed feedback to the authors, highlighting the rigor expected by our community. Authors were required to submit revised manuscripts, including a response to the reviewers and a marked manuscript to ensure all revised submissions adequately addressed reviewer concerns. For papers co-authored by one of the Program Chairs, all reviewer assignments, review processing, acceptance decisions, and rebuttal decisions were handled solely by the other Program Chair. The Springer review portal ensured that the chairing co-author could not see the reviewer names or scores and only received the reports for their papers as any other author would.

The conference included three workshops covering plant-inspired machines in soft robotics, communication, coordination, and control of neuromechanical systems, and preparing for human-biohybrid robot interactions. The main conference, held at the Field Museum in Chicago, IL, USA, consisted of three days of single-track plenaries, podium presentations, and poster sessions. Sixteen submissions were selected for podium presentations across eight sessions. The plenary speakers included John Rogers (Northwestern University), Mitra Hartmann (Northwestern University), Brian K. Taylor (Case Western Reserve University), C.J. Heckman (Northwestern University), and Ritu Raman (Massachusetts Institute of Technology). Session themes included Brain Network Modeling, Tools for Studying Behavior, Sensors, and others.

We wish to thank the many people who contributed to making Living Machines 2024 a reality. The ongoing mission and direction are guided by our wonderful Steering Committee. The continued quality and rigor of this conference owe substantial thanks to the reviewers who contributed their time and insights during the peer review process, and we would, of course, like to thank the authors and speakers for their submissions and participation in this year's program. Finally, we would like to thank our sponsors, volunteers, and partners who contributed their time, resources, and support to bring Living Machines 2024 to fruition.

July 2024

Nicholas S. Szczecinski
Victoria Webster-Wood
Matthew Tresch
Roger D. Quinn
William R. P. Nourse
Anna Mura

Organization

General Chair

Roger D. Quinn   Case Western Reserve University, USA

Program Chairs

Nicholas S. Szczecinski   West Virginia University, USA
Victoria A. Webster-Wood   Carnegie Mellon University, USA

Local Organization

Matthew Tresch   Northwestern University, USA

Communication Chair

William R. P. Nourse   Case Western Reserve University, USA

Workshop and Tutorial Chair

Kaushik Jayaram   University of Colorado – Boulder, USA

International Steering Committee

Minoru Asada   Osaka University, Japan
Joseph Ayers   Northeastern University, USA
Hillel Chiel   Case Western Reserve University, USA
Mark Cutkosky   Stanford University, USA
Marc Desmulliez   Heriot-Watt University, UK
José Halloy   Université Paris Cité, France
Koh Hosoda   Osaka University, Japan
Alexander Hunt   Portland State University, USA
Holger G. Krapp   Imperial College London, UK

Cecilia Laschi	National University of Singapore, Singapore
Nathan Lepora	University of Bristol, UK
Uriel Martinez-Hernandez	University of Bath, UK
Barbara Mazzolai	Istituto Italiano di Tecnologia, Italy
Fabian Meder	Istituto Italiano di Tecnologia, Italy
Anna Mura	Radboud University, The Netherlands
Tony Prescott	University of Sheffield, UK
Roger D. Quinn	Case Western Reserve University, USA
Masahiro Shimizu	Nagahama Institute of Bio-Science & Technology, Japan
Thomas Speck	Albert-Ludwigs-Universität Freiburg, Germany
Nicholas Szczecinski	West Virginia University, USA
Falk Tauber	Albert-Ludwigs-Universität Freiburg, Germany
Paul F. M. J. Verschure	Radboud University, The Netherlands
Vasiliki Vouloutsi	Technology Innovation Institute, United Arab Emirates
Victoria Webster-Wood	Carnegie Mellon University, USA

Reviewers

Emanuel Andrada
Henry Astley
Michael Bennington
Kevin Dai
Gesa Dinges
Volker Duerr
Jizhuang Fan
Camila Fernandez
Clarus Goldsmith
Lukas Groschner
Aung Htet
Jiaqi Huang
Alexander Hunt
Clayton B. Jackson
Sheldon Johnson
John Jutoy
Keiryo Kasai
Catherine Kehl
Isabella Kudyba
Yanjun Li
Ashlee Liao
Michael Mangan
Gary Marsat

Jeffrey McManus
Fabian Meder
Nathaniel Mengers
Jean-Michel Mongeau
Jasmine Nirody
William R. P. Nourse
Mingyu Pan
Aishwarya Pawar
Tony Prescott
Roger D. Quinn
Yauheni Sarokin
Ji Min Seok
Vivek Sharma
Masahiro Shimizu
Trevor Smith
German Orlando Romero Suarez
Anika Sun
Qin Sun
Gregory Sutton
Nicholas Szczecinski
Brian K. Taylor
Matt Tresch
Richard van Nieuwenhoven

Lorenzo Vannozzi
T. Thang Vo-Doan
Zhong Wang
Victoria Webster-Wood
Avery Williamson

Nicole Xu
Man Yang
Bohdan Zadokha
Xiaoting Zhong

Contents

Neural Networks for Computation

Bio-Inspired Neural Networks for Control

Biohybrid Systems

Biomechanics

Brain Network Modeling

BrainX3 3.0: Advancing Neuroinformatics and Artificial Brains for Living Machines

Man Yang[1](✉), Bas J. N. M. Drost[1], Dante Aviñó[1], Benedetta Felici[1],
Francisco Páscoa dos Santos[2,3], Raimon Bullich Vilarrubias[1], Vivek Sharma[1],
and Paul F. M. J. Verschure[1]

[1] Synthetic, Perceptive, Emotive and Cognitive Systems (SPECS) Lab, Donders
Institute for Brain, Cognition and Behaviour, Radboud University,
Nijmegen, The Netherlands
man.yang@donders.ru.nl
[2] Eodyne Systems S.L., Barcelona, Spain
[3] Department of Information and Communication Technologies, Universitat Pompeu
Fabra (UPF), Barcelona, Spain

Abstract. BrainX3 represents an integrated neuroinformatic platform
designed to facilitate the effective visualisation, analysis, semantic mapping, and simulation of whole brain dynamics. As the software evolves,
emphasis is placed on both studying biological and creating artificial
nervous systems; advancing to the needs of researchers. We present the
role of BrainX3 in facilitating a comprehensive understanding and exploration of brain data. Through a detailed exploration of its capabilities,
we demonstrate how BrainX3 serves as a tool for understanding the
brain's functioning. By bridging the gap between empirical data and
computational models, BrainX3 empowers users to delve deeper into the
complexities of the brain, ultimately advancing our understanding and
contributing to the development of living machines and artificial brains.
We also highlight recent advancements in the software, with a particular
emphasis on the modeling of artificial brains.

Keywords: BrainX3 · Neuroinformatics · Whole Brain Modeling ·
Signal Processing · Neurorobotics

1 Introduction

The operation of both biological and synthetic living machines is governed by
their respective neural networks. Hence, to understand the functions of these
systems we need to decipher how their brain transforms sensory and motivational states into action. This necessitates the development of specialised tools
to explore the intricate relationship between brain anatomy, physiology, and
behaviour, crucial for studying and engineering such systems [28]. Consequently,
a convergence in the methodologies used for analysing biological brains and synthesising artificial ones is anticipated. In this context, we introduce BrainX3,

---

M. Yang, B. J. N. M. Drost and D. Aviñó—Shared first authors.

© The Author(s), under exclusive license to Springer Nature Switzerland AG 2025
N. S. Szczecinski et al. (Eds.): Living Machines 2024, LNAI 14930, pp. 3–17, 2025.
https://doi.org/10.1007/978-3-031-72597-5_1

an interactive neuroinformatics platform exemplifying this integration. BrainX3 facilitates 3D visualisation, analysis, and simulation of human neuroimaging, electrophysiological data, and brain models [28]. This tool empowers neuroscientists and researchers in advancing the capabilities of living machines through pioneering strategies aimed at deepening comprehension and enhancing operational efficiency. Notably, BrainX3 enables users to directly explore and interact with brain datasets in an intuitive, semantically enhanced manner. The platform accommodates various data types such as Magnetic Resonance Imaging (MRI), Diffusion Tensor Imaging (DTI), Electroencephalography (EEG), Stereoelectroencephalography (SEEG), Magnetoencephalography (MEG), along with their derived data and semantic corpora from text databases and knowledge graphs. Its interactive 3D visualisations and advanced interaction techniques surpass conventional desktop tools, enhancing data exploration efficacy [3–5]. Furthermore, BrainX3 integrates empirical data with synthetic data generated through simulations. The software is designed with several guiding principles: human-in-the-loop interaction, ingestion of multi-modal data, simulation of neural models, immersive interfaces compatible with various display setups including virtual reality, cognitive interfaces supporting wearables and sensors, adherence to standards for data use and sharing, accuracy in visualisation and analysis methods, and applicability to research.

BrainX3 stands as a pioneering neuroinformatic platform to assist the comprehension of brain data. The software harnesses the capabilities of the Unity video game engine, for visualising and engaging with an array of brain data modalities [3]. From connectome datasets to MRI scans, electrophysiological recordings, simulations, and semantic annotations, BrainX3's versatility transcends conventional boundaries, fostering an immersive environment conducive to diverse research and clinical endeavours. While v1.0 showcased functionalities across desktop, VR, and immersive environments, it struggled with limitations inherent to the Unity environment, particularly in accommodating the complexities of neuroinformatic datasets [3]. In this article, we delve into the recent advancements tailored to meet the evolving demands of neuroscience, with a particular emphasis on the realms of modeling and digital twins [27]. We also emphasise and demonstrate the utilisation of whole brain models for simulating brain activity with the potential of replicating the complexities of the human brain and facilitating the creation of artificial systems based on its functionality. One specific challenge in living machines research is understanding the neural basis of adaptive behaviour. BrainX3 can be utilised to explore the neural connectivity patterns associated with adaptive learning in simulated environments. By mapping changes in brain activity before and after learning tasks, BrainX3 can assist in understanding the neural mechanisms, providing insights that are critical for developing adaptive artificial intelligence systems. BrainX3 emerges as an integrative neuroinformatic tool. It acts as a convergence point for generating and exploring brain-like data, poised to drive advancements in brain-inspired systems across a spectrum of domains.

2   BrainX3 3.0

BrainX3 is a layered architecture, comprising a Graphical User Interface (GUI), Application Core, Native, and Specific Plugins. The GUI layer orchestrates user interfaces and interactions across different platforms, while the core layer manages internal application logic and interfaces with plugin modules [3]. Native plugins handle data processing and visualisation, while specific plugins cater to neuroinformatic functionalities. BrainX3 3.0, implemented in Python, integrates external libraries like Qt [24] for GUI and VTK [26] for 3D visualisation. Its GUI framework facilitates multimodal exploration, providing access to logical dataset organisation, semantic corpora queries, 3D visualisation, and temporal signal plots. Utilising the Brain Imaging Data Structure (BIDS) format ensures universal compatibility of neuroimaging datasets [15]. BrainX3 adopts an iterative development strategy, guided by user feedback, to continually enhance and integrate components, driving innovation in neuroinformatics.

BrainX3 is distributed under an open-source model, allowing researchers and clinicians free access to the software. Users can request the latest version from the official BrainX3 website (https://www.brainx3.com/). Detailed installation instructions and user manuals are available on these platforms to facilitate easy setup and use.

3   New Additions to BrainX3

3.1   Brain Atlases

Cortical atlases are essential tools for delineating structurally consistent and meaningful brain regions, important for simulating brain function and behaviour in the design of living machines and the development of artificial brain models. With the incorporation of the Desikan-Killiany [11] atlas and Destrieux atlas [12], BrainX3 now supports five prevailing atlases (see Fig. 1), aligning with the latest advancements and prevalent usage in the literature on whole brain modeling and EEG data source reconstruction [2].

The Desikan-Killiany atlas is a structural brain atlas developed through the examination of the dataset comprising 40 MRI scans. In each hemisphere, 34 distinct cortical regions of interest (ROIs) were identified and annotated. It is widely used in the field of neuroimaging to measure cortical thickness, examine several facets of neurological health, including the course of neurodegenerative disorders, and analyse the anatomical structures of the brain.

On the other hand, the Destrieux atlas offers a more detailed parcellation of the cortex. It leverages an understanding of the sulcal and gyral architecture to identify 148 unique cortical regions (74 on each hemisphere), providing a greater level of detail compared to the Desikan-Killiany atlas. It is particularly useful for conducting detailed investigations of the cerebral cortex, specifically investigating the unique variances that characterise cortical folding patterns.

Through these atlases, BrainX3 can help to understand the connectivity patterns and functional networks between different brain regions, providing a neuroscientific foundation for the design and optimisation of living machines and artificial brains.

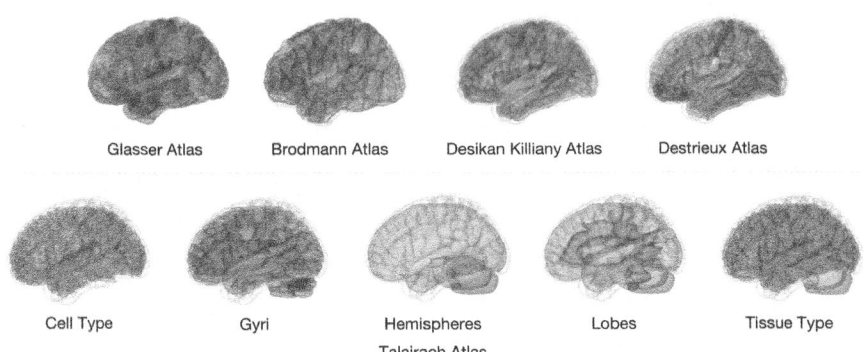

Fig. 1. BrainX3 visualises 3D structures from a variety of existing atlases. In addition to the recent integration of the Desikan-Killiany and Destrieux atlases, BrainX3 also provides access to a comprehensive range of other atlases, including the Brodmann [8], Glasser [14], and Talairach [31] atlases.

3.2   MRI Coordinates Mapping to 3D Atlases

For living machines, neuroimaging can be a crucial factor in understanding the anatomical information of the brain. However, the conventional implementation of neuroimaging, such as MRI, lacks explicit integration with parcellations, making extraction of information more difficult and time-consuming.

Therefore, a significant enhancement in BrainX3 is achieved with the addition of a new feature called 'MRI to Atlas'. This feature facilitates interaction with the MRI data by connecting the MRI widgets to the 3D atlas, thereby offering the user a powerful tool for anatomical localisation and visualisation. Mapping MRI coordinates to 3D atlases involves aligning the spatial information from MRI scans to standardised anatomical templates or atlases. This process allows researchers to precisely identify and localise brain structures and regions of interest within a common reference space. The feature uses coordinate extraction within the Montreal Neurological Institute (MNI) space, which is a standard coordinate system used in brain imaging. The feature utilises the affine transformation matrix, corresponding to the specific atlas file, and the MNI coordinates to compute the voxel coordinates, thereby facilitating the needed coordinates to find the corresponding brain area in the specific atlas file. The function also takes the direct neighbouring MNI coordinates when obtaining the clicked coordinates. This is to show all brain areas when clicking on a junction. The function then loads the areas in the 3D atlas. BrainX3 provides the user with the option to select an appropriate atlas to work with. Subsequently, the feature enables users to interact with the MRI widgets, which provide a dynamic interface for exploring the MRI space. When a region of interest is selected on MRI, the corresponding point of interest is highlighted within the 3D atlas, along with any brain regions it intersects with (see Fig. 2). This integrated functionality not only expedites the process of anatomical referencing but also may enhance the comprehension of MRI scans by providing a spatial context within the atlas framework. The 3D atlas framework comes with many tools for further investigation, such as connection exploration and a direct link to the whole brain simulation when operating right-click on the brain area. The connection exploration mode is a feature that is preserved from BrainX3 2.0 [28]. It allows the user to visualise the connections of the selected brain area. When utilising the direct link with the whole brain simulation, selecting a specific brain area via right-click operation will trigger the simulation to introduce a corresponding lesion in the selected region of interest. This allows researchers to explore brain areas and their consequences and study their significance.

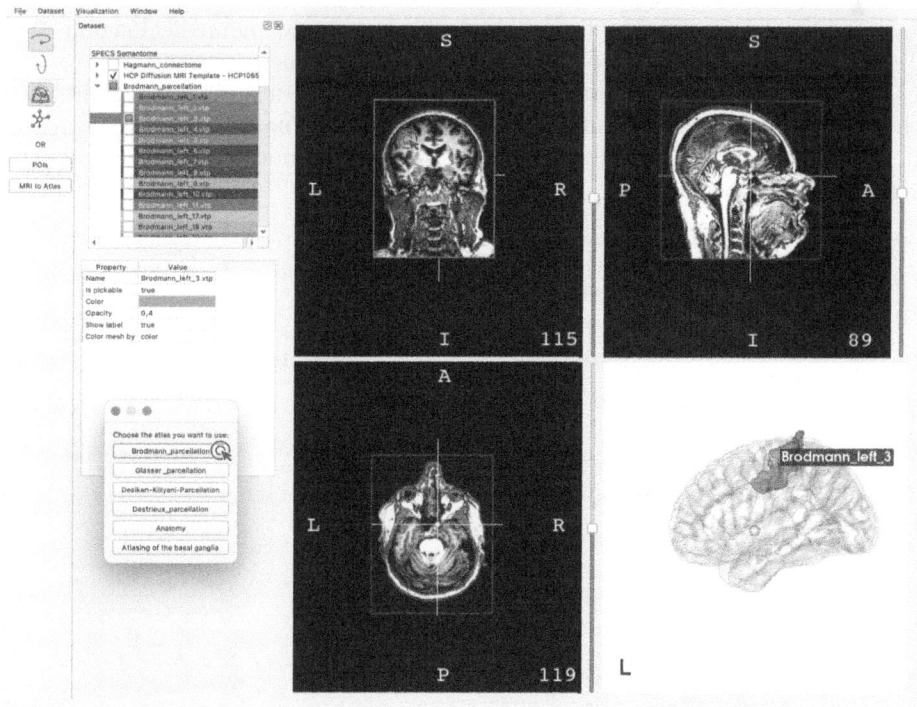

Fig. 2. Visualisation of the MRI to Atlas function. By selecting the desired atlas (here the Brodmann parcellation atlas is selected) and clicking on the region of interest in the MRI scans (here selected in the coronal view), the identified region on the scans can be mapped to the brain atlas on the 3D brain. The Brodmann area 3 on the left hemisphere is chosen here for demonstration.

This feature tackles the pressing challenge of translating MRI scans into 3D brain visualisation. Identifying specific areas on the atlas enables a researcher to model whole brain activity with various pathological and non-pathological conditions. For example, a researcher is looking into a certain neurological disorder where random brain areas are non-functional. Using the MRI to atlas function these areas can be determined and consequences can be studied in the whole brain model. This, in turn, enhances our understanding to mimic behaviour in living systems. The function allows researchers to utilise MRI scans for expedited study of the brain and look at brain areas in different parcellations. This feature therefore provides a streamlined method for acquiring anatomical information on brain regions and facilitating further investigation into interconnectivity using various tools.

3.3   Signal Processing

Signal processing is a fundamental tool used across diverse fields to extract hidden information from raw data. In biomedical signal processing, the focus is on analysing signals from various physiological and neural activities in living organisms, particularly within the human body. However, raw biomedical signals like EEG and MEG are often contaminated with noise, necessitating preprocessing, denoising, and feature extraction steps to derive meaningful insights. To achieve this goal, BrainX3 integrates a signal processing module based on the open-source MNE library [16], supporting the transformation of raw signals into actionable information.

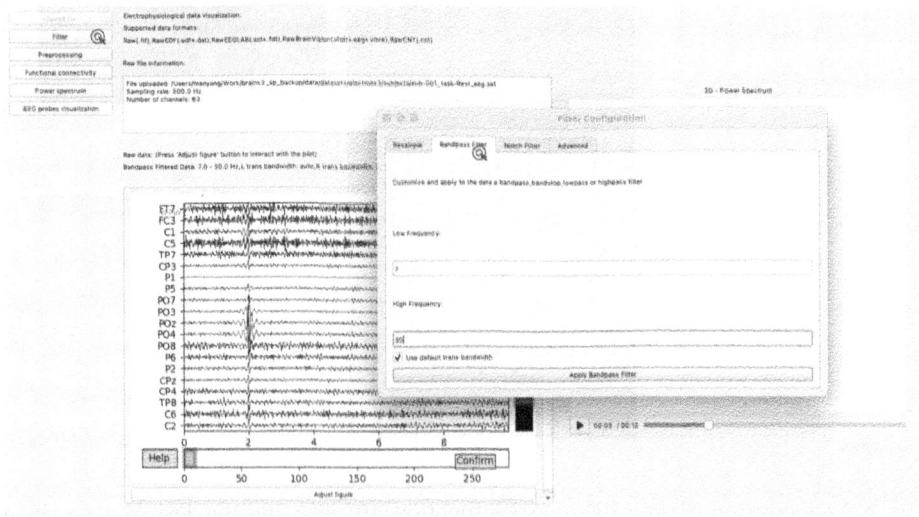

Fig. 3. Preprocessing window. This window allows the user to preprocess the raw data. For example, users can customise the filtering parameters and use the bandpass filter function to filter out EEG or MEG signals in the frequency band of interest [20].

The signal processing module empowers users to import EEG or MEG data in a variety of formats that are prevalent in scientific and clinical research (see Fig. 4). It offers a user-friendly visualisation of brain activity, together with essential details like sampling rate and number of channels, providing a foundational overview for subsequent analysis. Through interaction with raw data, BrainX3 enables users to observe changes in brain electrical or magnetic activities across various channels at specific time points and under designated labels. This functionality aids researchers in studying empirical data, which can inform the design of artificial brains.

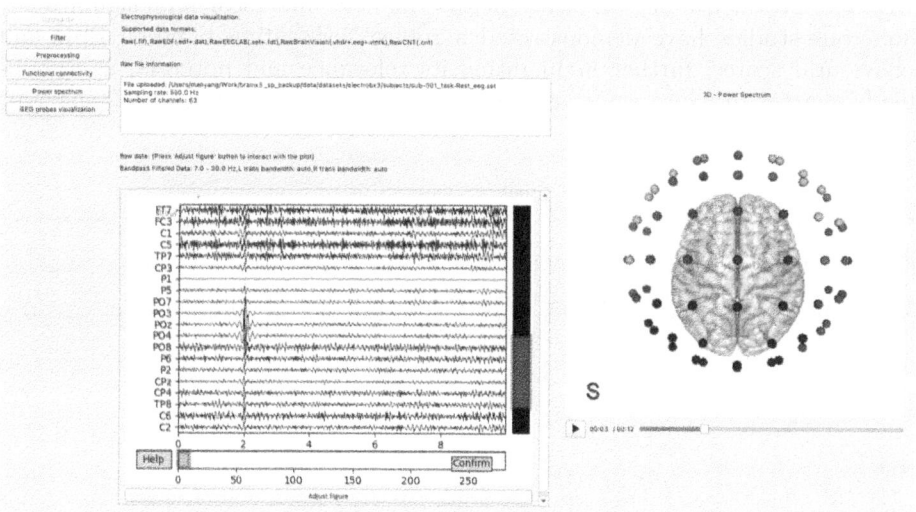

Fig. 4. Signal processing module of BrainX3. After uploading the raw data, this window displays brain activity, and other key information such as the file name, sampling rate, and number of channels. The 3D model displayed on the right illustrates the Power Spectral Density (PSD) across different locations on the scalp over time. For the representative purpose; an open source dataset is used [29].

To address the various interferences present in EEG or MEG signals obtained in hospitals or other medical facilities, often caused by external environmental factors (such as electromagnetic interference and power supply noise) and internal disturbances (such as muscle activity, heart activity, and respiration), BrainX3 features advanced preprocessing capabilities designed to improve the quality and usability of EEG or MEG data by minimising or eliminating unwanted signal components. For instance, the application of notch filters effectively eliminates interference caused by industrial frequency noise, while bandpass filtering filters out noise and interference outside the desired frequency spectrum (see Fig. 3), thereby improving the signal-to-noise ratio. Additionally, techniques like Independent Component Analysis (ICA) [1,6,18,21] allow for the extraction and removal of artifacts associated with eye movements and heartbeats. By cleaning the raw data in this manner [19], BrainX3 empowers researchers to extract meaningful brain activity, thereby augmenting the accuracy and reliability of subsequent analyses.

Moreover, the signal processing window integrates a three-dimensional visualisation feature for EEG or MEG montages of the loaded data in the user interface. The 3D rendering illustrates the PSD over the scalp through time. This visualisation facilitates the identification of unusual brain activity in particular spatial regions, allowing one to discern the relationship between distinct frequency bands and spatial locations and track any fluctuations or shifts in the PSD. The prevalence of PSD usage across the field underscores its significance. Numerous studies have demonstrated a robust correlation between PSD and behavioural scores, further highlighting its relevance and potential as a valuable biomarker in neuroscience research and its potential to facilitate behaviour emulation in machines [25].

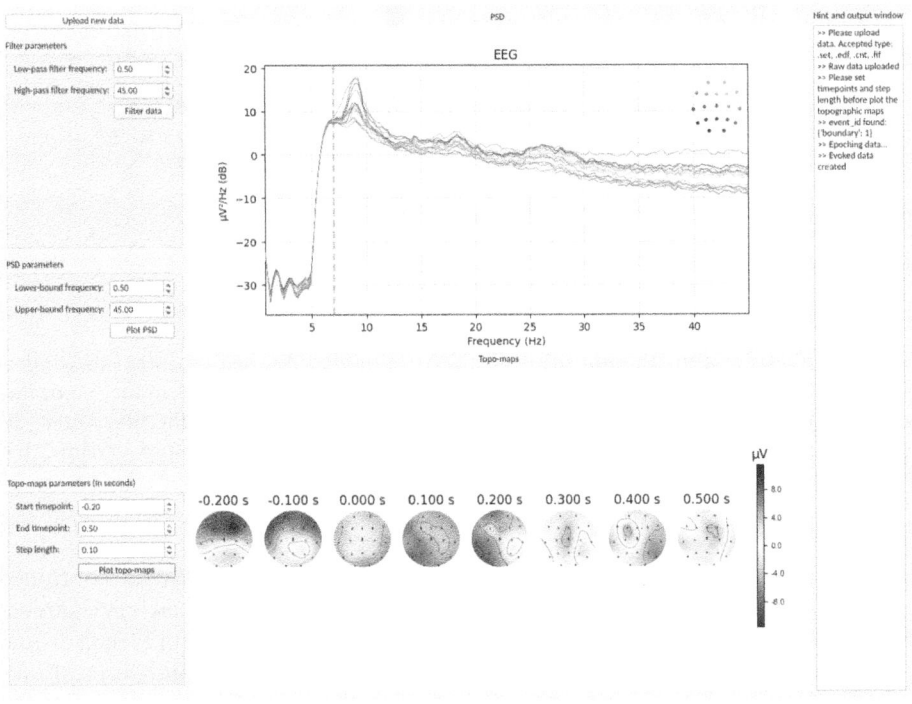

Fig. 5. PSD window. This window is utilised to display the spectral information of the data. Users can personalise the PSD parameters to suit their needs. Upon activation, it will automatically compute and provide the power spectral density curve of the original data, providing a clear representation of the energy distribution across various frequency components [20].

BrainX3 also features a specialised PSD visualisation that allows users to explore the frequency domain properties of brain activity [33]. This feature provides a concise representation of how power is distributed among various frequency components, making it easier to identify important characteristics such as dominating frequencies, peak frequencies, and frequency ranges (see Fig. 5). Gaining knowledge of these frequency characteristics is particularly advantageous for examining patterns of brain activity and identifying irregular rhythms.

With the integration of the signal processing module, BrainX3 unlocks a comprehensive pipeline for biomedical signal processing, which serves as a bridge between biological systems and artificial systems, enabling the translation of intricate brain activity into actionable insights essential for driving advancements in living machines.

3.4   Simulating Brain Activity

As research advances and so does the field of living machines, BrainX3 integrates whole-brain modeling into its core functionalities. This integration reflects the evolving landscape of neuroscience, facilitating the ability to construct biological brain simulations and control systems. Whole brain modeling has as its primary goal to give a better understanding of the intricate dynamics of brain function, offering insights into both normal cognitive processes and neurological disorders and the construction of brain-based control systems for living machines. The model is defined as a mathematical representation of the dynamical world. By using empirical structural data the neural activity across the brain can be represented. Whole brain modeling has in this example, applications which include modeling lesions, seizures and schizophrenia [23], but can also be used for the development of brain-based control systems.

We utilise the Stuart-Landau (SL) model to simulate MEG or functional Magnetic Resonance Imaging (fMRI) signals [9]. The SL equation (eq. 1) is applied to N brain areas that are represented as nodes by SL oscillators. They are coupled in the connectome, where the connectivity strength, C_{np}, and the conduction delays, τ_{np}, are both considered between each pair of nodes n and p. The conduction delays are defined in proportion to the fibre lengths between these brain areas, assuming a homogenous conduction speed v, such that $\tau_{np} = D_{np}/v$, where D_{np} is the real fibre length. To simulate how the activity in node n is affected by the behaviour of all other nodes $p \in N \wedge p \neq n$, the SL formula defines the interaction between nodes and is calculated for each time step.

$$\frac{dZ_n}{dt} = Z_n \left[a + i\omega - |Z_n^2| \right] + K \sum_{p \neq n}^{N} C_{np} \left[Z_p(t - \tau_{np}) - Z_n(t) \right] + \beta\eta_1 + i\beta\eta_2 \quad (1)$$

$Z_n(t)$ is a complex variable that describes the state of nth oscillator at time t. The first term of the equation describes the internal dynamics of the oscillator, where $\omega = 2\pi * f_f$ is the angular frequency, with f_f as the fundamental frequency. Parameter a determines the position of each unit concerning the limit cycle.

The second term of the equation represents the total input received from other oscillators, Z_p. This input is scaled by parameter K, which sets the strength of all network interactions with respect to the intrinsic node dynamics. The last term of the equation represents the real and imaginary part of uncorrelated white noise, where η_1 and η_2 are drawn from a Gaussian distribution with mean zero and standard deviation $\beta = 0.001$.

The integrated model in BrainX3 allows the user to utilise Desikan-Killiany [11] and Automated Anatomical Labeling (AAL) [32] parcellation to simulate brain activity informed by the structural organisation of the brain [17]. The amount of nodes in the Desikan parcellation is fixed at 70 nodes. In the AAL parcellation, there is an option to include the non-cortical areas, thereby adding nodes to the AAL parcellation, it has 90 nodes with non-cortical areas and 78 without those areas.

In BrainX3, we aim to position the whole brain model as a versatile research tool investigating brain simulations, and lesion-induced effects (see Fig. 6). The tool will help researchers explore the importance of different brain areas and better understand their interconnectivity. Furthermore, it allows the construction of a brain-based control system that can mimic real brain activities. Existing frameworks often lack the capability to integrate different data types or require

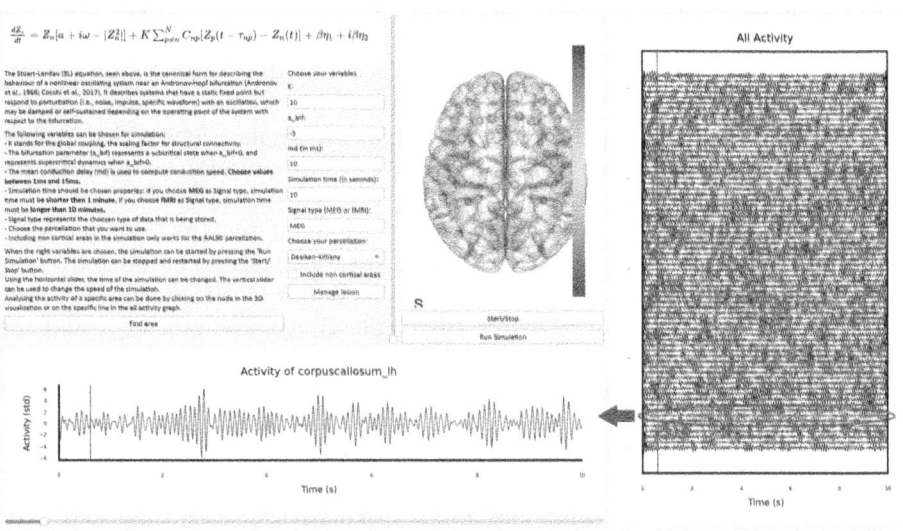

Fig. 6. The BrainX3 simulation window. Upon activation of the tool, the window appears providing users with the option to adjust the default settings such as changing the parcellation or adding lesions to the simulation. When the simulation is initiated, brain areas are depicted as nodes in the 3D space, colour-coded according to activity, while the activity plots are displayed in the graphs. Users are able to interact with both the All Activity plot and the 3D space by clicking on the plot or node of interest, allowing for a detailed view of the specific brain region. In the figure, the simulated brain activity is filtered in the alpha frequency band (8–13 Hz).

extensive manual preprocessing. The proposed BrainX3 approach improves upon these by offering preprocessing, and advanced visualisation tools. This enhances the accuracy and usability of whole brain models, facilitating more precise and comprehensive neuroimaging studies.

4 Discussion

While numerous solutions for visualisation and analysis abound, they often cater to specific acquisition systems, employing proprietary source code and file formats that hinder accessibility for the broader research community. In contrast, free alternatives such as Freesurfer [13], SPM [7], EEGLab [10], Fieldtrip [22], Brainstorm [30], and MNE tools [16] have widespread adoption. These open-source options offer mature and versatile solutions, empowering researchers with accessible and adaptable tools for neuroinformatics but lacking effective 3D visualisation and an integrated semantic search engine. BrainX3, as a neuroinformatics platform, now incorporates signal processing and whole-brain modeling functionalities, enhancing its capacity for patient-specific modeling. It serves as a comprehensive tool for constructing synthetic brains, offering support for decision-making in the development of living machines. Offering a rich array of features, BrainX3 enables researchers to visualise, analyse, and simulate various aspects of human neuroimaging, electrophysiological data, and brain models. This latest iteration of BrainX3, version 3.0, is characterised by a sophisticated layered architecture comprising a GUI to facilitate flexibility and scalability, allowing seamless integration of new functionalities and efficient management of the platform. Implemented using the Python programming language and leveraging external libraries such as Qt for the GUI and VTK for 3D visualisation, BrainX3 3.0 ensures high performance and usability.

In comparison to its predecessor, BrainX3 2.0 offers significant improvements in terms of architecture, making development and maintenance more streamlined and accessible. While numerous commercial and free alternatives exist in the neuroinformatics domain, BrainX3 stands out due to its unique capabilities and versatility. It not only empowers researchers and clinicians by providing comprehensive tools for neuroimaging analysis, brain modeling, and data integration but also facilitates collaborative research and education. These capabilities are crucial because they address the growing need for interdisciplinary approaches in neuroscience and artificial intelligence. By integrating multiple data types and analysis techniques, BrainX3 allows for more robust and nuanced insights into brain function and dysfunction. Researchers and clinicians frequently employ these features to streamline their workflows, enhance the reproducibility of their studies, and foster collaborative efforts across disciplines. The importance of these specific integrations lies in their ability to support the development of advanced computational models that mimic human brain function. In the context of artificial intelligence (AI) and artificial brains, BrainX3 provides tools for simulating whole brain activity, analysing brain connectivity patterns, and integrating AI algorithms with neuroimaging data. These functionalities are critical for advancing AI research, as they enable the creation of more sophisticated and biologically plausible AI models.

While BrainX3 offers comprehensive tools for brain visualisation and analysis, it has certain limitations. The current version may require high computational resources, making it less accessible for users with limited hardware capabilities. Additionally, while it integrates several data types, the system's performance might vary depending on the quality and consistency of the input data. Future versions will focus on optimising computational efficiency and enhancing data integration capabilities.

Furthermore, BrainX3 serves as a nexus for integrating neuroinformatics data into artificial systems, broadening the scope of brain-inspired technologies across various domains. Its adaptable nature accommodates the inclusion of novel models and the refinement of existing ones, enhancing the biological realism and efficacy of artificial brain models in diverse applications. BrainX3 not only enriches research and clinical practices in neuroinformatics but also spearheads advancements by connecting biological data with artificial brains. Its holistic functionalities and collaborative approach render it indispensable for researchers, clinicians, and educators while contributing to the advancement of artificial brain technologies.

Acknowledgements. The author(s) declare financial support was received for the research, authorship, and/or publication of this article. This work was funded by the European Commission's Counterfactual Assessment and Valuation for Awareness Architecture - CAVAA (European Commission, EIC 101071178), AI in Stroke Neurorehabilitation - AISN (European Commission, EIC 101057655), Personalised Health cognitive assistance for RehAbilitation SystEm - PHRASE (European Commission, EIC 101058240), eBRAIN-Health (European Commission, EIC 101058516) and European School of Network Neuroscience euSNN (MSCA-ITN ETN H2020-ID 860563). The funders had no role in the conceptualisation, analysis, decision to publish, or preparation of the manuscript.

References

1. Ablin, P., Cardoso, J.F., Gramfort, A.: Faster independent component analysis by preconditioning with hessian approximations. IEEE Trans. Signal Process. **66**(15), 4040–4049. https://doi.org/10.1109/TSP.2018.2844203. https://ieeexplore.ieee.org/document/8372626/
2. Alexander, B., et al.: Desikan-killiany-tourville atlas compatible version of m-crib neonatal parcellated whole brain atlas: the m-crib 2.0. Front. Neurosci. **13**, 34 (2019)
3. Arsiwalla, X.D., Betella, A., Martinez, E., Omedas, P., Zucca, R., Verschure, P.F.: The dynamic connectome: a tool for large-scale 3d reconstruction of brain activity in real-time. In: Rekdalsbakken, W., Bye, R.T., Zhang, H. (eds.) ECMS 2013 Proceedings, pp. 865–869 (2013). https://doi.org/10.7148/2013-0865, http://www.scs-europe.net/dlib/2013/2013-0865.htm
4. Arsiwalla, X.D., et al.: Connectomics to semantomics: Addressing the brain's big data challenge. Procedia Comput. Sci. **53**, 48–55 (2015). https://

doi.org/10.1016/j.procs.2015.07.278. https://linkinghub.elsevier.com/retrieve/pii/S1877050915017810

5. Arsiwalla, X.D., et al.: Network dynamics with BrainX3: a large-scale simulation of the human brain network with real-time interaction. Front. Neuroinf. **9** (2015). https://doi.org/10.3389/fninf.2015.00002. http://journal.frontiersin.org/Article/10.3389/fninf.2015.00002/abstract

6. Artoni, F., Delorme, A., Makeig, S.: Applying dimension reduction to EEG data by principal component analysis reduces the quality of its subsequent independent component decomposition. NeuroImage **175**, 176–187 (2018). https://doi.org/10.1016/j.neuroimage.2018.03.016. https://linkinghub.elsevier.com/retrieve/pii/S1053811918302143

7. Ashburner, J.: Computational anatomy with the spm software. Magn. Reson. Imaging **27**(8), 1163–1174 (2009). https://doi.org/10.1016/j.mri.2009.01.006. https://www.sciencedirect.com/science/article/pii/S0730725X09000149

8. Brodmann, K.: Vergleichende Lokalisationslehre der Grosshirnrinde in ihren Prinzipien dargestellt auf Grund des Zellenbaues. Barth (1909)

9. Castaldo, F., et al.: Multi-modal and multi-model interrogation of large-scale functional brain networks. NeuroImage **277**, 120236 (2023). https://doi.org/10.1016/j.neuroimage.2023.120236, https://linkinghub.elsevier.com/retrieve/pii/S1053811923003877

10. Delorme, A., Makeig, S.: Eeglab: an open source toolbox for analysis of single-trial eeg dynamics including independent component analysis. J. Neurosci. Methods **134**(1), 9–21 (2004) https://doi.org/10.1016/j.jneumeth.2003.10.009. https://www.sciencedirect.com/science/article/pii/S0165027003003479

11. Desikan, R.S., et al..: An automated labeling system for subdividing the human cerebral cortex on MRI scans into gyral based regions of interest. Neuroimage **31**(3), 968–980 (2006). https://doi.org/10.1016/j.neuroimage.2006.01.021. https://linkinghub.elsevier.com/retrieve/pii/S1053811906000437

12. Destrieux, C., Fischl, B., Dale, A., Halgren, E.: Automatic parcellation of human cortical gyri and sulci using standard anatomical nomenclature. Neuroimage **53**(1), 1–15 (2015). https://doi.org/10.1016/j.neuroimage.2010.06.010. https://linkinghub.elsevier.com/retrieve/pii/S1053811910008542

13. Fischl, B.: Freesurfer. NeuroImage **62**(2), 774–781 (2012). https://doi.org/10.1016/j.neuroimage.2012.01.021. https://www.sciencedirect.com/science/article/pii/S1053811912000389

14. Glasser, M.F., et al.: A multi-modal parcellation of human cerebral cortex. Nature **536**(7615), 171–178 (2016). https://doi.org/10.1038/nature18933. https://www.nature.com/articles/nature18933

15. Gorgolewski, K.J., et al.: The brain imaging data structure, a format for organizing and describing outputs of neuroimaging experiments. Sci. Data **3**(1), 160044 (2016). https://doi.org/10.1038/sdata.2016.44. https://www.nature.com/articles/sdata201644

16. Gramfort, A., et al.: MEG and EEG data analysis with MNE-Python. Front. Neurosci. **7**(267), 1–13 (2013). https://doi.org/10.3389/fnins.2013.00267

17. Jung, K., Eickhoff, S.B., Popovych, O.V.: Parcellation-based structural and resting-state functional whole-brain connectomes of 1000brains cohort (v1.1) (2022). https://doi.org/10.25493/8XY5-BH7. https://search.kg.ebrains.eu/instances/3f179784-194d-4795-9d8d-301b524ca00a

18. Lee, T.W., Girolami, M., Sejnowski, T.J.: Independent component analysis using an extended infomax algorithm for mixed subgaussian and supergaus-

sian sources. Neural Comput. **11**(2), 417–441 (1999). https://doi.org/10.1162/089976699300016719. https://direct.mit.edu/neco/article/11/2/417-441/6242

19. Maess, B., Schröger, E., Widmann, A.: High-pass filters and baseline correction in m/eeg analysis-continued discussion. J. Neurosci. Methods **266**, 171–172 (2016). https://doi.org/10.1016/j.jneumeth.2016.01.016. https://www.sciencedirect.com/science/article/pii/S0165027016000339

20. Miltiadous, A., et al.: A dataset of 88 EEG recordings from: Alzheimer's disease, frontotemporal dementia and healthy subjects (2023). https://doi.org/10.18112/OPENNEURO.DS004504.V1.0.6. https://openneuro.org/datasets/ds004504/versions/1.0.6

21. Montoya-Martínez, J., Cardoso, J.-F., Gramfort, A.: Caveats with stochastic gradient and maximum likelihood based ICA for EEG. In: Tichavský, P., Babaie-Zadeh, M., Michel, O.J.J., Thirion-Moreau, N. (eds.) LVA/ICA 2017. LNCS, vol. 10169, pp. 279–289. Springer, Cham (2017). https://doi.org/10.1007/978-3-319-53547-0_27

22. Oostenveld, R., Fries, P., Maris, E., Schoffelen, J.M.: Fieldtrip: open source software for advanced analysis of meg, eeg, and invasive electrophysiological data. Comput. Intell. Neurosci. **2011**, 156869 (2011).https://doi.org/10.1155/2011/156869

23. Pathak, A., Roy, D., Banerjee, A.: Whole-brain network models: from physics to bedside. Front. Comput. Neurosci. **16**, 866517 (2022). https://doi.org/10.3389/fncom.2022.866517. https://www.frontiersin.org/articles/10.3389/fncom.2022.866517/full

24. PyQT: Pyqt reference guide (2012). http://www.riverbankcomputing.com/static/Docs/PyQt4/html/index.html

25. Sahoo, B., Pathak, A., Deco, G., Banerjee, A., Roy, D.: Lifespan associated global patterns of coherent neural communication. Neuroimage **216**, 116824 (2020). https://doi.org/10.1016/j.neuroimage.2020.116824. https://linkinghub.elsevier.com/retrieve/pii/S1053811920303116

26. Schroeder, W.J., Martin, K., Lorensen, W.E., Avila, L.S., Martin, K.W., Lorensen, B.: The visualization toolkit: an object-oriented approach to 3D graphics; [visualize data in 3D - medical, engineering or scientific; build your own applications with C++, Tcl, Java or Python; includes source code for VTK (supports UNIX, Windows and Mac)], 4th edn. Kitware, Inc. (1998)

27. Sharma, V., Páscoa Dos Santos, F., Verschure, P.F.M.J.: Patient-specific modeling for guided rehabilitation of stroke patients: the BrainX3 use-case. Front. Neurol. **14**, 1279875 (2023). https://doi.org/10.3389/fneur.2023.1279875. https://www.frontiersin.org/articles/10.3389/fneur.2023.1279875/full

28. Sharma, V., Vilarrubias, R.B., Verschure, P.F.M.J.: BrainX3: a neuroinformatic tool for interactive exploration of multimodal brain datasets. In: Meder, F., Hunt, A., Margheri, L., Mura, A., Mazzolai, B. (eds.) Biomimetic and Biohybrid Systems, vol. 14158, pp. 157–177. Springer, Cham (2023). https://doi.org/10.1007/978-3-031-39504-8_11

29. Singh, A., Cole, R., Espinoza, A., Cavanagh, J., Narayanan, N.: Rest eyes open (2023). https://doi.org/10.18112/OPENNEURO.DS004584.V1.0.0. https://openneuro.org/datasets/ds004584/versions/1.0.0

30. Tadel, F., Baillet, S., Mosher, J.C., Pantazis, D., Leahy, R.M.: Brainstorm: a user-friendly application for MEG/EEG analysis. Comput. Intell. Neurosci. **2011**, 879716 (2011). https://doi.org/10.1155/2011/879716

31. Talairach, P.J.: Co-planar stereotaxic atlas of the human brain (1988)

32. Tzourio-Mazoyer, N., et al.: Automated anatomical labeling of activations in SPM using a macroscopic anatomical parcellation of the MNI MRI single-subject brain. Neuroimage **15**(1), 273–289 (2022). https://doi.org/10.1006/nimg.2001.0978. https://linkinghub.elsevier.com/retrieve/pii/S1053811901909784
33. Welch, P.: The use of fast fourier transform for the estimation of power spectra: a method based on time averaging over short, modified periodograms. IEEE Trans. Audio Electroacoust. **15**(2), 70–73 (1967). https://doi.org/10.1109/TAU.1967.1161901. http://ieeexplore.ieee.org/document/1161901/

Towards Biophysical Network Simulation of Stochastically-Formed Neurospheres

Michael J. Bennington[1] and Victoria A. Webster-Wood[1,2,3,4]($\boxtimes$)

[1] Department of Mechanical, Carnegie Mellon University, Pittsburgh, PA, USA
[2] Department of Biomedical Engineering, Carnegie Mellon University, Pittsburgh, PA, USA
[3] McGowan Institute for Regenerative Medicine, Carnegie Mellon University, Pittsburgh, PA, USA
[4] Robotics Institute, Carnegie Mellon University, Pittsburgh, PA, USA
vwebster@andrew.cmu.edu

Abstract. Biocomputing platforms, such as cultured neurospheres, have the potential to provide great advances in biohybrid computation and control systems. However, to design and fabricate neurospheres reliably and reproducibly, models that can accurately predict their computational behaviors are required. Towards the end of understanding how neurospheres perform higher-level computations, we present a model framework for simulating the dynamics of stochastically-connected neuron networks. Each neuron is modeled using biophysical models of neural excitability, and the system can be stimulated by a small number of simulated electrodes. The network response of the system is analyzed using Principal Components Analysis on the firing frequencies of the neurons. From preliminary simulations, we demonstrate the ability of these neurosphere networks to encode information about the magnitude of current stimuli. Future additions to this framework will incorporate the 3D geometry of both the neurosphere and individual dendritic trees.

Keywords: Neurospheres · Computational Modeling · Biophysics

1 Introduction

Neurospheres (spherical 3D cultures of neurons and other cells of the nervous systems [33,43]) and other neuron-based biocomputing platforms present great potential for next-generation computational tools. They can harness the natural capabilities of neural tissue to learn, adapt, and respond to environmental cues. Compared to other state-of-the-art machine learning and artificial intelligence systems, neurospheres operate using a fraction of the energy input, allowing for far more energy-efficient computing [17]. Current state-of-the-art systems have

This material is based on work supported by the National Science Foundation Graduate Research Fellowship under grant No. DGE1745016 and by the NSF Faculty Early Career Development Program under Grant No. ECCS-2044785.

already demonstrated the ability to control robotic systems [8,39,41], play simple video games [8,21], and perform recognition and prediction tasks [7,8,34]. Additionally, these neurospheres can serve as organic controllers for muscle-powered biohybrid systems, providing more naturalistic stimulation to the muscles, which has been shown to prolong performance [40].

However, these current systems rely on black-box approaches to tasks, relying on the ability to train neural systems to perform specific actions. If we hope to reliably and robustly design neurosphere systems to perform specific tasks, we must investigate how these systems encode and transform information and how the base units interact. In the case of electronic computers, these characteristics are known [4,24] - digital computers store information as transistor states (bits) and transform information through Boolean arithmetic; analog computers store information as voltages and currents and transform it using electronic circuit components (resistors, capacitors, etc.). Because of this understanding, designing systems to perform arbitrary tasks is tractable. However, in neural systems, the mechanisms by which individual neuron-to-neuron communication (in the form of temporal- or rate-coded messages) translates to the abstracted latent encodings observed in large neural systems remains unknown [22,25]. These questions could be investigated using appropriate biophysical simulations of these neurosphere systems.

Existing neurosphere models often focus on the self-organization of the system or the growth and change of these systems [28,33,43], related to using these neurospheres as disease models. Fewer models of neural cultures focus on modeling the electrical and computational aspects of these systems or do not model down to the neuron level, rather utilizing lumped approximations for many neurons [27], or other abstracted representations of neural computation, like reservoir computation models [15]. While useful in investigating higher-level dynamics in these systems [12,15], these abstracted models do not allow us to map these emergent phenomena to the properties at the cellular level as is needed to design computational systems built using living neurons. However, many models exist for modeling the biophysics of neural excitability [6,13,20,26,29,35]. By combining these biophysical models of excitability with models of formation and development, we can begin to understand how these neurosphere systems perform computations and how these computations can be designed into systems during formation and during training. In this work, we begin to establish a framework for modeling the electrical activity of stochastically generated neurosphere networks. We combine single-compartment Hodgkin-Huxley models of neuron excitability with a simplified model of stochastic network formation. Preliminary simulations were conducted on networks of various sizes to test the ability of these networks to encode information about input stimuli.

2   Methods

Biophysical simulations of stochastically generated networks were conducted to simulate the behavior of these neurosphere systems. Three neuron types - fast-spiking, regular spiking, and intrinsically bursting neurons - were connected in networks using both chemical and electrical synapses. The dynamics of each neuron type are modeled as a one-compartment Hodgkin-Huxley system with the ion channels varying between the cell types. An algorithm is developed to stochastically form network connections based on the spatial location of the neurons within the simulated neurosphere.

2.1   Biophysical Neuron Model

The governing dynamics of all three neuron types take the form of a single-compartment Hodgkin-Huxley system. Each cell type is differentiated by the ion channels present and the parameters of the equivalent circuit components. The form of the Hodgkin-Huxley dynamics for the different cell types are taken from [13, 29] (Eq. 1, Table 1). Briefly, the bilayer of the cell membrane acts as a capacitor, and the various ion channels act as dynamical, voltage-dependent resistors. Voltage sources in series with the ion channels model the electrochemical potential for the corresponding ion species. Finally, chemical and electrical synapses and stimulating electrodes can inject current into the compartment. Additionally, in our framework, we add background noisy currents [18].

The governing circuit equation for the compartment takes the form:

$$C_m \frac{dV}{dt} = I_{chem.}(t) + I_{elec.}(t) + I_{noise}(t) - \sum_c (\hat{g}_c A_c(t, V)(V(t) - E_c)) \quad (1)$$

where C_m and V are the membrane capacitance per unit surface area and the membrane voltage, $I_{chem.}$, $I_{elec.}$, and I_{noise} are the cumulative chemical and electrical synapse currents and noise currents, and the summation term represents the total ion channel currents. The form of the chemical and electrical synaptic currents are discussed in Sect. 2.2. The noise current is modeled as a piecewise-constant current source with duration τ_{noise} and magnitude sampled from a mean-zero normal distribution with standard deviation $2\sigma_{noise}$. The window width τ_{noise} is the reciprocal of the highest noise frequency.

The ion channels that are included in the summation term depend on the neuron type in question. For fast-spiking neurons, only two ion channels are present. These are fast-inactivating sodium ion channels and fast-activating potassium channels. These two channels are sufficient for generating action potentials. For regular spiking neurons, an additional slow potassium current is added. This allows the firing frequency of the regular neurons to adapt over time to a constant stimulus. A calcium ion channel is also present for the intrinsically bursting neurons, which allows for rapid bursting at the onset of stimulation, followed by slower spiking. Finally, all neurons contain a non-voltage-dependent leaky ion channel. For this channel, $A_c(t, V) = 1$. Representative single-neuron voltage traces for these cell types are shown in Fig. 1 for a 200 ms constant current stimulation.

For the ion channel c, $\hat{g}_c$ is the maximal conductance per unit surface area, $A_c(t, V)$ is the dynamical, voltage-dependent level of activation, and E_c is the electrochemical potential. The form that $A_c(t, V)$ takes depends on the ion channel, and the specific forms are found in Table 1. For all ion channels in this model, the activation function will consist of the product of gating variables [13]. The dynamics of these gating variables take the form:

$$\frac{dx}{dt} = \alpha_x(V)(1-x) + \beta_x(V)x \qquad (2)$$

where the specific forms of $\alpha_x(V)$ and $\beta_x(V)$ for the different gating variables are found in Table 1. This is true for all gating variables except for the gating variable for slow potassium currents, which follows dynamics characterized by:

$$\frac{dp}{dt} = \frac{p_\infty(V) - p}{\tau_p(V)} \qquad (3)$$

(see also Table 1 for the forms of $p_\infty(V)$ and $\tau_p(V)$). All parameters used in the present simulations are summarized in Table 2 in the Appendix.

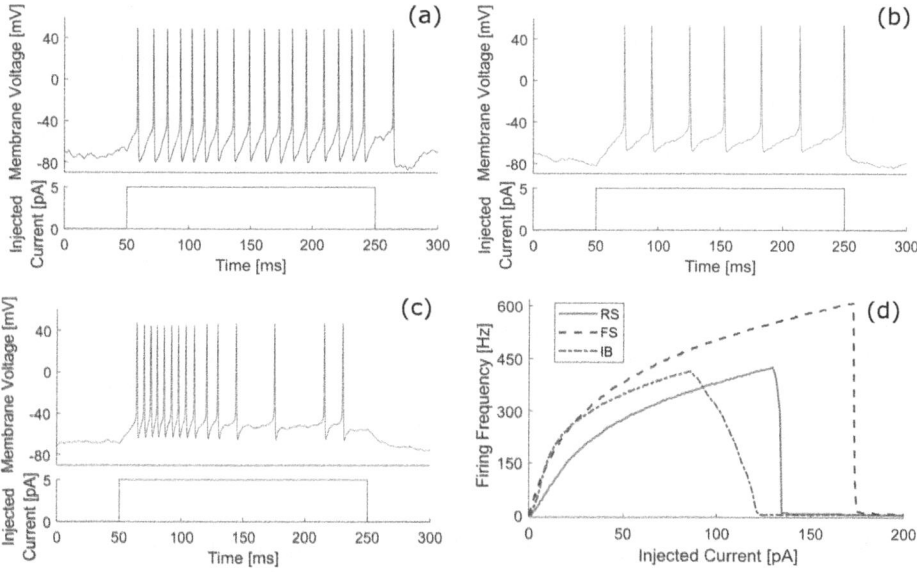

Fig. 1. Behavior of Different Neuron Types. (a)–(c) Representative simulation of each neuron type subjected to a 200 ms constant current injection of 5 pA. (a) Fast-spiking (FS) neuron. (b) Regular spiking (RS) neuron. (c) Intrinsically bursting (IB) neuron. Each neuron was also subject to a noise current with parameters $\tau_{noise} = 1$ ms and $\sigma_{noise} = 1$ pA. This noise current is responsible for the spike that occurs in the FS neuron after the deactivation of the current injection. (d) Frequency-current curves for the different neuron types. Each neuron type was subjected to a 300 ms constant current stimulation, and the average firing frequency across the full stimulation duration was calculated. No noise current was included in these simulations.

Finally, the parameters in the circuit equation are normalized per unit membrane surface area. To obtain the non-normalized values of the parameters, a

Table 1. Ion Channel Gating Dynamics. Here, V_T controls the threshold voltage of the neuron, and τ_{max} is the maximum time constant of the slow potassium ion channel. All gating variables are dimensionless and in the range $[0, 1]$.

Ion Channel	Activation Function	Gating Variable	$\alpha(V)$	$\beta(V)$
Fast-Inactivating Sodium	$A_{Na} = m^3 h$	m	$\dfrac{-0.32(V - V_T - 13)}{e^{-(V-V_T-13)/4} - 1}$	$\dfrac{0.28(V - V_T - 40)}{e^{(V-V_T-40)/5} - 1}$
		h	$0.128e^{-(V-V_T-17)/18}$	$\dfrac{4}{e^{-(V-V_T-40)/5} + 1}$
Fast-Activating Potassium	$A_K = n^4$	n	$\dfrac{-0.032(V - V_T - 15)}{e^{-(V-V_T-15)/5} - 1}$	$0.5e^{-(V-V_T-10)/40}$
Calcium	$A_{Ca} = q^2 s$	q	$\dfrac{-0.055(V + 27)}{e^{-(V+27)/3.8} - 1}$	$0.94e^{-(V+75)/17}$
		s	$0.000457e^{-(V+13)/50}$	$\dfrac{0.0065}{e^{-(V+15)/28} + 1}$
			$p_\infty(V)$	$\tau_p(V)$
Slow-Activating Potassium	$A_K^{slow} = p$	p	$\dfrac{1}{e^{-(V+35)/10} + 1}$	$\dfrac{\tau_{max}}{3.3e^{(V+35)/20} + e^{-(V+35)/20}}$

geometry for the neuron compartments is required. As a first-order approximation, here it is assumed that the dynamics are predominantly governed by the axon initial segment (AIS), where it has been shown that the post-synaptic currents are integrated and the actional potential is initiated [1,14,32]. For all neuron types, it is assumed that the AIS is approximately a cylinder with a diameter of 3 μm and a length of 30 μm [32].

2.2   Electrical and Chemical Synapse Model

The neurons in the neurosphere network can be connected by either chemical or electrical synapses (or both). Electrical synapses allow for bidirectional current exchange between the neurons, whereas chemical synapses only allow unidirectional currents. The synapse model utilized here is adopted from [13,16]. For electrical synapses, the current from pre-synaptic neuron j to post-synaptic neuron i takes the form:

$$I_{ij} = g_{ij}^e \left(V_j(t) - V_i(t) \right) \tag{4}$$

where g_{ij}^e is the synaptic strength (units: mS) between the two neurons. Because of the bi-directionality of the synapse, $I_{ij} = -I_{ji}$. For chemical synapses, the current from pre-synaptic neuron j to post-synaptic neuron i takes the form:

$$I_{ij} = g_{ij}^c r_j(t) \left(V_{syn}^j - V_i(t) \right) \tag{5}$$

where g_{ij}^c is the synaptic strength (units: mS), V_{syn} is the synaptic reversal potential, and r_j is the level of activation, modeling the fraction of bound neurotransmitter receptors. The dynamics of the receptor follow the kinetic equation:

$$\frac{dr_j}{dt} = \left(\frac{1}{\tau_r} - \frac{1}{\tau_d} \right) \frac{1 - r_j}{1 + e^{-V_j + V_0}} - \frac{1}{\tau_d} r_j \tag{6}$$

where τ_r and τ_d are the rise and decay time constants of the synapse, and V_0 is related to voltage at which the concentration of neurotransmitters reaches half of its maximal value [10]. All parameters related to the chemical synapses are summarized in Table 2.

2.3   Stochastic Network Formation

To model the formation of synaptic connection taking place in neurosphere cultures, stochastically-formed networks of the above-mentioned neuron types are constructed using the following process (summarized in Fig. 2):

First, a population of neurons, N, is drawn from a user-specified population prior using a Roulette Sampling technique [42]. Here, N is the user-specified number of neurons in the network. These neurons are placed in 2D space using a noisy sunflower seed pattern [38]. For neuron i, its position in polar coordinates is determined as:

$$[r_i, \theta_i] = \left[\sqrt{\frac{i}{N}}, \frac{2\pi}{\phi^2} i \right] \tag{7}$$

where $\phi = (1/2)(1+\sqrt{5})$ is the golden ratio. The Cartesian position of the neuron is then

$$[x_i, y_i]^T = [r_i \cos(\theta_i) + \xi_x, r_i \sin(\theta_i) + \xi_y]^T \tag{8}$$

where ξ_j is uniformly distributed random variable on the interval $[-0.01, 0.01]$, or 1% of the network size. Note that here the units of the 2D space are not considered. Without geometric consideration in the circuit model, it is not meaningful to prescribe dimensional geometry to the network.

With the neuron positioned in 2D space, we turn next to the formation of synaptic connections. For neuron i, the formation of its dendritic tree takes two steps. First, an axon projects in a randomly chosen direction. This direction is sampled from a normal distribution centered on the inverse-distance-weighted direction $\bar{\mathbf{n}}_i$ from neuron i to all other neurons in the network, calculated as:

$$\bar{\mathbf{n}}_i = \frac{\sum_j \frac{1}{|\mathbf{x}_j - \mathbf{x}_i|} \hat{\mathbf{n}}_{ij}}{\sum_j \frac{1}{|\mathbf{x}_j - \mathbf{x}_i|}} \tag{9}$$

where $\hat{\mathbf{n}}_{ij}$ is the unit vector from neuron i to neuron j. The standard deviation of the distribution is a user-specific parameter and defines the spread of the model "growth cone." This process takes inspiration from how neurons grow in response to chemical cues from other neurons and how the concentration of those cues will decay with distance [31, 36]. However, this model requires future validation in

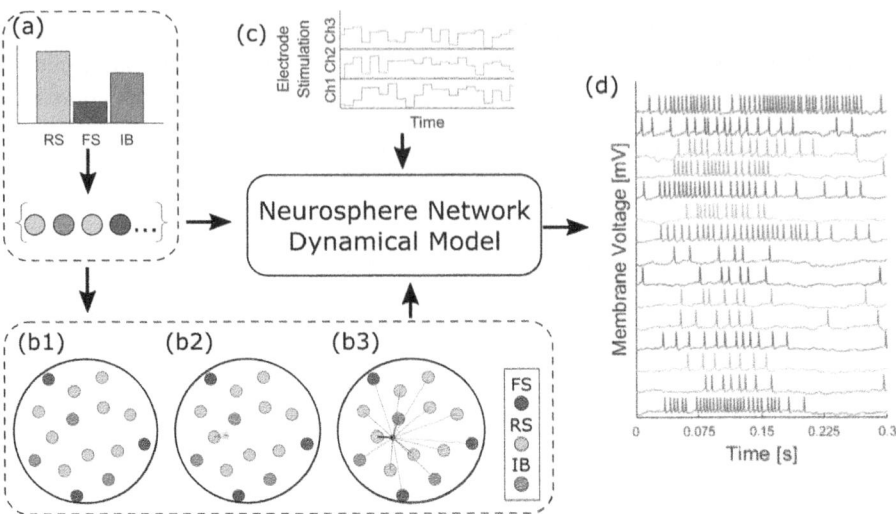

Fig. 2. Stochastic Neurosphere Network Framework. Here, the algorithm used to create and simulate neurosphere networks is summarized for a 15-neuron network. (a) Neuron types (see legend for color) are randomly sampled using user-specified prior and (b1) distributed in 2D space in a noisy sunflower-seed pattern. (b2) Direction of axonal growth is randomly sampled from a Gaussian distribution (red region shows $\pm 2\sigma$) centered on the inverse-distance-weight average direction to neighboring neurons. (b3) With the axon direction chosen (dark line), a branch location is specified (black dot). Connections are randomly made from the branch point to neighboring neurons, with the probability being proportional to the inverse distance to the branch point. The darkness of lines is proportional to the probability of synaptic formation. (c) To investigate neurosphere dynamics, randomly generated, piecewise-constant current stimulation is provided to three input neurons. The resulting membrane voltage of all neurons in the neurosphere is then calculated (d).

the context of 3D culture, as these previous works observed or modeled growth in planar culture. Next, the axon is projected a fixed distance[1] in the direction sampled above, and a branching point is placed at the end of the axon. Connections from neuron i to other neurons will originate at this branching point. To determine how many presynaptic connections neuron i will make with other neurons, a random integer m_{con} is sampled from the interval $[1, M_{con}]$, where $M_{con}(N)$ is the user-specified maximal number of presynaptic connections that a neuron can make based on the number of other neurons present. Then, neu-

---

[1] The distance of the pre-branching axon projection was chosen to be less than the typical spacing of neurons in the 2D model geometry. This would prevent neurons from intersecting. However, as mentioned above, there are no physical units for the system geometry, including this distance. This parameter can also be tuned in the future to better reflect a typical branching distance observed in neurons. In terms of the model units chosen for the graphical representation of the network, this distance was set to 50 model units.

rons in the network were randomly sampled (with replacement) again using a Roulette Sampling technique until a set of synaptic connections of size m_{con} was constructed. Here, the probability of forming a synapse between two neurons is proportional to the inverse distance between them. Each synapse formed between two neurons is randomly assigned to be either chemical or electrical via Roulette Sampling of a user-specified prior, and the synaptic strength is set to a fixed increment $\Delta g^j (j \in [\text{chemical, electrical}])$. If a duplicate synapse is formed between two neurons (e.g., a new chemical synapse is added where one already exists), the synaptic strength is simply increased by Δg^j.

The functional form of $M_{con}(N)$ was chosen to reflect the observation that neurons in 2D cultures tend to form fewer synapses per neuron in higher-density cultures [9]. For simplicity in these preliminary investigations, the following model was chosen:

$$M_{con}(N) = \text{round}\left(100\left(1 - \frac{N}{100}\right)\right) \tag{10}$$

However, in 2D neuron cultures, nonlinear relationships were observed [9], so the exact functional form should be further refined based on experimental measurements in 3D neurosphere cultures. Additionally, in its current form, this model is only meaningful for neurospheres of less than 100 neurons, as after this point, the number of connections would be negative. An updated model would be required for larger neurospheres. Similarly, it has also been observed that in higher-density cultures, the conductivity of synapses also decreases, seen as smaller post-synaptic potentials for the same stimulation [19]. As with the M_{con}, a simplified model is utilized here and requires further calibration for 3D neurosphere cultures. Specifically, the increment in synaptic conductivity is modeled as:

$$\Delta g^j(N) = (1 \times 10^{-8})\left(1 - \frac{N}{100}\right) \text{ mS} \tag{11}$$

The same functional form was used for chemical and electrical synapses. As mentioned for the model for M_{con}, this is limited to the case of less than 100 neurons and needs refinement informed by experimental measures.

2.4   Computational Experiments

To investigate the dynamics of these neurosphere networks, simulations were conducted with randomly generated input stimuli. Three neurons served as inputs to the system, those neurons being the ones located closest to the north-, west-, and south-most regions of the network. These neurons received trains of 60 ms current pulses, whose amplitude was sampled from a uniform distribution on the interval [0,20 pA].

Membrane voltage traces from simulated experiments were used to obtain spiking information from the neurosphere. To determine if a spike occurred, local peaks in the membrane voltage trace were identified using the MATLAB *findpeaks* function (MATLAB r2022b, MathWorks). To avoid obtaining false spikes due to subthreshold noise, a minimum voltage value for the peaks was set at 20 mV. From this spike train, an instantaneous firing frequency was calculated based on the number of spikes that occur in half-overlapping windows of width 20 ms. This window size was small enough that multiple samples could be taken within a single stimulation pulse. The instantaneous firing frequency was then smoothed with a 5-point moving average filter (*smooth*, MATLAB r2022b, MathWorks), giving a continuous firing frequency response for the neuron. This same analysis was conducted for all neurons in the neurosphere.

As a first step towards investigating possible latent encodings that are captured in these neurosphere networks, principal components analysis was performed on these firing frequency data. The value of the continuous firing frequency response was sampled in the same half-overlapping windows as above. From the time series firing frequency data for all neurons, the principal component axes and corresponding data projects were calculated (*pca*, MATLAB r2022b, MathWorks). The first three principal components were selected for further analysis. This number was chosen both to allow for graphical investigation and because it was observed that the amount of variance contained in subsequent components decayed rapidly. However, the number of information-containing components will likely change with the scale of the neurosphere and warrants its own investigation beyond the scope of this work.

2.5   Numerical Implementation

The present model was implemented using a custom MATLAB library. All simulations were solved using a variable-order, variable-step stiff differential equations solver (*ode15s*, MATLAB r2022b, MathWorks). For the present study, all simulations were conducted using an AMD Ryzen 5 5600X 6-core processor (3.70 GHz, 16 GB RAM). For the sake of reproducibility, all simulations were conducted starting with the same seed value for the MATLAB pseudorandom number generator of 200000 at the beginning of network formation. All code will be provided upon request. The current implementation of the solver scheme has not been optimized, as this was beyond the scope of this work. However, we plan to optimize for computational speed during the future development of this tool.

3   Results and Discussion

Using the proposed model framework, example simulations were conducted for networks of size $N = [15, 30, 45]$ (Fig. 3). Each simulation was run for 100 stimulation epochs, with a max stimulation current of 20 pA, and noise parameters $\sigma_{noise} = 5$ pA and $\tau_{noise} = 1$ ms. From the resulting time series membrane voltages (Fig. 4(a1–c1)), firing frequency was calculated, and principal components analysis was conducted on the firing frequency in fixed-width time bins. The first three principal components were considered for additional graphical analysis (Fig. 4(a2–c2)). These components covered 75.8%, 65.5%, and 44.2% of the variance for the N = 15, N = 30, and N = 45 cases, respectively.

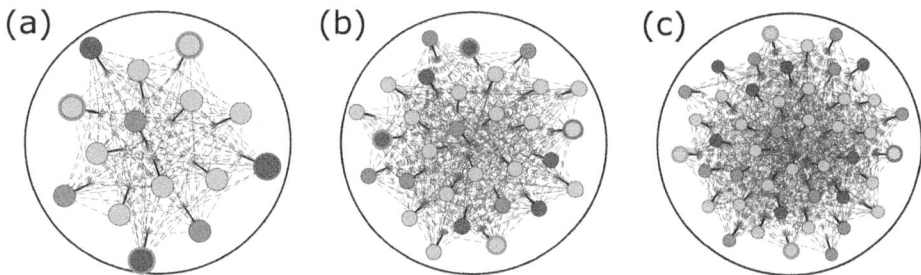

Fig. 3. Example Neurosphere Formation Network structures for size (a) N = 15, (b) N = 30, (c) N = 45. Colors correspond to the same neuron types as in Fig. 2, and the line style between two neurons showing the type of connection (dashed: chemical synapse only, dotted: electrical synapse only, dot-dashed: both electrical and chemical synapses). Green highlighting indicates the input neuron, and red highlighting indicates the output neuron. (Color figure online)

From a qualitative analysis of the membrane voltage time series, smaller networks showed higher firing frequencies with greater degrees of synchronicity between groups of neurons. Conversely, in larger networks, each individual neuron tended to show lower firing frequencies. This will be related to the choice of density-dependent maximum connectivity and synaptic conductivity increment. Additionally, observing the principal components of the firing frequencies, there appear to be input-current-related groupings (Fig. 4(a2–c2)). In these figures, the RGB values of the data point colors correspond to the stimulation current magnitude on input channels 1, 2, and 3, respectively. The input current-related groupings can be observed as clusters of similarly colored dots. This becomes more apparent in larger networks, where these groupings have more well-defined boundaries compared to the smaller networks. This suggests it is possible to encode input stimulus information in the firing frequency of these randomly connected networks. Further work is needed, however, to investigate the mapping between input and latent states, as well as the robustness of these encodings to stochasticity in the network. Additionally, it was observed that in the larger networks, more principal components contained a sizeable amount of the variance. Therefore, more components may need to be considered in these larger networks than the three that can be readily visualized.

The present model framework allows for preliminary simulations of neurosphere-like systems. However, multiple aspects require further refinement before it can be used as a predictive design tool. The first area of improvement concerns the system's lack of relevant geometry. Currently, neurons act as point compartments in dimensionless 2D space. In true neurospheres and neural systems in general, neurons have sprawling geometries that extend in all three dimensions [2]. This venture into the third dimension increases the degrees of freedom the neurons have to form synaptic connections. Additionally, this geometry means that neurons are not single components but consist of branching trees of axons and dendrites, the lengths and geometries of which contribute

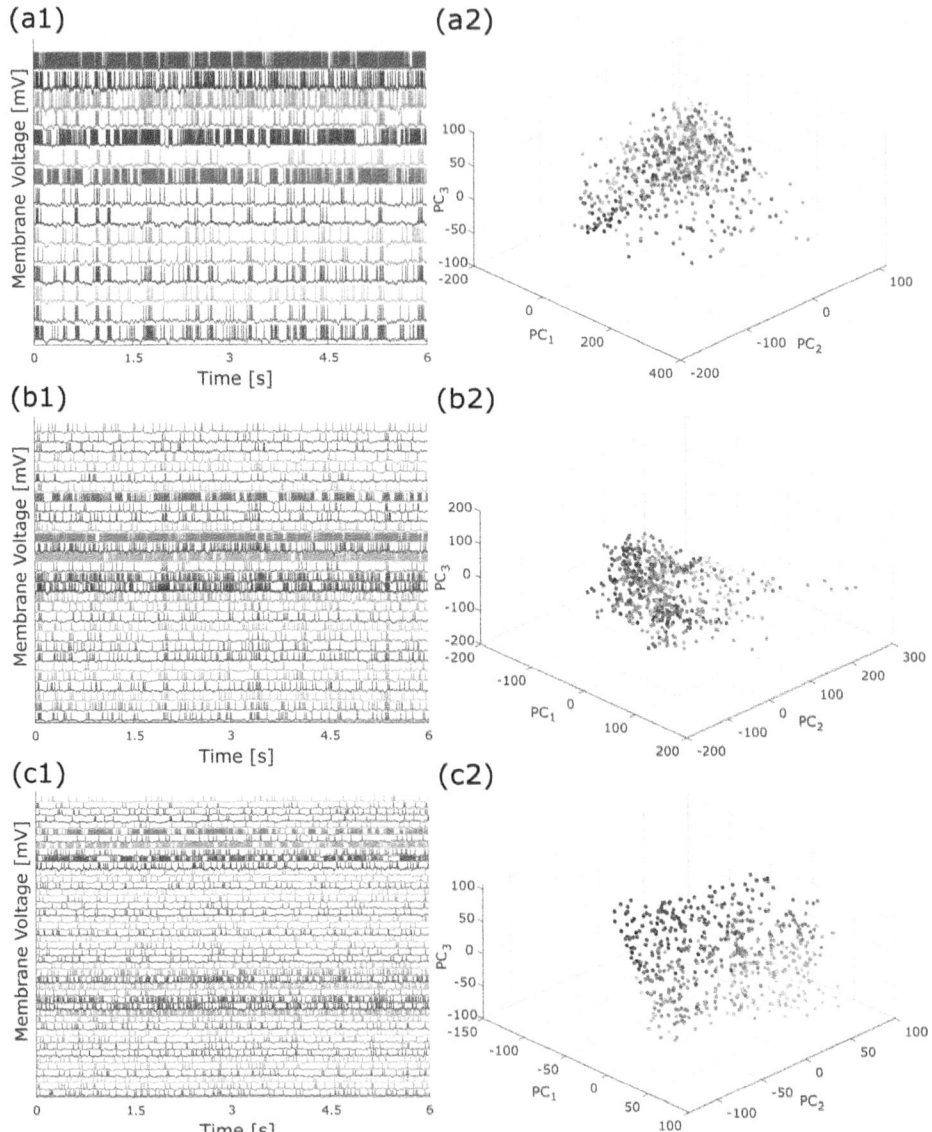

Fig. 4. Network Simulation Results. (a1–c1) Membrane voltage traces for the networks shown in Fig. 3. (a2–c2) Structure of first three principal components. The color of each dot corresponds to the input stimulus, with the red, green, and blue components corresponding to the normalized current magnitude on input channels 1, 2, and 3, respectively. (Color figure online)

to time delays in signal transmission [30] and other emergent electrical properties [11,23,37]. For more accurate modeling of these systems, these geometry-dependent effects should be incorporated either directly by incorporating multicompartment models of the axon and dendrites [3] or time-delay differential equations [5] for the synaptic connections. Finally, the spacing of neurons in the neurospheres will also be impacted by the volume fraction of non-neuronal cells in the culture. For smaller neuronal volume fractions, neurons will be, on average, farther apart from each other, changing their likelihood of connecting and the connection strength. This volume fraction and the stochastic arrangement of cells in packed 3D space could also be incorporated [33, 43].

The second area of improvement required for the model relates to the specific choice of sampling priors and parameter relationships. For these initial investigations, simplifications were made in the functional forms relating the maximal connectivity density and incremental synapse conductivity to the seeding density of neurons. The exact functional form can be refined from morphological and electrophysiological investigations of cultured neurospheres. Additionally, the various sampling priors used in this work were not calibrated to data. Finally, the types and parameters of the ion channels used in the circuit models were fixed and taken from the literature. To better reflect the cell sources utilized to build neurospheres, these parameters and their associated population distributions should be measured. These experimental results could be used to refine the model for the specific cell sources used. Finally, additional computational investigation could focus on the network's sensitivity to the different sampling and parameter priors. To maximize the impact of experiments, the parameters that are found to impact the model most could be prioritized. Additionally, if designers were able to customize the priors (using specific cell separation techniques or different mixtures of cell sources), then these sensitivities would allow them to predict the effect of a new prior and to begin optimizing these systems for specific tasks.

4 Conclusion

In this work, we present a model framework for simulating stochastically-formed neuron networks toward understanding the biophysics of neurosphere computation. Individual neurons are modeled using single-compartment Hodgkin-Huxley models with different combinations of ion channels, and we present a novel approach to model the stochastic formation of connections in neurospheres. Using this framework, we conduct preliminary simulations of networks of various sizes. In these simulations, it was observed that the current magnitude of input stimuli could be encoded in the principal components of firing frequencies. Future works will aim to increase the model's realism by incorporating the effects of 3D geometry and to increase the model's specificity through experimental characterization and validation of the constituent elements. This refined model will then be compared to experimentally measured neurosphere spikes trains.

Acknowledgement. The authors would like to thank Drs. Wayne Wu, Alison Barth, Joseph Najem, and Tzahi Cohen-Karni for their stimulating conversations during the formulation of this work.

Appendix

Table 2. Model Parameters. All parameters used in the model are summarized here. Most variables are taken verbatim from [13] and [29]. However, some are modified to better match the qualitative descriptions of the neurons proposed in those papers.

Parameter	Regular Spiking Neurons	Fast Spiking Neurons	Intrinsically Bursting Neurons
Neuron Parameters:			
C_m [uF/cm^2]	1	0.5	1
E_K [mV]		-90	
E_{Na} [mV]	56	50	50
E_{Ca} [mV]	——	——	120
E_L[mV]	-70.3	-70	-70
$\hat{g}_K$ [mS/cm^2]	6	10	10
$\hat{g}_{Na}$ [mS/cm^2]		56	
$\hat{g}_{Ca}$ [mS/cm^2]	——	——	0.2
$\hat{g}_K^{slow}$ [mS/cm^2]	0.075	——	0.075
$\hat{g}_L$ [mS/cm^2]	0.0205	0.015	0.0205
τ_p^{max} [ms]	608	——	608
V_T [mV]		-56.2	
Synapse Parameters:			
τ_r [ms]		0.5	
τ_d [ms]		8	
V_{syn} [mV]	20	-80	20
V_0 [mV]		-20	

References

1. Alcami, P., El Hady, A.: Axonal computations. Front. Cell. Neurosci. **13**(September), 1–19 (2019). https://doi.org/10.3389/fncel.2019.00413
2. Ascoli, G.A., Donohue, D.E., Halavi, M.: NeuroMorpho.Org: a central resource for neuronal morphologies. J. Neurosci. **27**(35), 9247–9251 (2007). https://doi.org/10.1523/JNEUROSCI.2055-07.2007

3. Bhalla, U.S.: Multi-compartment models of neurons. In: Computational Systems Neurobiology, vol. 7, pp. 1–570 (2012). https://doi.org/10.1007/978-94-007-3858-4

4. Block, F.E.: Analog and digital computer theory. Int. J. Clin. Monit. Comput. **4**(1), 47–51 (1987)

5. Bocharov, G.A., Rihan, F.A.: Numerical modelling in biosciences using delay differential equations. J. Comput. Appl. Math. **125**(1–2), 183–199 (2000). https://doi.org/10.1016/S0377-0427(00)00468-4

6. Burkitt, A.N.: A review of the integrate-and-fire neuron model: I. Homogeneous synaptic input. Biol. Cybern. **95**(1), 1–19 (2006)

7. Cai, H., et al.: Brain organoid reservoir computing for artificial intelligence. Nat. Electron. **6**(12), 1032–1039 (2023). https://doi.org/10.1038/s41928-023-01069-w

8. Chen, Z., et al.: An overview of *in vitro* biological neural networks for robot intelligence. Cyborg Bionic Syst. **4** (2023). https://doi.org/10.34133/cbsystems.0001

9. Cullen, D.K., Gilroy, M.E., Irons, H.R., Laplaca, M.C.: Synapse-to-neuron ratio is inversely related to neuronal density in mature neuronal cultures. Brain Res. **1359**, 44–55 (2010). https://doi.org/10.1016/j.brainres.2010.08.058

10. Destexhe, A., Mainen, Z.F., Sejnowski, T.J.: Models of synaptic transmission. In: Methods in Neuronal Modeling, pp. 1–25 (1998). https://doi.org/10.1007/978-3-642-46345-7_11

11. van Elburg, R.A., van Ooyen, A.: Impact of dendritic size and dendritic topology on burst firing in pyramidal cells. PLoS Comput. Biol. **6**(5), 1–19 (2010). https://doi.org/10.1371/journal.pcbi.1000781

12. Enel, P., Procyk, E., Quilodran, R., Dominey, P.F.: Reservoir computing properties of neural dynamics in prefrontal cortex. PLoS Comput. Biol. **12**(6), 1–35 (2016). https://doi.org/10.1371/journal.pcbi.1004967

13. Giannari, A.G., Astolfi, A.: Model design for networks of heterogeneous Hodgkin-Huxley neurons. Neurocomputing **496**, 147–157 (2022). https://doi.org/10.1016/j.neucom.2022.04.115

14. Goethals, S., Brette, R.: Theoretical relation between axon initial segment geometry and excitability. eLife **9**, 1–34 (2020). https://doi.org/10.7554/eLife.53432

15. Gürel, T., Rotter, S., Egert, U.: Functional identification of biological neural networks using reservoir adaptation for point processes. J. Comput. Neurosci. **29**(1–2), 279–299 (2010). https://doi.org/10.1007/s10827-009-0176-0

16. Hao, Y., Gong, Y., Wang, L., Ma, X., Yang, C.: Single or multiple synchronization transitions in scale-free neuronal networks with electrical or chemical coupling. Chaos, Solitons Fractals **44**(4–5), 260–268 (2011). https://doi.org/10.1016/j.chaos.2011.02.005

17. Howarth, C., Gleeson, P., Attwell, D.: Updated energy budgets for neural computation in the neocortex and cerebellum. J. Cereb. Blood Flow Metab. **32**(7), 1222–1232 (2012). https://doi.org/10.1038/jcbfm.2012.35

18. Huber, M.T., Braun, H.A.: Conductance versus current noise in a neuronal model for noisy subthreshold oscillations and related spike generation. Biosystems **89**(1–3), 38–43 (2007). https://doi.org/10.1016/j.biosystems.2006.05.009

19. Ivenshitz, M., Segal, M.: Neuronal density determines network connectivity and spontaneous activity in cultured hippocampus. J. Neurophysiol. **104**(2), 1052–1060 (2010). https://doi.org/10.1152/jn.00914.2009

20. Izhikevich, E.M.: Simple model of spiking neurons. IEEE Trans. Neural Netw. **14**(6), 1569–1572 (2003). https://doi.org/10.1109/TNN.2003.820440

21. Kagan, B.J., et al.: *In vitro* neurons learn and exhibit sentience when embodied in a simulated game-world. Neuron **110**(23), 3952-3969.e8 (2022). https://doi.org/10.1016/j.neuron.2022.09.001

22. Koren, V., Bondanelli, G., Panzeri, S.: Computational methods to study information processing in neural circuits. Comput. Struct. Biotechnol. J. **21**, 910–922 (2023) https://doi.org/10.1016/j.csbj.2023.01.009. https://www.sciencedirect.com/science/article/pii/S2001037023000119

23. Krichmar, J.L., Nasuto, S.J., Scorcioni, R., Washington, S.D., Ascoli, G.A.: Effects of dendritic morphology on CA3 pyramidal cell electrophysiology: a simulation study. Brain Res. **941**(1–2), 11–28 (2002). https://doi.org/10.1016/S0006-8993(02)02488-5

24. Lewin, D., Noaks, D.: Theory and Design of Digital Computer Systems. Springer, Dordrecht (1992). https://doi.org/10.1007/978-94-011-1576-6

25. Libedinsky, C.: Comparing representations and computations in single neurons versus neural networks. Trends Cogn. Sci. **27**(6), 517–527 (2023). https://doi.org/10.1016/j.tics.2023.03.002. https://linkinghub.elsevier.com/retrieve/pii/S1364661323000645

26. Long, L., Fang, G.: A review of biologically plausible neuron models for spiking neural networks. In: AIAA Infotech@Aerospace 2010. American Institute of Aeronautics and Astronautics, Atlanta, Georgia (2010)

27. Massobrio, P., Martinoia, S.: Modelling small-patterned neuronal networks coupled to microelectrode arrays. J. Neural Eng. **5**(3), 350–359 (2008). https://doi.org/10.1088/1741-2560/5/3/008

28. Poli, D., Magliaro, C., Ahluwalia, A.: Experimental and computational methods for the study of cerebral organoids: a review. Front. Neurosci. **13**(March), 1–13 (2019). https://doi.org/10.3389/fnins.2019.00162

29. Pospischil, M., et al.: Minimal Hodgkin-Huxley type models for different classes of cortical and thalamic neurons. Biol. Cybern. **99**(4–5), 427–441 (2008). https://doi.org/10.1007/s00422-008-0263-8

30. Puppo, F., George, V., Silva, G.A.: An optimized structure-function design principle underlies efficient signaling dynamics in neurons. Sci. Rep. **8**(1), 1–15 (2018). https://doi.org/10.1038/s41598-018-28527-2

31. Qian, K., Liao, A.S., Gu, S., Webster-Wood, V.A., Zhang, Y.J.: Biomimetic IGA neuron growth modeling with neurite morphometric features and CNN-based prediction. Comput. Methods Appl. Mech. Eng. **417**, 116213 (2023). https://doi.org/10.1016/j.cma.2023.116213

32. Rotterman, T.M., Carrasco, D.I., Housley, S.N., Nardelli, P., Powers, R.K., Cope, T.C.: Axon initial segment geometry in relation to motoneuron excitability. PLoS ONE **16**(11) (2021). https://doi.org/10.1371/journal.pone.0259918

33. Sipahi, R., Zupanc, G.K.: Stochastic cellular automata model of neurosphere growth: roles of proliferative potential, contact inhibition, cell death, and phagocytosis. J. Theor. Biol. **445**, 151–165 (2018). https://doi.org/10.1016/j.jtbi.2018.02.025

34. Sumi, T., et al.: Biological neurons act as generalization filters in reservoir computing. Proc. Natl. Acad. Sci. (2023). https://doi.org/10.1073/pnas.2217008120

35. Szczecinski, N.S., Hunt, A.J., Quinn, R.D.: A functional subnetwork approach to designing synthetic nervous systems that control legged robot locomotion. Front. Neurorobot. **11**, 1–19 (2017). https://doi.org/10.3389/fnbot.2017.00037

36. Tamariz, E., Varela-Echavarría, A.: The discovery of the growth cone and its influence on the study of axon guidance. Front. Neuroanat. **9**(MAY), 1–9 (2015). https://doi.org/10.3389/fnana.2015.00051

37. Vetter, P., Roth, A., Häusser, M.: Propagation of action potentials in dendrites depends on dendritic morphology. J. Neurophysiol. **85**(2), 926–937 (2001). https://doi.org/10.1152/jn.2001.85.2.926
38. Vogel, H.: A better way to construct the sunflower head. Math. Biosci. **44**, 179–189 (1979). https://doi.org/10.1016/0025-5564(79)90080-4
39. Warwick, K., et al.: Controlling a mobile robot with a biological brain. Defence Sci. J. **60**(1), 5–14 (2010). https://doi.org/10.14429/dsj.60.11
40. Won, P., Ko, S.H., Majidi, C., Feinberg, A.W., Webster-Wood, V.A.: Biohybrid actuators for soft robotics: challenges in scaling up. Actuators **9**(4), 1–11 (2020). https://doi.org/10.3390/act9040096
41. Yada, Y., Yasuda, S., Takahashi, H.: Physical reservoir computing with FORCE learning in a living neuronal culture. Appl. Phys. Lett. **119**(17) (2021). https://doi.org/10.1063/5.0064771
42. Younes, A., Elkamel, A., Areibi, S.: Genetic algorithms in chemical engineering : a tutorial. World (2008)
43. Zhdanov, V.P., Kasemo, B.: Simulation of the growth of neurospheres. Europhys. Lett. **68**(1), 134–140 (2004). https://doi.org/10.1209/epl/i2004-10170-1

Tools for Studying Behaviors

FlyWheel: A Robotic Platform for Modeling Fly Visual Behavior

William R. P. Nourse[1]([✉])(iD) and Roger D. Quinn[2](iD)

[1] Department of Electrical, Computer, and Systems Engineering, Case Western Reserve University, Cleveland, OH 44106, USA
`nourse@case.edu`
[2] Department of Mechanical and Aerospace Engineering, Case Western Reserve University, Cleveland, OH 44106, USA

Abstract. An ongoing problem in robotics is the calculation of body motion given motion in the visual field, also known as ego-motion estimation. This is a problem which has been solved in the visual system of most animals, including the fruit fly *Drosophila melanogaster*. Here we present FlyWheel, an open-source robotic platform for studying models of the visual motion-processing system in insects. We showcase a dataset of rotational motion data in real-world conditions using the robot, and use a simplified model of the motion pathway in *Drosophila* as a baseline for further comparison and development.

Keywords: Motion vision · Elementary movement detector · Synthetic nervous system

1 Introduction

An important problem which must be solved for navigation in both robotic systems and animals is visual ego-motion estimation, or the ability to use motion in the visual field to calculate how the body is moving through a fixed world [15]. Calculating ego-motion based on sequences of images has been a longstanding challenge in the field of computer vision, with the majority of successful solutions being built off of either measurements of optic flow or point correspondence. Initial methods estimated rotation then translation based on changing flows of point triplets [21], followed by methods which took the first derivative of image brightness in regions of interest [14]. Further methods were developed which used motion parallax between pairs of images, either to compute changes in depth [23] or image deformation [34]. In recent years convolutional neural networks have also been used, either as an end-to-end solution [9] or starting from an initial optical flow field [38].

This work was funded by National Science Foundation (NSF) DBI 2015317 as part of the NSF/CIHR/DFG/FRQ/UKRI-MRC Next Generation Networks for Neuroscience Program.

N. S. Szczecinski et al. (Eds.): Living Machines 2024, LNAI 14930, pp. 37–51, 2025.
https://doi.org/10.1007/978-3-031-72597-5_3

Fig. 1. FlyWheel, a mobile robot for testing models of motion control in flies.

An organism often studied for its motion-vision processing is the fruit fly *Drosophila melanogaster* [26,28,33], due to having a nervous system with significantly fewer neurons than vertebrates [4,17] as well as recent efforts to create a full brain connectome [25,36]. *Drosophila* and other insects generate an estimate of directional velocity throughout the visual field using the differences in timing between adjacent neurons in response to changing amounts of brightness, with sections being sensitive to increases in brightness and others to decreasing brightness [4]. Initial models of this mechanism for directional selectivity consisted of two-pixel (or input) detectors which either enhanced motion in the preferred direction [13] or suppressed motion in the opposite direction [3]. Many bio-inspired algorithms have been developed which are based on these two-pixel motion detectors, and have been successfully used for applications including quadrotor flight control [37] and target tracking [2]. It is also possible to estimate the velocity of natural images by combining multiple of these two-pixel detectors which are tuned to different spatial frequencies [7].

As more detailed information has become available about connectivity within the Drosophila optic lobe, it has become clear that the motion detectors are implemented as three-input detectors, not two, allowing the combination of preferred-direction enhancement and null-direction suppression within a single circuit [28]. For a detailed description of how a three-input detector creates directional selectivity, we refer the reader to its initial formulation by Haag et al. [12] or the detailed analysis presented by Groschner et al. [11]. In the work of Nourse et al. [19], a simplified version of this three-input detector was used to calculate the velocity of moving square-wave gratings using a network of neurons with bio-inspired dynamics. Currently however, no three-input detector system has been used for any robotics application.

In this work, we present the open-source robot FlyWheel, a platform for testing models of insect motion vision. We showcase a dataset of video clips collected during rotation on the robot, and provide results of a neural three-input motion detector as a baseline for further improvement (Fig. 1).

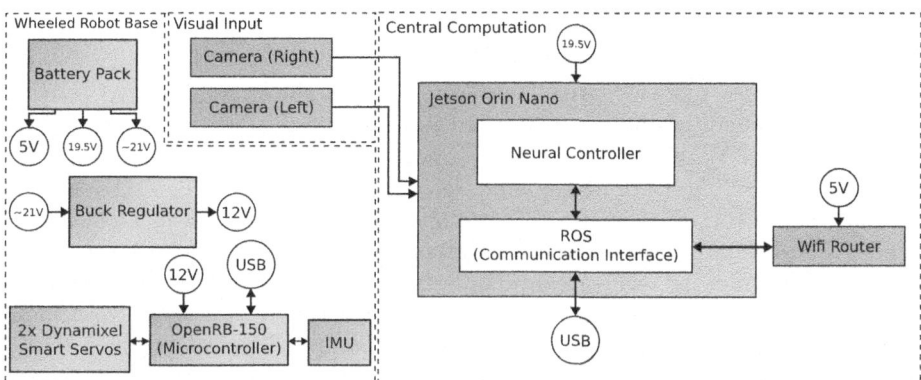

Fig. 2. System diagram of hardware and software components for FlyWheel. There are three subsystems: visual input, central computation, and a wheeled base. Each of these components is modular, and can be removed and replaced on the robot. The visual input consists of two 160 degree FOV cameras, arranged to have a similar stereo FOV as *Drosophila melanogaster*. The wheeled base provides power to the system, and has two Dynamixel (Robotis Co. Ltd., Seoul, South Korea) smart motors to provide propulsion. The central computing platform runs a ROS framework on an NVIDIA Jetson Orin Nano (NVIDIA, Santa Clara, CA), with a small wireless router as an external access point.

2   Robot Design

FlyWheel is built from three subsystems: central computation, a wheeled base, and visual input. Each of these components was designed to be modular, and can be removed and replaced on the robot. The robot body is fabricated using 3d-printed PLA on a consumer-grade printer. The hardware and software for FlyWheel is available at https://github.com/wnourse05/FlyWheel (Fig. 2).

2.1   Central Computation

The Central Computation module onboard FlyWheel is responsible for communicating with all of the sensors and actuators on the robot, as well as running any desired control algorithms. We chose to use an NVIDIA Jetson Orin Nano (NVIDIA, Santa Clara, CA) as our embedded computer due to its relative afford-ability and support for GPU acceleration, although the mechanical design would support the less expensive and less powerful Jetson Nano as well. For communi-cating with the cameras, motors, and any external computers, the Jetson Orin Nano uses a custom library built in the Robot Operating System (ROS) [22]. The combined camera feed is published as a rostopic, along with the status of a wireless game controller and commanded velocities for the motor system. Users can access the robot remotely via a miniature wireless router onboard.

2.2 Wheeled Base

The wheeled base has two primary roles: to move the robot, and to provide power to the embedded computer. Power comes from a lithium-ion battery bank, which provides 5 V DC for the wireless router, 19.5 V DC for the Jetson Orin Nano, and a 21–29 V DC output which is regulated down to 12 V DC for the motors. The motors are a pair of Dynamixel XL430 (Robotis Co. Ltd., Seoul, South Korea) smart motors, allowing precise control of the wheel rotational velocities. The motors receive commands from the Jetson Orin Nano using a Robotis OpenRB-150 microcontroller board. This board also sends rotational velocity information to the Jetson Orin Nano based on readings from a Bosch BNO055 inertial measurement unit (Robert Bosch GmbH, Gerlingen, Germany). The wheels are positioned in a unicycle-model configuration on either side of the robot, in order to reduce the distance between the axis of rotation and the cameras.

2.3 Visual Input

Since FlyWheel is designed for testing models of insect vision, it is important that the robot has a visual system which replicates that of the model insect as much as possible. Each of *Drosophila melanogaster*'s eyes has a field-of-view (FOV) of approximately 144° [35], and are combined to produce an overall FOV of 270° with a stereo overlap of 17° [30,31]. To replicate this, FlyWheel uses two 160 degree FOV IMX219 cameras from Yahboom (Yahboom, Shenzhen, China). These cameras are arranged to produce a net FOV of 286° with a stereo overlap of 34° as shown in Fig. 3.

Although flies are able to improve the resolution of their vision through vibrating their photoreceptors [10], they still have a fairly small visual resolu-tion compared to modern camera sensors. Each eye consists of approximately 800 facets or ommatidia [16] arranged in a hexagonal pattern [6], each with a recep-tive angle of five degrees [4]. In total, each eye can be approximated as having a visual resolution of 25×32 pixels. Additionally, most *Drosophila melanogaster* photoreceptors are sensitive to green wavelengths of light [8,29], although oth-ers are sensitive to blue light [24,27]. To replicate this on FlyWheel, we first strip the red and blue channels from the images captured by the cameras. We then concatenate the stereo pair of images side by side into a single image, and

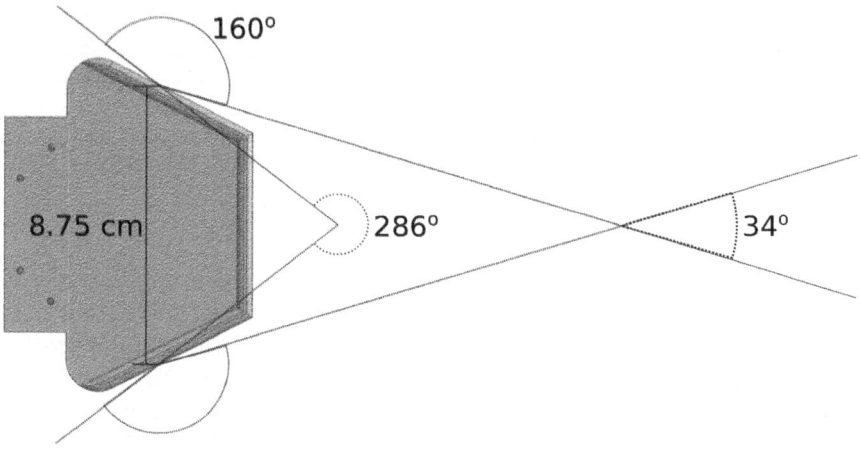

Fig. 3. FlyWheel field of view (FOV). Each eye has a 160° FOV, and is arranged to produce a net FOV of 286° with a stereo overlap of 34°. The inter-camera distance is 8.75 cm.

then downsample the image using nearest-neighbor interpolation. While not as accurate as area-based interpolation, the processing time of nearest-neighbor interpolation is significantly faster. For a comparison of latency between both interpolation methods across different final resolutions, please refer to Fig. 5A. The final resolution of the stereo image is 24 × 64 pixels, the dimensions which are closest to that of *Drosophila melanogaster* while still having satisfactory performance. The entire image processing pipeline runs at a rate of 30 frames per second (FPS), with a processing latency of 6 ms. For a visual example of the final images, please refer to Fig. 4.

The IMX219 cameras used in this work use a rolling shutter, which can produce distortion in moving images. Because of this, we chose to orient the cameras such that the rolling shutter effect is in the vertical direction. Since the robot is purely rotating in the horizontal/yaw direction, along with the slow speeds of our motion and the high degree of interpolation, we chose to not perform any additional postprocessing to correct any rolling shutter distortion as it is minimally present in the final frame sequences. We also did not incorporate a calibration procedure to account for any minor changes in pitch and roll between the two cameras, however this is something which can be done using standard image processing techniques in future work.

3   Motion Vision Dataset

A goal of FlyWheel is to test models of ego-motion estimation in *Drosophila melanogaster*, specifically for lateral steering. We collected a dataset of rotational

Fig. 4. Example stereo video frames after processing. Stereo pairs are concatenated into a single image, converted to greyscale, then downsampled from the native resolution of 1232×3280 to 24×64 pixels.

motion data by placing the robot in multiple different interior locations with varied lighting conditions and commanded it to spin in place while varying its rotational speed between 0.1 and 0.5 rad per second in the counter-clockwise direction. Using this paradigm, we created a dataset of 1,764 three-second long clips which are labeled with their corresponding rotational velocity, and where twenty percent of the clips are reserved for validation. This dataset is freely available at https://github.com/wnourse05/flywheel-rotation-dataset.

4   Motion Processing Network

As a base system of performance, we implemented a motion vision processing network based on the motion vision circuitry in the optic lobe of the fruit fly *Drosophila melanogaster*. We used the same techniques as Nourse et al. [19], with some adjustments to account for the use of natural images instead of simulated square gratings. The full network is shown in Fig. 6. In this section we will begin with an overview of the neural modeling techniques employed, and then will examine the design of each individual network section, emphasizing the changes made in this work. The network and all remaining support code can be found at https://github.com/wnourse05/FlyWheelBaseline-LivingMachines2024.

4.1   Neural Modeling

We choose to implement our motion-vision processing network as a Synthetic Nervous System (SNS) of non-spiking leaky integrator neurons, where the neural state U is updated as

$$\tau \cdot \dot{U} = -U + S + B + I, \tag{1}$$

where τ is the neural time constant, I is any external input, and B is a constant bias term. S is the synaptic input from any presynaptic neurons in the network,

$$S = \sum_{n}^{N} G_{syn,n}\left(U_n\right) \cdot \left(E_{syn,n} - U\right), \tag{2}$$

with U_n denoting a presynaptic neuron, and $E_{syn,n}$ denoting the synaptic reversal potential. Throughout the network, we design for neurons to communicate when their state is between 0 and R, with $R = 1$ in this work for numerical simplicity. All excitatory synapses in our model have $E_{ex} = 5R$, $E_{in} = -2R$ for inhibitory synapses, and modulatory synapses have a reversal potential of $E_{mod} = 0$. $G_{syn,n}(U_n)$ is a monotonic function which describes the incoming synaptic conductance, defined as

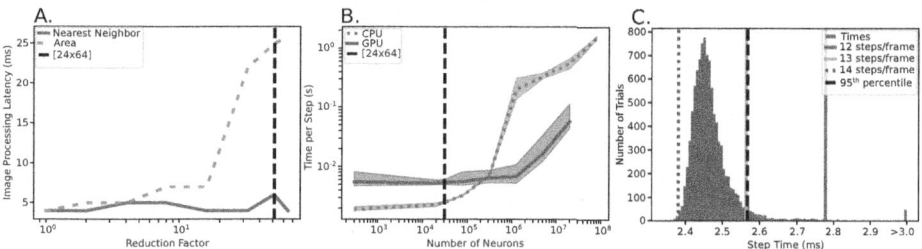

Fig. 5. Timing performance of image formatting and processing execution on target hardware. **A:** Latency in image processing as the target image reduces in size. Two different interpolation methods are compared, with nearest-neighbor interpolation shown in solid blue and area interpolation shown in dashed orange. A vertical dashed line is present at the image resolution 24×64, the scaled dimensions used in our dataset. **B:** Time per simulation step of our visual motion processing network, in seconds, as the dimensionality of the input increases. Execution on the Jetson Orin Nano CPU are shown in dotted green, and times for the Jetson Orin Nano GPU are shown in solid red. Dark lines correspond to the average, the shaded area corresponds to the 5th and 95th percentiles over 1000 steps. We use a vertical dashed line to denote the dimensionality corresponding to an input image size of 24×64 pixels. **C:** Detailed timing of our network with an input dimensionality of 24×64 pixels. Shown is a histogram of time per simulation step in milliseconds, over a testing run of 10,000 steps. A black dashed vertical line denotes the 95th percentile of the distribution. Shown in dashed green, solid orange, and solid red would be the time per step needed for 14, 13, or 12 simulation steps per video frame. In this work we chose to use 13 steps per frame for our simulations.

$$G_{syn,n} = g_{max,n} \cdot max\left(0, min\left(\frac{U_n - \theta_{lo}}{\theta_{hi} - \theta_{lo}}, 1\right)\right), \quad (3)$$

where $\theta_{lo} = 0$ and $\theta_{hi} = R$ are the lower and upper threshold states of synaptic activity.

Taking the model in Eq. 1, if we set $\dot{U}$ to 0 we find the steady-state response U^* [32] as

$$U^* = \frac{\sum_n^N g_{max,n}\frac{U_n^*}{R} \cdot E_{syn,n} + B + I}{1 + \sum_n^N g_{max,n}\frac{U_n^*}{R}}. \quad (4)$$

Synaptic Pathway Designs. In the SNS network, we tune many of the synapses using one of three analytic rules. The first is for signal transmission, where the target value of the postsynaptic neuron U^* from Eq. 4 is the steady-state voltage of the presynaptic neuron multiplied by a transmission gain K. As seen in Szczecinski et al. [32], this can be solved as

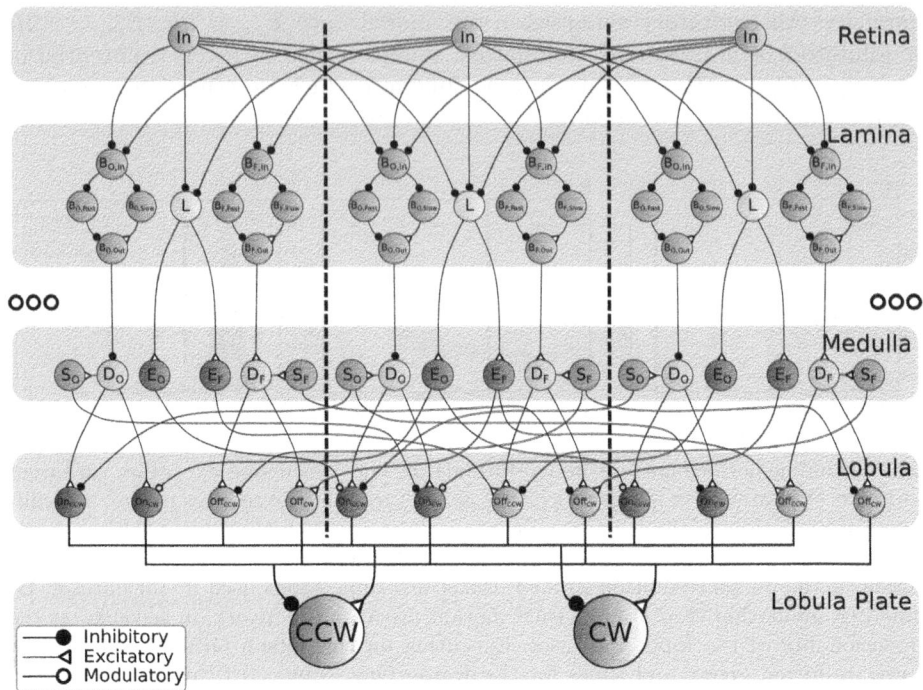

Fig. 6. Visual motion processing network used in this work, inspired by the anatomy of *Drosophila melanogaster* and adapted from [19]. Visual stimuli are encoded into a neural representation in the retina. They are then spatiotemporally filtered in the lamina, and temporally filtered again in the medulla. The lobula combines the neural activity in the medulla into estimates of motion at each pixel, and these estimates are summed across the entire visual field to generate a global estimate of motion in the lobula plate.

$$g_{max} = \frac{K \cdot R}{E_{syn} - K \cdot R}, \tag{5}$$

where E_{syn} is either E_{ex} or E_{in} depending on the role of the synapse.

An alternative formulation is to set a target state T of the postsynaptic neuron, depending on the presence of external inputs. This is shown in Nourse et al. [19] as

$$g_{max} = \frac{R \cdot (B - T)}{U_{pre}^* \cdot (T - E_{syn})}. \tag{6}$$

The other analytic synapse design in this work is a modulatory one, meant to modulate the sensitivity of a postsynaptic neuron to external and synaptic inputs. This can be designed following Szczecinski et al. [32], setting the synaptic conductance as

$$g_{max} = \delta - 1, \tag{7}$$

and using the modulatory reversal potential E_{mod}. In this formulation, the steady state U^* is divided by δ when $U^*_{pre} = R$.

For simulating these dynamics, we discretized Eqs. 1–3 into a forward-euler formulation, and simulated them as individual layers in the PyTorch numerical simulation software [20] in order to support execution on either a CPU or a GPU.

4.2   General Network Properties

Our first step in adapting the network from Nourse et al. [19] to this task was to determine how fast the network could run. To do this we evaluated the network over multiple different input image dimensions, and recorded the execution time for each simulation step over 1000 steps. We compared the step simulation time with increasing image size to the image processing latency with decreasing image size, and determined an input size of 24×64 pixels to be an appropriate balance of processing speed and biorealism. From here, we simulated the network for that input dimensionality for 10,000 steps in order to find a realistic time per step to base our simulations upon. We found that 95% of all trials could be accounted for with a timestep of $\Delta t = 2.56$ ms, equivalent to an update rate of 390 Hz or 13 steps per input frame. These results can be seen in Fig. 5.

4.3   Retina

The Retina converts the image stream into a neural representation. To do this, we create a layer of neurons the same size as the input image. For the temporal properties, we set the time constant from Eq. 1 as small as possible while maintaining numeric stability. We denote this as τ_{fast}, and empirically found this to be 15.4 ms.

4.4   Lamina

The Lamina takes the image representation from the retina and applies a bank of spatiotemporal filters. The visual processing system is also first split into the On and Off pathways, with each pathway having a bandpass network and sharing a lowpass filter.

Spatial Filtering. The most significant change in this work over that of Nourse et al. is that we implement the spatial filtering which was ommitted in that work. To perform spatial filtering of the image representation in the retina, each of the lamina input neurons integrates across a 5×5 grid of retinal neurons. This size was chosen based on the typical receptive field structure in *Drosophila* [4]. Given that the retina encodes the image brightness at each pixel as a neural state between zero and R, we want to ensure that the inputs into the lamina layer remain stable. Specifically, we aim to bound $U^* \in [0, R]$. In the trivial case where all presynaptic neurons are at rest, the steady-state postsynaptic voltage from Eq. 4 is $U^* = B$. When all presynaptic neurons are at a maximum state of R, Eq. 4 becomes

$$U^* = \frac{B + \sum_i^N g_{syn,i} E_i}{1 + \sum_i^N g_{syn,i}} \tag{8}$$

With the inputs to B_O, L, and B_F, we are interested in the inhibitory case, where $U^* \geq 0$ and $B = R$.

$$0 \leq \frac{R + \sum_i^N g_{syn,i} E_i}{1 + \sum_i^N g_{syn,i}} \tag{9}$$

Rearranging, we find that the sum of the synaptic conductances multiplied by the reversal potentials must be bounded by $-R$.

$$\sum_i^N g_{syn,i} E_i \geq -R \tag{10}$$

To do this, we choose to parameterize the sum on the left hand side of Eq. 10 as a probability density function (PDF) scaled by $-R$, as all PDFs by definition have a combined sum of 1. Any PDF could be chosen, but in order to replicate experimental results in *Drosophila melanogaster* we parameterize the sum as a difference of gaussians

$$g_{syn,ij} E_{ij} = -R \cdot \left(\frac{1}{\sigma_{cen}\sqrt{2\pi}} \cdot e^{\frac{-(\theta_i^2 + \phi_j^2)}{2\sigma_{cen}^2}} - \frac{A_{rel}}{\sigma_{sur}\sqrt{2\pi}} \cdot e^{\frac{-(\theta_i^2 + \phi_j^2)}{2\sigma_{sur}^2}} \right) \tag{11}$$

where σ_{cen} and σ_{sur} are the standard deviations of the center and surround gaussians, and $A_{rel} \in [0, 1]$ is a scaling coefficient [1]. As ΔE is constrained to a finite set of choices, we divide Eq. 11 by the corresponding E based on its sign to arrive at $g_{syn,ij}$.

Temporal Filtering. Within the lamina, the On and Off pathway each have a bandpass filter network and share a neuron acting as a lowpass filter. For the lowpass filter (L), for simplicity we set its membrane time constant to τ_{fast} since it will be further filtered later on in the Medulla. To implement a bandpass filter, we take the difference between two non-spiking neurons of different time constants (B_{Fast} and B_{Slow}). We parameterize both bandpass filters identically, with the fast pathway being set to τ_{fast} and the slow pathway being approximately five times slower.

4.5   Medulla

In the medulla, the spatiotemporal filtering performed in the lamina is temporally filtered again. In both the On and Off pathways, there are three neurons responsible for direct stimulation, suppression, and enhancement. The direct and enhancement (D and E) neurons receive synaptic input from the bandpass and lowpass (B and L) neurons, while the suppression (S) neuron receives input from the direct neuron. Each of these neurons behaves as a lowpass filter, with the temporal properties tuned following the procedure in Nourse et al. and assuming a spatial resolution of five degrees and a rotational speed of 0.1 to 0.5 rad per second.

4.6 Lobula

The role of the circuitry in the lobula is to convert the filtered representations in each column of the medulla into an estimate of the velocity at each pixel. The enhancement, direct, and suppression neurons from adjacent columns are combined to behave as a three-input elementary motion detector [12]. In the On pathway, D_O excites the motion detector whenever an increase in brightness passes over the column. This excitation is dampened by a modulatory synapse from E_O in the precending column (Eq. 7), and sharply inhibited by S_O in the next column in the preferred direction. The mechanism is nearly identical in the Off pathway, with the only difference being that E_F is excitatory instead of modulatory. As the velocity of the stimuli increases, the magnitude of the response in the motion detector decreases as the time between excitation and inhibition decreases.

4.7 Lobula Plate

In the final layer, we extend the network presented in Nourse et al. to include an approximation of the circuitry present in the *Drosophila melanogaster* lobula plate. We add two horizontal sensitive neurons, CCW and CW, one corresponding to counter-clockwise rotation and the other to clockwise rotation in the yaw direction. These neurons receive synaptic input from every motion detector neuron in the lobula, with the counter-clockwise sensitive detectors exciting CCW and inhibiting CW, and the inverse case for clockwise sensitive detectors [4]. These neurons have a time constant of τ_{fast}, and the synapses are tuned using Eq. 5 such that the sum of all the synaptic gains is one.

5   Results

Using the counter-clockwise clips in the test portion of the dataset described in Sect. 3, we evaluated the performance of the visual motion processing network described in Sect. 4. We simulated two different variants of the network, one with 5×5 pixel receptive fields and one with single-pixel receptive fields as in Nourse et al. [19]. For each sample clip, we let the network states stabilize to the first video frame and then recorded the neural state of the readout neurons CCW and CW over the remaining frames. Since all of the used clips correspond to counter-clockwise rotation, the network behaves correctly if the CCW neuron has a greater state than the CW. Across the test set, the network with single-pixel fields was correct for 93% of the clips and the 5×5 pixel network was correct 73% of the time. Performance for each velocity is shown in Fig. 7.

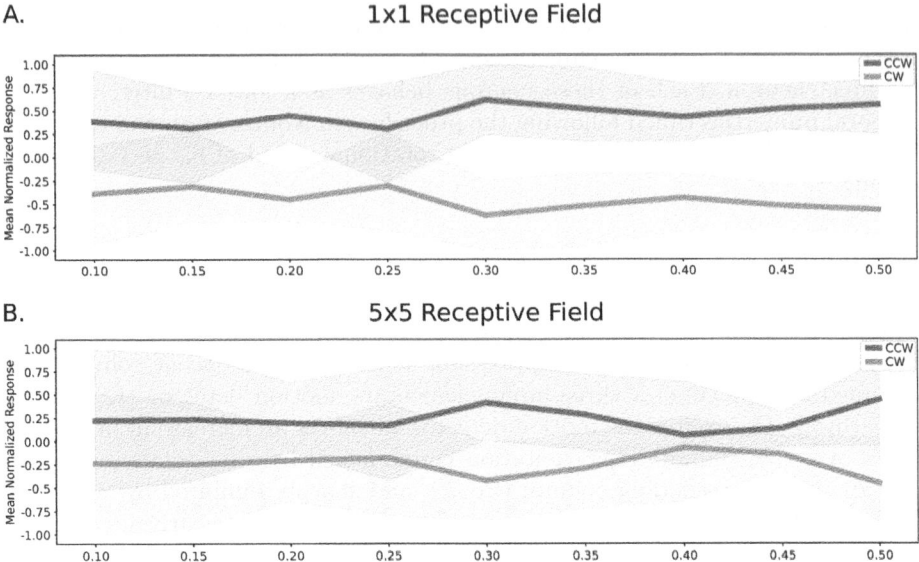

Fig. 7. Performance of the motion vision processing network on the 360 video clips in the test portion of the FlyWheel dataset. Each speed corresponded to 40 clips. **A.** Network with single-pixel receptive fields. The CCW neuron is greater than the CW neuron for counter-clockwise motion for 93% of the set. **B.** Network with 5×5 pixel receptive fields. The CCW neuron is greater than the CW neuron for counter-clockwise motion for 73% of the set. In both panels curves denote the mean neural response of all trials at each velocity, shaded area represents the 5th and 95th percentiles. All data is normalized to the maximum of the 95th percentile across all velocities.

6   Discussion

In this work, we present the robotic platform FlyWheel. FlyWheel is a wheeled robot with a binocular camera system designed to mimic the FOV of the fruit fly *Drosophila melanogaster*. We collected a dataset of video sequences across a range of turning velocities, and then implemented a visual motion processing SNS network to discriminate between counter-clockwise and clock-wise rotation over this dataset. The hardware and software for FlyWheel are open-source along with the dataset, and we believe that FlyWheel can be a valuable platform for benchmarking and studing models of motion processing and navigation in *Drosophila melanogaster* and other insects.

While our processing network was able to successfully identify the direction of global rotation, this estimate does not allow the discrimination of rotational speed. This is not surprising, given that the processing network was adapted from one made for square-wave gratings with little additional tuning. Additionally, performance of our network decreased as we added the more bio-realistic receptive fields to the input of our network. We provide this network as a base for comparison, but further work will use numerical optimization to better tune the network for natural image sequences. Other elements could also be added, such as additional inputs to the motion detectors [7] or synaptic feedback loops which are found within the Off pathway in *Drosophila* [5].

Finally, FlyWheel is only used in this work for collecting data when rotating in the yaw direction. Visual ego-motion consists of many other directional behaviors, including forward and backward motion as well as retreating from rapidly approaching stimuli [4]. FlyWheel could be used in future work to collect datasets of these other motion modalities, as well as test models of insect navigation in the mushroom body and central complex [18].

References

1. Arenz, A., Drews, M.S., Richter, F.G., Ammer, G., Borst, A.: The temporal tuning of the drosophila motion detectors is determined by the dynamics of their input elements. Curr. Biol. **27**, 929–944 (2017)
2. Bagheri, Z.M., Wiederman, S.D., Cazzolato, B.S., Grainger, S., O'Carroll, D.C.: Performance of an insect-inspired target tracker in natural conditions. Bioinspirat. Biomimetics **12** (2017)
3. Barlow, H.B., Levick, W.R.: The mechanism of directionally selective units in rabbit's retina. J. Physiol. **178**, 477 (1965)
4. Borst, A., Drews, M., Meier, M.: The neural network behind the eyes of a fly (2020)
5. Braun, A., Borst, A., Meier, M.: Disynaptic inhibition shapes tuning of off-motion detectors in drosophila. Curr. Biol. **33**, 2260–2269.e4 (2023)
6. Cagan, R.: Chapter 5 principles of drosophila eye differentiation. Curr. Topics Dev. Biol. **89**, 115–135 (2009)
7. Campbell, B.P., Lin, H.T., Krapp, H.G.: Weighting elementary movement detectors tuned to different temporal frequencies to estimate image velocity. In: Lecture Notes in Computer Science (including subseries Lecture Notes in Artificial Intelligence and Lecture Notes in Bioinformatics) **14157 LNAI**, pp. 398–410 (2023)
8. Clandinin, T.R., et al.: Drosophila lar regulates r1-r6 and r7 target specificity in the visual system (2001)
9. Costante, G., Mancini, M., Valigi, P., Ciarfuglia, T.A.: Exploring representation learning with cnns for frame-to-frame ego-motion estimation. IEEE Rob. Autom. Lett. **1**, 18–25 (2016)
10. Fenk, L.M., et al.: Muscles that move the retina augment compound eye vision in drosophila. Nature **612**(7938), 116–122 (2022)
11. Groschner, L.N., Malis, J.G., Zuidinga, B., Borst, A.: A biophysical account of multiplication by a single neuron. Nature **603**(7899), 119–123 (2022)
12. Haag, J., Arenz, A., Serbe, E., Gabbiani, F., Borst, A.: Complementary mechanisms create direction selectivity in the fly. eLife **5** (2016)
13. Hassenstein, B., Reichardt, W.: Systemtheoretische analyse der zeit-, reihenfolgen- und vorzeichenauswertung bei der bewegungsperzeption des rüsselkäfers chlorophanus. Zeitschrift für Naturforschung B **11**, 513–524 (1956)

14. Horn, B.K., Weldon, E.J.: Direct methods for recovering motion. Int. J. Comput. Vision **2**, 51–76 (1988)
15. Khan, N.H., Adnan, A.: Ego-motion estimation concepts, algorithms and challenges: an overview. Multimedia Tools Appl. **76**, 16581–16603 (2017)
16. Kumar, J.P.: Building an ommatidium one cell at a time (2012)
17. Leuba, G., Kraftsik, R.: Anatomy and embryolo changes in volume, surface estimate, three-dimensional shape and total number of neurons of the human primary visual cortex from midgestation until old age (1994)
18. Mitchell, R., Shaverdian, S., Dacke, M., Webb, B.: A model of cue integration as vector summation in the insect brain. Proc. R. Soc. B **290**(2001), 20230767 (2023)
19. Nourse, W.R., Szczecinski, N.S., Quinn, R.D.: A synthetic nervous system for on and off motion detection inspired by the drosophila melanogaster optic lobe. In: Lecture Notes in Computer Science (including subseries Lecture Notes in Artificial Intelligence and Lecture Notes in Bioinformatics), vol. 14157 LNAI, pp. 364–380 (2023)
20. Paszke, A., et al.: Pytorch: An imperative style, high-performance deep learning library. Curran Associates Inc. (2019)
21. Prazdny, K.: Egomotion and relative depth map from optical flow. Biol. Cybern. **36**, 87–102 (1980)
22. Quigley, M., et al.: Ros: an open-source robot operating system (2009)
23. Rieger, J.H., Lawton, D.T.: Processing differential image motion. JOSA A **2**(2), 354–359 (1985)
24. Rister, J., Desplan, C., Vasiliauskas, D.: Establishing and maintaining gene expression patterns: insights from sensory receptor patterning. Development **140**, 493–503 (2013)
25. Scheffer, L.K., et al.: A connectome and analysis of the adult drosophila central brain. eLife **9**, 1–74 (2020)
26. Serbe, E., Meier, M., Leonhardt, A., Borst, A.: Comprehensive characterization of the major presynaptic elements to the drosophila off motion detector. Neuron **89**, 829–841 (2016)
27. Sharkey, C.R., Blanco, J., Leibowitz, M.M., Pinto-Benito, D., Wardill, T.J.: The spectral sensitivity of drosophila photoreceptors. Sci. Rep. **10**(1), 1–13 (2020)
28. Shinomiya, K., et al.: Comparisons between the on-and off-edge motion pathways in the drosophila brain. eLife **8** (2019)
29. Stavenga, D.G.: Insect retinal pigments: spectral characteristics and physiological functions (1995)
30. Sten, T.H., Li, R., Otopalik, A., Ruta, V.: Sexual arousal gates visual processing during drosophila courtship. Nature **595**(7868), 549–553 (2021)
31. Strother, J.A., et al.: Behavioral state modulates the on visual motion pathway of drosophila. Proc. Natl. Acad. Sci. USA **115**, E102–E111 (2018)
32. Szczecinski, N.S., Hunt, A.J., Quinn, R.D.: A functional subnetwork approach to designing synthetic nervous systems that control legged robot locomotion. Front. Neurorobot. **11**, 37 (2017)
33. Takemura, S.Y., Nern, A., Chklovskii, D.B., Scheffer, L.K., Rubin, G.M., Meinertzhagen, I.A.: The comprehensive connectome of a neural substrate for 'on' motion detection in drosophila (2017)
34. Tomasi, C., Shi, J.: Direction of heading from image deformations. In: IEEE Computer Vision and Pattern Recognition, pp. 422–427 (1993)
35. Wang-Chen, S., et al.: Neuromechfly 2.0, a framework for simulating embodied sensorimotor control in adult drosophila (2023)

36. Winding, M., et al.: The connectome of an insect brain. Science (New York, N.Y.) **379**, eadd9330 (2023)
37. Zhang, L., Zhang, T., Wu, H., Borst, A., Khnlenz, K.: Visual flight control of a quadrotor using bioinspired motion detector. Int. J. Navigat. Observat. (2012)
38. Zhao, B., Huang, Y., Wei, H., Hu, X.: Ego-motion estimation using recurrent convolutional neural networks through optical flow learning. Electronics **10**, 222 (2021)

A Coupled-Oscillator Model of Human Attachment Dynamics Evaluated in a Robot Dyadic Interaction

Aung Htet[1]([✉])(iD), Alejandro Jimenez-Rodriguez[1](iD), Marcantonio Gagliardi[3], and Tony J. Prescott[2](iD)

[1] Department of Computing, Sheffield Hallam University, Sheffield, UK
aung.htet@student.shu.ac.uk, a.jimenez-rodriguez@shu.ac.uk
[2] Department of Computer Science, The University of Sheffield, Sheffield, UK
t.j.prescott@sheffield.ac.uk
[3] Institute for Lifecourse Development, University of Greenwich, London, UK
m.gagliardi@greenwich.ac.uk

Abstract. A better understanding of the nature of human relationships can aid the design of effective and appropriate social behaviour for robots. The investigation of human bonding via robotic modelling can also serve to test psychological theories in an embodied setting. In this work we present a robotic model of "attachment"—the primary bond between child and caregiver that shapes relationship behaviour throughout our lives. Following a dynamical systems approach, we model attachment as a behavioural coupling between motivational oscillators and show, by means of a dynamical analysis, that coupled robot dyads generate dynamical patterns that resemble caregiver-child interactions. By demonstrating coupling in an embodied model, we also show that measures of physical and emotional distance (a psychological variable), inferred from sensory data, can serve as effective control parameters for attachment behaviour. We find that this oscillator framework generates rich patterns of robot behaviours that can be associated with quantitative and qualitative observations of the "strange situation" procedure, an experimental paradigm that is widely studied in human relationship science, and of human avoidant and ambivalent attachment styles. The ability to estimate human attachment style and to generate appropriately-matched robot behaviours could be useful in social and companion robotics.

Keywords: Attachment · Human-Robot interaction · Dynamical systems

1 Introduction

People can form emotional bonds with intelligent artefacts, such as social and companion robots, that are complex and can be personally meaningful [1]. Some

N. S. Szczecinski et al. (Eds.): Living Machines 2024, LNAI 14930, pp. 52–67, 2025.
https://doi.org/10.1007/978-3-031-72597-5_4

forms of bonding could be beneficial in situations where the robot provides a valued service such as being physically or socially- assistive, at the same time, concerns have been raised that inappropriate bonding with a robot could cause harm (e.g. [2]). The nature of the behavioural interaction between human and robot is likely to be a determining factor in establishing any long-term bond. We have previously analysed human-robot relationships through the lens of social psychology and relationship science, proposing that there can be similarities between human-robot bonds and some forms of human-human and human-other bond [1,3]. In the current contribution, we present a dynamical systems account of the human attachment bond and explore its potential for understanding caregiver-child relationships through an embodied robotic model. We consider that this approach can both advance the understanding of human relationships and provide insights that could aid the future design of social and companion robots.

1.1 Attachment as a Motivational System

Attachment theory, developed by John Bowlby in the 1950s and 1960s [5] and expanded by Mary Ainsworth [6], highlights the importance of foundational relationships, particularly that between a child and its primary caregiver (typically the mother), as being critical in establishing ways of relating to others that persist through life. The classical theoretical approach uses different categories to classify attachment styles in children, as revealed by a laboratory procedure termed the "strange situation" procedure (SSP) [6,7]. In a typical experiment, a child and their caregiver are observed during multiple short episodes during which the caregiver is either absent, present alone, or present with a stranger. In the SSP, a child that is observed to have a weak emotional bond with the caregiver is characterised as having an *avoidant* attachment style and one that appears preoccupied about the caregiver's availability is characterized as *ambivalent*. A key dependent variable is the physical distance between child and caregiver, as illustrated in Fig. 1—a securely attached child typically shows bouts of exploratory behaviour, that involve moving away from, then returning to, the caregiver, on a quasi-periodic basis. In contrast the ambivalent child will typically stay close to the caregiver while the avoidant child will explore while paying little attention to the caregiver.

More recent work has proposed that the attachment styles identified by Bowlby and Ainsworth are best considered as emerging from a multi-dimensional motivational system [9,10]. For instance, Gagliardi [10], describes a 7-dimensional framework with three basic dimensions—avoidance, ambivalence and disorganisation—viewed as emerging during an early "imprinting" period (6 to 24 months). According to this approach, avoidance has an essentially emotional nature, meaning that it is primarily concerned with the affective bond between child and care-giver. Ambivalence, on the other hand, has a more situational or physical nature, meaning that it is concerned with the caregiver's availability. Gagliardi [11] recently described an information-theoretic model in which the child and caregiver were modelled as point agents in a two-dimensional space inspired by the SSP. The child's behaviour, derived from its attachment

 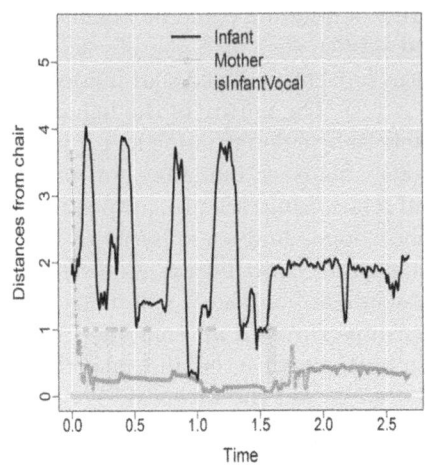

Fig. 1. Left: an SSP room with a mother (caregiver) and her child. Reprinted from [7] with permission from Elsevier. Right: Example behavior patterns displayed in the SSP, plots show distance of the child (black line) and mother (red line) from the chair during a reunion episode and illustrate the oscillatory movement patterns often seen with securely attached children. Reproduced from [8] with permission from Springer Nature. (Color figure online)

motivational system, was modelled as situated in the two-dimension avoidance-ambivalence space. The caregiver, whose behaviour was the manifestation of a caregiving motivational system, was modelled as situated in a two-dimensional sensitivity-responsiveness space. Robotic experiments with this model generated alternating patterns of exploration and approach behavior that were aligned with the attachment literature confirming the utility of the dimensional framework.

1.2   A Dynamical Systems Approach

In the current work, we propose a model of attachment that builds more directly on the dynamical system perspective in developmental psychology [12,13], modelling the child-caregiver relationship, as manifested in the SSP, as a system of coupled oscillators. This model builds on the dimensional view of avoidance and ambivalence, and the emphasis within the Gagliardi model [11] on physical and emotional distance, whilst more directly exploring the dynamical behaviour of the two coupled systems—a child that is motivated to attach and a caregiver that is motivated to provide care—both seeking to balance other motivations such as to explore. We adopt a novel approach that simplifies the information-theoretic model of Gagliardi into a set of differential equations that are more amenable to dynamical analysis while still capturing key characteristics of attachment phenomena. We also extend the approach from modelling point agents in a two-dimensional world, to a robotic implementation that operationalizes some of the elements of the Gagliardi model that assume the capacity of the two agents to infer each other's attachment state.

Our dynamical model stems from the motivated-behaviour-as-an-oscillation framework [14] in which the internal needs of the agents shape a dynamical landscape in a manner that can generate or extinguish attractors in the phase space. From this point of view, different motivational systems are activated depending upon the location of the agent's internal state in such a phase space by using attractor-centered readout functions. The results presented here are a natural corollary of such approach—if motivation is an oscillation, interaction becomes coupling. The coupling of dynamical oscillators has been widely studied. In the current work we use attractive and repulsive coupling to simulate ambivalent and avoidant tendencies. This kind of coupling generates a wide range of behaviours including inhomogenous steady states (IHSS), oscillation death, synchrony, antisynchrony and bi-stability [15]. Helm et al. [16] have previously used a couple-oscillator model to understand interpersonal synchrony with respect to physiological signals such as heartbeat and respiration (see [17]), the current work extends this methodology to the domain of interpersonal behavior.

1.3   Related Work

In originating attachment theory, Bowlby [5] was concerned with applying insights from both ethology and cybernetics—key scientific movements at the time he was working—to the understanding of human personality and relationships. A number of subsequent models have built on Bowlby's enthusiasm for computational accounts (see [18]), most notably, Petters [18], who developed a cognitive architecture for agents to implement and test aspects of attachment theory, and Gagliardi [11], who recently developed the information-theoretic account described above motivated by the emerging dimensional view. The current study complements this work by focusing on the dynamics of attachment behaviour, through a relatively minimal coupled oscillator model, an emphasis that might have appealed to Bowlby's search for concise explanations that can capture regularities underlying observable human behaviour. A previous dynamical account provided by Stevens [19], sought to cast attachment within the framework of homeostasis and modelled the development of attachment as a long-term process of adaptation. In contrast, the focus here is on short-term adaptation of caregiver-child dyad within timeframes comparable to the rich behavioural databases generated by the strange situation. The oscillator model developed here is particularly useful in capturing this kind of interaction. The use of robotics creates a focus on operationalising theories of coupling between agents while also generating a behavioural richness that can be absent in disembodied models. There are interesting parallels here with earlier work by Canamero et al. [22] who developed a model of imprinting in a physical robot. The robot we have used is animal-like rather than human-like, partly as our broader aim is understand the mammalian brain architecture for emotional and social behaviour. From this perspective human attachment can be seen as the expression of an underlying layered motivational control system that is present in all mammals

[23, 24]. We are also interested to explore similarities between attachment and other mammalian social behaviours such as filial huddling [24, 25].

1.4 Model Overview

In the first part of this contribution, we present our model, followed by an overview of the different attachment styles emerging as phenomena of synchronization and anti-synchronization. Finally, to test our model, we use the MiRo-e robotic platform [26]. In previous studies, we have demonstrated control of this platform with brain-inspired layered cognitive architecture [27], and have explored the robot's capabilities in affective communication [28]. In the current paper, we use a pair of MiRo-es to investigate the emergence of attachment-like behavior in a robot dyad modelling the caregiver-child character of the SSP.

2 The Model System

In previous work [14] we modelled motivational dynamics as a particle, here denoted x, moving within a one-dimensional motivational space so as to minimise energy. For two motivations, we define the potential $\Psi(x)$ such that:

$$\Psi(x, u, v) = \frac{1}{2}\left((x+1)^2(x-1)^2 + (x+1)^2\frac{(1-u)}{2} + (x-1)^2\frac{(1-v)}{2}\right), \quad (1)$$

Here u and v are two needs corresponding to the two motivations, these could relate to physiological variables, such as hydration or blood sugar level, or to more psychological constructs such as emotional needs. Equation (1) models an interaction between a fast gradient dynamics for the motivational state, x, and a slower accumulation of the needs. This system will evolve over time to minimise energy by following the negative gradient of the potential.

To model attachment, we assume each robot has two motivations: to receive or give care, and to explore. To simplify the model, we assume that both motivations are encoded by the same underlying need $u = -y$ and $v = y$. This remodels attachment as an approach-avoid conflict. Replacing in Eq. (1) we get:

$$\Psi(x, y) = \frac{x^4}{2} - \frac{x^2}{2} + xy + \frac{1}{2}.$$

Note that when $y = 0$, this potential has two minima (point attractors), however, as y becomes positive or negative, one of the minima disappears allowing the system to settle on the other one as illustrated in Fig. 2).

The slow need accumulation is modelled as

$$\dot{y} = bx + \text{coupling terms}.$$

We showed previously [14] that such a system generates relaxation oscillations therefore we obtain two coupled Van der Pol oscillators represented by the system:

$$\dot{x}_c = -\frac{\partial \Psi}{\partial x_c}(x_c, y_c) = x_c - 2x_c^3 - y_c,$$
$$\dot{y}_c = bx_c - \varepsilon_{Am}f(y_p, y_c) - k_0(\varepsilon_{Av}g(y_p, y_c) + \delta),$$
$$\dot{x}_p = -\frac{\partial \Psi}{\partial x_p}(x_p, y_p) = x_p - 2x_p^3 - y_p,$$
$$\dot{y}_p = bx_p + \varepsilon_{Am}f(y_p, y_c) - k_0(\varepsilon_{Av}g(y_p, y_c) + \delta).$$

$$(2)$$

Here x_i, where $i \in \{c, p\}$ (c representing child and p representing parent/caregiver), is the current motivational state based on receiving or giving care, and the variable y_i, where $i \in \{c, p\}$, is the accumulated need. ε_{Am} and ε_{Av}, referred to below as the *ambivalence* and *avoidance* terms respectively, are parameters that weight the contributions of the two coupling functions and that link the accumulated needs of the two agents. These are defined as:

$$f(y_p, y_c) = y_c + y_p$$
$$g(y_p, y_c) = y_c - y_p.$$

$$(3)$$

The functions f and g are inspired by the "repulsive" and "attractive" coupling used in [15]. The rationale behind that choice is explained in the following section. Note that ε_{Am} and ε_{Av} are parameters of the caregiver-child dyad. k_0 and δ are chosen so that the parameters change in the interval $[0, 1]$ in an interpretable way. The dynamics of these caregiver-child dyad parameters and how the model behaves will be explained further below.

3   Dynamics of the Disembodied Model

Figure 2 shows the phase space geometry under different coupling regimes for the caregiver and the child. In all the figures, we show the nullclines for each oscillator (a nullcline is a curve in the phase plane where one of the variables undergoes no change). In the absence of any coupling, the two nullclines intersect in a unstable fixed point and a relaxation oscillation emerges as an attractor for the system (Fig. 2, left).

In the fully ambivalent scenario, the ambivalence term will push the two oscillators apart by the repulsion mechanism (Fig. 2, center). On the other hand, the avoidance term will draw them together towards a common fixed point which corresponds to a state of perpetual exploration (Fig. 2, right).

We now proceed to analyze the full system as the ambivalence and avoidance parameters change.

3.1   Ambivalent Regime

When $\varepsilon_{Av} = 0$, we are in the ambivalent regime. The system has 3 fixed points, the trivial one at the point $(0, 0, 0, 0)$ an in-homogenous steady state (IHSS) at

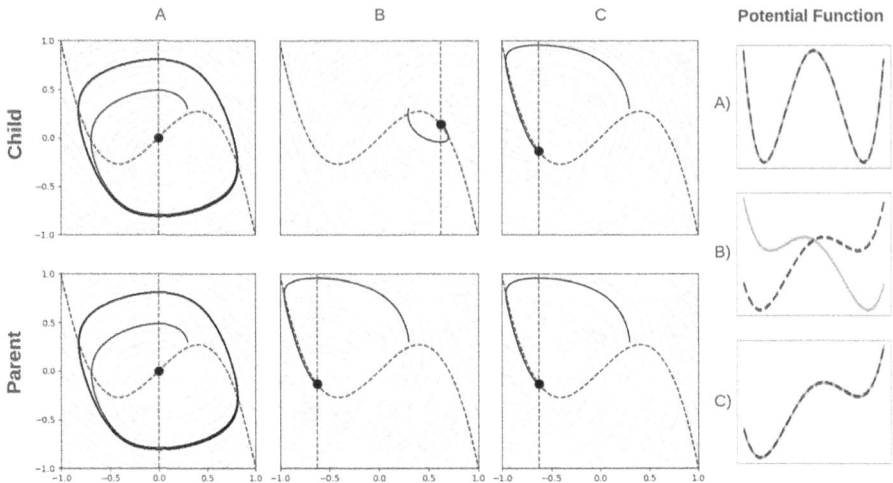

Fig. 2. Illustration of the mechanisms of attachment in the coupled oscillator model. We assume $f(x,y) = g(x,y) \equiv k$ to illustrate the attraction and repulsion effects for illustration purposes. We show the solution to (2) as a closed trajectory in the xy phase space for the child (top row) and for the caregiver (bottom row). The blue curve corresponds to the nullcline $\dot{x} = 0$, th red line is $\dot{y} = 0$. The black dot is a fixed point of the system. A. The first column shows the behaviour of the uncoupled oscillators and illustrates the existence of closed trajectories (i.e. relaxation oscillations). B. Shows the putative ambivalent behaviour with $\epsilon_{Am} = 1$ and $\epsilon_{Av} = 0$. Notice that the system is attracted to opposite fixed points that correspond to perpetual exploration and approach. C. Putative avoidant behaviour, with $\epsilon_{Av} = 1$ and $\epsilon_{Am} = 0$, showing how both agents are attracted to an exploration fixed point. Right column shows the corresponding potential functions $\Psi(x)$ for the child (purple) and for the parent/caregiver (yellow) at the fixed points. (Color figure online)

$FP = (\bar{x}, \bar{y}, -\bar{x}, -\bar{y})$, with

$$\bar{x} = \sqrt{\frac{\varepsilon_{Am} - b}{2\varepsilon_{Am}}} \tag{4}$$

$$\bar{y} = \frac{b}{\varepsilon_{Am}} \sqrt{\frac{\varepsilon_{Am} - b}{2\varepsilon_{Am}}}, \tag{5}$$

which are obtained by setting $\dot{x}_i = 0$ and $\dot{y}_i = 0$, and solving he resulting quadratic equation. The later is of interest to us. It can be observed that, as ε_{Am} increases, there is a sub-critical Hopf bifurcation (a transition in the behavior of the system) such that the existing limit cycle loses stability at $\varepsilon_{Am} = b$ and the system settles in an ambivalent steady state in which the needs are opposite to each other. Figure 3 shows the dynamics of the model as the ambivalence parameter increases in the interval $[0, 1]$, (Fig. 3b) shows the sub-critical Hopf bifurcation.

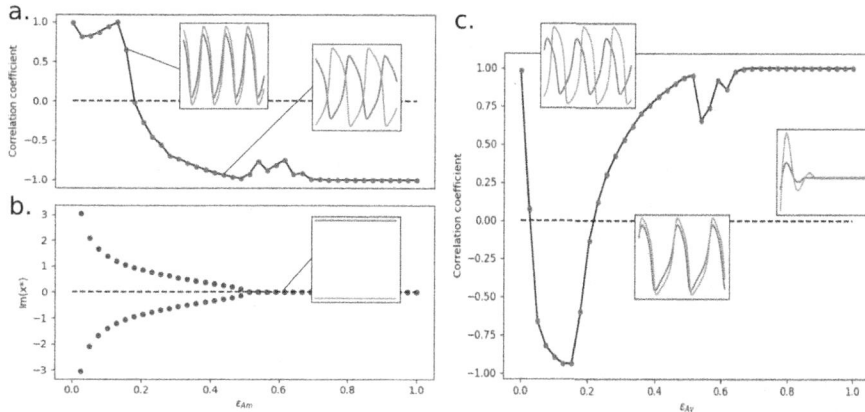

Fig. 3. a. Correlation coefficient of the needs of the parent and the child as the ambivalence parameter ϵ_{Am} increases. For lower values, the dyad is synchronized (inset). As the parameter increases, it becomes quickly uncorrelated until it collapses in an inhomogenous steady state in which the parent is not able to satisfy the needs of the child. b. Subcritical Hopf bifurcation. A limit cycle loses stability and a steady state appears as the parameter increases. Shown in the graph is the imaginary part of the roots in 5. c. The correlation coefficient in the avoidant regime drops quickly for small values of the parameter. This region is characterized by the needs of the child tracking the needs of the parent. Half way through the interval, the system becomes synchronized just before settling into the only steady state: one of continuous exploration or complete avoidance.

In order to understand the interaction between the needs of the caregiver-child dyad, we compute correlation coefficient between the two needs:

$$r(x_c, x_p) = \frac{\sum_i (x_c^i - \bar{x}_c)(x_p^i - \bar{x}_p)}{\sqrt{\sum_i (x_c^i - \bar{x}_c)^2}\sqrt{\sum_i (x_p^i - \bar{x}_p)^2}}. \qquad (6)$$

The dyad starts synchronized but promptly becomes desynchronized and then antisynchronized as the parameter increases in the oscillatory regime; when the child needs care, the parent is not available to provide it.

3.2   Avoidant Regime

When $\varepsilon_{Am} = 0$ we are in the avoidance regime. The system has a unique fixed point at $(\bar{x}, \bar{x}, \bar{y}, \bar{y})$; the dyad tend towards the same steady state. This state is given by the solutions of the cubic equation:

$$x^3 + \frac{1-q}{2q}x + \frac{\delta}{2} = 0,$$

with $q = \frac{k_0 \epsilon_{Av}}{b}$. We have chosen k_0 and δ such that

$$-\Delta = -4\left(\frac{1-q}{2q}\right)^3 - 27\left(\frac{\delta}{2}\right)^2 < 0,$$

for all $\epsilon_{Av} \in [0,1]$, so that there is only one fixed point. Δ is the discriminant obtained from solving the depressed cubic equation. Similar to the ambivalent case, this fixed point becomes stable as the parameter increases, however, in this case, it is shared by both agents in the system. Figure 3c shows the dynamics of the correlations in the avoidant dyad.

4   Robotic Implementation

We implement the attachment dynamical model in a robot-robot dyad, where one robot assumes the role of the parent/caregiver and the other the role of the child.

4.1   Action Selection

To select actions, we use readout functions that indicate whether the approach or explore behavioural systems should be activated. When the motivational state is positive, the approach behavioural system controls the robot, and when it is negative, the exploration system takes over. Mathematically, we express the activation level of each system as:

$$A_{\text{approach}}(x_i) = \Theta(x_i), \tag{7}$$
$$A_{\text{explore}}(x_i) = \Theta(-x_i), \tag{8}$$

where $\Theta(\cdot)$ is the Heaviside function (a form of step discontinuity). Following [11], we define a way of influencing the other agent's motivational state by the perceived physical (d_p) and emotional distances (d_e) between them. To achieve this, we modify equations in (9) to include those behavioural estimates:

$$\begin{aligned} f(y_p, y_c) &= y_c + y_p \pm d_p \\ g(y_p, y_c) &= y_c - y_p - d_e. \end{aligned} \tag{9}$$

Therefore, the physical distance influences the ambivalent coupling while the emotional distance influences the avoidant coupling. The emotional distance (d_e) increases over time following the first order equation:

$$\dot{d_e} = \kappa_e(1 - d_e), \tag{10}$$

when there is no care being given, and is reset to $d_e = 0$ once a care-giving interactions is successful. κ_e is the rate of accumulation of the emotional distance. The emotional distance here is considered as emotional connectivity, which we treat here as similar to physiological needs such as thirst or hunger. This need is considered to be satisfied through interactions such as care-giving interactions.

The physical distance is the normalized euclidean distances from the parent:

$$d_p = \min\left(1, \frac{d_x(p_c, p_p)}{L}\right), \tag{11}$$

where $d_x = \|p_c - p_p\|_2$, p_c and p_p are the position vectors of the child and the parent, estimated from odometry data, and L is the size of the arena.

In this work, both agents have access to the internal accumulated needs of the other agent as required for the coupling of the oscillators, therefore the effects of d_p and d_e are only modulatory. Future work will focus on the estimation of these variables from behaviour. Here, we consider responsiveness and availability to the other agent as a measure of physical distance, thus we base this calculation on the caregiver and child's respective positions.

4.2 Giving Care

The caregiving interaction happens by means of vocalizations performed using MiRo's biomimetic voice synthesis [30]. Each agent accumulates evidence about the interaction using a simple drift diffusion process (see Fig. 4):

$$dX_i = (-aX_i + I) + \sqrt{\sigma}dW, \tag{12}$$

where a is the rate of accumulation and σ the variance of the random process. The parameters of the stochastic equation are chosen empirically to match the rates and time scale of the oscillation. The input I is defined through a simple template matching algorithm: each robot's audio input is continuously sampled by the approach motivational system for energy peaks in the preferred frequency bands of each agent. Those bands correspond to the bands and harmonics where the biomimetic vocalization is more likely to occur depending upon the mass of the animal being simulated [30].

Because both the vocalization and the environment are noisy, the caregiving interaction is only complete after enough evidence is accumulated following the procedure described in Fig. 4 (right).

The caregiving interaction for the caregiver has been designed to start from the first threshold where it simultaneously makes and expects audio responses until it crosses a threshold where it deems the child's responses satisfactory. In the case of the child, it will begin from below the first threshold, and either randomly drifts towards it or cross over it when it receives enough stimulation from the caregiver. The architecture of the system along with the dynamics of the caregiving interactions are shown in Fig. 4.

5 Results

5.1 Robot Implementation

The two MiRo-e robots [26]—one representing the parent/childgiver and other the child—were placed in a enclosed square arena with wide field camera record-

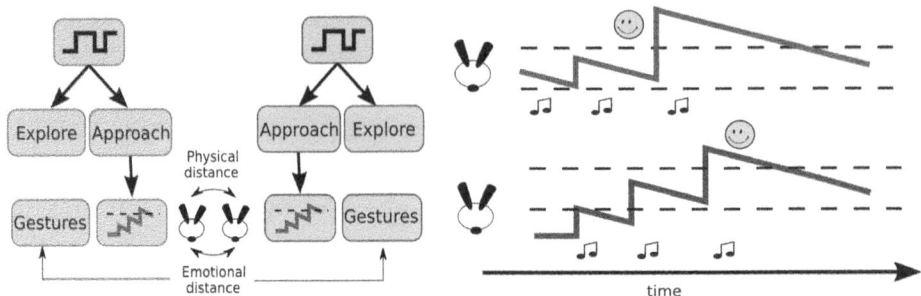

Fig. 4. Left. Cognitive architecture of the child and caregiver robots. The oscillator controller acts as a motivational switch that activates one of the two parallel behavioural systems—approach and explore (see Fig. 5)—depending on need state. Right. Evidence accumulation for the caregiving interaction. The process has two thresholds. The first one initiates vocalizations for each agent. Once the accumulation is above the first threshold, the agent will respond with a new vocalization each time it detects a potential response. The process finishes after crossing the second threshold at which point the emotional distance is reset to 0.

ing their interaction and with a reflective marker on the head of the child robot for tracking (see Fig. 5). The caregiver robot was located in a box surrounded by april tags that the child could easily detect. The parent/caregiver attends to the child as part of its exploration routine but giving/receiving of care was based solely on vocalizations (as explained above).

We tested the model system over multiple episodes of X minute duration, initialising the model each time, and using appropriate parameter values to generate behavior patterns relating to the different attachment regimes–secure, avoidant and ambivalent (See figures below and supplementary videos).

Based on our disembodied model (specifically, the correlations between oscillators shown in Fig. 3), we identified three regions of parameter space corresponding to putative secure, ambivalent and avoidant regimes.

For lower values of the parameters (secure regime), the child explores the arena and uses the caregiver as a secure base. Each caregiving interaction is successfully completed (Fig. 6). Note that interactions tend to be short and happen only when the infant is close to the caregiver.

A putative avoidant attachment is achieved for mid-range parameter values $\epsilon_{Av} \approx 0.6$ where the two oscillators are synchronized but the avoidant state dominates. The child spends more time away from the parent having short bouts of vocalizations before switching back to exploration (Fig. 7, left).

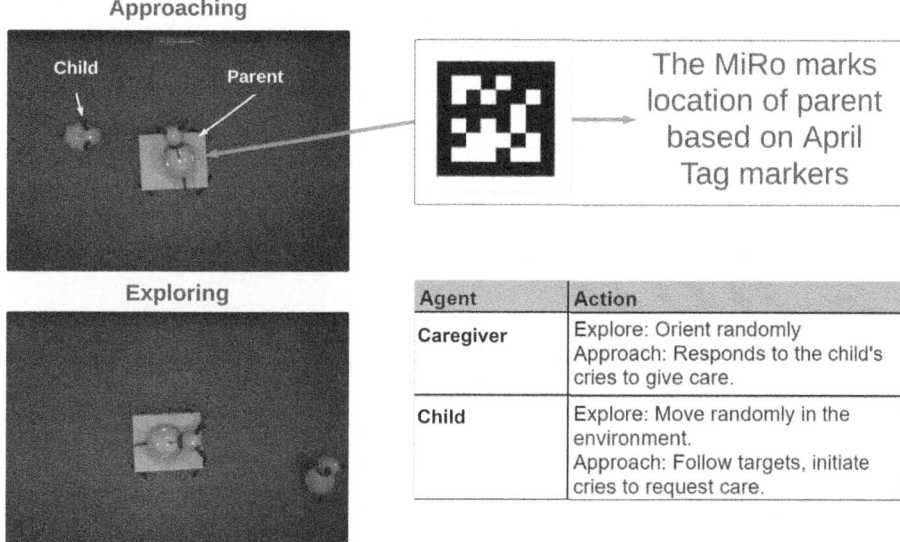

Fig. 5. Experimental setup of the robot-robot SSP. The arena is an enclosed region in the robotics lab with a box in the middle, on top of which sits the caregiver. The child is tracked with a reflective marker. The box is surrounded with April tag markers that serve as targets for the child's approach behaviour. Once the child is close to an April tag it starts asking for care by vocalising. The approach routine of the caregiver consists of orienting towards the child and responding to care requests. The exploration routine of the child consists of choosing random points in the arena to explore; for the caregiver, it consists of random orientations withing the box. The table in the figure shows the different actions available to the caregiver and child robots.

Finally, an ambivalent dyad is observed for higher values of the parameter $\epsilon_{Am} > 0.6$, where the oscillators are anti-synchronized. Calls for care are not reciprocated by the caregiver and the child spends increasing amounts of time close to the base, in need of care, while the caregiver ignores its calls (Fig. 7 right).

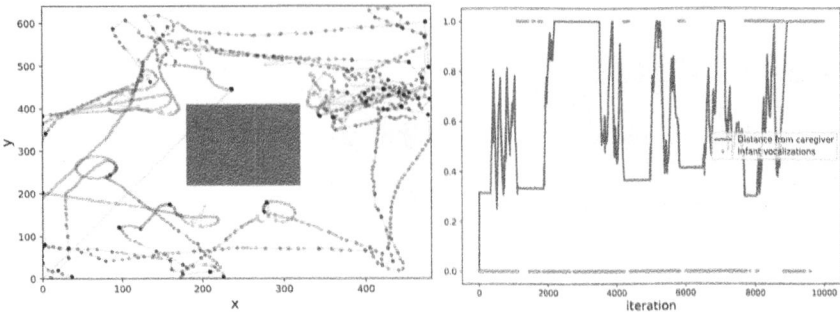

Fig. 6. Left. Trajectory of the child relative to the caregiver located at the blue square in a secure scenario $\epsilon_{Am} = 0.1$ corresponding to a parameter regime in which both oscillators are synchronized. The child explores the space safely and returns to base regularly. Right. Distance from the base (center of the arena) normalized and plotted in blue, higher values indicate exploration bouts. Vocalizations are indicated in orange, where a value of 1 indicates a request for care. In the secure regime, vocalizations occur close to the caregiver and are attended to immediately (as indicated by their length). (Color figure online)

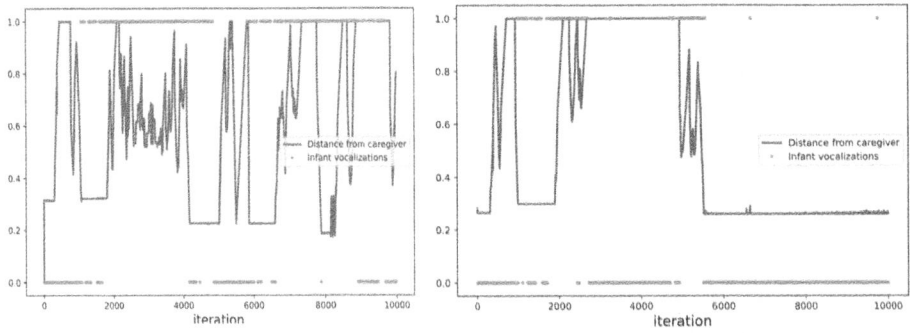

Fig. 7. Distance and vocalizations as in Fig. 6 for avoidant and ambivalent regimes. Left. Avoidance—the child spends most of the time far from the parent and the exploration bouts are punctuated by short care request attempts before switching back to exploration. Right. Ambivalence—the calls for care are usually unattended. The child spends increasing time close to the base while the parent ignores the care requests.

6   Conclusions and Future Work

This research advances the understanding of human relationships by presenting a novel dynamical model of human attachment viewed as the behavioural coupling of two oscillators. Moreover, we have demonstrated, in an embodied implementation using a robot dyad, that clear patterns of attachment can be detected for different parameters values that resemble the results of quantitative studies on human attachment [8]. For instance, we show in Fig. 6, a pattern of oscillatory behavior, for the secure attachment scenario, with alternating bouts of exploration and care-seeking, that resembles that illustrated in Fig. 1 for the SSP. Interestingly, the patterns of distances and vocalizations, in our robot model, vary greatly for different parameter regimes, with episodes of low and high proportions of vocalizations as observed in human dyads when placed in the strange situation. Our dynamical model predicts clear regions of synchronicity, antisynchronicity, and steady states in the phase space. Additionally, just before the transition to a steady state, we observe non-periodic regimes (critical fluctuations). Future work could test these predictions directly by careful tracking of parent-child interactions.

A limitation of the current model, that we are working to understand, is that the bifurcation in the original dynamical model is not reproduced in our robotic implementation. Future work will also focus on improving the estimation of the physical and emotional distances based on observed behaviour and care received. This aspect relies on an accurate estimate of the robots' physical location relative to each other, the detection of each other and their gestures, and the capacity to learn the correct parameter values over time. Improvements in coupling between the agents may help in matching the dynamics of the theoretical model, alternatively, the theoretical model could be modified in recognition that coupling will always be noisy and imperfect.

The results of studies also show that a coupled oscillator model of attachment can generate visually-appealing and temporally-rich patterns of human-robot interaction that could be useful in developing application of social and companion robots, whose behavior can otherwise appear stereotyped (leading to loss of interest). Robillard and Hoey [4] have proposed that assistive technologies, such as robots, can usefully align their emotional expression with the emotional state of the user; our study suggests methods for implementing alignment in robot behavior, which could lead to advances in the development of therapeutic robots.

Acknowledgements. This work was supported by the UK Research and Innovation (UKRI) under the UK government's Horizon Europe funding guarantee for the Horizon Europe EIC Pathfinder CAVAA project.

Declaration of Interest. TJP is a director and shareholder of Consequential Robotics Ltd which develops the MiRo robot, and Bettering Our Worlds (BOW) ltd which develops robot software. Other authors have no competing interests.

References

1. Prescott, T.J., Robillard, J.M.: Are friends electric? the benefits and risks of human-robot relationships. iScience **24**(1) (2021). https://doi.org/10.1016/j.isci.2020.101993
2. Sharkey, N., Sharkey, A.: The crying shame of robot nannies: an ethical appraisal. Interact. Stud. Social Behav. Commun. Biol. Artif. Syst. **11**(2), 161–190 (2010)

3. Collins, E.C., et al.: Attachment to assistive technology: a new conceptualisation. Assist. Technol. Res. Ser. **33**, 823–828 (2013)
4. Robillard, J.M., Hoey, J.: Emotion and motivation in cognitive assistive technologies for dementia. Computer **51**(3), 24–34 (2018)
5. Bowlby, J.: Attachment, vol. 1, 2nd edn. Basic Books, New York (1982)
6. Ainsworth, M.D.S., et al.: Patterns of Attachment: A Psychological Study of the Strange Situation. Lawrence Erlbaum, Oxford (1978)
7. Prince, E.B., et al.: Continuous measurement of attachment behavior: a multimodal view of the strange situation procedure. Infant Behav. Dev. **63**, 101565 (2021). https://doi.org/10.1016/j.infbeh.2021.101565
8. Chow, S.-M., et al.: Representing sudden shifts in intensive dyadic interaction data using differential equation models with regime switching. Psychometrika **83**(2), 476–510 (2018). https://doi.org/10.1007/s11336-018-9605-1
9. Fraley, R.C., Spieker, S.J.: Are infant attachment patterns continuously or categorically distributed? a taxometric analysis of strange situation behavior. Dev. Psychol. **39**(3), 387 (2003)
10. Gagliardi, M.: How our caregivers shape who we are: The seven dimensions of attachment at the core of personality. Front. Psychol. **12**, 657628 (2021)
11. Gagliardi, M.: Human attachment as a multi-dimensional control system: a computational implementation. Front. Psychol. **13**, 844012 (2022)
12. Thelen, E., Smith, L.B.: A Dynamic Systems Approach to the Development of Cognition and Action. MIT Press, Cambridge (1994)
13. Kelso, J.A.S.: Dynamic Patterns: The Self-organization of Brain and Behaviour. MIT Press, Cambridge (1995)
14. Jimenez-Rodriguez, A., Prescott, T.J., Schmidt, R., Wilson, S.: A framework for resolving motivational conflict via attractor dynamics. In: Living Machines 2020. LNCS (LNAI), vol. 12413, pp. 192–203. Springer, Cham (2020). https://doi.org/10.1007/978-3-030-64313-3_19
15. Dixit, S., et al.: The dynamics of two coupled van der pol oscillators with attractive and repulsive coupling. Phys. Lett. A **383**(32), 125930 (2019)
16. Helm, J.L., Sbarra, D., Ferrer, E.: Assessing cross-partner associations in physiological responses via coupled oscillator models. Emotion (Washington, D.C.) **12**(4), 748–762 (2012). https://doi.org/10.1037/a0025036
17. Palumbo, R.V., et al.: Interpersonal autonomic physiology: a systematic review of the literature. Pers. Social Psychol. Rev. **21**(2), 99–141 (2017)
18. Petters, D.D.: The attachment control system and computational modeling: origins and prospects. Dev. Psychol. **55**(2), 227 (2019)
19. Stevens, G., Zhang, J.: A dynamic systems model of infant attachment. IEEE Trans. Auton. Mental Dev. **1**, 196–207 (2009). https://doi.org/10.1109/TAMD.2009.2038190
20. Atkinson, L., et al.: Mathematical Models of Mother/Child Attachment (2006)
21. Lomas, J.D., et al.: Resonance as a design strategy for AI and social robots. Front. Neurorob. **16**, 850489 (2022). https://doi.org/10.3389/fnbot.2022.850489
22. Canamero, L., et al.: Attachment bonds for human-like robots. Int. J. Humanoid Rob. **3**(3), 301–320 (2006)
23. Craig, A.D.: How do you feel? Interoception: the sense of the physiological condition of the body. Nat. Rev. Neurosci. **3**(8), 655–666 (2002). https://doi.org/10.1038/nrn894
24. Wilson, S.P., Prescott, T.J.: Scaffolding layered control architectures through constraint closure: insights into brain evolution and development. Phil. Trans. Royal

Soc. Lond. Ser. B Biol. Sci. **377**(1844), 20200519 (2022). https://doi.org/10.1098/rstb.2020.0519

25. Wilson, S.P.: Modelling the emergence of rodent filial huddling from physiological huddling. Royal Soc. Open Sci. **4**(11), 170885 (2017). https://doi.org/10.1098/rsos.170885

26. Prescott, T.J., et al.: MiRo: an animal-like companion robot with a biomimetic brain-based control system (2017). https://doi.org/10.1145/10.1145/3029798.3036660

27. Mitchinson, B., Prescott, T.J.: MIRO: a robot "mammal" with a biomimetic brain-based control system. In: Lepora, N.F.F., Mura, A., Mangan, M., Verschure, P.F.M.J.F.M.J., Desmulliez, M., Prescott, T.J.J. (eds.) Living Machines 2016. LNCS (LNAI), vol. 9793, pp. 179–191. Springer, Cham (2016). https://doi.org/10.1007/978-3-319-42417-0_17

28. Collins, E., Prescott, T.J.: Saying it with light: a pilot study of affective communication using the MIRO robot (2015). https://doi.org/10.1007/978-3-319-22979-9_25

29. Paxton, B., et al.: Modules for experiments in stellar astrophysics (MESA): time-dependent convection, energy conservation, automatic differentiation, and infrastructure. ApJS **192**, 3 (2011). https://doi.org/10.1088/0067-0049/192/1/3

30. Moore, R., Mitchinson, B.: A biomimetic vocalisation system for MiRo, pp. 363–374 (2017). https://doi.org/10.1007/978-3-319-63537-8_30

Creating an Artificial No-Fly Zone with Sensory Disruptions

Andrew Taylor Giang[iD] and Brian K. Taylor[✉][iD]

Case Western Reserve University, Cleveland, OH 44106, USA
{atg39,bkt2}@case.edu

Abstract. Migrating birds are subject to building collisions and changes to their stopover ecology in urban centers containing sprawling skyscrapers with transparent glass windows and artificial light. We devised a theoretical solution to prevent birds from entering building dense areas ('No-Fly Zones') by targeting the avian sensory system to induce a deterring effect through the use of artificial sensory noise. In our simulation, we introduced artificial noise into a virtual environment with an agent navigating along a predetermined vector and observed the probability of successfully avoiding the no-fly zone in two- and three-dimensions. We found that introducing artificial noise can improve the likelihood of avoiding the no-fly zone. Results from this simulation should be compared to future real-world behavioral data to help determine implementation and feasibility of creating areas with increased sensory noise to reduce biological entry into established no-fly zones and curtail physical structure interactions. Potential sensory systems that can be targeted include vision, olfaction, and magnetoreception.

Keywords: Bird-building collision · Ecological intervention · Sensory disruption

1 Introduction

1.1 Bird-Building Collisions: Anthropogenic Threat to Avian Welfare

Bird-building collisions are a poignant example of the unintended consequences of urbanization on wildlife. Millions of birds fatally collide with man-made structures each year [17–19,21], especially glass windows. These incidents are not merely isolated accidents but reflect a deeper, systemic issue at the interface of human development and wildlife conservation. The primary cause of bird-building collisions is the inability of birds to perceive glass as a barrier, often due to its reflective properties that mimic surrounding environments [2,15]. Factors such as building design, the surrounding vegetation, and the intensity of artificial indoor lighting can exacerbate this issue, particularly for nocturnally migrating bird species. Building collisions contribute significantly to mortality rates in bird populations, affecting both common and threatened avian groups.

© The Author(s), under exclusive license to Springer Nature Switzerland AG 2025
N. S. Szczecinski et al. (Eds.): Living Machines 2024, LNAI 14930, pp. 68–79, 2025.
https://doi.org/10.1007/978-3-031-72597-5_5

1.2   Existing Solutions for Avoiding Bird-Building Collisions

Several solutions have been put forward for preventing bird-building collisions. Visible markers like nets, screens, and grills placed in front of windows and large structures are currently being used to varying degrees of success. However, these solutions can diminish building aesthetics in some cases, making their mass implementation difficult [13,15]. Acoustic lighthouses, playing a loud, audible noise right before impact, have shown some promise as well, but a potential concern from this solution is the additive effect to local sound pollution [3,23,24]. Another current solution that targets the avian visual system is a light pollution reduction method which relies on humans to variably reduce artificial lighting at night to reduce attracting mass migrating birds to areas where birds would be subject to a greater risk of collision, predation, and changes to their stopover ecology [4]. These current solutions all have some potential drawback which led our research group to devise a solution that involves reducing entry into structurally dense areas altogether.

1.3   Sensory Disruption – A Potentially Novel Mitigation Strategy

One solution to preventing bird-building collisions is to have birds avoid human structures altogether by effectively creating a no-fly zone around an area of interest, such as a city. A possible method for accomplishing this would to cause mild and temporary disorientation by disrupting the sensory cues that birds use. If a bird or other migratory animal has a city in its path, disruption of the animals' migratory senses at the right time could steer the animal off course, away from the city. If this can be done at a series of locations, it may be possible to effectively push an animal around a city. Potential sensory cues that could be altered include visual cues [15], olfactory cues [5,7,14,27], and magnetic cues, as several bird species use the earth's magnetic field to navigate from one point to another [9–11,16,20,22,25,26,28].

1.4   Paper Goals

In this paper, we explore the feasibility of maneuvering migratory birds around cities and other human structures by introducing an artificial noise intervention that disrupts orientation. We developed an agent-based computational model to simulate the behavior of a migratory bird navigating through a virtual environment. While the bird has a baseline level of stochasticity in its motion, the noise intervention increases this stochasticity in particular regions. The objective of this experiment was to determine whether artificial noise could disorient a migratory agent enough to direct its path away from a fictive city. We note here that in this study, we omit a specific navigation algorithm or sensory modality, and instead focus on baseline motion that is primarily aimed in one direction, with environmental noise causing disruptions to the motion. This approach allowed us to focus purely on whether increased random motion could influence an organism around a region of interest. We plan to use the results of the present study in future explorations where the effects of noise on specific navigation algorithms and sensory modalities are explored (see Sect. 4 for details).

2   Methods

2.1   Computational Model and Agent Characteristics

The migratory agent was modeled as a point entity that moves in three-dimensional Cartesian space (x, y, z). The agent migrates along the y direction, and can veer off course by moving in the x (lateral) or z (altitude) directions. (Fig. 1).

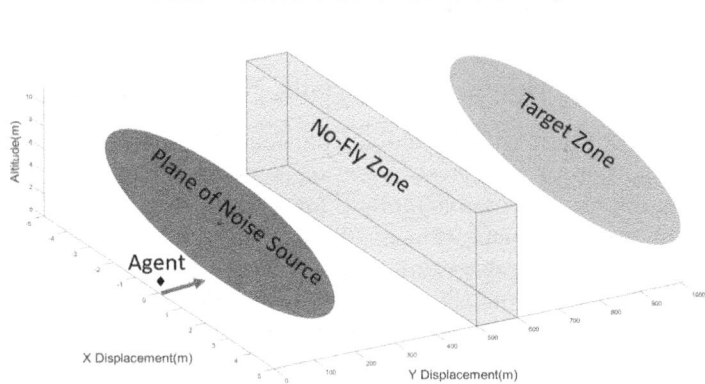

Fig. 1. No-Fly Zone Environment with no plotted trajectories. The blue sphere represents the area of effect induced by the noise source. The red rectangular prism represents the user-defined 'no-fly zone'. The green circle represents a user-defined "target zone" that can be used to observe the final spatial distribution of agents several hundred meters beyond the no-fly zone under control and experimental conditions. (Color figure online)

The agent has a predetermined mean vector heading that does not rely on any form of dynamic navigational algorithm. The agent's movement is characterized by specified step lengths and a fixed direction, mimicking a simplified version of migratory flight towards a goal location. Step lengths can be influenced by baseline environmental noise, and artificial noise under experimental conditions. The agent moves from a defined start point to a specified endpoint.

2.2   Motion Model

At each timestep, the agent's position is updated based on its movement in the x, y, and z directions with the potential addition of noise due to external environmental factors, and deflection effects due to the artificial sensory noise intervention.

The position update equations had the following general form:

$$\boldsymbol{x}_{i+1} = \boldsymbol{x}_i + \Delta\boldsymbol{x} + \boldsymbol{x}_{deflect}. \tag{1}$$

Here, $\boldsymbol{x}$ is a vector for an (x, y, z) location, and i is the current time step. $\Delta\boldsymbol{x}$ is a change in position that happens at every time step. In this experiment, $\Delta\boldsymbol{x}$ is defined as $(0, 1, 0)$, where the predetermined vector heading is $+1$ in the y-dimension. $\boldsymbol{x}_{deflect}$ modifies the motion of the agent based on the current distance d from a source of sensory noise. In this way, the agent has a mean motion direction (i.e., $\Delta\boldsymbol{x}$) that can be altered by sensory noise (i.e., $\boldsymbol{x}_{deflect}$). In Eq. 1, we use a change in position $\Delta\boldsymbol{x}$ for simplicity rather than specifying a change in speed and a specific time step size (i.e., $\boldsymbol{v}dt$). Future studies can implement velocities to better understand how our intervention responds to changes in velocity, and how species with different motion capabilities might be affected by our intervention.

$\boldsymbol{x}_{deflect}$ has the following general piece-wise linear form (Fig. 2):

$$\boldsymbol{x}_{deflect} = \begin{cases} N \cdot mult_{min}, & d > d_{max}, \\ N \cdot \left(mult_{max} + \frac{mult_{max} - mult_{min}}{d_{min} - d_{max}} (d - d_{min}) \right), & d_{min} \leq d \leq d_{max}, \\ N \cdot mult_{max}, & d < d_{min}. \end{cases} \tag{2}$$

Here, d is the current Euclidean distance from the noise source. d_{min} is the distance from the source at which the maximum noise is present (generated by the scaling factor $mult_{max}$), and d_{max} is the distance from the source at which the minimum noise is present (generated by the scaling factor $mult_{min}$) (Fig. 2). N is a random number drawn from a normal distribution (see Table 1). Equation 2 deflects the agent's motion 1) by a minimal amount when far away from the source (i.e., $d > d_{max}$), 2) by an amount that depends on distance when $d_{min} \leq d \leq d_{max}$, and 3) by a maximal amount when close to the source (i.e., $d < d_{min}$). The parameters can be set to different values to independently control motion in the x, y, or z directions, and to turn the noise intervention on or off. In this way, the agent always has elements of random motion far from the noise source, but can be influenced by a source of noise in the vicinity of the no fly zone. A piece-wise linear function based on normally distributed random numbers was used for simplicity. However, in future studies that examine interventions that target specific sensory modalities, different nonlinear functions and random number distributions would likely be necessary (e.g., magnetoreception would respond differently at different distances than vision). For the current study, parameters were set to the same value for each direction. However, they could be set to different values in future investigations.

Table 1. Parameters that are used for the artificial noise intervention.

N		$mult_{min}$	$mult_{max}$	d_{min}	d_{max}
x	$\mathcal{N}(\mu_x = 0, \sigma_x^2 = 0.0005)$	1	5	0	500
y	$\mathcal{N}(\mu_y = 0, \sigma_z^2 = 0.0005)$	1	5	0	500
z	$\mathcal{N}(\mu_z = 0, \sigma_z^2 = 0.0005)$	1	5	0	500

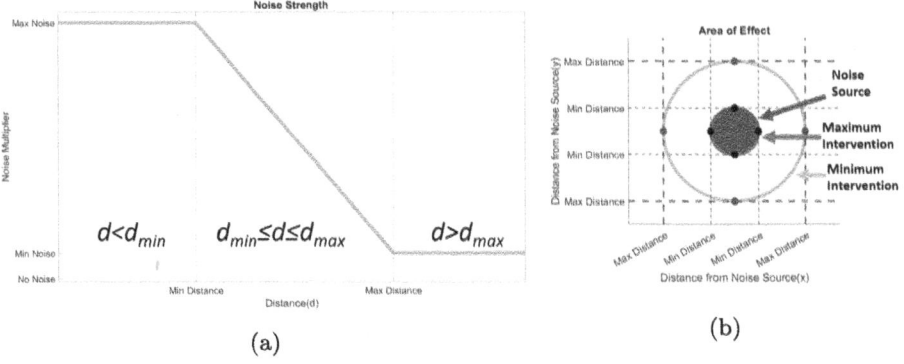

(a)   (b)

Fig. 2. Relationship between the strength of noise and the distance between the agent and noise source (not to scale). The agent experiences the maximum strength of noise when adjacent to the source of noise. The strength of noise diminishes as the agent moves further away from the source of noise.

2.3 Simulation Setup and Experiments

The simulation runs until the agent reaches a y value of 1000 m. Because our simulation is not deterministic, we employed a Monte Carlo approach, which involved running multiple simulations to observe statistical patterns in the agent's heading disruptions and pathways. We varied the position of the noise source in x while holding its y coordinate constant at 10 m, and then varied the position in y while holding the x coordinate constant at 0 m.

3 Results

Figure 3 shows overhead projections of agents migrating from the starting location to the goal in both the control (i.e., no induced noise) and experimental (i.e., induced noise) scenarios. As can be seen, noise disorients the agent to the point that it bypasses the city.

Figures 4 and 5 show 3D plots for multiple trials. As can be seen, in Fig. 4 , the agents mostly move through the city when there is no induced noise. With induced noise, the city is not visible because many agents avoid the city due to disorientation (Fig. 5). Figures 6 and 7 show a top-down and front view of the trajectories. Figure 8 quantifies the proportion of agents that avoid the city

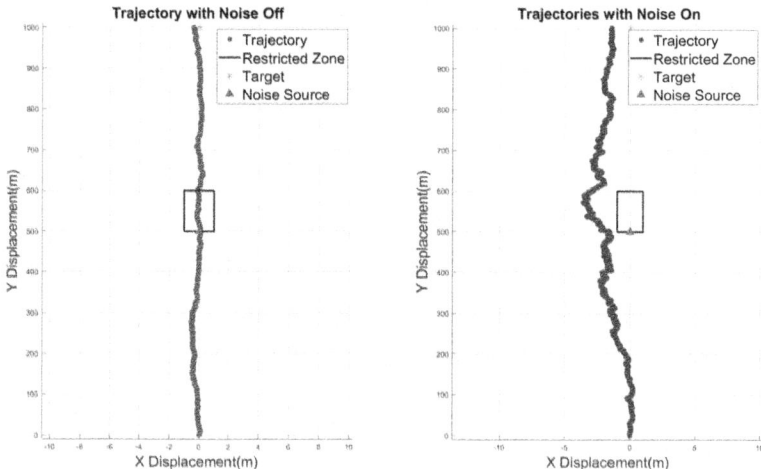

Fig. 3. A sample 2D representation of a trial comparing control (left) to experimental (right) conditions where the noise source induces a 'disorienting' effect on the agent. Here, the agent moves through the no-fly zone in the control conditions, but avoids the no-fly zone in the experimental conditions.

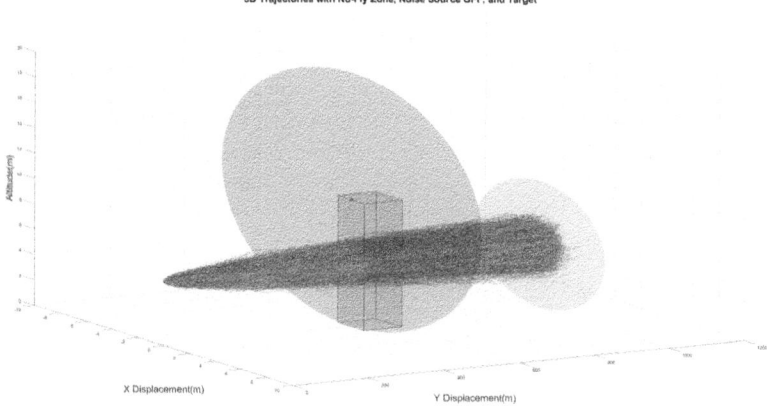

Fig. 4. Control: 10,000 trials visualized in three dimensions. Each line represents a single agent navigating through the virtual environment.

due to disorientation. The induced noise causes the spread of agents to be more pronounced visually.

For different noise source locations in both X and Y, we compared successful no-fly zone avoidance between conditions with noise turned off (Noise OFF) and

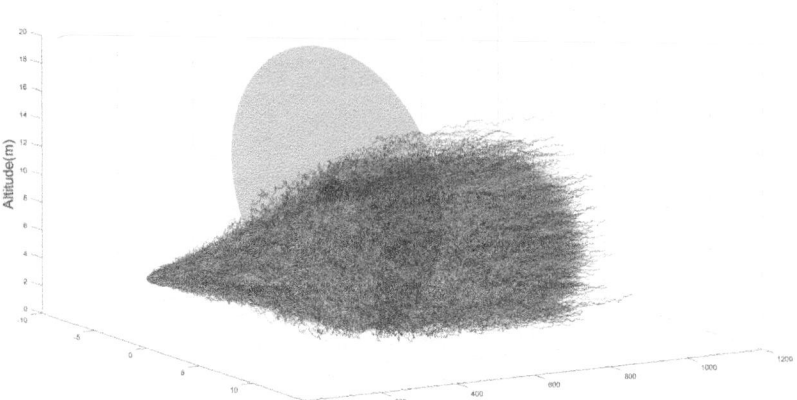

Fig. 5. Experimental: 10,000 trials visualized in three dimensions with the noise source turned on.

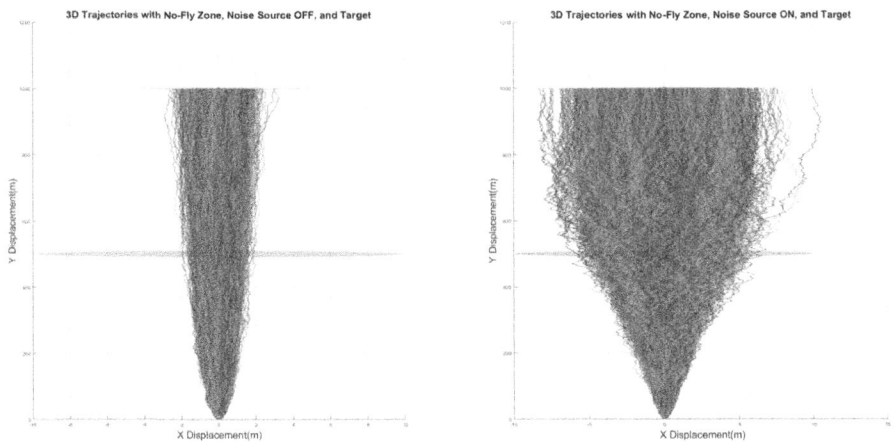

Fig. 6. Control and experimental conditions visually compared with a top-down view.

conditions with noise activated (Noise ON). Our analysis revealed statistically significant differences in successful no-fly zone avoidance when comparing the Noise OFF with X Noise ON (p < 0.00001) and Noise OFF with Y Noise ON (p < 0.00001), indicating a pronounced effect of introduced sensory noise on obstacle avoidance. Specifically, the introduction of artificial sensory noise, irrespective of noise source location (X or Y), was associated with success in avoiding the no-fly zones, as evidenced by the independent t-tests.

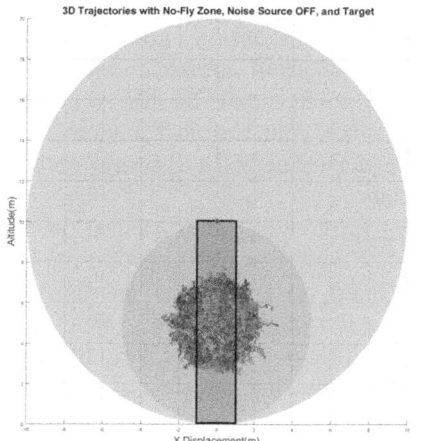 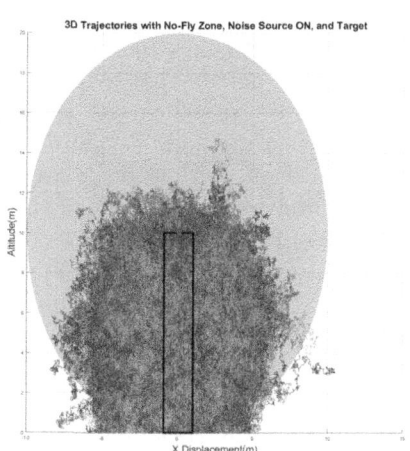

Fig. 7. Control and experimental conditions visually compared when viewed from Y plane.

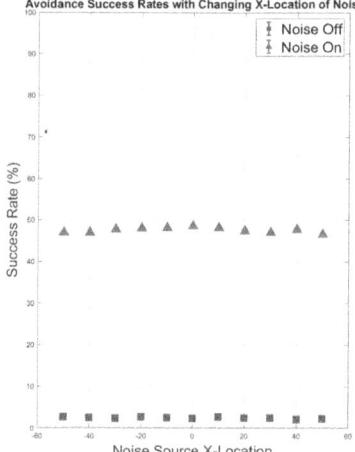 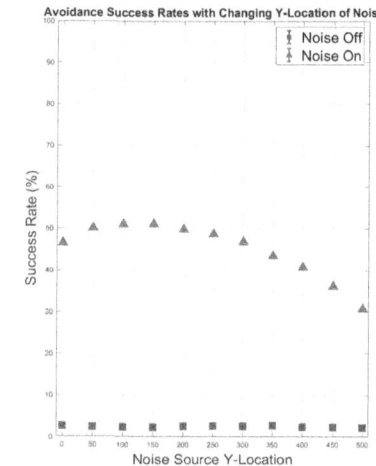

Fig. 8. Success rates for agents avoiding entry into established boundaries within a virtual environment. When varying the noise source location along the X-axis under experimental conditions, there is some difference in success rates. When varying the Y-axis locations, there is a slight peak in success rates around $y = 150$, with a decline as the noise source moves closer to the specified no-fly zone suggesting a point of diminishing return in successful no-fly zone avoidance.

4   Discussion

Our study investigated the feasibility of maneuvering migrating animals around specified regions using artificial sensory noise interventions. Our findings indicate that an artificial noise intervention can influence an agent to avoid a zone of interest. In particular, based on Fig. 8, the noise intervention can increase the percentage of agents that avoid a particular region from approximately 3% to 50%. The rate at which the agent avoids the no fly zone did not vary with the x location of the noise source. The ability to avoid the no fly zone varied with y location, with a peak avoidance rate occurring with the noise source approximately 400 m in front of the no fly zone.

While our study demonstrates the concept of navigation disorientation as a means of preventing animals from entering zones of interest, the question remains of *how* one might practically implement such an intervention. For migratory birds, a potential intervention could be disruption of the magnetic field sense (i.e., magnetoreception). A variety of animals use the earth's magnetic field as a source of navigation information to assist with navigating across continents and oceans. While the specific sensory mechanisms associated with magnetoreception remain an issue of active investigation, many migratory birds are believed to use a chemically-based magnetoreception mechanism in which the products of a chemical reaction are influenced by the magnetic field [12, 20]. Radio frequency electromagnetic waves are thought to disrupt this particular magnetosensory mechanism [6, 9]. Our study demonstrates the concept of navigation disorientation to prevent animals from entering building dense areas. However, practical implementation in the future remains a challenge due to additional alterations needed to be applied to future iterations of the model. For migratory birds, potential intervention could involve using low-frequency radio waves to disrupt their magnetoreceptive senses. Future studies should aim to implement a navigational algorithm based on magnetoreception and examine the effects of varying the properties of the noise sources including but not limited to number of sources, location(s), amplitude(s), frequencies.

Birds modeled in our simulation experienced zero-mean Gaussian noise which resulted in temporary spatial deviations without systematic course changes. If birds exit the disruption zone confused and displaced, they are expected to reorient using innate navigational cues like olfactory, celestial, and visual cues as noted in past studies [14, 15, 20, 28]. The disruption zone aims to be sensorially displeasing, encouraging birds to avoid it. Future work will model-post disruption behavior using real-life data to better understand flight reorientation based on inherent navigational abilities. The magnitude of deviation is limited by the noise strength and the duration of exposure. While all initial trials are uncertain and novel, larger-scale trials with additional noise sources could reveal the true impact artificial noise can have on migratory trajectories. Unlike the current study, future investigations that are specific to a particular sense might require using alternatives to normally distributed noise to properly capture the sensory modality in question.

In terms of electromagnetic interference and its effects on consumer spectrum usage, research has shown that birds are most disoriented by broadband electromagnetic noise with frequencies between 0.1 MHz–10 MHz, which do not overlap with the higher frequencies used by human communication networks [6]. Future implementation should ensure minimal interference with electronic infrastructure, potentially requiring better shielding of electronics. Additionally, bird-bird interactions in flocks, which were not tested in our simulation, could either stabilize or amplify the effects of sensory noise [1]. Increasing the noise strength might counteract the flock's stabilizing effect, leading to increased migratory vagrancy or trajectory variability. There is also the possibility that combining sensory noise intervention with traditional bird-friendly measures such as bird-safe glass and artificial light reduction could enhance mitigation effectiveness while minimizing potential ecological disruption [4, 15].

It will be important to implement a navigational algorithm based on magnetoreception and repeat the study with a radio frequency noise source targeting the magnetoreceptive sense in future studies [9]. This would allow us to correlate different levels of radio frequency noise to different rates of city avoidance and determine whether this approach would be feasible in real animals. It is conceivable that intentional disruption is only possible in a localized region smaller than the area of effect studied in our model, necessitating multiple noise sources distributed throughout an area to achieve a similar impact. Additionally, a distribution of varying noise sources and the behavior of the agent relative to the x, y, z footprint of a city could be analyzed. Our simulation is agnostic to sensor modality, allowing to similar investigations across additional sensory modalities like vision, olfaction, and audition, both individually and in combination with each other. Further investigations specific to a particular sense might require alternatives to normally distributed noise to properly capture the sensory modality in question.

Contributing to additional ecological costs, our simulation assumes no external sensory disruptions once the animal passes the disruption zone, with only minimal inherent system noise. However, the potential for indirect mortality exists if successfully sensory disruption does not include measures to redirect migrating agents back to their intended trajectories. Mature birds may reorient themselves using inherent navigational senses and past experiences, while juvenile birds may experience greater risks due to never experiencing altered magnetic fields before [1, 8]. Complementary measures to minimize ecological disruption include designing localized zones of influence targeting critical areas of high collision risk, combined with creating safe passage corridors and bird glass to help balance successful mitigation and disruption.

Acknowledgments. BKT is partially funded by a grant from the Air Force Office of Scientific Research (grant number FA9550-20-1-0399).

Disclosure of Interests. We declare we have no competing interests.

References

1. Alerstam, T.: Ecological causes and consequences of bird orientation. Experientia **46**(4), 405–415 (1990). https://doi.org/10.1007/BF01952174
2. Basilio, L.G., Moreno, D.J., Piratelli, A.J.: Main causes of bird-window collisions: a review. Anais da Academia Brasileira de Ciências **92**(1) (2020). https://doi.org/10.1590/0001-3765202020180745. https://www.scielo.br/j/aabc/a/4QCVMKjDPsyMSvjWDnvDv7S/?lang=en

3. Boycott, T.J., Mullis, S.M., Jackson, B.E., Swaddle, J.P.: Field testing an "acoustic lighthouse": Combined acoustic and visual cues provide a multimodal solution that reduces avian collision risk with tall human-made structures. PLOS ONE **16**(4) (2021). https://doi.org/10.1371/journal.pone.0249826. https://journals.plos.org/plosone/article?id=10.1371/journal.pone.0249826
4. Doren, B.M.V., Horton, K.G., Dokter, A.M., Klinck, H., Elbin, S.B., Farnsworth, A.: High-intensity urban light installation dramatically alters nocturnal bird migration. Proc. Natl. Acad. Sci. **114**(42) (2017). https://doi.org/10.1073/pnas.1708574114. https://www.pnas.org/doi/10.1073/pnas.1708574114
5. Eder, S.H., et al.: Magnetic characterization of isolated candidate vertebrate magnetoreceptor cells. Proc. Natl. Acad. Sci. **109**(30) (2012). https://doi.org/10.1073/pnas.1205653109. https://www.pnas.org/doi/full/10.1073/pnas.1205653109
6. Engels, S., et al.: Anthropogenic electromagnetic noise disrupts magnetic compass orientation in a migratory bird. Nature **509**(7500) (2014). https://doi.org/10.1038/nature13290. https://www.nature.com/articles/nature13290
7. Gagliardo, A., Bried, J., Lambardi, P., Luschi, P., Wikelski, M., Bonadonna, F.: Oceanic navigation in cory's shearwaters: evidence for a crucial role of olfactory cues for homing after displacement. J. Exp. Biol. **216**(Pt 15) (2013). https://doi.org/10.1242/jeb.085738. https://pubmed.ncbi.nlm.nih.gov/23842626/
8. Hall-Karlsson, K.S.S., Thord, F.: How far do birds fly during one migratory flight stage? Ringing Migrat. **24**(2), 95–100 (2008). https://doi.org/10.1080/03078698.2008.9674381
9. Hiscock, H.G., Mouritsen, H., Manolopoulos, D.E., Hore, P.J.: Disruption of magnetic compass orientation in migratory birds by radiofrequency electromagnetic fields. Biophys. J. **113**(7) (2017). https://doi.org/10.1016/j.bpj.2017.07.031. https://pubmed.ncbi.nlm.nih.gov/28978441/
10. Holland, R.A.: True navigation in birds: from quantum physics to global migration. J. Zool. **293**(1) (2014). https://doi.org/10.1111/jzo.12107. https://zslpublications.onlinelibrary.wiley.com/doi/full/10.1111/jzo.12107
11. Holland, R.A., Helm, B.: A strong magnetic pulse affects the precision of departure direction of naturally migrating adult but not juvenile birds. J. Royal Soc. Interface **10**(81) (2013). https://doi.org/10.1098/rsif.2012.1047. https://royalsocietypublishing.org/doi/10.1098/rsif.2012.1047
12. Hore, P.J., Mouritsen, H.: The radical-pair mechanism of magnetoreception. Ann. Rev. Biophys. **45**(1), 299–344 (2016). https://doi.org/10.1146/annurev-biophys-032116-094545. https://pubmed.ncbi.nlm.nih.gov/27216936/
13. Håstad, O., Odeen, A.: A vision physiological estimation of ultraviolet window marking visibility to birds. PeerJ **2** (2014). https://doi.org/10.7717/peerj.621. https://pubmed.ncbi.nlm.nih.gov/25320684/
14. Jorge, P.E., Marques, P.A.M., Phillips, J.B.: Activational effects of odours on avian navigation. Proc. Royal Soc. B: Biol. Sci. **277**(1678) (2010). https://doi.org/10.1098/rspb.2009.1521. https://royalsocietypublishing.org/doi/10.1098/rspb.2009.1521
15. Klem, D.: Preventing bird-window collisions. Wilson J. Ornithol. **121**(2) (2009). https://doi.org/10.1676/08-118.1. https://bioone.org/journals/the-wilson-journal-of-ornithology/volume-121/issue-2/08-118.1/Preventing-BirdWindow-Collisions/10.1676/08-118.1.full
16. Kullberg, C., Henshaw, I., Jakobsson, S., Johansson, P., Fransson, T.: Fuelling decisions in migratory birds: geomagnetic cues override the seasonal effect. Proc. Royal Soc. B: Biol. Sci. **274**(1622) (2007). https://doi.org/10.1098/rspb.2007.0554. https://royalsocietypublishing.org/doi/10.1098/rspb.2007.0554

17. Longcore, T., et al.: Avian mortality at communication towers in the United States and Canada: which species, how many, and where? Biol. Conservat. **158**, 410–419 (2013). https://doi.org/10.1016/j.biocon.2012.09.019. https://www.sciencedirect.com/science/article/abs/pii/S0006320712004144

18. Loss, S.R., Lao, S., Eckles, J.W., Anderson, A.W., Blair, R.B., Turner, R.J.: Factors influencing bird-building collisions in the downtown area of a major North American city. PLOS ONE **14**(11) (2019). https://doi.org/10.1371/journal.pone.0224164. https://journals.plos.org/plosone/article?id=10.1371/journal.pone.0224164

19. Loss, S.R., Will, T., Loss, S.S., Marra, P.P.: Bird-building collisions in the United States: estimates of annual mortality and species vulnerability. Condor **116**(1) (2014). https://doi.org/10.1650/CONDOR-13-090.1. https://academic.oup.com/condor/article/116/1/8/5153098

20. Mouritsen, H.: Long-distance navigation and magnetoreception in migratory animals. Nature **558**(7708), 50–59 (2018) https://doi.org/10.1038/s41586-018-0176-1. https://www.nature.com/articles/s41586-018-0176-1

21. Parkins, K.L., Elbin, S.B., Barnes, E.: Light, glass, and bird-building collisions in an urban park. Northeast. Naturalist **22**(1) (2015). https://doi.org/10.1656/045.022.0113. https://bioone.org/journals/northeastern-naturalist/volume-22/issue-1/045.022.0113/Light-Glass-and-BirdBuilding-Collisions-in-an-Urban-Park/10.1656/045.022.0113.short

22. Ritz, T., et al.: Magnetic compass of birds is based on a molecule with optimal directional sensitivity. Biophys. J. **96**(8) (2009). https://doi.org/10.1016/j.bpj.2008.11.072. https://www.ncbi.nlm.nih.gov/pmc/articles/PMC2718301/

23. Swaddle, J.P., Ingrassia, N.M.: Using a sound field to reduce the risks of bird-strike: an experimental approach. Integrat. Comparat. Biol. **57**(1) (2017). https://doi.org/10.1093/icb/icx026. https://academic.oup.com/icb/article/57/1/81/3958321?login=false

24. Thady, R.G., Emerson, L.C., Swaddle, J.P.: Evaluating acoustic signals to reduce avian collision risk. PeerJ **10** (2022). https://doi.org/10.7717/peerj.13313. https://peerj.com/articles/13313/

25. Tonelli, B.A., Youngflesh, C., Tingley, M.W.: Geomagnetic disturbance associated with increased vagrancy in migratory landbirds. Sci. Rep. **13**(1) (2023). https://doi.org/10.1038/s41598-022-26586-0. https://www.nature.com/articles/s41598-022-26586-0

26. Wiltschko, R., Wiltschko, W.: The magnetite-based receptors in the beak of birds and their role in avian navigation. J. Comparat. Physiol. A Neuroethol. Sensory Neural Behav. Physiol. **199**(2), 89–98 (2013). https://doi.org/10.1007/s00359-012-0769-3. https://www.ncbi.nlm.nih.gov/pmc/articles/PMC3552369/

27. Wiltschko, R., Wiltschko, W.: Considerations on the role of olfactory input in avian navigation. J. Exp. Biol. **220**(23), 4347–4350 (2017). https://doi.org/10.1242/jeb.168302. https://journals.biologists.com/jeb/article/220/23/4347/33711/Considerations-on-the-role-of-olfactory-input-in

28. Wiltschko, R., Wiltschko, W.: Animal navigation: how animals use environmental factors to find their way. Eur. Phys. J. Spec. Topics **232**(2), 237–252 (2022). https://doi.org/10.1140/epjs/s11734-022-00610-w. https://link.springer.com/article/10.1140/epjs/s11734-022-00610-w

Sensors and Sensing

Maximizing Robotic Limb Rigidity and Strain Sensing Capabilities Through Localized Kevlar Fiber Reinforcement

Gesa F. Dinges[1] , Isabella Kudyba[1] , Sasha N. Zill[2] ,
and Nicholas S. Szczecinski[1]([envelope])

[1] Neuro-Mechanical Intelligence Laboratory, Department of Mechanical, Materials and Aerospace Engineering, West Virginia University, Morgantown, WV 26506, USA
imk00001@mix.wvu.edu, nicholas.szczecinski@mail.wvu.edu
[2] Department of Anatomy and Pathology, Joan C. Edwards School of Medicine, Marshall University, Huntington, WV 25704, USA

Abstract. Strain can provide important sensory information for locomotor control in both robots and insects. Strain measurements in limbs can indicate forces that resist movements generated by actuators or muscle. Key time points in stepping can be monitored through changes in strain and inform the neuromuscular or robotic control system of the step cycle phase, allowing for modifications during unplanned events. For both systems, there is a trade-off between the limb rigidity and thus accuracy of limb positioning, and the magnitude (i.e., sensitivity) of strain measurements. Rigid limb segments enable precise end effector (e.g., foot) placement but reduce the strain magnitude when force is resisted; compliant limb segments increase the strain magnitude, but extreme compliance can potentially decrease precision in determination of limb position and movement. Robotic limb segments typically have homogeneous material properties, requiring the choice between rigidity and compliance. In contrast, insect limbs have spatial gradients of material properties. We show the benefits of localized Kevlar fiber reinforcement for strain sensing in robotic limb segments. While full-segment Kevlar reinforcement solely increases rigidity, the most effective reinforcement format for increasing both rigidity and strain magnitude is partial fiber supplementation encompassing the majority of the limb segment but not the area where strain is monitored. We propose that future robotic additive manufacturing should incorporate material heterogeneity to optimize rigidity and strain sensing capabilities.

Keywords: 3D-printing · Kevlar · heterogeneous materials · legged locomotion

1 Introduction

Traversing rugged terrain using legs benefits from the measurement of forces acting on the limbs. Animals make use of force information in the control of walking by monitoring the strain of compliant body parts in series between the actuator and the

---

G. F. Dinges, I. Kudyba and S.N. Zill—These authors contributed equally to this work.

N. S. Szczecinski et al. (Eds.): Living Machines 2024, LNAI 14930, pp. 83–93, 2025.
https://doi.org/10.1007/978-3-031-72597-5_6

point of force application. Vertebrates monitor tendon strain using Golgi tendon organs [1] and insects monitor exoskeletal strain using campaniform sensilla (CS) [2, 3]. The nervous systems of these animals use this sensory feedback to adapt motor output in a context-appropriate manner [4]. To produce robots whose motions are as agile and adaptable as those of animals, we seek to incorporate this type of force feedback into their control systems.

In insects, campaniform sensilla, which detect deformations of the exoskeleton that occur when contractions of leg muscles are resisted, monitor strain. Information from the sensilla is used to adapt muscle forces in posture and locomotion. In walking robots, force can be monitored using load cells or strain gauges [5–7]. Load cells are extremely rigid and linearly encode strain, which requires high signal amplification and, consequently, makes them susceptible to noise. Strain gauges applied to polymer robot parts, on the other hand, allow high-resolution encoding of directional strain and have been utilized in walking robots [5–7]. While classic strain gauge rosettes are beneficial in locomoting robots, the development of novel strain gauge techniques, such as strain gauges developed using gradient stiffness sliding [8] and stretchable pressure sensors [9] may prove to be beneficial in future application due to their high sensitivity.

Both insect and robotic force measurement systems are affected by their material make-up and its effects on strain propagation (e.g., during contact with the ground). Furthermore, for both systems to have the most predictable kinematics possible, maximally stiff limbs are most beneficial. The exoskeleton of adult insects is stiff due to both the presence of rigid chitin fibers and the crosslinking and sclerotization of the protein matrix in which the fibers are embedded. In robot manipulators, kinematics and dynamics assume that the bodies that make up the arm are rigid [10]. However, the material stiffness of both cuticle and robotic parts has the potential to decrease strain signals, making the utilization of this important sensory information difficult. In insects, stiffness is elegantly incorporated with strain sensing capabilities through the heterogeneous material properties of the cuticle [11, 12]. For example, in some insects the exoskeleton is thin at the locations of the campaniform sensilla [13, 14]. However, the chitin fibers in the cuticle surrounding the receptor caps are concentrated and oriented to distribute the effects of stresses around the sense organ [15]. This ensures that each sensillum has exquisite sensitivity in detecting strain while maintaining high stiffness in the surrounding leg cuticle. For robust robotic control, similar stiffness maximization while ensuring strain measurability could also be beneficial.

In line with advancements in 3D-printing techniques for robotic parts, altering the fiber ratios in robotic limb segments may improve strain sensing capabilities while maintaining limb stiffness for kinematic control. Kevlar fiber reinforcement has a higher impact resistance than carbon fiber [16]. To investigate how this reinforcement may benefit distributed sensing in walking robots, we analyzed strain sensing in dynamically scaled robotic models of insect tibias. We used three different tibias, each with different proportions of Kevlar reinforcement. We displaced the distal end of each tibia transversal to the tibia's long axis (i.e., as a cantilever beam) and measured the restoring force applied by the tibia and the strain at a proximal site at a similar location to where CS would be located in the insect.

Our results clearly showed that partial Kevlar reinforcement of the tibia distal to the strain gauge site is the beneficial solution for maintaining tibial rigidity while increasing the magnitude of strain at the sensor location. The strains monitored in a partially fiber reinforced limb segment (i.e., distal to the strain gauge) were greater than those monitored in a non-reinforced limb segment. However, the signal to noise ratio was not improved through fiber supplementation compared to no fiber reinforcement. Consequently, fiber supplementation increases rigidity but not the signal to noise ratio. The partially reinforced segment was more rigid than no fiber reinforcement. The fully reinforced limb segment showed significantly reduced strain signals compared to partial and no fiber reinforcement and its surface was always in tension, never in compression. Based on these results, we propose the consideration of partial Kevlar reinforcement in additively manufactured components in future walking robots to enhance force sensing.

2 Material and Methods

We utilized a dynamically scaled, biomimetic stick insect leg segment for all experiments. The robotic limb used for these experiments was first published in Zyhowski et al., 2022. Each leg segment sample was a hollow square tube, which modeled the hollow exoskeleton of an arthropod while remaining easy to manufacture. Most Markforged 3D-printers have the capability to add reinforcement fibers to increase the part's strength while simultaneously printing the part out of plastic. Using Eiger software (Markforged Inc., Waltham, MA, USA), we 3D-printed (Mark 2; Markforged Inc.) limb segments out of Onyx® ([17]; Markforged Inc.) with and without Aramid Fiber (*Kevlar* [16]; Markforged Inc.) reinforcement. We created three versions of the tibial leg segment (n = 1) with varying amounts of fiber reinforcement. As this is a preliminary study and due to the high cost of strain gauges each model was tested once. The first model had no Kevlar fiber reinforcement (*no-fiber model*, Fig. 1A). The second model had Kevlar fiber throughout the complete shaft (*full-fiber model*; 118.5 mm of Kevlar, Fig. 1A). The third model was printed with Kevlar fiber throughout the shaft from the distal end up to 20 mm from the proximal end (*partial-fiber model*, 98.5 mm of Kevlar, Fig. 1A). Reinforcement fibers are added and controlled in the Eiger software under the "XRAY" tab. All layers of the part were selected. The Kevlar fibers were printed with an isotropic solid fill and fibers were aligned with the axial direction of the leg segment (Fig. 1B). In the *partial-fiber* model, the region of reinforcement fiber is selected in the software by selecting the distal end of the leg segment to a small bump in the design that is later sanded off.

On all legs, we manually glued strain gauge rosettes (Micro-Measurements C5K-06-S5198–350-33F; Vishay Intertechnology, Malvern, PA, USA; Grid resistance, 350.0 Ω ± 0.5%) on the dorsal side, 10 mm distal to the proximal end of the shaft (Fig. 1A). They were aligned along the transverse and axial axes of the segment. In order to compare strain measurements between models, we aligned the strain gauges and tibia using a 3D-printed guide. The strain gauge signals were amplified using operational amplifiers (Texas Instruments, Dallas, Tx., USA; IC OPAMP GP 4 CIRCUIT 14SOIC) and converted to 12-bit digital signals using a microcontroller OpenCM 9.04 Board (Robotis Inc., Lake Forest, CA, USA).

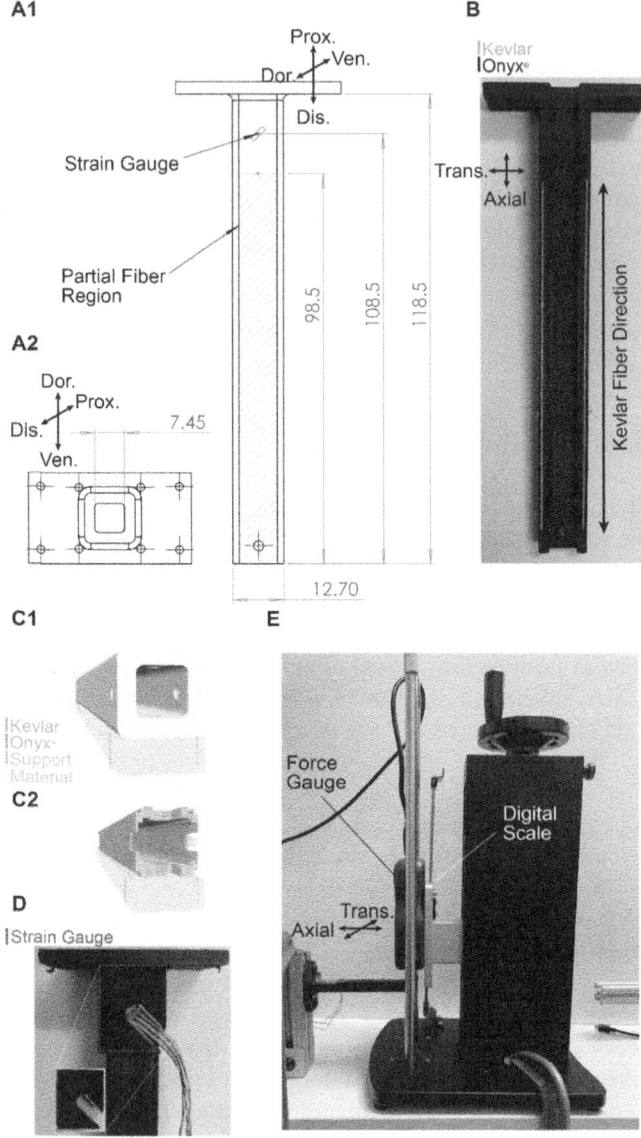

Fig. 1. Models and setup design; **A1** schematic of the robotic tibia leg segment; the shaft was printed in three different manners: 1) the full 118.5 mm were printed using Onyx® only (*no-fiber* model); 2) the full 118.5 mm were printed using Onyx® and Kevlar reinforcement (*full-fiber* model); 3) the distal most 98.5 mm were printed using Onyx® and Kevlar reinforcement (area marked with hatch marks), while the remaining 20 mm were printed using Onyx® only (*partial-fiber* model). The strain gauges were placed 10 mm from the proximal shaft end, with an axial and transverse axis orientation. Prox.: proximal, Dis.: distal, Dor.: dorsal, Ven.: ventral; **A2** front view of the model's proximal end; **B** partially printed *partial-fiber* model; yellow fibers are Kevlar; **C1** model as seen in Eiger software, without Kevlar; **C2** model as seen in Eiger software, with Kevlar; **D** proximal end of tibia with strain gauge guide and attached stain gauge rosette; magenta lines mark the axes of the strain gauge rosette; insert shows strain gauge guide; **E** image of the general setup; each model's distal end is aligned with the force probe.

To test the effects of Kevlar on strain measurements and limb displacement during loading, we utilized a manual hand wheel-operated test stand (FGS-250W; Nidec-Shimpo, Kyoto, Japan). The force was monitored with a digital force gauge (1000 N ± 0.3% full scale accuracy; FG-3009; Nidec-Shimpo). The hand wheel included a tensile frame kit (FGS-250W-TFK; Nidec-Shimpo) to monitor displacement. Each model was attached to a slotted t-rail at its proximal end using a 3D-printed bracket (Fig. 1A). The distal end was aligned with the force probe (Fig. 1B, C). We displaced the distal end of each model in 0.05–0.10 mm increments to a maximum displacement of 4.5 mm. At this peak displacement, the models underwent a constant displacement test for 180 s. Following this phase, the displacement was reduced back to the starting value of 0 mm. The mechanical displacement was performed manually while displacement values, force, and strain were monitored using MATLAB (2021b; MathWorks, Natick, MA, USA).

We performed a least-squares fit of the hysteresis of the force probe measurement over time with a Generalized Maxwell model [18], which predicts force relaxation as an exponential decay,

$$F = a_1 \cdot \exp(b_1 \cdot t) + c_1, \tag{1}$$

where a is the magnitude of the stress relaxation, b describes the time course of stress relaxation, and c is the force at which stress relaxation ends. This model was chosen because of the observed decay profile of the force probe measurement over time. The time constant of hysteresis is $\tau = -1/b$. To correct the fit in the *no-fiber* model that had low force changes over time, we prolonged the hold phase to 360 s and used this data exclusively for curve fitting.

To analyze the signal-to-noise ratio (SNR) of the strain measurements, we performed a least-squares fit of the strain data over time with an exponential curve similarly to force using the Generalized Maxwell model,

$$\varepsilon = a_2 \cdot \exp(b_2 \cdot t). \tag{2}$$

The noise was calculated by comparing the data with the least-squares fit, then the SNR was calculated by dividing the power of the fit over the power of the noise.

3   Results

All models showed changes in monitored strain during displacement (Fig. 2A). All three models showed axial elongation during displacement, while transverse compression was only observed in the *no-fiber* and *partial-fiber* models. In contrast, the transverse axis of the *full-fiber* model elongated during displacement. Along both the axial and transverse axes, the *partial-fiber* model had the greatest strain gauge measurements. The lowest overall strain was monitored in the *full-fiber* model.

There was a clear correlation between Kevlar reinforcement and monitored force during displacement (i.e., segment rigidity; Fig. 2B). The greatest force was monitored in the *full-fiber* model, while the lowest force was monitored in the *no-fiber* model. The peak measured force (at 4.5 mm of transverse, distal deflection) was 32 N in the *full-fiber* model, 22 N in the *partial-fiber* model, and 11 N in the *no-fiber* model.

The strain measurements during displacement showed clear hysteresis loops, and thus energy dissipation, between loading and unloading (Fig. 3A1–2). The greatest difference between strain measurements during loading and unloading was seen within both the transverse and axial axes of the *partial-fiber* model. The least change in strain was seen in the *full-fiber* model. All models had greater strain gauge magnitudes during load application (Fig. 3A1–A2).

During the constant displacement test at peak displacement, all three models showed stress relaxation (Fig. 3B1–3). The *no-fiber* model had a force relaxation of 9.2%; the *full-fiber* model of 13.5%; and the *partial-fiber* model of 12.5%. The fastest force decay was present in the *no-fiber* model followed by the *full-fiber* model and the *partial-fiber* model (Table 1 [b]). The force magnitude decreased most in the *full-fiber* model followed by the *partial-fiber* model and the *no-fiber* model (Table 1 [a]).

Table 1. Fit coefficient results [Eq. 1].

	No-Fiber Model	Full-Fiber Model	Partial Fiber Model
a_1	2.055	4.263	2.778
b_1	−0.009708	−0.01133	−0.01186
c_1	8.892	27.33	19.53
$a_1/(a_1 + c_1)$	0.188	0.135	0.125
τ	103 s	88.3 s	84.3 s

The SNR in the *no-fiber* model was 48.5 dB along the axial axis and 44.7 dB along the transverse axis. In the *full-fiber* model, the SNR was 26.3 dB along the axial axis and 29.3 dB along the transverse axis. In the *partial-fiber* model, the SNR along was 42.5 dB the axial axis and 44.1 dB along the transverse axis.

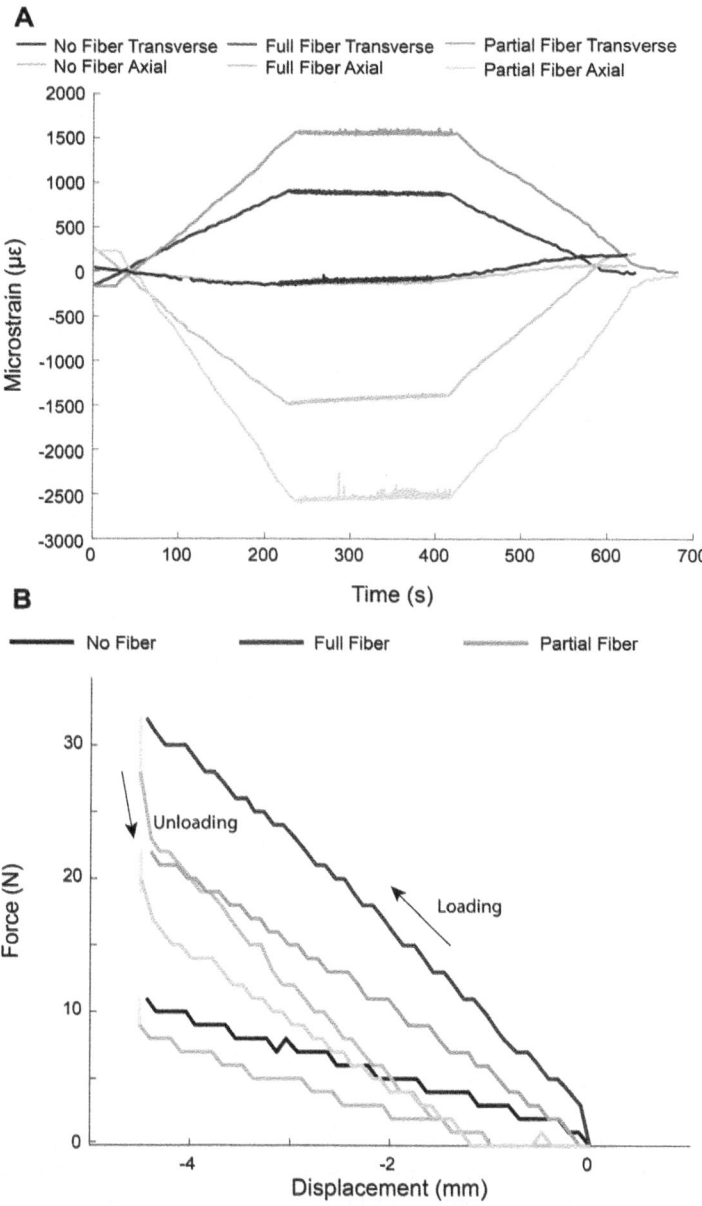

Fig. 2. Microstrain and force measurements of each limb segment during displacement; **A** micros-train measurements along the axial and transverse axis of the three different models during a 4.5 mm displacement of the distal end (positive values represent compression); **B** monitored force at the distal end of each model during displacement. Gray lines represent the decrease in force during the constant displacement phase.

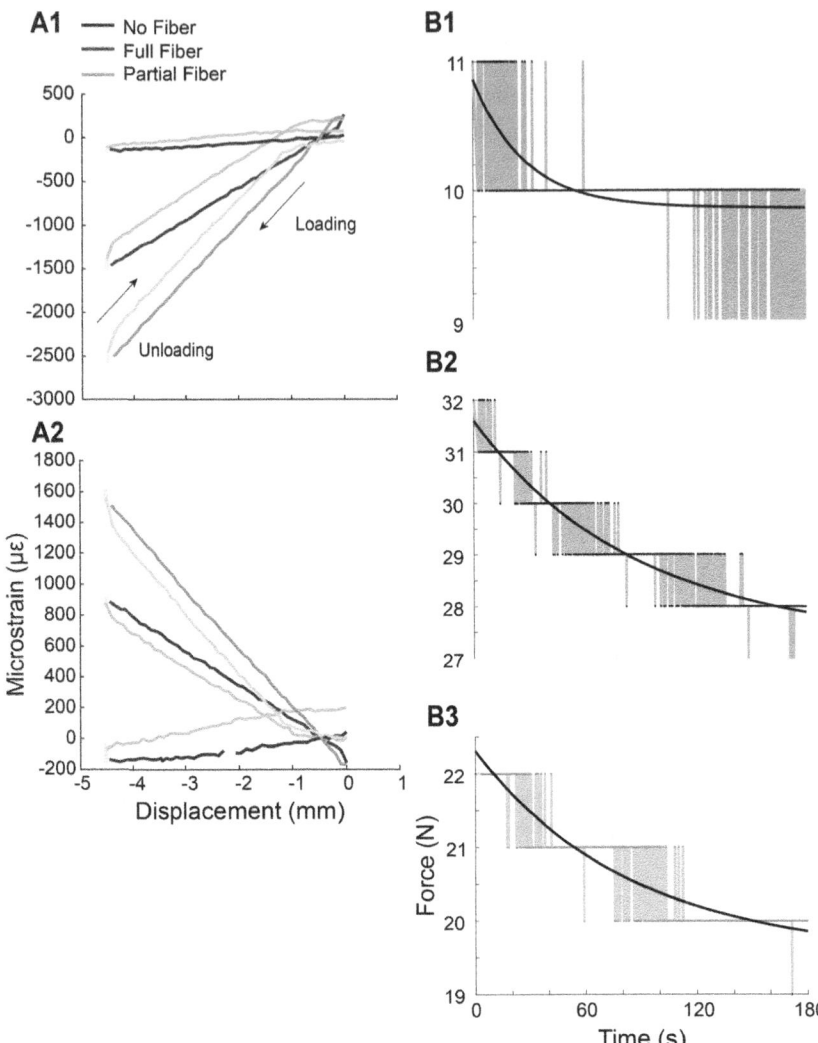

Fig. 3. Strain and force measurements during displacement; **A** microstrain measurements during displacement in each model; low opacity marks increasing displacement, high opacity marks decreasing displacement, grey marks constant displacement; **A1** axial axis; **A2** transverse axis, **B** force measurements during constant displacement test; at a peak displacement of 4.5 mm, the displacement was kept constant for 180 s, allowing the force to vary due to stress relaxation; each force trajectory was fitted using an exponential decay fit; **B1** *no-fiber* model; **B2** *full-fiber* model; **B3** *partial-fiber* model

4 Discussion

To advance the field of distributed sensing in locomoting robotics and to shed light on the effects of material properties on strain sensing, we investigated the effects of Kevlar fiber reinforcement on both displacement and strain sensing in robot limb segments. We utilized a previously published insect-inspired robotic limb and modified it to incorporate Kevlar at different locations. We compared *no-fiber*, *partial-fiber*, and *full-fiber* reinforcement. Fiber reinforcement was placed in the *partial-fiber* model from the distal end to 10 mm from the strain gauge to increase strain measurement while reducing the overall compliance of the limb segment.

Our data clearly showed that the stiffest model was the *full-fiber* model, with the *partial-fiber* model exhibiting about 69% of the *full-fiber* model's stiffness and the *no-fiber* model exhibiting about 34% of the *full-fiber* model's stiffness (Fig. 2B). Despite these differences in stiffness, the strain gauge measurement was highest in the *partial-fiber* model. This strain showed the same trajectory as in the non-fiber model and was, thus, not artificially altered through the partial Kevlar inclusion, unlike the *full-fiber* model, which showed no tension along the transverse axis (Fig. 3A1–2). The *partial-fiber* model, which had no Kevlar fiber in the area of the strain gauge, produced the highest-amplitude strain measurements while maintaining reasonably high rigidity.

The highest SNR was seen in the *no-fiber* model and the lowest SNRs were seen in the *full-fiber* model. The *partial-fiber* models axial SNR was 12.3% lower than the *no-fiber* models axial axis (Table 1). This may be due to error in the application of the strain gauge rosettes, as both the connection to the operational amplifiers and their adherence to the model itself may influence their measurements. Additionally, the constitution of the *partial-fiber* model may amplify environmental noise, such as vibration from the floor. Further study should include a higher number of samples. Another limitation to this study is that the force gauge used to measure the applied force has a resolution of 1 N. In future experiments, a force gauge with more precision should be used.

These findings are not only of interest for robotic manufacturing but also highlight the relevance of the highly complex biological insect cuticle for strain sensing. The cuticle of an insect varies within and between locations in thickness, composition, and layering [12]. Further, recent findings from stick insects have highlighted that mechanical stress relaxation in the cuticle affects the adaptation rates of strain sensors [19]. The present data suggest that the incorporation of more rigid fibers throughout limb segments can affect both hysteresis and strain magnitude, while also indicating that the reinforcement of rigid elements must be nuanced to increase the sensitivity of strain monitoring. Similarly, to the Kevlar fiber-reinforced models used herein, insect cuticle contains anti-parallel alpha-chitin fibers that contribute to overall stiffness through their morphology [11]. As within our *partial-fiber* model, the size of these chitin nanofibrils can vary in locations with high resistance to compression [11, 20], which highlights the benefits of bioinspired, spatially planned fiber reinforcement in robotic limbs. Consequently, to better understand strain sensing in insects, we propose analyzing the material properties of the cuticle surrounding CS and their effects on the purely mechanical aspects of sensor activation.

In conclusion, we analyzed the benefits of Kevlar reinforcement in robotic limbs for walking legs. The data show advantages of partial fiber supplementation for an increase in rigidness and strain sensing magnitude. Utilizing these findings will further advance the resiliency and robustness of robots.

Funding. IK and NSS were supported by NSF DBI 2015317 as part of the NSF/CIHR/DFG/FRQ/UKRI-MRC Next Generation Networks for Neuroscience Program. IK, NSS, and SNZ were supported by NSF IIS 2113028. GFD was supported by DFG DI 2907/1-1 (Project number 500615768).

Disclosure of Interests. The authors have no competing interests to declare that are relevant to the content of this article.

References

1. Houk, J., Simon, W.: Responses of golgi tendon organs to forces applied to muscle tendon. J. Neurophysiol. **30**, 1466–1481 (1967). https://doi.org/10.1152/jn.1967.30.6.1466
2. Pringle, J.W.S.: Proprioception in Insects: I. A new type of mechanical receptor from the palps of the cockroach. Journal of Experimental Biology **15**, 101–113 (1938)
3. Pringle, J.W.S.: Proprioception in Insects II. The Action of the Campaniform Sensilla on the Legs (1937)
4. Zill, S., Schmitz, J., Büschges, A.: Load sensing and control of posture and locomotion. Arthropod Struct. Dev. **33**, 273–286 (2004). https://doi.org/10.1016/j.asd.2004.05.005
5. Zyhowski, W.P., Zill, S.N., Szczecinski, N.S.: Adaptive load feedback robustly signals force dynamics in robotic model of *Carausius Morosus* stepping. Front. Neurorobot. **17**, 1125171 (2023). https://doi.org/10.3389/fnbot.2023.1125171
6. Dinges, G.F., Zyhowski, W.P., Goldsmith, C.A., Szczecinski, N.S.: Comparison of Trochanteral Strain in Locomotor Model Organisms Using Robotic Legs. Springer (2023)
7. Zyhowski, W.P., Zill, S.N., Szczecinski, N.S.: Load Feedback from a Dynamically Scaled Robotic Model of *Carausius Morosus* Middle Leg. In: Conference on Biomimetic and Biohybrid Systems, pp. 128–139. Springer International Publishing, Cham (2022)
8. Xue, F., et al.: Ultra-Sensitive, Highly Linear, and Hysteresis-Free Strain Sensors Enabled by Gradient Stiffness Sliding Strategy. npj Flex Electron **8**, 1–8 (2024). https://doi.org/10.1038/s41528-024-00301-7
9. Li, P., et al.: Wide range compressed sensing structure based on tension-compression conversion and variable stiffness slope structure. Sci. China Mater. **67**, 871–878 (2024). https://doi.org/10.1007/s40843-023-2748-8
10. Lynch, K.M., Park, F.C.: Modern Robotics: Mechanics, Planning, and Control. Cambridge University Press, Cambridge, UK (2017). ISBN 978-1-107-15630-2
11. Vincent, J.F.V.: Arthropod Cuticle: A Natural Composite Shell System. Compos. A Appl. Sci. Manuf. **33**, 1311–1315 (2002). https://doi.org/10.1016/S1359-835X(02)00167-7
12. Rajabi, H., Jafarpour, M., Darvizeh, A., Dirks, J.-H., Gorb, S.N.: Stiffness distribution in insect cuticle: a continuous or a discontinuous profile? J. R. Soc. Interface **14**, 20170310 (2017). https://doi.org/10.1098/rsif.2017.0310
13. Moran, D.T., Chapman, K.M., Ellis, R.A.: The fine structure of cockroach campaniform sensilla. J. Cell Biol. **48**, 155–173 (1971). https://doi.org/10.1083/jcb.48.1.155
14. Jafarpour, M., Eshghi, S., Darvizeh, A., Gorb, S., Rajabi, H.: Functional significance of graded properties of insect cuticle supported by an evolutionary analysis. J. R. Soc. Interface **17**, 20200378 (2020). https://doi.org/10.1098/rsif.2020.0378

15. Vincent, J.F.V., Wegst, U.G.K.: Design and mechanical properties of insect cuticle. Arthropod Struct. Dev. **33**, 187–199 (2004). https://doi.org/10.1016/j.asd.2004.05.006
16. Kevlar 3D Printing - Specialized Continuous Fiber Available online: https://markforged.com/materials/continuous-fibers/kevlar, Accessed on 5 March 2024
17. Onyx - Composite 3D Printing Material Available online: https://markforged.com/materials/plastics/onyx. Accessed on 22 February 2023
18. Xu, Q., Engquist, B.: A mathematical model for fitting and predicting relaxation modulus and simulating viscoelastic responses. Proceedings of the Royal Society A: Mathematical, Physical and Engineering Sciences **474**, 20170540 (2018). https://doi.org/10.1098/rspa.2017.0540
19. Harris, C.M., Szczecinski, N.S., Büschges, A., Zill, S.N.: Sensory signals of unloading in insects are tuned to distinguish leg slipping from load variations in gait: experimental and modeling studies. J. Neurophysiol. **128**, 790–807 (2022). https://doi.org/10.1152/jn.00285.2022
20. Gardiner, B.G., Khan, M.F.: A new form of insect cuticle. Zool. J. Linn. Soc. **66**, 91–94 (1979). https://doi.org/10.1111/j.1096-3642.1979.tb01903.x

Flexible Strain Gauge Sensors as Real-Time Stretch Receptors for Use in Biomimetic BPA Muscle Applications

Rochelle Jubert[1]([✉]), Alexander Hunt[1], and Michael Hopkins[2]

[1] Department of Mechanical and Materials Engineering, Portland State University, Portland, OR, USA
rjubert@pdx.edu
[2] Liquid Wire, Portland, OR, USA

Abstract. This paper presents a novel approach to real-time length sensing for biomimetic Braided Pneumatic Actuators (BPAs) in soft robotics applications. Flexible strain gauge sensors from LiquidWire are ironed onto a sewn Nylon sleeve for external placement on BPAs. Calibration equations that include voltage rate and hysteresis are developed to convert strain gauge resistance into muscle displacement. Experimental results demonstrate the efficacy of the proposed method, achieving low error rates and high biomimicry. The non-linear calibration outperforms linear methods, showcasing its suitability for artificial proprioceptive neural networks. This approach offers accurate real-time feedback for enhanced robotic control, addressing the need for low-profile, modular sensors that mimic muscle stretch receptors. Future research may explore further refinements and applications of this technique.

1 Introduction

Artificial muscles, such as braided pneumatic actuators (BPAs), are frequently used to develop biomimetic robots due to their muscle-like properties [7,8,10, 15]. These actuators provide variable stiffness and often exhibit similar force-length and force-velocity dependencies that are found in biological muscles. The use of artificial muscles enables the development of more interesting robotic designs that no longer depend on single rotation joints controlled by motors; other joint designs, such as ball-and-socket and compact, four-bar mechanisms can be created [16,17]. Additionally, artificial muscles can be arranged in complex geometries and cross multiple joints. Developing robots with these capabilities, however, produces more complexities in control and sensing. Joint encoders, the mainstay of robotic feedback, can no longer be used. New methods of sensing are needed to get feedback on muscle behavior to implement intelligent controls.

Here again, we can take inspiration from how biological systems provide sensory feedback of muscle movement and contraction in the body. Animals sense movement in their bodies through proprioceptive feedback [19]. These sensory neurons include spindles and stretch receptors that are wrapped around and embedded in muscle and tendon tissues [13]. They are known to sense muscle

N. S. Szczecinski et al. (Eds.): Living Machines 2024, LNAI 14930, pp. 94–108, 2025.
https://doi.org/10.1007/978-3-031-72597-5_7

velocity, tension, and length, also referred to as Types Ia, Ib, and II. This feedback is then integrated into the nervous system and used for control of individual muscles, and coordination of muscle groups [11]. The development of sensors that mimic this feedback could significantly improve the controllability of artificial muscles.

Several methods have been explored to incorporate real-time length sensing abilities into BPA design, aiming to mimic the function of muscle stretch receptors and complete the artificial proprioceptive feedback loop. This can be achieved by weaving sensors within the fabric of the BPA, placing sensors inside, or by attaching sensors externally. While structural sensors that are integrated directly into the fabric provide a low-profile and biomimetic solution, the muscle fabrication processes are labor-intensive and inaccessible to research being conducted with stock BPAs [5,18,20]. Sensors that are placed inside of the BPA bladder produce a low-profile design, however, these methods suffer from poor noise-to-signal ratios, making them less suitable for precise soft robotic control [1,3,6]. Therefore, the use of flexible external sensors made from piezoelectric materials such as Gallium-Indium or ElectroLycra has been increasing due to their modularity, biomimetic characteristics, and low-profile application methods [4,12]. Although these methods have developed some clever techniques for capturing strain rate and hysteresis, they experience some challenges with noise and material choice such that they are unable to produces length measurements at a high enough accuracy that would be useful for feedback control.

This research sets out to fill this gap by developing a reliable method for sensing artificial muscle length for use as feedback in a BPA-actuated robot. Similar to previous research [12], we consider strain rate and hysteresis when generating calibration equations to convert the strain gauge resistance to muscle length. We test this calibration against both slow motions and fast motions that replicate signals that may be sent to the robot during locomotion. We demonstrate that the proposed design, signal processing, and calibration provide a promising method for producing precise muscle-length sensing ability that is biomimetic, low-profile, modular, and suitable as feedback in artificial robotic proprioceptive control.

2 Methods

To collect consistent real-time length data while minimizing noise, a sturdy length-sensing test rig was built, as seen in Fig. 1.

The extruded aluminum frame held a sliding crossbeam that displaced as an attached 180 cm long, 10mm diameter stock Festo BPA was inflated and deflated with two respective orientations of valves, as seen in Fig. 2–one inflation orientation with a Kelly Pneumatics Miniature Proportional valve upstream of a 3/2 way AirTAC solenoid valve to modulate muscle inflation and one deflation orientation with the proportional valve downstream of the binary solenoid valve to modulate deflation. These two configurations allowed for more precise control of muscle inflation and deflation rate to better characterize sensor strain rate and hysteresis.

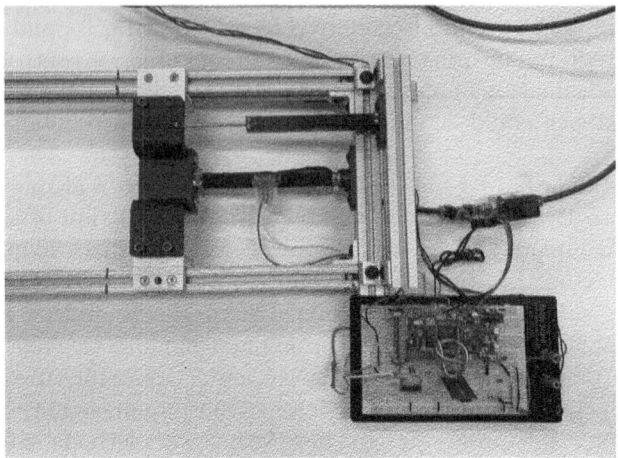

Fig. 1. Real-time length sensing test rig. The extruded aluminum frame holds a sliding crossbeam that displaces as an attached 180 cm long, 10 mm diameter stock Festo BPA is inflated and deflated with two respective inflation and deflation configurations of a binary solenoid valve and a proportional valve. A linear potentiometer collects precise experimental length measurements for comparison with the Liquid Wire strain gauge sensor.

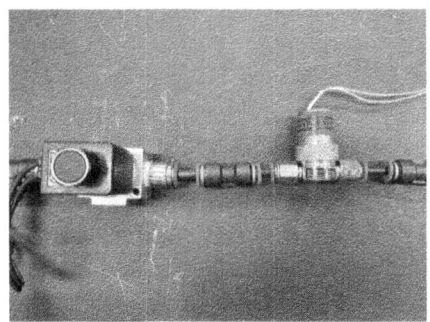 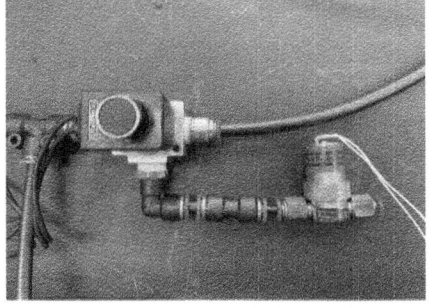

(a) Inflation Valve Configuration   (b) Deflation Valve Configuration

Fig. 2. Valve configurations to regulate muscle inflation (a) and muscle deflation (b). This was done to account for sensor strain rate and hysteresis.

A P3 America LMC13 linear motion potentiometer collected precise experimental length measurements for comparison with the Liquid Wire flexible strain gauge sensor.

2.1   Liquid Wire Strain Gauge Sensor

This study explores the application of flexible strain gauge sensors developed by Liquid Wire in Portland, Oregon [9] for use in biomimetic research. These sensors consist of channels within Thermoplastic Polyurethane (TPU) filled with a proprietary Gallium-Indium-Tin Metal Gel ™, as depicted in Fig. 3. The selected

TPU exhibits high elasticity, supporting over 30% strain, and demonstrates rapid recovery capabilities that contribute to reduced hysteresis. The Metal Gel ^{TM} is a shear-thinning gel featuring specifically engineered cross-linked oxide structures [14]. This composition provides a dual nature—solid yet flowable—enabling the gel to stretch with the material, thereby linearly increasing resistance as it extends the conductive path. Upon retraction, the gel returns to its original shape, effectively maintaining low hysteresis with the TPU.

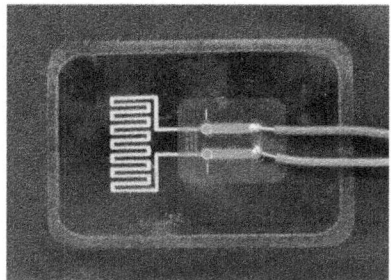

Fig. 3. Liquid Wire flexible strain gauge sensor consisting of channels within Thermoplastic Polyurethane filled with a proprietary Gallium-Indium-Tin Metal Gel ^{TM}.

2.2 Strain Gauge Application Method

The priorities in determining an application method for attaching the Liquid Wire sensor to the BPA were durability, modularity, biomimicry, and a low profile. The method that proved most successful and was ultimately pursued was heat-pressing the sensor onto nylon fabric and sewing the fabric into a flexible, modular cuff that could be mounted onto the BPA, with the strain gauge parallels perpendicular to the displacement of the muscle, as seen in Fig. 4. This method satisfied the desired design priorities, making it suitable for BPA soft-robotics applications.

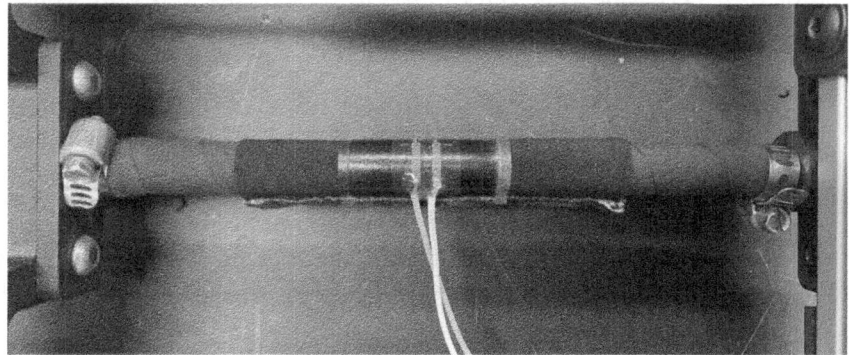

Fig. 4. Flexible Strain Gauge Sensor Sewn Sleeve

2.3   Circuitry

The strain gauge sensor was installed in a quarter Wheatstone bridge configuration, using a Spectrol 70Y-100 trimming potentiometer to balance the bridge and an INA125 instrumentation amplifier to amplify the signal by a gain of 10 for reading on an Arduino Due. A bridge input voltage over 1.5 V resulted in drift of the strain gauge signal, so this voltage was kept below 1.5 V. As mentioned, a separate P3 America LMC13 linear motion potentiometer was used as a true length measurement for comparing to the strain gauge signal. It was calibrated by using a tape measure to measure the muscle length at its inflated and deflated states and using those measured values to linearly interpolate. The proportional valve was configured using a current driver circuit and controlled using a PWM signal [2].

2.4   Actuation Trials

In order to examine the effect of strain rate and hysteresis on the characterization of the Liquid Wire sensor, displacement from the potentiometer and amplified change in voltage across the wheatstone bridge were sampled at 100 Hz for six muscle inflation and deflation rates. For the inflation trials, the inflation valve configuration from Fig. 2 was used to modulate the flow of air into the muscle by adjusting the proportional valve PWM value to change the inlet cross-sectional area. For the six trials, PWM values corresponding to a 0.25, 12.5, 25, 50, 75, and 100% open cross-sectional inlet area were used. For the deflation trials, the deflation valve configuration from Fig. 2 was used to control the flow of air out of the muscle by similarly calling PWM values corresponding to a 0.25, 12.5, 25, 50, 75, and 100% cross-sectional outlet area. These two valve configurations were necessary due to the proportional valve not being able to control both inflation and deflation within the same trial.

   To later validate the effectiveness of the flexible strain gauge attachment and calibration methods, two trials were conducted actuating the BPA, one where the BPA was inflated and deflated arbitrarily at a range of strain rates and the other using repeating pulses to simulate neuron firing as a more biomimetic method of BPA actuation. The pulses used in these trials were two sequential pulses with a consistently decreasing pulse gap to investigate the effect of the pulse gap on the strain gauge sensor accuracy.

2.5   Data Processing and Strain Gauge Calibration

To characterize the flexible strain gauge, two calibration methods where pursued: one two-dimensional linear fit that does not account for hysteresis and strain rate and one three-dimensional non-linear fit that does. For the two-dimensional linear fit, the potentiometer displacement values were converted to strain, then

the values for strain and voltage across the wheatstone bridge were both normalized by their total ranges. Normalized strain was plotted against normalized
voltage for all inflation and deflation data sets and a linear best fit equation
was generated using MATLAB, taking voltage as an input and generating strain
as an output. The calibration equation was generated using normalized values
to facilitate visualizing the relationships between the different variables and to
standardize the equation for future use. To examine the success of the linear calibration method, the collected strain gauge voltage data from both the arbitrary
actuation trial and the repeating pulse trial were normalized by their total ranges
and inputted into the linear calibration equation to yield normalized strain as an
output. This normalized strain was converted to represent displacement of the
muscle in millimeters and was plotted against the potentiometer displacement
data. Average error between the strain gauge displacement calculation and the
potentiometer displacement data was calculated using the equation below:

$$err = \frac{(d_p - d_s)}{\delta} \cdot 100$$

where err is percent error, d_p is the potentiometer displacement signal, d_s is
the strain gauge displacement signal, and δ is the range of the strain gauge
displacement values. Root mean squared error was calculated using the following
equation:

$$RMSE = \sqrt{\frac{1}{n} \cdot \sum_{i=1}^{n}(d_p - d_s)^2}$$

where n is the number of data points in the set.

For the three-dimensional non-linear fit, the potentiometer displacement values were converted to strain, the strain was then differentiated over time to yield
instantaneous strain rate, and strain, strain rate, and voltage were all normalized
by their total ranges. First, all inflation trials were plotted on a three-dimensional
plot with normalized strain rate as the x-axis, normalized voltage as the y-axis,
and normalized strain as the z-axis. A polynomial fit was generated in the MAT-
LAB curve fitting tool with one degree in the x-axis and three degrees in the
y-axis. This fit acted as the strain gauge non-linear inflation calibration equation,
taking normalized strain rate and bridge voltage as inputs and generating normalized strain as an output. Second, the plotting and curve fitting was repeated
for the deflation trials, producing a similar strain gauge non-linear calibration
equation for muscle deflation. To examine the success of the non-linear calibration method for real-time BPA actuation, the collected strain gauge voltage data
from both the arbitrary actuation trial and the repeating pulse trial were first
normalized by dividing by their total ranges. Instantaneous voltage rate was calculated by differentiating strain gauge voltage over time. Voltage rate was then

normalized by dividing by its total range. Using normalized voltage and voltage rate as inputs, the non-linear inflation and deflation calibration equations were used to produce normalized strain as the output. This normalized strain was redimensionalized to represent displacement of the muscle in millimeters and was superimposed with the potentiometer displacement data. Average error and root mean squared error were calculated using the same equations as above.

3   Results

A Liquid Wire flexible strain gauge sensor, ironed onto a Nylon sleeve and mounted to an artificial BPA muscle, was used as a means of measuring real-time displacement. Figure 5 shows raw data from the strain gauge and potentiometer for the arbitrary actuation trial (top) and repeated pulse trial (bottom). For the arbitrary actuation trial, the calculated average percent error was 14.10% and the RMSE was 2.169% normalized strain. For the repeated pulse trial, the calculated average percent error was 5.180% and the RMSE was 0.9266% normalized strain. It can be seen that the strain gauge roughly follows the potentiometer displacement reading, though it exhibits considerable noise, irregular behavior, and delay.

From here, two methods of calibration were considered: a linear calibration that excludes strain rate and hysteresis and a non-linear calibration that considers inflation or deflation of the muscle and accounts for strain rate.

3.1   Linear Calibration

The relationship between muscle strain, as calculated by the potentiometer, and the voltage across the Wheatstone bridge can be seen in Fig. 6.

A linear approximation was fit to this data as the simplest possible calibration and as a point of comparison, even though clear non-linearities can be seen. The best fit linear approximation equation was found to be

$$\varepsilon = 0.9744 \cdot V + 0.1757$$

and had a r^2 value of 0.9680.

3.2   Non-linear Calibration

For the non-linear calibration, two separate calibrations equations were generated, one for inflation and one for deflation. To generate the inflation and deflation calibration equations, three-dimensional plots were generated with strain

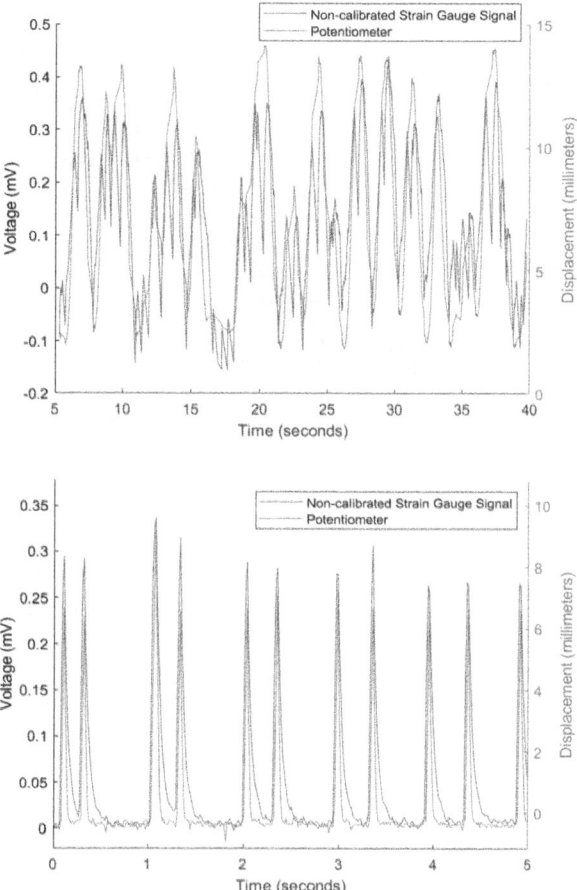

Fig. 5. Liquid Wire sensor reading pre-calibration for random actuation (top) and pulse based actuation (bottom)

rate as the x-axis, bridge voltage as the y-axis, and strain as the z-axis. A polynomial best fit of one degree in the x-axis and three degrees in the y-axis was generated as the non-linear calibration equation for each curve. The inflation and deflation calibration curves can be seen in Fig. 7.

The corresponding best fit equation for inflation is:

$$\varepsilon = 0.058 + 0.001 \cdot \dot{\varepsilon} + 0.774 \cdot V - 0.121 \cdot V \cdot \dot{\varepsilon} + 2.30 \cdot V^2 + 0.094 \cdot \dot{\varepsilon} \cdot V^2 - 2.26 \cdot V^3$$

where $\dot{\varepsilon}$ is equal to strain rate, V is voltage across the wheatstone bridge, and ε is strain. The R^2 value for the fit is 0.9934 and the RMSE is 2.851% normalized strain. This fit was chosen because it was the lowest order fit that produced an

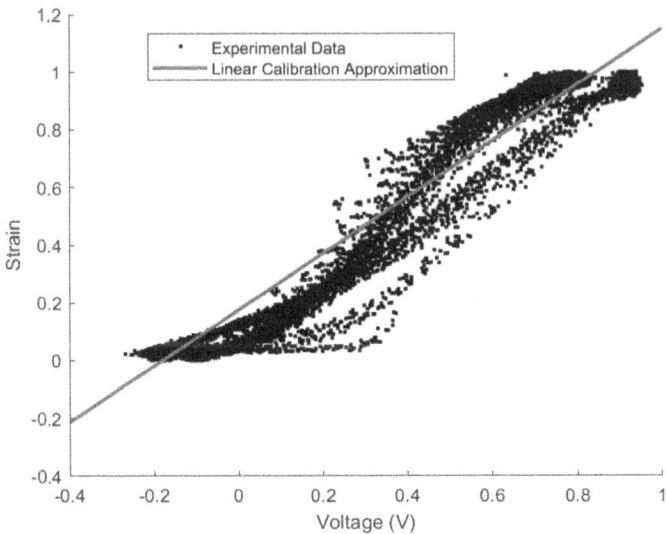

Fig. 6. Strain vs. voltage data and accompanying linear calibration approximation

impactful R^2 value, with the next lowest order fit having an R^2 value of 0.9806 and an RMSE of 4.890% normalized strain, while the next highest order fit had an R^2 value of 0.9938 and an RMSE of 2.765% normalized strain.

The corresponding best fit equation for deflation is:

$$\varepsilon = 0.225 - 0.218 \cdot \dot{\varepsilon} + 0.825 \cdot V - 0.773 \cdot V \cdot \dot{\varepsilon} - 0.481 \cdot V^2 + 1.05 \cdot \dot{\varepsilon} \cdot V^2 + 0.564 \cdot V^3$$

The R^2 value for the fit is 0.9943 and the RMSE is 1.821% normalized strain. This fit was chosen because it was the lowest order fit that produced an impactful R^2 value, with the next lowest order fit having an R^2 value of 0.9895 and an RMSE of 2.467% normalized strain, while the next highest order fit had an R^2 value of 0.9945 and an RMSE of 1.798% normalized strain.

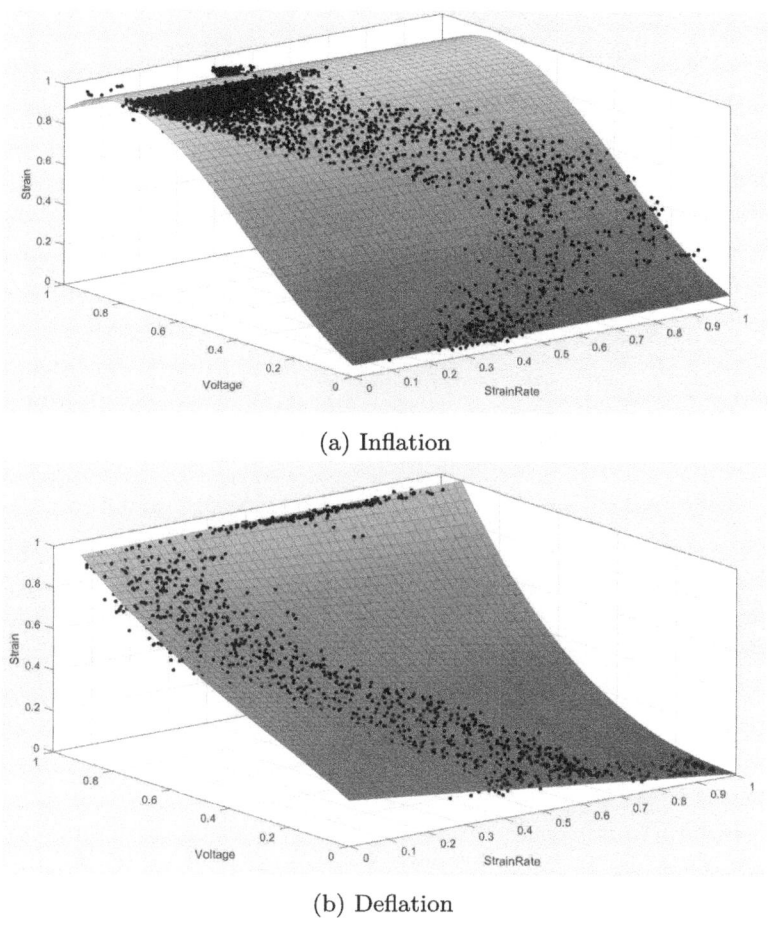

(a) Inflation

(b) Deflation

Fig. 7. Non-Linear Calibration Curves

3.3 Applied Linear Calibration

The results of applying the linear calibration equation show an average error of 18.62% and an RMSE of 3.807% normalized strain for the random actuation data and an average error of 5.875% and RMSE of 1.845% normalized strain for the pulse data, as seen in Fig. 8.

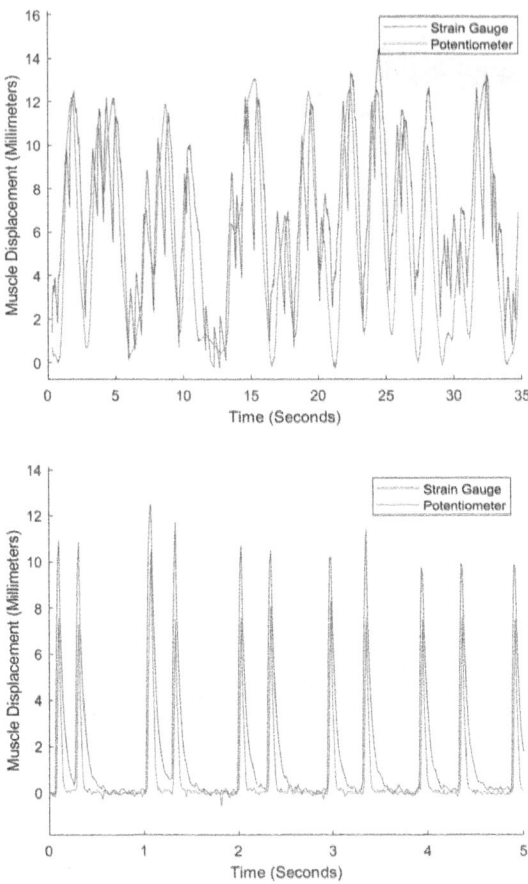

Fig. 8. Linearly calibrated random actuation (top) and pulse based actuation (bottom)

In the random actuation trials, the strain gauge signal exhibits a similar amount of noise as the raw data and does not reach the full magnitude of the potentiometer length reading. The pulsing actuation trials show minimal error in the strain gauge sensor reading but does demonstrate some delay and overshoot in comparison to the potentiometer signal.

3.4   Applied Non-linear Calibration

The results of applying the non-linear calibration equations show an average error of 16.05% and an RMSE of 2.777% normalized strain for the random actuation data and an average error of 4.863% and an RMSE of 1.550% normalized strain for the pulse data, as seen in Fig. 9.

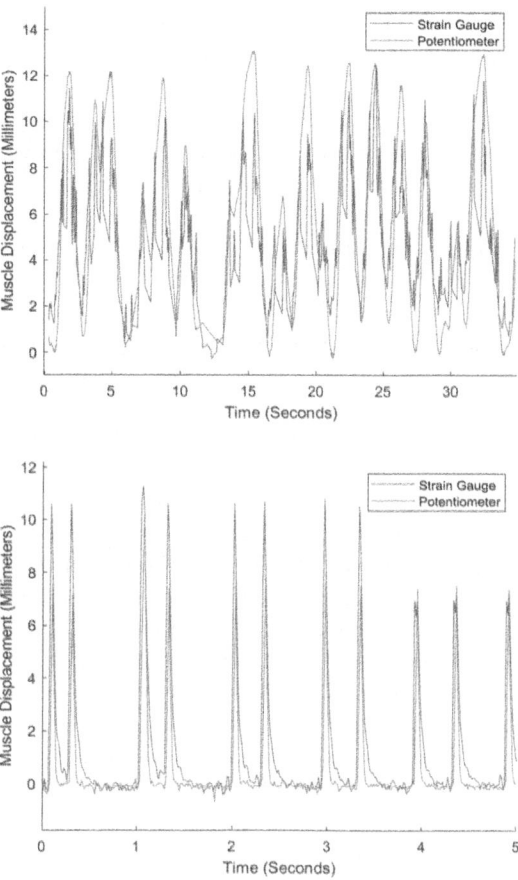

Fig. 9. Non-Linearly calibrated random actuation (top) and pulse based actuation (bottom)

The non-linearly calibrated strain gauge signal demonstrates a comparable amount of noise to the raw data and similarly to the linear calibration, the strain gauge signal does not reach the full magnitude of the potentiometer length reading. The non-linear calibration appears to perform well in the pulse-based actuation trials, though also shows some delay and overshoot in comparison to the potentiometer signal. In comparison with the linearly-calibrated signal, the non-linearly calibrated signal exhibits less overshoot of the potentiometer signal.

4   Discussion

This research examines the validity of using Liquid Wire flexible strain gauges as a means for measuring real-time length feedback of BPA artificial muscles.

The success of the proposed methods is highlighted by the modularity and consistency of the sensor sleeve, the low-profile and biomimetic nature of the strain gauge sensor, and the performance of two calibration methods–one linear calibration that neglects strain rate and hysteresis and one non-linear calibration that does not. The clear victory in the methods is seen especially in quantifying the pulse-based actuation, where for both calibration methods, the strain gauge signal exhibits low average percent error and low RMSE. The two methods are nearly interchangeable for this trial due to their similar error values, though the non-linear calibration does outperform the linear calibration and provides a higher level of accuracy. A paired T-test examining the two methods in the pulse-based actuation trials revealed a two-tailed P-value of less than 0.0001, demonstrating that this difference can be considered extremely statistically significant. Overall, the performance of the proposed methods in the pulse-based actuation trials demonstrates a two-fold biomimetic success: a low-profile and flexible real-time BPA length sensor that mimics the function of muscle stretch receptors, especially for pulse-based BPA actuation that simulates neuron firing for muscle activation.

The low average error and RMSE in the pulse-based actuation trials could be due to the periods of rest between the pulses. The displacement of the muscle during these periods is very low, ultimately decreasing the overall average error and RMSE. This prompts further examination of the relationship between pulse width and strain gauge sensor accuracy, where generally within this trial, the success of the strain gauge was unaffected. In comparison with the non-calibrated signal, low significant improvement was made using either calibration method and further analysis is required to determine the impact of the calibration equations for pulse-based actuation. Ultimately, a better understanding of the success of these methods could be achieved through more thorough characterization of sensor responses and understanding of the frequency response. Further analysis of the voltage rate should equally be investigated, especially in conjunction with pulse-based actuation pulse width.

While the linear and non-linear calibration methods vary slightly in their successes for the pulse-based actuation, both methods equally failed to outperform the non-calibrated strain gauge signal for the random actuation trial. It is hypothesized that the higher frequency of rapid changes in direction and inflation rate produced more error for this trial. This high error warrants pursuing signal filtering in future work to further investigate the application of the flexible strain gauges and proposed calibration methods in random BPA muscle actuation.

In comparison to a similar experiment that examines the impact of strain rate and hysteresis on piezoresistive real-time BPA length sensing, the methods proposed in this work demonstrate a similar success in random BPA actuation. In the study, the found RMSE value for the proposed piezoresistive flexible sensor signal was 1.27 mm, about 20% of entire axial displacement of the actuator [12]. While the methods proposed vary in their sensor construction, the similarities between their sensor characterization methods provide an opportunity to compare their results. Overall, the measured error in the Liquid Wire flexible strain gauge signal is slightly lower than in the proposed piezoresistive flexible sensor, potentially highlighting the high elasticity, and therefore generally low hysteresis, of the Liquid Wire sensor. Ultimately, this research shows that using Liquid Wire flexible strain gauges for real-time BPA length-sensing highlights a unique application of this genre of sensor: measuring pulse-based BPA actuation.

Acknowledgements. This work could not have been accomplished without the help of Connor Blankenau and Ben Bolen. Partially-funded by NSF grant for NeuroNex: C3NS 2015317.

Disclosure of Interests. Author Michael Hopkins is an employee of Liquid Wire.

References

1. Antonelli, M.G., Zobel, P.B., De Marcellis, A., Palange, E.: Design and characterization of a mckibben pneumatic muscle prototype with an embedded capacitive length transducer. Machines **10**, 1156 (2022)
2. Chakravarthy, S., Kapilavai, A., Ghosal, A.: Experimental characterization and control of miniaturized pneumatic artificial muscle. J. Med. Dev. **8**, 041011 (2014)
3. Chung, J.: Real-time length sensing of braided pneumatic actuator using ir time-of-flight sensor (2023)
4. Dai, K., Elangovan, A., Whirley, K., Webster-Wood, V.A.: Soft tubular sensors for contact detection. In: 12th International Conference, Living Machines 2023, Proceedings, Part I (2023)
5. Felt, W., Chin, K.Y., Remy, D.: Contraction sensing with smart braid mckibben muscles. IEEE/ASME Trans. Mechatron. **21**, 1201–1209 (2015)
6. Goulbourne, N.C., Son, S.: Numerical and experimental analysis of mckibben actuators and dielectric elastomer sensors. In: ASME 2007 International Mechanical Engineering Congress and Exposition (2009)
7. Hosoda, K., Sakaguchi, Y., Takayama, H., Takuma, T.: Pneumatic-driven jumping robot with anthropomorphic muscular skeleton structure. Auton. Rob. **28**(3), 307–316 (2010). https://doi.org/10.1007/s10514-009-9171-6
8. Hosoda, K., Takuma, T., Nakamoto, A., Hayashi, S.: Biped robot design powered by antagonistic pneumatic actuators for multi-modal locomotion. Rob. Auton. Syst. **56**(1), 46–53 (2008). http://www.sciencedirect.com/science/article/pii/S0921889007001352
9. https://www.liquidwire.com/ . Accessed 12 Apr 2024
10. Hunt, A., Szczecinski, N., Quinn, R.: Development and training of a neural controller for hind leg walking in a dog robot. Front. Neurorob. **11** (2017). http://journal.frontiersin.org/article/10.3389/fnbot.2017.00018/abstract
11. Jankowska, E.: Spinal interneuronal networks in the cat: elementary components. Brain Res. Rev. Netw. Motion **57**(1), 46–55 (2008)
12. Maselli, M., Zrinscak, D., Magliola, V., Cianchetti, M.: A piezoresistive flexible sensor to detect soft actuator deformation. In: 2019 2nd IEEE International Conference on Soft Robotics (RoboSoft) (2019)
13. Prochazka, A.: Quantifying proprioception. Prog. Brain Res. **123**, 133–42 (1999)
14. Ronay, M.: wO2017151523A1 (2017)

15. Scharzenberger, C., Mendoza, J., Hunt, A.: Design of a canine inspired quadruped robot as a platform for synthetic neural network control. In: Martinez-Hernandez, U., et al. (eds.) Living Machines 2019. LNCS (LNAI), vol. 11556, pp. 228–239. Springer, Cham (2019). https://doi.org/10.1007/978-3-030-24741-6_20

16. Steele, A.G., Etoundi, A., Hunt, A.J.: Experimental verification of kinematics and kinetics in a biomimetic bipedal robot. J. Mech. Rob. **15**, 014503 (2022). https://doi.org/10.1115/1.4054441

17. Steele, A.G., Hunt, A., Etoundi, A.C.: Biomimetic knee design to improve joint torque and life for bipedal robotics. In: Giuliani, M., Assaf, T., Giannaccini, M.E. (eds.) TAROS 2018. LNCS (LNAI), vol. 10965, pp. 91–102. Springer, Cham (2018). https://doi.org/10.1007/978-3-319-96728-8_8

18. Wakimoto, S., Suzumori, K., Kanda, T.: Development of intelligent mckibben actuator. In: IEEE/RSJ International Conference on Intelligent Robots and Systems (IROS) (2005)

19. Windhorst, U.: Muscle proprioceptive feedback and spinal networks. Brain Res. Bull. **73**(4-6), 155–202 (2007). https://linkinghub.elsevier.com/retrieve/pii/S0361923007001037

20. Wirekoh, J., Valle, L., Pol, N., Park, Y.L.: Sensorized, flat, pneumatic artificial muscle embedded with biomimetic microfluidic sensors for proprioceptive feedback. Soft Rob. **6**, 768–777 (2019)

Sensory Feedback Cancellation: Developing Resonator Networks to Mimic *A. leptorhynchu's* Cerebellar Processing of Sensory Feedback

Sheldon P. Johnson[1]($\boxtimes$) (ID), Gary Marsat[2] (ID), and Nicholas S. Szczecinski[1] (ID)

[1] Neuro-Mechanical Intelligence Laboratory, Department of Mechanical, Materials and Aero-Space Engineering, West Virginia University, Morgantown, WV 26506, USA
spj00006@mix.wvu.edu, nss00001@mail.wvu.edu
[2] Department of Biology, West Virginia University, Morgantown, WV 26506, USA

Abstract. Sensory feedback allows animals to read, react, and adapt to an environment. However, the sensory information received by the body could become overwhelming, thus overloading the brain. Yet, animals are able to process all this information by canceling redundant signals from their surroundings. One species in which this phenomenon has been explored is the *Apteronotus leptorhynchu* (brown ghost knife fish), a small electric fish that generates a bioelectric field. Sensory signals from electrical sensing organs are passed through granular cerebellar cells, which then feedback onto the primary sensory neurons to cancel low-frequency components of the sensory information. This enables the canceling of redundant sensory information and noise and makes downstream networks more sensitive to changes in sensory input. In this preliminary study, we take the first step of replicating this functionality using a series of neural resonators. Each resonator has a unique preferred frequency and then should feed back onto the sensory signal with a frequency-specific phase delay. Our resonator is a neural "differentiator" from our prior work, which amplifies frequencies up to the cutoff frequency of the network. We propose how sensory feedback cancellation could be incorporated into bioinspired robot control.

Keywords: Resonator · Synthetic Nervous System-toolbox · Functional Subnetwork Approach · Cerebellum · Ghost Knife Fish

1 Introduction

Neural systems perform functions that can inspire engineered systems. Cerebellar networks are particularly interesting in that regards and we focus here on a circuit in which feedback input allows to filter out redundant sensory signals. More specifically, we draw inspiration from the parallel fiber feedback onto primary sensory neurons in gymnotid fish [1]. These fish are exposed to continuous inputs of sensory signals, including self-generated signals (e.g. from movement) or from nearby fish. The low frequency and redundant signals are particularly inconvenient because they can interfere with their capacity to perceive important novel signals by masking them [2]. To cope with these noisy background signals, their sensory system has a mechanism to filter redundant low-frequency signals without filtering novel important signals.

© The Author(s), under exclusive license to Springer Nature Switzerland AG 2025
N. S. Szczecinski et al. (Eds.): Living Machines 2024, LNAI 14930, pp. 109–118, 2025.
https://doi.org/10.1007/978-3-031-72597-5_8

This mechanism relies on a feedback pathway through granular cerebellar cells that provides a canceling signal to subtract the redundant noise in the primary sensory neurons [3]. To generate this canceling signal, the feedback pathway consists of a delay line with frequency-tuned channels [1] that returns a copy of the sensory input. The synapses between the feedback and the primary sensory neurons (parallel fibers onto ELL pyramidal cells) are plastic and therefore only the fibers with the correct delay for a given input frequency remain strong. This feedback input is thereby shaped into a negative image of the redundant sensory input. A key aspect of this mechanism is the presence of frequency-specific channels [1] which must rely on a resonance mechanism to be selective to specific frequencies. In this paper, we create a realistic neural circuit that could underly the frequency-tuned resonator that could be present in the feedback pathway described above.

In particular, we seek to capture the functionality of these feedback-canceling mechanisms mathematically without the complexity of detailed biological modeling (e.g., specific ion channels). Because we plan to incorporate them into a real-time robot controller, we use simple neural models that can be simulated rapidly. Furthermore, because we wish to understand how the network functions, we use models that are tractable to analyze. For this reason, we are creating our model using the Synthetic Nervous System (SNS) framework [4] and implementing it with the SNS-Toolbox Python library [5].

In this preliminary study, we simulate the response of a number of neural "resonator" circuits. Multiple resonators were constructed because the system we draw inspiration from- the electrosensory system- relies on multiple frequency-specific cerebellar channels to provide feedback independently different frequencies [1]. We apply a series of sinusoidal inputs of varying frequencies to each network in order to generate its frequency response spectrum. Each circuit is tuned differently to have a different resonant frequency, replicating the functionality of the parallel fibers in the cerebellum. We show that as an ensemble, the activity of these resonators reflects the frequency of the incoming signal. This preliminary result supports our plans for future work, in which each resonator will feed back onto the incoming signal with a specific phase delay in order to cancel components of the input signal.

2   Materials and Methods

Using the SNS-Toolbox library [5] in Python, we developed six resonators each containing three non-spiking neurons: one fast-responding one slow-acting, and one postsynaptic neuron (Fig. 2). The fast and slow-acting neurons make an excitatory and inhibitory synapse connection, respectively, to the postsynaptic neuron. For the neurons in the neural network, the dynamics are as follows:

$$C_m \cdot \frac{dV}{dt} = -G_m \cdot (V - E_r) + I_b + I_{syn} + I_{ext} \tag{1}$$

where C_m is the membrane capacitance, G_m is the membrane conductance, V is the voltage, E_r is the resting potential, I_b is the bias current, I_{syn} is the synaptic current, and I_{ext} is the external current. With the voltage, and currents already being set values we can alter the resting potential and the membrane capacitance. Our resting potential value was set to 0 so our current is changed. The values for the membrane capacitance for each neuron can be found in Table 1. The synapse is what allows our network to differentiate the incoming signal and just as the neuron, the SNS-Toolbox has built-in synapse dynamics which are defined by the equations,

$$G = G_{\max} \cdot \max\big(0, \min\big(1, U_{pre}/R\big)\big) \tag{2}$$

$$I_{syn} = G \cdot (E_{rev} - U_{post}) \tag{3}$$

where G is the conductance, $G_{\max}$ is the max conductance, U_{pre} is the presynaptic voltage or the membrane potential of the presynaptic neuron relative to its rest potential (i.e., $U = V - E_r$), R is the expected range of fluctuation in the membrane voltage, E_{rev} is the reversal potential relative to the postsynaptic neuron's rest potential, and U_{post} is the postsynaptic neuron's membrane potential. Changing the reversal potential of the synapse allows us to define the role of the synapse, e.g., excitatory ($E_{rev} > 0$) or inhibitory ($E_{rev} \leq 0$).

The SNS-toolbox simulates the network response using the Forward Euler method,

$$y(t_0 + n\Delta t) \approx y(t_0) + \sum_{i=0}^{n-1} f(t_0 + i\Delta t)\Delta t$$

where t_0 is the initial time, n is the number of timesteps at which to calculate the response, Δt is the time step, which we set at 0.1 ms. Using this we can update and observe the responses of our system in terms of time. For further implementation see [Nourse et al. 2023].

2.1   Functional Subnetwork Approach to Creating a Resonator

To create a network that functions as a differentiator, we pass the input current signal through two neurons with different time constants in parallel. The neuron with the shorter time constant is called the "fast" neuron, and that with the longer time constant is called the "slow" neuron. Then, the fast neuron excites the network's third, output neuron and the slow neuron inhibits the output neuron. As shown previously, the output neuron's voltage reflects the rate of change of the input current [4]. For an appreciable output voltage, the time constant of the slow neuron needs to be substantially longer than that of the fast neuron. The resulting network performs as a high-pass filter because rapidly changing inputs depolarize the fast neuron before the slow neuron can respond, temporarily activating the output neuron.

However, one aspect of this network that was not addressed in previous work is that every neuron in the network is a low-pass filter, itself. Therefore, the differentiator network really functions as a band-pass filter: When the input changes slowly, both the fast and slow neurons are activated at the same rate and the network output is 0; when the input changes rapidly, neither the fast nor the slow neuron are activated and the network output is 0; when the input changes at the appropriate rate, the fast neuron is activated before the slow neuron and the output is temporarily positive. Because the network has a frequency at which its output is greatest, we call this network a "resonator".

The fast neuron in each resonator possesses a small membrane capacitance value with 5 nF being the smallest and increasing by 5 nF per resonator up to 30 nF. For the slow neurons, the membrane capacitance must be much larger than the fast-acting neuron, so each neuron's membrane capacitance is 10 times more than the fast neuron's (Table 1). We can calculate the time constants for every pair of neurons by using the equation,

$$\tau = \frac{C_m}{G_m}, \tag{4}$$

where τ is the time constant, C_m is the membrane capacitance, and G_m is the membrane conductance, which we set to 1 μS (or $(M\Omega)^{-1}$). Setting $G_m = 1$ μS makes each neuron's time constant equivalent to its membrane capacitance (Table 1).

Table 1. Each resonator's fast and slow time constants

Resonator	Fast time constant	Slow time constant
Resonator 1	5 ms	50 ms
Resonator 2	10 ms	100 ms
Resonator 3	15 ms	150 ms
Resonator 4	20 ms	200 ms
Resonator 5	25 ms	250 ms
Resonator 6	30 ms	300 ms

To determine the frequency response of each network and ensure that these "differentiators" possess a resonant frequency as expected, the neurons were excited with an input current with the shape of a sine wave with frequencies ranging from 10^{-5} to 10^{31} kHz. This frequency range was chosen to characterize the resonator responses over their most sensitive frequencies.

Finally, to obtain the resonant frequencies of each resonator, the gain (i.e., the ratio of the output neuron's voltage to the input current) was needed. The gain was procured by taking the peak of the amplitude of the response in the frame of,

$$t > (c - 1) \cdot \tau_L, \tag{5}$$

where t is the amount of time the input current is being applied, c is the number of cycles of the current stimulus, and τ_L is the longest neuron time constant in the network. This was to ensure that the simulated network's response had achieved a steady state. The number of cycles for testing was 15 and the longest time constant was 300 ms.

Lastly, to simulate the response of a parallel fiber in response to continuous sensory feedback, e.g., as a fish moves through different environments, we tested how the resonators would respond to a current that changes its frequency during one of its cycles.

3   Results

The resonant frequency for each resonator was found (Fig. 3). They are represented as the peak of the amplitude from each resonator's response curve. All the values for the resonant frequencies are very small (Table 2). This tells us that the resonators do not have resonance outside the range of the frequencies that we want our system to respond to which can range from 0 to 30 Hz (Fig. 1).

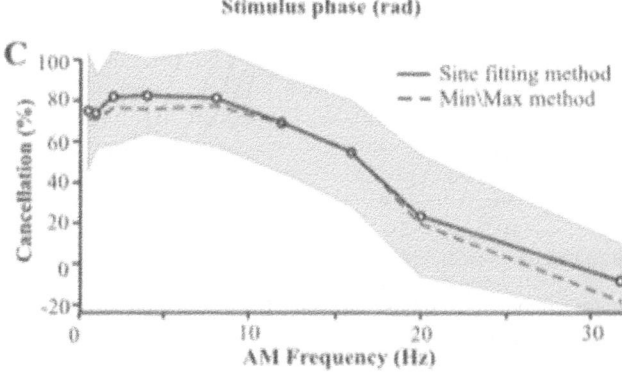

Fig. 1. "Cancellation of the stimulus-response due to feedback as a function of stimulus frequency". Using the "Sine Fitting method" reveals the resemblance the shape of the stimulus-response has to a sine wave when given the same frequency [1].

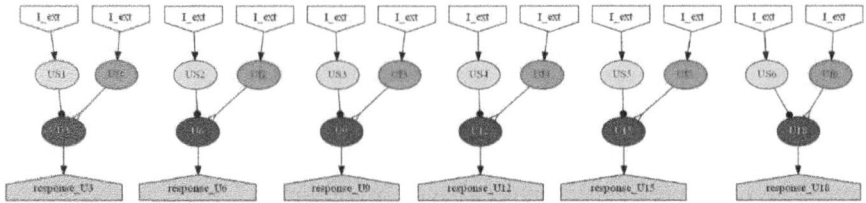

Fig. 2. Configuration of the resonator(s). Each resonator has its respective time constants for its fast and slow-acting neurons. The time constants increase from left to right.

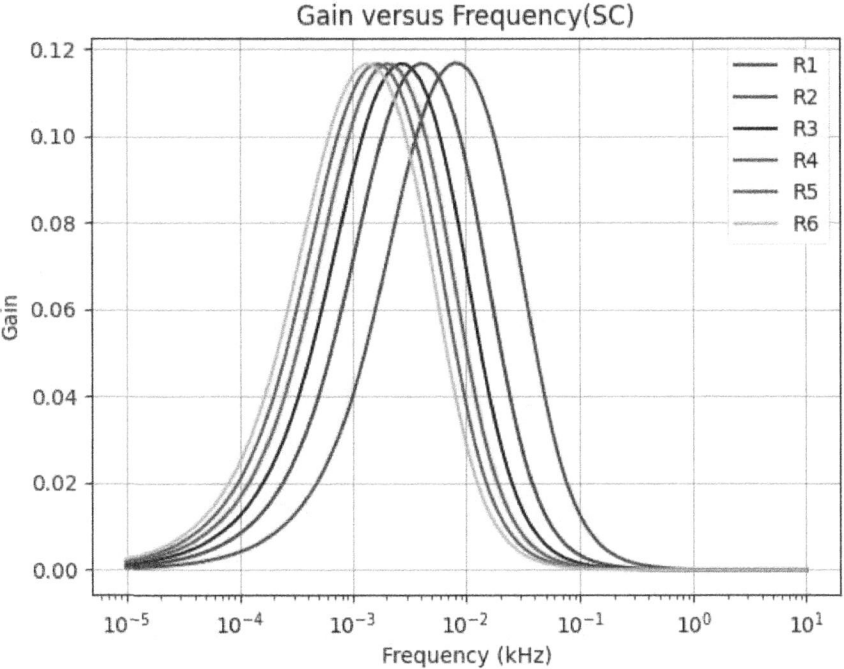

Fig. 3. The resonator's frequency response spectrum. Each peak represents the resonant frequency to which each resonator responds.

Being able to see how our system responds to a change in frequency is crucial. So, to mimic the sudden shift in the frequencies of the signal, we increase our input current frequency partway through the simulation (Fig. 4). The system is responding as expected of our differentiator. The frequency shift can be seen by the decrease in the amplitude of resonators 4, 5, and 6 and the increase in the voltage values for resonators 1, 2, and 3 (Fig. 5). This has let us confirm that when the frequency is within the range of the resonant frequencies the response of the resonator changes accordingly (i.e., the change seen in resonator 3's response). These changes can also be seen clearer when plotted as a bar graph (Fig. 6).

Table 2. Resonators resonant frequencies associated gain from constant sine wave input.

Resonator(s)	Gain	Resonant frequencies
Resonator 1	1.16×10^{-1} dB	8.11 Hz
Resonator 2	1.16×10^{-1} dB	4.04 Hz
Resonator 3	1.16×10^{-1} dB	2.66 Hz
Resonator 4	1.16×10^{-1} dB	2.01 Hz
Resonator 5	1.16×10^{-1} dB	1.75 Hz
Resonator 6	1.16×10^{-1} dB	1.32 Hz

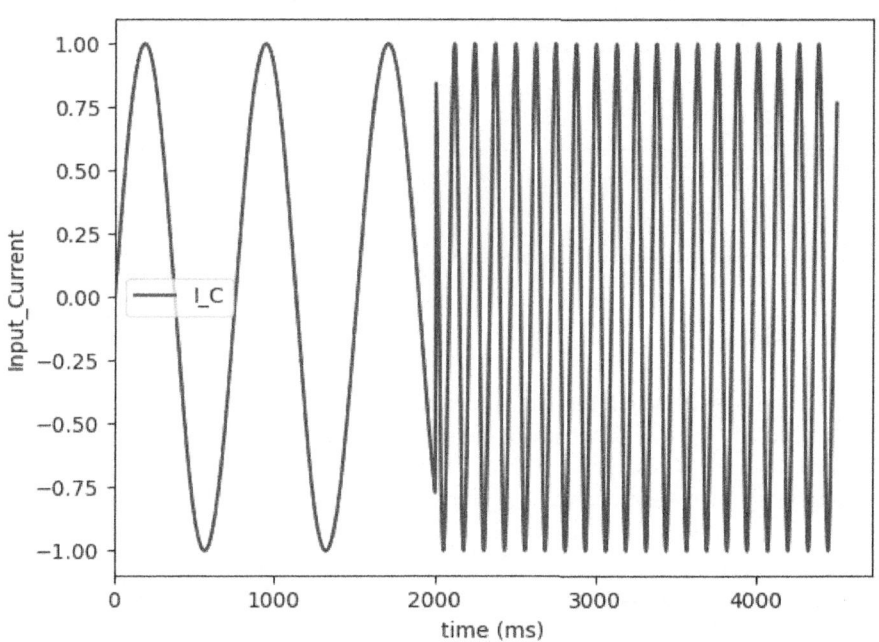

Fig. 4. The sinusoidal input that changes its frequency mid-period.

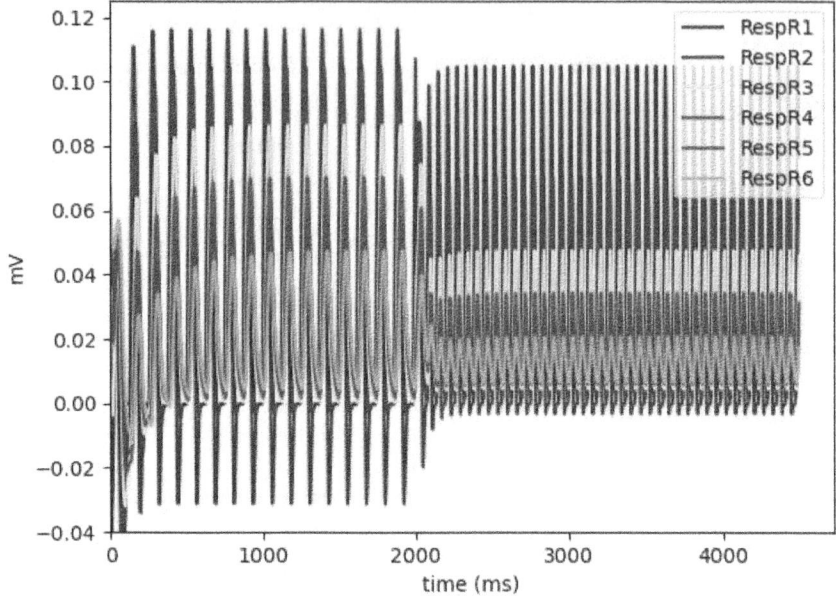

Fig. 5. The resonators' response to a sinusoidal wave that had its frequency changed mid-cycle.

4 Discussion

To abstract the way in which parallel fibers in the brown ghost knife fish's cerebellum cancel "expected" sensory feedback and apply it to a bioinspired robot control system, we created a series of resonators, each of which had a unique resonant frequency. In this preliminary investigation, we designed the resonator as a differentiator because the network functions as a high-pass filter, but every neuron in the network functions as a lowpass filter, resulting in a preferred frequency at which the response has the greatest [4]. As expected, each resonator in the group has a unique response to the input. The activity of the ensemble corresponds to the frequency of the input. In the future, we will extend the model such that each resonator inhibits the input with a unique synaptic delay, replicating some features of the parallel fibers in the cerebellum [1]. We will also test our system in more complex scenarios such as using noisy inputs with multiple-frequency components since the inputs we used for our preliminary work were an unnoisy, single-frequency sinusoid.

We anticipate that canceling redundant sensory information in this way will enable a robot to focus on novel, unexpected sensory stimuli. Such stimuli could be self-generated. In a ghost knife fish, moving the tail or the presence of another fish will alter the electrical feedback it receives in a way that can be predicted [6] and the feedback needs to adapt its prediction as these redundant signals change. Analogously, the movement of our robots can activate sensors along the leg that are intended to measure contact forces with the ground but can also be fooled by vibrations of the leg [7]. This results in temporary "false positive" detections of ground contact. We plan to build on this preliminary model to

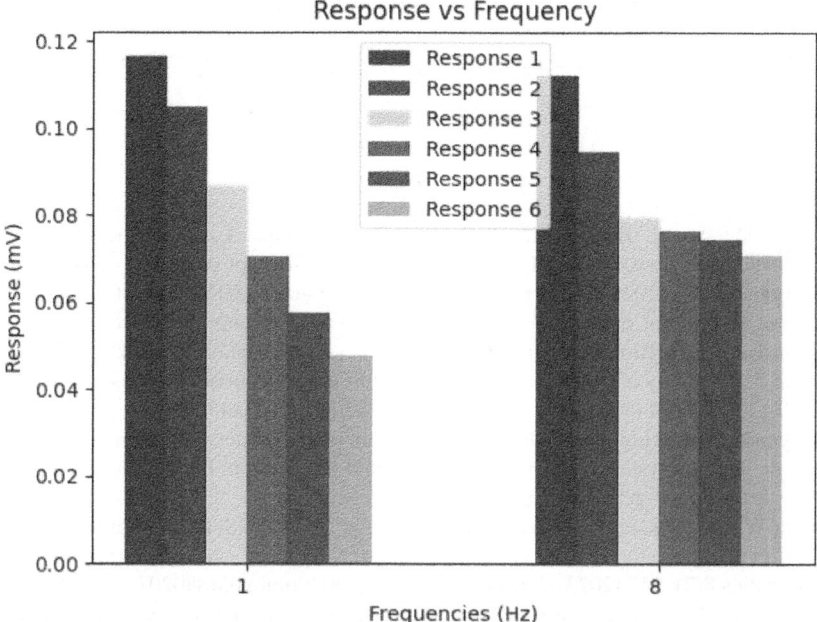

Fig. 6. The resonators' response to a sinusoidal wave that had its frequency changed mid-cycle. Displays the changes between the maximum value of the original frequency and the maximum value after it has been altered.

predict the force feedback in response to the movement of the legs and cancel unwanted force feedback, which may eliminate false positives.

Canceling redundant sensory information may also make the robot more aware of changes in the environment. If it is already predicting forces in response to motion as described in the previous paragraph, it should be able to detect some environmental changes, e.g., walking from pavement onto ice. Canceling the expected force feedback from walking on pavement may make small changes in force feedback more apparent. Such changes in the environment could then trigger autonomous changes in robot behavior, e.g., trotting across firm ground but walking carefully over ice.

We hypothesize that a robot may learn to distinguish these scenarios through unsupervised learning mechanisms, in which it "clusters" similar sensory experiences together and applies the same behavior in response to similar experiences. We believe that canceling redundant sensory feedback as performed by parallel fibers in the cerebellum will facilitate such learning in the future. Also, we expect our system to function as an artificial cerebellum for the robot, integrating the sensory information received from an environment. We want to observe different factors that could help with real-time adaptation. We plan to look at joint angles, strain measurements, touch, and any other physical alterations the robot experiences externally from the environment that generates sensory information that can be measured. This would allow the robot to eventually discern the difference between falling off a cliff or trudging through water.

Acknowledgments. This work was funded by NSF EFRI BRAID 2223793 to GM and NSS.

References

1. Bol, K., Marsat, G., Harvey-Girard, E., Longtin, A., Maler, L.: Frequency-tuned cerebellar channels and burst-induced LTD lead to the cancellation of redundant sensory inputs. J. Neurosci. **31**(30), 11028–11038 (2011). https://doi.org/10.1523/JNEUROSCI.0193-11.2011
2. Metzner, W.: Neural circuitry for communication and jamming avoidance in gymnotiform electric fish. J. Exp. Biol. **202**(10), 1365–1375 (1999). https://doi.org/10.1242/jeb.202.10.1365
3. Bastian, J.: Plasticity of feedback inputs in the apteronotid electrosensory system. J. Exp. Biol. **202**(10), 1327–1337 (1999). https://doi.org/10.1242/jeb.202.10.1327
4. Szczecinski, N.S., Hunt, A.J., Quinn, R.D.: A functional subnetwork approach to designing synthetic nervous systems that control legged robot locomotion. Front. Neurorobotics **11**, 37 (2017). https://doi.org/10.3389/fnbot.2017.00037
5. Nourse, W.R.P., Jackson, C., Szczecinski, N.S., Quinn, R.D.: SNS-Toolbox: an open source tool for designing synthetic nervous systems and interfacing them with cyber– physical systems. Biomimetics **8**(2), 247 (2023). https://doi.org/10.3390/biomimetics8020247
6. Kennedy, A., Wayne, G., Kaifosh, P., Alviña, K., Abbott, L.F., Sawtell, N.B.: A temporal basis for predicting the sensory consequences of motor commands in an electric fish. Nat. Neurosci. **17**(3), 416–422 (2014). https://doi.org/10.1038/nn.3650
7. Szczecinski, N.S., Quinn, R.D. : Leg-local neural mechanisms for searching and learning enhance robotic locomotion. Biological Cybernetics, 1–14 (2017). https://doi.org/10.1007/s00 422-017-0726-x

Navigational Systems

Binocular Vision and Vector-Summation Based Integration of Bilateral Innate and Learned Visual Cues in Insect Navigation

Qin Sun[1,2]($\boxtimes$), Xuelong Sun[1,2], and Haiyang Li[1,2]

[1] School of Mathematics and Information Science, Guangzhou University,
Guangzhou, China
xsun@gzhu.edu.cn
[2] Machine Life and Intelligence Research Centre, Guangzhou University,
Guangzhou, China
2112215058@e.gzhu.edu.cn

Abstract. Insects rely extensively on visual information for navigation, utilizing a combination of innate instincts and learned behaviors. The mushroom body (MB) has been identified as a key player in insect visual learning, with insects possessing bilateral MBs. However, the mechanisms underlying the interaction between the left and right MBs, and how innate and learned visual cues are integrated for accurate navigation, remain elusive. In this study, we employ a novel approach wherein visual models fusing MB and innate are initially provided with binocular (left and right) visual inputs, followed by the application of a bio-plausible vector-summation method to integrate binocular innate and learned (MB) visual guidance. We verify the efficacy of this integration method by reproducing recently published data from biologists, thus providing computational support for empirical findings. This research not only sheds light on the potential mechanism for integrating bilateral innate and learned visual cues in the insect brain but also offers insights that could inspire efficient solutions for information fusion in robotics.

Keywords: Insect Navigation · Visual Navigation · Binocular Vision · Vector Summation · Innate and Learned Behavior · Bilateral Processing

1 Introduction

Insects exhibit remarkable flexibility in utilizing vision for navigation, showcasing a rich array of visual behaviors [9,12]. From the intricate flight patterns of bees [4] to the precision-guided movements of ants [7,15], insects demonstrate a sophisticated understanding of their visual environment. These behaviors encompass

Application Demonstration and Industrialization of Reconfigurable Digital Intelligent Control Technology for Flexible Platforms (Grant No.CXTD2020001); National Natural Science Foundation of China under the Grant No.62206066.

© The Author(s), under exclusive license to Springer Nature Switzerland AG 2025
N. S. Szczecinski et al. (Eds.): Living Machines 2024, LNAI 14930, pp. 121–134, 2025.
https://doi.org/10.1007/978-3-031-72597-5_9

both innate and learned components, reflecting the complex interplay between genetic predispositions and environmental experiences [11,13]. While learned behaviors, such as visual homing and route following, have been extensively studied and modeled using Mushroom Body (MB) models [1,23,27], the underlying mechanisms governing its integration with innate visual guidance remain elusive. Moreover, the mechanisms by which the left and right MBs process binocular visual inputs [14] and integrate their outputs to enhance navigation guidance remain unclear. Despite some existing models attempting to explain these integration processes [11,13], certain observed behaviors still lack comprehensive explanations [8,16,19].

One promising approach to address this challenge is the concept of *vector summation* [18,21,26], which offers a bio-plausible solution for integrating multiple cues in insect navigation. Previous models have successfully utilized vector summation (with its neural implementation resembling that of a ring attractor [20]) to simulate a wide range of navigation behaviors [22,28], suggesting its potential utility in explaining the integration of innate and learned visual guidance. In this study, we apply the vector summation method to integrate bilateral innate and learned visual guidance. Specifically, to capture innate visual behavior, we model the tracking of a vertical bar in retinal images, as there is limited biological data regarding the neural processing of this behavior [13]. For learned visual navigation, we employ the established MB model [1,27], acknowledging its role in learning and memory processes [1,29]. To replicate bilateral visual processing, we employed a weighted-average method to amalgamate the binocular visual inputs before subjecting them to bilateral innate and learned visual processing [13].

To validate our approach, we define a navigation task identical to that used in biological experiments [8]. We adjusted the parameters and simulation settings to closely mirror the experimental conditions experienced by real ants. For instance, simulating a left-MB lesion in real ants involved disconnecting the left MB's output from the left MB in our bilateral model. By systematically and quantitatively comparing the performance of our model-guided agents with that of real animals, we observed that our model successfully replicated the majority of key navigation behaviors. Our results demonstrate the effectiveness of the proposed bilateral cue integration method in replicating insect navigation behaviors. Our findings suggest that this integration mechanism could potentially underlie various cue integration processes in the insect brain and provide bio-inspired solutions for sensor fusion in robotics.

In addition, to further explore how changes in the environment of the navigation task would bring about changes in the experimental results. We changed the defined navigation task and came back with a similar experiment. The results show that the experimental results remain almost unchanged even when the environment is changed. See the result section for a detailed description.

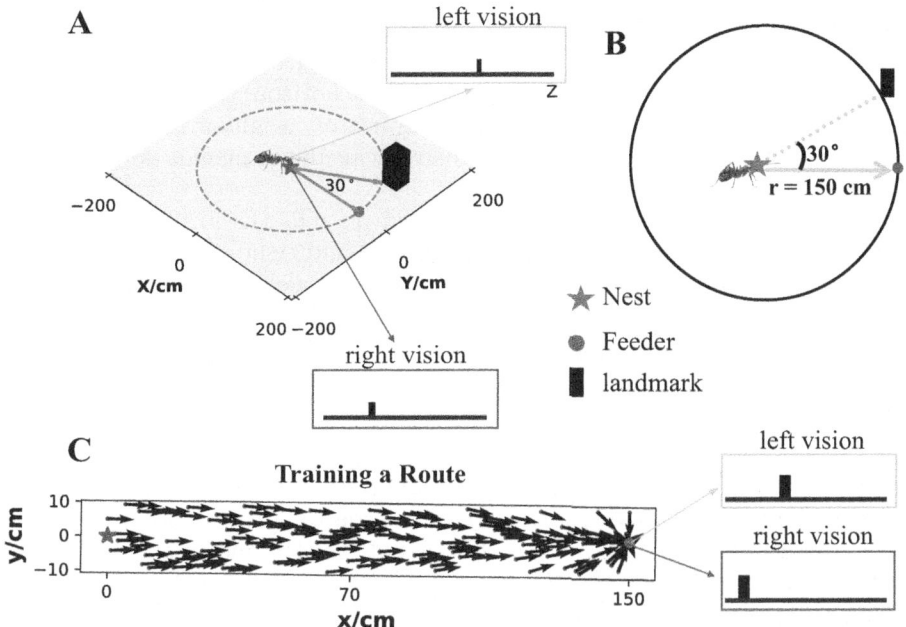

Fig. 1. Simulated 3D environment depicting the sampled image of the world and a training route for agents. A: The simulated 3D environment utilized in experiments. The two images inserted in A represent the views of the left and right compound eyes of the ant agent at the nest position. Refer to Sect. 2.2 for the acquisition of vision images. In this and subsequent diagrams, the green star denotes the position of the nest, while the red dot indicates the position of the feeder. B: A view of the arena from the X-axis direction. C: The route employed to train the agents, consisting of 150 randomly selected points indicated by arrows pointing toward the feeder in the figure. The two figures on the right display the left and right compound eye vision with the agent at the feeder and a positive heading direction. (Color figure online)

2   Methods and Materials

2.1   Navigation Environments

To mirror the experimental conditions outlined in [8], we designed the simulated 3D environment (Fig. 1A) with a circular platform measuring 150 cm in radius. A solitary visual cue, represented by a distinctive black cuboid, is positioned at the edge of the platform, with a virtual food source (feeder) located 30° to the right of this landmark.

2.2   Binocular Visual Input

The binocular vision of the agent at a specific position $[x, y]$ and heading direction θ is reconstructed as follows: for the left view, it is located at $[x - 1.5 \cos(\frac{\pi}{2} - \theta), y +$

$1.5\sin(\frac{\pi}{2} - \theta)]$ with $\theta + \frac{\pi}{4}$, while for the right view, it is at $[x + 1.5\cos(\frac{\pi}{2} - \theta), y -$ $1.5\sin(\frac{\pi}{2} - \theta)]$ with $\theta - \frac{\pi}{4}$, adhering to the 3 cm distance between the eyes [5]. The eyes are situated 1 cm from the ground, with a horizontal field of view of 360° and a vertical field of view of 104° (centered on the horizon) [1,27]. Subsequently, the images are resized to 72 × 20 pixels using nearest neighbor interpolation, as illustrated in Fig. 1A and C. Finally, each greyscale image pixel is normalized by dividing by 255 and subtracting it by 1.

Recent research has pointed out that Kenyon cells (KCs) of both left and right MB receive visual projections from the left and right compound eyes [14]. Therefore before being fed into subsequent visual models, we used linear fusion of left and right visual inputs for simplicity, as depicted in Fig. 2C.

$$\begin{cases} PN_L &= \alpha V_L + \beta V_R \\ PN_R &= \beta V_L + \alpha V_R \\ \alpha + \beta &= 1 \end{cases} \tag{1}$$

where PN_L and PN_R denote the fused left and right visual inputs, while α and β represent the weights assigned to ipsilateral and contralateral vision, respectively. And in this study $\alpha = \beta = 0.5$. V_L and V_R denote the left and right visual inputs before fusion.

2.3   Learned Visual Navigation Model

The insect's mushroom body (MB) is widely regarded as the primary learning center in the insect brain [2,3]. To ensure biological plausibility, we employ an MB model to simulate learned visual navigation behaviors. Following a similar approach to [1], we flatten the previously described 2D images (PN_L and PN_R in Eq. 1 whose size is 72 × 20) into 1D vectors denoted as F (size 1440 × 1) to provide visual inputs to the visual projection neurons (vPNs) of the MB network. Consequently, the first layer comprises 1440 vPNs and is represented as follows:

$$C_{vPN}^i = F^i, \quad i = 0, 1, \dots, N_{vPN} \tag{2}$$

where N_{vPN} is the number of the vPN neurons and F^i represents the ith of pixel in the image 1D vector.

The second layer consists of 10,000 Kenyon cells (KCs). The vPNs project to KCs through randomly generated binary connections which causes each KC to receive input from 10 randomly selected vPNs:

$$I_{KC}^i = \sum_{i=0}^{N_{vPN}} W_{vPN-KC}^{ji} C_{vPN}^i \tag{3}$$

where I_{KC}^i represents the total input current received by KC from the vPNs, the KCs are then modeled using certain threshold $\mathcal{E}$ (Note that the threshold is chosen to activate a certain number of KCs and in this study $\mathcal{E} = 0.04$) :

$$C_{KC}^i = \begin{cases} 0, & \text{if } I_{KC}^i \le \mathcal{E} \\ 1, & \text{if } I_{KC}^i > \mathcal{E} \end{cases} \tag{4}$$

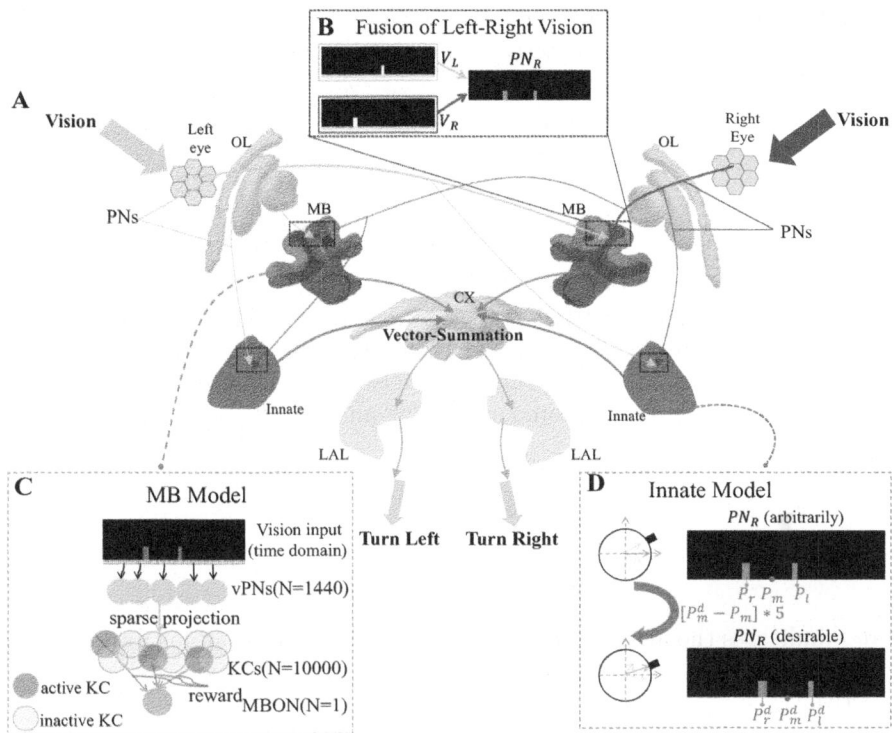

Fig. 2. Schematic diagram of the proposed integrated bilateral innate and learned visual navigation model with binocular visual inputs. A: Information flow in the insect eyes and brain regions, including the optic lobe (OL), mushroom bodies (MBs), abstracted innate processing region, lateral accessory lobe (LAL), and central complex (CX). B: Example of left-right vision integration, utilized as input for later visual models. C: MB-based learned visual navigation model, generating a valence for the current view (visual novelty). N denotes the number of neurons in each layer used in this paper's model. D: Innate visual navigation model. In the polar plot in the left column, the black object denotes the landmark, arrows in the middle indicate the agent's heading direction and arrows on the sides denote the direction of the left and right compound eyes. Binocular visual inputs received by the agents are depicted in the right column, with the blue dot representing the midpoint between the two bars. Pictures of the brain regions were downloaded from insectbraindb.org [17]. (Color figure online)

The final layer consists of one MBON that receives input from all active KCs via a plastic connections matrix $W_{KC-MBON}$ which uses an anti-Hebbian learning rule:

$$C_{MBON} = \sum_{i=0}^{N_{KC}} W_{KC-MBON}^{i} C_{KC}^{i}$$ (5)

$$W_{KC-MBON}^{i,t} = W_{KC-MBON}^{i,t-1} - \delta, \quad \text{if } C_{KC}^{i,t-1} = 1$$

where δ denotes the learning rate and learning only occurs when the reward signal is on. The value of MBON C_{MBON} denotes the novelty of the current visual inputs. Typically, smaller values indicate higher familiarity and vice versa.

The left and right MB share the same network architecture and their final desired heading outputs are denoted as $\gamma_L^{learned}$ and $\gamma_R^{learned}$, which are computed by:

$$\gamma_L^{learned} = \min_{\beta}[C_{MBON}^{L}(\beta)]$$

$$\gamma_R^{learned} = \min_{\beta}[C_{MBON}^{R}(\beta)]$$ (6)

$$\beta \in [-180°, -135°, \dots, 135°, 180°]$$

where β indicates the angle of scanning from $-180°$ to $180°$ at $45°$ intervals [31]. $C_{MBON}^{L}(\beta)$ and $C_{MBON}^{R}(\beta)$ denote outputs of the left and right MB at angle β, respectively.

2.4 Innate Visual Navigation Model

In contrast to learned visual behavior, which is believed to occur within the mushroom body (MB) [8,19], there exists limited biological data concerning the neural processing of innate visual behavior [24,30]. In the navigation environment depicted in Fig. 1A and B, the compound eyes perceive two vertical bars alongside a predominantly featureless background. Consequently, the change between the vertical bars in the retinal image serves as a tracking model in this study, with the middle pixel of the two vertical bars selected. This tracking model is employed to orient the agent towards the landmark, as illustrated in Fig. 1D.

As depicted in the top of Fig. 2D, the horizontal positions of the pixels representing the centers of the two vertical bars are denoted as P_r and P_l, respectively. The pixel in the middle of these bars P_m, is computed as:

$$P_m = P_r + (P_l - P_r)/2$$ (7)

Similarly, when the agent's heading direction faces the landmark, it receives the visual input as shown at the bottom of Fig. 2D. The horizontal positions of the pixels representing the centers of the two vertical bars are P_r^d and P_l^d. The position of the pixel in the middle, P_m^d, is modelled as:

$$P_m^d = P_r^d + (P_l^d - P_r^d)/2$$ (8)

The angle at which the agent's innate visual behavior suggests to head is a certain proportion of the difference between these two equations, with that proportion set to 5 due to the 72×20 pixel image representing a 360-degree horizontal field of view. The left and right innate models share the same calculation, and their final desired heading outputs are denoted as γ_L^{innate} and γ_R^{innate}, calculated by:

$$\gamma_L^{innate} = 5[P_m^d(L) - P_m(L)] \tag{9}$$

$$\gamma_R^{innate} = 5[P_m^d(R) - P_m(R)] \tag{10}$$

2.5   Integration of Learned and Innate Visual Navigation Model

We integrate bilateral innate and learned visual navigation using a weighted-average method, employing vector summation where the length of the vector represents its weight. Therefore, we got four vectors from the bilateral innate and learned visual guidance:

$$\begin{cases} \mathbf{V}_L^{innate}(t) &= [\cos(\gamma_L^{innate}(t)), \sin(\gamma_L^{innate}(t))], \\ \mathbf{V}_R^{innate}(t) &= [\cos(\gamma_R^{innate}(t)), \sin(\gamma_R^{innate}(t))], \\ \mathbf{V}_L^{learned}(t) &= [\cos(\gamma_L^{learned}(t)), \sin(\gamma_L^{learned}(t))], \\ \mathbf{V}_R^{learned}(t) &= [\cos(\gamma_R^{learned}(t)), \sin(\gamma_R^{learned}(t))] \end{cases} \tag{11}$$

Then these four vectors determine the moving direction (i.e., the direction of the velocity) of the agent as formulated by:

$$\mathbf{V}(t) = K_1[\mathbf{V}_L^{innate}(t) + \mathbf{V}_R^{innate}(t)] + K_2[\mathbf{V}_L^{learned}(t) + \mathbf{V}_R^{learned}(t)] \tag{12}$$

The coefficients K_1 and K_2 were used to adjust the weights of the desired heading direction from the left-right innate and learned guidance, respectively. In each experiment, these two coefficients were randomly selected from the intervals $[1, 1.1]$ and $[2, 2.2]$, respectively, which ensured a uniform distribution. Then the position $\mathbf{X}(t)$ of the agent is updated by:

$$\mathbf{X}(t+1) = \mathbf{X}(t) + C_v\mathbf{V}(t) \tag{13}$$

where $\mathbf{X}(t)$ represents the position of the agent in the Cartesian coordinates at time t; C_v denotes the constant velocity of the agent measured in centimetres per time step.

2.6   Data Analysis

In our study, we employ navigation trajectories and the 95% confidence intervals of the heading directions as evaluation indices to elucidate the agent's navigation ability. This approach aligns with the methodology employed in the corresponding biological experiments.

To calculate the confidence intervals, we utilize the bootstrap distribution of the median final heading direction of the agent, generating 10,000 samples. Subsequently, we select the 2.5th and 97.5th percentile values from this distribution as the confidence intervals [10].

Throughout this study, we conduct a total of 30 experiments for each case, ensuring robustness and reliability in our analysis.

3   Results

A series of simulations have been conducted to reproduce the results from the biological experiments [8]. The following experiments were simulated in our study: 1) Granting the agent the ability to navigate to the landmark and training the agent to navigate to the feeder relative to the landmark; 2) Exploring the effect of left or right MB lesion on the agent's visual navigation ability; 3) Exploring the effect of left or right compound eye occlusion on the agent's navigation ability. For each set of simulations, we executed $n = 30$ trials and the positions and headings of the agent during navigation were recorded and analysed.

3.1   Innate and learned visual navigation performance

Agents guided by our model are initialized from the nest, and the simulation experiments reveal that the agents successfully navigate to the landmark. The 95% confidence intervals of the heading directions ($[32.24°, 32.58°]$) encompass the landmark position, indicating successful reproduction of the biological experiments where insects (wood ants) exhibit innate attraction to large visual cues [8] (see the left panel of Fig. 3).

Subsequently, agents undergo an artificial training phase, familiarizing themselves with the route from the nest to the feeder, as depicted in Fig. 1C. Upon completion of the training phase, agents commence navigation from the nest again. Notably, they no longer navigate towards the landmark but instead successfully navigate to the feeder. However, the 95% confidence interval ($[8.17°, 8.37°]$) does not encompass the feeder position for we adjusted the weights of K_1 and K_2 in Eq. (12) to render more realistic navigation performance under the case of lesion unilateral MBs (i.e., Sect. 3.2). While this, our simulations replicate the biological experiments, demonstrating that ants learn to navigate to a food source (feeder) relative to a landmark (see the right panel of Fig. 3).

3.2   Effects of Mushroom Body Lesions on Agent Navigation

Biological experiments have shown that damaging either the left or right mushroom body (MB) prompts insects, previously trained to navigate to a feeder, to revert to navigating toward a landmark. To replicate this scenario, during the unilateral MB lesion simulations (note that simultaneous damage to both MBs would mimic the pre-training phase), we silence the injured MB's output by setting $C_{MBON} = 0$ (actually, the case of complete MB silencing is simulated).

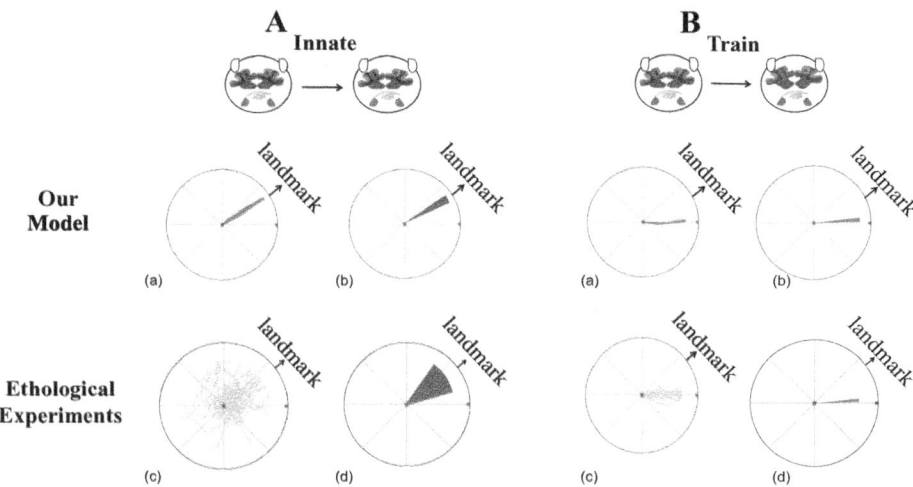

Fig. 3. Comparison of the results of biological experiments with our model. Each case presents agent trajectories and the 95% confidence interval for agent heading direction from our model (upper part) and the biological experiments (lower part). The left panel represents innate visual behavior, while the right panel represents learned visual behavior. Confidence intervals are depicted as sectors in the figures. The upper sketch illustrates the head of the simulated insect, as in Fig. 2A, with corresponding color coding. Grey coloring indicates no involvement of MBs, while red coloring indicates MB involvement. Biological experiment data sourced from published data in [8]. (Color figure online)

Following the simulation, agents, starting from the nest, exhibit a bias towards the landmark position, akin to observations in biological experiments [8].

Notably, the 95% confidence interval ($[12.30°, 13.44°]$) does not encompass the feeder, as depicted in the left panel of Fig. 4. In contrast to biological experiments, our confidence intervals are biased towards the landmark, rather than encompassing it. The extent of this bias towards the landmark position can be adjusted by tuning the weights of K_1 and K_2 in Eq. (12). Although we maintain constant values of them for individual simulations, adaptive tuning of these weights could render more realistic navigation performance akin to real ants. Despite this, our model successfully replicates key behaviors observed when MBs are unilaterally injured, indicating that damage to a unilateral MB suffices to impact an insect's learned visual navigation (see the left panel of Fig. 4).

3.3 Effects of Eye Occlusion on Agent navigation

To assess the experimental effects of our model under compound eye occlusion, similar to biological experiments [8], we passed only monocular vision into the learned and innate visual navigation model. That's to say, if the left compound eye was occluded, only the vision corresponding to the right compound eye was utilized, and vice versa.

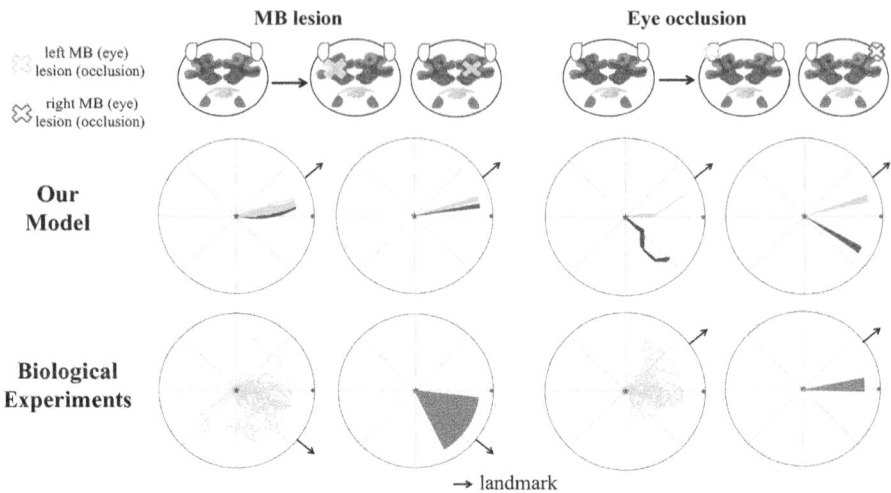

Fig. 4. As depicted in Fig. 3. The left panel illustrates visual behavior following left or right MB lesion. Notably, the biological experiments were performed with the landmark located on the contralateral side of the damaged MB to study the navigation of ants during unilateral MB damage. Therefore, the navigation trajectories and confidence intervals of the ants when the landmark was located on the contralateral side of the damaged MB are depicted in the figure. The right panel displays visual behavior following left or right eye occlusion.

In our simulations, we observed that if the left compound eye was occluded, the agent navigated toward the landmark but did not reach it completely. However, the 95% confidence interval ($[19.56°, 19.63°]$) did not contain the feeder position. Conversely, if the right compound eye was occluded, the agent navigated to the right of the feeder, with the 95% confidence interval ($[-37.95°, -38.17°]$) also not encompassing the feeder position.

In summary, our model predicts that if the left compound eye is occluded, the agent navigates to the left of the feeder, while if the right compound eye is occluded, the agent navigates to the right of the feeder, as illustrated in the right panel of Fig. 4.

These findings diverge from biological experiments. However, recent biological research [25] has revealed that post-training eye occlusion does impact the learned visual navigation behavior of real ants. Specifically, ants must recognize vision learned in both compound eyes, and monocular ants show an immediate decrease in their ability to navigate familiar routes but can compensate for the lack of vision after a re-learning process.

Given these insights, we speculate that in biological experiments, ants with covered eyes compensated for their visual impairments before exhibiting navigation behavior, thus navigating towards the feeder, as illustrated in the right panel of Fig. 4.

3.4   Effects of Navigational Environment on Agent navigation

To investigate the effect of the change in the position of the landmark and feeder on the experimental results, We change the navigation environment in Sect. 2.1 to place the landmark 30° below the feeder, but nothing else changed. See more information in Fig. 5.

Similar to the setup of the previous experiments, in this section, we also do four sets of experiments on the simulated agents: simulating the navigation of the innate ants - innate, simulating the navigation of the innate ants after being trained - train, simulating the navigation of the trained ants after MB lesion - MB lesion, and simulating the navigation of the trained ants after eye occlusion - eye occlusion.

The experiments find that: placing the landmark 30° below the feeder, the agents guided by our model can navigate to the landmark (95% confidence interval is $[-29.88°, -30.37°]$); after training, the agents can navigate to the feeder (95% confidence interval is $[-4.54°, -4.31°]$). The left and right MB of the trained agents are damaged; and find that the corresponding 95% confidence interval ($[-9.45°, -9.41°]$) of the agents is in favor of the landmark, even though it does not encompass the landmark. The left and right eyes of the trained agent are occluded. The experiments find that the 95% confidence interval ($[32.80°, 33.32°]$) corresponding to agents with the left eye occlusion is biased to the left side of the feeder, while the 95% confidence interval ($[-18.69°, -17.54°]$) corresponding to agents with the right eye occlusion is biased to the right side of the feeder. These are consistent with the landmark placing the feeder 30° above it. These are depicted in Fig. 5.

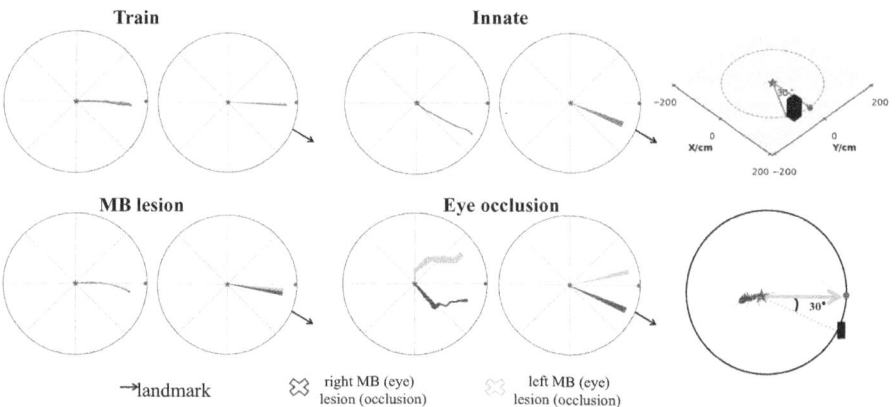

Fig. 5. Four experimental scenarios with landmark located 30° below the feeder. All indicators are the same as in the previous paper except for the change in landmark position. For example, the green star indicates nest, and the red dot indicates feeder. The far right column is the navigation environment.

Thus, regardless of whether the landmark is placed above or below the feeder, the navigation of agents guided by our model is similar. Untrained agents can navigate to the landmark, and trained agents navigate to the feeder. Whereas in MB lesion, agents are biased toward the landmark; in left eye occlusion, agents navigate to the left of the feeder; and in right eye occlusion, the agents navigate to the right side of the feeder.

4   Conclusion and Discussion

This study addresses the complex integration of bilateral innate and learned visual cues in insect navigation. Leveraging a combination of binocular vision and vector summation, we developed a computational model to simulate this integration process. By replicating key navigation behaviors observed in real ants, our model demonstrates its efficacy in accurately representing insect navigation mechanisms. The outcomes contribute to the understanding of how insects navigate their environment by integrating both innate and learned visual cues, offering a potential method for information fusion in robots.

The results from our eye occlusion experiments imply a difference in navigation performance compared to that reported by [8]. Specifically, while monocular eye occlusion did not affect the visual navigation of real ants, we observed an ipsilateral bias in navigation orientation in our model (see right panel of Fig. 4). However, more recent studies suggest that eye occlusion does impact ants' learned visual navigation [25]. Therefore, further investigation is needed to determine the extent to which eye occlusion affects visual inputs, low-level visual pre-processing, high-level visual computation, and even the motor commands generated by the central complex [6].

Another issue lies in the simplistic approach we employed for fusing binocular vision, which entailed a linear fusion method. However, the processing of binocular vision in the compound eyes of insects is highly intricate in biological reality. Thus, this aspect warrants further consideration to align more closely with biological principles.

References

1. Ardin, P., Peng, F., Mangan, M., Lagogiannis, K., Webb, B.: Using an insect mushroom body circuit to encode route memory in complex natural environments. PLoS Comput. Biol. **12**(2), e1004683 (2016)
2. Aso, Y., et al.: The neuronal architecture of the mushroom body provides a logic for associative learning. elife **3**, e04577 (2014)
3. Aso, Y., et al.: Mushroom body output neurons encode valence and guide memory-based action selection in drosophila. elife **3**, e04580 (2014)
4. Bairlein, F., et al.: Cross-hemisphere migration of a 25 g songbird. Biol. Let. **8**(4), 505–507 (2012)
5. Brenner, E., Smeets, J.B.: Two eyes in action. Exp. Brain Res. **170**, 302–311 (2006)

6. Buehlmann, C., Dell-Cronin, S., et al.: Impact of central complex lesions on innate and learnt visual navigation in ants. J. Comp. Physiol. A **209**(4), 737–746 (2023). https://doi.org/10.1007/s00359-023-01613-1
7. Buehlmann, C., Mangan, M., Graham, P.: Multimodal interactions in insect navigation. Anim. Cogn. **23**(6), 1129–1141 (2020)
8. Buehlmann, C., Wozniak, B., Goulard, R., Webb, B., Graham, P., Niven, J.E.: Mushroom bodies are required for learned visual navigation, but not for innate visual behavior, in ants. Curr. Biol. **30**(17), 3438–3443 (2020)
9. Collett, M., Chittka, L., Collett, T.S.: Spatial memory in insect navigation. Curr. Biol. **23**(17), R789–R800 (2013)
10. Efron, B., Tibshirani, R.J.: An Introduction to the Bootstrap. Chapman and Hall/CRC (1994)
11. Eschbach, C., et al.: Circuits for integrating learned and innate valences in the insect brain. elife **10**, e62567 (2021)
12. Freas, C.A., Spetch, M.L.: Varieties of visual navigation in insects. Anim. Cogn. **26**(1), 319–342 (2023)
13. Goulard, R., Buehlmann, C., Niven, J.E., Graham, P., Webb, B.: A unified mechanism for innate and learned visual landmark guidance in the insect central complex. PLoS Comput. Biol. **17**(9), e1009383 (2021)
14. Habenstein, J., Amini, E., Grübel, K., El Jundi, B., Rössler, W.: The brain of cataglyphis ants: neuronal organization and visual projections. J. Comp. Neurol. **528**(18), 3479–3506 (2020)
15. Heinze, S.: Unraveling the neural basis of insect navigation. Curr. Opin. Insect Sci. **24**, 58–67 (2017)
16. Heinze, S.: Visual navigation: ants lose track without mushroom bodies. Curr. Biol. **30**(17), R984–R986 (2020)
17. Heinze, S., et al.: A unified platform to manage, share, and archive morphological and functional data in insect neuroscience. eLife **10**, e65376 (2021)
18. Hoinville, T., Wehner, R.: Optimal multiguidance integration in insect navigation. Proc. Natl. Acad. Sci. **115**(11), 2824–2829 (2018)
19. Kamhi, J.F., Barron, A.B., Narendra, A.: Vertical lobes of the mushroom bodies are essential for view-based navigation in Australian myrmecia ants. Curr. Biol. **30**(17), 3432–3437 (2020)
20. Kim, S.S., Rouault, H., Druckmann, S., Jayaraman, V.: Ring attractor dynamics in the drosophila central brain. Science **356**(6340), 849–853 (2017)
21. Le Moël, F., Stone, T., Lihoreau, M., Wystrach, A., Webb, B.: The central complex as a potential substrate for vector based navigation. Front. Psychol. **10**, 380097 (2019)
22. Mitchell, R., Shaverdian, S., Dacke, M., Webb, B.: A model of cue integration as vector summation in the insect brain. Proc. R. Soc. B **290**(2001), 20230767 (2023)
23. Müller, J., Nawrot, M., Menzel, R., Landgraf, T.: A neural network model for familiarity and context learning during honeybee foraging flights. Biol. Cybern. **112**, 113–126 (2018)
24. Rayshubskiy, A.: Neural Control of Steering in Walking Drosophila. Ph.D. thesis, Harvard University (2020)
25. Schwarz, S., Clement, L., Haalck, L., Risse, B., Wystrach, A.: Compensation to visual impairments and behavioral plasticity in navigating ants. bioRxiv (2023)
26. Sun, X., Mangan, M., Yue, S.: An analysis of a ring attractor model for cue integration. In: Biomimetic and Biohybrid Systems: 7th International Conference, Living Machines 2018, Paris, France, July 17–20, 2018, Proceedings 7, pp. 459–470. Springer (2018)

27. Sun, X., Yue, S., Mangan, M.: A decentralised neural model explaining optimal integration of navigational strategies in insects. Elife **9**, e54026 (2020)
28. Sun, X., Yue, S., Mangan, M.: How the insect central complex could coordinate multimodal navigation. Elife **10**, e73077 (2021)
29. Takemura, S., et al.: A connectome of a learning and memory center in the adult drosophila brain. Elife **6**, e26975 (2017)
30. Thiagarajan, D., Sachse, S.: Multimodal information processing and associative learning in the insect brain. Insects **13**(4), 332 (2022)
31. Wystrach, A., Philippides, A., Aurejac, A., Cheng, K., Graham, P.: Visual scanning behaviours and their role in the navigation of the Australian desert ant Melophorus bagoti. J. Comp. Physiol. A **200**, 615–626 (2014)

Bioinspired Magnetic Navigation for Exploring Celestial Bodies

Renzhi Li[1], Thao Quynh Ngo[2], Jeffrey P. Gill[3]📖, Catherine Kehl[2]📖,
and Brian K. Taylor[2,3(✉)]📖

[1] University of Southern California, Los Angeles, CA 90007, USA
[2] The University of North Carolina at Chapel Hill, Chapel Hill, NC 27599, USA
`quynhngo@live.unc.edu, cekehl@email.unc.edu`
[3] Case Western Reserve University, Cleveland, OH 44106, USA
`{jpg18,bkt2}@case.edu`

Abstract. Modern navigation strategies on Earth often rely on predeployed artificial global navigation satellite systems (GNSS) for positioning, navigation, and timing information (PNT). This is impractical when navigating through space or on other celestial bodies. Current methods for space navigation require presurveyed information about naturally occurring signals and patterns from other celestial bodies and communication with Earth-based manned systems. Occlusions from other celestial bodies combined with the physical inaccessibility of deployed space vehicles limit the autonomy and potential scope of navigating space vehicles. While other sensory cues may be useful to enhance space vehicle navigation and autonomy, this information may not be practical to obtain ahead of time. In contrast, animals on Earth are able to autonomously migrate across long distances, often encountering phenomena they have never seen by using the Earth's magnetic field as a navigation cue. In this paper, using the planet Uranus as a case study, we develop a biologically inspired method for navigating around the surface of another planet by using its magnetic field for relative navigation. Navigation along and about the magnetic pole is explored. The findings suggest that a planet's magnetic field appears to be a feasible method for enabling autonomous navigation on other planets.

Keywords: Magnetoreception · GPS free navigation · Mapless navigation · Space navigation

1 Introduction: The "Attraction" of Magnetic Navigation

1.1 Navigation Around Celestial Bodies

Modern navigation strategies on Earth rely on predeployed artificial global navigation satellite systems (GNSS), such as the United States' Global Positioning System (GPS) [1]. Receivers on Earth calculate their positions based on positioning, navigation, and timing information (PNT) sent by GNSS. This approach is

N. S. Szczecinski et al. (Eds.): Living Machines 2024, LNAI 14930, pp. 135–147, 2025.
https://doi.org/10.1007/978-3-031-72597-5_10

not viable for space vehicles such as orbiters or landers traveling through space on other celestial bodies, as there is no predeployed network of satellites. Current approaches for navigation in space rely on detecting signals from objects not collocated with a space vehicle(e.g., reference points in the solar system or star patterns). They also require knowledge about the exact orientation of sensors relative to other objects [2]. For example, ground-based radiometric approaches [2] measure a space vehicle's motion from Earth. Additionally, a space vehicle may need to maintain an orientation that enables communication with Earth to receive commands, including position and orientation changes. Undesired orientations or occlusions from other celestial bodies can interfere with Earth-space vehicle communication. Together, these factors limit space vehicle autonomy, as operating space vehicles are often inaccessible to direct human intervention, and may pass through regions where communication with Earth-based stations is unavailable. Thus, it is vital to establish more autonomous space vehicle navigation methods that do not require communication with Earth, or information from distant celestial bodies.

1.2   Magnetic Fields for Navigation

Biological Magnetoreception. Biology has demonstrated itself to be a source of inspiration for a host of man-made challenges with natural analogues (e.g., autonomy, locomotion, sensory processing, materials [3–5]). A range of species that includes vertebrates such as sea turtles and birds [6], and invertebrates such as insects [7,8], are able to successfully navigate towards attractive targets (e.g., food, mates) by using the Earth's magnetic field (i.e., magnetoreception) to aid in determining position or orientation [6,9–14]. While magnetoreception's sensory mechanisms, transduction to the nervous system, and connection to animal behavior remain enigmatic and an area of active investigation, current evidence suggests that some animals use combinations of the magnetic field's properties (e.g., intensity and angle relative to the surface of the planet, called inclination) to determine location relative to a goal [15–18], while others use inclination alone as a means of transequatorial navigation ([11,12], Fig. 1). In this paper, we refer to a combination of magnetic intensity and inclination as a magnetic signature.

Especially for marine species, the magnetic field may help to navigate an environment that is largely devoid of regular features and landmarks. Note that intrinsic magnetic mapping may not be necessary for these migratory animals. Animals could sense the magnetic field in relation to other reference points during navigation, allowing them to complete their maiden migratory voyage solely based on their magnetoreception. Some animals even use the magnetic field to initiate physiological changes that prepare them for migration [6].

Engineered and Biologically Inspired Magnetoreception. Engineers have been interested in using the magnetic field to reduce dependence on satellite-based navigation because the magnetic field is naturally occurring, available

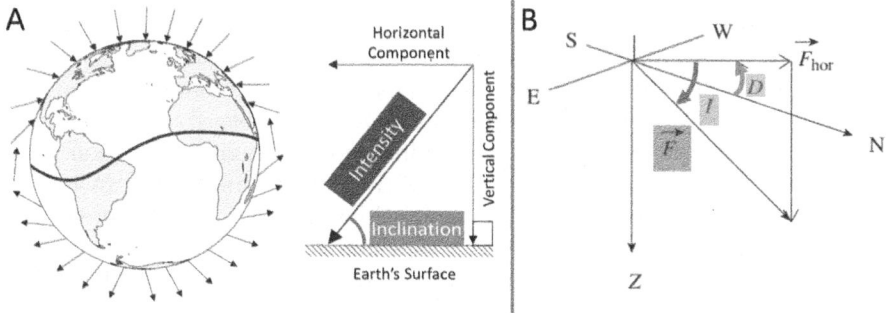

Fig. 1. Illustration of the Earth's magnetic field (A) and its various components (B). In panel A, vectors on the globe show how the inclination angle varies with latitude on Earth. Panel B) The field can be represented by its intensity, inclination, and declination, or resolved into different orthogonal coordinate systems (e.g., North-East-Down). Panel A is adapted from [6], while Panel B is adapted from [21].

above or underwater, and inexpensive to access. Strides have been made in this domain via engineered and bioinspired approaches. One method proposed requires online estimation of various magnetic field sources that can then be subtracted from a measurement of the total magnetic field [19]. Another approach requires measuring of the magnetic field and computing its gradients [20]. Bioinspired approaches have used magnetic signatures to generate and help explain the migratory behaviors observed in animals such as sea turtles [22], and the transequatorial navigation behavior observed in some birds [23].

1.3 Connecting Magnetoreception to Space Navigation

For space applications in which there are strong magnetic fields, magnetic navigation may be a viable step toward enabling autonomous space vehicle navigation. In space, navigation approaches that do not require detailed presurveyed maps are preferred as this information may be difficult to collect and could become outdated. Consider a mission to a planet with a strong magnetic field such as Jupiter or Uranus. Even if a vehicle was sent ahead of time to collect data on the planet's magnetic field for mission planning purposes, by the time the actual mission to that planet commences, the magnetic field may have changed. By the time the mission-specific space vehicle arrives, its magnetic field data and navigation algorithm may not allow it to successfully navigate around the planet. Thus, it may be advantageous to use a navigation approach that only requires a gross understanding of a planet's magnetic field as this is easier to obtain and adjust to. This is a property that is inherent to all migratory animals that use the Earth's magnetic field to navigate. Even if an animal inherits some spatial representation of the magnetic field, this representation may not match the current magnetic field at the time of the first migratory journey. Animals that are unable to cope with this difference face decreased odds of survival.

1.4 Goals for This Paper

In this study, using animal navigation based on magnetic signatures as an inspiration, we attempt to demonstrate the ability of magnetic-based navigation to successfully guide a space vehicle around another planet. To accomplish this goal, we adapt our previous for understanding animal magnetoreception [22, 23] to navigating from one point to another on the planet Uranus. NASA is in the process of planning missions to ice giants such as Uranus [24]. One of the challenges and benefits of using Uranus as a case study is that while Uranus does have a magnetic field, it differs from the field found on Earth. Specifically, Uranus' magnetic field is not oriented with the spin axis of the planet and appears to be offset from the center of the planet [25]. Biological navigation approaches working on Uranus would demonstrate the generality of bioinspired navigation approaches on other celestial bodies.

Our paper is organized as follows. Section 2 describes our magnetic field model, the components of the model that our strategy uses, and the navigation algorithm. Section 3 shows the outcomes of our navigation algorithm from several different starting locations. Section 4 concludes with a discussion of our present study and potential future directions.

2 Methods

2.1 Magnetic Field Model

The model of Uranus' magnetic field was built using Magpylib, a Python library for modeling magnetic fields [26]. It consists of a sphere, with a dipole (modeled as a long cylinder with a radius of 5% of the diameter of the planet) displaced 31% of the length of the radius from the center (Fig. 2). For ease of interpretation, figures throughout this paper have the magnetic axis in a vertical orientation. However, it should be kept in mind that the magnetic axis is neither parallel to the axis of spin nor perpendicular to the direction of the sun.

2.2 Construction of a Bi-coordinate Map from the Magnetic Field

The magnetic field is a vector field that can be described using a multitude of components and/or angles (Fig. 1). In this paper, we use magnetic inclination angle and intensity. Magnetic inclination angle is typically defined as the angle between the magnetic field vector at a point, and the plane that is tangent to the planet at that point (i.e., the local horizontal). For ease of computation and implementation, we use the complementary angle by computing the angle between the magnetic field vector, and the vector that is normal to the tangent plane (i.e., a vector that points to the center of the planet, or *down*). Magnetic intensity (also known as magnetic strength) is the magnitude (i.e., Euclidean norm) of the magnetic field vector at a given point.

Plotting lines of constant inclination and intensity on the surface of the planet reveals a grid-like structure, though the grid is spatially nonlinear and nonorthogonal (i.e., not perpendicular—Fig. 3). As more perpendicular contours create a

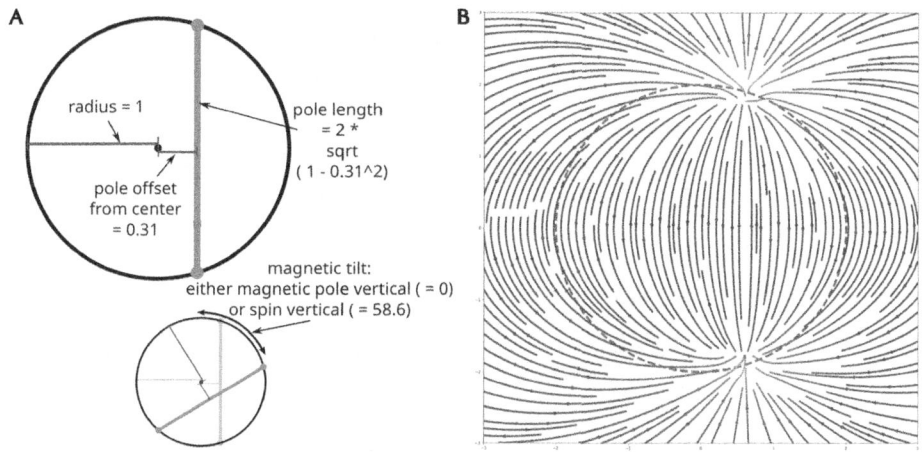

Fig. 2. The Magnetic Model A) The arrangement of the magnetic model, with the magnetic pole on the vertical, deviated by 31% of the radius from the center of the planet. B) The resultant magnetic field. Note that the area within the red circle that represents the planet shows the field on the surface of the planet, whereas outside of the circle shows the field on a plane that cuts through the center of the planet (Color figure online).

more navigable grid, it is our prediction that the areas of higher orthogonality will be more navigable than the areas in which the two coordinate system components run more parallel to each other.

2.3 Navigation Algorithm

Our navigation algorithm uses a modified version of the strategies presented in our previous studies [22, 27–29]. These prior studies aimed to test hypotheses regarding how animals might use magnetic signatures to move from point to point while simultaneously extracting principles that might serve future engineered systems. In the algorithm below, steps 1, 2, 5, and 6 are based on our previous studies, while steps 3 and 4 are novel introductions. In this paper, the agent measures the field directly, and does not use any form of neuromorphic computing or computational neuroscience, although this is a potential research direction [30].

We defined a simulated agent's current position, $\mathbf{x} = (r, \theta, \phi)$, and goal location, $\mathbf{x}_g = (r, \theta_g, \phi_g)$, in spherical coordinates.

The agent's distance from the center of the planet, r, is held constant. Additionally, the agent knows the magnetic inclination, $I_g = I(\mathbf{x}_g)$, and intensity, $F_g = F(\mathbf{x}_g)$, at the goal location. At each time step, the following navigation algorithm is executed:

1. The agent measures the local magnetic inclination, $I(\mathbf{x})$, and total magnetic field intensity, $F(\mathbf{x})$.

Fig. 3. Portions of the magnetic field on Uranus' surface (orthographic projection). The contours of inclination angle (degrees) are shown in white and those of the logarithm of intensity (arbitrary units) are shown in black. The magnetic equator is shown in red. Highly orthogonal regions are shown in bright yellow, while more parallel ones are shown in darker purple (Color figure online).

2. The agent computes a differences vector in polar coordinates from the differences between the goal and local magnetic inclination and intensity:

$$\mathbf{d} = \begin{bmatrix} 0 \\ I_g - I(\mathbf{x}) \\ F_g - F(\mathbf{x}) \end{bmatrix}. \tag{1}$$

3. The agent computes the L^1 length (Manhattan distance) of the vector $\mathbf{d}$,

$$\|\mathbf{d}_1\| = |I_g - I(\mathbf{x})| + |F_g - F(\mathbf{x})|, \tag{2}$$

as well as the L^2 length (Euclidean distance),

$$\|\mathbf{d}_2\| = \sqrt{(I_g - I(\mathbf{x}))^2 + (F_g - F(\mathbf{x}))^2}. \tag{3}$$

4. The agent computes its step size, s, according to a piecewise linear formula, with a minimum step size of 0.005 and a maximum step size of 0.05:

$$s = \begin{cases} 0.005 + 0.045 \cdot \dfrac{\|\mathbf{d}\|_1}{0.12}, & \|\mathbf{d}\|_1 \leq 0.12 \\ 0.05, & \|\mathbf{d}\|_1 > 0.12 \end{cases}. \tag{4}$$

5. The agent moves by subtracting the scaled differences vector, $s \frac{\mathbf{d}}{\|\mathbf{d}\|_2}$, from its current position:

$$\mathbf{x} \leftarrow \mathbf{x} - s \frac{\mathbf{d}}{\|\mathbf{d}\|_2}. \tag{5}$$

6. Return to step 1 and repeat until the maximum number of time steps is reached (500) or when the agent reaches its goal, according to the following criteria:

$$I_g - I(\mathbf{x}) \leq 0.0005 \quad \text{and} \quad F_g - F(\mathbf{x}) \leq 0.0005. \tag{6}$$

We note here that any constants used were obtained empirically. For this initial study, we focused on setting the constants to prevent the agent from taking small steps that prevented ever reaching a goal, and large steps that caused the agent to consistently overshoot goals. This was coarsely done for several randomly selected navigation paths, and then extended for all other paths. Optimizing these parameters to extremize some metric (e.g., minimizing distance or travel time) will be the subject of future studies.

2.4   Experiments

We performed several experiments to test our navigation strategy in this magnetic field environment. Each experiment took on the order of seconds to minutes to run. First, we had our simulated agent attempt to migrate from points near the planet's magnetic north pole towards points near the planet's south pole (i.e., along the magnetic axis) to determine how well the strategy executed transequatorial navigation along the axis of the magnetic dipole, similar to [23] (Fig. 4). Borrowing terminology from Earth's geometry and magnetic field, we refer to this as the "North-South" paradigm because the agent is migrating from the northern magnetic pole to the southern magnetic pole.

Next, we had our agent attempt to migrate about the axis of the magnetic pole from different starting locations (Fig. 4). Again, borrowing terminology from Earth's geometry and magnetic field, we refer to this as the "East-West" paradigm because the agent is migrating about the magnetic axis. It should be noted that in all of these experiments the agent is working from perfect data, rather than the noisier data of real world sensors.

Using these two paradigms, we identified regions of successful and unsuccessful navigation. Based on these results, we had our agent navigate from a number of starting points to a number of goal points in the region of apparent navigability (see Sect. 3.3, Fig. 7). We refer to this as the "Arbitrary" paradigm because in this case, the agent is trying to migrate to arbitrary points.

3   Results

3.1   North-South

For the North-South paradigm, while the routes taken by the agent are not the shortest distance between the two points, the agent appears to successfully reach the specified goal points (Fig. 5).

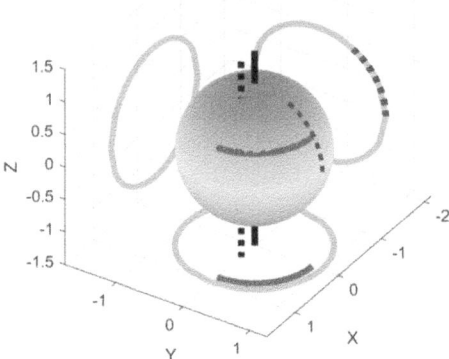

Fig. 4. Plot to illustrate "North-South" motion (blue dashed line), and "East-West" motion (red solid line) about the magnetic axis of the planet (black dashed line) (Color figure online).

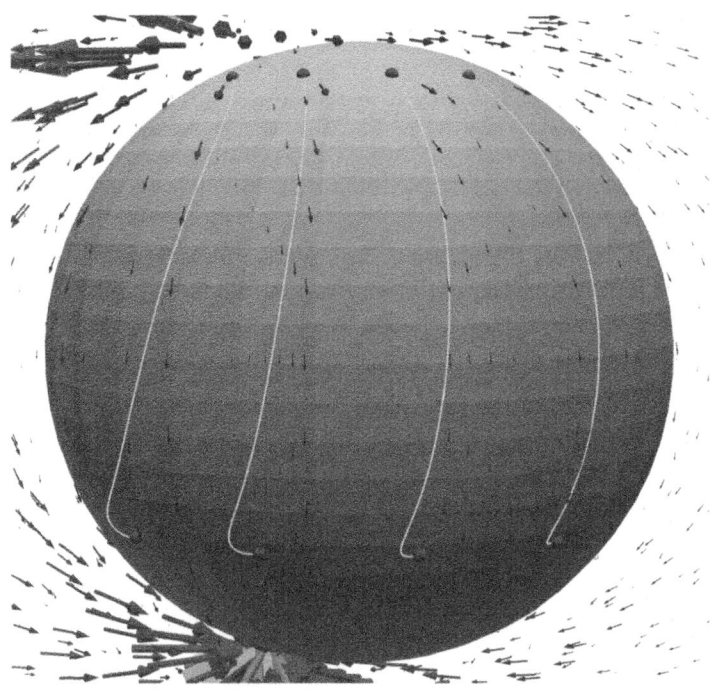

Fig. 5. Pictured are four trajectories that each run along the North-South axis of the planet. In this and all other plots, trajectories start at the red dots on the top of the sphere, move along the cyan paths, and end at the blue dots at the bottom of the sphere. The arrows represent magnetic field vectors at different locations around the planet. In this plot, the navigation routes shown are successful (Color figure online).

3.2   East-West

For the East-West paradigm, the agent was able to successfully navigate the majority of these excursions (Fig. 6A). However, if the agent was too close to either magnetic pole, it was unable to find its goal (Fig. 6B).

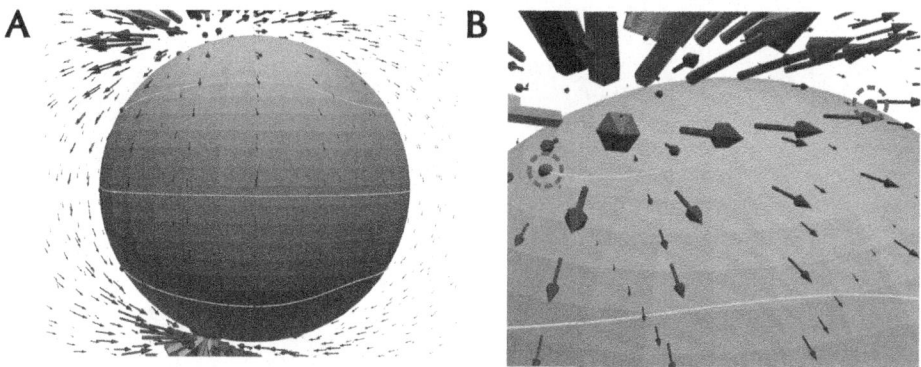

Fig. 6. Here we show four trajectories that parallel the magnetic equator. A While the three nearer to the equator are all successful, B the one starting (Red dot surrounded by red dotted line) and ending near the pole goes off track and does not reach its goal (blue dot surrounded by purple dotted line) (Color figure online)

3.3   Arbitrary-Paths

For the Arbitrary paradigm, we gave the agent a number of starting and end points that started near one extreme of the navigable area, and ended near the other (Fig. 7A and B). It should be observed that our current magnetic model produces twin magnetic signatures reflected to either side of the planet. This being the case, we counted navigation to either goal as a success. By these measures, the majority of the trajectories were successful.

To better characterize which trajectories were and were not successful, we ran an automated series of trajectories to see if they could reach their goal locations within 500 time steps. We found that the majority of goal locations could be reached from most points other than a relatively small number of locations near the magnetic pole (e.g., Fig. 7C and D). As an example, for a starting point on the magnetic equator (i.e., Fig. 7C and D), the agent is able to reach $\sim 77\%$ of the goal points (blue dots). The shape of the navigable area varies slightly depending on the location of the starting point, a finding we intend to investigate and quantify in future studies.

A small number of these failure cases resulted in what appeared to be limit cycles for those goal locations. This needs further analysis, though it may be a property of the navigation algorithm as it is currently implemented. Fixed point stability analysis would likely indicate that these goal locations have spiral source fixed points (complex eigenvalues with positive real parts) [27].

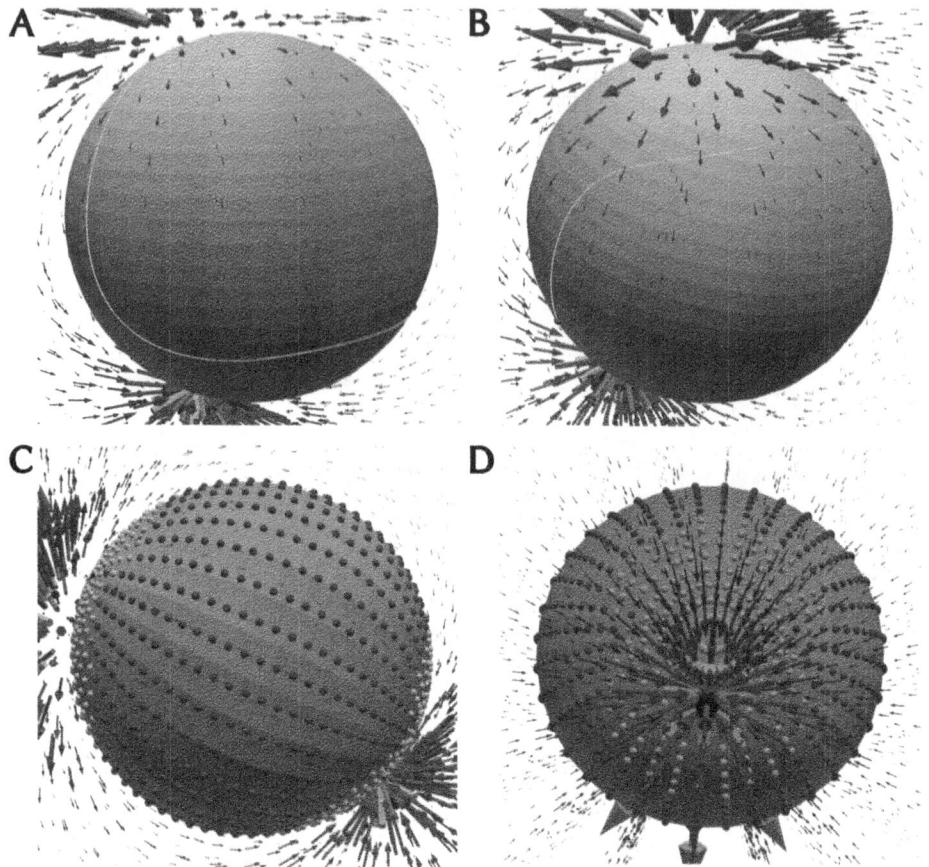

Fig. 7. A, B: Examples of successful arbitrary paths. C, D: Example plots of reachable (blue dots) and unreachable (yellow dots) points for a starting point on the magnetic equator. Navigation paths that approach the poles tend to fail, but there are far more successful trajectories than otherwise (Color figure online).

4   Discussion and Future Work

4.1   Findings and Implications

Our study's results suggest that bioinspired magnetoreception can be used to successfully navigate over most of the surface of another planet, even when that planet's magnetic field that differs from Earth's. This might be especially useful for surveyors on planets without fixed surfaces or landmarks, or to facilitate navigation by orbiting space vehicles with limited processing ability during the time gaps in communication with distant control facilities. In this case, the vehicles in question may be able to autonomously continue their mission even during intermittent communications losses.

Of particular note is that our model does not rely on an explicit, detailed, presurveyed magnetic map of the environment being explored. Rather, it only uses implicit gross knowledge of the magnetic field. Furthermore, the model uses only local sensors and does not require extensive processing resources (e.g., state estimation, or registration to a presurveyed map). These factors are critical for the development of autonomous navigation methods in unexplored areas. Note that with our current algorithm, as is seen in Fig. 7, the paths our agent takes are not necessarily straight lines from one point to another. This matches the behavior of several animals, such as loggerhead sea turtles that migrate around the Atlantic Ocean, or birds that migrate from Europe to Northern Africa via. the Iberian peninsula, a path that may enable them to avoid ecological barriers [6].

4.2 Current Limitations

Our current navigation algorithm is not reliable in the areas near the poles. This appears to be because lines of constant intensity and inclination are close to parallel in those regions, making the location of a specific point more difficult due to ambiguity. Also, the current algorithm cannot distinguish between magnetic signatures that are not unique and exist at multiple locations around the planet [28, 29]. This may mirror challenges that animals could face on Earth, as a species that has evolved in one location could be disoriented if placed in another location [27]although the use of multimodal sensing may help to alleviate this problem [29].

4.3 Future Work

In the immediate future work regarding Uranus, we have three primary goals. First, we wish to better quantify the results we have obtained and observed in this study. As stated in Sect. 3.3, the shape of the reachable area varies based on the starting location of the agent, and there appear to be limit cycles that occur for different goal locations. While the present study addresses these features in a qualitative way, we would like to employ more quantitative measures. Additionally, we want to modify the model such that it can tolerate non-unique magnetic signatures around the planet. We hope to gather more information about the behavior of our navigation strategy near the poles so that we may improve the navigation algorithm and extend its range. Furthermore, we would like to add the effects of noise into our model to better reflect the data from real world sensors. On a longer time span, we wish to create a more realistic model of the magnetic field of Uranus, and other planets in the solar system with strong magnetic fields. We would also like to incorporate orbital dynamics into our model. Our current model is kinematic and assumes that the agent can maneuver on demand with a constant thrust, similar in concept to a ground vehicle or aircraft. An orbiting space vehicle is constrained to only provide thrust at specified times, relying on orbital dynamics the rest of the time. Finally, it is our hope that improvements we make to the algorithm might also apply to navigation approaches for Earth that do not rely on satellites.

Acknowledgments. JPG, CEK, and BKT are partially funded by a grant from the Air Force Office of Scientific Research (grant number FA9550-20-1-0399).

Disclosure of Interests. We declare we have no competing interests.

References

1. USA: (2024). GPS.gov from https://www.gps.gov/
2. Turan, E., Speretta, S., Gill, E.: Autonomous navigation for deep space small satellites: scientific and technological advances. Acta Astronaut. **193**, 56–74 (2022)
3. Webb, B.: Robots with insect brains. Science **368**(6488), 244–245 (2020)
4. Ijspeert, A.J.: Biorobotics: using robots to emulate and investigate agile locomotion. Science **346**(6206), 196–203 (2014)
5. Lepora, N.F., Verschure, P., Prescott, T.J.: The state of the art in biomimetics. Bioinspiration Biomimetics **8**(1), 013001 (2012)
6. Lohmann, K.J., Lohmann, C.M.F., Putman, N.F.: Magnetic maps in animals: nature's GPS. J. Exp. Biol. **210**(21), 3697–3705 (2007)
7. Dreyer, D., et al.: The earth's magnetic field and visual landmarks steer migratory flight behavior in the Nocturnal Australian Bogong Moth. Curr. Biol. **28**(13), 2160-2166.e2165 (2018)
8. Reppert, S.M., Gegear, R.J., Merlin, C.: Navigational mechanisms of migrating monarch butterflies. Trends Neurosci. **33**(9), 399–406 (2010)
9. Wiltschko, W., Wiltschko, R.: Migratory orientation: magnetic compass orientation of garden warblers (Sylvia borin) after a simulated crossing of the magnetic equator. Ethology **91**(1), 70–74 (1992)
10. Wiltschko, W., Munro, U., Ford, H., Wiltschko, R.: Magnetic inclination compass: a basis for the migratory orientation of birds in the Northern and Southern Hemisphere. Experientia **49**, 167–170 (1993). https://doi.org/10.1007/BF01989423
11. Wiltschko, W., Wiltschko, R.: Magnetic compass of European robins. Science **176**(4030), 62–64 (1972)
12. Beason, R.C.: You can get there from here: responses to simulated magnetic equator crossing by the Bobolink (Dolichonyx oryzivorus). Ethology **91**(1), 75–80 (1992)
13. Lohmann, K., Pentcheff, N., Nevitt, G., Stetten, G., Zimmer-Faust, R., Jarrard, H., Boles, L.: Magnetic orientation of spiny lobsters in the ocean: experiments with undersea coil systems. J. Exp. Biol. **198**(10), 2041–2048 (1995)
14. Putman, N.F.: Magnetosensation. J. Comp. Physiol. A **208**(1), 1–7 (2022)
15. Lohmann, K.J., Putman, N.F., Lohmann, C.M.F.: The magnetic map of hatchling loggerhead sea turtles. Curr. Opin. Neurobiol. **22**(336), 342 (2012). https://doi.org/10.1016/j.conb.2011.11.005
16. Scanlan, M.M., Putman, N.F., Pollock, A.M., Noakes, D.L.G.: Magnetic map in nonanadromous Atlantic salmon. Proc. Natl. Acad. Sci. **115**(43), 10995–10999 (2018). https://doi.org/10.1073/pnas.1807705115
17. Naisbett-Jones, L.C., Putman, N.F., Stephenson, J.F., Ladak, S., Young, K.A.: A magnetic map leads juvenile European eels to the Gulf Stream. Curr. Biol. **27**, 1236–1240 (2017). https://doi.org/10.1016/j.cub.2017.03.015

18. Putman, N.F., et al.: An inherited magnetic map guides ocean navigation in juvenile Pacific salmon. Curr. Biol. **24**, 446–450 (2014)
19. Canciani, A.J.: Magnetic Navigation on an F-16 Aircraft Using Online Calibration. IEEE Trans. Aerosp. Electron. Syst. **58**(1), 420–434 (2022)
20. Qi, X., et al.: Geographic true navigation based on real-time measurements of geomagnetic fields. IEEE Trans. Geosci. Remote Sens. **61**, 1–10 (2023)
21. Knecht, D., Shuman, B.: The Geomagnetic Field. Handbook of Geophysics and the Space Environment. A, Jursa, Air Force Geophysics Laboratory (1985)
22. Pizzuti, S., et al.: Uncovering how animals use combinations of magnetic field properties to navigate: a computational approach. J. Comp. Physiol. A **208**(1), 155–166 (2022)
23. Taylor, B.K., Lohmann, K.J., Havens, L.T., Lohmann, C.M.F., Granger, J.: Long-distance transequatorial navigation using sequential measurements of magnetic inclination angle. J. R. Soc. Interface **18**(174), 20200887 (2021)
24. Origins, Worlds, and Life: A Decadal Strategy for Planetary Science and Astrobiology 2023-2032 — The National Academies Press
25. Ness, N.F., Acuña, M.H., Behannon, K.W., Burlaga, L.F., Connerney, J.E.P., Lepping, R.P., Neubauer, F.M.: Magnetic Fields at Uranus. Science **233**, 85–89 (1986)
26. Ortner, M., Coliado Bandeira, L.G.: Magpylib: a free Python package for magnetic field computation. SoftwareX **11**, 100466 (2020). https://doi.org/10.1016/j.softx.2020.100466
27. Gill, J.P., Taylor, B.K.: Navigation by magnetic signatures in a realistic model of Earth's magnetic field. Bioinspiration Biomimetics **19**(3), 036006 (2024). https://doi.org/10.1088/1748-3190/ad3120
28. Taylor, B.K.: Bioinspired magnetoreception and navigation using magnetic signatures as waypoints. Bioinspiration Biomimetics **13**(4), 046003 (2018)
29. Brian Kyle, T., Sabrina, C.: Bioinspired magnetoreception and navigation in nonorthogonal environments using magnetic signatures. Bioinspiration Biomimetics **14**, 066009 (2019)
30. Nichols, S., Havens, L., Taylor, B.: Sensation to navigation: a computational neuroscience approach to magnetic field navigation. J. Comp. Physiol. A **208**(1), 167–176 (2022)

Bioinspired Navigation Based on Distributed Sensing in the Leech Using Dynamic Neural Fields

Sebastian T. Nichols[1], Jeffrey P. Gill[2], Bruno Mota[3],
Cynthia M. Harley[4], and Brian K. Taylor[2]([✉])

[1] The University of North Carolina at Chapel Hill, Chapel Hill, NC 27599, USA
`seb.nichols399@gmail.com`
[2] Case Western Reserve University, Cleveland, OH 44106, USA
`{jpg18,bkt2}@case.edu`
[3] Universidade Federal do Rio de Janeiro, Rio de Janeiro 21941, Brazil
[4] Metropolitan State University, Saint Paul, MN 55106, USA
`cindy.harley@metrostate.edu`

Abstract. Water waves can help aquatic animals to distinguish between predators and prey. Previous studies suggest that leech sensory receptors have evolved to respond to relevant wave frequencies. While these studies examined how sensory information affects animal behavior, the underlying neural processing remains unclear. In this study, we present a model that mimics leech goal seeking behavior using an agent-based simulation. Our model uses neural fields, a Winner-Take-All framework from computational neuroscience, to process sensory data. A simulated leech was placed in a simulated environment containing artificial water waves. A distributed sensor array around the agent detected the wave motion, which was then processed via a computational neuroscience approach called a neural field. This sensory information was used to compute motion directions. Modeled behavioral data aligned with data from previous animal experiments. Our model can complement animal experiments by allowing us to pose questions that would be challenging to address directly in an animal. Also, our results may provide insights into novel processing approaches that can be leveraged by man-made sensory systems to process data from multiple sensors.

Keywords: leech · mechanoreception · neural fields

1 Introduction

1.1 Distributed Sensing Background

Animals ranging from invertebrates such as leeches to vertebrates such as humans use arrays of individual sensors, a phenomenon known as distributed sensing, to detect sensory stimuli (Fig. 1). To provide some examples, humans have mechanoreceptors dispersed across the epidermis to detect mechanical stimuli

N. S. Szczecinski et al. (Eds.): Living Machines 2024, LNAI 14930, pp. 148–162, 2025.
https://doi.org/10.1007/978-3-031-72597-5_11

[1] while insects use fields of campaniform sensilla to detect limb loads [2]. It is hypothesized that magnetoreception could be distributed [3,4]. Understanding distributed sensing is essential for understanding how data from multiple sensors is combined and used to direct behavior. Beyond scientific understanding, distributed sensing and computational neuroscience/neuromorphic computing approaches could benefit man-made systems in several ways [6]. Some of these benefits include 1) robustness because many sensors must fail to cause total system failure, 2) using less complex sensors [5], and 3) developing systems with lower size, weight, cost, and power requirements.

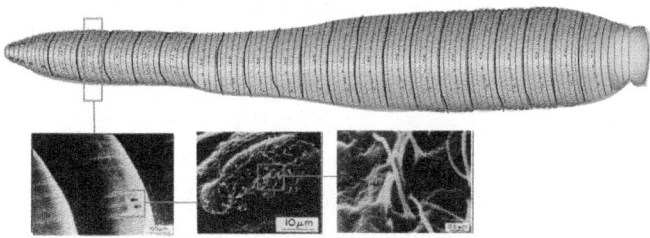

Fig. 1. Leeches have 14 sensilla on each of their 21 segments. These sensilla are positioned around the circumference of a single annulus, or segmental ring. Below the leech schematic there are SEM images from Derosa and Friesen [22] showing increasingly zoomed in images of a mechanosensory sensillum.

1.2 Leeches as a Model for Distributed Sensing

Leeches are an attractive organism for studying distributed sensing. They have over 294 distributed sensilla, and a relatively simple nervous system (10^4 neurons vs. 10^5 for the common fruit fly). The leech has 14 visual and mechanosensory sensors per each of its 21 segments which wrap around the segment in a regular pattern. Previous studies have sought to elucidate the relationship between sensory stimulation, neural responses (i.e., spike rate frequency), and motor commands and organism level behavior [7–10]. However, the mechanisms a leech uses to convert sensory information to a direction of travel are still unknown. Here, we investigate possible mechanisms through the creation of a computational model that is based on previous biological data, and mathematics that have been shown to accurately represent neuronal processes [11]. While these possibilities may not be the exact mechanism(s) that the leech employs, they provide a reference point to guide future biological experimentation, and present a potential template for employing distributed sensing in engineered systems.

Previous studies have examined the sensory capabilities of the medicinal leech, *Hirudo verbana* [12,14]. Leeches were exposed to water waves of various temporal frequencies to examine their response to both mechanical and visual elements of the wave. Certain wave frequencies produced peak find rates for both unimodal (i.e., mechanical or visual) and multimodal (i.e., mechanical and visual) stimuli. In this study, we focus on the mechanical stimulus of water waves.

1.3 Neural Processing

Several models have attempted to simulate an animal's neural response to sensory input [4, 15–20]. In our previous work [21], we used a simplified representation of spike rate distributions to mimic the leech's nervous system, inspired by work on modeling the integration of light and magnetic sensory information in animals [15]. The present study advances this model by using dynamic neural fields to simulate neural processing. Neural fields have been used to replicate nervous system responses, and provide a framework to model the behavior of populations of distributed neurons [11, 19, 23].

1.4 Paper Goals

In this study, we employ the winner-take-all (WTA) framework used by Wilson [11, section 7.2] to enable a simulated leech to navigate to a goal. The WTA network focuses on the neural inhibition between different neural populations, or neural nodes. WTA networks have been previously used for tasks such as path integration [11]. We chose this model formulation because of its demonstrated biological relevance and ability in navigation and orientation contexts.

Using this model, we tasked a simulated agent that uses a neural field to perform distributed sensing while navigating from a starting point to a goal. This task was performed using different neural thresholds (an intrinsic neural feature), water depths and water wave frequencies (extrinsic environmental features). Our model reproduced the find rates (i.e., percentage of leeches that successfully navigate to a target location) observed in animal experiments. Our model's find rate vs. frequency aligns with frequencies at which real leeches most successfully find targets [12]. Much of our work is based on work developed in Nichols [24], which was later adapted for magnetoreception in Nichols et al. [33].

2 Methods

Figure 2 provides a flow-chart summary of our model. A simulated agent (representing a leech from the species *Hirudo verbana*) sensed a mechanically generated water wave stimulus (Fig. 2A) via distributed sensing (Fig. 2B). Distributed sensory information was processed using a neural field (Fig. 2C). A behavioral algorithm transformed the neural responses into behavioral actions that were used to move towards the source of the stimulus (Fig. 2D).

Note that in this study, as a starting point, we restrict sensing to mechanoreception, similar to unimodal sensation experiments with real world animals [12].

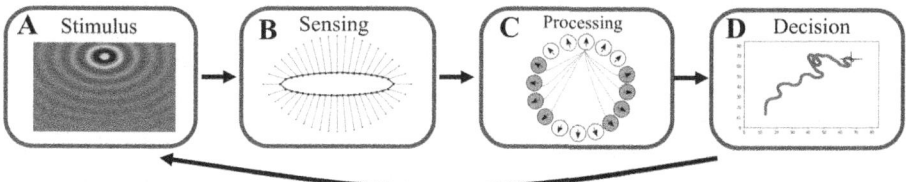

Fig. 2. General flowchart displaying the core components of the model and how they interact with each other. These simulated sensors are arranged in a distributed manner, spanning around the perimeter of the agent (B). The sensors detect and gather information from the environment (A). This information is the input for the neural field (C). The neural field computes an angle that the agent uses to orient itself and navigate towards the target location (D).

2.1 Water Wave Simulation

Water waves were modeled as 2D surface waves with physical properties satisfying the dispersion relation: a relationship that defines how wavelength depends on wave frequency. The surface elevation of these waves can be modeled with the following equations [25–28]:

$$\eta(\boldsymbol{x}, t) = A(\boldsymbol{x}) \sin(\theta(\boldsymbol{x}, t)) \tag{1}$$

$$A(\boldsymbol{x}) = \frac{A_1}{|\boldsymbol{x} - \boldsymbol{x}_g| + \varepsilon} \tag{2}$$

$$\theta(\boldsymbol{x}, t) = \boldsymbol{k} \cdot \boldsymbol{x} - \omega t \tag{3}$$

$$k = |\boldsymbol{k}| = \frac{2\pi}{\lambda}, \quad \omega = \frac{2\pi}{T} \tag{4}$$

Equation 1 defines the wave's elevation η at time t and position $\boldsymbol{x} = \{x, y\}$. Equation 2 describes the wave amplitude A as decreasing with distance from the wave source, located at $\boldsymbol{x}_g = \{x_g, y_g\}$; the constants $A_1 = 33.6$ cm^2 and $\varepsilon = 10^{-4}$ cm in this study, chosen to produce 4-cm waves near the source (as will be seen in Sect. 2.2, the agent's sensors are insensitive to wave amplitude, so these constants have no bearing on the behavior of the agent). Equation 3 represents the phase of the wave in both space and time. Equation 4 shows the relationships between the wavenumber k and spatial wavelength λ, and between the angular frequency ω and temporal period T. A visual representation of this point source water wave is shown in Figs. 2A and 5. In both figures, λ is the distance between two peaks. The next section gives a description of the wave vector $\boldsymbol{k}$.

We chose to model water waves as gravity waves, i.e., wave motion that depends on gravity (g) and water depth (h), to generate baseline behavioral data in response to the simplest form of a mechanosensory stimulus. Future studies will explore other water wave regimes such as capillary waves (water waves with motion dominated by surface tension). To replicate realistic water waves, ω and k must satisfy the dispersion relation

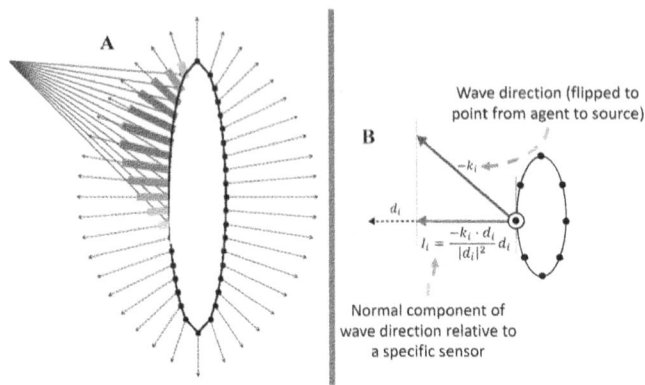

Fig. 3. The mechanosensory detection method is illustrated through an agent with its distributed sensors (dashed black arrows, radiating from elliptical agent) and sample mechanosensory inputs shown as wave vectors (solid blue arrows, originating from a common source in A). The wave vectors carry information about the direction and magnitude of the oncoming water wave, which the agent can sense and process to orient itself towards the target location. Each sensor detects the component of the wave vector normal to it via vector projection (B). The magnitude of these projected vectors vary from strong detection (large red bars in A) to low detection (small yellow bars in A) depending on the alignment difference between the sensor detection vector d_i and the wave vector k_i. (Color figure online)

$$\omega^2 = gk \tanh(kh) \tag{5}$$

where "tanh" is the hyperbolic tangent. The dispersion relation in Eq. 5 shows the spatial relationship for water movement based on g and h. Since there is already data on leech navigational performance as a function of wave frequency [12], we used these frequencies as inputs into the dispersion relation (Eq. 5) to calculate wavelength at specific water depths and wave frequency inputs.

2.2 Sensor Detection

We modeled the leech as a 2D ellipse that is 10 cm long and 1 cm wide; measurements based approximately on the size of an adult in the leech species *Hirudo verbana* [13]. While a 2D model removes our ability to examine leech depth regulation, this approach was deemed acceptable for mirroring Harley et al. [12], which primarily examined behavior in 2D. Whereas real leeches are highly flexible, our ellipse is rigid and of constant size, and we leave more realistic body kinematics to future studies. Using the model presented by Wilson [11, section 7.2] as a template, we equipped our simulated leech with 24 neural populations (i.e, nodes) equally spaced around its perimeter at 15° increments, the same arrangement presented in Wilson [11]. Each population represents an aggregate of individual sensors that are sensitive to a particular range of directions.

Real leeches sense water waves via sensory hairs (i.e., cilia) distributed along their body [12]. Properly simulating all aspects of water wave mechanosensation and processing is an area of active investigation, and can be computationally intensive [29]. Because we are concerned with organism-level behavior, we use a simplified approach for water wave detection.

To measure the direction of the oncoming stimulus, the agent calculates the angle (ϕ) between the stimulus direction and the sensor location. For mathematical convenience, this is done using the sensor detection vector (d_i) (i.e., a line pointing from the agent's center towards the ith sensor's location (black dashed arrows in Fig. 3)), and the wave vector (k_i)(i.e., a line pointing from the stimulus origin $x_g = \{x_g, y_g\}$ to the ith sensor's location $x_i = \{x_i, y_i\}$ (blue arrows in Fig. 3) with magnitude $k = \frac{2\pi}{\lambda}$).

The wave vector k_i is given as

$$k_i = \frac{x_i - x_g}{|x_i - x_g|} k \tag{6}$$

Equation 6 is then used to calculate the incidence angle ϕ_i and signal intensity I_i (red arrow in Fig. 3B) of the wave with respect to the ith sensor.

$$\phi_i = \arccos \frac{-k_i \cdot d_i}{|k_i||d_i|} \tag{7}$$

$$I_i = (-k_i \cdot d_i) \frac{d_i}{|d_i|^2} \tag{8}$$

$$I_i = |I_i| \tag{9}$$

Equation 7 calculates the angle between the two vectors. If the angle is less than 90° then the wave is within the sensor's range of detection and it can continue to measure the wave's magnitude. We calculate the magnitude at the ith sensor by first projecting the wave vector onto the sensory detection vector with Eq. 8 and then finding the magnitude of that projected vector (I_i) with Eq. 9. This magnitude value (I_i) approximates the stimulus strength at the given sensor and also measures the sensor's alignment with the oncoming wave. Because the magnitude of I_i depends on the wavenumber k (through Eqs. 6, 8, and 9), and I_i serves as an input to our neural field (see Sect. 2.3 for details), we would expect the activity of the neural field to increase as the wavenumber increases.

We note here that information was detected and processed among all sensors simultaneously (see Sect. 2.3 for details). In the future, as we refine and improve both our sensor and neural models, we would like to incorporate phenomena akin to interaural time differences to examine how differences in both spatial and temporal processing impact the ability to detect frequency, wavelength, or a mixture of both.

2.3   Sensory Processing: Neural Field Model

At a high level, a neural field is composed of nodes that each represent a population of neurons that responds to a preferred input. These populations can interact with each other through excitatory and inhibitory connections. Neural fields are useful for studying the behavior of populations of neurons, vs. examining the performance of individual neurons [11,30]. While details of our neural field approach can be found in Wilson [11, section 7.2], we summarize here.

To provide a conceptual description, in our study, the neural field has 24 neural nodes. Each node is paired with and receives excitation from a set of sensors sensitive to specific directional inputs. Nodes inhibit neighboring nodes at intermediate distance by convolving the activity of the network via negative weights in a weighting array (Fig. 4). This results in the nodes having a distribution of activity, with one or some of the nodes having activity that exceeds a threshold (i.e., a "winning" neuron or set of neurons). Because each node represents a physical direction, as illustrated in Fig. 4, the winning neuron and its neighbors encode a perceived direction, which the agent uses to control its motion. Mathematically, these events are represented in Eqs. 10, 11, and 12:

$$E_j = \sum_{i=1}^{n} I_i \big(\cos(\Omega_j - \Omega_i + \text{noise}) \big)_+ \tag{10}$$

$$\tau \frac{dR_j}{dt} = -R_j + (E_j - \boldsymbol{W} * \boldsymbol{R})_+ \tag{11}$$

$$\Omega_{\text{interp}} = 15° \frac{R_{\text{select}-1} - R_{\text{select}+1}}{2(R_{\text{select}+1} - 2R_{\text{select}} + R_{\text{select}-1})} + \Omega_{\text{select}} \tag{12}$$

The jth neural node may receive excitation from each of the $n = 24$ sensors. The excitation from the ith sensor to the jth node scales with the stimulus strength I_i (Eq. 9) and with the similarity in the preferred direction Ω_j of the jth node and the preferred direction Ω_i of the ith sensor. The + subscript indicates a nonlinear activation function that sets equal to zero any excitation from sensors that differ in preferred angle from that of the node by more than 90°. In this way, a sensor that is aligned with the node's preferred direction will provide maximum stimulation to that node, while sensors that are not aligned with the node's preferred direction will provide minimal or no stimulation. Gaussian noise with mean 0° and standard deviation 90° is also added to the cosine term to represent noise in neural processing. All sensory inputs are summed to compute the total excitatory sensory input for the jth node, E_j, in Eq. 10.

The activation level of the jth neural node, R_j, is governed by a differential equation with time constant $\tau = 0.5$ s (Eq. 11). The node receives excitatory sensory inputs (E_j), as well as inhibitory inputs from other neural nodes ($-\boldsymbol{W} * \boldsymbol{R}$). $\boldsymbol{W}$ is a synaptic weighting array that is convolved with the array of all neural node activations, $\boldsymbol{R}$. Per Wilson [11, section 7.2], $\boldsymbol{W}$ inhibits intermediate-distance nodes, but does not affect near or far neighboring nodes (Fig. 4).

To model the biological phenomena of over- and under-stimulation, we set a constant, called the neural threshold, which is varied between simulations in this study. A node with activation level R_j that exceeds this threshold is considered salient, and the preferred direction Ω_j encoded by the node may influence the perceived direction of the wave source. Under ideal conditions, just one or a few nodes with preferred directions corresponding to the true direction of the wave source will reach this threshold. If the threshold is set too low, too many nodes may produce salient signals, leading to over-stimulation. When the threshold is set too high, no direction may be salient, leading to under-stimulation.

At each time step, one neural node is selected at random from among all nodes with activations above the neural threshold parameter (see Sect. 2.4 for handling the case when no neural node activations exceed the threshold). The activation level of the selected node (R_{select}) with preferred direction Ω_{select}, along with the activations of its two nearest neighbors ($R_{\text{select}-1}, R_{\text{select}+1}$), are used together to estimate the perceived direction of the stimulus wave source, Ω_{interp}, via parabolic interpolation (Eq. 12), which is more accurate than the 15° intervals encoded by the nodes' preferred directions. The perceived direction is used to determine bearing changes for our motion model (see Sect. 2.4).

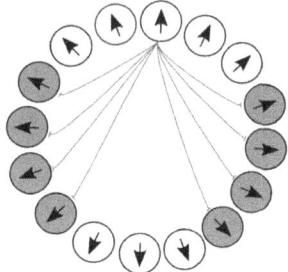

Fig. 4. Visual representation of a winner-take-all (WTA) neural field network (adapted from Wilson [11, fig. 7.5]). In this example the upper middle node receives a sensor input and inhibits neighbors at intermediate distance (red). Nearby nodes (top) and very distant nodes (bottom) are not inhibited. Each node inhibits its intermediate-distance neighbors like this, but only one set of inhibitory connections, from the upper middle node, is shown for clarity. In our implementation, one node is selected at random among nodes with activations above a neural threshold parameter. The selected node's activation (R_{select}) along with the activations of its nearest neighbors ($R_{\text{select}+1}$ and $R_{\text{select}-1}$) are used together via parabolic interpolation to obtain an accurate estimate of the direction of a wave source (perceived direction). (Color figure online)

The activity of all nodes (i.e., R_j's) is updated every time step. Based on both preliminary observations and biological considerations, the sensors take measurements for 2 s, and are inactive for 6 s. In Eq. 11, this corresponds to the excitatory and inhibitory input terms being active with nonzero values for 2 s, and then both being set to a value of zero for 6 seconds (see next section for motion model, as this section only deals with neural processing). This 6-second rest period allows neural node activity to decay, preventing the winner-take-all network from becoming "stuck" with one winning node inhibiting all others even as the agent turns and sensory inputs change. This simplistic approach helped ensure that later measurements are not corrupted by information from earlier measurements, and is also biologically inspired as a neuron's response can decay over time after a stimulus is presented. This also reflects spiking patterns commonly observed in single celled neuron responses [31].

2.4 Motion Model

The agent's orientation and position at time t are defined by its bearing β_t, its center of mass $\{x_{c,t}, y_{c,t}\}$, and the positions of its 24 sensors $\{x_{i,t}, y_{i,t}\}$. During each time step, the agent first rotates around its center of mass by a change in bearing, $\Delta\beta$, and then travels forward at a constant speed s for the full duration of the time step, $\Delta t = 0.1$ s. New values are calculated for the next discrete time, $t + \Delta t$, according to Eqs. 13–17:

$$\Delta\beta = k_p \Omega_{interp} \Delta t \tag{13}$$

$$\beta_{t+\Delta t} = \beta_t + \Delta\beta \tag{14}$$

$$\begin{bmatrix} \Delta x \\ \Delta y \end{bmatrix} = \begin{bmatrix} s\Delta t \cos\left(\beta_{t+\Delta t}\right) \\ s\Delta t \sin\left(\beta_{t+\Delta t}\right) \end{bmatrix} \tag{15}$$

$$\begin{bmatrix} x_{c,t+\Delta t} \\ y_{c,t+\Delta t} \end{bmatrix} = \begin{bmatrix} x_{c,t} \\ y_{c,t} \end{bmatrix} + \begin{bmatrix} \Delta x \\ \Delta y \end{bmatrix} \tag{16}$$

$$\begin{bmatrix} x_{i,t+\Delta t} \\ y_{i,t+\Delta t} \end{bmatrix} = \begin{bmatrix} \cos\left(\Delta\beta\right) & -\sin\left(\Delta\beta\right) \\ \sin\left(\Delta\beta\right) & \cos\left(\Delta\beta\right) \end{bmatrix} \left(\begin{bmatrix} x_{i,t} \\ y_{i,t} \end{bmatrix} - \begin{bmatrix} x_{c,t} \\ y_{c,t} \end{bmatrix} \right) + \begin{bmatrix} x_{c,t} \\ y_{c,t} \end{bmatrix} + \begin{bmatrix} \Delta x \\ \Delta y \end{bmatrix} \tag{17}$$

Assuming at least one neural node's activation exceeded the neural threshold, the neural field returns a perceived direction (Eq. 12). Using Eq. 13, the agent converts the perceived angle Ω_{interp} into a change in bearing, $\Delta\beta$, using the constant $k_p = 0.4$ s^{-1} (chosen somewhat arbitrarily to avoid oscillations when too large and overslow turning when too small). Equation 14 updates the agent's bearing. Based on our agent's size and behavioral studies that suggest leeches crawl their body length about every 6.4 s [14], our simulated leech moves at $s = 1.56$ cm/s. Using Eqs. 15 and 16, and its new bearing, the agent calculates the distances $\{\Delta x, \Delta y\}$ that its center of mass travels, and updates its center of mass. Eq. 17 updates the positions of the agent's sensors, first by rotating them around the previous center of mass, and then by translating them by $\{\Delta x, \Delta y\}$.

If none of the neural field's activations exceeds the neural threshold, which can occur especially during the 6-second windows when sensors are inactive, the agent chooses a uniformly random integer angle in $[-45°, +45°]$ for Ω_{interp}, rotates via Eqs. 13 and 14, and then has a 40% chance of not moving forward at all. This model behavior is inspired by the real behavior of the leech when a stimulus is too weak to be detected, and the leech may not move or may turn randomly. The 45° angle was chosen for simplicity, but can be adjusted in future studies that aim to improve model fidelity.

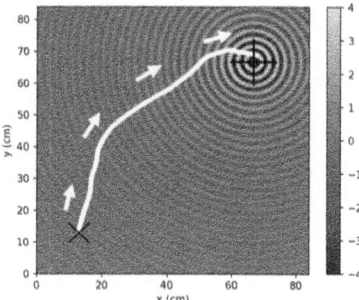

Fig. 5. Sample trajectory plot showing the path taken by an agent to reach the origin of a simulated water wave. The color bar represents the water elevation (cm). The distributed sensors are updated at each time step with new wave vector quantities depending on the agent's position and bearing. The simulation terminates once the agent stays within 4 cm of the target continuously for 5 s. The experiment outlined in Sect. 2.5 performs this navigation task 50 times per parameter combination.

We note here that this model of motion is greatly simplified from a leech's actual crawling or swimming behavior. We plan to incorporate more detailed and physically relevant forms of locomotion in future studies.

2.5   Simulation Setup and Quantification

We compared the performance of our simulated agent to real-world leech behavior observed in Harley et al. [12]. Our experiments take place in a square behavioral arena that is 7,056 cm^2 (84 cm by 84 cm). This roughly matches the size of the behavioral arena from Harley et al. [12]. The only difference is that the real world animal experiments used a circular shaped arena, while we used a square shaped arena to simplify boundary collisions [12], which were modeled in this study by simply having the agent turn 180° if it encountered a boundary.

We gave the simulated agent 180 s to explore and sense the behavioral arena. It had to stay within 4 cm of the target location for at least 5 s to count as a successful find. While these times were shortened from the animal experiments to reduce simulation run time, they produce similar trajectories.

A point source gravity wave propagated outwards from a northeastern position in the arena (Fig. 5), while our agent always started at a southwestern position relative to the wave source.

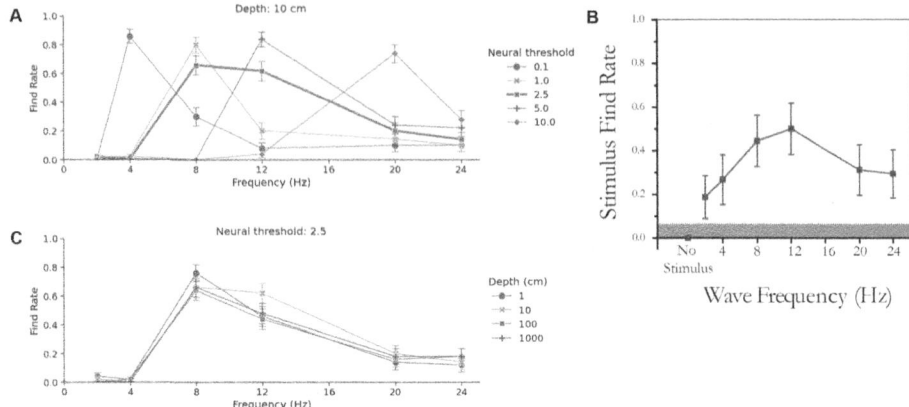

Fig. 6. Find rate data for the validation simulations and prior animal experiments. (A) For a fixed water depth of 10 cm, the neural threshold parameter and stimulus wave frequency were systematically varied, and the find rate was measured across 50 trials for each combination. As neural threshold increases, the wave frequency that the agent responds to most successfully also increases. For the values tested here, the find rate function most closely resembles animal data (B) when the threshold is 2.5 (bold green line with square markers in A), when the find rate peaks at 8–12 Hz. (B) Animal data taken from Harley et al. [12]. (C) For a fixed neural threshold of 2.5, the water depth and wave frequency were systematically varied, and the find rate was measured across 50 trials for each combination. In general, water depth does not significantly impact the find rate or the approximate range of frequencies with peak find rate (8–12 Hz). Across all three panels, each error bar represents the binomial standard deviation, a measure of uncertainty that decreases as the number of trials increases. Animal experiments in B were limited to 15–18 trials per wave frequency level. (Color figure online)

To compare our model to Harley et al. [12], we ran our model for six water wave stimulus frequencies (2, 4, 8, 12, 20, and 24 Hz), four depths (1, 10, 100, and 1000 cm), and five neural thresholds (0.1, 1.0, 2.5. 5.0, 10.0). Navigational performance was measured by computing the find rate across 50 trials for each parameter combination. A 'find' is defined as the agent successfully locating the source, and the find rate is the proportion of successful finds across all of the trials for a given combination of water wave frequency, depth, and neural threshold. When a find occurs during the simulation, the trial terminates and is marked as a success. Similar to Harley et al. [12], we plot find rate against wave frequency so that we may compare our simulation to real animal behavior. These simulations were performed in batches using cloud computing provided by Google Colab, collectively taking several hours to run.

3   Results

Figure 5 shows an example of navigational behavior for an agent with 24 sensors.
    Figure 6 shows plots of find rate vs. wave frequency for our simulated agent across different neural thresholds (Fig. 6A) and real-world leeches (Fig. 6B).

Figure 6A shows that for any fixed neural threshold, the agent tends to find its goal most successfully when the water waves originating from the goal have a particular frequency (i.e., each line has a peak). As the neural threshold is increased, this "preferred" wave frequency increases too. Real-world adult leeches have been shown to have a wave frequency that they respond best to as well, in the range of 8–12 Hz (see Fig. 6B, reproduced from Harley et al. [12]). We attempted to find a neural threshold that qualitatively replicates this real-world animal behavior. We found that with a neural threshold of 2.5, our simulated leeches respond most successfully to waves in the range of 8–12 Hz, similar to real-world animals. While we have not optimized the neural threshold to match behavioral data from real animals, the results demonstrate that our model qualitatively captures this aspect of leech sensation and navigation. For a neural threshold of 2.5, we also plot find rate vs. frequency for multiple depths (Fig. 6C). As can be seen, the find rate (varying by no more than 18% for a given frequency) and especially preferred frequencies (always in the approximate range 8–12 Hz) are relatively insensitive to depth, which matches studies from our group on the behavior of a single leech cilium [29]. For a depth of 10 cm and a neural threshold of 2.5, we plot sample trajectories for each frequency tested (Fig. 7). As can be seen, for this combination of parameters, the agent has the best chance of finding the target for waves of 8 Hz and 12 Hz.

4   Discussion

Our study suggests two main conclusions and points of interest. First, neural fields can process sensory information from water waves and qualitatively reproduce leech navigation behavior. Namely, peak find rates can be generated for water wave frequencies approximately 8–12 Hz. Second, depth of the water column does not appear to affect navigation behavior. A previous modeling study made this prediction looking at the neural activity of one sensory neuron and one single hair sensor [29]. The current study, which uses a completely different approach (i.e., modeling populations of neurons) generates the same result.

We believe our results are encouraging, given all of the important features that our simulation lacks. Our simulation does not have an explicit mechanoreception hair sensor model, and instead infers information about wave intensity and direction relative to each sensor. Also, our simulation does not attempt to replicate a leech's detailed neurobiology or physiology (e.g., segmental ganglia, flexible body plan, sensation frequency and temporal response). Finally, we did not attempt to optimize any of our model's parameters to obtain a "best fit" to behavioral data. Despite these limitations and simplifications, our simulation can generate results that qualitatively mirror real-world animal behavior. By improving its fidelity in the future, our model can serve as a tool to address future questions about distributed sensing and processing.

From an engineering perspective, especially in the future, we would like to explore the fidelity of our model by adding noise to, or zeroing out individual sensors. This would simulate the failure of individual sensors, and allow us

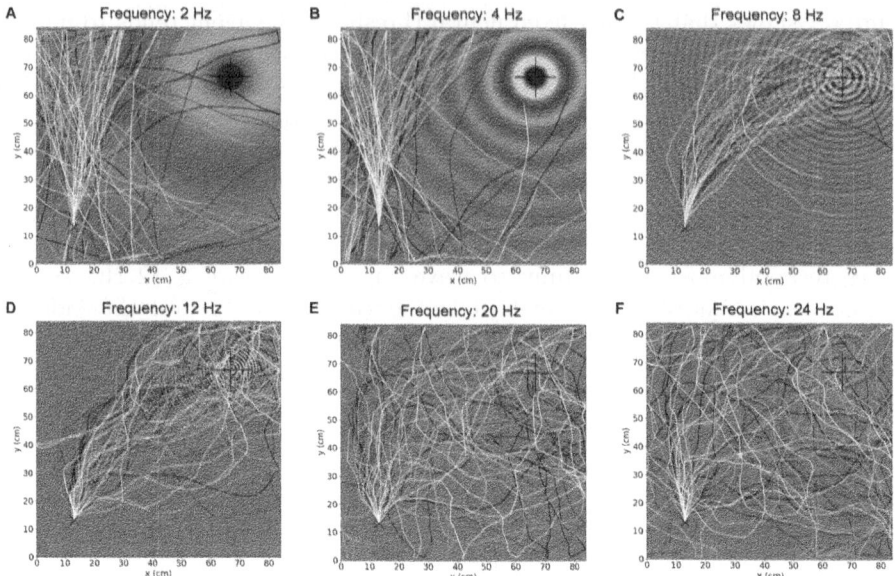

Fig. 7. Sample trajectories for a range of stimulus wave frequencies. Here, the water depth was fixed at 10 cm and the neural threshold at 2.5. Each plot shows 50 trials. At low wave frequencies (A, B), the neural field is under-stimulated, and the agent fails to turn, traveling in straight lines. At moderate frequencies (C, D), the agent finds the wave source most of the time. At high frequencies (E, F), the neural field is over-stimulated, and the agent turns too often, choosing new directions at random.

to investigate how robust the system is to sensor failure, or data corruption. This could be useful in the development of future engineered systems. In our model, each sensor is relatively simple. A collection of simple sensors providing usable information even when a subset of these sensors is disabled would enable the development of sensor systems that are lower cost and more robust than what is currently available. A future area of interest is comparing this and other approaches based on computational neuroscience and neuromorphic computing to engineered approaches in terms of quantities such as computational complexity. Our work is part of the growing trend of using computational neuroscience and neuromorphic engineering to better understand biological systems and develop novel engineered systems [6,32].

Acknowledgments. This work was partially supported by a grant from the Air Force Office of Scientific Research (FA9550-20-1-0399). B. Mota is supported by Fundação Serrapilheira Institute (grant Serra-1709-16981) and CNPq (PQ 2017 312837/2017-8).

Data Accessibility. Code is provided as electronic supplementary material (please note that this script may take several hours to run): https://github.com/qbeslab/ LeechNavigationNeuralFields.

Disclosure of Interests. We declare we have no competing interests.

References

1. Zimmerman, A., Bai, L., Ginty, D.D.: The gentle touch receptors of mammalian skin. Science **346**(6212), 950–954 (2014)
2. Zill, S., Schmitz, J., Büschges, A.: Load sensing and control of posture and loco-motion. Arthropod Struct. Dev. **33**, 273–286 (2004)
3. Walker, M.: A model for encoding of magnetic field intensity by magnetite-based magnetoreceptor cells. J. Theor. Biol. **250**, 85–91 (2007)
4. Taylor, B.K.: Validating a model for detecting magnetic field intensity using dynamic neural fields. J. Theor. Biol. **408**, 53–65 (2016)
5. Hochner, B.: An embodied view of octopus neurobiology. Curr. Biol. **22**(20), R887-92 (2012)
6. McDonnell, M.D., et al.: Engineering intelligent electronic systems based on com-putational neuroscience. Proc. IEEE **102**(5), 646–651 (2014)
7. Lockery, S.R., Kristan, W.B.: Distributed processing of sensory information in the leech. I. Input- output relations of the local bending reflex. J. Neurosci. **10**(6), 1811–1815 (1990)
8. Kristan, W.B., Calabrese, R.L., Friesen, W.O.: Neural control of leech behavior. Prog. Neurobiol. **76**, 279–327 (2005)
9. Wagenaar, D.A.: A classic model animal in the 21st century: recent lessons from the leech nervous system. J. Exp. Biol. **218**, 3353–3359 (2015)
10. Moshtagh-Khorasani, M., Miller, E.W., Torre, V.: The spontaneous electrical activ-ity of neurons in leech ganglia. Physiol. Rep. **1**, e00089 (2013)
11. Wilson, H.: Spikes, Decisions, and Actions: the Dynamical Foundations of Neuro-science. Oxford University Press, New York (1999)
12. Harley, C.M., Cienfuegos, J., Wagenaar, D.A.: Developmentally regulated multi-sensory integration for prey localization in the medicinal leech. J. Exp. Biol. **214**, 3801–3807 (2011)
13. Kutschera, U., Elliott, J.: The European medicinal leech Hirudo medicinalis L.: morphology and occurrence of an endangered species. Zoosyst. Evol. **90**(2), 2 (2014)
14. Harley, C.M., Wagenaar, D.A.: Scanning behavior in the medicinal leech Hirudo verbana. PLoS One **9**(1), e86120 (2014)
15. Jensen, K.K.: Light-dependent orientation responses in animals can be explained by a model of compass cue integration. J. Theor. Biol. **262**, 129–141 (2010)
16. Taylor, B.K., Johnsen, S., Lohmann, K.J.: Detection of magnetic field proper-ties using distributed sensing: a computational neuroscience approach. Bioinspir. Biomim. **12**, 3 (2017)
17. Hunt, A., et al.: Development and training of a neural controller for hind leg walking in a dog robot. Front. Neurorobot. **11**, 18 (2017)
18. Zhang, K.: Representation of spatial orientation by the intrinsic dynamics of the head-direction cell ensemble: a theory. J. Neurosci. **16**(6), 2112–2126 (1996)
19. Coombes, S., et al.: Neural Fields: Theory and Applications. Springer-Verlag, Berlin Heidelberg (2014)
20. Kasabov, N.K.: Time-Space, Spiking Neural Networks and Brain-Inspired Artificial Intelligence. Springer-Verlag, Berlin (2019)

21. Nichols, S.T., Kekl, C.E., Taylor, B.K., Harley, C.: Bioinspired navigation based on distributed sensing in the leech. In: Proceedings of Living Machines, pp. 275–287 (2020)
22. Derosa, Y.S., Friesen, W.O.: Morphology of leech sensila: observations with the scanning electron microscope. Biol. Bull. **160**, 383–393 (1981)
23. Amari, S.: Dynamics of pattern formation in lateral-inhibition type neural fields. Biol. Cybern. **27**, 77–87 (1977)
24. Nichols, S.: Bioinspired Navigation Based on Distributed Sensing in the Leech Using Dynamic Neural Fields. Senior Honors Thesis, University of North Carolina, Chapel Hill. https://doi.org/10.17615/6yz9-6d68
25. Haberman, R.: Applied Partial Differential Equations: with Fourier Series and Bounary Value Problems. Prentice Hall, New Jersey (2004)
26. Plawsky, J.L.: Transport Phenomena Fundamentals. Taylor and Francis (2001)
27. Dingemans, M.W.: Water Wave Propagation Over Uneven Bottoms: Linear Wave Propagation (Vol 13). World Scientific (1997)
28. Craik, A.D.D.: Wave Interactions and Fluid Flows. Cambridge University Press (1988)
29. Piephoff, F., Taylor, B.K., Kehl, C.E., Mota, B., Harley, C.M.: Biomechanics of transduction by mechanosensory cilia for prey detection in aquatic organisms. J. Theor. Biol. **583**, 111782 (2024)
30. Izhikevich, E.M.: Dynamical Systems in Neuroscience. MIT Press (2010)
31. Lehmkuhl, A.M., Muthusamy, A., Wagenaar, D.A.: Responses to mechanically and visually cued water waves in the nervous system of the medicinal leech. J. Exp. Biol. **221**(4), jeb171728 (2018)
32. Webb, B.: Robots with insect brains. Science **368**(6488), 244–245 (2020)
33. Nichols, S., Havens, L., Taylor, B.: Sensation to navigation: a computational neuroscience approach to magnetic field navigation. J. Comp. Physiol. A **208**(1), 167–176 (2022)

A Comparative Study of Reinforcement Learning and Insect-Inspired Visual Navigation Methods

Xiaoting Zhong[1,2]([⊠]), Xuelong Sun[1,2], and Haiyang Li[1,2]

[1] School of Mathematics and Information Science, Guangzhou University,
Guangzhou, China
2394781676@qq.com, xsun@gzhu.edu.cn
[2] Machine Life and Intelligence Research Centre, Guangzhou University,
Guangzhou, China

Abstract. Navigation capability is crucial for the functionality of living machines across various domains. Recently, two types of approaches have been pursued to address navigation tasks: reinforcement learning (RL) based methods and insect-inspired approaches focusing on insect navigation expertise. Recent advancements in insect navigation studies have provided valuable insights, inspiring the development of efficient navigation solutions. In this study, we present a systematic comparison between RL and insect-inspired visual navigation methods in solving identical navigation tasks. Our findings, for the first time, demonstrate that insect-inspired methods exhibit superior cost-efficiency. These methods require significantly less computational resources and storage while achieving performance levels comparable to state-of-the-art RL techniques. This comparative analysis underscores the remarkable potential of insect-inspired models in navigation tasks, highlighting their exceptional cost-effectiveness. Such findings not only advance our understanding of navigation strategies but also emphasize the viability of insect-inspired approaches in engineering living machines.

Keywords: Reinforcement learning · Proximal policy optimization · Long short-term memory · Mushroom body · Insect-inspired · Insect visual navigation

1 Introduction

Navigation plays a pivotal role in the functionality of living machines across a spectrum of applications, from autonomous vehicles to mobile robots. Over the years, reinforcement learning (RL) based methods [5,27] have emerged as a popular approach to address navigation tasks, leveraging iterative learning techniques to optimize navigation policies [25,28]. Sax et al., 2018 efficiently performs

Application Demonstration and Industrialization of Reconfigurable Digital Intelligent Control Technology for Flexible Platforms (Grant No.CXTD2020001); National Natural Science Foundation of China under the Grant No.62206066.

N. S. Szczecinski et al. (Eds.): Living Machines 2024, LNAI 14930, pp. 163–175, 2025.
https://doi.org/10.1007/978-3-031-72597-5_12

visual navigation tasks using the proximal policy optimization (PPO) algorithm of RL and learning policies based on visual biases [17]. An actor-critic model was proposed by [32], in which the policy function setting was related to the goal and the current state in order to make a better generalization to new goals, but the model lacked memory storage and was difficult to adapt to more complex environments. Mirowski et al., 2016 constructed a stacked LSTM framework that trained a goal-driven reinforcement learning problem jointly with an assisted deep prediction and closed-loop classification task using raw sensory information as input, and successfully solved the dynamic goal problem in 3D mazes [14]. Mnih et al., 2016 proposed an asynchronous RL method with combined Actor-Critic and LSTM [6,7,9] networks, which has been successful in various continuous motion control problems as well as 3D maze navigation [15]. However, RL methods often entail substantial computational demands and struggle with generalization across diverse environments.

In contrast to RL, insect-inspired navigation approaches draw inspiration from the remarkable navigation abilities exhibited by insects [2,3]. Notably, insect-inspired models, particularly those based on the neuroinsectlogical architecture of Mushroom Bodies (MBs) [1,22] and Central Complex [20,21], offer promising avenues for efficient navigation. These models capitalize on the remarkable efficiency and adaptability of insect navigation strategies, offering a cost-effective alternative to RL methods.

Despite the advancements in both RL and insect-inspired navigation models, a systematic and quantitative comparison of their performance and cost-efficiency remains conspicuously absent. To bridge this gap and given the fact that vision stands out as a fundamental sense for navigation [31], we defined a purely vision-based navigation task and employ RL and insect-inspired methods to solve it. Upon trial and error, PPO was found to have better performance in handling visual navigation tasks, so we initially utilize PPO [18] as the RL method, supplemented with Long Short-Term Memory (LSTM, [16]) networks to enhance performance. Concurrently, we implement an MB-based visual homing model [19,22] as the insect-inspired navigation approach.

To evaluate the efficacy of these navigation models, we subject them to three distinct settings: fixed start position and heading, fixed start position with random heading, and random start position and heading. Remarkably, our results reveal that the insect-inspired model consistently outperforms the RL approach to a larger extent when the highest degree of generalization is required. This comparative analysis sheds light on the strengths and limitations of RL and insect-inspired navigation models, emphasizing the potential of insect-inspired strategies as cost-effective alternatives in navigation tasks [4,12,29].

2 Methods and Materials

2.1 Navigation Environment and Task

The simulated 3D environment employed in this study mirrors that of prior works [19,22]. Comprising randomly generated shrubs, trees, and tussocks, this world

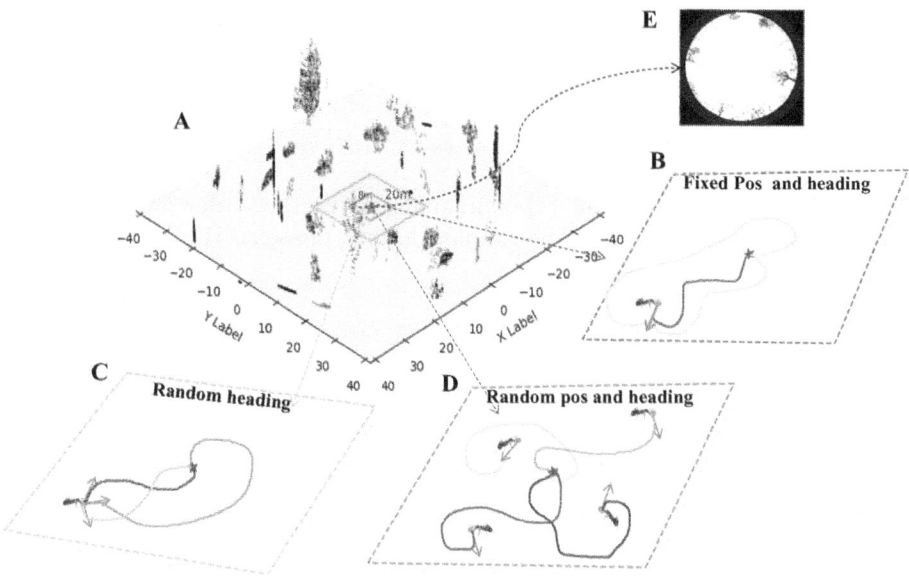

Fig. 1. Simulated 3D World and navigation tasks. (A) The simulated 3D world with visible objects, A square of 8 m serves as the bounded area for navigation. (B–D) Three visual navigation tasks implemented in an 8 m × 8 m empty space with different start conditions.The ant's position is the starting position,and the center pentagram is the end.The test routes are sample trajectories with different headings.(E) Example of a reconstructed image view perceived by the agent at position [0, 0] with heading direction of 0°.

serves as the visual backdrop for navigation tasks (Fig. 1A). In this environment, the navigation task requires the agent to start from an arbitrary position (start point) with an arbitrary heading direction and navigate to a predefined destination (typically located at $[x = 0, y = 0]$ in our experiments) solely depend on visual input.

2.2   Image Reconstruction and Pre-processing

The visual input of the agent at a particular position (x, y) with a particular heading direction α is reconstructed at 1 cm from the ground with a field of view of 360° horizontally and 105° vertically (centred on the horizon), with a resolution of 1 degree/pixel, generating a 360 × 105 pixel panoramic image. Following suit with previous modeling studies [19,22], we extracted rotational-invariant features from the reconstructed panoramic views using Zernike Moments (ZM).The panoramic image is transformed by ZM, generating a 208 × 208 pixel image (Fig. 1E). Zernike Moments are obtained by projecting a function onto orthogonal basis polynomials known as Zernike polynomials [11, 24]. For a given visual image $f(x, y)$, the ZM coefficients can be calculated as follows:

$$Z_{nm}(\rho) = \frac{n+1}{\pi} \sum_x \sum_y f(x, y) V_{nm}^*(\rho, \theta) \tag{1}$$

where $V_{nm}^*(\rho, \theta)$ is orthogonal polynomials, n is the order and m is the repetition($m \in N, |m| \leq n$). The amplitude and phase of the ZM coefficients satisfy :

$$\begin{cases} |Z_{nm}^{\theta_r}| = |Z_{nm} e^{-jm\theta_r}| = |Z_{nm}|, \quad \text{i.e.,} \ A_{nm}^{\theta_r} = A_{nm}, \\ \Phi_{nm}^{\theta_r} = \Phi_{nm} - m\theta_r \end{cases} \tag{2}$$

Clearly, the amplitude $A = |Z|$ remains invariant for the panoramic image viewed with different headings at the same position, while the phase Φ_{nm} varies.

2.3   Insect-Inspired Solution: MB Model

The applied MB model closely resembles that in previous studies [19, 22], comprising three main layers: vPNs, KCs, and MBON (see Fig. 2 upper right). Initially, amplitude coefficients A^u are transmitted to the vPNs as activation signals,

$$O_{PN}^u = \begin{cases} A^u, & A^u > 0 \\ 0, & A^u \leq 0 \end{cases} \tag{3}$$

where $u = 1, 2, \ldots, N_{PN}$ and N_{PN} denotes the number of vPNs neurons. Subsequently, a sparse connection matrix M_{PN2KC} between vPNs and KCs facilitates the summation operation:

$$I_{KC}^v = \sum_{u=0}^{N_{PN}} M_{PN2KC}^{vu} O_{PN}^u \tag{4}$$

Here, I_{KC}^v represents the input of KCs, which is processed by an activation function to yield the KC output O_{KC}^u. Similarly, a randomly generated connection matrix $M_{KC2MBON}$ from KCs to MBON computes the output:

$$O_{MBON} = \sum_{u=0}^{N_{KC}} M_{KC2MBON}^u O_{KC}^u \tag{5}$$

Upon activation of the reward signal (Fig. 2), the network is trained to update the connection matrix between KCs and MBON using the learning rate $\alpha_{KC2MBON}$:

$$M_{KC2MBON}^{u,t} = M_{KC2MBON}^{u,t-1} - \alpha_{KC2MBON} \quad \text{if } O_{KC}^{u,t-1} = 1 \tag{6}$$

Note that O_{MBON} (MBON) signifies the novelty of the current vision to the environment, with larger values indicating greater novelty with the current vision.

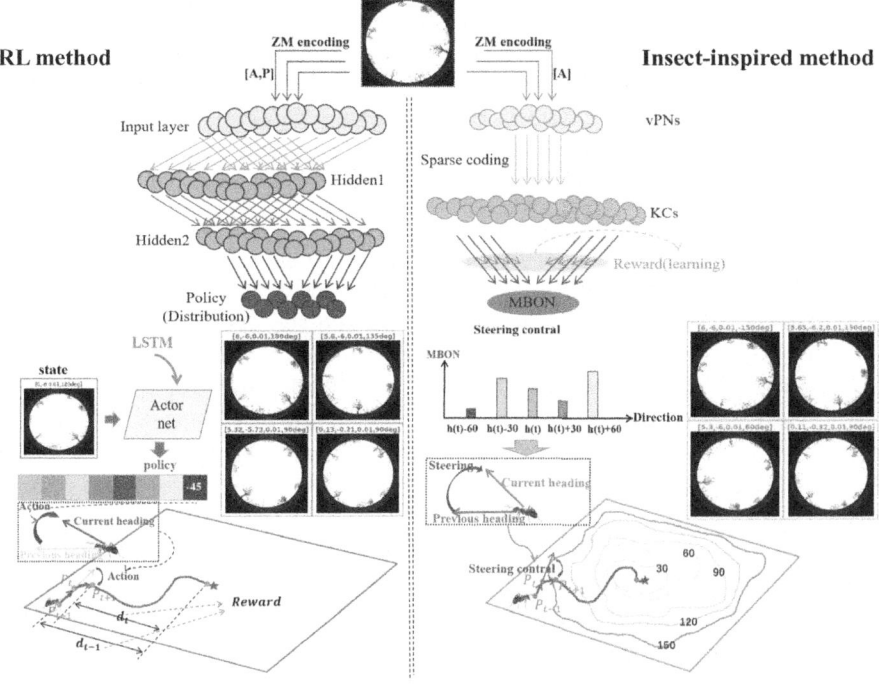

Fig. 2. Reinforcement learning and insect-inspired methods for solving the navigation task. *Left, RL:* The upper half depicts the structure of the policy network (Actor net). The lower section shows the navigation zone, with the red pentagram denoting the home (target). P_t represents the agent's position at time t, and d_t indicates the Euclidean distance from home at time t. The reconstructed view from four positions along the navigating route is shown above the empty space. The left portion illustrates the agent's steering control. The colored rectangles at the bottom of the network represent the probability distribution of discrete actions, with darker colors indicating higher probability values. *Right, Insect-inspired:* The upper half presents a schematic of the mushroom body (MB)-based visual homing network structure of the insect-inspired model. The lower half displays a schematic diagram of the agent navigating in the environment driven by the insect-inspired model, with the size matching that of the left depiction. Note that the steering control here is obtained by predicting the degree of directional novelty obtained by taking a step forward from the five directions of the current heading, $\pm 30°$ and $\pm 60°$, then by selecting the minimum direction of novelty as the next heading.

To utilize MBON more effectively during testing, this study employs multi-directional MBON comparison to select the heading instead of steering control [22]. Predictions of the novelty output are made for the current heading, as well as the left and right $30°$ and $60°$ directions, with the direction exhibiting the smallest novelty chosen as the next heading (Bottom right of Fig. 2).

For model training, home memory was established by sampling 25 locations near the home (all facing home), which were trained as inputs to the model to derive a gradient distribution with home as the lowest point of the visual gradient (Bottom right of Fig. 2).

2.4   Reinforcement Learning Solution: PPO and LSTM

PPO Model. The Proximal Policy Optimization (PPO) algorithm stands out as one of the most robust algorithms in RL, offering a model-free, on-policy, actor-critic, policy-based approach [10]. In this study, the PPO model is constructed based on the RL-PPO algorithm to tackle the insect visual navigation task within an unknown environment. Considering the visual navigation task, the PPO model defines states, actions, and rewards as follows.

State Setting: The current state x_t comprises the amplitude and phase of the current visual image:

$$x_t = [A, P] \tag{7}$$

Action Setting: The action set includes eight possible turns. The Actor network outputs the probability distribution of actions and samples the action accordingly (Bottom left of Fig. 2).

Reward Setting:

$$r = \begin{cases} 0, & \text{initial} \\ 20, & \text{homing} \\ 4[d(P_{t-1}, N) - d(P_t, N)], & \text{others} \end{cases} \tag{8}$$

Here, d represents the euclidean distance function, N denotes the position of home, and P_t is the agent's position at moment t. The network utilized for the PPO model is the Actor-Critic network.

Actor-Critic Network: In PPO, the Actor-Critic network [23] is a common deep reinforcement learning model for learning policies in the environment. The Critic network is responsible for evaluating the value function of the state:

$$Adv_t = r_{t+1} + \gamma V_\phi(x_{t+1}) - V_\phi(x_t) \tag{9}$$

$$F(\phi) = E_t[(Adv_t)^2] \tag{10}$$

The Critic network enables the predicted value to be approached to the true value by minimizing $F(\phi)$. Where Adv is Advantage function, ϕ is Critic network's parameters, $V_\phi(x_t)$ is the state prediction value. The Actor is responsible for learning the policy:

$$L(\theta) = E_t[\min\{Adv_t \cdot r_t(\theta), Adv_t \cdot Clip(r_t(\theta), 1 - \epsilon, 1 + \epsilon)\}] \tag{11}$$

$$r_t(\theta) = \frac{\pi_\theta}{\pi_{\theta_{old}}} \tag{12}$$

The Actor network by maximizing the objective function $L(\theta)$ enabled to learn better policies. where $'Clip'$ is clipping function, θ is Actor network's parameters, π_θ is the probability distribution of actions.

PPO-LSTM Model. To preserve and extract the memory, a hidden layer LSTM network is inserted between the hidden layers of the actor-critic network(as shown in the bottom left of Fig. 2). LSTM network has three neural layers which are forget gate, input gate and output gate. First, the forget gate determines how many hidden state cells C_{t-1}(memory) are discarded at the time step t:

$$f_t = \sigma(W_f \cdot [x_t, h_{t-1}] + b_f) \tag{13}$$

where b_f and W_f are the offset and input weight of forget gate f_t, x_t is the input of the LSTM as well as the output of Hidden1 at t, h_{t-1} indicates the output of LSTM at t-1, σ indicates the sigmoid activation function. Next, the input gate determines how much valid information to extract at the t and to filter this information:

$$I_t = \sigma(W_i \cdot [x_t, h_{t-1}] + b_i) \tag{14}$$

$$C'_t = tanh(W_c \cdot [x_t, h_{t-1}] + b_c) \tag{15}$$

$$C_t = f_t \cdot C_{t-1} + I_t \cdot C'_t \tag{16}$$

where C'_t represents candidate cell state (ensure gradient stability). After updating the cell state at moment t, the neural layer that calculates the output value through the output gate:

$$h_t = \sigma(W_o \cdot [x_t, h_{t-1}] + b_o) \cdot tanh(C_t) \tag{17}$$

Then h(t) as input to Hidden2. All other network connectivity calculations (e.g., input layer to Hidden1, Hidden2 to output layer) are in fully connected form, and the activation function is uniformly tanh.

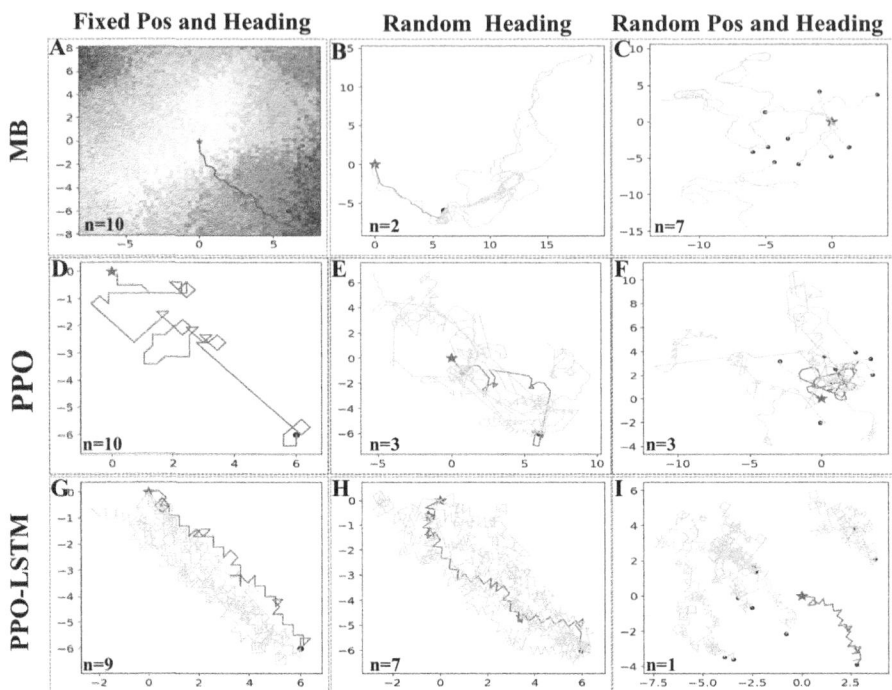

Fig. 3. Navigation trajectories of agents guided by different models under various start position and heading settings. The black dot indicates the initial position, while the red pentagram marks the home position. In the very top-left figure, the blue background illustrates the visual familiarity gradient generated from the MB model's output, where lighter shades indicate higher levels of familiarity. n denotes the success (arrive the nest/target) count out of 10 trials (Color figure online).

3   Results

3.1   Evaluating Model Performances

To gain deeper insights into the performance of the insect-inspired and RL models, we devised three navigation tasks varying in randomness: fixed position and heading, random heading, and random position and heading (Fig. 1B–D). Additionally, we gathered 10 trajectories for each model across these tasks to provide an intuitive observation of the agent's behavior within the environment (Fig. 3).

For a more quantitative assessment of the models' performances, we subjected each model to continuous testing with 100 trails. Subsequently, we collected and computed the returns achieved by each model over the navigating period (Fig. 4B–D).

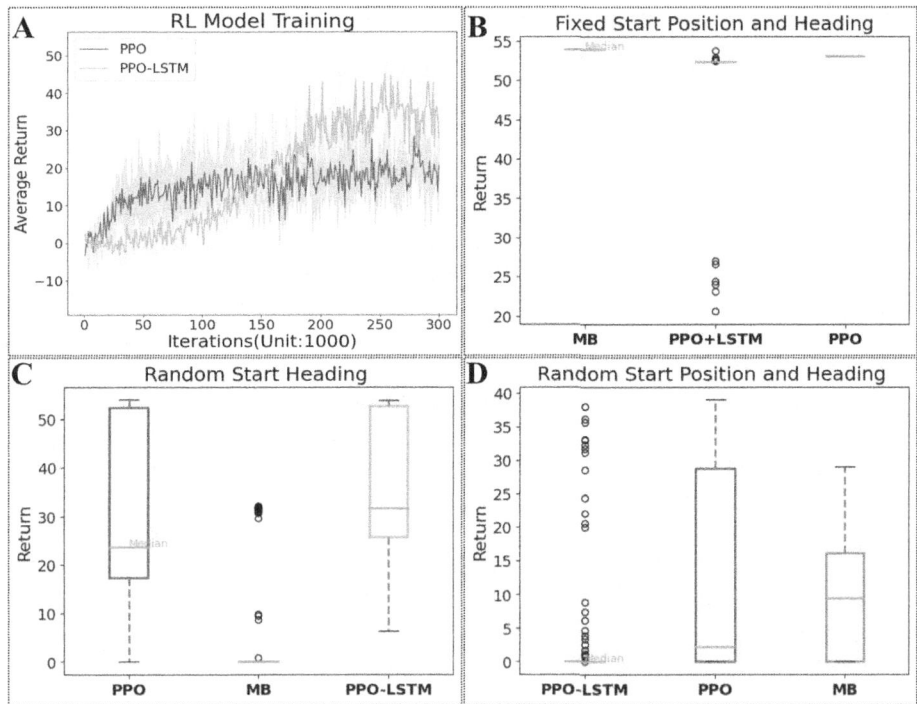

Fig. 4. Model Performance. (A) Convergence plot of average return for RL model training. The average return is calculated as the mean value from the returns of agents navigating three trajectories, with evaluations conducted every 1000 steps. (B–D) Return distributions for 100 tests under the test conditions of fixed position and heading, fixed position with random heading, and random position and heading.

Fixed Start Position and Heading. Under this condition, all three models exhibited a high success rate, with the PPO-LSTM model achieving shorter routes (Fig. 3).

The PPO and MB model trajectories remain unchanged after selecting a fixed heading, with the MB model reaching the destination more efficiently. Conversely, the PPO models, lacking trajectory adjustments, may not find the shortest route but consistently reach the target. Unlike others, the PPO-LSTM model is more flexible in trajectory adjustment, which leads to the result that it reaches the destination efficiently. In 100 tests, the returns of all models are close to perfect (Fig. 4B). Note that the reward setting in the RL model not only encourages forward movement and a certain amount of exploration, which gives better training results. However, it also makes it possible to get higher rewards for detours. To be fair, the same rewards are set for all models, and the inconsistency between the corresponding cumulative rewards and trajectory lengths in Fig 4B is due to the RL reward settings.

Fixed Start Position with Random Start Heading. As the task's difficulty increased, the success rates of the models decreased. The MB model's performance relies on visual gradient stability, affected by visual information, noise, and environmental complexity (Fig. 3). Trajectories of the PPO model (Fig. 3) often converge near home but not to it, suggesting better navigation but insufficient policy training. Introducing LSTM improved the PPO-LSTM model's exploration and success rates (Fig. 3). It is worth noting that the MB model is trained to be obtained with regularly distributed data near the target location, so facing tests with random headings at fixed positions places greater limitations on the model. In contrast, the RL model is trained under this condition and thus has relatively high returns(Fig. 4C).

Random Start Position and Heading. Under increased randomness, the MB model benefited from its training on diverse visual gradient distributions, improving performance (Fig. 3). We have tried training the PPO-LSTM model in this condition, but the results are difficult to converge. Therefore, the limitation of the training condition makes the trajectories of the PPO-LSTM in this condition consistent at different initial positions (Fig. 3), indicating its limited exploration ability Comparing performances, the MB model demonstrated superior generalization (Fig. 4D), suggesting its advantageous position in this navigation task.

3.2   Evaluating the Cost Computation Resources

The RL models used for testing were trained for 30,000 iterations under random heading, which helped to improve the generalization ability of the model (Fig. 4A). The PPO-LSTM model exhibited stronger learning ability, indicating that processing memorized information is crucial for solving navigation tasks. However, despite achieving better learning results, the PPO-LSTM model showed inefficient training efficiency (Table 1). The high number of parameters in the RL method led to significant time costs for effective policy learning. In contrast, while the RL method does not require additional training data, it suffers from inefficient training, high time costs, and large storage requirements, making it impractical for real-world applications.

The above RL models used for testing were all obtained after 30,000 iterations under random heading(Fig 4A). It shows that the PPO-LSTM model has stronger learning ability, which suggests that the processing of memorized information is one of the key factors in solving the navigation task. Although the PPO-LSTM model achieved better learning results, it had an inefficient training efficiency (Table 1). The high number of navigation model parameters in the RL method means that the RL model needs to spend a lot of time cost to learn an effective policy. Compared with the insect-inspired method, RL method suffers from inefficient training, high time cost, and large storage requirement, which makes it inconvenient for practical application.

Combining test and train results, the insect-inspired model not only achieves comparable behavioral performance to the RL model with efficient training but

Table 1. Model Training Information

Model	Parameter	Training time
PPO	147409	20.5 h
PPO-LSTM	306057	31.3 h
MB	48081	0.38 s

* The training was conducted on an Intel i5-10500 CPU @ 3.10 GHz with 16 GB RAM on a 64-bit Windows 11 system

also exhibits stronger generalization. This superiority suggests its potential for development in complex tasks like visual navigation. In contrast, the RL approach appears more limited; without the introduction of the LSTM network, it struggles to improve strategy behavior. However, when LSTM is introduced, training fails to converge under tasks with high generalization requirements,while the model may learn noise and details during training, leading to overfitting behaviors that disregard general patterns or regularities in the data.

4   Conclusion and Discussion

This study presents a comparison between reinforcement learning (RL) and insect-inspired visual navigation methods, aiming to evaluate their performance and cost-efficiency in solving identical navigation tasks. Through rigorous experimentation and analysis, we demonstrate that the insect-inspired navigation model, particularly based on Mushroom Bodies (MBs), outperforms RL-based approaches in various navigation settings. Notably, the insect-inspired model makes the model present superior performance in highly generalized scenarios with less training data. Conversely, the RL model, which requires a large amount of data to be acquired for training through interactions, fails to converge in the face of highly generalized training, and only performs well under less generalized tasks. Navigating in unstructured environments with limited visual features, akin to those encountered by insects [26,30], poses a significant challenge for living machines. Our findings indicate that current RL-based models are not as effective as the solutions evolved by insects for such tasks. This underscores the importance of appropriate information encoding and integration mechanisms tailored to specific navigation objectives. Learning from nature offers invaluable insights and strategies for overcoming complex navigational obstacles encountered by living machines [4,12,13].

Moreover, the potential for integrating insect-inspired neural mechanisms with RL principles emerges as a promising avenue for future research. By combining the navigational capabilities encoded in insect neural architectures [8,26] with the adaptive learning mechanisms of RL, it may be possible to develop more robust and efficient solutions for autonomous navigation [29]. Such an integrative approach holds the promise of leveraging the advantages of both paradigms, ultimately leading to enhanced navigation performance and adaptability in diverse environmental conditions.

References

1. Ardin, P., Peng, F., Mangan, M., Lagogiannis, K., Webb, B.: Using an insect mushroom body circuit to encode route memory in complex natural environments. PLoS Comput. Biol. **12**(2), e1004683 (2016)
2. Bing, Z., Nitschke, D., Zhuang, G., Huang, K., Knoll, A.: Towards cognitive navigation: a biologically inspired calibration mechanism for the head direction cell network. J. Autom. Intell. **2**(1), 31–41 (2023)
3. Clement, L., Schwarz, S., Wystrach, A.: An intrinsic oscillator underlies visual navigation in ants. Curr. Biol. **33**(3), 411–422 (2023)
4. De Croon, G.C.H.E., Dupeyroux, J.J.G., Fuller, S.B., Marshall, J.A.R.: Insect-inspired AI for autonomous robots. Sci. Robot. **7**(67), eabl6334 (2022)
5. Ernst, D., Louette, A.: Introduction to Reinforcement Learning (2024)
6. Gers, F.A., Schmidhuber, J., Cummins, F.: Learning to forget: continual prediction with LSTM. Neural Comput. **12**(10), 2451–2471 (2000)
7. Graves, A., Graves, A.: Long Short-Term Memory. Supervised Sequence Labelling with Recurrent Neural Networks, pp. 37–45 (2012)
8. Heinze, S.: Unraveling the neural basis of insect navigation. Curr. Opin. Insect Sci. **24**, 58–67 (2017)
9. Hochreiter, S., Schmidhuber, J.: Long short-term memory. Neural Comput. **9**(8), 1735–1780 (1997)
10. Jiawei, X., Xufang, Z., Zhong, L., Qingtao, X.: Lstm-dppo based deep reinforcement learning controller for path following optimization of unmanned surface vehicle. J. Syst. Eng. Electron. **34**, 1343–1358 (2023). https://doi.org/10.23919/JSEE.2023.000113
11. Khotanzad, A., Hong, Y.H.: Invariant image recognition by Zernike moments. IEEE Trans. Pattern Anal. Mach. Intell. **12**(5), 489–497 (1990)
12. Manoonpong, P., et al.: Insect-inspired robots: bridging biological and artificial systems. Sensors **21**(22), 7609 (2021)
13. Matsiko, A.: Taking inspiration from nature is a no-brainer. Sci. Robot. **8**(78), eadi2720 (2023)
14. Mirowski, P., et al.: Learning to Navigate in Complex Environments (2016). arXiv preprint: arXiv:1611.03673
15. Mnih, V., et al.: Asynchronous methods for deep reinforcement learning. In: International conference on machine learning, pp. 1928–1937. PMLR (2016)
16. Piao, C., Liu, C.H.: Energy-efficient mobile crowdsensing by unmanned vehicles: a sequential deep reinforcement learning approach. IEEE Internet Things J. **7**(7), 6312–6324 (2019)
17. Sax, A., Emi, B., Zamir, A.R., Guibas, L., Savarese, S., Malik, J.: Mid-Level Visual Representations Improve Generalization and Sample Efficiency for Learning Visuomotor Policies (2018). arXiv preprint: arXiv:1812.11971
18. Schulman, J., Wolski, F., Dhariwal, P., Radford, A., Klimov, O.: Proximal Policy Optimization Algorithms (2017). arXiv preprint: arXiv:1707.06347
19. Stone, T., Mangan, M., Wystrach, A., Webb, B.: Rotation invariant visual processing for spatial memory in insects. Interface focus **8**(4), 20180010 (2018)

20. Stone, T., et al.: An anatomically constrained model for path integration in the bee brain. Curr. Biol. **27**(20), 3069–3085 (2017)
21. Sun, X., Fu, Q., Peng, J., Yue, S.: An insect-inspired model facilitating autonomous navigation by incorporating goal approaching and collision avoidance. Neural Netw. **165**, 106–118 (2023)
22. Sun, X., Yue, S., Mangan, M.: A decentralised neural model explaining optimal integration of navigational strategies in insects. Elife **9**, e54026 (2020)
23. Sutton, R.S., McAllester, D., Singh, S., Mansour, Y.: Policy gradient methods for reinforcement learning with function approximation. Adv. Neural Inf. Process. Syst. **12**, (1999)
24. Teague, M.R.: Image analysis via the general theory of moments. JOSA **70**(8), 920–930 (1980)
25. Wang, X., Xiong, W., Wang, H., Wang, W.Y.: Look before you leap: bridging model-free and model-based reinforcement learning for planned-ahead vision-and-language navigation. In: Proceedings of the European Conference on Computer Vision (ECCV), pp. 37–53 (2018)
26. Webb, B., Wystrach, A.: Neural mechanisms of insect navigation. Curr. Opin. Insect Sci. **15**, 27–39 (2016)
27. Wiering, M.A., Van Otterlo, M.: Reinforcement learning. Adapt. Learn. Optim. **12**(3), 729 (2012)
28. Wijmans, E., et al.: Dd-ppo: Learning Near-Perfect Pointgoal Navigators from 2.5 Billion Frames (2019). arXiv preprint arXiv:1911.00357
29. Wystrach, A.: Movements, embodiment and the emergence of decisions. Insights from insect navigation. Biochem. Biophys. Res. Commun. **564**, 70–77 (2021)
30. Young, F.J., et al.: Enhanced long-term memory and increased mushroom body plasticity in heliconius butterflies. Iscience **27**(2), (2024)
31. Zeng, F., Wang, C., Ge, S.S.: A survey on visual navigation for artificial agents with deep reinforcement learning. IEEE Access **8**, 135426–135442 (2020)
32. Zhu, Y., Mottaghi, R., Kolve, E., Lim, J.J., Gupta, A., Fei-Fei, L., Farhadi, A.: Target-driven visual navigation in indoor scenes using deep reinforcement learning. In: 2017 IEEE International Conference on Robotics and Automation (ICRA), pp. 3357–3364. IEEE (2017)

Control and Mechanics of Soft and Continuum Systems

Erodium Awn's Water Transport Insights for Controlled Swelling Agent Rearrangement in Anisotropic Structures

Yauheni Sarokin$^{(\boxtimes)}$ (ID), Alvo Aabloo (ID), and Indrek Must (ID)

University of Tartu, 50411 Tartu, Estonia
{yauheni,alvo.aabloo,indrek.must}@ut.ee

Abstract. Naturally evolved plant hygroactuation mechanism involves an opti-mised capillary system for fast liquid distribution in a swellable cellulose fibrous anisotropic structure, which is a source of inspiration for the design of efficient hydromorphs. In particular, the relative contributions, mobility, and transition kinetics of free water contained within the capillaries and water bound to the cellular walls are crucial optimisation parameters in engineering systems based on controlled internal swelling agent dislocation. We introduce a methodology to detect free water accumulated in the centre of the awn based on internal light scattering. Free liquid transfered across the awn half-thickness (32 μm) in 24 s, evidenced by decreased light scattering. Optical scattering data was compared to swelling kinetics, expressed as awn (un)coiling, that primarily associates with bound water. After stopping the water influx, the awn proceeded uncoiling for approximately 12 s due to highly mobile free water still reservoired in the cap-illary structure. The insight into internal water rearrangement kinetics in awns allows the design of more efficient anisotropic robotic systems that actuate and change stiffness by combining internal liquid displacement and liquid exchange with the environment.

Keywords: *Erodium* awn · Hygroscopic actuation · Swelling

1 Introduction

Understanding the mechanism and associated kinetics of liquid displacement within plants is crucial for comprehending various physiological processes. The ascent of water from the roots through the xylem to the leaves showcases a remarkable natural process driven by capillary action, root pressure, and the transpiration pull mechanism [1]. For instance, turgor pressure, which results from the osmotic flow of water into cells, provides the necessary force for cell expansion and plant growth. This osmotic mechanism allows for the stiffening of plant tissues, which is vital for the plant's structural integrity and upright posture [2].

In contrast, while the role of water and associated mechanisms in dead plant tissues, particularly in structural components like xylem vessels, has received less attention, it is a natural source of insights, inspiring engineering the hygroscopically driven systems.

© The Author(s), under exclusive license to Springer Nature Switzerland AG 2025
N. S. Szczecinski et al. (Eds.): Living Machines 2024, LNAI 14930, pp. 179–192, 2025.
https://doi.org/10.1007/978-3-031-72597-5_13

The movements of plants due to water content alternation, such as *Erodium cicutarium* awn, stem from volumetric alterations attributed to the hygroscopic characteristics of materials within them, i.e., the plant cell walls, a complex ordered structure composed of cellulose, hemicellulose, proteins, and other compounds [3, 4].

Water, in non-living plant tissues, exists in two states: free and bound water. Free water in dead plant tissues is the bulk water found within the vascular system, including the xylem and phloem, and within the intercellular spaces [5]. This water is not chemically bound to macromolecules and can move freely within the plant. Bound water, on the other hand, is molecularly associated with macromolecules, such as polysaccharides, within cell walls [6]. This water is bound within macromolecular structures, limiting its mobility. Water in its bound state within plant tissues is necessary for actuation and stiffening mechanisms [2, 7].

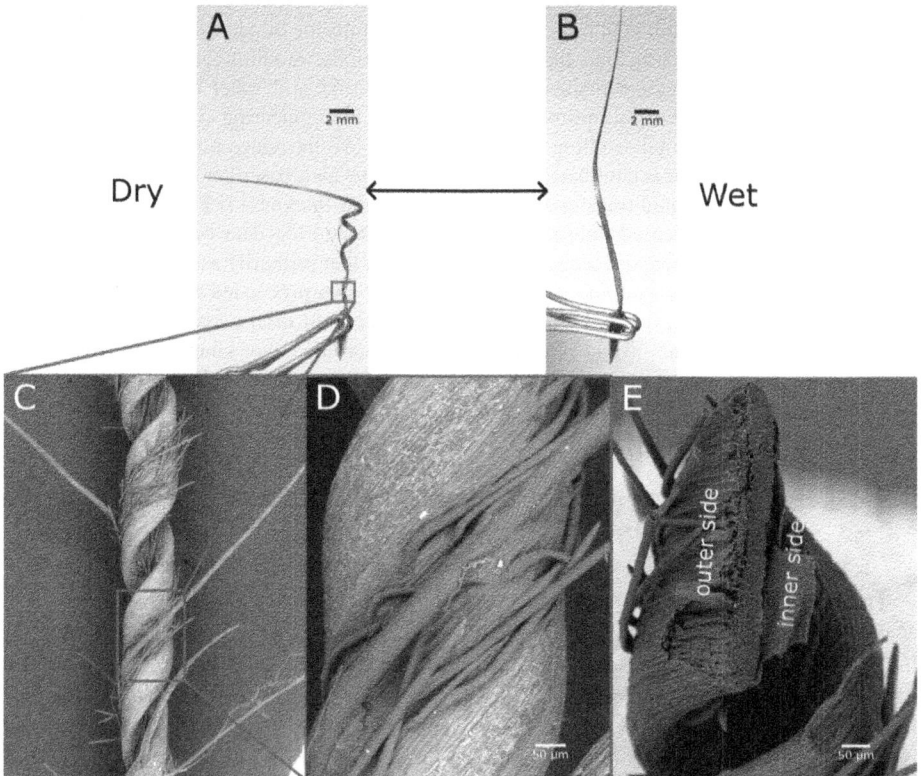

Fig. 1. Erodium *cicutarium* awn. Optical photographs of the (A) fully coiled dry and (B) fully uncoiled wet awn. (C, D) SEM micrographs of the coiled awn. (E) SEM micrograph of the cross-section of the awn.

Grasping the interplay between free and bound water within porous hygroscopic structures, such as plant tissues, is necessary for the development of actuators based on internal liquid rearrangement. In our recent study, we explored the impact of pore fill ratio on the kinetics of liquid redistribution within a synthetic swellable porous structure where a constant amount of electrohydrodynamic medium (electrolytic solution) is transferred between electrodes binding to the porous polymeric membrane and forming a swelling gradient [8]. Our findings identified optimal conditions in terms of transient liquid content, highlighting medium pore fill ratios (~30%) in terms of total liquid content, resulting in efficient liquid displacement within the porous structure. Also, in the studied synthetic structure, liquid existed in both bound and free states; however, our methodology enabled us to analyse the dynamics of liquid movement without differentiating between the bound and free liquid. The working principle of this system implies a controlled displacement of constant liquid volume within the porous structure, yet is different from the hygroactuation principle, where the humidity of the atmosphere conditions a transient amount of liquid. Also, the previously developed synthetic structure is isotropic and, therefore, is not optimised for elevated hygroactuation, which does not allow for the direct assessment of bound liquid content from the hygroactuation extent. Natural structures with an anisotropic actuation-optimized structure give insights into understanding the contributions of different binding states and intrastructural transport of water.

The intensity of internally scattered light in porous materials depends on the refractive index mismatch between the porous material and the medium inside its cavities. The higher the refractive index mismatch, the more light is scattered. Considering that the refractive index of any liquid medium is higher than that of air, the intensity of scattered light in a porous medium decreases with liquid content. *Erodium cicutarium* awn (Fig. 1A-B) is an exemplary natural structure for studying the variation in refractive index upon hydration due to its porous structure and the ability to absorb water efficiently. As the free water content increases (the refractive index mismatch between water (1.31) and cellulose (1.56) [9] is lower than between air (1) and cellulose), free water within the lumens of the wood cells alters the light scattering [10, 11]. Bound water, on the other hand, is chemically attached to the wood's cell walls. The light scattering by porous cellulosic structure saturated only with bound water is not expected to differ considerably from the light scattering in dry conditions. While saturation of the wood with bound water changes the refractive index slightly, the mismatch between refractive indexes of the swollen cellulose and of air does not pronouncely vary. Compact wood soaking with water has indicated a negligible effect on light scattering [12]. Optical scattering offers a promising approach for detecting free water content in *Erodium* awn, capitalising on the refractive index mismatch decrease between porous cellulosic structure versus voids upon free water content increase. A corresponding methodology for free water content assessment is presented in this work.

Seed awns have naturally developed a hygroscopic actuation mechanism involving a complex dynamic interplay of hygroscopic material properties and porous structure. In biological structures, hygroactuation involves low strains in complex geometries, making local and absolute strain measurement challenging. *Erodium cicutarium* awns are composed of cellulose fibres arranged in a tilted helical pattern (Fig. 1C-E) [13]. This composition allows for anisotropic expansion and contraction, driven by swelling and deswelling, leading to coiling and uncoiling motions with relative strain amplified geometrically [14]. Free water in the awn's porous cavities moves relatively freely since it is not bound to the cellulose, thus allowing for fast hydration or dehydration (i.e., transition to become bound and released, respectively) [15]. The hygroscopic actuation of *Erodium cicutarium* awns, which uncoil progressively, quickly, and drastically with water absorption, provides a convenient and widely available case study system to gauge the amount of bound water (i.e., hygroactuation gauges bound water); the more water absorbed, the more the awn uncoils [16]. Differentiation between free and bound water promises a better understanding of the water transport kinetics and structural aspects of hygroactuation and interaction with ambient humidity. However, free water detection appears to be more involved than bound. Total water content could be assessed gravimetrically [17], yet at a limited resolution and not applicable in some *in situ* scenarios. Electrical impedance could be complementarily used [8], yet in a biological structure that simultaneously develops strain and the electrolyte concentration varies, e.g. by evaporation, it does not accurately estimate free or total water content. Free water amount would give us more insight into the contribution of water intrastructural transport on strain development. Here, we suggest optical methods for free liquid detection. The optical scattering technique is non-invasive and applicable *in situ* at depths permeable to light. To our knowledge, optical scattering has not been previously used for local strain analysis. By integrating strain difference analysis (by visual observation) and optical scattering, it becomes possible to separately and effectively detect the absolute quantities of bound and free water content in liquid displacement based actuating systems and locally induced strain, offering a comprehensive understanding of its hydration dynamics and associated liquid transport system.

We explored the dynamic interplay between hydration levels and seed awns' mechanical and optical properties. Mounted to an experimental setup and periodically exposed to intensive humidification, the seed awn's body underwent a series of hydration, allowing for the simultaneous determination of scattered light intensity and the extent of hygroactuation during humidification. The increase in the volume of free water occurred linearly and was registered as an abrupt decrease in the intensity of scattered light. The water reaction with cellulose is expressed in an increase in its volume, enabling the quantification of the amount of bound water separately from free water.

2   Methods

2.1   Samples

Erodium cicutarium achenes were collected near Tartu and used without pretreatment.

2.2   Light Scattering Measurements

The location of light scattering measurements was chosen at the concave surface approximately in the middle of the responsive section of the awn (Fig. 2A, 2E). The cut ends of two OM1 optical fibre cables (Fibrmart, SMA5-SMA5-DX-OM1-FM, core diameter: 62.5 μm, cladding diameter: 125 μm) were stripped to cladding by approximately 1 cm. The cables' ends were aligned parallel to each other, with a narrow gap between the claddings of optical fibres. This position was fixed using UV adhesive (QIAO QIAO DIY Hard UV Resin). The resulting assembly was smoothened on fine-grit sandpaper

(Fig. 2D) perpendicularly to the direction of the optical fibres so that a planar surface was formed. One of the optical fibres is connected to a Fabry-Perot Benchtop Laser Source (Thorlabs S1FC660, 660 nm, 2.5 mW, FC/PC). The other optical fibre was connected to a spectrometer (Thorlabs, CCS200). The integration time of the spectrometer was set to 2 s. The laser power was adjusted to 0.1 mW. The change in scattered light intensity over time is defined as the area under the light intensity curve registered by the spectrometer in the 632–669 nm range.

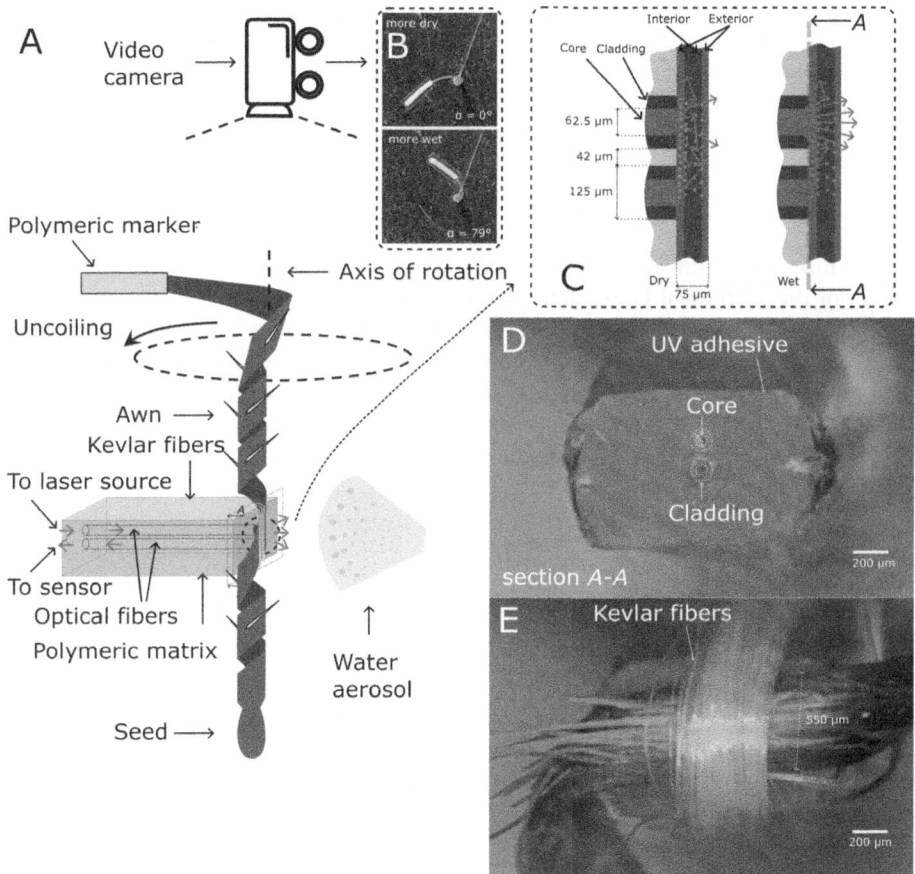

Fig. 2. Setup for simultaneous detection of backscattered light intensity and awn's coiling degree. (A) Schematic of the setup. (B) Representative video frames in two different hydration states, used for the quantification of the rotation angle. The yellow visual marker is shown. (C) Schematic of light scattering in a porous awn's structure in dry (left) and in hydrated state (right). (D) The surface for the awn fixation point with two optical fibres oriented perpendicularly to the surface. (E) The awn fixation using Kevlar fibres.

2.3 Attachment of the Awn

The awn was first fully uncoiled by saturating it with water. The fully uncoiled awn was positioned on the smoothened surface of the optical fibre assembly so that both ends of the optical fibres were in direct contact with the awn's surface. To prevent dislocation upon hygroactuation, the position of the seed awn on the sensor was fixed using Kevlar fibres, as shown in Fig. 2E.

2.4 Humidification

An ultrasonic nebuliser was placed approximately five centimetres from the awn seed to apply water aerosol periodically. The water aerosol was timed using an Arduino UNO development board. The humidity level and temperature in the room where the experiment was conducted were 45% and 23 °C, respectively.

2.5 Hygroactuation Measurement

A PVC tube (0.75 mm diameter, 6.1 mm length) was used as an optical marker at the end of the seed awn. Upon humidification, the *Erodium cicutarium* awn uncurled clockwise (Fig. 2B, supplementary video 1), rotating in a single plane. However, as the awn's capacity to store water approached saturation, the marker's movement transitioned from circular motion to axial rotation. In our experiment, the awn has not been fully saturated with water, and the rotation of the awn was preserved in a single plane. A video camera (iPhone) was positioned orthogonally to the plane of rotation of the awn to detect the optical marker (Fig. 2A-B). During hygroactuation, the angular position of the marker was extracted from video frames using an image recognition module in National Instruments LabVIEW 21 software.

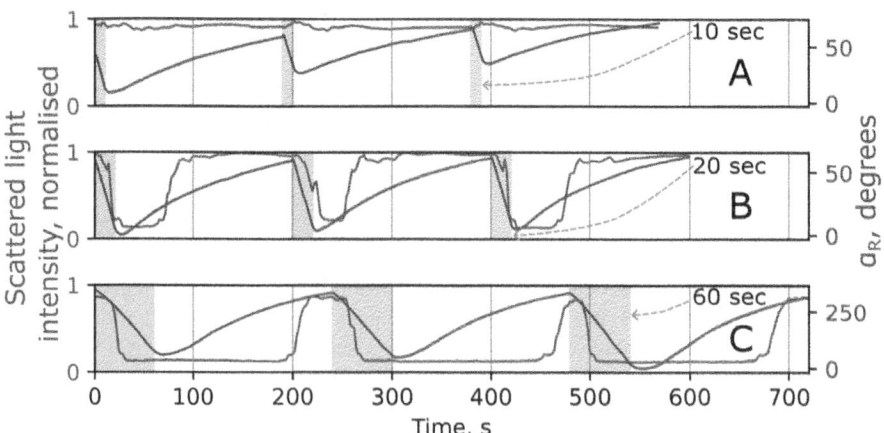

Fig. 3. Typical transient course for scattered light intensity and rotation angle α_R during awn periodically hydrated for in (A) 10 s; (B) 20 s; (C) 60 s. The humidification period is depicted as an orange area.

3 Results and Discussion

3.1 General Observations on Light Scattering in the Awn Structure

Five different humidification periods were selected: 10 (Fig. 3A), 20 (Fig. 3B), 30, 45, and 60 (Fig. 3C) seconds. The uncoiling extent increased with the humidification time, indicating a transient bound water content increase within the structure. After each humidification period, the awn was dried for three minutes. This duration was selected to allow the return to the same state at the onset of each humidification cycle. A 60-s humidification resulted in approximately 300° uncoiling, well confined in a single plane (Fig. 3C). The increased free water content throughout the awn resulted in more matched refractive indexes between water and cellulose and, consequently, lower internal light scattering. The uncoiling response to the humidification of the awn was immediate. After stopping the humidification, no additional water was introduced to the awn; however, the awn continued to uncoil, indicating a continuously increasing bound water content, achievable only by the presence of free water content, which is continuously depleted by both evaporation and swelling (thus becoming bound water).

Light scattering intensity variation did not occur gradually with the change in the amount of free water but abruptly (see Fig. 3A-3C) upon accumulating a particular free water amount threshold in the centre of the awn.

The authors assume that the light path, when passing through a porous structure with liquid content, deviates less from the initial trajectory (Fig. 2C) in comparison to a dry porous structure, where light is mostly scattered. Upon awn's intense humidification, the free liquid content in the awn capillaries increases unevenly throughout the body (from the exterior towards the interior). Thus, a gradient of free water is formed throughout the thickness of the awn, with the highest content of free water outside and the lowest content of free water at the centre of the awn. Correspondingly, a gradient of refractive index mismatch is formed, the lowest where the amount of liquid is the highest. According to our interpretation, since the amount of free liquid in the centre of the awn is the lowest during humidification, the refractive index mismatch is the highest, and light is scattered the most locally. The overall drop in scattered light intensity during humidification is thus expected to be observed as soon as the threshold amount of free liquid is accumulated in the centre of the awn.

To be able to assess the scattering in interior layers, the structure needs to be transmissive enough to the light. We measured the awn of the seed to absorb most of the laser's monochromatic light: the transmittance at the used laser's wavelength (660 nm) through the awn's thickness (75 μm) was approximately 0.061%. However, the low absolute transmittance is not critical for water state analysis, as we are only recording the relative intensities between more and less scattering conditions.

In a uniform media, the whole volume between the light entry and exit would contribute. However, as we hypothesise that in our experiment, the scattering originates from the middle of the structure where the open pores are filled the latest, the scattering method allows for localised measurements, enabling the registration of variations in free liquid without detecting bound water in a few tens of μm resolution. Reaching similar non-invasive resolution with, e.g., impedance tomography would be considerably more difficult.

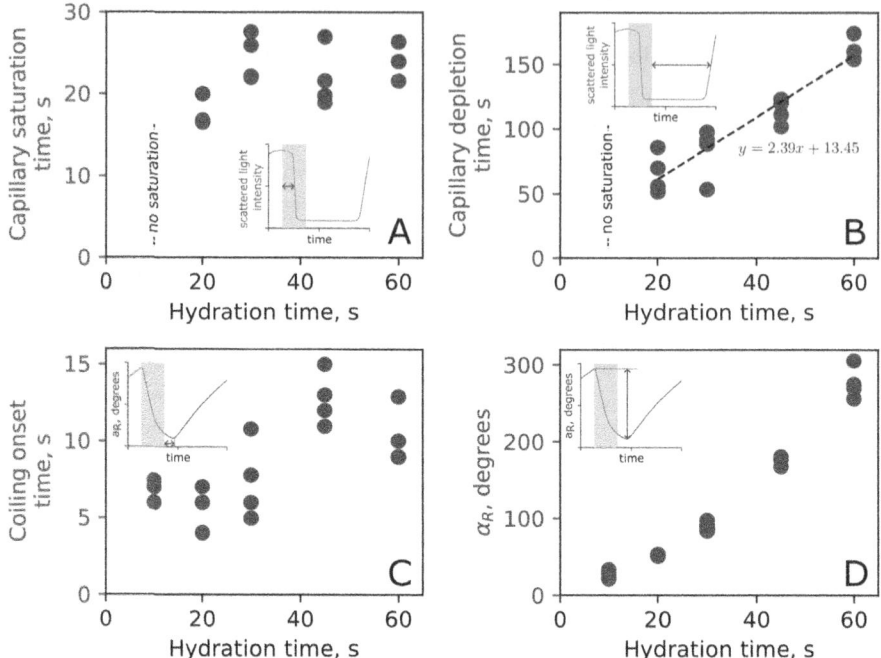

Fig. 4. Responsiveness of the Erodium awn to hydration time. (A) Capillary saturation time (B) Capillary depletion time. (C) Evaporation delay. (D) The angle of rotation α_R. The insets in all panels illustrate the corresponding parameter definitions.

At the site of optical observations, the rate of water variation locally is not expected to be the same as in the rest of the awn. Upon humidification and evaporation, free water is transferred throughout the structure within capillaries and introduced and evaporated from the surface. The water evaporation is hindered locally at the assessment point since one side of the awn is in contact with the experimental assembly, and the other is covered with the kevlar fibres, which predictably reduces water evaporation and free water depletion from the capillaries locally. Consequently, registered scattered light intensity corresponded to free water content in the centre of the awn locally at the observation site, where the kinetics of water depletion are lower with respect to the rest of the awn. This feature is used in further analysis to suggest global and localised water content variation.

3.2 Characteristic Parameters for Liquid Intrastructural Transport

To better understand the mechanism of water accumulation and their proportional relationship, we characterised the system using four parameters: capillary saturation and depletion time, coiling onset time, and swelling extent expressed as angular rotation in relation to hydration time. The capillary saturation time (Fig. 4A) was defined as the interval between the start of humidification and the decrease in scattered light intensity to 50% of its initial value. According to our interpretation, this parameter reflects the kinetics of free water accumulation, indicating that a threshold amount of free water has been accumulated at the centre of the awn, conditioned by the variation in refractive index mismatch in this region. This partially confirms our hypothesis above on the scattering threshold corresponding to the innermost layer. Since the humidification conditions were consistent throughout the experiments, this parameter, approximately 24 s, was not dependent on the hydration time. The ten-second hydration time did not cross the threshold value for free water content - the water introduced in this period was either bound or evaporated. The gap between the awn and the plane surface of the measurement assembly is comparable to the pore size and is immediately exposed to the water upon hydration. The surface water layer is unlikely to have had an effect on scattering measurement, as the surface layer is expected to emerge almost immediately, but the capillary saturation time recorded by scattering is more than 20 s.

Capillary depletion (Fig. 4B) determines the time interval between the end of humidification and the increased scattered light intensity to 50% of its initial value. This parameter is dependent on the humidification time because the amount of free liquid within the awn's interior increased over time, which, in turn, extended the time required for the evaporation of water. This parameter depends on the amount of water accumulated during hydration; therefore, its value is directly proportional to the hydration time, confirmed by linear fitting in Fig. 4B. Linear fitting also showed a close-to-zero intercept value, as expected.

The coiling onset (Fig. 4C) indicates that the awn continued uncoiling because, after humidification cessation, the bound water content was still continuously increasing, and this parameter had a slight dependency on the hydration time because the free water content, although increasing with the hydration time, was quickly depleted due to concurrent evaporation.

The relationship between the rotation angle and hydration time (Fig. 4D) is nonlinear, indicating that the bound water content in the awn does not increase linearly with hydration time but rather exponentially. As the water aerosol reaches the awn's surface, free water rearranges within the awn through capillaries, and the free water transition into the bound state begins. The swelling kinetics of cellulose is higher at the onset of interaction with free water and decreases exponentially with water saturation. However, the amount of free water infiltrating inward consistently increases, continually accelerating the water's transition into the bound state, resulting in the exponential growth of this parameter with humidification time.

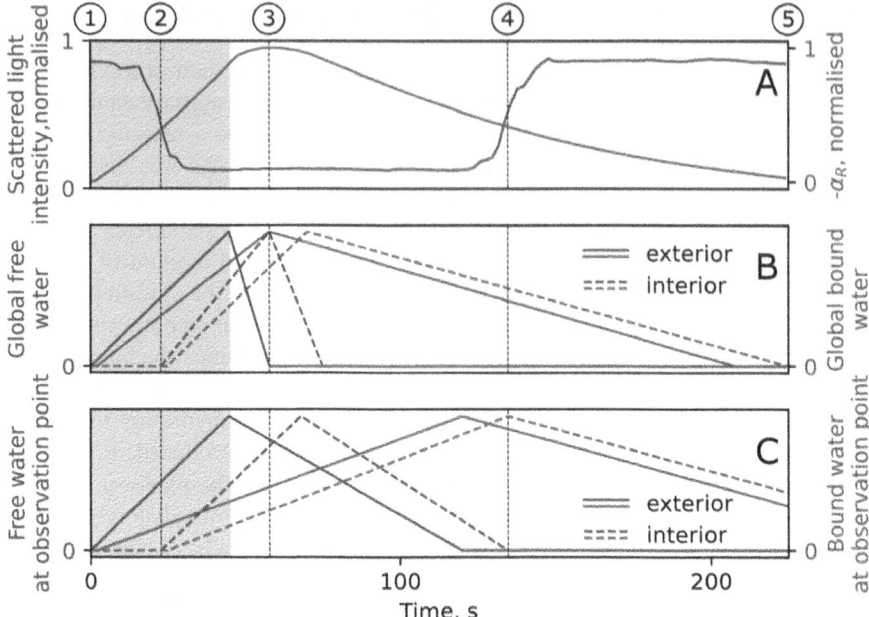

Fig. 5. Proposed sequential water content variation with respect to type and localisation. (A) A typical transient course for scattered light intensity variation versus normalised awn's angular rotation $-\alpha_R$. (B) Predicted variation of the free and bound water content in the awn's interior and exterior of the whole awn during the cycle shown in (A). (C) Predicted variation of the free and bound water content in the awn's interior and exterior locally at the site of optical observation during the cycle shown in (A).

3.3 Free and Bound Water Content Variation

Figure 5A shows a representative variation in scattered light intensity and the normalised extent of the awn's rotation during the experiment, reflecting the variation in the amount of bound and free water, respectively. As mentioned above, the scattered light intensity quickly (almost a binary transition) alters its value, reflecting the accumulation of a certain amount of free water in the centre of the awn. $-\alpha_R$ indicates bound water content as the degree of swelling and is directly proportional to the hygroactuation extent. This parameter is represented as the negative value of α_R, normalised to the maximum value across the experimental data range. As previously discussed, the experimental assembly's direct contact with the awn's surface features hindered water evaporation kinetics, and thus, it differs locally from the rest of the awn. Eventually, the results of the two measurements did not synchronously reflect changes in the ratio of free water to bound water and were also utilised to formulate a hypothesis on the qualitative water composition within the awn during the experiment.

By integrating the findings from two experiments and the thermodynamic principles, we propose a simplified and hypothetical representation of qualitative and quantitative water content variation in the awn as a whole and locally to the observation site. Initially, the seed awn is in a dry state, characterised by an absence of free water and a negligible amount of bound water within its structure. This condition is marked by the awn being fully coiled and the optical sensor registering maximum light intensity due to the high level of light scattering (Fig. 5, time event 1).

Upon introducing water aerosol, non-equilibrium humidification starts. As water aerosol is applied, water begins to bind with cellulose starting from the awn's surface. This initial absorption phase results in the relatively quick bound water content increase in the exterior, leading to uncoiling due to the awn's humidification. Despite the increase in water content, light scattering initially remains high due to the water not yet absorbed by the awn's interior (refractive index mismatch in the centre of the awn is high because threshold free water amount has not been accumulated).

The experiment progresses as intense humidification (Fig. 5, first 45 s) facilitates rapid free water transport through the capillaries, extending the hydration process (bound water increase) from the exterior to the awn's interior, which continues to uncoil in response to the increasing hydration. Correspondingly, there is a noticeable drop in light scattering as the awn's as the free water exceeds the threshold for optical detection (Fig. 5, time event 2).

As the amount of free water content is proportional to the humidification time, and immediately after stopping the directed spraying of water aerosol, the exterior's free water content begins to decline. The awn's maximum free water content has been reached by the end of each humidification phase.

The subsequent dehydration stage introduced a reverse process where the awn began to coil back. Hygroactuation is the result of all swelling and deswelling actions through-out the awn's bulk, and its direction and kinetics depend on which process is prevailing. However, the awn continued to uncoil after the cessation of the humidification phase, indicating ongoing water absorption due to the abundance of free water within the awn. Approximately 12 s after the humidification phase, the awn starts to coil back (Fig. 5, time event 3). The degree of coiling correlated with the total bound water content, sug-gesting that bound water content has reached its maximum value and free water available for absorption was depleted. However, the authors do not attribute the coiling onset to the complete depletion of free water from the awn but instead to the combination of fading swelling in the awn's interior and the ongoing deswelling in the awn's exterior. As the free water content changes gradually from the exterior towards the interior of the awn (decreasing toward the interior upon humidification), the swelling gradient is formed accordingly across the awn's thickness.

The bound water is depleted from the material by evaporation, and therefore, free water is to be depleted beforehand locally. As detected optically, the threshold amount of free water was still present in the centre of the awn after the whole awn was already coiling back. This behaviour is attributed to hindered evaporation at the observation site (Fig. 5 time event 4). As shown in the hypothetical graph in Fig. 5B, the free water content in the awn reaches threshold free water content locally much faster (approximately 60 s) when evaporation is not hindered from one side of the awn. Correspondingly, the kinetics of bound water variation is slowed down at the site of observation (Fig. 5B-C). At the end of the dehydration phase, bound water content becomes depleted from the awn interior (Fig. 5, time event 5). This endpoint reflects the awn's return to its initial condition, completing the cycle of hygroactuation.

The very effective hygroactution is not solely due to hygroscopic properties. The other two key factors responsible for efficient actuation are the anisotropic orientation of cellulose fibres and capillaries. Distribution of the free liquid in this type of actuator is always associated with the swelling gradient formation and features unequal swelling response throughout the swelling medium. Kinetics associated with the liquid free-to-bound transition and morphology of the liquid transport system are the critical parameters for efficient hygroactuating system development.

The optical technique developed in this work is mostly suitable for biological samples, with a particular focus on determining liquid content near the surface (within the optical transparency range, as light intensity fades exponentially with thickness). This technique is sensitive to contributions from external light sources and may provide inaccurate values in non-laboratory conditions. Although the binary response in the scattering experiment is associated to the threshold liquid amount, it should be verified using more sensitive apparatus in the upcoming studies. The current results allow for detecting free water accumulation and depletion, but not its precise amount. Combining this technique with gravimetric measurements will allow for absolute water content determination and, consequently, free-to-bound water proportion. Combined with a controlled internal liquid displacement mechanism, it allows for the production of very efficient and quick hygroscopic anisotropic robotic systems where the operating principle involves the redistribution of a constant amount of swelling agent within the interior, not the absorption of a transient amount of water from the external environment. Our previous work successfully incorporated an actively controlled liquid displacement mechanism based on electrohydrodynamic medium displacement in porous swellable structures and characterised its efficiency [6]. However, the porous structure in this work has yet to be optimised for anisotropic actuation; the pores and polymeric fibres are isotropically oriented throughout the bulk. According to our knowledge, the mechanism of hygroscopic actuation in a porous anisotropically oriented swellable system, similar to *Erodium cicutarium* awn, has yet to be combined with a controlled internal liquid displacement system.

4   Conclusions

To develop an efficient hygromorphic system, understanding the kinetics associated with swelling and liquid displacement is essential. The methodologies developed in this work give insights into the assessment of the amount of liquid, as well as its state and displacement kinetics. The reported methods involve optical detection of the threshold amount of free water accumulated at the centre of the porous cellulosic structure and visual observation of the extent of hygroactuation to track free and bound water state transitions. The naturally occurring hygroactuators based on water exchange with the external environment, such as *Erodium cicutarium* awn, serve as exemplary models for internal liquid rearrangement analysis within the optimally developed hygroscopic anisotropic porous structure. Free and bound water content in the awn was assessed simultaneously during humidification and recovery.

A liquid-saturated porous structure has a lower refractive index mismatch than a dry one. This statement is correct if water is uniformly distributed; in our experiment, humidification creates a liquid gradient across the awn's thickness, causing a varying refractive index mismatch, highest at the awn's centre. Consequently, the scattered light intensity changed abruptly, not gradually, indicating the time for water to transfer from the surface to the centre, thus characterising the efficiency of the capillary transport system. As demonstrated in the experiment, closing the surface pores locally reduces the kinetics of water displacement due to limited access to the surface, where evaporation occurs. Due to the awn's low transparency, most light is scattered and absorbed, allowing for liquid identification in up to tens of μm. The findings of this experiment allow for the kinetics of liquid movement in capillaries to be determined independently of the evaporation process.

The transition of free water to bound water occurs through the chemical bonding of water with polysaccharides and results in a change in the volume of the swelling object. The anisotropic awn structure maximises swelling in one direction, while its helical tilt allows easy determination of hygroactuation extent through the rotation angle of an optical marker and, consequently, the amount of bound water. The awn was observed to continue uncoiling after the cessation of humidification for some time, indicating kinetics associated with the depletion of accumulated water and the capacity of the awn to store water. The free water content has been observed to increase linearly with humidification time despite the bound water content increasing exponentially. This increase is associated with the kinetics of free liquid transport through the capillary system, the kinetics of water transition from a free to a bound state, and the rate of its propagation within the structure, which is an essential property as it determines the efficiency of the hygroscopic system. Cues from this experiment suggest combining visual observation with gravimetric measurements to accurately determine the quantity of water and its qualitative composition and, therefore, the kinetics associated with the transition of water from a free to a bound state and evaporation from the bound state. In addition to the capillary system, the surface of the awn is covered with trichomes. This configuration of numerous fibres effectively increases the surface area available for evaporation, suggesting a strategy for engineered solutions.

Together with previously conducted analysis on the optimal conditions of liquid transport within synthetic porous structures with constant and transient liquid content reported a methodology for the localised determination of the kinetics of liquid transport based on electro impedance, we report a set of characterisation methods for investigation of optimal conditions of liquid transport in a porous structure for hygroscopically conditioned actuation. The developed technique enables a non-invasive approach to detect free water content locally in porous structures for, e.g., plant health monitoring, analogous to photoplethysmography that uses light absorption for blood volume and oxygen content monitoring in medical applications. However, it extends its capabilities by allowing both quantitative and qualitative analysis, distinguishing between bound and free liquid states. Moreover, investigating the properties of anisotropic structures inspires the adaptation of a similar approach for the hygroactuating systems with a constant amount of swelling agent. For instance, in our previous work, electrohydrodynamic medium displacement caused lateral expansion of the isomeric polymeric structure and pore distribution was not oriented. The authors intend to integrate the engineered anisotropic structure optimised for unidirectional expansion with controlled internal liquid distribution and apply the developed technologies to characterise the resulting actuation system.

Acknowledgements. This research was supported by the Estonian Research Council grants PRG1498 and PRG1084.

References

1. Taiz, L., Zeiger, E., Møller, I.M., Murphy, A.: Plant physiology and Development (2015)
2. Dumais, J., Forterre, Y.: Vegetable dynamicks: the role of water in plant movements. Annu. Rev. Fluid Mech. **44**, 453–478 (2012)
3. Pettolino, F.A., Walsh, C., Fincher, G.B., Bacic, A.: Determining the polysaccharide composition of plant cell walls. Nat. Protoc. **7**(9), 1590–1607 (2012)
4. Evangelista, D., Hotton, S., Dumais, J.: The mechanics of explosive dispersal and self-burial in the seeds of the filaree, Erodium cicutarium (Geraniaceae). J. Exp. Biol. **214**(4), 521–529 (2011)
5. Pittermann, J., et al.: The Structure and Function of Xylem in Seed-Free Vascular Plants: An Evolutionary Perspective. Functional and Ecological Xylem Anatomy, 1–37 (2015)
6. Cosgrove, D.J.: Loosening of plant cell walls by expansins. Nature **407**(6802), 321–326 (2000)
7. Hatakeyama, T., Iijima, M., Hatakeyama, H.: Role of bound water on structural change of water insoluble polysaccharides. Food Hydrocoll. **53**, 62–68 (2016)
8. Sarokin, Y., Aabloo, A., Must, I.: Plant-inspired rearrangement of liquid in a porous structure for controlled swelling. Bioinspir. Biomim. **18**(6), 066005 (2023)
9. Saarela, J.M.S., Heikkinen, S.M., Fabritius, T.E.J., Haapala, A.T., Myllylä, R.A.: Refractive index matching improves optical object detection in paper. Meas. Sci. Technol. **19**(5), 055710 (2008)
10. Juttula, H., Makynen, A.: Determination of refractive index of softwood using immersion liquid method. 2012 IEEE International Instrumentation and Measurement Technology Conference Proceedings, pp. 1231–1234 (2012)
11. Chen, H., et al.: Refractive index of delignified wood for transparent biocomposites. RSC Adv. **10**, 40719–40724 (2020)
12. Simonaho, S.P., Tolonen, Y., Rouvinen, J., Silvennoinen, R.: Laser light scattering from wood samples soaked in water or in benzyl benzoate. Optik **114**(10), 445–448 (2003)
13. Abraham, Y., et al.: Tilted cellulose arrangement as a novel mechanism for hygroscopic coiling in the stork's bill awn. J. R. Soc. Interface. **9**(69), 640–647 (2012)
14. Jung, W., Kim, W., Kim, H.Y.: Self-burial mechanics of hygroscopically responsive awns. ICB **54**(6), 1034–1042 (2014)
15. Kulasinski, K.: Free energy landscape of cellulose as a driving factor in the mobility of adsorbed water. Langmuir **33**(22), 5362–5370 (2017)
16. Shrestha, S., Diaz, J.A., Ghanbari, S., Youngblood, J.P.: Hygroscopic swelling determination of cellulose nanocrystal (CNC) films by polarized light microscopy digital image correlation. Biomacromol **18**(5), 1482–1490 (2017)
17. Eger, C.J., et al.: The structural and mechanical basis for passive-hydraulic pine cone actuation. Adv. Sci. **9**(20), 2200458 (2022)

Simulated Control of an Aquatic Serpentine Robot with Stable Heteroclinic Channels

Nathaniel Mengers$^{(\boxtimes)}$ ⓘ, Natasha Rouse ⓘ, and Kathryn A. Daltorio ⓘ

Case Western Reserve University, Cleveland, OH, USA
nnm22@case.edu

Abstract. Stable Heteroclinic Channels (SHCs) are a novel framework for creating central pattern generators (CPGs). In MATLAB 2022a, we implement an SHC controller for lateral undulation in a simulated aquatic serpentine robot with six segments. We demonstrate that anguilliform locomotion, wherein lateral displacement during undulation increases from head to tail, can also be achieved by scaling SHC parameters. When compared with a sine controller, SHCs achieve equivalent velocity and 42% lower overall COT for the same lateral undulation gait. COT improvements are attributable to lower startup energy consumption. We propose a method for integrating tactile sensing into the SHC trajectory planner by scaling the kernel activation rate. We show that the sensorized SHC controller exhibits faster, lower amplitude gait cycles, enabling progression in a narrow crevice. Compared with a sensorized sine controller, the sensorized SHC controller achieves 41% greater speed, but 52% lower efficiency. This research demonstrates that SHCs benefit from intuitive tuning like sine control, while also producing smooth trajectories representative of other CPG frameworks.

Keywords: heteroclinic channels · central pattern generator · control · snake robot.

1 Introduction

Biological systems effectively navigate complex, variable environments. Snakes are a prolific example, as their kinematic redundancy permits a broad range of locomotion patterns. Snakes have evolved to maneuver through both aquatic and terrestrial conditions, including confined spaces. Their adaptability may make serpentine morphologies advantageous for robots performing ecological exploration, pipeline inspection, and search and rescue.

Snake-like robots commonly employ sine-based joint trajectories, such as the serpenoid curve proposed by Hirose in 1994, to achieve lateral undulation [16,20, 22]. [26] similarly uses the serpenoid curve for lateral undulation in polychaete annelid worm robots. Sinusoids have also been used for sidewinding, rectilinear [23], and concertina gaits [4]. While simple and flexible, sine controllers may produce non-smooth kinematic outputs on startup or when sensory information

N. S. Szczecinski et al. (Eds.): Living Machines 2024, LNAI 14930, pp. 193–207, 2025.
https://doi.org/10.1007/978-3-031-72597-5_14

modulates gait parameters [12,15]. Abrupt trajectories demand large motor commands, which fatigue actuators and increase energy consumption.

As an alternative, researchers have explored Central Pattern Generators (CPGs), which are bio-inspired controllers that produce rhythmic output in the absence of rhythmic input. CPGs occur naturally in the central nervous system of many organisms, controlling heartbeats, breathing, and locomotion [1,3,21,28]. Several neural CPG formulations have been investigated for lateral undulation and concertina locomotion in serpentine robots [8,13,15].

Abstractions of neural CPGs based on coupled differential equations have also been developed for robotic control [5,6,25,27]. These mathematical approaches generate stable oscillation without the complexity of modeling individual neurons. Integrating the differential equations filters high frequency sensory signals, producing smooth trajectories [12]. Dynamic Movement Primitives (DMPs) are a popular CPG framework consisting of a proportional derivative controller plus a set of weighted, periodically activated Gaussian kernels. The weights are typically learned such that the controller produces a desirable gait. Unfortunately, the weights do not map explicitly to the intended trajectory [19]. Consequently, DMPs behave as a black box and operators cannot easily alter the system behavior without retraining the controller.

Stable Heteroclinic Channels (SHCs) have been proposed as another tool for creating dynamical state oscillators. SHCs involve connected saddle points such that the unstable manifold of one flows into the stable manifold of the next. SHC control has been demonstrated for slip reduction in peristaltic robots [7] and task switching in humanoid robots [2]. In [19], the authors replace Gaussian kernels in DMPs with SHCs. They reveal that the weights in SHC movement primitives visually represent the desired trajectory, improving transparency.

We posit that SHC control offers intuitive trajectory modulation like sine controllers, while generating smooth trajectories like other CPGs. We show that the SHC controlled robot achieves similar swimming speed while reducing cost of transport (COT) when compared to a robot with sinusoidal control in an obstacle-free environment. We scale SHC weights such that the robot switches from lateral undulation to anguilliform swimming, where lateral displacement and joint amplitudes increase from head to tail. Lastly, we integrate tactile sensing into an SHC controller and characterize performance as the robot swims through a crevice.

2   Materials and Methods

2.1   Simulation Dynamics

Fluid Modeling. To simulate an aquatic serpentine robot, we adopt the framework in [10]. The model addresses a submerged planar robot comprised of discrete linkages with elliptical cross sections. Fluid is viscous, incompressible, and irrotational in the robot's reference frame. The authors develop equations of motion for the center of mass (X_{CM}, Y_{CM}) and absolute linkage orientation θ including linear drag, nonlinear drag, and added mass in open water (Fig. 1). The relative joint angles ϕ are derived from kinematics. Parameters used in our study are listed in Table 3.

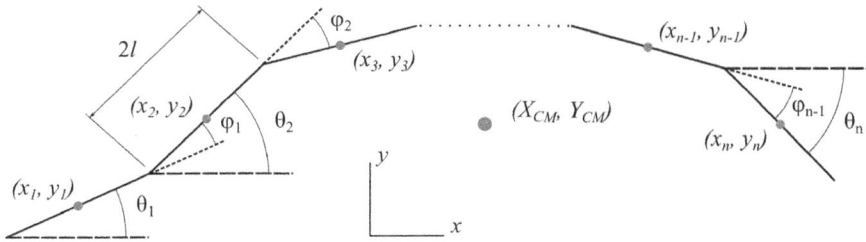

Fig. 1. Kinematic diagram of n segmented snake robot. Variable names from [11].

Obstacle Modeling. Along with interactions between the robot and the fluid, we model collisions between the robot and surrounding objects. Obstacles are treated as a series of points connected by flat surfaces with stiffness $k_{wall} = 30,000\frac{N}{m}$ and damping $c_{wall} = 500\frac{N}{m \cdot s}$. We approximate each robot segment as a set of points spaced $dx_{segment} = 0.001\,m$ apart and assume that points inside an obstacle penetrated the nearest surface. The distance d_n and velocity v_n of the point normal to the surface are computed, then the local force is calculated as $dF_n = (k_{wall} \cdot d_n + c_{wall} \cdot v_n) \cdot dx_{segment}$. We adopt a linear friction model with stiction as described in [14]. Torques are obtained by integrating contact forces over displacement from the link center of mass. Effects of obstacles on fluid behavior are ignored for simplicity.

2.2 Control

Sinusoidal Control without Tactile Sensing. Let us consider the serpenoid controller as described by Hirose in [22]. To maintain consistency, we adopt the variable naming scheme from the fluid dynamics model [10]. For joint i, the desired trajectory $\phi_i^*(t)$ at time t is computed with the desired amplitude, frequency, and relative phase offset $\alpha_h = \frac{\pi}{6}$, $\omega_h = \frac{5\pi}{9}$ rads/s, and $\delta_h = \frac{2\pi}{9}$ rads respectively (Eq. 1). Similar to [10], we apply PID steering control ϕ_0 to ensure locomotion along the x axis (Eq. 2). The robot heading is computed as the average of all linkage angles $\psi = \frac{1}{n}\sum_{i=1}^{N}\theta_i$. We define the reference heading $\psi_{ref} = -atan\left(\frac{Y_{CM}}{\delta}\right)$, where $\delta = 4l$. With all joint amplitudes the same, this controller emulates the lateral undulation gait observed in terrestrial snakes. The joint torque u_i for any joint i is computed using PD control (Eq. 3). Controller parameters can be found in Tables 4 and 3.

$$\phi_i^* = \alpha_h sin(\omega_h t + \delta_h(i-1)) + \phi_0 \tag{1}$$

$$\phi_0 = -k_{I,0}\int (\psi_{ref} - \psi)\,dt + k_{p,0}(\psi_{ref} - \psi) + k_{d,0}(\dot{\psi}_{ref} - \dot{\psi}) \tag{2}$$

$$u_i = k_p(\phi_i^* - \phi_i) + k_d(\dot{\phi}_i^* - \dot{\phi}_i) \tag{3}$$

Sinusoidal Control with Tactile Sensing. Decreasing joint amplitudes yields a narrower body shape, which may reduce collisions for a snake robot in narrow channels. In [17], authors define shape control, wherein differential equations are used to adapt sine parameters. In [17,24], shape controllers are used for pipe climbing and navigating peg arrays, respectively. We apply a simple shape controller to decrease joint amplitudes from a reference value of $\alpha_{ref} = \frac{\pi}{6}$ during contact (Eq. 4). We choose amplitude gain $k_\alpha = 1.5$, amplitude damping $c_\alpha = 0.05$, and tactile input gain $k_T = 0.5$. Tactile input $z_T = 1$ if any linkages contact an obstacle and $z_T = 0$ otherwise. This controller adjusts joint amplitudes uniformly, although future work may explore more targeted approaches.

$$\dot{\alpha}_{h,t+dt} = k_\alpha \left(\alpha_{ref} - \alpha_{h,t} \right) - c_\alpha \left(\dot{\alpha}_{h,t} \right) - k_T z_T \tag{4}$$

Lateral Undulation SHC Control In lateral undulation, each joint repeats the behavior of the one ahead of it with a time delay. We view the gait as a repeating pattern of waves passing down the robot, increasing and decreasing the joint angles. With SHCs, waves are constructed by K cyclically arranged saddle points, or kernels, whose activation $x_{1 \times K}$ is described by Eq. 5 [19]. Unhindered, a kernel's activity x_i grows exponentially according to its growth rate, α_i and the time scaling factor $\tau = 1$. However, we select the connection matrix $\rho_{K \times K}$ such that each kernel moderately inhibits itself and strongly inhibits all other kernels except the next one in the sequence. The inhibition causes kernels to momentarily activate ($x_i > 0.9$) in a cyclic pattern [9]. Normally distributed noise $\mathcal{N}$ with magnitude $\eta\sqrt{dt} = 10^{-9}\sqrt{0.001}$ reduces dwell time in the vicinity of saddle points by creating deviations along the unstable dimension of the saddles [7]. Parameter values are listed in Table 5.

$$\tau dx = x \left(\alpha^T - x\rho \right) dt + \left(\eta\sqrt{dt}\mathcal{N}\left(0, 1 \right) \right)^T \tag{5}$$

Since the proposed SHC controller includes one cycle for increasing joint angles and a second cycle for decreasing them, we define the relationship between kernels in a block diagonal connection matrix (Eqs. 6 and 7). We structure the SHC controller to perform the same lateral undulation gait as the sinusoidal controller. With joint offset of $\frac{2\pi}{9}$ radians and two kernels per joint, $K = 18$ kernels are required. With the guidelines in [18], we tune the growth rate $\alpha_i = 23.2$ for every kernel i such that the frequency is consistent with the sinusoidal controller. We set the SHC magnitude $\beta_i = 1$ and noise insensitivity $\nu_i = 1$.

$$\rho_{i,j}^s = \begin{cases} \alpha_i/\beta_i & if \ i = j \\ \frac{\alpha_i - \alpha_i/\nu_i}{\beta_j} & if \ i = j \oplus 1 \\ \frac{\alpha_i + \alpha_j}{\beta_j} & otherwise \end{cases} \tag{6}$$

$$\rho = \begin{bmatrix} \rho^s & 0 \\ 0 & \rho^s \end{bmatrix} \tag{7}$$

The effect of kernel activation on joint accelerations is defined by the forcing term $f(x)$ (Eq. 8). For a robot with n segments, the weight submatrix $w^s_{n-1 \times K/2}$ is chosen according to Eq. 9 with $\lambda_1 = 3$ and $\lambda_2 = 7$, then the overall weight matrix $w_{n-1 \times K}$ is constructed (Eq. 10). For convenience, a weight matrix heatmap is included in Fig. 2. This formulation encodes the upward and downward trends in joint accelerations as the corresponding kernels activate and deactivate. We also adapt the method from [19] to include PID steering, with gain matrix P and steering sensor data $z = \left[\psi, \dot{\psi}, \ddot{\psi} \right]$. As in Sect. 2.2, the PID is tuned using Ziegler Nichols closed loop method (See Table 5). The desired joint accelerations $\ddot{\phi}^*$ are computed as in Eq. 11 including $f(x)$ and a PD control term for reference tracking with $\alpha_\phi = 4$, $\beta_\phi = 1$, and $\phi_{goal} = 0$. Joint torques are computed as in Sect. 2.2.

$$f(x) = \frac{x \left(w^T + Pz \right)}{\sum_{i=1}^{K} x_i} \tag{8}$$

$$w^s_{i,j} = \begin{cases} \lambda_1 & if \ i = j \oplus 1 \ or \ i = j \ominus 2 \\ \lambda_2 & if \ i = j \ or \ i = j \ominus 1 \\ 0 & otherwise \end{cases} \tag{9}$$

$$w = [w^s, -w^s] \tag{10}$$

$$\ddot{\phi}^* = \alpha_\phi \left(\beta_\phi \left(\phi_{goal} - \phi^* \right) - \dot{\phi}^* \right) + f(x) \tag{11}$$

Anguilliform SHC Control. During swimming, snakes transition from the lateral undulation gait with near constant amplitudes for all joints to anguilliform locomotion with smaller amplitudes in anterior joints. In a recent publication on SHC based movement primitives, Rouse et al assigned the kernel weights to a desired trajectory for a planar kinematic model, then performed batch learning to reduce trajectory error [19]. The paper demonstrated that unlike in DMPs, the optimal weights visually represent the trajectory. The results suggest that by scaling weights, operators can intuitively modify SHC controller outputs. We apply the scaling property to generate anguilliform locomotion. The weights for anguilliform locomotion w^a are obtained from the lateral undulation weights using Eq. 13, based on the method for sine controllers in [10].

$$g = \frac{n - i}{n + 1} \tag{12}$$

$$w^a_{i,j} = w_{i,j} g(i) \tag{13}$$

SHCs with Tactile Sensing. The controller introduced in Sect. 2.2 does not include tactile sensing and therefore may perform poorly in confined spaces. We introduce the term $k_T z_T$ into the SHC canonical state equation, where $k_T = 0.55$ (Eq. 14). As in the Sect. 2.2, we assign $z_T = 1$ if any linkage contacts an obstacle and $z_T = 0$ otherwise. During contact, kernels progress more quickly such that joints have less time to accelerate and joint amplitudes decline. The

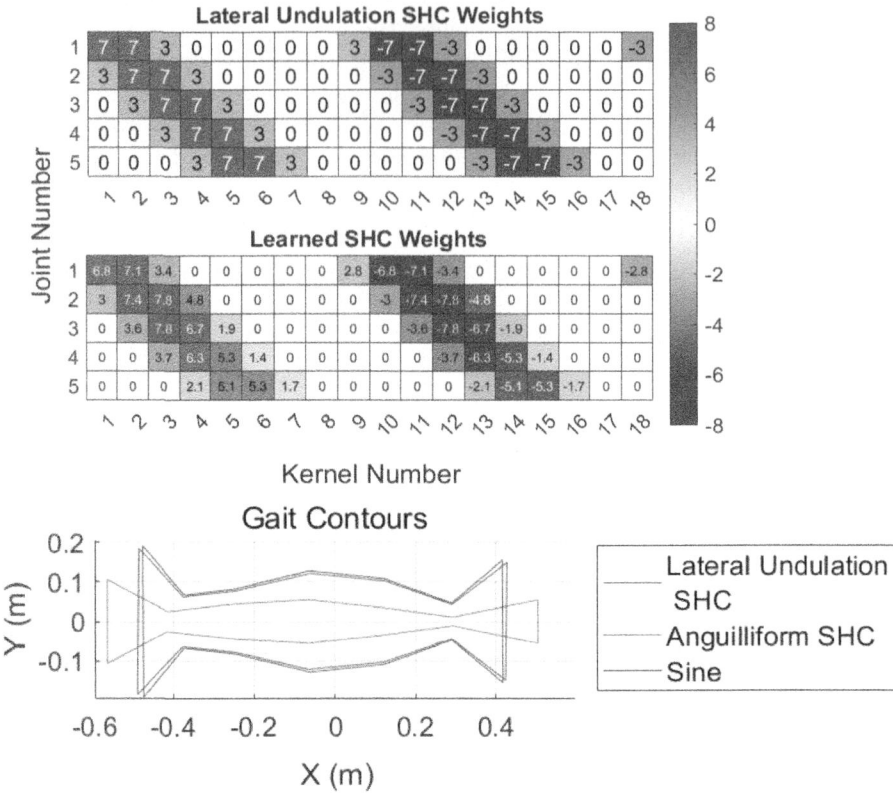

Fig. 2. (a) Heatmap of weights for lateral undulation and anguilliform SHC controllers. Weight magnitude in the anguilliform controller decreases with joint number, corresponding to smaller anterior joint amplitudes. (b) Boundaries of the robot's center line over one gait cycle. The anguilliform controller produces a narrower body shape, and lateral displacement increases tailward.

increased kernel progression rate also corresponds to increased joint oscillation frequency. Since all tactile sensors affect every kernel, phase differences between joints remain the same and coordinated locomotion is maintained.

$$\tau dx = x\left(1 + k_T z_T\right)\left(\alpha^T - x\rho\right)dt + \left(\eta\sqrt{dt}N\left(0,1\right)\right)^T \tag{14}$$

2.3   Experimental Design

Open Water. We first consider a robot swimming in quiescent water with no obstacles using the sine, lateral undulation (LU) SHC, and anguilliform SHC controllers. We record the position of the center of mass, joint torques, and joint velocities for $t_{max} = 30$ seconds of swimming, with all linkages beginning at rest and

$\theta_{i,t=0} = 0$. Then, we compare the cost of transport (Eq. 15) for each controller with power consumption at time t approximated as $P_t = \sum_{i=1}^{n_{joints}} \left| u_{i,t} \dot{\phi}_{i,t} \right|$. Energy consumption is normalized by gravitational acceleration $G = 9.81\,m/s^2$, total mass of the robot m_T, and forward displacement, $X_{CM}(t_{max})$. If displacement is negative, the COT is undefined. Additionally, we examine the kernel activations and forcing term $f(x)$ for the SHC controllers.

$$COT = \frac{\sum_{t=0}^{t_{max}} P_t}{Gm_T X_{CM}(t_{max})} \tag{15}$$

Straight Channel. Next, we investigate how the lateral undulation controllers perform with and without tactile sensing in structured terrain. We simulate swimming for 30 s in a straight, 0.3 m wide channel (Fig. 3). The robot begins the experiment with its entire body in the channel with $\theta_i = 0$ and no wall contact. We evaluate the the COT and mean velocity for each controller.

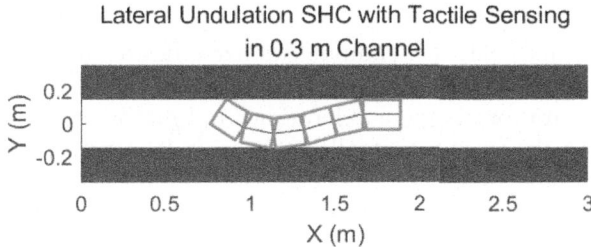

Fig. 3. The robot performing lateral undulation in a 0.3 m channel.

3 Results

3.1 Open Water

The lateral undulation SHC controller effectively replicates the lateral undulation gait, achieving comparable velocity to the sine controller (Table 1). The anguilliform controller locomotes more slowly, as frontal segments generate less thrust due to lower joint oscillation amplitude. Progression of the robot through both open water and the confined space for all controllers is found in Fig. 4.

Table 1. Controller performance in open water

Controller	Average Velocity (m/s)	COT	COT after t = 1 s
Lateral Undulation SHC	0.261	0.09	0.088
Anguilliform SHC	0.137	0.073	0.072
Sine	0.271	0.16	0.098

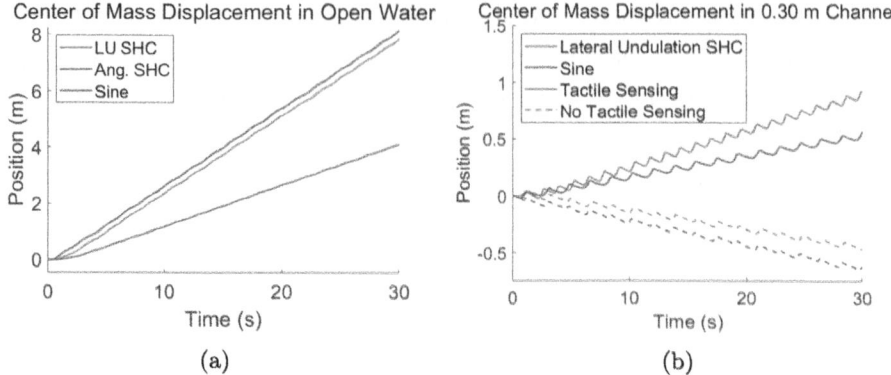

Fig. 4. (a) In open water, the lateral undulation (LU) SHC controller performs similarly to the sinusoidal controller. The anguilliform swimmer moves slower due to reduced joint amplitude and thrust near the head. (b) Tactile feedback improves speed in confined spaces, particularly for the SHC controller.

On startup, the sine controller computes nonzero desired joint velocities. The robot begins at rest such that there is a large discrepancy between the desired and actual initial configuration. Large accelerations and motor torques are required to reduce the error, decreasing controller efficiency. In contrast, the SHC controllers compute desired joint accelerations, then obtain the desired velocities and angles by integration. This approach yields produce smooth, differentiable trajectories. Consequently, SHC trajectories achieve more efficient locomotion. After this transient phase, trajectories for all controllers are smooth, so the lateral undulation SHC and sine controller produce similar steady state COTs.

To elucidate how weight scaling impacts the robot's behavior, the trajectories for the anterior joint ϕ_5 for each controller are depicted in Fig. 5. The sine controller and lateral undulation SHC exhibit joint oscillation with an amplitude of nominally $\frac{\pi}{6}$ radians. In contrast, anterior joint of the anguilliform controller undergoes smaller oscillations due to weight scaling. Joint trajectory trends are reflected in the forcing term $f(x)$. Furthermore, we normalize the peak to peak amplitudes (p-p) of $f(x)$ and ϕ for the anguilliform controller against the same for the lateral undulation controller. These amplitude ratios correlate closely with the weight scaling factor g, indicating that tuning the weights is an intuitive tool for modulating the gait of the robot (Fig. 6).

3.2   Straight Channel

Alongside open water performance, Fig. 4 in Sect. 3.1 shows the robot's forward displacement for the sine and lateral undulation SHC controllers with and without sensing. Obstacles deter locomotion for all controllers. During contact, the sine controller reduces joint oscillation amplitude. In contrast, the SHC controller increases the frequency of the kernel activation, allowing less time for the joints to accelerate. This generates higher frequency and lower amplitude trajectories, as shown in Fig. 7. The combined frequency and amplitude adaptation enhances speed more than amplitude reduction alone (Table 2).

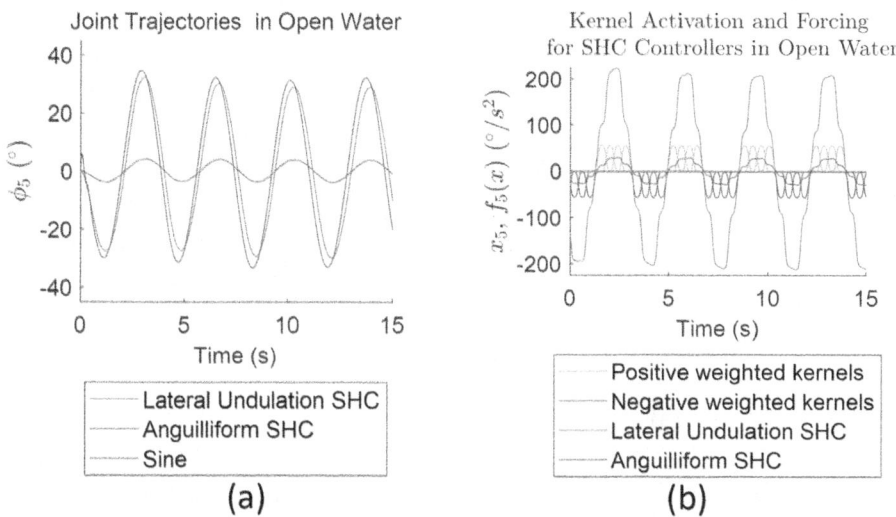

Fig. 5. (a) Anterior joint trajectories (ϕ_5) of SHC controllers in open water. (b) The progression of kernels that impact the anterior joint and $f_5(x)$. Kernel activations are consistent for all SHC controllers in the absence of sensory input. The oscillation amplitude of $f(x)$ is smaller for the anguilliform locomotion, corresponding to the lower amplitude in ϕ_5.

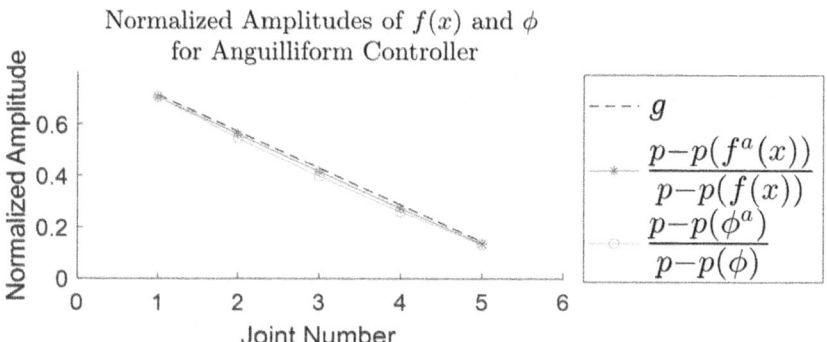

Fig. 6. The ratio of peak to peak (p-p) amplitudes of $f(x)$ and ϕ before and after scaling are strongly correlated with the scaling factor g.

Table 2. Performance in 0.3 m channel. Tactile sensing denoted with (T).

Controller	Average Velocity (m/s)	COT	COT after t = 1 s
Lateral Undulation SHC	−0.011	−	−
Lateral Undulation SHC (T)	0.06	1.99	2.02
Sine	−0.016	−	−
Sine (T)	0.039	1.31	1.28

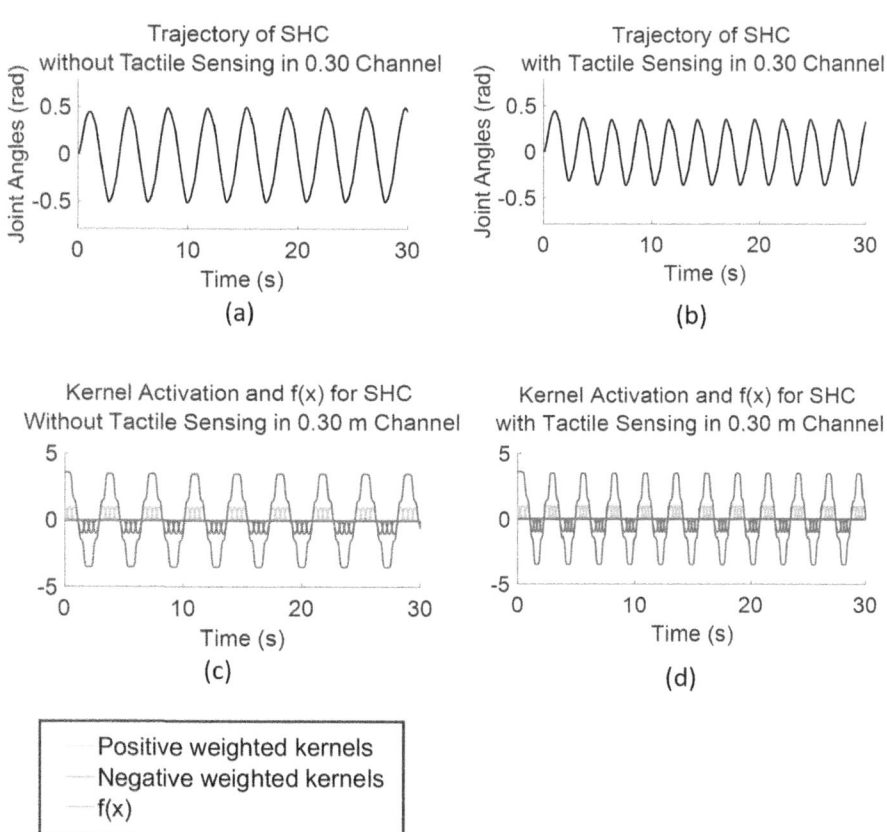

Fig. 7. Kernel activations and trajectory for joint 1 in narrow crevice. Obstacle detection speeds up kernel progression, increasing frequency and decreasing amplitude of joint trajectories.

By assessing the velocity and COT for each controller, we obtain a more detailed understanding of how sensing impacts performance. Compared with the sensorized sine controller, the sensorized SHC exhibits 41% higher velocity, although overall cost of transport also increases by 52%. Our results suggest that in confined spaces, tactile sensing is crucial for trajectory planning. While kernel modulation is useful for incorporating sensing in SHCs, more research is required to reduce energy consumption of SHC controllers in obstacle laden environments.

4   Conclusions and Future Work

In this paper, we implement a novel CPG framework based on SHCs on a simulated serpentine swimming robot. We show that SHC controllers can produce similar velocity compared with traditional sine controllers in open water. We also demonstrate that SHC control improves overall efficiency in open water because it produces smooth, differentiable kinematic trajectories, reducing torque requirements on startup. As with sine control, operators can easily modulate SHC trajectories by scaling weight parameters.

Our work additionally establishes a method for tactile sensor integration with SHC based controllers. By increasing the kernel activation rate when the robot contacts obstacles, we achieve a higher frequency, narrower gait. This approach significantly improves velocity and efficiency over unsensorized controllers, as well as improving speed in comparison with sine controllers that incorporate tactile sensing. Further research is needed to improve efficiency in sensor equipped SHC controllers. Having demonstrated basic control of a serpentine robot with SHCs in simulation, we can develop a physical robot and examine real-world performance. In both simulation and with a physical system, we will conduct parametric studies to assess controller behavior in channels of various widths and textures. We will also explore learning SHC weights to discover optimal gaits. Future research may characterize how the phase of SHC kernels can be manipulated to modify gaits, which would allow tactile sensors to adapt individual joint trajectories rather than whole body motion patterns.

Acknowledgments. This research was supported by the Department of Defense through the National Defense Science and Engineering Graduate Fellowship Program. Research was also supported by the National Science Foundation's CAREER award (2047330).

Disclosure of Interests. The authors have no competing interests to declare that are relevant to the content of this article.

A   Appendix

Table 3. Parameters for fluid dynamics, obstacle modeling, and kinematics.

Variable	Description	Value
ρ_f	Fluid density (kg/m^3)	1000
C_f	Drag coefficient along link axis	0.03
C_D	Drag coefficient perpendicular to link axis	2
C_A	Added mass coefficient	1
e_1	major radius (m)	0.09
e_2	minor radius (m)	0.035
m	link mass (kg)	0.05
l	link half-length (m)	0.09
n	Number of links	6
dt	Simulation time step (s)	0.001
$\phi(t)$	Relative joint angles (rad)	–
$\phi^*(t)$	Desired relative joint angles (rad)	–
$\theta(t)$	Absolute angle of linkages (rad)	–
k_{wall}	Obstacle stiffness coefficient (N/m)	7000
u	Joint torque (N · m)	–
ψ	Robot heading (rad)	–
c_{wall}	Obstacle damping coefficient (N · s/m)	1000
dx_{wall}	Feature width for obstacles (m)	0.001
$dx_{segment}$	Point resolution for collision dynamics (m)	0.001
μ_s	Coefficient of static friction	0.8
μ_k	Coefficient of kinetic friction	0.6
k_p	Motor proportional gain	50
k_d	Motor derivative gain	0.5
G	Gravitational acceleration (m/s^2)	9.81

Table 4. Sine Controller Parameters

Variable	Description	Value
α_h	Amplitude (rad)	$\pi/6$
ω_h	Frequency (rad/s)	$5\pi/9$
δ_h	Angular offset between joints	$2\pi/9$
k_α	Amplitude gain (rad)	1.5
α_{ref}	Equilibrium amplitude (rad)	$\frac{\pi}{6}$
c_α	Amplitude damping for sensorized controller (rad/s)	0.05
k_T	Tactile sensing amplitude gain (rad)	0.5
z_t	Tactile sensing signal	1 if contact, 0 otherwise

Table 5. SHC Controller Parameters

Variable	Description	Value
τ	Temporal scaling factor	1
x	Kernel Activation	$0.004 - 1$
K	Number of kernels	18
α_ϕ	Damping coefficient	4
β_ϕ	Gain coefficient	1
ϕ_{goal}	Joint trajectory goal	0
α	Growth rate	23.2
β	Magnitude	1
ν	Insensitivity to noise	1
λ_1	Weight parameter	3
λ_2	Weight parameter	7
K_u	Steering ultimate gain	2
T_u	Steering ultimate period	1
K_p	Steering proportional gain	$0.2K_u$
T_d	Steering derivative period	$0.333T_u$
T_i	Steering integral period	$0.5T_u$
P	Steering gain matrix	$\left([K_p/T_i, K_p, K_pT_d]^T 1_{1\times K}\right)^T$
k_t	Tactile sensing gain	0.65
η	Noise magnitude	$1 \times 10^{-9} \cdot 1_{K \times n_{sensors}}$
$x_{t=0}$	Initial conditions of kernels	$[0.0093, 0.9756, 0_{1\times6}, 0.0093, 0_{1\times5}, 0.45, 0.5, 0, 0]$
z_t	Tactile sensing signal	1 if contact, 0 otherwise

References

1. Bellingham, M.C.: Driving respiration: the respiratory central pattern generator. Clin. Exp. Pharmacol. Physiol. **25**(10), 847–856 (1998). https://doi.org/10.1111/j.1440-1681.1998.tb02166.x
2. Brecelj, T., Petrič, T.: Stable heteroclinic channel networks for physical human-humanoid robot collaboration. Sensors **23**(3), 1396 (2023). https://doi.org/10.3390/s23031396
3. Brown, T.G., Sherrington, C.S.: The intrinsic factors in the act of progression in the mammal. Proc. R. Soc. Lond. Ser. B Contain. Pap. Biol. Char. **84**(572), 308–319 (1997). https://doi.org/10.1098/rspb.1911.0077
4. Chen, S.,Roth, A.: Gait Design of a Novel Arboreal Concertina Locomotion for Snake-like Robots (2023). arXiv:2309.06000 [cs]
5. Cohen, A.H., Holmes, P.J., Rand, R.H.: The nature of the coupling between segmental oscillators of the lamprey spinal generator for locomotion: a mathematical model. J. Math. Biol. **13**(3), 345–369 (1982). https://doi.org/10.1007/BF00276069
6. Crespi, A., Ijspeert, A.J.: AmphiBot II: an amphibious snake robot that crawls and swims using a central pattern generator. In: Proceedings of the 9th International Conference on Climbing and Walking Robots (CLAWAR 2006) (2006)

7. Daltorio, K.A., Boxerbaum, A.S., Horchler, A.D., Shaw, K.M., Chiel, H.J., Quinn, R.D.: Efficient worm-like locomotion: slip and control of soft-bodied peristaltic robots. Bioinspiration Biomimetics **8**(3), 035003 (2013). https://doi.org/10.1088/1748-3182/8/3/035003

8. Gul, M., Samad, A., Ullah, A., Abbas, Z., Masood, J.: Concertina gait learning for snake robot using artificial neural network. In: 2019 International Conference on Electrical, Communication, and Computer Engineering (ICECCE), pp. 1–5 (2019). https://doi.org/10.1109/ICECCE47252.2019.8940791

9. Horchler, A.D., Daltorio, K.A., Chiel, H.J., Quinn, R.D.: Designing responsive pattern generators: stable heteroclinic channel cycles for modeling and control. Bioinspiration Biomimetics **10**(2), 026001 (2015). https://doi.org/10.1088/1748-3190/10/2/026001

10. Kelasidi, E., Pettersen, K.Y., Gravdahl, J.T., Strømsøyen, S., Sørensen, A.J.: Modeling and propulsion methods of underwater snake robots. In: 2017 IEEE Conference on Control Technology and Applications (CCTA), pp. 819–826 (2017). https://doi.org/10.1109/CCTA.2017.8062561

11. Kelasidi, E., Jesmani, M., Pettersen, K.Y., Gravdahl, J.T.: Locomotion efficiency optimization of biologically inspired snake robots. Appl. Sci. **8**(1), 80 (2018). https://doi.org/10.3390/app8010080

12. Liljebäck, P., Pettersen, K.Y., Stavdahl, Ø., Gravdahl, J.T.: A review on modelling, implementation, and control of snake robots. Robot. Auton. Syst. **60**(1), 29–40 (2012). https://doi.org/10.1016/j.robot.2011.08.010

13. Liu, X., Gasoto, R., Onal, C., Fu, J.: Learning to Locomote with Deep Neural-Network and CPG-based Control in a Soft Snake Robot (2020). arXiv:2001.04059 [cs, math]

14. Marques, F., Flores, P., Claro, J.C., Lankarani, H.: A survey and comparison of several friction force models for dynamic analysis of multibody mechanical systems. Nonlinear Dyn. **86**, 1407–1443 (2016). https://doi.org/10.1007/s11071-016-2999-3

15. Norman-Tenazas, R.: Robust Snake Robot Control Via A Spiking Neuron Central Pattern Generator. PhD thesis, Johns Hopkins University (2021). URL http://jhir.library.jhu.edu/handle/1774.2/64215

16. Ostrowski, J., Burdick, J.: Gait kinematics for a serpentine robot. In: Proceedings of IEEE International Conference on Robotics and Automation, vol. 2, pp. 1294–1299 (1996). https://doi.org/10.1109/ROBOT.1996.506885

17. Rollinson, D., Choset, H.: Gait-based compliant control for snake robots. In: 2013 IEEE International Conference on Robotics and Automation, pp. 5138–5143 (2013). https://doi.org/10.1109/ICRA.2013.6631311

18. Rouse, N., Daltorio, K.: Stable Heteroclinic Channel-Based Movement Primitives: Tuning Trajectories using Saddle Parameters (2024)

19. Rouse, N.A., Daltorio, K.A.: Visualization of stable heteroclinic channel-based movement primitives. IEEE Robot. Autom. Lett. **6**(2), 2343–2348 (2021). https://doi.org/10.1109/LRA.2021.3061382

20. Sato, M., Fukaya, M., Iwasaki, T.: Serpentine locomotion with robotic snakes. IEEE Control Syst. Mag. **22**(1), 64–81 (2002). https://doi.org/10.1109/37.980248

21. Selverston, A.I.: Invertebrate central pattern generator circuits. Philos. Trans. R. Soc. B Biol. Sci. **365**(1551), 2329–2345 (2010). https://doi.org/10.1098/rstb.2009.0270

22. Shigeo, H.: Biologically inspired robots: snake-like locomotors and manipulators by Shigeo Hirose Oxford University Press, Oxford: 220pages, incl. index (£40). Robotica **12**(3), 282–282 (1993). https://doi.org/10.1017/S0263574700017264

23. Tesch, M., Lipkin, K., Brown, I., Hatton, R., Peck, A., Rembisz, J., Choset, H.: Parameterized and scripted gaits for modular snake robots. Adv. Robot. **23**, 1131–1158 (2009). https://doi.org/10.1163/156855309X452566
24. Travers, M., Gong, C., Choset, H.: Shape-constrained whole-body adaptivity. In: 2015 IEEE International Symposium on Safety, Security, and Rescue Robotics (SSRR), pp. 1–6 (2015). https://doi.org/10.1109/SSRR.2015.7442945
25. Travers, M., Whitman, J., Choset, H.: Shape-based coordination in locomotion control. Int. J. Robot. Res. **37**(10), 1253–1268 (2018). https://doi.org/10.1177/0278364918761569
26. Tsakiris, D.P., Sfakiotakis, M., Menciassi, A., la Spina, G., Dario, P.: Polychaete-like Undulatory Robotic Locomotion. In: Proceedings of the 2005 IEEE International Conference on Robotics and Automation, pp. 3018–3023 (2005). https://doi.org/10.1109/ROBOT.2005.1570573
27. Wang, Z., Gao, Q., Zhao, H.: CPG-inspired locomotion control for a snake robot basing on nonlinear oscillators. J. Intell. Robot. Syst. **85**(2), 209–227 (2017). https://doi.org/10.1007/s10846-016-0373-9
28. Weaver, A.L., Roffman, R.C., Norris, B.J., Calabrese, R.L.: A role for compromise: synaptic inhibition and electrical coupling interact to control phasing in the leech heartbeat CPG. Front. Behav. Neurosci. **4**, 38 (2010). https://doi.org/10.3389/fnbeh.2010.00038

A Comparison of Model-Free Controllers for Trajectory Tracking in a Plant-Inspired Soft Arm

Muhammad Sunny Nazeer[1]($\boxtimes$) (ID), Yasmin Tauqeer Ansari[2](ID),
Egidio Falotico[3](ID), and Cecilia Laschi[1](ID)

[1] Department of Mechanical Engineering, College of Design and Engineering,
National University of Singapore, Singapore, Singapore
{m.nazeer,mpeclc}@nus.edu.sg
[2] Bioinspired Soft Robotics Lab, Istituto Italiano di Tecnologia, Genoa, Italy
yasmin.ansari@iit.it
[3] The Biorobotics Institute, Scuola Superiore Sant'Anna, Pontedera, Italy
e.falotico@santannapisa.it

Abstract. The field of soft robotics is experiencing a transformative phase with the emergence of self-supporting modular soft robot arms, inspired by design principles drawn from climbing plants, which are gaining recognition as a rich source of bio-inspiration. The vision to deploy these systems in highly unstructured environments, qualifies the need to investigate model-free algorithms that facilitate motion capabilities based solely on data regarding system-environment interactions. This paper delves into the development of model-free controllers to enable tracking capabilities in these systems. While the trajectory tracking task is already recognized as challenging in the context of redundant continuum/soft arms, the difficulty is compounded when aiming to generate control policies solely from sequential feedback from the environment. The novelty of this work lies in the development of both learning-based and learning-free model-free computational frameworks to address this task. Both controllers are validated on a 9-DoF modular cable-driven plant-inspired soft arm for moving through multiple trajectories in 3D space. The comparison of these controllers holds significant insights to future directions for the practical applicability of these systems in real-world scenarios, and are promising to pave way for novel application scenarios.

Keywords: Control of Soft Robots · Robot Control · Bio-inspired Control · Machine Learning · Adaptive Control · Behavior-based Control

1 Introduction

Continuum soft robot arms (SRAs) represent a novel generation of robotic manipulators capable of flexibly bending at any point along their length, thereby,

---

M.S. Nazeer and Y.T. Ansari—The following authors contributed equally in this paper.

© The Author(s), under exclusive license to Springer Nature Switzerland AG 2025
N. S. Szczecinski et al. (Eds.): Living Machines 2024, LNAI 14930, pp. 208–220, 2025.
https://doi.org/10.1007/978-3-031-72597-5_15

facilitating a wide range of dexterous movements and adaptability to external loads [1]. These desirable properties are promising to address major challenges in robotic manipulation within extreme and unstructured environments, resulting in their rapidly increasing development since the early 1990s [2].

The design of SRAs was primarily inspired by the remarkable abilities of muscular hydrostats, such as the elephant trunk and the octopus' arm, to efficiently manipulate natural environments [3]. These biological continuum structures exploit the elasticity and internal arrangement of muscles to achieve their impressive flexibility and control. Engineering solutions have translated these properties into hardware platforms by integrating lightweight flexible actuators into an actuation unit, which is typically capable of omnidirectional bending along with elongation/contraction and/or torsion, as extensively elaborated in previous studies [4]. These actuation units are then concatenated to form the overall structure where the wall thickness of the subsequent units is generally tapered. The resulting systems, while dexterous, are often bulky and lack the ability to support self-weight. Consequently, these systems are orientated downward in the neutral position during operation. This limitation has been addressed for the first time in [5], where the authors investigate a novel source of bioinspiration from the plant-kingdom, i.e., the climbing plant. These species are especially effective at supporting their own weight while increasing in height and also generating motion strategies that usually cover a large volume of space. In particular, this comes from the property of flexural rigidity that decreases from the base towards the tip, allowing for flexibility at the tip to manipulate objects while maintaining sufficient stiffness at the base to support the structure [6]. By translating and incorporating this biological property, the authors have developed the first self-supporting cable-driven SRA that is oriented in the upward position during operation. It is worthy to note that the property of decreasing flexural rigidity is also present in animal counterparts [7,8], but has not been taken into account in existing designs so far.

This article investigates the practical application of this novel self-supporting modular SRA, which will rely on controllers that can generate appropriate actuator commands (i.e. control policies) in order to achieve a desired task, and is a research topic in its nascency. In general, the long-term vision is to deploy these systems in natural settings, and thus, qualifies the need to investigate the development of algorithms capable of autonomous adaptation to these environments based solely on data regarding system-environment interactions. To the best of the authors' knowledge, current solutions have taken inspiration from the decentralized computational capability of plants to formalize a Behavior-Based Controller (BBC), which is able to achieve a task without mapping the kinematic operating spaces, but rather, through sequential decision-making based on interactions with the environment and sensory feedback. This controller has been tested and validated on the platform under consideration in order to enable reaching set-points in 3D space [9]. The central focus of this work is to further advance this research area by investigating and comparing multiple model-free methods that can, in a similar manner, enable trajectory tracking in the SRA under quasi-static/kinematic operating conditions. In general, enabling trajectory tracking in modular SRAs formulates a non-trivial problem [10] since the redundant arrangement of actuators limits the formulation of a control solution in closed form. To exacerbate this challenge, the material properties of SRAs introduce nonlinearities which results in unpredictable behavior [11].

1.1 Literature Review

Traditional control approaches to enable trajectory tracking in SRAs employ iterative analytical methods that have proven effective for rigid-link counterparts. The widely investigated method requires to invert a tractable approximation of the forward kinematic mapping, i.e., the analytical model [12–14]. However, a key limitation of traditional methods lies in the parameterization and update of environmental factors, which unavoidably affects the behavior of the system. An alternative method is finite element analysis, which provides a numerically exact technique for statics modeling with frictional considerations, with a trade-off of high computational complexity [15].

In contrast to traditional approaches, data-driven algorithms developed for enabling trajectory tracking in SRAs aim to correlate input activation and sensory feedback through computational formulations, and thus, are commonly known as model-free control strategies [16,17]. This is promising to overcome limitations of the previous method, and also are easily scalable to a wide range of actuation technologies. Furthermore, it is also easier to implement and faster to deploy [18]. The widely investigated methodology is to employ supervised-learning algorithms to use a labelled dataset to learn a continuous mapping between operating spaces, and is inspired by the biological notion of internal models. Its potential lies in its ability to generalize between observed data even in the presence of noise. Existing solutions have investigated the formulation of different types of mappings, including, forward and inverse kinematics, and forward and inverse dynamics [16,19]. These mappings are then embedded in controllers [10]. However, it is non-trivial to formulate these controllers in closed-loop with high accuracy. Another model-free approach that has started to gain traction in the community is reinforcement learning (RL), which addresses the problem of how a computational agent can learn to approximate an optimal behavioral strategy through sequential interaction with the environment [11,17]. The agent performs an action at each state, and receives rewards from the environment. The agent derives the effectiveness of the state–action pairs until a policy is learned [20]. The primary advantage of this technique, inspired from the neuroscientific reactive motor control theory, is to deal with highly unstructured environments in order to generate control policies based on data from interaction with the environment, without collecting any prior dataset.

The central contribution of this work is three-fold: (i) to develop a model-free learning-based control strategy, i.e., an RL-based approach; (ii) to develop a model-free learning-free control strategy, i.e., a behavior-based approach; (iii) to test and validate both strategies on the modular plant-inspired SRA for trajectory tracking of multiple trajectories in 3D space. Furthermore, to compare and analyze the experimental results of the different control strategies. The manuscript is arranged in the following manner: Sect. 2 presents the experimental setup and the control architectures employed followed by Sect. 3 which describes the achieved results and their performance analysis as validated on a nine Degrees of Freedom (DoF) modular cable-driven continuum arm for tracking multiple trajectories. The future outlooks presented in Sect. 4, respectively.

2   Materials and Methods

This section presents the experimental setup used, the experimental task description, and the description of the proposed controllers.

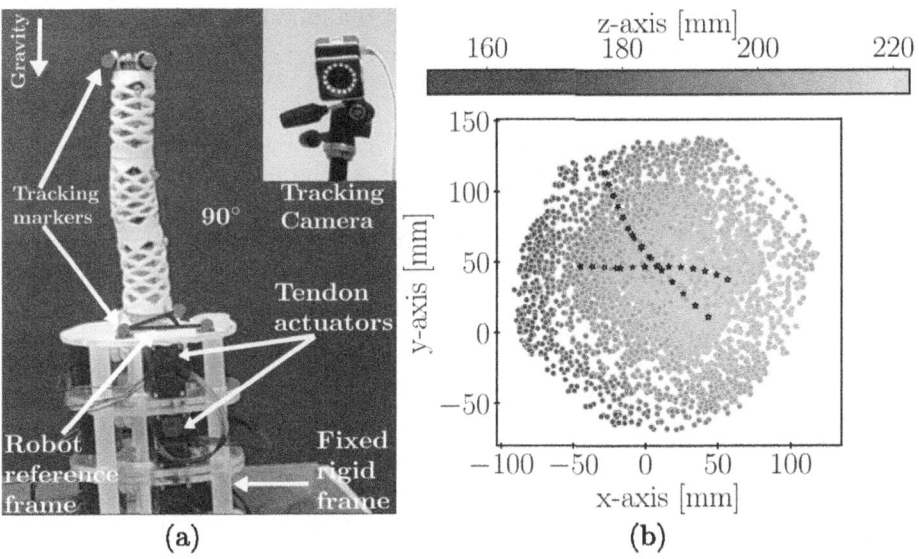

Fig. 1. **(a)** The soft continuum arm used as the test-bed for the experiments. It is a 9-DoF modular tendon-driven soft arm, where each module comrpises of three tendons spaced at 120° relative to one another. The soft arm is mounted on a rigid frame in an upright manner. The lower portion of the rigid frame houses the motors driving the tendons **(b)** The workspace of the system, recorded via the motion capture system (vicon) in response to a random actuation-space trajectory designed separately for all the nine motors of the soft arm. Four random trajectories, not along any principal direction of motion of the robotic arm, are extracted from workspace which serve as test trajectories for the controllers. Two such trajectories, discretized into 20 points, are highlighted in black color in the figure.

2.1   Experimental Setup

A modular SRA, presented in [5] and shown in Fig. 1a, was employed as the validation test-bed. The soft arm draws inspiration from climbing plants, designed to decrease flexural rigidity from the base to the tip which enables it to support its own weight and maintain an upright posture. The hollow structure of the arm modules and the tapering body further aids in reducing the overall weight of the system. Comprising of three modules arranged sequentially, each module consists of tendons aligned longitudinally at 120° intervals. This configuration allows for omnidirectional bending of the arm sections with differential input and uniform contraction with equal force on all tendons. The tendons were independently activated by Dynamixel XM430-W210-R motors, which also provided feedback on position, velocity, and torque. A rigid 3D-printed frame was used to encase all the motors and securely anchor the arm upright while ensuring its tendons were taut. For environmental feedback, a vision-based tracking system (Vicon) was employed. Three retro-reflective markers placed at the arm's tip enabled the computation of its pose in 3D Cartesian space by averaging the positions of markers belonging to the same cross-section of the module.

2.2   Task Description

The workspace of the robot is illustrated in Fig. 1b. Four random trajectories were extracted from the robot workspace to act as the reference trajectories for the proposed controllers. The figure highlights two of these trajectories in black. Each trajectory is discretized into 20 points. The desired objective (task) is to track the reference trajectory with minimal tracking error with each controller discussed in the subsequent sections.

2.3   Reinforcement Learning-Based Controller (RLC)

RL algorithms are a popular choice when it comes to learning a control solution without requiring any expert knowledge of the platform or the task at hand, especially for sophisticated environments involving highly non-linear systems [21]. Due to the trial-and-error approach of these algorithms, they tend to be very sample inefficient [21,22], requiring millions of time-steps to train a control policy. Since, it is virtually impossible to provide dataset of such a magnitude in the real-time, in-silico training environments are used to train the initial policies [17] and then optimized in real-time to achieve desired behavior on the physical platform of choice [11,23]. Similar task-learning setting was also adopted in the current work, and is depicted in Fig. 2 Top. Specifically, the in-silico training environment included a data-driven Forward Kinematics Model (FKM) of the SRA and a reward function describing the underlying task requirements, and is discussed subsequently.

The FKM was trained, based on the random state-actions dataset collected as follows: a dynamically saturating random actuation space trajectory was designed. The soft arm was actuated at 5 Hz using the actuation space trajectory. Consequently, the movement of the tip of the soft arm (the task space of the soft arm) was recorded via the motion capture system. The resultant movement of the soft arm is shown in Fig. 1b. In total 6000 data samples were recorded. The randomness among the nine actuation space trajectories was meant to record a variety in the soft arm movements, avoid redundancy, and to provide an estimate of the task space state transition of the soft arm in response to nine motor values as input. A simple Artificial Neural Network (ANN), involving a single hidden layer of Long Short Term Memory (LSTM) and a dense output layer, was used to train the FKM. In total, 60% of the random state-action pairs, presented in Sect. 2.2, were used for training with a batch size of 10, *softsign* activation for the input, hidden and output layer, epoch size of 50, and a learning rate of 0.001. The training took less than two-minutes on a personal laptop with Python-based environment, 64 bit Linux-based operating system, 32 GB RAM (with additional 32 GB virtual RAM), Intel core i7-10750H CPU@2.60 GHz, and NVIDIA GeForce RTX 4080 GPU.

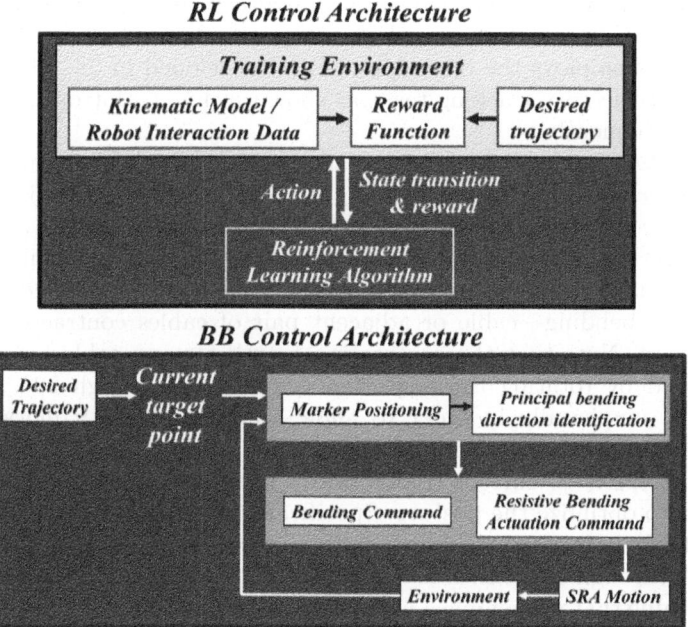

Fig. 2. Control Architectures for the Reinforcement-learning Controller (RLC) and the Behavior-based Controller (BBC)

The reward function was based on a negative of the Mean Absolute Error (MAE) between the policy-reproduced trajectory and the reference trajectory. Soft Actor Critic (SAC) algorithm, presented in [24], was employed to train the control policy using an implementation provided by stable-baselines [25]. The training was performed with the following hyper-parameters: off-policy replay buffer of size 500000 data samples, linearly varying learning rate from 0.001 to 0.0001 for both agents (the actor and critic network), episode length of 200 time-steps, batch-size of $\frac{1}{8}$ time-steps of episode length, gamma of 0.95, and a total of 7 millions time-steps. The training took approximately 3 h on a personal laptop with Python-based environment, 64 bit Linux-based operating system, 32 GB RAM (with additional 32 GB virtual RAM), Intel core i7-10750H CPU@2.60 GHz, and NVIDIA GeForce RTX 4080 GPU.

2.4   Behavioral-Based Controller (BBC)

In the spectrum of artificial intelligence, distributed controllers refer to frameworks that comprise of autonomous computing agents that can act independently and asynchronously, thereby, offering a computationally efficient approach to problem solving without requiring prior knowledge of the platform or the task at hand. This underlies their applicability in dynamically changing environments. In particular, distributed control architectures were pioneered through the development of the behaviour-based architecture [26], which comprises of task-achieving modules, known as behaviours, combined in a bottom-up manner. This work employs the bio-inspired BBC developed in [9], which has been modified for trajectory tracking tasks as shown in Fig. 2 Bottom, and is briefly recapped subsequently.

It is well-known that a triad of radially arranged flexible actuators can generate six principal directions of bending, i.e., by activating any single cable or activating any pairs of adjacent cables. Furthermore, the bending angle in each principal direction can be reduced by contracting the adjacent pair of cables or cable antagonistic to the given configuration. Based on this, we define two basic behaviors: (i) bending—cable or adjacent pair of cables contracted in a principal direction. Note that the contraction length for any cable for a time-step is pre-defined by rotating the respective servomotor through 20°. This value was selected empirically in order to allow minimum smooth motion without backlash; (ii) resistance to bending—contracting a cable or an adjacent pair of cables antagonistic to current configuration to reduce the bending angle from (i) in order to optimize the posture. Specifically, the cables in (ii) are shortened by a pre-defined constant resistive length as a result of rotating the respective servomotor through 10°, which has also been chosen empirically considering the minimum value that will enable a noticeable resistance. The significance of incorporating this resistive pull has been extensively investigated in [27]. These two basic behaviors are combined in a bottom-up manner to formulate the overall controller, which operates at 1 Hz.

The input to the controller is a desired point in the target trajectory described in Sect. 2.2. Specifically, each point in the discretized trajectory is provided to the controller, for a single time-step. In response to this input, the controller will generate activation commands that result in a bending configuration of the soft arm via a two-step sequential decision-making process explained as follows:

(i) six points corresponding to the principal bending directions are identified at the end-effector. Three of these points are visible through the placement of retroreflective markers (from tracking software), whereas the remaining three are computed geometrically. The point closest to the desired target at a given time-step is identified.

(ii) A command is sent to actuators to bend in the corresponding principal bending direction. Simultaneously, the cable or pairs of adjacent cables antagonistic to the current configuration are contracted to optimize the posture of the system.

The effectiveness of the generated solution at each time-step will be measured by the distance between arm's tip and the desired target.

3   Results and Discussion

This section presents the experimental results of the performance of the RL and BB controllers on the SRA, followed by the comparison and discussion of the proposed approaches.

3.1   Architecture Formulation

As mentioned in Sect. 2.3, the RLC controller was formalized through the in-silico training of the control policies using the learning-based-FKM (of the SRA), which achieved an MAE of ≤ 5 mm. Note that the RLC was trained to sequentially reach all the points of the reference trajectory. Then the RLC was validated on the SRA in a closed-loop setting, which means that for a given trajectory, the trained RLC predicted an action for the starting point in the trajectory which was then applied directly to the SRA. In turn, the new state of the SRA was recorded via the vision-based tracking system and provided back to the trained RLC. In the next step, the RLC generated the solution for the next point in the trajectory, and so on. Note that the controller was given a single time-step to reach each point in a given trajectory. In regards to the BBC, the controller did not require any offline formulation, but rather, it was validated directly on the SRA in a closed-loop setting to reach the points in a desired trajectory sequentially, similarly to as done for the RLC. Both controllers were tested at 1 Hz. Additionally it is important to note that the robot is at the neutral position as shown in Fig. 1a at the beginning of each experimental trial.

3.2   Performance Criteria

The performance criteria for the controllers was evaluated as follows: for a given trajectory, the reaching error was measured between the current position of the SRA and the desired position of the trajectory. To guarantee the robustness of generated solutions, the controller was tested for a given trajectory 10 times. The overall performance when then an average error for the 10 trajectories, calculated according to Eq. (1), as,

$$\mu_d = \frac{1}{T} \sum_{t=1}^{T=10} \text{MAE}(s_t^r, \ s_t^i) \tag{1}$$

where, (s^r) refers to the reference trajectory, (s^i) refers to the obtained trajectory, T refers to the number of times the experiment was repeated (in this case, 10), and (μ_d) refers to the mean tracking error over 10 trials for a given trajectory.

3.3   Experimental Results

As an example, the performance of the RLC and BBC along one desired trajectory is illustrated in Figs. 3 and 4, respectively. In particular, Figs. 3(a-b-c) and 4(a-b-c) represent the instantaneous control solution-reproduced 3D trajectories comparison in three different perspectives (xy, yz and xz) in relation to the desired trajectory, for the RLC and BBC respectively. Similarly, Figs. 3(d) and 4(d) highlights the mean tracking error, for the RLC and BBC respectively. It is important to remember that these results are the mean of 10 experimental trials.

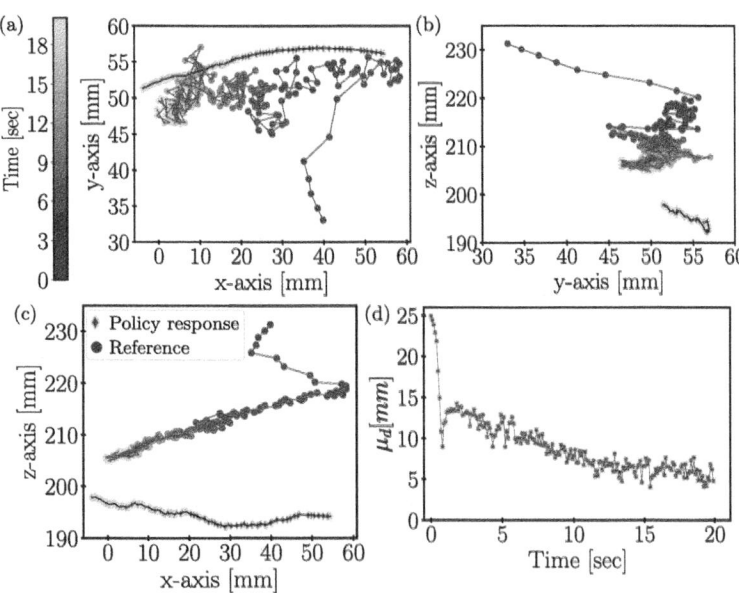

Fig. 3. The performance of RL-trained controller with the three-module soft robot arm (shown in Fig. 1a) along one reference trajectory. **(a-b-c)** the obtained response in relation to the desired trajectory in the x-y-z directions, respectively, **(d)** the tracking error over the entire trajectory. Note that these results have been obtained by taking the mean of 10 experimental trials.

It can be observed that the response of RLC is more chaotic as compared to BBC due to the probabilistic decision-making capability of the SAC-trained policies. This nature, while seems noisy, helps adapt to variations in the evaluation environments as was presented in our previous works in [11,16,17]. However, if task constraints change, for instance, a new trajectory is introduced,

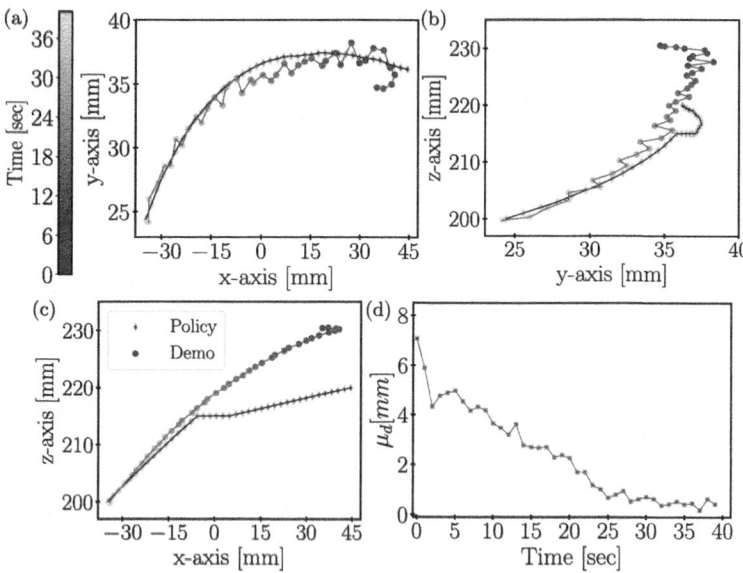

Fig. 4. The performance of behavior-based controller with the three-module soft robot arm (shown in Fig. 1a) along one unseen trajectory. **(a-b-c)** the obtained response in relation to the desired trajectory in the x-y-z directions, respectively, **(d)** the tracking error over the entire trajectory. Note that these results have been obtained by taking the mean of 10 experimental trials.

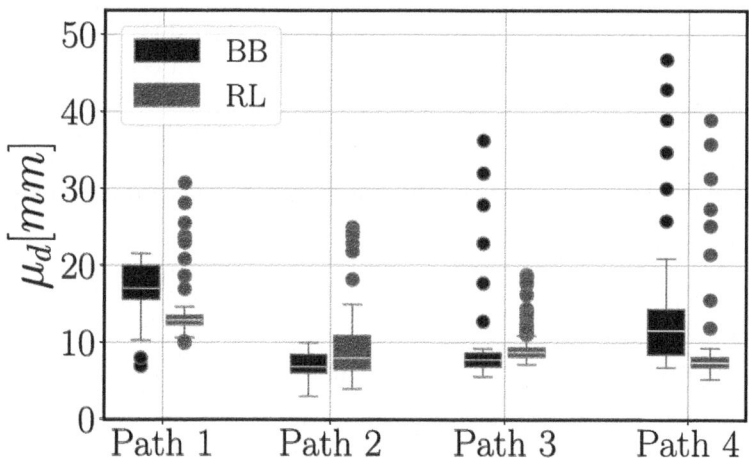

Fig. 5. The figure presents the population statistics of the responses of RLCs and BBCs for four independent reference trajectories extracted from the soft robot's workspace.

RLC will have to be re-trained to meet new task constraints while BBC may be able to generalize with degraded accuracy. An RLC-type of learning-based approaches have additional merits and de-merits associated to them as compared to BBC-type of solutions. For instance, RLC-type of solutions tend to be sample-inefficient (thereby requiring significant more time to derive the control solution) as compared to BBC, making them more practical for real-time control derivation; Their accuracy can be controlled in a wide range of environments irrespective of the mode or number of actuation channels of the testbed while BBC can only work through a handful of actuation-primitives and the complexity may drastically increase with increasing number of actuation channels; Finally, RLCs require substantial storage memory during policy derivation as compared to BBCs.

These experimental protocols were then adopted for four different trajectories. The overall population statistics for the response of RLC and BBC for all four reference trajectories is presented in Fig. 5. It can be observed that there accuracy of the controllers and outperform each other depending upon the trajectory. One reason for this is the fact that the BBC controller is highly dependent upon the initial position of the trajectory, while this is not true for the RLC.

Specifically, if the initial position of the trajectory is close to the initial position of the robot, the BBC will quickly reach the trajectory and continue along the path with an overall lower accuracy. In this case, and also considering it has lower variance along the trajectory as shown previously, it will have an overall lower tracking error. On the other hand, if the initial position of the trajectory is far away, it will take BBC time to reach the trajectory, but once it starts to follow the path, the tracking error will reduce significantly. Another aspect of the BBC is the fact that it only operates by contracting the cables, so there is a limit at which the controller can generate a solution along a trajectory, after-which it will stop to move and the error will undeniably increase. Future works will consider to take a larger action-space into account for this controller. Considering the obtained results, the performance of the controllers have been quantified and compared in Table 1. In particular, the comparison has been done for the follow-

Table 1. Comparison of the RL and BB controllers

Properties	BBC	RLC
Actuation limits	Works only in contraction	Continuous action space
Memoryless control-policies	Yes	Yes
Online method	Yes	No
Computational efficiency	High	Low
Smoothness of the control policy	Jerky motion	Jerky motion
Accuracy	High	High
Real-time solution generation	Yes	No

ing criteria: (i) Architecture Formulation—the actuation limits exploited by the controllers, the nature of the generated control-policies memory-less, the ability of the controllers to work online and/or offline, the computational complexity of the controller; (ii) Performance—the smoothness of the generated control policies, the accuracy of the tracking error, the ability of the controller to generate solutions in real-time. Based on these results, it can be induced that the BBC has more potential to be deployed to real-world scenarios and generalize to unseen circumstances.

4   Conclusions

Establishing safe interaction with the real world through soft robotics is among the primary motivations behind this class of robotics, making the problem of control solutions development, including environmental interaction, a necessary objective. Such a problem setting requires either sophisticated sensory information inclusion or adaptive decision-making. The current work is intended to contribute towards real-time control solutions' development with online adaptive decision-making.

Acknowledgements. The current work was supported in part by NUS startup Grant under *RoboLife – Soft robots with morphological adaptation and life-like abilities*, in part by an EU MSCA ITN Project *SMART - Soft, Self-responsive, Smart MAterials for RoboTs* with grant agreement no. 860108, and in part by an EU Project *GROWBOT - Towards a new generation of plant-inspired growing artefacts* under grant agreement no. 824074.

Disclosure of Interests. The authors have no competing interests to declare that are relevant to the content of this article.

References

1. Laschi, C., Mazzolai, B., Cianchetti, M.: Soft robotics: technologies and systems pushing the boundaries of robot abilities. Sci. Robot. **1**(1), eaah3690 (2016)
2. Ansari, Y., Hassan, T., Manti, M., Falotico, E., Cianchetti, M., Laschi, C.: Soft robotic technologies for industrial applications. In: European Projects in Knowledge Applications and Intelligent Aystems-EPS Lisbon, pp. 35–64 (2016)
3. Laschi, C., Cianchetti, M., Mazzolai, B., Margheri, L., Follador, M., Dario, P.: Soft robot arm inspired by the octopus. Adv. Robot. **26**(7), 709–727 (2012)
4. Walker, I.D.: Continuous backbone "continuum" robot manipulators. International Scholarly Research Notices (2013)
5. Naselli, G.A., Scharff, R.B., Thielen, M., Visentin, F., Speck, T., Mazzolai, B.: A soft continuum robotic arm with a climbing plant-inspired adaptive behavior for minimal sensing, actuation, and control effort. Adv. Intell. Syst., 2300537 (2023)
6. Speck, T., Rowe, N.P.: In: Kurmann, M.H., Hemsley, A.R. (eds.) The Evolution of Plant Architecture, pp. 447–479. Royal Botanic Gardens, Kew, UK (1999)
7. Dagenais, P., Hensman, S., Haechler, V., Milinkovitch, M.C.: Curr. Biol. **31**, 4727 (2021)

8. Xie, Z., Domel, A.G., An, N., Green, C., Gong, Z., Wang, T., Knubben, E.M., Weaver, J.C., Bertoldi, K., Wen, L.: Soft Robot. **7**, 63 (2020)
9. Donato, E., Ansari, Y.T., Laschi, C., Falotico, E.: Plant-inspired behavior-based controller to enable reaching in redundant continuum robot arms. In: 2023 IEEE International Conference on Soft Robotics (RoboSoft), pp. 1–6. IEEE (2023)
10. George Thuruthel, T., Ansari, Y., Falotico, E., Laschi, C.: Control strategies for soft robotic manipulators: a survey. Soft Robot. **5**(2), 149–163 (2018)
11. Nazeer, M.S., Laschi, C., Falotico, E.: RL-based adaptive controller for high precision reaching in a soft robot arm. IEEE Trans. Robot. (2024)
12. Jones, B.A., Walker, I.D.: Kinematics for multisection continuum robots. IEEE Trans. Robot. **22**(1), 43–55 (2006)
13. Camarillo, D.B., Carlson, C.R., Salisbury, J.K.: Task-space control of continuum manipulators with coupled tendon drive. In: Experimental Robotics, pp. 271–280. Springer, Berlin, Heidelberg (2009)
14. Bailly, Y., Amirat, Y.: Modeling and control of a hybrid continuum active catheter for aortic aneurysm treatment. In: Proceedings of the 2005 IEEE International Conference on Robotics and Automation, 2005. ICRA 2005, pp. 924–929. IEEE (2005)
15. Coevoet, E., et al.: Software toolkit for modeling, simulation, and control of soft robots. Adv. Robot. **31**(22), 1208–1224 (2017)
16. Nazeer, M.S., Laschi, C., Falotico, E.: Soft dagger: sample-efficient imitation learning for control of soft robots. Sensors **23**(19), 8278 (2023)
17. Nazeer, M.S., Bianchi, D., Campinoti, G., Laschi, C. and Falotico, E.: Policy adaptation using an online regressing network in a soft robotic arm. In: 2023 IEEE International Conference on Soft Robotics (RoboSoft), pp. 1–7. IEEE (2023)
18. George Thuruthel, T., Falotico, E., Manti, M., Pratesi, A., Cianchetti, M., Laschi, C.: Learning closed loop kinematic controllers for continuum manipulators in unstructured environments. Soft Robot. **4**(3), 285–296 (2017)
19. Szadkowski, R., Nazeer, M.S., Cianchetti, M., Falotico, E., Faigl, J.: Bootstrapping the dynamic gait controller of the soft robot arm. In: 2023 IEEE International Conference on Robotics and Automation (ICRA), pp. 2669–2675. IEEE (2023)
20. Ansari, Y., Manti, M., Falotico, E., Cianchetti, M., Laschi, C.: Multiobjective optimization for stiffness and position control in a soft robot arm module. IEEE Robot. Autom. Lett. **3**(1), 108–115 (2017)
21. Wiering, M.A., Van Otterlo, M.: Reinforcement learning. Adapt. Learn. Optim. **12**(3), 729 (2012)
22. Cianchetti, M., Laschi, C., Menciassi, A., Dario, P.: Biomedical applications of soft robotics. Nat. Rev. Mater. **3**(6), 143–153 (2018)
23. Nazeer, M.S., Laschi, C., Falotico, E.: Imitation and reinforcement learning to control soft robots: a perspective. In: IOP Conference Series: Materials Science and Engineering, vol. 1292, no. 1, pp. 012010. IOP Publishing (2023)
24. Haarnoja, T., et al.: Soft Actor-Critic Algorithms and Applications (2018). arXiv preprint: arXiv:1812.05905
25. Raffin, A., Hill, A., Gleave, A., Kanervisto, A., Ernestus, M., Dormann, N.: Stable-baselines3: reliable reinforcement learning implementations. J. Mach. Learn. Res. **22**(268), 1–8 (2021)
26. Arkin, R.C., Arkin, R.C.: Behavior-Based Robotics. MIT Press (1998)
27. Donato, E., Ansari, Y.T., Laschi, C., Falotico, E.: To Enabling Plant-like Movement Capabilities in Continuum Arms (2022)

Pulse Modulation in Braided Pneumatic Actuators Mimics Contractile Behavior of Biological Muscles

Mohammad Elzein$^{(\boxtimes)}$ and Alexander Hunt

Portland State University, Portland, OR 97201, USA
melzein@pdx.edu

Abstract. Advancements in robotics and bioengineering have steered toward the emulation of biological muscle systems with robotic actuators to achieve a synthesis of mechanical strength and biological adaptability. One area that has been the subject of relatively few investigations, however, is mimicking the pulse-like control of muscles. Muscles contract in response to action potentials generated in motoneurons. Previous investigations have found that muscle contractile force is highly dependent on the timing between action potentials. This study investigates the influence of pulse lengths and the inter-pulse gap on the performance of braided pneumatic actuators (BPAs), devices characterized by their nonlinearity and dynamic response akin to biological muscles. Our research hypothesizes that pulse-based control strategies used in artificial muscles will closely resemble the same force dependence on inter-pulse intervals that is seen in biological muscles. We present an analysis of the maximum force output of BPAs as a function of pulse length and pulse timing, illustrating a discernible pattern of force augmentation related to pulse durations and inter-pulse gaps. The pulse lengths tested were 10, 15, 20, 25, 30, 35, and 40 ms. In these tests, two pulses were provided to the artificial muscles with varying inter-pulse intervals, ranging from 500 ms to 1 ms. The force and pressure in the muscles were recorded during the pulses. The corresponding max recorded forces were 71, 105, 136, 158, 182, 204, and 205 N. When these max forces were normalized by the force the muscle produced under a single short pulse, the max forces were 3.55, 3.38, 3.16, 2.63, 2.52, 2.41, and 2.2, respectively. Our findings suggest that using artificial muscles with a bio-inspired pulse-based control scheme may provide increased biomimetic capabilities when compared to other control schemes, with the maximum force being recorded with a pulse gap interval of approximately 27 ms, regardless of the pulse duration. The experimental design did not include a full factorial test, and the scope of our claims is limited to the specific pulse durations and gaps tested. Future research should explore a wider range of pulse combinations to fully understand the optimal control strategies for BPAs.

Keywords: Actuator · Artificial Muscles · Biomimicry

N. S. Szczecinski et al. (Eds.): Living Machines 2024, LNAI 14930, pp. 221–235, 2025.
https://doi.org/10.1007/978-3-031-72597-5_16

1 Introduction

The development of robotic actuators that emulate the dynamic capabilities of biological muscle systems represents a frontier in robotics and bioengineering. This endeavor seeks not only to replicate the mechanical prowess of natural muscles but to integrate the nuanced control and adaptability inherent in biological systems. The foundational work of Griffin, Godfrey, and Thomas [1] on muscle activation patterns has been pivotal, offering insights into the optimal stimulation strategies to maximize muscle force. Another study on trunk muscle activation patterns during hip abduction tests highlights the importance of understanding how muscles coordinate to maintain stability and function [12], thus providing a critical bridge between biological flexibility,artificial constraints and applications of these concepts [1, 12].

In nature, muscles contract when they receive signals from the nervous system that cause their fibers to shorten, pulling on bones and creating movement. In the study by Griffin et al. [1], they explored how electrical pulses can be used to stimulate muscle contractions, specifically in muscles that are paralyzed due to spinal cord injuries. They discovered that a specific pattern of quick pulses of electricity followed by short pauses maximized the force of muscle contractions, as shown in Fig. 1 below.

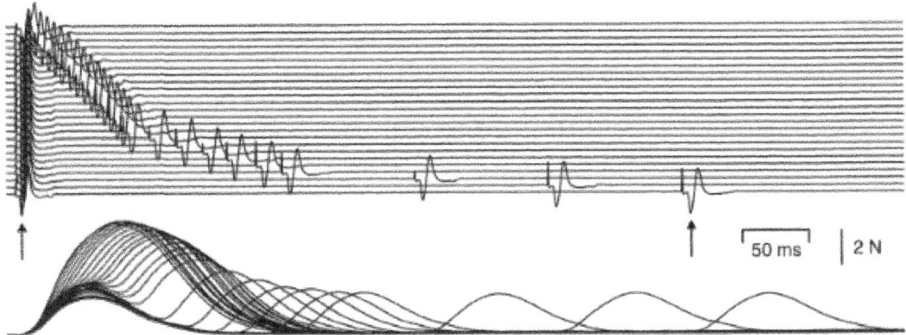

Fig. 1. 50 μs 2-pulse train force results from a paralyzed thenar muscle, it shows the results from the response of the test subjects muscle, recording resultant force evoked from the paralyzed thenar muscles of a spinal cord–injured (SCI) subject by trains of 2 pulses of 50 μs length. The top portion of the figure represents the sent electrical pulse signals while the bottom portion represents the resultant force from the pulses. Used with permission from Dr. Griffin from her 2002 paper "Stimulation pattern that maximizes force in paralyzed and control whole thenar muscles" [1].

Recent advancements in the field have underscored the potential of human muscle activation patterns to enhance the functionality of braided pneumatic actuators (BPAs). These actuators, noted for their nonlinearity, hysteresis, and time-varying behaviors, necessitate sophisticated control strategies that can emulate the adaptability and precision of biological muscles [2, 3]. For instance, the biologically inspired control of humanoid robots using McKibben pneumatic artificial muscles, such as demonstrated by Hosoda et al. in their design of a jumping robot with an anthropomorphic muscular skeleton structure, has proven the feasibility of mimicking human muscle activation patterns to achieve human-like movements and adaptability to load changes [4, 8]. Furthermore, the exploration of hybrid actuation principles, inspired by the antagonistic muscle action in animals, for soft robotic manipulators, indicates a promising direction for enhancing robotic adaptability and precision [5, 6]. The work by Asano et al. on Kenshiro, a humanoid that closely mimics the human musculoskeletal system, exemplifies how these principles can be integrated to improve the dynamic capabilities of robots, thereby contributing significantly to the field of bio-inspired robotics [9].

Our hypothesis builds upon this work, proposing that pulse-based control strategies used on artificial muscles will closely resemble the same force dependence on inter-pulse intervals that is seen on biological muscles. We attempt this by pulsing a braided pneumatic actuator for a short, specified amount of time while it is connected to a force sensor to capture the results. We shorten the amount of time between 2 separate pulses of a specified length to see the effect of the time between pulses and their resultant force. This is important as it can shed light on the use of pulse width modification (PWM) in controlling the BPAs.

2 Methods

2.1 Experimental Setup

The experimental apparatus consisted of braided pneumatic actuators (BPAs) connected to a controlled building air supply, at a pressure of 6.205 Bar, that could vary the pulse length and inter-pulse gap with the use of Festo VUVG-B14-T32C-AZT-F-1T1L air solenoid valves on a VTUG valve manifold. Loadstar RAS1 S-beam force sensors were attached to the BPAs to measure the output force in Newtons (N). NXP MPX5700AP Pressure sensors were placed parallel to the BPA to confirm pulse pressure. The structure, as shown in Fig. 2, consists of 80/20 T-slot bars holding a Loadstar RAS1 S-beam 1000 lb load cell connected to one end of the 10 mm diameter, 312 mm long Festo MXAM-10 BPA. The sensor readings and control of the Festo air solenoid valves were implemented with the use of an Elegoo Uno R3 board and Arduino coding, and the data processing was implemented with the use of MATLAB. The load cell data was calibrated to be zero force while the setup was at rest, and all reported force values are in reference to this no-load force.

2.2 Braided Pneumatic Actuator

McKibben braided pneumatic actuators (BPA), also known as pneumatic artificial muscles, are widely utilized in robotics and bioengineering for their ability to mimic the behavior of biological muscles [10]. The McKibben braided pneumatic actuator, also known as a pneumatic artificial muscle, originated from the work of Joseph L. McKibben in the 1950 s. It was initially developed as an assistive device for polio patients to help them regain muscle function [17]. These BPA's consisted of a rubber tube within a braided mesh that when inflated would cause the radius of the tube to increase while causing a decrease in its length [13], as shown in Fig. 2b.

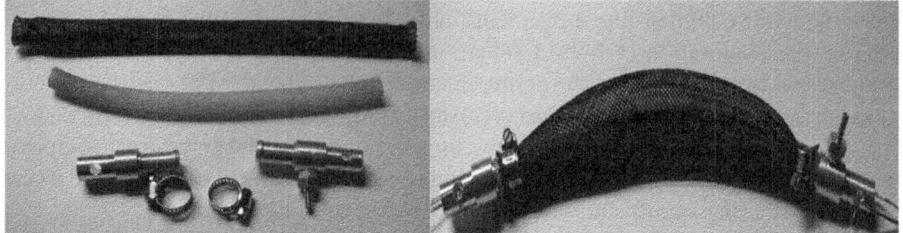

Fig. 2. A. McKibben braided pneumatic actuator parts that consists of a braided mesh, inflatable rubber tube, and valve end stops. **B.** assembled and inflated McKibben BPA [11].

Fig. 3. Festo fluidic muscle cross section

The Festo fluidic muscles are a variant of McKibben BPAs. Unlike traditional McKibben actuators that have a rubber bladder inflating within a braided mesh, these actuators consist of a rubber bladder with braids embedded at specific angles, as shown in Fig. 3. When pressurized, the bladder expands, causing the braided structure to contract longitudinally and generate force, as illustrated in Fig. 2b. Human muscles follow a similar behavior, generally contracting to about 80% of their resting length when fully flexed [16]. This mirrors the operation of Festo fluidic muscles, which contract to 70–80% of their original length when inflated, exhibiting the same dynamic behavior [17].

2.3 Pulse Modulation Protocol

Pulse lengths were modulated using Festo VUVG-B14-T32C-AZT-F-1T1L Solenoid valves, as shown in Fig. 4, which allowed for precise control over the timing of air pulses delivered to the BPAs. These solenoid valves are known for their high flow rates and compact design, making them ideal for applications requiring quick response times and reliable performance. These 2 × 3/2-way, monostable, closed valves are a type of pneumatic valve with two positions and three ports. In its default (monostable) state, it blocks the flow of air, and when activated, it allows air to pass through one of the ports to another. This type of valve is typically used to control the direction of air flow in pneumatic systems. These valves have a reported switch on time of 10 ms and switch off time of 27 ms [14, 15].

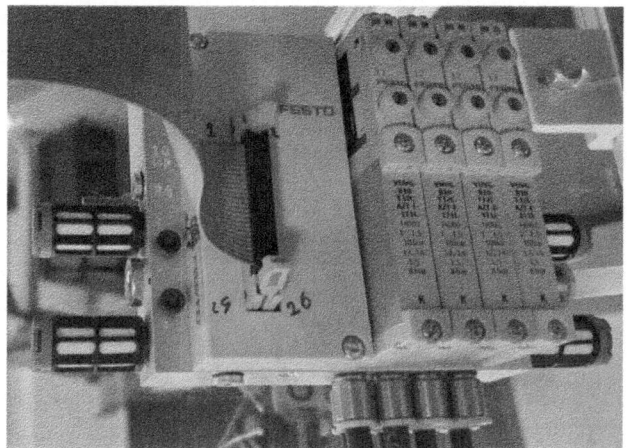

Fig. 4. Festo VUVG-B14-T32C-AZT-F-1T1L Solenoid valves

The supply pressure was set to 6.205 Bar. The pulse lengths tested were 10, 15, 20, 25, 30, 35, and 40 ms. The inter-pulse gap was also systematically varied between 1 ms and 500 ms. To manage data collection efficiently, the inter-pulse gap was varied according to the size of the gap. For inter-pulse gaps, 500 ms and 250 ms, the change in inter-pulse gap was set at 25 ms, for delays between 250 ms and 100 ms, the change in inter-pulse gap was set to 15 ms, for those between 100 ms and 70 ms, the change was set to 10 ms. For the shortest delays, those under 70 ms, the change in gap size was minimized to 2 ms. This range of timing variables was chosen as the output force started to change at a much higher rate when the pulses were closer together in comparison to when they were further apart. This nuanced approach allowed for an exploration of the effects of pulses proximity to one another on the resultant force exerted by the BPAs. By recording the force and analyzing the impact of both pulse lengths and the duration between pulses, we aimed to uncover the relationships between timing of both parameters for use in pneumatic actuation system controls (Fig. 5).

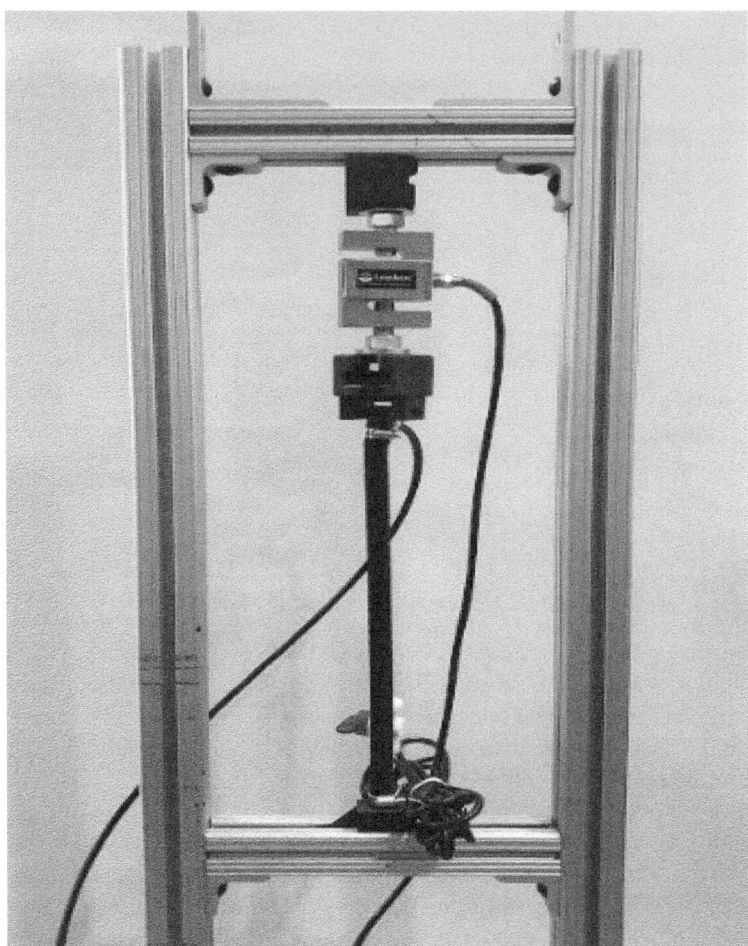

Fig. 5. Testing structure holding the BPA. The artificial muscle, long tube in black, is secured using 3D printed parts to the bottom of the frame and an S-shaped load cell for force data collection.

2.4 Data Analysis

The data was subjected to quantitative signal analysis using MATLAB. To ensure accurate representation and reduce noise, a 12th order Butterworth filter was applied with a 1000 Hz sampling rate and a 120 Hz cutoff frequency. This filtering process was critical to eliminate high-frequency noise that could distort the results, particularly important when dealing with sensitive measurements of force. For normalization, each maximum force value was divided by the highest maximum force recorded in the experiment, resulting in normalized data representing the efficiency relative to pulse length. The normalized maximum force data was then plotted against pulse length using MATLAB to visualize trends. The Butterworth filter was utilized because of its maximally flat frequency response in the passband, ensuring that the filtered signal retained its shape, thus providing a clear and accurate analysis of the relationship between pulse length and actuator efficiency without the interference of unwanted high-frequency components.

3   Results

3.1   Force Response to Varying Pulse Lengths

Figure 6 shows the results for the braided pneumatic actuators (BPAs) subjected to air pulses of varying lengths: 10, 15, 20, 25, 30, 35, and 40 ms. When the pulse gap is 500 ms, the force profiles do not overlap for any of the pulse lengths, however as the pulse gap gets smaller, the force responses from the pulses begin to overlap, increasing the force output. The maximum force was found with 40 ms pulses spaced 27 ms apart. This is 2.2 times higher than a single 40 ms pulse, which results in a force of 205 N. For the 10 ms pulse, the maximum force was found with pulses spaced 27 ms apart, with a resultant force of 71 N. This was found to be 3.55 times larger than the single pulse. For the 15 ms pulse, the maximum force was found also with a pulse gap of 27 ms with a resultant force of 105 N, which is 3.38 times larger than the single pulse. The 20 ms pulse had a similar pulse gap of 27 ms with a resultant force of 136 N, which is 3.16 times larger than a single pulse max. The 25 ms pulses also had maximum force at a pulse gap of 27 ms with a force output of 158 N, which is 2.63 times larger than a single pulse. The 30 ms pulses had a similar pulse gap of 27 ms for the maximum resultant force of 182 N, this was found to be 2.53 times greater than the single pulse output. For the 35 ms pulses, the pulse gap was also found to be 27 ms with the resultant force of 204 N, which is 2.41 times greater than the single pulse maximum. This information is summarized in Table 1.

Table 1. Varying pulse lengths and their corresponding single pulse and double pulse maximum force outputs and the normalized force results.

Pulse length (ms)	Single pulse maximum force (N)	Double pulse maximum force (N)	Normalized maximum force
10	20	71	3.55
15	31	105	3.38
20	43	136	3.16
25	60	158	2.63
30	72	182	2.53
35	84.5	204	2.41
40	93	205	2.20

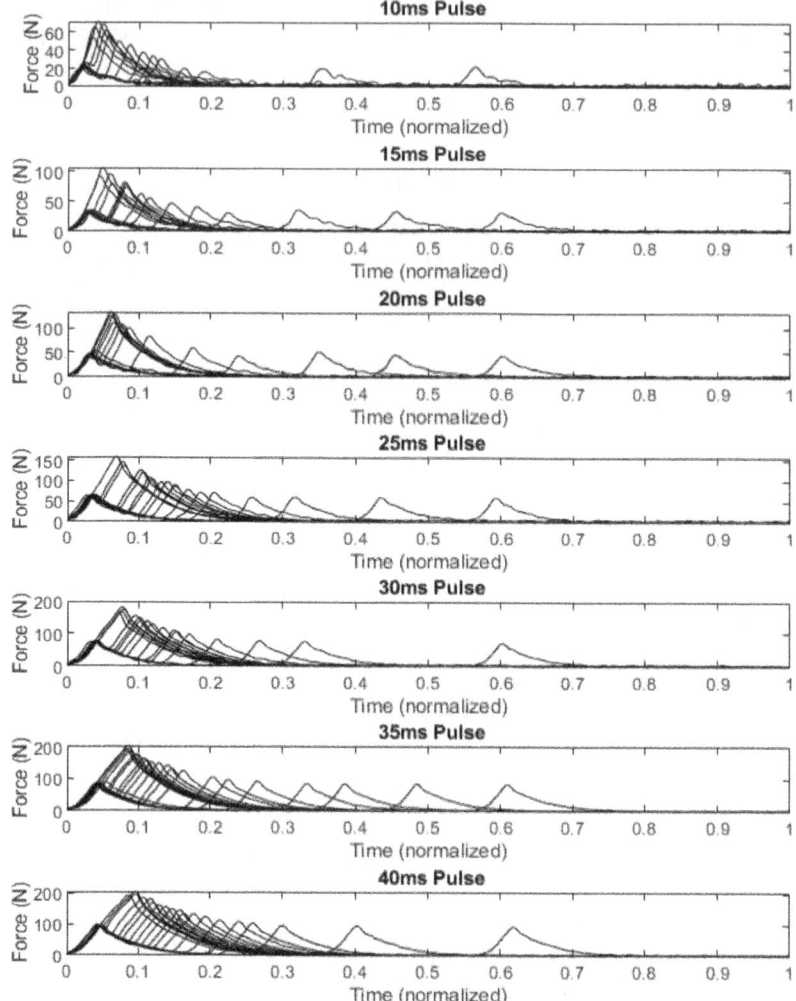

Fig. 6. Force responses for each pulse length ranging from 10 ms to 40 ms. Not every pulse is depicted, the portions of data used for the graphs were selected to best represent the general behavior shown in the results.

Figure 6 presents a comprehensive subplot arrangement, displaying the force response for each pulse length, ranging from 10 ms to 40 ms, the portions of data used for the graphs were selected to best represent the general behavior shown in the results.

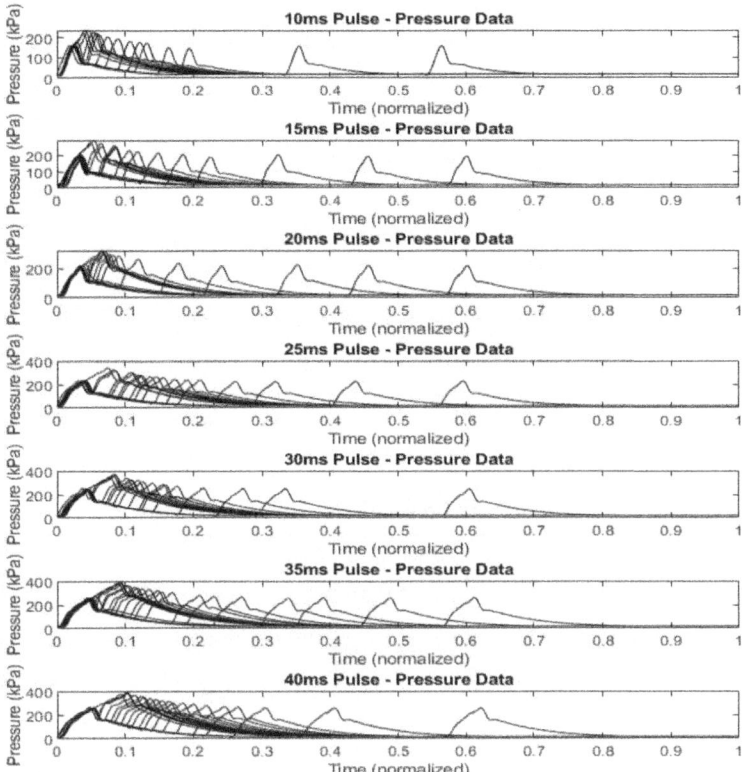

Fig. 7. Pressure responses for each pulse length ranging from 10 ms to 40 ms. Not every pulse is depicted, the portions of data used for the graphs were selected to best represent the general behavior shown in the results.

The resemblance of the results shown in Figs. 1 and 6 helps to show that the pulse mechanisms found in nature can have a similar output when applied to mechanical designs. Figure 7 is like Fig. 6 but is concentrating only on the pressure output. Which shared the semi similar results but was not a sum greater than its inputs.

3.2 Detailed Examination of Maximum Force Points

Figure 8 shows a graph of 2 40 ms pulses with a 0.5 s gap between the end of the first pulse and the start of the second pulse alongside the square wave pulses to represent the time when the command to open the valves to inflate the BPA is sent in comparison to the time it takes for it to be achieved. It is highlighting the pulse gap, where it is the time from when the valve close command is sent at the end of the first pulse and the open command is sent to begin the second pulse. It also shows the length of the pulse on the right which depicts the time the valve first opens, building pressure, to the time it closes, after which the pressure in the BPA escapes.

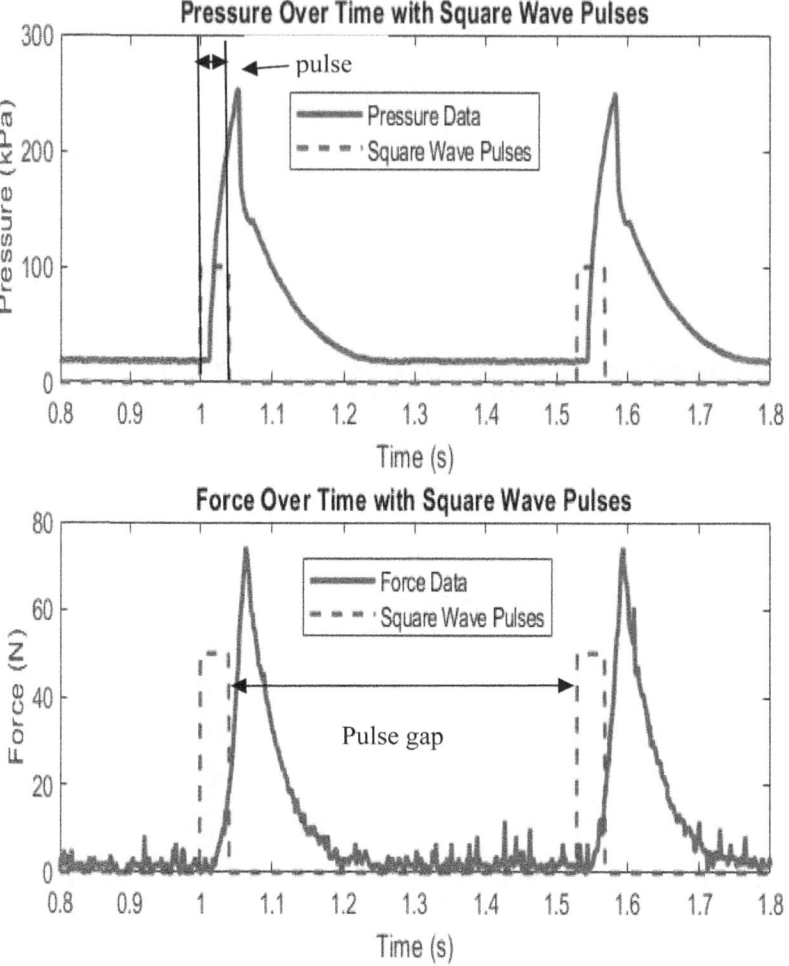

Fig. 8. 2 40 ms pulses with a 0.5 s gap between the end of the first pulse and the start of the second pulse alongside the square wave pulse to represent the time the commands to open and close the valves are sent.

Figure 9, below, focuses on the critical moments where maximum force is achieved for a 40 ms pulse length. This figure details the segment of the plot immediately surrounding the peak force output for the 40 ms pulse duration tested.

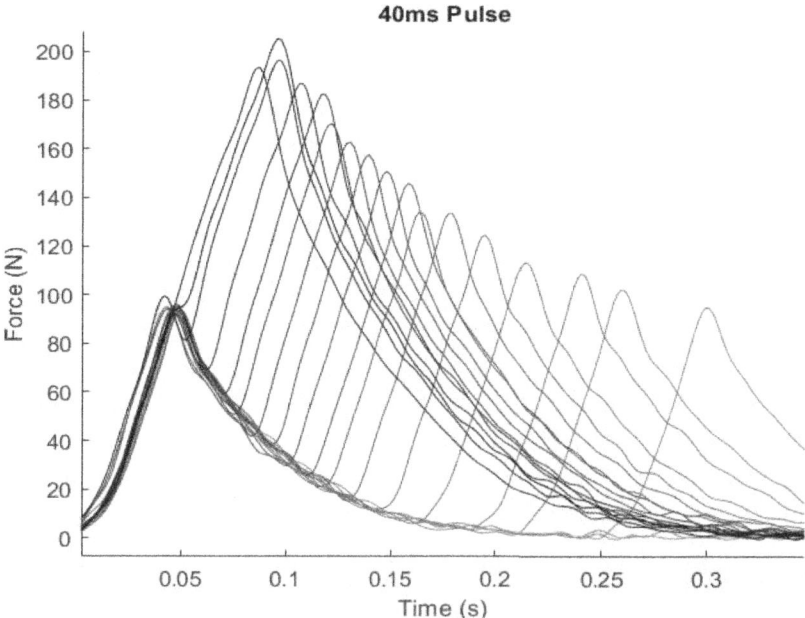

Fig. 9. Close up view of the force produced with a Pulse Length of 40 ms. A maximum force 205 N was produced with a Pulse Gap of 27 ms. This pulse gap is seen across the various pulse lengths and corresponds the amount of time it takes to fully close the valve before reopening.

3.3   Analysis of Maximum Force Output

We further analyzed the data to assess both the absolute maximum force output across the varying pulse lengths and the force output, normalized against the peak force observed for each pulse length, as shown in Fig. 10. One notable trend: shorter pulse lengths demonstrated superior normalized maximum force values, with 10 ms pulses achieving a value of 3.55. Several notable trends can be observed in this data. First, the maximum force increases fairly linearly with the pulse length, for both single and double pulses. However, the effect of timing a second pulse is more significant for smaller pulse lengths than larger pulse lengths, as can be seen in Fig. 8b. This trend indicates a decreasing normalized force with increasing pulse lengths, where 15 ms pulses have a normalized value of 3.38 when compared to a single pulse, 20 ms pulses have a value of 3.16, 25 ms pulses have a value of 2.63, 30 ms have a value of 2.52, and the 40 ms pulses exhibited the lowest normalized maximum force value of 2.2. This observation underscores the intricacies of pulse duration on actuator performance, revealing that shorter pulses, while less forceful in absolute terms, can result in a significantly higher proportion of force when the pulses are timed properly.

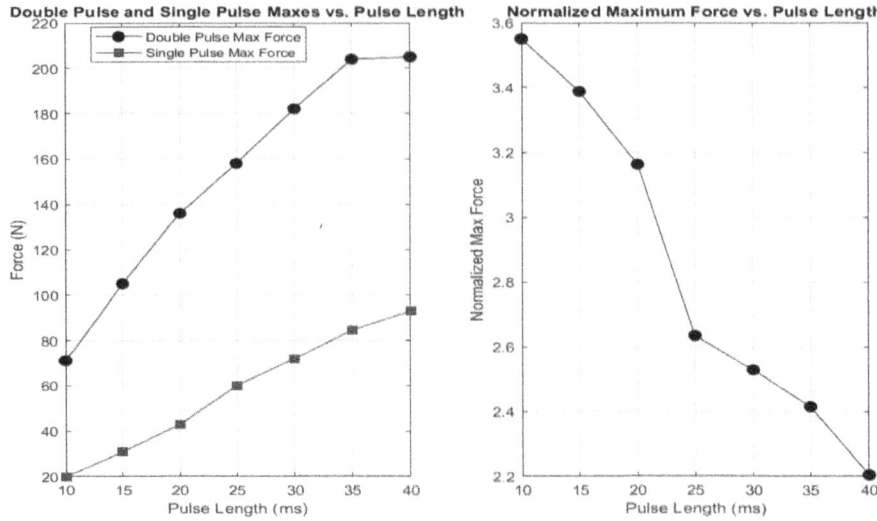

Fig. 10. A, Maximum Pulse Force Output (N) vs. Pulse Length (ms) **B,** Normalized Max Force vs Pulse length

4   Discussion

The results of this study have unveiled insights into the performance characteristics of BPAs under various pulse modulation schemes. By examining the relationship between pulse length and maximum force output, we observed a clear pattern of force augmentation with increased pulse durations. Specifically, pulse lengths ranging from 10 ms to 40 ms exhibited a progressive increase in maximum force output, with values starting from 71 N at 10 ms and reaching a maximum around 205 N at 40 ms. This pattern is indicative of the BPAs' sensitivity to pulse modulation, showcasing a relatively linear relationship between pulse length and actuator force output [7]. Both 35 ms and 40 ms exhibit similar force contractions, showing a non-linear effect at the longest pulses. It is unclear if this is the beginning of a new trend, or just an artifact of having limited data. More data at longer pulse lengths should be collected to clarify this result. An interesting find from this study is that a double pulse can have a higher output force than a single pulse of the same duration. This can be seen with the 10 ms double pulse having a maximum force of 71 N in comparison to the 20 ms single pulse having a maximum force of 43 N.

Another one of the more intriguing findings was the normalized maximum force data, which provides a nuanced view of actuator performance relative to pulse length variations. Similar to biological muscles, the force output from the artificial muscle can be amplified by correctly timing the pulses between activation. In biological muscles, this likely occurs due to enhanced calcium release and mechanical advantage due to the elimination of slack in the system [1]. For our artificial system, this force is increased because the pressurized air does not have time to completely escape the BPA before the valve controlling the air flow receives another command to open again. Consequently, this cumulative effect enhances the force output of the BPA.

Shorter pulse lengths demonstrate an amplified response to multiple pulses in a row when compared to longer pulses. This is evidenced by the higher normalized maximum force values for 10 ms pulses being 3.55 vs a maximum normalized force value of 2.2 for 40 ms pulses. These results are to be expected as the increased time that the valve is open becomes a smaller percent of time overall for longer pulse durations. Interestingly, biological muscles showed a peak normalized force value of around 2.8 [1]. This falls right in the middle of the pulse lengths tested in this work and would be similar to what would occur for a pulse length of 20–25 ms.

Furthermore, these results highlight the role of the inter-pulse gap in achieving optimal actuator performance, with a notable observation that the average pulse gap required to reach maximum force without being perceived as a continuous single pulse was approximately 27 ms. This finding emphasizes the importance of timing in the control strategies of BPAs, suggesting that beyond the duration of stimulation, the recovery or rest period between pulses is pivotal in determining force output.

The implications of these findings are important for the design and control of soft robotic systems, particularly in applications requiring high adaptability and precision, such as humanoid robotics and rehabilitation devices. The ability to fine-tune actuator performance through pulse modulation opens new avenues for developing more responsive and efficient robotic systems that better mimic the complex dynamics of biological muscle systems. Additionally, the control of vibration resulting from the rapid pulses should be considered to ensure the stability and smooth operation of the actuators, as excessive vibration could lead to wear and tear or affect the precision of the system.

Moreover, our study highlights another mechanism by which to replicate the behavior of biological muscles, offering a promising direction for the future of soft robotics. By further exploring the intricate balance between pulse length and inter-pulse gap, researchers can explore how the nervous system optimizes motoneuron behavior to produce effective and efficient control.

One notable limitation of our study stems from the mechanical constraints of the Festo Solenoid valves employed in our pulse modulation protocol. Specifically, these valves were experimentally found to require approximately 7 ms to fully open and 25 ms to close. Consequently, the results presented here are specific to the valves used in this study. Valves with different opening and closing timing will necessarily get different results. However, because of how these results are produced, these results should follow the same trends. That is, there should exist an optimal inter-pulse gap that results in maximal forces being larger than the addition of force from two pulses. Researchers using alternative valve technologies with different response times may seek to perform their own tests or to develop novel strategies that account for and mitigate these mechanical limitations. Additionally, valves with faster response times may enable more fine control over the forces produced using this activation methodology. This adaptation could enable a more precise emulation of the rapid muscle activation and relaxation cycles observed in biological systems, thereby enhancing the bio-inspired fidelity and functional versatility of braided pneumatic actuators.

In light of these findings, future research should focus on expanding the range of pulse lengths and inter-pulse gaps explored, as well as investigating the effects of varying air pressure and actuator configurations. Such studies would contribute to a deeper understanding of the fundamental mechanisms governing BPA performance and facilitate the development of more sophisticated control algorithms tailored to specific application needs.

5   Conclusion

In conclusion, our study underscores the potential of bio-inspired pulse modulation in advancing the design and functionality of pneumatic actuators. As we continue to bridge the gap between biological inspiration and robotic application, the insights from this research will undoubtedly play a role in shaping the future of soft robotics, paving the way for more adaptive, efficient, and capable robotic systems.

Acknowledgments. I would personally like to thank the members of Portland State University's Agile and Adaptive Robotics Lab for providing guidance and help, when necessary, with the collection and management of data. I would also like to thank Dr. Griffin for her work in inspiring the goals of this paper.

Disclosure of Interests. The authors have no competing interests to declare that are relevant to the content of this article.

References

1. Griffin, L., et al.: Stimulation pattern that maximizes force in paralyzed and control whole thenar muscles. Journal of Neurophysiology **87**(5), 2271–2278 (2002). https://doi.org/10.1152/jn.2002.87.5.2271
2. Robinson, R.M., et al.: Model-based feedforward control of a robotic manipulator with pneumatic artificial muscles. Volume 1: Development and Characterization of Multifunctional Materials; Modeling, Simulation and Control of Adaptive Systems; Structural Health Monitoring (2012). https://doi.org/10.1115/smasis2012-8084
3. Yang, T., et al.: Learning-based error-constrained motion control for pneumatic artificial muscle-actuated exoskeleton robots with hardware experiments. IEEE Trans. Auto. Sci. Eng. **19**(4), 3700–3711 (2022). https://doi.org/10.1109/tase.2021.3131034
4. Northrup, S.G.: Biologically -inspired control of a humanoid robot with nonlinear actuators. Vanderbilt University, United States -- Tennessee (2001). ProQuest, https://stats.lib.pdx.edu/proxy.php? url= https://www.proquest.com/dissertations-theses/biologically-inspired-control-humanoid-robot-with/docview/304726910/se-2
5. Stilli, A., et al.: Shrinkable, stiffness-controllable soft manipulator based on a bio-inspired antagonistic actuation principle. In: 2014 IEEE/RSJ International Conference on Intelligent Robots and Systems (2014). https://doi.org/10.1109/iros.2014.6942899
6. Park, Y.-L., et al.: Design and control of a bio-inspired soft wearable robotic device for ankle–foot rehabilitation. Bioinspiration & Biomimetics **9**(1), 016007 (2014). https://doi.org/10.1088/1748-3182/9/1/016007

7. Colbrunn, R.W., et al.: Modeling of braided pneumatic actuators for robotic control. Proceedings 2001 IEEE/RSJ International Conference on Intelligent Robots and Systems. Expanding the Societal Role of Robotics in the the Next Millennium (Cat. No.01CH37180) (2001). https://doi.org/10.1109/iros.2001.976361

8. Hosoda, K., Sakaguchi, Y., Takayama, H., Takenaka, T.: Pneumatic-driven jumping robot with anthropomorphic muscular skeleton structure. Auton. Robot. **28**(3), 307–316 (2009). https://doi.org/10.1007/s10514-009-9171-6

9. Asano, Y., Okada, K., Inaba, M.: Musculoskeletal design, control, and application of human mimetic humanoid Kenshiro. Bioinspir. Biomim. **14**(3), 036011 (2019). https://doi.org/10.1088/1748-3190/ab03fc

10. Aschenbeck, K.S., Kern, N.I., Bachmann, R.J., Quinn, R.D.: Design of a quadruped robot driven by air muscles. The First IEEE/RAS-EMBS International Conference on Biomedical Robotics and Biomechatronics, pp. 875–880. Pisa, Italy (2006). https://doi.org/10.1109/BIOROB.2006.1639201

11. How to make air muscles! (2007). Instructables. Retrieved from https://www.instructables.com/How-to-make-air-muscles/

12. Murata, N., et al.: Trunk muscle activation patterns during active hip abduction test during remission from recurrent low back pain: an observational study. BMC Musculoskelet. Disord. **22**, 395 (2021). https://doi.org/10.1186/s12891-021-04538-5

13. Chou, C.P., Hannaford, B.: Measurement and Modeling of McKibben Pneumatic Artificial Muscles. IEEE Trans. Robot. Autom. **12**(1), 90–102 (1996). https://doi.org/10.1109/70.481753

14. Datasheet: Solenoid valve VUVG-B14-T32C-AZT-F-1T1L (2024.). Festo. Retrieved from https://www.festo.com/tw/en/a/download-document/datasheet/573476

15. Datasheet: Valve manifold VTUG (2024). Festo. Retrieved from https://www.festo.com/us/en/a/download-document/datasheet/573606

16. Anatomy & Physiology: Nervous System Control of Muscle Tension, OpenStax, https://pressbooks-dev.oer.hawaii.edu/anatomyandphysiology/chapter/nervous-system-control-of-muscle-tension/

17. Gurstelle, W.: Making a Simple Air Muscle. Make (2015). https://makezine.com/projects/joseph-mckibben-and-the-air-muscle/

System Design

Design of a Rat Robotic Forelimb

Huy Pham[1]([✉]), Clayton B. Jackson[1], Benjamin Armstead[1],
William R. P. Nourse[3], Emanuel Andrada[2], and Roger D. Quinn[1]

[1] Department of Mechanical and Aerospace Engineering, Case Western Reserve
University, Cleveland, OH 44106, USA
hbp16@case.edu
[2] Institute of Zoology and Evolutionary Research, Friedrich-Schiller University, Jena,
Germany
[3] Department of Electrical, Computer, and Systems Engineering, Case Western
Reserve University, Cleveland, OH 44106, USA

Abstract. This paper presents the design of robotic rat forelimbs, scaled
to 2.5 times the size of a female Sprague-Dawley rat. Based on a previous rat hindlimb model, significant enhancements were implemented to
facilitate manufacturing, robustness, improve overall performance, and
enhance biological accuracy. The two front legs are each equipped with
five motors to enable sagittal rotations of the scapula, elbow, and wrist
joints, along with scapula abduction and adduction. The leg segment
dimensions are based on a scanned rat bones model, but the shapes are
modified for 3D printing and assembly. Parts are printed using micro carbon fiber filled nylon, strengthened by various amounts of continuously
inlaid carbon fiber. Revolute joints are driven by motors, and a pulley-belt transmission system is incorporated to move wrist and elbow motors
higher up in order to reduce the inertia of the leg. Furthermore, the foot
structure comprises two segments that are passively controlled by two
torsion springs to enhance flexibility and facilitate a more naturalistic
movement. Additionally, a new electrical board is integrated to enhance
operational smoothness and align with the control scheme.

Keywords: Rat Forelimb · Robot · Locomotion · Synthetic Nervous
System

1 Introduction

Robot locomotion is advancing, with today's robots showing improved capabilities in navigating complex environments thanks to sophisticated mechanical
designs and control systems [16]. A principal inspiration for robot development
lies in the animal kingdom as animals have evolved over time to move with
ease through various environments—a trait that engineers are still working to

This work was supported by DFG FI 410/16-1 and NSF DBI 2015317 as part of
the NSF/CIHR/DFG/FRQ/UKRI-MRC Next Generation Networks for Neuroscience
Program

N. S. Szczecinski et al. (Eds.): Living Machines 2024, LNAI 14930, pp. 239–253, 2025.
https://doi.org/10.1007/978-3-031-72597-5_17

replicate in robots. As a result, advances in animal neuromechanics research can lead to the development of more efficient and adaptable robots, capable of navigating complex terrains. For instance, understanding how walking insects adapt their motion to their environment without extensive computational methods can inform the design of new systems for controlling insect-like robots [15]. Conversely, biomimetic robots also benefit biologists. Biorobots may serve as models for understanding animal behaviour. By replicating aspects of animal physiology and behaviour in robots, researchers can test hypotheses about the mechanisms underlying these functions. This approach allows for controlled experiments and manipulation of variables that may not be possible with living organisms, providing a deeper understanding of biological systems [15]. For example, by combining wet (laboratory-based) and computational neuroscience with robotic validation methods, researchers have been able to uncover the structure and function of core circuits in the insect brain. These circuits are responsible for navigation and swarming capabilities observed in foraging insects. Insect-like robots serve as physical manifestations of these core circuits, allowing researchers to observe and study them in action [15]. Some robots, such as Drosophibot, Puppy, and MIT Cheetah 3, draw inspiration from biology, mimicking the movements of the fruit fly, whippet, and cheetah, respectively [3, 10, 12].

However, there is limited research done on rat robots. Rats are appealing candidates for biologically inspired robots for a variety of reasons. Specifically, the rat size is large enough to allow actuation with commercial motors without significant scaling up for robot design, which makes dynamic scaling more straightforward. Dynamic scaling predicts the dominant force that governs a specific behaviour based on an animal's size and speed, considering the interaction between muscle forces and limb mechanical properties. The dominant forces resisting actuation during behavior include inertia, elastic forces, gravity, and viscosity, and these forces have significant implications for behavior control [21]. Also, data on rats is readily available due to their widespread use in research and, although their nervous systems are extremely complex, they are much less so than humans [8]. Previous robotic rats include two rat robotic hindlimbs developed by Donnelly-Power et al. and Aronhalt et al., a model produced by Shi et al., and a climbing rat robot created by Andrada et al. [1, 2, 8, 18]. However, the forelimb has yet to be modeled with biological accuracy due to the complex behavior of the scapula [23]. This paper explains the design principles and decisions behind a set of robotic rat forelimbs that will be incorporated into a four legged rat robot in future work.

The latest robotic rat hindlimb model was developed by Aronhalt et al., which consists of two legs with three limb segments each: the femur, tibia, and foot, a pelvis, and an electronics mount on top (Fig. 1). Each leg has four degrees of freedom: sagittal rotation at the hip, knee, and ankle, and femoral long-axis rotation at the hip. The limbs were created in the shape of rat bones, and they are actuated by Robomaster M2006 motors with C610 speed controllers. The two legs are connected by a connector piece located where the pelvis would exist. This connector piece is then free to translate vertically but not horizontally or rotationally through two rods in the center of the assembly. The mount allows for self-supported walking movements while keeping the robot in place by restraining the pelvis with a rod and spring to provide support and allow vertical motion through clamping the base [2].

Some design principles of Aronhalt's model, such as using motors as actuators, approximating robot size, and motor connection design, were carried over to the robotic forelimb described in this paper. However, the leg segments will no longer resemble the shape of rat bones but will be modified to accommodate 3D printing and assembly. Additionally, pulley-belt systems are implemented to move lower joints motors higher up, closer to the scapula, reducing the inertia of the legs. The foot is designed as a multi-segmented part, with a torsion spring incorporated to mimic rat toes, allowing the foot to conform to the ground while walking. In addition, a new electrical board is developed to enhance the motor performance. Previously, Aronhalt's robot experienced electrical noise when attempting to control multiple motors, making command transmission and feedback reception difficult. To address this challenge, all electrical components are now connected to a single circuit board. This measure effectively minimizes noise interference and streamlines the wiring.

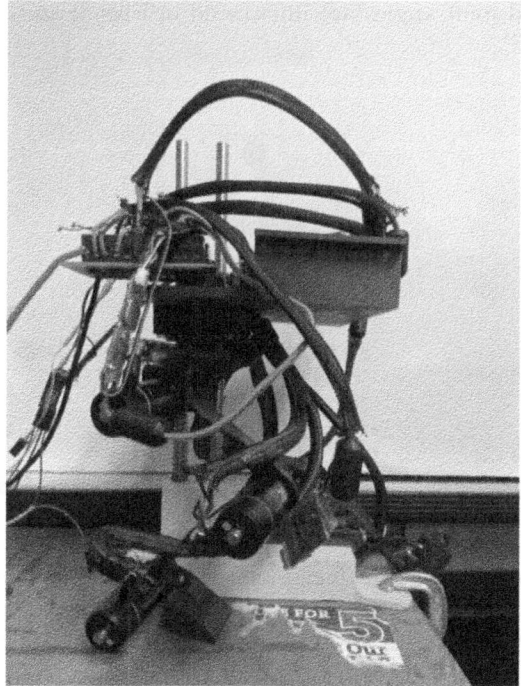

Fig. 1. Robot rat hindlimb model created in Aronhalt et al [2]. All leg segments except for the foot are in the shape of rat bones. All joints are actuated by motors, and the foot is rigid.

2   Mechanical and Hardware Design

2.1   Kinematic Degrees of Freedom and Scaling

The first part of dynamic scaling is to match the kinematics of the animal. The movement of a rat forelimb while walking is composed of a 23-degrees-of-freedom (DOF) in total: scapula (6 DOFs), shoulder (3 DOFs), elbow (2 DOFs), wrist (2 DOFs), metacarpal joints (5 DOFs), and interphalangeal joints (5 DOFs) [23]. While an ideal robot to mimic rat mechanics should have all of these DOFs, there is a trade-off between biomimicry and complexity. Adding more actuators and transmission systems increases the weight of the legs and consumes more space in the design. Therefore, we reduce the number of DOFs in our robot design following Stark et al.'s findings that the forelimb movement of quadruped animals can be simplified to 5 DOFs, excluding scapula translations, while still capturing the walking motion of the animal [20]. The robot described in this paper comprises a pair of legs, each composed of four segments: the scapula, upper arm, lower arm, and hand. Each leg has 7 DOFs: sagittal rotations at the scapula (protraction/retraction), shoulder, elbow, wrist, and distal joint, transversal rotation at the scapula (abduction/adduction), and vertical translation of the scapula. Rat kinematic data during trotting has been collected as presented in Aronhalt et al. [2]. Cardian and joint angles are illustrated in Figs. 2 and 3, respectively.

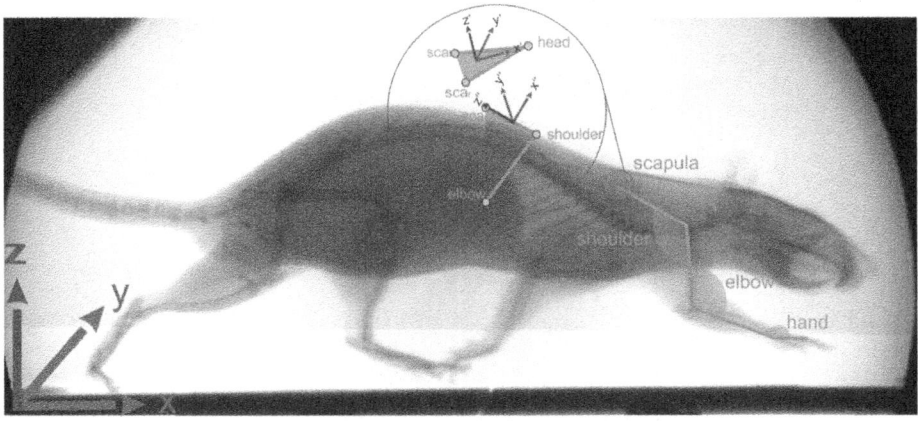

Fig. 2. Joint angles of a rat's front leg during walking. Shoulder, elbow and hand joint angles were computed as three-point angles. The leg rotations about the scapular pivot were estimated by computing the Cardian angles between the ribcage (composed by both scapula joints and the ribcage cranial marker) and a plane created by the scapula joint, the shoulder joint, and the elbow joint.

The robot is 2.5 times larger than a female Sprague-Dawley rat, which was chosen for practical purposes. At this size, the robot is large enough to be compatible with various mechanical components and motors available on the market,

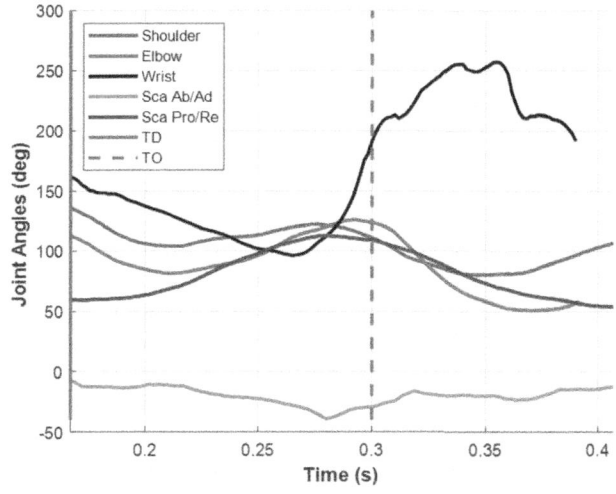

Fig. 3. Joint angles data for the rat forelimb over one step. The motion of the plane created by the scapula, shoulder, and elbow relative to the ribcage displays three-dimensional rotations about the scapular pivot. "Sca Ab/Ad" refers to scapula abduction/adduction joint angles, and "Sca Pro/Re" refers to scapula protraction/retraction joint angles (in the sagittal plane). "TD" and "TO" are touch-down and toe-off, respectively.

helping to avoid the challenges associated with prototyping. Furthermore, relationships can be found in [21] to scale the 2.5 times larger robot to be dynamically similar to the rat.

2.2   Skeleton Design and Fabrication

The design of the leg segments is also important for kinematic similarity with the animal. The goal is to replicate biological accuracy while also ensuring ease of manufacturing and assembly. To achieve this balance, the leg segments were designed to closely resemble the lengths of the scanned rat bones model found by Hunt et al. [11], scaled by 2.5, while accommodating the limitations of 3D printing and assembly. The previous attempt to replicate the bone structure proved impractical due to complex features and thin sections, which are vulnerable to breakage during assembly or operation. In the revised design, the 2.5-scaled lengths of the rat bones were retained, while complicated features of the bones were modified such that there are more flat faces to accommodate 3D printing and assembly, and more room is created for carbon fiber reinforcement (Fig. 4). This change affects the inertia and stiffness of the leg segments; however, the motors are much heavier than the leg segments and dominate the leg's inertia, and the joint properties dominate the leg's compliance. Therefore, these changes have little effect on dynamic scaling. See Sect. 2.6 below.

The structural components were manufactured utilizing the Markforged Mark Two 3D printer (Markforged Inc, Waltham, MA). The primary material used is the company's specialized filament, Onyx, which is a thermoplastic filled with short-strand chopped carbon fibers, reinforced by incorporating differing amounts of continuously inlaid long-strand carbon fiber. Carbon fiber reinforced plastic has a high strength-to-weight ratio, which allows for creating lighter and stronger parts compared to plastics or metals.

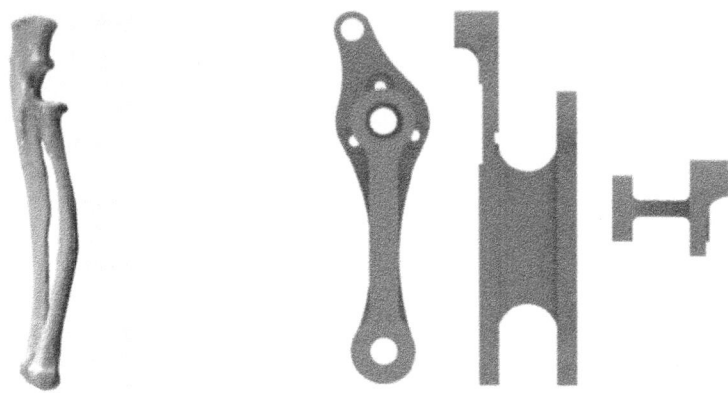

Fig. 4. Example of the rat lower arm bone model scaled by 2.5 (grey) versus the robot upper arm model (green). The length is retained, but the shape is modified for prototyping. (Color figure online)

2.3   Drivetrain and Actuators Selection

The rotation of the joints is achieved through the integration of electric motors. The selected motor is the RoboMaster M2006 Brushless DC Gear Motor, the same one used in Aronhalt's model. This motor has been proven to achieve the desired torque, back drivability, and feedback [2].

The motor responsible for movement along the sagittal plane is attached to the proximal limb segment through a circular mounting interface. The driven limb segment is connected to the motor through the motor's shaft, which fits into a hole in the limb segment and aligns with a flat surface on the shaft. To ensure stability and minimize slipping between the shaft and limb segment, a bolt is inserted through a hole on the flat surface of the motor shaft and the limb segment hole.

The scapula abduction/adduction motors were mounted onto the ribcage (the red part in Fig. 7). A connector piece was then used to connect this motor to the scapula sagittal rotation motor. A ball bearing is embedded inside the ribcage to support this motor holder. The mount was designed to allow for self-supported walking movements while keeping the robot in place by restraining the ribcage with two rods and two springs to provide support and allow vertical motion through clamping the base. In addition, linear bearings are implemented inside the ribcage to minimize friction while translating. Two rods were used instead of one to prevent the entire ribcage from rotating during walking.

In the robotic rat hindlimb (Fig. 1), each joint is actuated by a single motor attached directly to the joint [2], which poses many issues. For instance, the hip motor bears the burden of lifting the weights of multiple other motors during leg lifting, contributing to torque-related noise, feedback delays, and instability in motion. Additionally, a large moment acting on the hip motor shaft can lead to significant deflection, and even failure during operation. This problem can be addressed by using two pulley-belt transmission systems and relocating the motors responsible for driving lower joints higher and closer to the scapula motors. Specifically, the wrist motor is repositioned near the elbow joint, while the elbow motor is situated closer to the shoulder joint. This new motor distribution reduces the weight further down the leg, thus reducing inertia of the leg about the scapula protraction/retraction joint. Figure 5 illustrates two different motor configurations, detailing the distances from each motor to the scapula protraction/retraction joint.

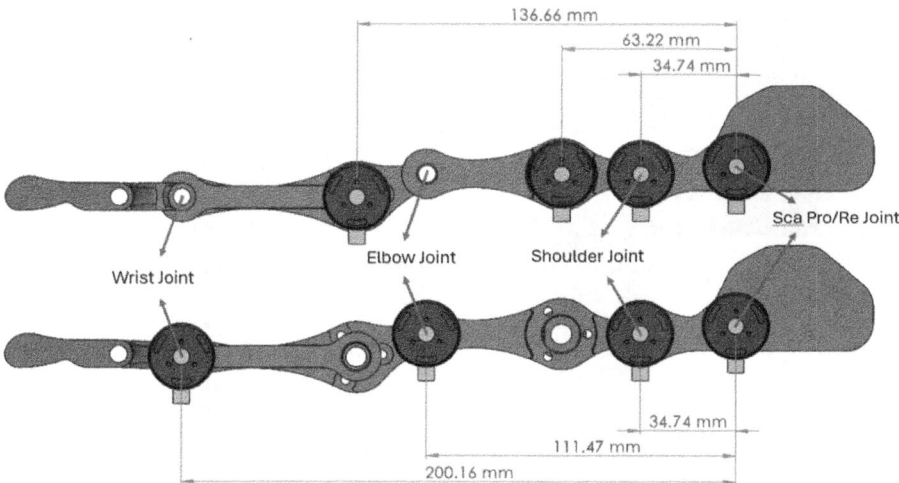

Fig. 5. Two different motor setups. The first setup, shown at the top, uses pulley-belt systems, allowing the motors to be positioned closer to the scapula. The second setup, depicted at the bottom, drives each joint directly with an individual motor.

The weight of each RoboMaster M2006 motor is 90 g. Considering that the motors primarily contribute to the leg's inertia, we can calculate the moment of inertia about the protraction/retraction joint for each case as follows:

$$I_{\text{top}} = 0.09 \times \left(34.74^2 + 63.22^2 + 136.66^2\right) = 2149.24 \text{ kg} \cdot \text{mm}^2 \quad (1)$$

$$I_{\text{bottom}} = 0.09 \times \left(34.74^2 + 111.47^2 + 200.16^2\right) = 4829.62 \text{ kg} \cdot \text{mm}^2 \quad (2)$$

Therefore, using pulley-belt systems can reduce the maximum inertia of the leg about the scapula protraction/retraction joint by:

$$\frac{I_{\text{bottom}} - I_{\text{top}}}{I_{\text{bottom}}} = \frac{4829.62 - 2149.24}{4829.62} = 55.6\% \tag{3}$$

However, achieving proper belt tension is also a challenge because belt tensioners cannot be implemented due to limited space. Therefore, the belt length is determined based on the theory of timing belt length:

$$L = 2C + \frac{\pi}{2}(D + d) + \frac{(D - d)^2}{4C} \tag{4}$$

where L is the belt length, C is the center-to-center distance between two pulleys, D and d are the diameters of the pulleys.

Another potential issue of using the pulley-belt transmission is the deflection of motor shafts due to large bending moments caused by belt tension. This issue is addressed by introducing an H-shaped (Fig. 6), carbon fiber reinforced leg segment, which can effectively support bending at the end of the motor shafts by integrating bearings into each shaft.

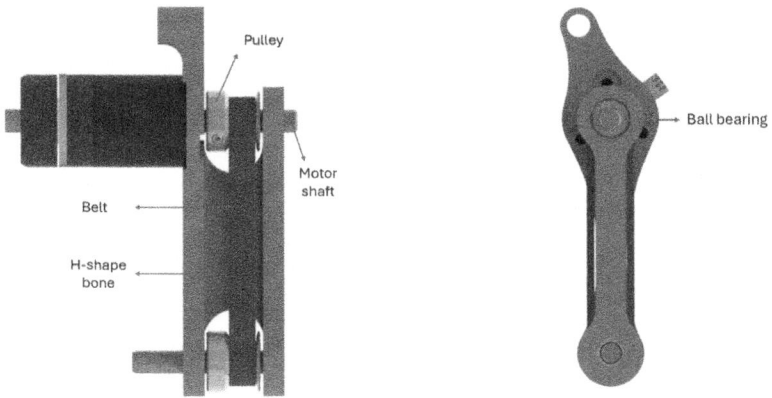

Fig. 6. H-shape bone with embedded bearings supports belt tension.

2.4   Compliant Feet

The design of the hand (or front foot) draws inspiration from the biomechanics of natural rat toes and feet, aiming to replicate their functionalities for improved locomotion and adaptability [24]. In biomechanics, the foot is a complex structure comprising multiple bones, joints, ligaments, and muscles that work together to provide stability, flexibility, and propulsion during movement [14]. The toes, in particular, play a crucial role in maintaining balance, providing grip, and adapting to uneven surfaces [9]. In rats and other quadrupeds, distal joints which connect the bones at the tips of the fingers are known to be the most important contributors to spring-like leg behavior [1,13]. Previous work done on compliant feet includes Drosophibot, which mimics insect feet, and the bird-inspired robotic leg developed by Chatterjee et al. [4,10]. In this rat robotic forelimb, the foot structure comprises two segments that are passively controlled by two torsion springs to enhance flexibility and facilitate a more natural movement. Furthermore, the arch is slightly curved to conform to the ground, and also to make it thick enough to be carbon fiber reinforced (Figs. 7 and 8).

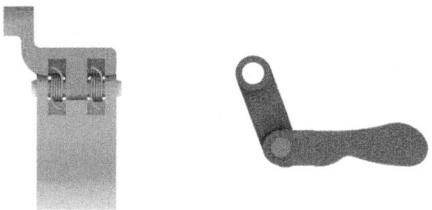

Fig. 7. Two-segment foot with torsion spring incorporated increases compliance.

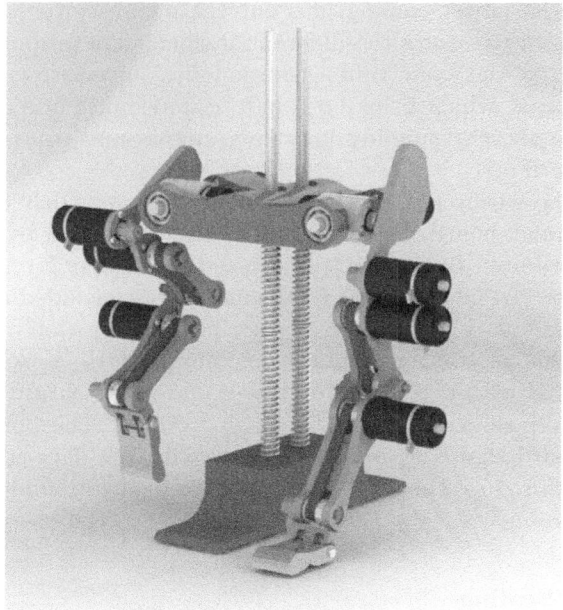

Fig. 8. Rat forelimbs and ribcage (red) model in SolidWorks. The CAD file and hardware schematics can be accessed at https://github.com/HuyPham0304/Rat-Robot-Design.git. (Color figure online)

2.5   Hardware Design

The electronics for the rat hindlimb consists of a Teensy microcontroller and a CANbus transceiver mounted on a custom-printed circuit board (PCB), which connects to the aforementioned RoboMaster M2006 brushless motors and their corresponding electronic speed controllers. The Teensy microcontroller serves as an interface between the control system and the hardware of the robot. The motor controllers for the selected M2006 motors communicate via the Controller Area Network (CAN) protocol. The CAN protocol allows us to communicate both ways, sending commands and receiving position data from a chain of motors with only two pins on the Teensy. While we could theoretically connect as many motors as we want to a single CAN chain, we choose to limit our design to one limb (five motors) per chain. This reduces the effects of electrical noise and helps to increase modularity.

In early development, we saw erratic behavior in motor responses due to electrical noise on the CAN chains, which our custom PCB design seeks to eliminate. Several measures have been taken to reduce signal noise and interference from external sources. These include incorporating termination resistors at the ends of the CAN chain to minimize reflected signal, adding decoupling capacitors to smooth the power coming into our CAN transceivers, matching trace length on our board to ensure the differential signals are properly lined up and reach the motors at the same time. Additionally, our entire circuit board has a ground plane layer, which helps both reduce impedance and shield electronic components from the surrounding brushless motors and controllers that have high switching currents.

To simplify the wiring of our legs, we integrate power delivery to the limbs into the same circuit board. Power is supplied to the board by an XT-60 connector, then distributed to the electronic speed controllers for each motor with XT-30 connectors. An additional XT-60 connector is included on the board to allow for a second board to be connected for later integration of the hindlimbs. Each of the M2006 motors can draw a maximum of 10 A, so we design this section of our PCB with 0.1-inch wide traces and manufacture our board with a 2-oz copper layer thickness to better dissipate heat. The power distribution section of the board shares a common ground with the data section but has a thin connection to reduce the noise in the section of the ground plane closest to the sensitive components.

2.6   Dynamic Scaling

The field of dynamics consists of kinematics and kinetics. We designed the leg to be kinematically similar to the rat front leg as described above. It has the primary joint degrees of freedom found in the rat leg and the leg segments are scaled to be 2.5 times larger than those in the rat. Kinetic scaling requires that the relationships between inertia, stiffness and damping be scaled similarly to the animal. If inertia is larger, then stiffness and damping must also be increased according to the relationships in [21]. Motors are much heavier than muscles, therefore, we placed the motors more proximal to the scapula to reduce inertia. Geared motors have passive stiffness and damping that can be measured [2]. Proportional-derivative control can be used to increase these properties such that they are related to inertia in the same way as in the animal. This will be done in future work.

3 Results

To assess the performance of the robotic rat forelimb, we used the kinematic data from a rat leg's walking movement illustrated in Fig. 3 as the input command for the motors. The commanded data represents the ideal joint angles that the robot should achieve, while the actual position data was recorded from the motors on the robot's joints during the execution of these commands. The primary objective was to replicate the precise movements of a rat's front limb during walking, encompassing both the swing and stance phases of walking.

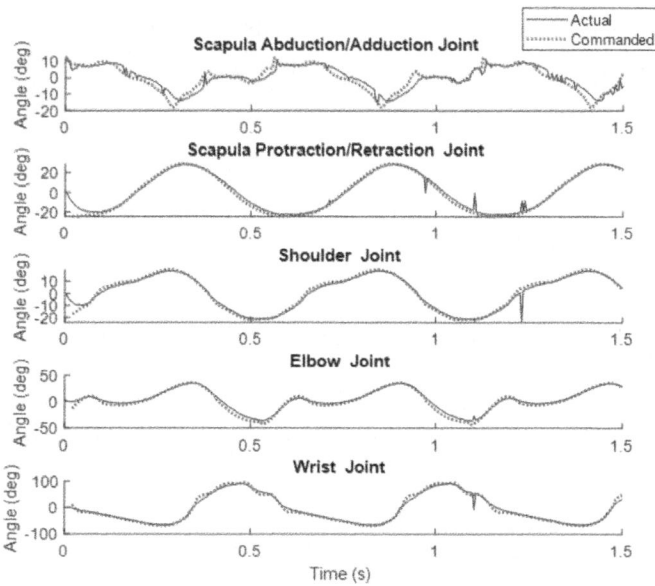

Fig. 9. Results from position control testing. The commanded position data is based on the animal data shown in Fig. 3. The actual data is the position feedback from the motors.

As shown in Fig. 9, the robot's joint angles closely follow the commanded angles, demonstrating the system's capability to accurately replicate the desired limb movements. The graph shows that the actual data tracks the commanded data with minimal deviation, indicating high precision in motor control and the effectiveness of the mechanical design in reducing inertia.

To quantify the accuracy of the robot's movements, we calculated the root mean square error (RMSE) and the normalized RMSE (nRMSE) between the commanded and actual joint angles for each degree of freedom. The RMSE value provides a measure of the average deviation between the desired and actual positions, while the nRMSE, which is expressed as a percentage of the range of motion for each joint, allows for a comparison of error relative to the joint's overall movement. These error analyses provide insights into the performance of the motors and the effectiveness of the hardware.

Table 1. RMSE and nRMSE for each joint angle

Joint	RMSE (deg)	nRMSE (%)
Scapula Abduction/Adduction	2.863	9.56
Scapula Protraction/Retraction	5.986	11.16
Shoulder	4.835	11.59
Elbow	9.638	12.34
Wrist	19.112	11.72

Tables 1 and 2 summarize the RMSE and nRMSE for each joint. The results indicate that all joints, except for the wrist which has a much broader range of motion, maintain an RMSE of less than $10°$. The nRMSE values, all below 15%, confirm that the deviations are small relative to the joints' ranges of motion, indicating the accuracy of the motor control system.

These minor deviations can be attributed to the inherent mechanical tolerances, the dynamics of the pulley-belt transmission system, and an artifact of the motor calculating the position. The nRMSE values provide a clearer understanding of the precision of each joint's movements in the context of their respective ranges of motion.

4   Conclusions and Future Development

In this project, a robotic rat forelimb model was successfully created and tested. Overall, the results demonstrate that the robotic rat forelimb can accurately replicate the kinematic movements of a real rat's forelimb, attributed to the combination of precise motor control, robust mechanical design, and minimal electrical noise. Additionally, the compliant foot enhances the robot's biomimicry, resulting in more natural and effective foot-ground contact. These findings validate the design and control strategies employed in this study and provide a solid foundation for future work on a complete robotic rat. rat. When completed the robot .will be used for experiments in neural control (Fig. 10).

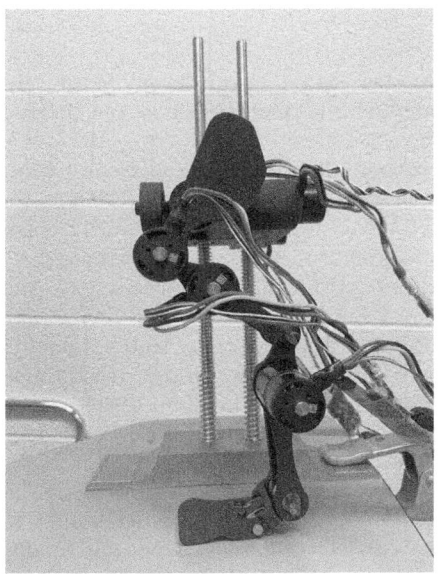

Fig. 10. The current rat robotic forelimb prototype

A synthetic nervous system (SNS) will be constructed to control the fore-limbs as we already have done for the hind legs [5]. An SNS is a dynamical, mathematical model of parts of an animal's nervous system applied to control a robot [22]. The SNS used to control the rat forelimb will be inspired by the two-layer central pattern generator (CPG) model proposed by Rybak et al. and further tested and developed by Deng et al. [5,6,17]. The goal is to fine-tune the type Ia, Ib, and II feedbacks of each joint, which corresponds to position, velocity, and torque feedbacks respectively, as well as the parameters of neurons and synapses. The data generated by the SNS will then be compared with actual rat walking data illustrated in Fig. 3. The more similar the robot's kinematics and scaled dynamics are to the real rat's locomotion, the more closely the SNS may resemble the function of the real rat's nervous system. As previously mentioned, joint angles can be measured through existing sensors in the motors. The motors can also provide a measure of active joint torque. However, for future control experiments, integration of a ground contact sensor into the foot is necessary.

Song et al. have proposed an alternative model that utilizes groups of slow, intermediate, and fast V2a interneurons to modulate locomotion speed. This model may offer a more accurate representation of vertebrate spinal control and can be potentially explored in the future [19].

After developing SNS control for the robot, control experiments will be performed with the robot walking on a split belt treadmill to mirror experiments performed with animals. The ultimate goal is to combine both front legs and hind legs to create a whole rat robot capable of walking similarly to the animal.

References

1. Andrada, E., Mämpel, J., Schmidt, A., Fischer, M.S., Karguth, A., Witte, H.: From biomechanics of rats' inclined locomotion to a climbing robot. Int. J. Des. Nat. Ecodyn. **8**(3), 192–212 (2013)
2. Aronhalt, E.: Development of a Robotic Rat Hindlimb Model and Neural Controller. MA thesis, Case Western Reserve University, Cleveland, Ohio (2023)
3. Bledt, G., Powell, M.J., Katz, B., Di Carlo, J., Wensing, P.M., Kim, S.: MIT cheetah 3: design and control of a robust, dynamic quadruped robot. Other repository. Institute of Electrical and Electronics Engineers (IEEE) (2019). Accessed 17 Aug 2020. ISBN: 9781538680940
4. Chatterjee, A., Mo, A., Kiss, B., Gönen, E.C., Badri-Spröwitz, A.: Multisegmented adaptive feet for versatile legged locomotion in natural terrain. In: 2023 IEEE International Conference on Robotics and Automation (ICRA), London, United Kingdom, pp. 1162–1169 (2023). https://doi.org/10.1109/ICRA48891.2023.10161515.
5. Deng, K., Szczecinski, N.S., Arnold, D., Andrada, E., Fischer, M.S., Quinn, R.D., Hunt, A.J.: Neuromechanical model of rat hindlimb walking with two-layer CPGs. Biomimetics (Basel) **4**(1), 21 (2019). https://doi.org/10.3390/biomimetics4010021
6. Deng, K., et al.: Biomechanical and sensory feedback regularize the behavior of different locomotor central pattern generators. Biomimetics **7**(4), 226 (2022). https://doi.org/10.3390/biomimetics7040226
7. Dienes, J., Hicks, B., Slater, C., Janson, K.D., Christ, G.J., Russell, S.D.: Comprehensive dynamic and kinematic analysis of the rodent hindlimb during over ground walking. Sci. Rep. **12**(1), 19725 (2022). https://doi.org/10.1038/s41598-022-20288-3
8. Donnelley-Power, E.: Design of a rat hindlimb robot and neuromechanical controller. Master's thesis, Case Western Reserve University, Cleveland, Ohio (2022)
9. Fong, D.T.P., Mao, D.W., Li, J.X., Hong, Y.: Greater toe grip and gentler heel strike are the strategies to adapt to slippery surface. J. Biomech. **41**(4), 838–844 (2008). https://doi.org/10.1016/j.jbiomech.2007.11.001
10. Martinez-Hernandez, U., et al. (eds.): Living Machines 2019. LNCS (LNAI), vol. 11556. Springer, Cham (2019). https://doi.org/10.1007/978-3-030-24741-6
11. Wilson, S.P., Verschure, P.F.M.J., Mura, A., Prescott, T.J. (eds.): Biomimetic and Biohybrid Systems. Lecture Notes in Computer Science (Lecture Notes in Artificial Intelligence), vol. 9222. Springer, Cham (2015). https://doi.org/10.1007/978-3-319-22979-9
12. Hunt, A.J., Szczecinski, N.S., Quinn, R.: Development and training of a neural controller for hind leg walking in a dog robot. Front. Neurorobot. **11**, 18 (2017). https://doi.org/10.3389/fnbot.2017.00018
13. Lee, D.V., McGuigan, M.P., Yoo, E.H., Biewener, A.A.: Compliance, actuation, and work characteristics of the goat foreleg and hindleg during level, uphill, and downhill running. J. Appl. Physiol. **104**, 130–141 (2008). https://doi.org/10.1152/japplphysiol.01090.2006
14. MacGregor, R., Byerly, D.W.: Anatomy, Bony Pelvis and Lower Limb: Foot Bones. StatPearls Publishing, Treasure Island (FL) (2023)
15. Mangan, M., Floreano, D., Yasui, K., Trimmer, B.A., Gravish, N., Hauert, S., Webb, B., Manoonpong, P., Szczecinski, N.: A virtuous cycle between invertebrate and robotics research: perspective on a decade of Living Machines research. Bioinspir. Biomim. **18**(3), 035005 (2023). https://doi.org/10.1088/1748-3190/acc223

16. Rubio, F., Valero, F., Llopis-Albert, C.: A review of mobile robots: concepts, methods, theoretical framework, and applications. Int. J. Adv. Robot. Syst. **16**(2), (2019). https://doi.org/10.1177/1729881419839596

17. Rybak, I.A., Shevtsova, N.A., Lafreniere-Roula, M., McCrea, D.A.: Modelling spinal circuitry involved in locomotor pattern generation: insights from deletions during fictive locomotion: modelling spinal circuitry involved in locomotor pattern generation. J. Physiol. **577**(2), 617–639 (2006). https://doi.org/10.1113/jphysiol.2006.118703

18. Shi, Q., et al.: Development of a small-sized quadruped robotic rat capable of multimodal motions. IEEE Trans. Robot. **38**(5), 3027–3043 (2022). https://doi.org/10.1109/TRO.2022.3159188

19. Song, J., et al.: Multiple rhythm-generating circuits act in tandem with pacemaker properties to control the start and speed of locomotion. Neuron **105**(6), 1048–1061 (2020). https://doi.org/10.1016/j.neuron.2019.12.030

20. Stark, H., Fischer, M.S., Hunt, A., et al.: A three-dimensional musculoskeletal model of the dog. Sci. Rep. **11**, 11335 (2021). https://doi.org/10.1038/s41598-021-90058-0

21. Sutton, G.P., Szczecinski, N.S., Quinn, R.D., Chiel, H.J.: Phase shift between joint rotation and actuation reflects dominant forces and predicts muscle activation patterns. In: PNAS Nexus, vol. 2, no. 10, pgad298 (2023). https://doi.org/10.1093/pnasnexus/pgad298

22. Szczecinski, N.S., Hunt, A.J., Quinn, R.D.: A functional subnetwork approach to designing synthetic nervous systems that control legged robot locomotion. Front. Neurorobot. **11**, 37 (2017). https://doi.org/10.3389/fnbot.2017.00037

23. Tata Ramalingasetty, S., et al.: A whole-body musculoskeletal model of the mouse. IEEE Access **9**, 163861–163881 (2021). https://doi.org/10.1109/ACCESS.2021.3133078

24. Varejão, et al.: Motion of the foot and ankle during the stance phase in rats. Muscle Nerve **26**(5), 630–5 (2002). https://doi.org/10.1002/mus.10242

Cellular Plasticity Model for Bottom-Up Robotic Design

Trevor R. Smith[1]([✉])[iD], Thomas J. Smith[2][iD], Nicholas S. Szczecinski[1][iD], Sergiy Yakovenko[1][iD], and Yu Gu[1][iD]

[1] West Virginia University, Morgantown, WV 26505, USA
trs0024@mix.wvu.edu
[2] The University of Texas at Dallas, Richardson, TX 75080, USA

Abstract. Traditional top-down robotic design often lacks the adaptability needed to handle real-world complexities, prompting the need for more flexible approaches. Therefore, this study introduces a novel cellular plasticity model tailored for bottom-up robotic design. The proposed model utilizes an activator-inhibitor reaction, a common foundation of Turing patterns, which are fundamental in morphogenesis-the emergence of form from simple interactions. Turing patterns describe how diffusion and interactions between two chemical substances-an activator and an inhibitor-can lead to complex patterns and structures, such as the formation of limbs and feathers. Our study extends this concept by modeling cellular plasticity as an activator-inhibitor reaction augmented with environmental stimuli, encapsulating the core phenomena observed across various cell types: stem cells, neurons, and muscle cells. In addition to demonstrating self-regulation and self-containment, this approach ensures that a robot's form and function are direct emergent responses to its environment without a comprehensive environmental model.

In the proposed model, a *factory* acts as the activator, producing a *product* that serves as the inhibitor, which is then influenced by environmental stimuli through consumption. These components are then regulated by cellular plasticity phenomena as feedback loops. We calculate the equilibrium points of the model and the stability criterion. Furthermore, simulations are utilized to examine how varying parameters affect the system's transient behavior and the impact of competing functions on its overall functional capacity. Results show the model converges to a single stable equilibrium tuned to the environmental stimulation. Such dynamic behavior underscores the model's utility for generating predictable responses within robotics and biological systems, showcasing its potential for navigating the complexities of adaptive systems.

Keywords: Cellular Plasticity · Robot Design · Morphogenesis · Activator-Inhibitor

This study was supported in part by the National Science Foundation Graduate Research Fellowship Award #2136524 to Trevor R. Smith, the National Science Foundation EFRI BRAID Award #2223793 to Nicholas S. Szczecinski, and the DOD Restoring Warfighters with Neuromusculoskeletal Injuries Research Award (RESTORE) W81XWH-21-1-0138 to Sergiy Yakovenko. Trevor R. Smith and Thomas J. Smith contributed equally to this work.

N. S. Szczecinski et al. (Eds.): Living Machines 2024, LNAI 14930, pp. 254–268, 2025.
https://doi.org/10.1007/978-3-031-72597-5_18

1   Introduction and Background

Robots today are typically designed through a top-down process to determine their form and function to meet specific design requirements. However, the vast space of potential solutions presents significant challenges in identifying acceptable, let alone optimal, solutions without significantly constraining design freedoms [1,2]. Despite extensive research on robotic design, human experience and creativity play vital roles, rendering today's design process arguably more of an art than a science [3–5]. Because of this synthetic approach, robots often struggle to adapt to the complexities of the natural world [6]. In contrast, biological organisms, which extensively inhabit this world, are shaped by bottom-up interactions within nature, a phenomenon that is challenging to emulate. Nevertheless, the emergence of biological organisms through bottom-up interactions has been extensively studied through the lens of morphogenesis, where low-level chemical interactions between cells lead to complex emergent structures [7–9].

A common methodology within morphogenesis research utilizes Turing patterns, which model the diffusion and reaction of two chemicals (activator and inhibitor) as a set of partial differential equations [10]. Subsequent studies have applied this methodology to describe various biological phenomena, such as the formation of limbs, fingers, patterns on seashells, feathers, etc. [11–13]. This concept has been extended to robotics, with systems like Kilobots and Loopy employing Turing patterns for designing their formation from the bottom-up [14,15]. For instance, Loopy, consisting of a closed-loop chain of motor cells, utilizes the activator quantity in each cell to dictate the corresponding motor angle, collectively forming its shape. These formations demonstrate inherent resilience, such as Loopy correcting self-intersecting shapes and the Kilobots' ability to reform post-damage. While robotic studies have primarily focused on the developmental phase of morphogenesis to generate steady-state robot morphologies, it is essential to recognize that organisms are not static; they constantly adapt their form and behavior to changes in environmental stimuli.

At the cellular level, this adaptability has been captured by cellular plasticity, another aspect of morphogenesis. Cellular plasticity describes how cells enhance their abilities in response to environmental changes. This phenomenon has been observed throughout many cell types including stem cells [16–18], muscle cells [19–21], and neurons [22–24], each demonstrating unique responses. However, the complexity and high variability of these responses has hindered the development of a simplified, widely applicable model, complicating cellular plasticity's integration into bottom-up robotic design frameworks despite complex models existing for specific biological processes [25–27].

Recognizing this challenge, our work does not aim to develop a universal model that applies to all facets of cellular plasticity. Instead, we focus on distilling core phenomena from stem cells, muscle cells, and neurons into a simplified model tailored for robotic design. This model aims to replicate key aspects of cellular plasticity: 1) the enhancement of total capacity through specialization—demonstrated by stem cell differentiation [16–18], 2) growth is spurred by product scarcity—demonstrated by muscle cell hypertrophy [19–21], and 3) exposure to sustained stimuli modulates functional capacity—demonstrated by long-term potentiation/depression of synaptic strength between neurons [22–24]. Furthermore, these phenomena, which are governed by self-regulated processes that respond to immediate environmental stimuli, contrast with traditional engineering approaches that depend on fixed setpoints and comprehensive environmental models.

To model the targeted cellular plasticity phenomenon, an activator-inhibitor reaction, typical of Turing patterns, is augmented with environmental stimuli, thus enabling a uniform description of developmental and cellular plasticity morphogenesis for bottom-up design. By incorporating cellular plasticity into the morphogenesis processes demonstrated on robotic platforms, we could potentially enhance robots' abilities to adapt their emergent form and behavior based on environmental stimuli. For instance, if the Kilobot robots repeatedly experience damage (i.e., losing neighboring connections), they could increase their density and rate of cohesion. Moreover, to limit the scope of this problem, we will focus on the cellular plasticity of an individual cell. Therefore, our contributions to the literature are:

- Creation of a simplified cellular plasticity model for the bottom-up design of robots.
- Expansion of the model to describe multi-functional cells by incorporating various competing processes.
- Providing analytical and simulation analysis of this model's equilibrium points, stability, and parametric effects on its transient response.

2 Methodology

The proposed cellular plasticity model for bottom-up robotic design includes a *factory*, analogous to an organelle, that produces a *product* molecule consumed by the environment. This factory-product pair represents a cell's ability to perform a function, where the factory's size/quantity dictates the function's intensity, and the product quantity describes the immediate readiness to perform the function. This relationship can be mapped to robotic systems; for instance, a factory-product pair could represent a motor applying torque to a joint in response to angular displacement, with the factory as the torque gain, the product as the available torque, and the consumption rate as the applied torque. Furthermore, the interactions of these components are regulated by the biological phenomena from Sect. 1 manifested as feedback loops. Moreover, to simulate multi-functional cells (i.e., robots with more than one ability), the model is expanded to include multiple pairs of factories and products.

2.1 Single Factory

Referring to Fig. 1, at the heart of the cellular plasticity model is the factory quantity (F), which functions as the activator and not only self-replicates at rate G but also produces the inhibitory product quantity (P) at rate R. This inhibitor modulates the factory by slowing product synthesis and factory growth at respective rates I and K. Additionally, the product is consumed by the environment at a rate of $C \cdot P$, where C is the environmental stimulus and the product's quantity, or availability, proportionally affects how fast it can be consumed. This consumption represents a negative stimulus on the product, which reduces its inhibitory effect on the factory and modulates the equilibrium between the factory (F) and product (P) quantities with the environmental demand (C). This relationship for the cellular plasticity model is mathematically described in (1) and (2).

$$\frac{dF}{dt} = (G - K \cdot P) \cdot F \tag{1}$$

$$\frac{dP}{dt} = (R - I \cdot P) \cdot F - C \cdot P \tag{2}$$

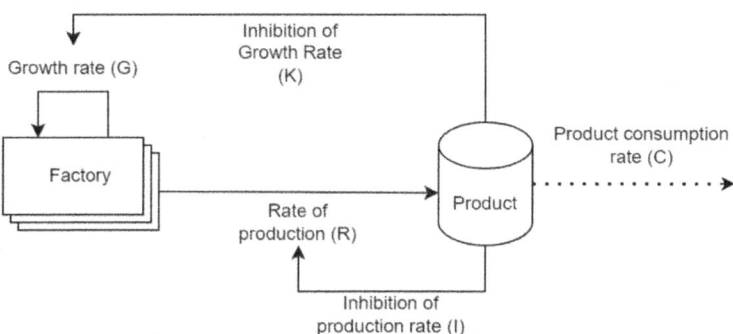

Fig. 1. Cellular plasticity model for bottom-up robotic design. This model utilizes a self-replicating factory that produces a product consumed by the environment. This product also inhibits the production and growth rate of the factory, allowing for stable self-regulated adaption to the environmental changes in product consumption.

This model, (1) and (2), describes two of the three core phenomena of cellular plasticity from Section 1-growth is spurred by product scarcity, and sustained stimuli modulate functional capacity-via two negative feedback loops depicted in Fig. 1. These loops increase the net production rate $(R - I \cdot P)$ and net factory growth $(G - K \cdot P)$ in response to reduced product levels (P), capturing the first phenomenon. Next, if the net factory growth feedback loop reacts slower than the net production rate feedback loop, only prolonged consumption rate changes will significantly modify factory capacity, capturing the second phenomenon. Furthermore, this model captures self-containment and self-regulation, as it does not rely on an external environment model to regulate factory capacity.

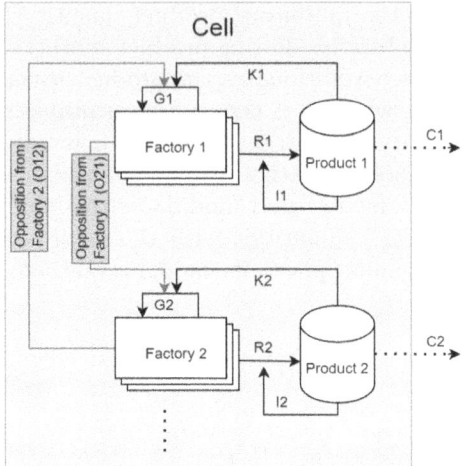

Fig. 2. Expansion of the cellular plasticity model to multiple unique functions within a single cell, via multiple competing factories that oppose each other at a rate of O_{ij}

2.2   Multi-factory

Next, to capture the phenomenon from stem cells that specialization improves total capacity, the cellular plasticity model is expanded to multiple unique processes competing for space in the cell, as shown in Fig. 2. This phenomenon is achieved by introducing an opposition rate, O_{ij} that reduces the net growth rate of the ith factory proportionally to the quantity of the opposing j^{th} factory; thus, (1) becomes (3), where N is the total number of factories in the cell. This opposition rate emulates resource competition, encouraging the cell to specialize by allocating production capabilities to higher-demand products.

$$\frac{dF_i}{dt} = \left(G_i - K_i \cdot P_i - \sum_{j \neq i}^{N} O_{ij} \cdot F_j\right) \cdot F_i \tag{3}$$

2.3   Model Constraints

Multiple constraints must be specified to ensure the model captures the cellular plasticity phenomena outlined in Sect. 1. The first constraint is that the parameter values of G, K, R, I, and O_{ij} are positive constants. Secondly, to ensure that only sustained stimuli lead to changes in functional capacity, the model's parameters must be constrained such that the factory's net growth response (i.e., its time constant τ_f), is slower than the production rate's response, τ_p, to changes in the consumption rate ($\tau_f > \tau_p$). Furthermore, the factory (F) and product (P) quantities are also restricted to positive values, as negative values lack physical meaning. Lastly, the consumption rate stimulus (C) is limited to positive values, thus restricting the model from considering external production sources. Section 4 further describes the relevance of these constraints in relation to the analyses conducted in Sect. 3.

3   Analysis

Utilizing the methodology from Sect. 2, this study investigates the system's response to immediate and extended environmental demand surges through step changes in consumption rate. Specifically, this analysis focuses on determining steady-state product and factory levels, stability criteria, and the impact of parameter variations on the time response of the system. Moreover, the study also explores the parametric effects of opposition on the capacities of factories within a multi-factory cell configuration.

3.1   Steady State and Stability Criteria

To get a representative overview of the system dynamics and analyze the effects of initial conditions on the steady-state value of the product and factory, an example phase portrait, with factory and product nullclines (4) and (5), respectively, is shown in Fig.3.

$$\frac{dF}{dt} = 0 : P = \frac{G}{K}, \quad F = 0 \tag{4}$$

$$\frac{dP}{dt} = 0 : F = \frac{C \cdot P}{R - I \cdot P} \tag{5}$$

Analyzing the vector field along the factory and product axes reveals that any state starting in the positive quadrant stays there, ensuring positive factory and product levels. This behavior results from the vertical factory nullcline blocking trajectories from crossing into the negative factory domain and a positive production rate when the product is zero (2). Next, by observing the equilibrium point designated by the red star, it is a stable spiral node that attracts all positive states. In addition, due to the horizontal factory nullcline (4) and inverse proportional product nullcline (5), the system will only exhibit one non-zero equilibrium point independent of system parameters. Furthermore, by evaluating the denominator of (5) to zero, we find that the limit of the product nullcline as the factory capacity approaches infinity is finite and equal to $P_{lim} = R/I$, which is the ratio of the product synthesis rate R and product inhibition rate I and is displayed in Fig. 3.

The steady-state values for product and factory quantities were found by intersecting the nullclines (4) and (5), solving for the non-zero equilibrium point (6) and (7), where the minimum factory quantity required to support the consumption stimulus is $F_{min} = C/R$, which is the ratio of the consumption stimulus C and product synthesis rate R.

$$P_{\infty} = \frac{G}{K} \tag{6}$$

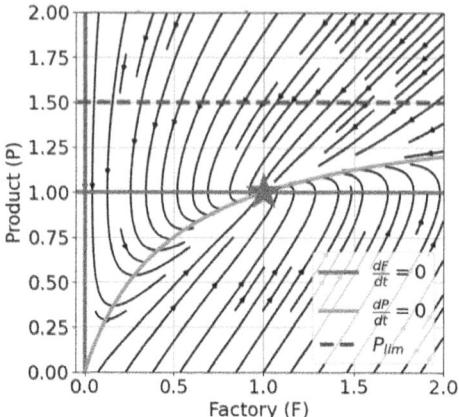

Fig. 3. A Representative phase portrait of the single factory's response with the product (orange) and factory (blue) nullclines, and a single non-zero equilibrium (red star) with parameters of $G = K = I = 1.0$, $C = 0.5$, and $R = 1.5$. P_{lim} describes the limit product level as the product nullcline approaches infinity. The inward spiral of the phase portrait signifies a stable equilibrium that attracts from any positive state. (Color figure online)

$$F_\infty = \frac{C/R}{K/G - I/R} = \frac{F_{min}}{1/P_\infty - 1/P_{lim}} \tag{7}$$

Inspection of (6) and (7) shows that only the steady-state factory quantity depends on the environmental consumption rate, while the steady-state product level depends on the ratio of intrinsic parameters, specifically the factory growth rate (G) and the inhibition of factory growth (K). This analysis was extended to the multi-factory steady state using (2) and (3) to derive (8) and (9).

$$F_{i,\infty} = \frac{F_{min,i}}{K_i/(G_i - \sum_{j\neq i}^{N} O_{ij} \cdot F_{j,\infty}) - 1/P_{lim,i}} \tag{8}$$

$$P_{i,\infty} = \frac{G_i - \sum_{j\neq i}^{N} O_{ij} \cdot F_{j,\infty}}{K_i} \tag{9}$$

In a multi-factory cell, the steady-state levels of the product and the factories are interdependent on the steady-state values of other factories. However, the presence of additional factories invariably reduces the capacity of each factory and product compared to the cell's unopposed single-factory configuration.

Next, to assess the stability of the single factory model, we evaluated the system's Jacobian matrix's trace (δ) and determinant (Δ) at equilibrium points: the origin $(0,0)$ in (10) and the non-zero equilibrium (F_∞, P_∞) (11), respectively. The equilibrium point is stable only if both the trace is negative and the determinate is positive.

$$\delta_{(0,0)} = G - C < 0, \quad \Delta_{(0,0)} = -C \cdot G \not> 0 \tag{10}$$

$$\delta_{(F_\infty, P_\infty)} = \frac{-C \cdot R/I}{R/I - G/K} < 0, \quad \Delta_{(F_\infty, P_\infty)} = C \cdot G > 0 \qquad (11)$$

Analysis of (10) shows the origin is inherently unstable due to the always negative determinate, thus directing the system towards positive values. However, for the non-zero equilibrium (F_∞, P_∞) to be stable (11) must have a positive denominator, establishing the stability criterion (12). Where the steady state product level (P_∞) must be less than the limit product level (P_{lim})

$$\frac{G}{K} = P_\infty < \frac{R}{I} = P_{lim} \qquad (12)$$

3.2 Parametric Effects on Time Constants

Now that the stability criterion and steady-state values for the factory and product have been established, the parametric effects on the model dynamics are examined via simulations to evaluate the time constants of the factory (τ_f) and product (τ_p) in response to step changes in consumption rate. To simplify analysis The system is reparameterized from (G, K, R, I, C) to steady-state product level $(P_\infty = G/K)$, limit product level $(P_{lim} = R/I)$, and minimum factory quantity $(F_{min} = C/R)$, by dividing (1) by G and (2) by R. This parameter reduction simplifies analysis from five parameters to two when applying a unit step input to F_{min}. In Fig. 4, P_{lim} and P_∞ were varied from [0.1 to 5] with the time constant ratio (τ_f/τ_p) plotted as a heatmap.

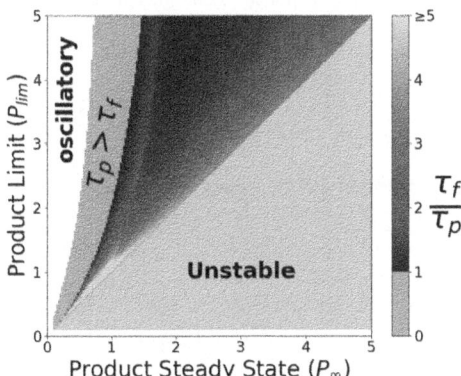

Fig. 4. Parametric effects on the relative time constants of the product (τ_p) and factory (τ_f), particularly as system parameters near zero or instability τ_f becomes much larger than τ_p. The orange region displays where the product time constant exceeds the factory time constant. Damped oscillatory modes emerge when P_{lim} significantly exceeds P_∞, marked by the white region. (Color figure online)

From Fig.4, it is observed that as P_{lim} and P_∞ approach zero and the insta-bility threshold, the relative time constant between the factory and the prod-uct becomes very large. As P_{lim} and P_∞ move away from instability, the fac-tory time constant eventually becomes smaller than the product time constant (orange region in Fig. 4). This indicates that the factory responds faster than the product, adapting to short-term changes while the product adapts to long-term changes, violating the core phenomenon of sustained stimuli modulating functional capacity. Furthermore, as P_{lim} increases relative to P_∞, the system exhibits a damped oscillatory response (white region in Fig. 4). This causes the factory capacity (F) to overshoot its steady state, leading to an over-response to stimuli. Despite being stable when $P_\infty << P_{lim}$, the model constraint that the factory time constant be slower than the product time constant ($\tau_f > \tau_p$) further restricts the valid parameter range to the heat map region.

3.3 Transient Response to Short- and Long-Term Changes in Consumption

Next, to analyze the system response to short- and long-term changes in the consumption rate of the environment, the system with parameter values of $G = K = I = 1.0$ and $R = 1.1$ was subjected to a significant increase in the consumption rate (2 product/time unit) for a short duration (2 time units) and long duration (50 time units) and plotted in Fig. 5 along with the net pro-duction rate $PR = R - I \cdot P$, the minimum factory quantity F_{min}, and steady state factory (F_∞) and product levels (P_∞).

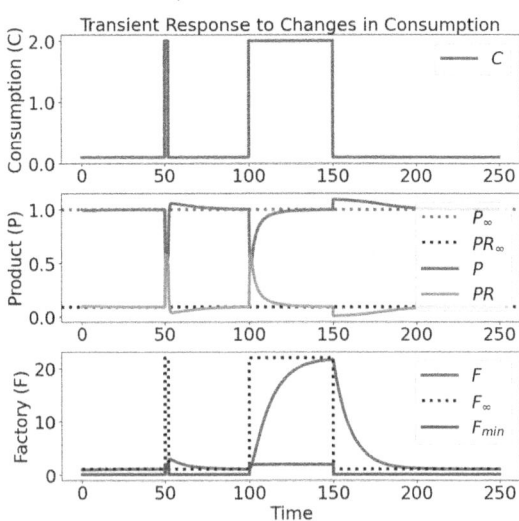

Fig. 5. Product (P) and Factory (F) transient response to short (at $t = 50$) and long (at $t = 100$) periods of increased in consumption (C). In addition to the net production rate (PR) and minimum factory capacity (F_{min}). Furthermore, the steady-state factory, product, and production rate are plotted with dotted lines. Parameter values are $G = K = I = 1.0$ and $R = 1.1$

The first observation of Fig. 5 is that the model exhibited distinct behaviors on different time scales of resource fluctuation. For short-term deficits (at $t = 50$), the production rate increased rapidly with only a small increase in factory capacity. However, if the deficit is prolonged (at $t = 100$), only then will the factory capacity increase significantly. Furthermore, a higher quantity of the factory persists after the removal of the heightened consumption rate until it eventually decays and the factory capacity returns to the new steady state of the environment. The following observation of Fig. 5 shows that the steady-state factory level is approximately ten times larger than the minimum required to support the consumption rate.

3.4 Effects of Opposition on Identical Factories

To assess the opposition parameter's impact on factory steady-state levels, we analyzed two factories with identical parameters under varying consumption rates ([.1 - 1]) across three scenarios: low-symmetric opposition ($O_{12} = O_{21} = .001$), high-symmetric opposition ($O_{12} = O_{21} = 0.05$), and asymmetric opposition ($O_{12} = 0.05, O_{21} = .001$). Figure 6 displays the factory steady-state levels for each of these scenarios at the intersection of the curves of constant consumption of each product: vertical curves for C_1 and horizontal curves for C_2.

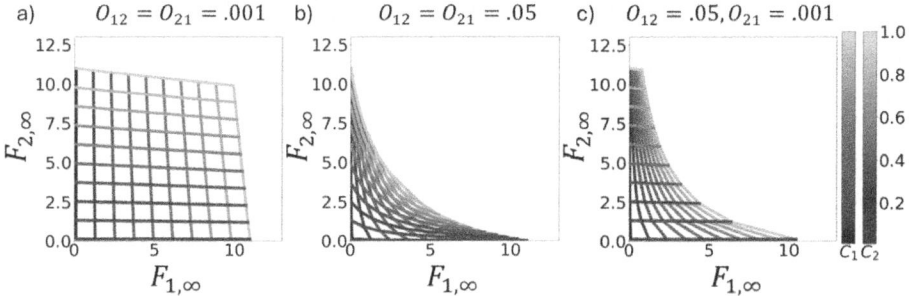

Fig. 6. Effects of low (a), high (b), and asymmetrical (c) opposition rates (O_{ij}) on the steady-state factory quantities of a multi-factory cell. More vertical lines are curves of constant consumption of factory 1's product (C_1), while more horizontal lines are curves of constant consumption of factory 2's product (C_2)

The initial analysis of Fig. 6 reveals that with rising symmetric opposition rates, the constant consumption lines transition from nearly square shapes-indicating no inter-factory dependence-to shapes increasingly skewed towards zero. This deformation indicates that high opposition rates significantly restrict factory capacities when both products have high consumption rates; however, the impact is minimal if either factory's product consumption rate is low. Furthermore, applying opposition asymmetrically results in the steady-state capacity surface stretching towards the factory with lesser opposition. This adjustment suggests that asymmetric opposition directly influences factory capacities, favoring the less opposed factory in the allocation of resources.

Next, to analyze the effects of opposition on the total capacity of the multifactory cell, the consumption rates for a cell with two identical factories were varied from [0.1 to 1.0], and the total capacity was plotted as a heat map along with contours of total consumption ($Totcon = C_1 + C_2$) and total capacity ($Total\ capacity = F_1 + F_2$).

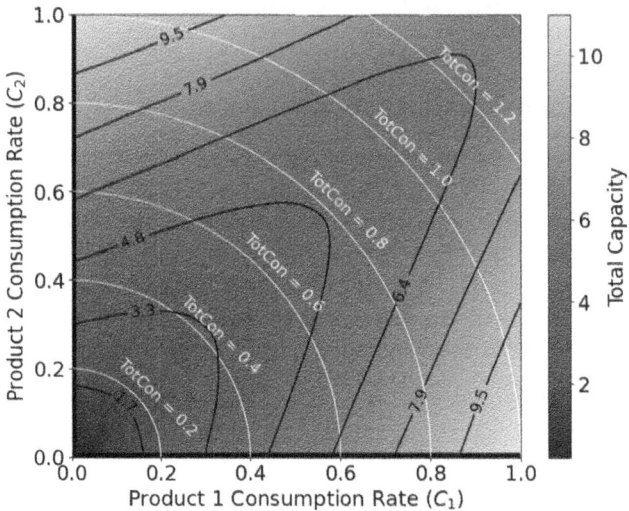

Fig. 7. Heatmap of the total capacity of a two factory cell relative to the consumption rates of factory 1 (C_1) and factory 2 (C_2). Black lines are contour lines of total factory capacity, while white lines are contours of constant total consumption (TotCon)

In Fig. 7, it is evident that as a cell specializes (increases one factory's capacity over the other), its total capacity rises. This observation is readily seen by tracing the total consumption line equal to 0.8 from the center towards either factory 1 or 2, where the total capacity grows from approximately 5 to over 7.9.

4   Discussion

Based on the results of Sect. 3, the proposed cellular plasticity model imitates the generalized biological phenomena: 1) growth is spurred from product scarcity, 2) sustained stimuli modulate functional capacity, and 3) specialization increases total capacity, in addition to being self-contained and self-regulating, provided its constraints are met. However, the model's constraint for positive factory and product quantities is mild due to any initially positive factory and product pair remaining positive, as shown in Fig. 3. Furthermore, the constraint requiring slower factory growth compared to product synthesis is partially mitigated by Fig. 4, illustrating a range of valid parameter values.

The proposed model displays how growth is driven by product scarcity in (7) and (8), where the factory's steady-state capacity expands in proportion to the environmental demand (C). This behavior is visualized in Fig. 5, where factory growth is initiated only when product levels fall below their steady-state value. This response is reminiscent of muscle strengthening, where cells increase oxygen uptake or Adenosine triphosphate (ATP) production in response to deprivation [20, 21]. Furthermore, this approach emphasizes self-containment, where adaptations rely on internal factors (e.g., factory and product quantities) rather than a simplified environment model. By using real-world stimuli to influence product levels and factory capacities, the robot could adapt to the complexities of unpredictable real-world conditions that a human-specified model might neglect.

The phenomenon of functional capacity modulation by sustained stimuli is effectively demonstrated in Fig. 5, where only prolonged demand changes influence factory capacity, not short-term spikes. Initially, the system leverages on-hand product reserves to address sudden increases in demand C, subtly adjusting its production rate to meet the new consumption rate. However, a significant increase in factory capacity only occurs if the product deficit is prolonged, similar to the biological mechanism of long-term potentiation/depression, where sustained activity is essential for synaptic strength modulation [22, 24]. This dual-response adaptation, along with the system's ability to exceed minimal needs (Fig. 5), equips the cell for prolonged and dynamic demand surges without excessively responding to temporary spikes.

Also, the model exhibits self-regulation by converging to a stable equilibrium specifically tuned to environmental stimulation, as illustrated in Fig. 3 and supported by Eqs. (6) and (7). This single equilibrium shows that a cell's capacity directly responds to environmental stimuli, reflecting the environment's impact on cellular functions. Such dynamic behavior underscores the model's utility for generating predictable responses within robotics and biological systems, showcasing its potential for understanding these complex systems.

The next phenomenon, specialization increases total capacity, is exhibited by this model due to the single factory steady state capacity (7) being higher than the multi-factory steady state capacity (8), thus the highly specialized single factory cell has more capacity than a generic multi-factory cell. In addition, this insight is displayed in Fig. 6 by the steady-state factory capacity being largely unaffected by the opposition of the other factory if the consumption rate is much higher for one compared to the other. Furthermore, from Fig. 6, the asymmetric opposition rates predispose the cell to specialize into the lesser opposed factory. This response is similar to the histone effects on stem cells, where the cells are pre-biased to form into their parent cell types [18]. Furthermore, from Fig. 6, the deformation of the upper right corner of the equilibrium surface towards zero emulates a limited-resources constraint, where it is more difficult to perform two tasks equally than to specialize in one task. Moreover, Fig. 7 directly displays that the model captures this phenomenon due to the total capacity of the cell being minimal when the consumption rate is equal between the two factories (i.e., on the 45-degree diagonal). This specialization mechanism underscores the importance of adaptability and efficiency in robotics, indicating that robots initially equipped with multiple functions can dynamically adjust their functional capacity to prioritize higher-demand functions, effectively designing themselves from the bottom up.

Since this model utilizes the activator-inhibitor framework, it can be integrated into existing morphogenesis-based bottom-up design frameworks such as [14,15], potentially similar to the multi-factory cell configuration. A simple application of this model is in adapting the rigidity of a robot's morphology to the environment. Specifically, this could be done utilizing the Loopy platform, which is constructed as a chain of servo motors [15], by modifying the response of each motor to its angular error. Therefore, in this scenario, the factory could be a proportional gain to the angular error, and the consumption rate could be the supplied torque, with the product representing the available torque. Thus, based on (7), the servo motor's response to perturbations would vary with the external load: under lighter loads, it would demonstrate increased flexibility, whereas, under heavier loads, its response would become more rigid due to a higher gain. Furthermore, this example can be extended to the multi-factory case, where each motor also regulates its response to angular velocity, thus modifying Loopy's viscosity (i.e., the fluidity of its response to perturbations). Thus, macroscopically, the rigidity and viscosity of Loopy's morphology would be designed from the bottom up as an emergent response to its environment. This application highlights the model's potential to inspire further bottom-up designs for more responsive and adaptable robotic systems based on principles observed in cellular plasticity.

5   Conclusions and Future Work

In this work, we successfully developed a cellular plasticity model for morphogenesis-based bottom-up robotic design. This model captures general phenomena observed in various cell types: 1) growth stems from product scarcity from muscle cells, 2) sustained stimuli modulate functional capacity from neurons, and 3) specialization increases total capacity from stem cells, in addition to being self-contained and self-regulating. Furthermore, the singular stable equilibrium point for a given environment demonstrates that a cell's distribution of functional capabilities is a direct emergent response to the environment. Moreover, by utilizing the activator-inhibitor framework augmented with environmental stimuli, this model can be readily incorporated into existing morphogenesis-based bottom-up robotic designs. Therefore enhancing robots' abilities to adapt their emergent form and behavior to their environment.

This study is limited by simplifying complex biological processes to general phenomena and assuming that factories can grow indefinitely given adequate time. Additionally, it focuses solely on how a single cell adapts its morphology without analyzing diffusion effects or external production sources of the product. Furthermore, the lack of experimental validation with physical robots restricts the empirical confirmation of the model's applicability. Future endeavors aim to address these gaps by undertaking experimental validations with physical robots to examine the influence of cellular plasticity on the robot's emergent morphology. In addition to enhancing the model to include a defined factory capacity limit per cell and incorporating a model for cellular division and death. Furthermore, this model will adjust the parameters of the spawning cell (similar to evolutionary algorithms [28] and stem cell histones [18]) to bias specialization towards the additional capacity needed by the parent cell, introducing another layer of adaptive response at a longer time scale. Moreover, this work will extend to multiple cells with varied parameters and redundant factories, incorporating diffusion effects to better emulate multicellular behaviors and possibly create Turing patterns. The goal is to explore specialization and collaboration among cells to aid multi-robot teams in task selection and specialization from the bottom up, making them more responsive and versatile.

References

1. Kang, E., Jackson, E.K., Schulte, W.: An approach for effective design space exploration. In: Monterey Workshop, vol. 6662, pp. 33–54. Springer (2010)
2. Nardi, L., Koeplinger, D., Olukotun, K.: Practical design space exploration. In: IEEE 27th International Symposium on Modeling, Analysis, and Simulation of Computer and Telecommunication Systems (MASCOTS) 2019, pp 347–358 . IEEE (2019)
3. Gericke, K., Blessing, L.: Comparisons of design methodologies and process models across domains: a literature review. In: DS 68-1: Proceedings of the 18th International Conference on Engineering Design (ICED 11), Impacting Society through Engineering Design, vol. 1: Design Processes, Lyngby/Copenhagen, Denmark (2011)
4. Tomiyama, T., Gu, P., Jin, Y., Lutters, D., Kind, C., Kimura, F.: Design methodologies: industrial and educational applications. CIRP Ann. **58**(2), 543–565 (2009)
5. Kapurch, S.J.: NASA Systems Engineering Handbook. Diane Publishing (2010)
6. Pollack, J.B., Lipson, H., Ficici, S., Funes, P., Hornby, G., Watson, R.A.: Evolutionary techniques in physical robotics. In: Evolvable Systems: from Biology to Hardware: Third International Conference, ICES: Edinburgh, Scotland, UK, April 17–19, 2000 Proceedings 3, pp. 175–186. Springer (2000)
7. Mamei, M., Vasirani, M., Zambonelli, F.: Experiments of morphogenesis in swarms of simple mobile robots. Appl. Artif. Intell. **18**(9–10), 903–919 (2004)
8. Sayama, H.: Robust morphogenesis of robotic swarms [application notes]. IEEE Comput. Intell. Mag. **5**(3), 43–49 (2010)
9. Jin, Y., Meng, Y.: Morphogenetic robotics: an emerging new field in developmental robotics. IEEE Trans. Syst. Man Cybernet. , Part C (Applications and Reviews) **41**(2), 145–160 (2010) , Part C (Applications and Reviews) **41**(2), 145–160 (2010)
10. Turing, A.M.: The chemical basis of morphogenesis. Bull. Math. Biol. **52**(1–2), 153–197 (1990)
11. Marcon, L., Sharpe, J.: Turing patterns in development: What about the horse part? Curr. Opin. Genet. Dev. **22**(6), 578–584 (2012)
12. Nakamasu, A., Takahashi, G., Kanbe, A., Kondo, S.: Interactions between zebrafish pigment cells responsible for the generation of turing patterns. Proc. Natl. Acad. Sci. **106**(21), 8429–8434 (2009)

13. Boettiger, A., Ermentrout, B., Oster, G.: The neural origins of shell structure and pattern in aquatic mollusks. Proc. Natl. Acad. Sci. **106**(16), 6837–6842 (2009)
14. Slavkov, I., et al.: Morphogenesis in robot swarms. Sci. Robot. **3**(25), eaau9178 (2018)
15. Smith, T., Butts, R.M., Adkins, N., Gu, Y.: Swarm of one: bottom-up emergence of stable robot bodies from identical cells. In: 2023 IEEE/RSJ International Conference on Intelligent Robots and Systems (IROS), pp. 4683–4689. IEEE (2023)
16. Huang, B., Lu, M., Galbraith, M., Levine, H., Onuchic, J.N., Jia, D.: Decoding the mechanisms underlying cell-fate decision-making during stem cell differentiation by random circuit perturbation. J. R. Soc. Interface **17**(169), 20200500 (2020)
17. Kaitsuka, T., Hakim, F.: Response of pluripotent stem cells to environmental stress and its application for directed differentiation. Biology **10**(2), 84 (2021)
18. Nair, N.U., Lin, Y., Bucher, P., Moret, B.M.: Phylogenetic analysis of cell types using histone modifications. In: Algorithms in Bioinformatics: 13th International Workshop, WABI: Sophia Antipolis, France, September 2–4, 2013. Proceedings 13, pp. 326–337. Springer (2013)
19. Aguilar-Agon, K.W., Capel, A.J., Martin, N.R., Player, D.J., Lewis, M.P.: Mechanical loading stimulates hypertrophy in tissue-engineered skeletal muscle: molecular and phenotypic responses. J. Cell. Physiol. **234**(12), 23547–23558 (2019)
20. Feriche, B., García-Ramos, A., Morales-Artacho, A.J., Padial, P.: Resistance training using different hypoxic training strategies: a basis for hypertrophy and muscle power development. Sports Med. Open **3**, 1–14 (2017)
21. de Freitas, M.C., Gerosa-Neto, J., Zanchi, N.E., Lira, F.S., Rossi, F.E.: Role of metabolic stress for enhancing muscle adaptations: practical applications. World J. Methodol. **7**(2), 46 (2017)
22. Turrigiano, G.G., Nelson, S.B.: Homeostatic plasticity in the developing nervous system. Nat. Rev. Neurosci. **5**(2), 97–107 (2004)
23. La Rosa, C., Parolisi, R., Bonfanti, L.: Brain structural plasticity: from adult neurogenesis to immature neurons. Front. Neurosci. **14**, 75 (2020)
24. Jiang, F., Bello, S.T., Gao, Q., Lai, Y., Li, X., He, L.: Advances in the electrophysiological recordings of long-term potentiation. Int. J. Mol. Sci. **24**(8), 7134 (2023)
25. Shen, S., Clairambault, J.: Cell plasticity in cancer cell populations. F1000Research, vol. 9 (2020)
26. Oliveri, H., Goriely, A.: Mathematical models of neuronal growth. Biomech. Model. Mechanobiol. **21**(1), 89–118 (2022)
27. Stiehl, T., Marciniak-Czochra, A.: Characterization of stem cells using mathematical models of multistage cell lineages. Math. Comput. Model. **53**(7–8), 1505–1517 (2011)
28. Floreano, D., Urzelai, J.: Evolutionary robots with on-line self-organization and behavioral fitness. Neural Netw. **13**(4–5), 431–443 (2000)

Vertical Closure Constraint for Self-replicating Machines

Alex Ellery[✉]

Centre for Self-Replication Research (CESER), Department of Mechanical and Aerospace Engineering, Carleton University, 1125 Colonel By Drive, Ottawa, ON K1S 5B6, Canada
aellery@mae.carleton.ca

Abstract. In examining the implementation of a physical self-replicating machine on the Moon, we explore the implications of vertical closure as a constraint on the design of such. We describe the design of this self-replicating machine from its demandite list of in-situ sourced materials, a lunar industrial ecology to extract those materials, electrochemical and other chemical processes to purify desired materials and additive manufacturing methods for 3D printing the major components of the self-replicator. We then turn to the vertical closure issue defined through metrics based on resource-returned-on-investment, i.e. physical output/input ratios, and how this drives the design of the self-replicator. Several biological phenomena emerge suggesting that physical self-replicating machines can provide insights into biological life, terrestrial or extraterrestrial.

Keywords: Self-replicator · Universal constructor · Vertical closure

1 Introduction

Self-replicating machines are the ultimate expression of biomimetics in imitating the most fundamental property of life, hitherto unique to biological life. There have been many definitions of life but we pick one that emphasises physicality but not its medium. For example, it has been shown that in chemical space, there are over a million possible backbone configurations to nucleic acids of which DNA/RNA is just one set (Butch et al 2021). This suggests that life is medium-tolerant. There are seven fundamental characteristics of life (Koshland 2002): (i) genetic program of instructions that encodes construction of the biological organism; (ii) evolution of the genetic program through generational mutation; (iii) compartmentalisation of the organism by a boundary; (iv) energy input from the environment; (v) continuous material synthesis of the organism; (vi) behavioural adaptability through learning; (vii) catalytic specificity of metabolic chemical reactions.

Genetic program of instructions is common to the von Neumann self-replicator concept (von Neumann & Burks 1966). Notably missing from this list is self-replication as a specific property but it is implied by the genetic evolution property. Indeed, we would argue that the evolution property is derivative from the more fundamental self-replication property through inevitable copying mutations. We suggest that compartmentalisation in

N. S. Szczecinski et al. (Eds.): Living Machines 2024, LNAI 14930, pp. 269–283, 2025.
https://doi.org/10.1007/978-3-031-72597-5_19

differentiating between self and the environment is a functional property but is realized in biological organisms as a physical selectively permeable boundary. Metabolic processing of energy input from the environment is considered fundamental to physical life (Boden 1999). This is uncontroversial. However, we suggest that metabolic processes do not necessarily have to be autopoietic (property (v) above) – autopoiesis implies continuous synthesis but we suggest that there may be discrete phase(s) of synthesis. Von Neumann's self-replicator did not address these metabolic aspects by employing discrete self-assembly in an abstract formalism which excluded energy considerations. Behavioural adaptability is uncontroversial (an example being bacterial motility in the presence of sugar) but learning implies a neural substrate which is peculiar to animals. Nevertheless, plants are information processing systems which measure environmental parameters such as humidity, gravity, etc. They exhibit anticipatory nocturnal reorientation of their leaves in sun-tracking behaviour in the absence of daylight suggesting internal modelling of daily rhythms (Garzon 2007). Furthermore, plants can select from three different strategies for coping with local competition for sunlight – vertical growth for competitive dominance against dense short competitors, shade tolerance to maximise leaf area-to-weight ratio under shade against dense tall competitors and lateral root growth to avoid competition with sparse tall competitors (Gruntman et al 2017). These behaviours occur over developmental timescales but the mediation of mechanosensitive Ca^{2+} ion channels is unclear (Monshausen & Gilroy 2009). However, auxin transport between plant cells as an analogue of vesicle-based neurotransmitter transport between synapses is unlikely (Alpi et al 2007). Although there appears to be decision-making, there appears to be no "neural" learning aspect in higher plants. We suggest that catalytic specificity is peculiar to isothermal metabolism of biological organisms which are limited by the temperature tolerance of their specific material substrate – carbon-based biomolecules. There is no physical reason to omit high temperature thermal processes for metabolism based on engineering materials. We argue here that this and other lists of properties of life omit a fundamental physical property of life – vertical closure constraints. Vertical closure is the constraint that the material, energy and information cost to build the self-replicator cannot exceed that produced by it – this is a statement of the first law of thermodynamics.

The concept of vertical closure as a defining constraint on life has not been addressed in any substantive way. Before exploring this, we briefly mention several notions of closure that apply to biological life – there are several types of closure that mean different things in different contexts. In philosophy, causal closure maintains that no physical event can be caused by a non-physical event. We are not concerned with this. Closure may have a physical thermodynamic interpretation. Biological life is required to be thermodynamically open to energy and material flow; physical artificial life has the same requirement. Closure can refer to the flow of matter and energy within an ecology constrained by adiabatic walls, i.e. no energy transfer from outside the ecosystem (Morowitz et al. 2005). Within adiabatic walls, a closed ecology will degrade to a state of maximum entropy. Such cannot support life as life persists only in far-from-equilibrium states requiring a flow of energy. The Earth is effectively materially closed but open to energy input from the sun. Even applied to organisms, closure has a multitude of different interpretations. Life itself must be open to both energy flow and material flux. Closure may define constraints on such thermodynamically open (dissipative) systems in which energy is converted into structural complexity (self-organisation). Autopoiesis is the balance between processes of production (anabolism) and destruction (catabolism) in the continuous synthesis of a self-producing biological body (Villalobos & Razeto-Barry 2020). Closure may be defined by the principle of a self-maintained, self-constraining boundary between a biological entity and its environment that is consistent with generative autopoiesis (Mossio & Moreno 2010, Montevil & Mossio 2015). Closure in a metabolic cycle in this case delays the production of entropy. A living organism must be (catalytically) closed to efficient causation, i.e. it must synthesise its catalysts internally (Cardenas et al. 2010). This is a necessary property of autocatalytic sets, i.e. every catalyst is a product of metabolism (Lehman & Kauffman 2021). The self-replicating machine must implement a similar chemical closure and closed boundedness through its replication lifecycle. This means that it is closed to efficient causes originating outside the system, reliant instead only on efficient causes within the system. Autocatalysis is one type of chemical closure but an industrial ecology with chemical recycling is another. In autopoietic theory, two different types of boundaries may be defined – a physical boundary that separates the physical organism from its environment (cognitive boundary) and a more abstract boundary of extra-body processes (non-cognitive boundary) (Di Paolo 2009). A self-replicating machine's boundaries are determined by its rovers that acquire resources from the environment and so are pseudopodic and reside within the cognitive boundary despite separation from any physical boundary.

Replicative (M,R) systems are input-output formal models of primitive cells with metabolism M and repair R augmented by replication (Vega 2023). Inputs are nutrients and outputs are nucleotides, amino acids and waste. The concept of closure to efficient causation has been asserted to imply that (M,R)-systems as formal models of life are non-computable by a Turing machine in a Godelian sense (Korbak 2023). However, this cannot be the case. The Turing-Church thesis dictates that universal Turing machine operations are computations. Indeed, Turing machine operations on biomolecules are the basis for molecular DNA parallel computing (Benenson et al 2001). The chemoton is a simplified model of a primitive cell and is an extension of the (M,R) model that embodies closure concepts – it incorporates a metabolic chemical network, template-based self-replication and an enclosing bilipid membrane (Csendes 1984). We may characterize living organisms as a network of interacting feedback and feedforward control systems that integrate sensing the environment and effecting the environment (Bich & Bechtel 2022). In biological cells, genetic regulatory networks of complex hierarchies of feedback mechanisms impart robustness to uncertain environments (Csete & Doyle 2002). Such complexity evolved hierarchically from simpler modules (Lenski et al 2003). Signal processing in such control systems must be computable to function effectively. We can see that closure has been applied as different concepts in biology that are rather abstract. We adopt a more concrete concept of closure that has its roots in systems engineering (von Tiesenhausen & Darbro 1980). Biological information can flow in two directions – horizontal gene transfer between peers and vertical gene transfer through generations. There are closure constraints that apply to the self-replication process which apply in the vertical direction, i.e. through generations rather than horizontally through peers. Vertical closure refers to constraints applicable over generations. Vertical closure is thus fundamental to self-replicating machines.

2   Synthesis by Throughput

The context for this exploration of vertical closure is a self-replicating machine on the surface of the Moon that exponentially constructs a lunar industrial infrastructure from local lunar resources as far as practicable with minimum supplies from Earth (Freitas & Gilbreath 1980, Chirikjian et al. 2002, Ellery 2016). The population p of self-replicating modules may be given by:

$$p = (1 + r)^n \tag{1}$$

where r = number of offspring per generation, n = number of generations. If $r = 2$ and $n = 13$, $p > 1.5 \times 10^6$, illustrating the power of exponential growth for rapid lunar industrialisation. The initial capital cost of investment in the first module is effectively amortised through the exponential growth in productive capacity of subsequent generations (Ellery 2017). As self-repair is a subset of self-replication, population growth will be fully exponential without restraint. Currently, the self-replication property is currently unique to biological organisms, so if imparted to a technological realisation, such a self-replicating machine might be regarded as a lifeform (Ellery 2018).

2.1   Demandite

The first constraint is imposed by the availability of materials on the Moon, a celestial body that has not been subjected to significant alteration – especially by liquid water – since it was formed. The Moon has a simple geology comprising a handful of common rock-forming minerals of interest: (i) anorthite plagioclase ($CaAl_2Si_2O_8$) is the dominant mineral in the highlands representing a source of alumina, aluminium, quicklime, calcium, silica, silicon and oxygen; (ii) orthoclase feldspar ($KAlSi_3O_8$) is comparatively rare but represents a valuable source of potassium and kaolinite clay; (iii) ilmenite ($FeTiO_3$) is common in the mare regions representing a source of iron, rutile, titanium and oxygen; (iv) olivine ($(Mg,Fe)_2SiO_4$) is commonly associated with impact basins representing a source of magnesia, magnesium, silica, silicon and oxygen; (v) the commonest rock-forming minerals on the Moon are pyroxenes which are widespread but of little use as ores; (vi) much rarer spinels such as chromite are challenging to process; (vii) there will be localized deposits of nickel-iron meteoritic material on and below the surface of large impact craters representing a source of iron, nickel, cobalt, troilite and rare sources of selenium (with troilite) and tungsten (as micro-inclusions); (viii) water ice as a source of hydrogen is widespread at the poles and in other dark regions. We do not address physical processing here but a series of comminution and beneficiation techniques will be required to separate minerals of interest. From these resources, we can construct a suite of functional materials to build all the basic subsystems of a generic spacecraft (Table 1). This constitutes the demandite materials list with their respective proportions required to build an unfuelled spacecraft (Ellery 2022a, 2022b, 2022c, 2022d). Some variants on a spacecraft that require additional material are lunar bases (requiring excess compressive structures) and launchers (with sufficient fuel to reach the Gateway).

Table 1. Lunar demandite list of functional materials with estimated proportions required to build a typical unfuelled spacecraft (excess percentages refer to additional mass required to build a lunar base and propellant required to launch to the Gateway in orbit around the Moon)

Functionality (mass fraction)	Lunar-Derived Material
Tensile structures (25%)	Wrought iron Aluminium
Compressive structures (+50%)	Cast iron Regolith + binder
Elastic structures (trace)	Steel springs/flexures Silicone elastomers
Hard structures (3%)	Alumina
Thermal conductor straps (1%)	Fernico (e.g. kovar) Nickel Aluminum
Thermal radiators (3%)	Aluminium
Thermal insulation (3%)	Glass (SiO_2 fibre) Ceramics such as SiO_2
High thermal tolerance (4%)	Tungsten Alumina
Electrical conduction wire (7%)	Aluminium Fernico (e.g. kovar) Nickel
Electrical insulation (1%)	Glass fibre Ceramics (SiO_2, Al_2O_3 and TiO_2) Silicone plastics Silicon steel for motors
Active electronics devices (vacuum tubes) (12%)	Kovar Nickel Tungsten Fused silica glass
Magnetic materials for actuators (5%)	Ferrite Alnico Silicon steel Permalloy
Sensory transducers (5%)	Resistance wire Quartz Selenium
Optical structures (11%)	Polished nickel/aluminium Fused silica glass lenses
Lubricants (trace)	Silicone oils Water
Power system (20%)	Fresnel lens + thermionic conversion Flywheels
Combustible fuels (+250%)	Oxygen Hydrogen

Clearly, some materials are multifunctional such as aluminium for tensile structures, thermal conductors, thermal radiators, electrical conductors, alnico magnets, optical reflectors, thermite welding and solid propellant. It is worth noting that glass fibres as thermal and electrical insulation may be manufactured from local mare basalt or alkaline earth aluminosilicate (anorthite) glass where optical properties are not relevant. Optical transparency favours fused silica glass to eliminate contaminants such as Fe which causes darkening.

2.2 Industrial Ecology

The next step is to utilise chemical and electrochemical techniques to extract the desired materials from their mineral forms. The concept behind the industrial ecology is sustainability. The IPAT equation applied to industrial processes quantifies environmental impact I to be minimized (Chertow 2000): $I = PAT$ where P = population of industrial products produced, A = material consumed/unit product, T = waste/unit resource consumed. The population defines the industrial productivity of the system which is to be maximized through growth. For sustainability, the only parameters we can reduce are A and T: (i) minimise resource consumption A through dematerialization and reuse; (ii) minimise waste T through recycling into resource.

In building a lunar industry, the problem is that reactive reagents are scarce on the Moon necessitating employment of Earth-imported NaCl salt as the source of a variety of reagents. As these are not consumed, they are recycled (except for special applications such as Sorel cement for manufacturing lunar bases and electrolyte replenishment which is expected to be minor). A lunar industrial ecology is shown in the Appendix (Table A1) that implements sets of chemical processes characterized by minimizing waste by implementing full recycling (Ellery 2020a, 2020b). To illustrate a portion of the industrial ecology, anorthite may be artificially chemically weathered with HCl in a two-stage process that yields silica and alumina respectively:

$$CaAl_2SiO_8 + 5HCl + H_2O \rightarrow CaCl_2 + 2AlCl_3.6H_2O + \mathbf{SiO_2}$$
$$AlCl_3 \cdot 6H_2O \rightarrow Al(OH)_3 + 3HCl + H_2O$$
$$Al(OH)_3 \rightarrow \mathbf{Al_2O_3} + 3H_2O$$

All ceramic oxides such as alumina may be reduced through the FFC electrochemical process. The FFC process is a general-purpose electrolytic reduction process using molten salt ($CaCl_2$) in which the oxide reactant and metal product remain in the solid state (with modest temperatures of 900–1100 °C yielding > 99% metallurgical purity metal (Ellery et al 2022). Oxygen is stripped out and may be recovered at inert anodes. The metal output is in sintered powder form suitable for input to powder-bed metal additive manufacturing such as selective laser sintering.

2.3 Additive Manufacturing

Additive manufacturing (commonly referred to as 3D printing) represents a general-purpose manufacturing method capable of great versatility. It is capable of fabricating complex structures unachievable through subtractive manufacturing. There are several approaches. Fused deposition modelling is used for plastics primarily. An example of this is the RepRap (Replicating Rapid-Prototyper) 3D printer (Jones et al 2011). The RepRap can print a significant number of its own (ABS or PLA) plastic parts. All additive manufacturing machines (and milling machines) are cartesian configuration robots. To complete the self-replication process, RepRap would have to enhance its functionality significantly beyond plastic extrusion: (i) print metal through selective laser sintering/melting or electron beam additive manufacturing; (ii) print its computational electronics such as neural circuitry based on vacuum tube technology rather than solid-state technology (Ellery 2022a, 2022b, 2022c, 2022d); (iii) print its sensors including piezoelectric quartz for tactile sensing arrays and vision sensors using photosensitive selenium as the active component in small arrays of photomultiplier tubes controlled through active vision (Ellery 2022a, 2022b, 2022c, 2022d); (iv) print its electric motors as general purpose actuators which can be reconfigured into any robotic kinematic machine including machines of production (Elaskri & Ellery 2020; Freitas & Merkle 2004); (v) self-assemble using reconfigurable manipulators (Zykov et al. 2005), environmental structuring (Chirikjian et al 2002) or any combination thereof. By 3D printing material layer-by-layer, 3D printing minimises waste compared with subtractive fabrication (which can waste 90% of material resources). It requires no special tooling. We proffer that the key ability for self-replication (and indeed, universal construction) is additive manufacturing of the mechatronic components of (kinematic) machines of production. Of course, 3D printing through plastic extrusion cannot be used on the Moon where carbon is scarce (though silicone plastics exhibit reduced carbon content). Plastics may be substituted by ceramics and glass – e.g. porcelain (derivable from lunar orthoclase) insulating mounts and flexible glass fibre electrical insulation were used in knob-and-tube electrics.

2.4 Artificial Metabolism

The industrial ecology/fabrication process exhibits a bow-tie architecture characteristic of biological metabolic networks in which a large number of inputs are funnelled through just a few reaction pathways and then yield a large number of outputs (Csete & Doyle 2004; Ellery 2020a, 2020b). Biological metabolism evolved from simple chemical networks. Primary biological synthesis from CO_2 is based on just five metabolites (acetate, pyruvate, oxaloacetate, succinate and α-ketoglutarate) at the core of anabolic and catabolic pathways. These and derivative metabolites of the Krebs cycle may have evolved from a pre-ATP biosynthetic metabolic network involving two metabolites pyruvate and glyoxalate (undergoing just four reactions – aldol/retro-aldol, hydration/dehydration, reduction/oxidation and oxidative decarboxylation) mediated by ferrous iron Fe^{2+} and hydroxylamine (Muchowska et al 2019). The lunar industrial ecology similarly comprises a small set of chemical pre-processes, many of which feed into a single general-purpose oxide reduction process – the FFC electrochemical molten salt process. Together with the carbonyl process, a large range of metal alloys may be manufactured from a significant range of the Moon's mineral resources fed into a modest suite of 3D printers. The versatility of 3D printing yields a vast number of potential components from which to assemble complex systems – motors, circuit boards, sensor arrays – into robotic (and non-robotic) systems of any configuration including their power systems (Ellery 2021a, 2021b). This suggests structural commonalities between the industrial ecology/fabrication facility and biochemical processes.

3   Closure by Return on Investment

The universal constructor is the basis of the von Neumann self-replicator – a machine that can construct anything if provided with the appropriate resources of matter, energy and information to do so (von Neumann & Burk 1966). This includes the matter, energy and genetic instruction to build a copy of itself. The self-replicator imposes stringent conditions of vertical closure to matter, energy and information required to construct itself and to output itself. We can express vertical closure conditions as resource return on investment RROI, defined as the ratio of resource output R_{out} to resource input R_{in}. For a self-replicator, the most immediate constraint is $R_{out} = R_{in}$ so RROI = 1. However, this is grossly simplified and the vertical closure constraints are more severe. We examine the implications for each type of resource – matter, energy and information – in turn. However, as shall become apparent, they are tightly interdependent.

3.1   Material Return on Investment

Biological materials are based dominantly on C, H, O, N, P, S – such volatile resources are deficient on the Moon. We employ engineering materials for constructing a self-replicating machine. Every component of the self-replicating machine is constructed from a portfolio of materials, physical and chemical processes, reactors and machines required for its manufacture. For example, a mobile phone comprises of over 30 different materials (Franz 2011). All these materials required mining by machines, physical comminution and beneficiation machines, stages of (electro)chemical processing, suites of manufacturing processes by a variety of specialised manufacturing machines (including those associated with electronics) and then assembled into a single product by assembling machines. The birth and embryonic growth of a mobile phone is characterised by a diffuse set of different origins that fan-in into a single product – a funnel. Indeed, all terrestrial products comprise a complex interlocking network of funnels that yield a suite of different components that comprise the supply side of the market. The fan-out is provided by the distribution system that transports products through the world via hubs to meet the demand side of the market. Lunar facilities will not have access to this complex web of supply chains and distribution system that exist on Earth. This is why the bowtie architecture must be implemented locally on the Moon – the self-replicating machine has precisely this architecture. Material return on investment (MROI) refers to material and parts closure. Analogous to the earlier expression, we define MROI as the ratio of material output to the material input to the self-replicator. The material input includes the suite of materials, processes and machines and their manufacture required to generate the product. For a self-replicating machine, the product is itself by definition – the product is its machines of production. The self-replicator must be able to manufacture all aspects of itself, i.e. MROI = 1 as a minimum condition. To achieve this stringent condition, there are several approaches we can enforce.

First, we restrict the required raw materials inventory to minimise mining and chemical processing requirements. The demandite list forces this process where we can turn the Moon's restricted mineralogy to advantage by forcing substitutions. For example, we substitute copper with aluminium for electrical conduction. The paucity of carbon on the Moon eliminates plastics as a resource (though under certain circumstances, we may employ silicones which embody carbon only in their sidechains). The restricted demandite list of materials minimises the mining and chemical processing (and its associated reagents) required. A single general purpose artificial chemical weathering process based on HCl leaching has been adopted and applied to all the major indigenous lunar minerals in the lunar industrial architecture. Similarly, a single process – the carbonyl process – has been adopted for purifying asteroidal iron-nickel-cobalt metals. Finally, the FFC electrochemical process is a single general-purpose process that reduces any bulk oxide to > 99% metallurgical purity – alumina to aluminium, rutile to titanium, etc.

Secondly, we wish to minimise parts inventory to minimise manufacturing and assembly processes. 3D printing is one approach to this – it requires no specialised tooling (which suffer wear-and-tear) and minimises material consumption and material waste over subtractive methods such as milling and turning. Unused material may be recycled as feedstock. Furthermore, 3D printing reduces the requirements for assembly of systems due to its ability to construct complex parts in elaborate morphologies unachievable using subtractive manufacturing. We have focused on two basic components required of a self-replicating machine – vacuum tubes as the core component of computational electronics and electric motors as the core component of robotic actuation. We can exploit these components for a wide variety of functions. For example, vacuum tubes are the basis for active electronics, photomultiplier tubes, magnetrons (with motor components within them), thermionic converters, electron guns (for electron beam processing including additive manufacturing), etc.

Return on assets (ROA) is a common terrestrial manufacturing metric that is the ratio of income to value of assets. Though it is a financial measure, it may be thought as a useful proxy for return on mass investment, i.e. ratio of mass of produced goods to mass of production machines. However, ROA ~ 20% is considered excellent suggesting that this is not a good proxy for return on mass investment. Furthermore, almost all manufacturing efficiency metrics are of this nature yielding percentages under 100%. The manufacturing metrics that involve throughput over time do not consider lifecycles of machines (nominally 10,000 h) except EROI discussed below. It would be expected that the mass of product over the lifecycle of the productive asset to exceed unity by a considerable margin otherwise it is not sustainable.

3.2 Energy Return on Investment

Energy for self-replication was not explored by von Neumann nor von Tiesenhausen though it is often, at least partially, implicit in artificial life worlds in the form of a proxy as computational resources. Energy closure is commonly quantified through energy return on investment (EROI) commonly used in terrestrial energy accounting in renewable energy lifecycle analysis (Bardi et al 2011). EROI is the ratio of energy output E_o by an energy system to the energy input E_i required to build it. For energy accounting, $E_o > E_i$. The same metric applies to the self-replicator with the constraint of energy closure, i.e. EROI ≥ 1.

There are several approaches we can adopt to maximise energy output on the Moon. Firstly, we can exploit renewable energy sources on the Moon, i.e. solar energy that is available without atmospheric distortion at 1370 W/m^2. And so it is at the base of the biological food web on Earth (though photosynthetic efficiency is poor at $< 1\%$). Given that most energy required for constructing the self-replicating machine is thermal for chemical/electrochemical processing and thermal-based 3D printing, solar concentrators are favoured over photovoltaic conversion. Nevertheless, electrical energy will be required favouring high efficiency energy conversion methods. Photovoltaic conversion efficiency of Si is capped at ~15% which degrades with temperature. However, on the Moon, pn junction manufacture requires precise doping which is unlikely without microtechnology, limiting conversion efficiencies to <5%. Thermionic conversion within vacuum tubes exploits high temperatures offering ~ 10–15% (Ellery 2021). Photon-enhanced thermionic efficiency potentially offers enhanced conversion efficiencies ~ 30–50% (Schwede et al 2010). Unlike the isothermal conditions characteristic of biological energy conversion, the self-replicating machine requires the high temperatures of the hearth to power its metabolism.

To minimise the energy inputs required to manufacture the self-replicating machine, we must employ energy savings to reduce energy consumption. The lunar industrial ecology treats waste as feedstock so negligible energy is wasted in processing of waste. This also favours the adoption of effective comminution and physical beneficiation methods to remove physical waste material as early as possible from the processing chain (though very little would be wasted – lunar highland regolith is ~90% anorthite mineral which is utilised almost entirely for alumina, silica and quicklime). The FFC process itself minimises energy consumption in that 97% of its energy requirement is thermal and can be supplied through solar concentrators directly from solar flux while only 3% is electrical for the electrolysis circuit (Ellery et al 2022). This minimises the losses in electrical energy conversion. 3D printing minimises energy wasted by eliminating material waste inherent in subtractive manufacturing. There are several potential approaches – a Fresnel lens-based approach that uses concentrated solar energy directly to 3D print metals, ceramics and glass and precision electron beam additive manufacturing for 3D printing metals – electron beam generation is much more efficient than laser generation. It is conceivable that the electron beam and laser may be throttled to provide minor subtractive and surface finishing processes within the same machine offering reduced material consumption.

3.3 Information Return on Investment

Information closure is essential – the information required for specification of the self-replicator (information input I_i) cannot exceed the information storage capacity of the self-replicator (information output I_o), i.e. $I_i \leq I_o$. In fact, this is guaranteed by the von Neumann approach of copying and interpreting the same genetic instructions so information return on investment, IROI = 1. There have been detractions to the practical possibility self-replication technology (Sewell 2023) but they suffer from a misapplication of the infinite regress problem that was resolved by von Neumann and through the imposition of vertical closure of information. Similarly, in biological self-replication, the genetic code is translated into a semantic (phenotypic) form for construction but it is transcribed only in syntactic (genetic) form for copying for (vertical) transmission to offspring. Biological information is based on an arbitrary coding relation – through tRNA – between DNA/RNA sequences and amino acid sequences. The amino acid sequence is a linear code that through molecular interactions folds into a specific 3D shape that dictates its chemical function. The physics of protein folding is not required to be stored genetically as this is a result of the laws of physics. Pragmatics is applied at the level of evolutionary success of the organism's construction. This constitutes the principle of semantic closure (Rocha 2001). This implies that DNA/RNA as a genetic medium is not universal.

The problem that does arise is that information costs energy for processing and storage plus the energy consumed in the manufacture of hardware substrates such as memory stores and logic gate processing. If we wish to minimise the information output requirements of the physical substrate, we must minimise information input, i.e. compress the genetic instruction code for the self-replicating machine. One of the chief problems is that to maximise fidelity in copying to minimise copying errors, we must implement error detection and correction codes that add redundancy to prevent evolutionary change through mutation (Ellery & Eiben 2019). This expands the genetic code rather than compressing it. There are several strategies that we might explore to implement such approaches to compression but we mention one. We can maximise parts re-use similar to biological exaptation. This minimises information specification length (in a Chaitin-Kolmogorov complexity sense). An example of this is in adopting electric motors for energy storage as flywheels and vacuum tubes for thermionic energy conversion on the Moon. By exapting the pre-existing vacuum tube (active electronic device) and motor (actuator) for energy generation and storage respectively, we are utilising pre-existing assets and their genetic specifications. Another example would be for electromagnetic launchers on the Moon. Given that the coil gun is a rolled-out dc motor writ large, its specification is based on that of the motor but with a different configuration and size. This is one means through which to modularise the genetic instructions for multiple re-use to compress it. An intriguing issue is that biological information storage appears to be unconstrained with accumulation of so-called "junk" DNA.

3.4   Resource Return on Investment

If $R = MROI = EROI = IROI = 1$, we have a self-replicating machine that equates to a physical version of Langton's loop (Langton 1984). Its universal construction capability is in fact constrained to the $R = 1$ capacity – it can construct anything asymptotically less complex than the self-replicator itself. It is questionable that this is true universal construction. Universal construction requires reconfigurability of the self-replication architecture. For instance, if the self-replicator were to be reprogrammed to construct solar power satellites, the industrial ecology and fabricators must be reconfigured. One possibility is reconfiguration through artificial genetic regulatory networks to impart both adaptability and robustness (Ellery 2021a, 2021b). Universal construction requires more stringent conditions beyond full vertical closure, i.e. $MROI \geq 1$, $EROI \geq 1$ and $IROI \geq 1$. Furthermore, an $R = 1$ machine can copy itself but would have no capacity for self-repair. The commonality of DNA polymerase suggests that replicative DNA synthesis evolved from DNA repair mechanisms, i.e. repair preceded replication. Growth may be considered the main function of biological organisms –growth may be separate from reproduction (determinate growth) or simultaneous with it (indeterminate growth) (Lika & Kooijman 2003).

To permit exponential growth of self-replication, there are three further principles we must employ: (i) maximised utilisation of common rock-forming minerals rather than enriched ores to ensure plentiful supplies; (ii) we employ multifunctional materials as much as possible; (iii) indigenous approach of utilising everything and wasting nothing. From anorthite, we extract calcium chloride (as this is required in only small quantities for FFC electrolyte leakage, we more commonly reconstitute HCl and/or NaCl), alumina, silica, aluminium, silicon and oxygen. This is the deployment of materials for multifunctional applications. In the lunar industrial ecology, a single metal extraction and purification process – the carbonyl process – is adopted to treat nickel-iron asteroid material. Troilite inclusions in such material are used to supply the catalyst for the carbonyl process. This is also our source of selenium (through sulphide substitution in troilite) and tungsten. We waste nothing of the rarer sources of nickel-iron meteorites. These limits need to be explored further but are suggestive of the importance of ecological efficiency.

To exploit the universal construction facility, it is essential to design R to be as large as possible as this determines universal construction capacity. We can impose some minimum estimates to R. For instance, it is reckoned that a society with healthy growth, EROI must be in the range $15 < EROI < 30$ (Lambert et al 2014). A minimum R (without universal construction) has R as the product of the number of offspring per generation (r) and the number of generations of self-replication required (n), i.e. $R = nr$. Every self-replicator contributes to all subsequent generations. We need to add in 100% self-repair capability which doubles this on the basis that this equates to a full copy, i.e. $R = 2nr$. For our nominal lunar self-replicator, $R = 2(13)(2) = 52$ for 1.5 million units after 13 generations. This effectively imposes a counting mechanism similar to telomeres imposing a Hayflick limit to the number of replication cycles (Ellery 2022a, 2022b). To add universal construction, we require $R > 2nr$ but this is arbitrarily unbounded within the laws of physics depending on the scope of universal construction (e.g. constructor theory in physics (Deutsch & Marletto 2015) as applied to life (Marletto 2015)). We may accept that there is a limit to the sophistication of universal construction to enable self-replication so $R = 2nr$ is a reasonable margin for a self-replicating machine.

4   Conclusions

Vertical closure conditions impose significant strictures on the design of physical self-replicating machines. In applying some of these constraints, some well-known biological principles are derived – bowtie metabolic architectures, energy accounting, mutation rates, exaptation, Hayflick limits and ecological efficiency. In exploring the physicality of self-replicating machines, we may gain insights into biological life from a more general perspective without the anthropomorphism of terrestrial biochemistry – perhaps to the extent of providing insights into extraterrestrial life (Ellery 2018).

Acknowledgments. This study was not funded.

Disclosure of Interests. The authors have no competing interests to declare that are relevant to the content of this article.

Appendix: Lunar Industrial Ecology

Table A1. Lunar industrial ecology which extracts from lunar minerals a suite of demandite-listed functional materials with some potential applications (emboldened oxides may be reduced by the FFC process into pure metals

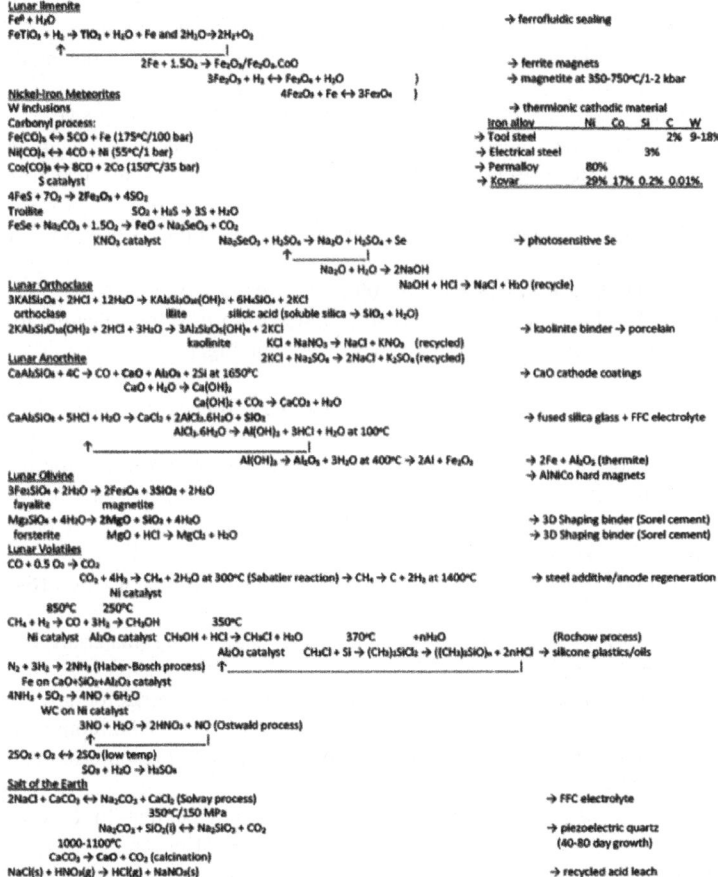

References

Alpi, A., et al.: Plant neurobiology: no brain, no gain? Trends in Plant Sciences **12**(4), 135–136 (2007)

Bardi, U., Lavacchi, A., Yaxley, L.: Modelling EROEI and net energy in the exploitation of non-renewable resources. Ecol. Model. **223**, 54–58 (2011)

Benenson, Y., Paz-Elizur, T., Adar, R., Kelnan, E., Livneh, Z., Shapiro, E.: Programmable and autonomous computing machine made of biomolecules. Nature **414**(6862), 430–434 (2001). https://doi.org/10.1038/35106533

Bich, L., Bechtel, W.: Control mechanisms: explaining the integration and versatility of biological organisms. Adaptive Behaviour **30**(5), 389–407 (2022)

Boden, M.: Is metabolism necessary? Br. J. Philos. Sci. **50**, 231–248 (1999)

Butch, C., Meringer, M., Gagnon, J.-S., Cleaves, J.: Open questions in understanding life's origins. Commun. Chem. **4**, 11 (2021)

Cardenas, M., Letelier, J.-C., Gutierrez, C., Cornish-Bowden, A., Soto-Andrade, J.: Closure to efficient causation, computability and artificial life. J. Theor. Biol. **263**, 79–92 (2010)

Chertow, M.: IPAT equation and its variants. J. Ind. Ecol. **4**(4), 13–29 (2000)

Chirikjian, G., Zhou, Y., Suthakorn, J.: Self-replicating robots for lunar development. IEEE/ASME Trans. Mechatron. **7**(4), 462–472 (2002)

Csendes, T.: Simulation study of the chemoton. Kybernetes **13**(2), 79–85 (1984)

Csete, M., Doyle, J.: Bow ties, metabolism and disease. Trends Biotechnol. **22**, 446–450 (2004)

Csete, M.E., Doyle, J.C.: Reverse engineering of biological complexity. Science **295**(5560), 1664–1669 (2002)

Deutsch, D., Marletto, C:: Constructor theory of information. Proc. Royal Soc. A **471**(Feb), 20140540 (2015)

Di Paolo, E.: Extended life. Topoi **28**, 9–21 (2009)

Elaskri, A., Ellery, A.: 3D printed electric motors as a step towards self-replicating machines. In: Proceedings of the International Symposium Artificial Intelligence, Robotics and Automation in Space, paper no 5020 (2020)

Ellery, A.: Are self-replicating machines feasible? AIAA J. Spacecraft Rockets **53**(2), 317–327 (2016)

Ellery, A.: Space exploration through self-replication technology compensates for discounting in NPV cost-benefit analysis – a business case? New Space J. **5**(3), 141–154 (2017)

Ellery, A.: Engineering a lunar photolithoautotroph to thrive on the Moon – life or simulacrum? Int. J. Astrobiol. **17**(3), 258–280 (2018)

Ellery, A.: Sustainable in-situ resource utilisation on the Moon. Planet. Space Sci. **184**(4), 104870 (2020)

Ellery, A.: How to build a biological machine using engineering materials and methods. Biomimetics J. **5**(3), 35 (2020)

Ellery, A.: Are there biomimetic lessons from genetic regulatory networks for developing a lunar industrial ecology? Biomimetics **6**(3), 50 (2021). https://doi.org/10.3390/biomimetics6030050

Ellery, A.: Generating and storing power on the Moon using in-situ resources. Proc IMechE J. Aerospace Eng. **236**(6), 1045–1063 (2021)

Ellery, A.: "Lunar demandite – you gotta make this using nothing but that. In: Proceedings of teh ASCE Earth & Space Conference Colorado School of Mines, Denver, pp, 743–758 (2022)

Ellery, A.: Bootstrapping neural electronics from lunar resources for in-situ artificial intelligence applications. In: Proceedings of the 42nd SGAI International Conference on Artificial Intelligence – Lecture Notes in Artificial Intelligence, vol. 13652, pp. 83–97 (2022)

Ellery, A.: Curbing the fruitfulness of self-replicating machines. Int. J. Astrobiol. **21**(4), 243–259 (2022). https://doi.org/10.1017/S1473550422000246

Ellery, A.: The "sensible" way to construct robots from lunar resources. In: Proceedings of the 73rd International Astronautics Congress, Paris, IAC-22.D3.2B.x68580 (2022)

Ellery, A., Eiben, A.: To evolve or not to evolve: that is the question. In: Proceedings of the Artificial Life Conference 357–364 (2019)

Ellery, A., Mellor, I., Wanjara, P., Conti, M.: Metalysis FFC process as a strategic lunar in-situ resource utilisation technology. New Space J. **10**(2), 224–238 (2022)

Franz, R.: *Life Cycle of Materials in Mobile Phones*, Underwriters Laboratories White Paper (2011)

Freitas, R., Gilbreath, W.: Advanced Automation for Space Missions, NASA CP-2255 (1980)

Freitas, R., Merkle, R.: Kinematic Self-Replicating Machines. Landes Bioscience, Austin, TX (2004)

Garzon, F.: Quest for cognition in plant neurobiology. Plant Signal. Behav. **2**(4), 208–211 (2007)

Gruntman, M., Groß, D., Májeková, M., Tielbörger, K.: Decision-making in plants under competition. Nat. Commun. **8**, 2235 (2017). https://doi.org/10.1038/s41467-017-02147-2

Jones R, Haufe P, Sells E, Iravani P, Olliver V, Palmer C, Bowyer A (2011) "RepRap – the replicating rapid prototyper" *Robotica* **29** (Jan), 177–191

Korbak, T.: Self-organisation, (M, R)-systems and enactive cognitive science. Adapt. Behav. **31**(1), 35–49 (2023)

Koshland, D.E.: The seven pillars of life. Science **295**(5563), 2215–2216 (2002)

Lambert, J., Hall, C., Balogh, S., Gupta, A., Arnold, M.: Energy, EROI and quality of life. Energy Policy **64**, 153–167 (2014)

Langton, C.: Self-reproduction in cellular automata. Physica D **10**(1–2), 135–144 (1984)

Lehman, N.E., Kauffman, S.: Constraint closure drove major transitions in the origins of life. Entropy **23**(1), 105 (2021). https://doi.org/10.3390/e23010105

Lenski, R., Ofria, C., Pennock, R., Adami, C.: Evolutionary origin of complex features. Nature **423**(May), 139–144 (2003)

Lika, K., Kooijman, S.: Life history implications of allocation to growth versus reproduction in dynamic energy budgets. Bull. Math. Biol. **65**, 809–834 (2003)

Marletto, C.: Constructor theory of life. J. Royal Soc. Interface **12**, 20141226 (2015)

Monshausen, G., Gilroy, S.: Feeling green: mechanosensing in plants. Trends Cell Biol. **19**(5), 228–235 (2009)

Montevil, M., Mossio, M.: Biological organisation as closure of constraints. J. Theor. Biol. **372**, 179–191 (2015)

Morowitz, H., Allen, J., Nelson, M., Alling, A.: Closure as a scientific concept and its application to ecosystem ecology and the science of the biosphere. Adv. Space Res. **36**, 1305–1311 (2005)

Mossio, M., Moreno, A.: Organisational closure in biological organisms. Hist. Philos. Life Sci. **32**, 269–288 (2010)

Muchowska, K., Varma, S., Moran, J.: Synthesis and breakdown of universal metabolic precursors promoted by iron. Nature **569**(May), 104–107 (2019)

Rocha, M.: Evolution with material symbol systems. BioSystems **60**, 95–121 (2001)

Schwede, J., et al.: Photon-enhanced thermionic emission for solar concentrator systems. Nat. Mater. **9**, 762–767 (2010)

Sewell, G.: Human-engineered self-replicating machines. Biocosmos **1**, 12–15 (2023)

Vega, F.: The cell as a realization of the (M, R) system. Biosystems **225**, 104846 (2023). https://doi.org/10.1016/j.biosystems.2023.104846

Villalobos, M., Razeto-Barry, P.: Are living beings extended autopoietic systems? An embodied reply. Adapt. Behav. **28**(1), 3–13 (2020)

von Neumann, J., Burks, A.: Theory of Self-Reproducing Automata. University of Illinois Press, Champaign, USA (1966)

von Tiesenhausen, G., Darbro, W.: Self-replicating systems – a systems engineering approach. NASA TM-78304, Marshall Space Flight Centre, Alabama (1980)

Zykov, V., Mytilinaios, E., Adams, B., Lipson, H.: Self-reproducing machines. Nature **435**, 163–164 (2004)

Mechanical Design of a Feline Robot for Dynamic Scaling Testing

Amy Budzichowski[1], Shane Riddle[1], Rucha Batchu[1], Tina Chen[1], Clayton B. Jackson[1], William R. P. Nourse[2]($\boxtimes$), and Roger D. Quinn[1]

[1] Department of Mechanical and Aerospace Engineering, Case Western Reserve University, Cleveland, OH 44106-7222, USA
[2] Department of Electrical, Computer, and Systems Engineering, Case Western Reserve University, Cleveland, OH 44106-7222, USA
wnourse05@gmail.com

Abstract. Animal size impacts locomotion, due to its effect on the influence of gravity, inertia, and an animal's internal elasticity and damping. We are developing a cat robot to further explore the impact of these four characteristics on animal locomotion. This paper details the mechanical design of this cat robot's rear limbs, as well as the simulated validation of this design. In future work, we plan to design forelimbs with a floating scapula and test the robot in split-belt treadmill experiments similar to those done in mammalian experiments as we develop its synthetic nervous system controller.

Keywords: Legged robot · Dynamic scaling · Feline

1 Introduction and Background

Animals of different sizes move differently. This is because different forces dominate a creature's movement depending on how large it is. There are four primary forces which affect locomotor strategy: gravitational, inertial, viscous, and elastic forces. Often, two or three forces will dominate an animal's motion, and the others will be negligible [1, 16, 19, 23, 33]. Elastic and viscous forces dominate the locomotion of smaller creatures such as insects, while larger animals such as dogs, humans, and horses experience more prominent gravitational and inertial effects. This is due to both their size and the construction of the animals' anatomy. Insects are small enough that gravitational and inertial effects are negligible, and their anatomy contains significant built-in elasticity and damping [22]. Conversely, larger animals' size means that gravitational and inertial effects dominate their locomotion, and any elastic or damping effects from their anatomy are negligible in comparison [18]. We are building a cat robot in order

This work was funded by National Science Foundation (NSF) DBI 2015317 as part of the NSF/CIHR/DFG/FRQ/UKRI-MRC Next Generation Networks for Neuroscience Program.

to augment prior research on the effect of scale in animals of intermediate size. In modeling the fundamental biomechanics of a cat, we can use this cat robot to further explore feline locomotion.

Given that animal locomotion depends on size, and an animal's nervous system controls its motion, it follows that an animal's size affects the structure and function of its nervous system [33]. Our work seeks to explore this interplay between animal size and nervous system structure. Biomimetic robots are uniquely positioned to explore this interaction, as they allow us to validate scientific hypotheses surrounding animal locomotion [26]. By building robots based on leading theories of biomechanics and neural control, we can reverse-engineer animal locomotion, and emulate live animal experiments with robots which operate on similar principles. Because robots do not get tired or have animal experimental use considerations, experiments involving robotic animals can be carried out at far greater scale than those involving live animals. While this does not aim to replace animal testing entirely, the experiments on robots can be used to test theories and design future experiments on the animals. This allows preliminary research into animal locomotion to be carried out at greater scale for comparatively less cost, allowing live animal trials to be used more economically.

Prior work within our lab has explored the biomechanics and neural control of animals at several different scales: Drosophibot [13], MantisBot [34], Puppy [21], and most recently the rat robot [2]. The creation of this cat robot aims to augment the prior scaling work done within the lab by providing a biomimetic robot at a scale in between rat and dog. Additionally, cats are one of the smaller animals to walk upright [7] rather than in a crouched posture, like rats [15], which makes them an interesting animal for scaling studies. This paper explores the mechanical design of the rear limbs of our cat robot, as well as some preliminary testing and validation of the design and motor control algorithm.

2   Methods and Materials

2.1   Motor Selection and Torque Requirements

The motors selected for this robot are the Westwood Robotics Koala BEAR (Westwood Robotics LLC, Westwood, MA) model. These were chosen for their low gear ratio, back-drivability, and torque feedback capabilities, as well as their relatively small form factor ($6.4 \times 6.2 \times 3.7$ cm) and high torque output (3.5 Nm static, 10.5 Nm dynamic). Additionally, the motors have a speed constant of 27.3 RPM/V. With our 24 V power supply, the maximum velocity of the motors is well above the maximum cat joint velocity of 149 RPM [29]. These motors are quasi-direct drive, which allows for relatively straightforward torque control [30]. Thus, the motors are capable of emulating variable stiffness and damping within the motor control code, something that normally requires physical springs and dampers to be added in series with other motors. Other works which have used these motors have reported sufficient control frequencies [24], however it should be noted that the motors are still limited and cannot emulate infinite stiffness or damping properties. Further testing is needed to characterize the valid regions of stiffness and damping for these motors, as simulated tests show that too large damping commands require motor torques beyond the maximum dynamic torque of the motors. An alternative is to implement discrete passive springs and dampers at the joints. The ability to dynamically change these properties greatly reduces the robot's design complexity and allows these parameters to be changed dynamically instead of requiring physical replacement of components. Thus, these motors allow us to perform studies on the dynamic scale of the robot without changing the hardware. It is important to note that the dynamic scale of the robot refers to the relationship between inertia, stiffness, damping, and temporal properties, along with the kinematic configuration and scale [33]. Changing any one of these properties impacts the dynamic scale of the robot.

A joint torque analysis was performed to determine the expected loads each joint of the robot would experience during a cat-like walking gait, and whether the Koala motor specifications would be sufficient. We used dynamic motion tracking data of a cat walking on a treadmill from Prilutsky et al. [29]. This data consisted of the limb joint angles and the dynamic force experienced at each joint over time. It also included the mass, length, and center of mass of each part of the limb (digits, tarsal, tibia/fibula, and femur). The vertical force experienced at the metatarsophalangeal (MTP) joint was used to approximate the ground reaction force (GRF), as this element is in contact with the ground during the entirety of stance phase, excluding toe-off.

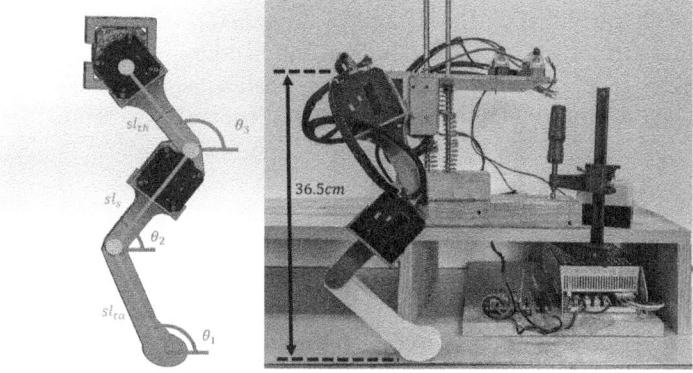

Fig. 1. On the left is a CAD model of the robotic leg. On the right is the physical robotic leg. Green dots represent pivot points, Blue lines represent the limb length. (Color figure online)

The joint torque analysis was performed using forward kinematic, static torque calculations on the model shown in Fig. 1 for each timestep of the collected data tracking the MTP joint angle, the ankle angle, and the knee angle. The static torque calculations used for the initial design phase incorporate the dynamic forces recorded in the motion tracking data giving us the instantaneous torque at each timestep. We recognize that while this provides an estimate for preliminary design work a true dynamic analysis will need to be performed prior to finalizing the design. To accommodate the use of absolute coordinates in the models, the joint angle data was converted from its initial relative coordinates to absolute coordinates $(\theta_1, \theta_2, \theta_3)$. The robot shown in Fig. 1 has its mass concentrated at the motors, which are located near the joints. This is a reasonable approximation for the purposes of this analysis as the robot limbs are composed of 3D printed carbon fiber and are thus negligibly light compared to the motor mass (250 g).

$$
\tau_{\text{ank,c}} = -F_c l_{\text{ta}} \cos(\theta_1) + g \left[m_{\text{ta}} l_{\text{com,ta}} \cos(\theta_1) + m_s (l_s - l_{\text{com,s}}) \cos(\theta_2) \right.
$$
$$
\left. + m_{\text{th}} \left(l_s \cos(\theta_2) + (l_{\text{th}} - l_{\text{com,th}}) \cos(\theta_3) \right) \right] \tag{1}
$$

$$
\tau_{\text{knee,c}} = -F_c \left[l_{\text{ta}} cos(\theta_1) + l_s cos(\theta_2) \right] + g \left[m_{\text{ta}} \left(l_{\text{com,ta}} cos(\theta_1) + l_s cos(\theta_2) \right) \right.
$$
$$
\left. + m_s l_{\text{com,s}} cos(\theta_2) + m_{\text{th}} \left(l_{\text{th}} - l_{\text{com,th}} \right) cos(\theta_3) \right] \tag{2}
$$

$$
\tau_{\text{hip,c}} = -F_c \left[l_{\text{ta}} cos(\theta_1) + l_s cos(\theta_2) + l_{\text{th}} cos(\theta_3) \right]
$$
$$
+ g \left[m_{\text{ta}} \left(l_{\text{com,ta}} cos(\theta_1) + l_s cos(\theta_2) + l_{\text{th}} cos(\theta_3) \right) \right.
$$
$$
\left. + m_s \left(l_{\text{com,s}} cos(\theta_2) + l_{\text{th}} cos(\theta_3) \right) + m_{\text{th}} l_{\text{com,th}} cos(\theta_3) \right] \tag{3}
$$

Equations 1–3 describe the torque about each joint of the biological cat which inspired our robot, while Eqs. 5–7 describe the torque about each joint of the modeled cat robot. Descriptions and values for each parameter used in these equations can be found in Table 1.

$$
F_r = F_c \frac{m_{\text{robot}}}{m_{\text{cat}}} \tag{4}
$$

$$
\tau_{\text{ank,r}} = s \left[-F_r l_{\text{ta}} cos(\theta_1) + mg l_s cos(\theta_2) \right] \tag{5}
$$

$$
\tau_{\text{knee,r}} = s \left[-F_r \left(l_{\text{ta}} cos(\theta_1) + l_s cos(\theta_2) \right) + mg l_s cos(\theta_2) \right] \tag{6}
$$

$$
\tau_{\text{hip,r}} = s \left[-F_r \left(l_{\text{ta}} cos(\theta_1) + l_s cos(\theta_2) + \right. \right.
$$
$$
\left. \left. l_{\text{th}} cos(\theta_3) \right) + mg \left(l_s cos(\theta_2) + 2 l_{\text{th}} cos(\theta_3) \right) \right] \tag{7}
$$

To account for the difference in lengths between the robot and the animal, a scaling factor, s, was incorporated into Eqs. 5–7. To adjust the ground reaction forces (GRFs), the contact forces measured in testing [29], F_c, were scaled by the ratio of the mass of the robot to the mass of the cat. While compact, the motors were still too large to fit on a frame the size of a typical cat so a length increase was necessary. The length scaling factor allowed us to analyze the increased joint torques the system would experience at larger scales and determine a size that accommodated ease of manufacturing without exceeding the motor torque limits all while trying to keep the scale as close to 1 as possible. The motor masses were placed at the distal end of the femur and tibia of the model for this analysis.

Table 1. The parameters and variables used in the joint torque equations. Variables without listed values are time dependent.

Param.	Description	Value	Param.	Description	Value
θ_1	MTP Joint Angle	–	l_{ta}	Tarsal Length	6.15 cm
θ_2	Ankle Angle	–	l_s	Shank Length	9.5 cm
θ_3	Knee Angle	–	l_{th}	Thigh Length	9.4 cm
m_{ta}	Tarsal Mass	19.1 g	$l_{com,ta}$	Tarsal COM	2.99 cm
m_s	Shank Mass	56.1 g	$l_{com,s}$	Shank COM	4.02 cm
m_{th}	Thigh Mass	142 g	$l_{com,th}$	Thigh COM	4.16 cm
m_{robot}	Robot Mass	10 kg	τ_c	Cat Joint Torque	–
m_{cat}	Cat Mass	3.02 kg	τ_r	Robot Joint Torque	–
F_c	Contact Force	–	s	Length Scaling Factor	1.75

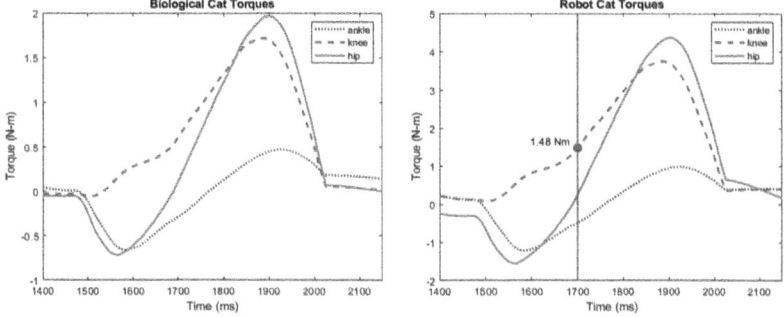

Fig. 2. Hip, knee, and ankle torques through a single stance phase for a cat hind leg and robotic cat leg analogue. The gray line indicates the timestep we considered to be standing position and the maximum torque at that time. The torque profiles are similar in shape but differ in magnitude.

The joint torques over the course of a single stance phase are shown in Fig. 2 for the animal and robot models, respectively. The length scale for the robot model used was 1.75 and the mass of the robot was set to its expected total of 10 kg. Preliminary testing and prototyping revealed that a scale factor of roughly 1.75 was the minimum length increase needed to fit our motors on the robot without requiring us to manufacture custom drive components, such as the belts and pulleys. To check that this scale produced joint torques within the motor limits we identified a timestep in the stance data where the joint angles correlated to those of a typical standing position (t = 1700 ms). The maximum joint torque calculated at this standing position was 1.48 Nm, well below the motor's static loading limit of 3.5 Nm. Furthermore, the maximum torque experienced over the entirety of stance was under 4.5 Nm, which is well below the motor's dynamic loading limit of 10.5 Nm. With both conditions satisfied, a length scale of 1.75 was chosen for the design of the cat robot. Assuming the motors are placed at the ankle and knee of the robot, this provides enough space to fit them without overloading the motors beyond their torque specification. While the scaling factor would ideally be closer to 1, increasing the amount of space for the motors, without exceeding their torque capabilities, was crucial for manufacturability. An increase in size still allows for the robot to be dynamically similar to the cat because the stiffness and damping in the motors can be increased relative to the inertia of the leg according to scaling laws. Additionally, the robot at a 1.75 scale is still within the size range of domestic felines, falling around the size and weight of a Maine Coon.

2.2   Mechanical Design of Rear Limbs

The mechanical design of the cat robot aims to mimic feline morphology as accurately as possible without introducing unnecessary complexity. For our purposes, this means that the hip, knee, and ankle joints are actuated by motors, and a passively compliant MTP joint allows the foot to conform to the ground throughout stance. Analyses of feline locomotion generally focus on the hip, knee, and ankle, and excludes the MTP joint in the foot [10,31]. Using these active and passive degrees of freedom allows us to capture the main components of locomotion.

The knee and ankle of the robot are simplified to be hinge joints, so each has one motor controlling flexion and extension. The hip in the animal is a ball-and-socket joint, though it has been shown that motion in the sagittal plane alone is sufficient to produce locomotive behavior [25]. However, it was found that abduction/adduction motion in the hip plays a significant role in the stability of walking [25,28]. Therefore, we have included motors to control motion of the hip joints in both the sagittal and frontal planes of motion. Future works may require a redesign of the ankle to include additional degrees of freedom.

Final Design. Our final design is scaled up by a factor of 1.75 from the size of the biological cat used in our torque analysis. This places our design within the acceptable limits of the torque capabilities of the motor as discussed in the Sect. 2.1. We decided to implement a belt-driven system, with a motor at the hip actuating the knee, and motor at the knee actuating the ankle. Thus, there is no concentrated mass load at the end of the tibia, reducing the inertia of the leg with respect to the hip joint.

Our belt-drive system uses Fingertech timing belts (Fingertech Robotics Ltd., Saskatoon, CA), with custom 3D-printed gears adapted from the Fingertech 16T gears. The gear ratio from driving motor at the hip to actuated joint at the knee is 1:1, as is the gear ratio from the driving motor at the knee to the actuated joint at the ankle. The purpose of having the ankle and knee belt-driven is to allow for the motors to be placed higher up on the limb, reducing the inertia of the robot about the hip. The Koala BEAR motors do not have a driveshaft. Rather, they have an actuated faceplate to which objects can be fastened. Our driving gears were adapted to bolt directly to the faceplate, with mounting holes matching that on the faceplate of the motor. These gears were 3D printed without supports.

The current version of the cat robot, depicted in Fig. 1, consists of only the rear limbs, so the pelvis need not be fully actuated or anatomically accurate. As we have no front limbs to support the robot, the pelvis is currently mounted to a platform with two vertical rods, with ball bearings ensuring smooth vertical motion. For ease of design, manufacturing, and to provide a place to mount electronics, the base of the pelvis consists of a flat plate with two large holes cut out for placement of linear ball bearings, and eight smaller holes above the point where the abduction/adduction motor is mounted. The motor is attached to the bottom of the pelvis, enclosed in a 3D-printed structure with tapped M3 holes so that the full weight of the motor is not being supported by the four M3 mounting holes on its top face.

An enclosure for the flexion/extension motor mounts directly to the faceplate of the abduction/adduction motor. Mounted to the flexion/extension motor is a connector piece, which creates an offset between the head of the femur and the outside of the pelvis in order to allow the femur to rotate 360° without contacting the pelvis when the flexion/extension motor is vertical.

Femur. The final femur design is shown in Fig. 3. The eight holes on the face of the head of the femur allow it to mount directly to the connector piece, and thus it is directly driven by the flexion/extension motor. A belt channel runs through the center of the femur, with significant cutouts along the shaft to allow for easy access to and maintenance of the timing belt and gears. The cutouts along the shaft are also far enough apart to accommodate the head of the tibia, which mounts at the circular hole at the distal end of the femur. The platform extending out from the head of the femur houses the motor, which is bolted on from below and is used to belt-drive the knee.

Tibia. The head of the tibia is longer than that of the femur so that there is room for both the driven gear (at the point where the D-slot is located) and the driving gear within the head of the tibia. Because providing enough vertical clearance to prevent collision of the bottom of the femur and the top of the knee-mounted motor would require that the motor be placed too low on the tibia, the motor is mounted at a 5 mm offset from the face of the head of the tibia to allow full range of motion of the tibia about the knee. Aside from the changes mentioned above, the tibia design is largely the same as the femur design.

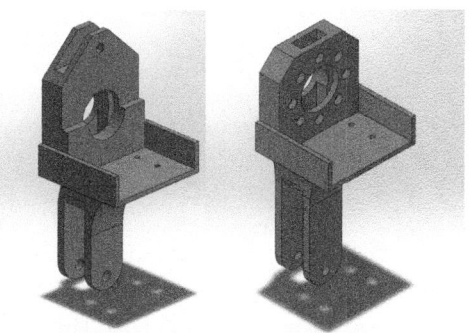

Fig. 3. Left: Isometric view of robot tibia. Right: Isometric view of robot femur.

2.3   Mechanical Design of the Foot

While many quadrupedal robots exist, few use compliant mechanisms for their feet. Most quadrupedal robots use peg or rounded ball feet for simplicity [17]. However, these designs do not move like the feet of a cat. A compliant foot design may enable the cat robot to better mimic cat gait by allowing the foot to conform to the ground throughout stance without the additional complexity of a fully actuated foot. It has also been shown that the use of passive compliance in the feet of robots increases the stability of the robot [3, 4, 27]. The compliant foot must be compatible with the femur and tibia described above. It must be able to handle stresses during locomotion and have a range of motion comparable to that of a biological cat.

Before generating concepts for the compliant foot design, we conducted research on cat anatomy and preexisting robotic feet [5, 14]. The hind feet of a cat have three main sections: the tarsals, metatarsals and the phalanges [6]. The basic shape of the compliant foot was designed to closely approximate the shape of a biological cat foot, with a focus on retaining the joint between the tarsals and phalanges. For ease of manufacturability and stability, the design does not include individual movable toes.

We chose a design which used silicone rubber as a passive spring housed between the digits and tarsals. The toe and tarsal sections of the hind foot were fabricated as separate parts and joined through casting silicone in an appropriate shape. The shape of the toe and tarsal components was modified in consideration for the appropriate range of motion for the hind foot. The foot is expected to have a joint range of 0 to 90°.

Mathematical Models. To analyze the flexure and stress of the joint, we modeled the compliant foot as a small-length flexural pivot [20]. Using a beam length of L and a flexural segment of length l, the stiffness, movement, and stress can be modeled using the following equations:

$$c = \frac{h}{2} \tag{8}$$

$$\theta_0 = \frac{M_0 l}{EI} \tag{9}$$

$$K = \frac{EI}{l} \tag{10}$$

$$\sigma_{max} = \frac{M_0 c}{I} \tag{11}$$

where c refers to half of the beam height, I refers to the area moment of inertia, M_0 refers to the moment applied at the end of the beam, and E is the Young's modulus. The moment approximation was used due to available estimated motor torques. Based on the joint torque calculated for the ankle motor, a moment value of 0.744 N · m was used. The silicone beam length, width, and height were chosen based on its fit in the tarsal and toe components. The beam length is approximated using the length of the tarsal component, as the moment is applied from the end of the tarsal. Table 2 lists these values used in this model. Using this model, we calculated a stress of 2.3 MPa at the joint. These equations are rough approximations, especially for the degree of bending observed during prototyping. However, they were deemed close enough for initial design (Fig. 4).

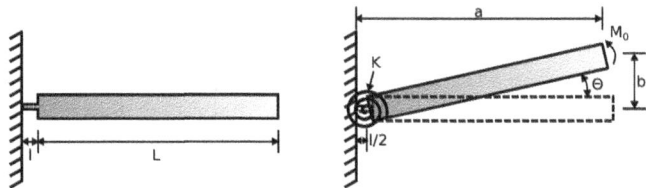

Fig. 4. Pseudo Rigid Body Model of Small Length Flexural Pivot [20].

Table 2. Values used for the model of the Metatarsophalangeal Joint.

Parameter	Value
Moment, M_0	0.744 Nm
Beam Length, L	0.107 m
Silicone Length, l	0.015 m
Silicone Width, w	0.016 m
Silicone Height, h	0.0115 m
Area Moment of Inertia, I	2.03E−9 kg · m^4
Neutral Axis Location, c	0.0125 m

The dimensions of the compliant foot are based on data obtained from a biological cat. The robot is scaled to 1.75 times the size of this cat, so the tarsal and toe components were restricted to 0.108 m and 0.048 m long, respectively.

We modeled the silicone joint concept in SolidWorks. The phalanges were grouped together as a single toe component. The tarsals and metatarsals were grouped together as one tarsal component. The end of the toe component which faces the tarsal has a curve to guide the movement range of the tarsal. In order to decrease stress on the overhang, we added a flare to the end of the tarsal which faces the toe. This spreads out the area that the tarsal is in contact with the toe component when the joint is in a 90° position.

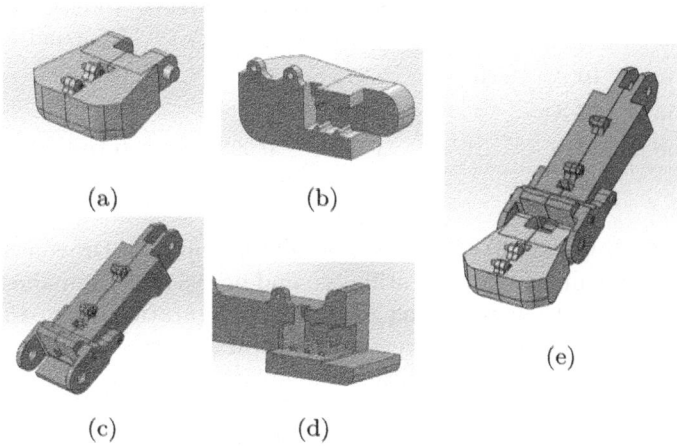

Fig. 5. Tarsal model with compliant MTP joint. (a) Toe Component. (b) Cut view of toe. (c) Tarsal component. (d) Cut view of tarsal. (e) Fully assembled tarsal model with compliant MTP joint.

Both the toe and tarsal components include a hollow chamber for the silicone rubber. We added teeth to both chambers to grip the silicone and prevent it from sliding out after casting. There are 4 teeth in the chamber in the toe, with two on the top and two on the bottom. There are 5 teeth in the tarsal chamber, with two on the top and three on the bottom. These teeth are rounded to prevent potential tear damage. These features as well as the assembled model of the tarsal and toes is shown in Fig. 5

Materials. We 3D printed the main components of the compliant foot for ease of manufacture. Dragon Skin brand (Smooth-On, Macungie, PA) silicone rubber was chosen for use at the joint due to its flexibility and durability. This brand of silicone is located on the middle to lower range of the hardness scale, which allows it the flexibility to bend without cracking. In addition, it has the strength to withstand the expected loads on the joint. We bought and tested 3 variants of Dragon Skin silicone rubber—Dragon Skin 10 Medium, Dragon Skin 20, and Dragon Skin 30—to compare their characteristics. These variants were chosen due to their tensile strength being higher than the stress we calculated of 2.3 MPa. A simplified list of their properties is shown in Table 3. In addition, the torsional stiffness was estimated for all three variants using the first iteration of the foot. These estimated values were calculated by measuring the bend angle of the foot under the weight of the tarsal.

Table 3. Silicone Rubber Properties [32].

Variant	Hardness	Cure Time (h)	Tensile Strength (MPa)	100% Modulus (E, MPa)	Estimated Torsional Stiffness (K, N*m/rad)
Dragon Skin 10	10 A	5	3.275	0.152	0.0128
Dragon Skin 20	20 A	4	3.792	0.338	0.0110
Dragon Skin 30	30 A	16	3.447	0.593	0.104

In the end, Dragon Skin 30 was chosen for the joint, as Dragon Skin 10 and 20 both had very similar torsional stiffness, and occasionally remained in a bent configuration rather than returning to a flat configuration when the foot was moved around. Additionally, the weight of the tarsal component alone was able to bend the 10 and 20 feet a significant amount ($>70°$), which meant that they are too compliant and would not hold up well under the weight of the full robot. While the material of the foot should be able to handle the stresses from the robot weight itself, the bending mechanism would not behave as desired. In this scenario, the foot may immediately go from a 0 to 90° configuration without much resistance. In comparison, Dragon Skin 30 was stiff enough to return to a flat configuration after bending in preliminary tests, and the weight of the tarsal component only bent the foot below 45°. Additionally, the amount of silicone in the foot can be adjusted to the stiffness needs of the robot in future designs.

3   Results

Before beginning experiments with the cat robot, we implemented a simulated model of our design in the physics simulator Mujoco [35]. This model allowed us to validate the joint controller which will be used to control the robot, and to get an idea of the results we could expect from our Koala BEAR motors.

One of the primary motivations behind using quasi-direct drive actuators for our robot was their ease of torque control [30], which allows us to dynamically adjust the stiffness and damping of any joint on the robot in order to test theories about dynamic scaling in animal joints. We can do this by directly controlling the torque at each joint to mimic a rotational system with stiffness and damping

$$\tau = -k \cdot (\theta - \theta_0) - c \cdot \dot{\theta} \tag{12}$$

where θ is the motor position, θ_0 is the motor resting position, $\dot{\theta}$ is the motor velocity, k is the rotational stiffness coefficient, c is the rotational damping coefficient, and τ is the motor torque. As the focus of these simulations was on the motor controller, a more traditional, rigid foot was used rather than the foot with compliant toes. Further testing will be done to evaluate various designs of the feet as they relate to the normal gait cycle.

We subjected the simulated leg to multiple drop tests where the leg fell from a height of 0.55 m and collided with the ground. For each test we varied the stiffness and damping coefficients for all of the joints. Results can be seen in Fig. 6. The simulations use a forward Euler method, with a time step matching a reasonable control frequency for the motors [24,30]. As expected, setting the stiffness to large values results in underdamped oscillations and setting the damping to large values results in an overdamped behavior.

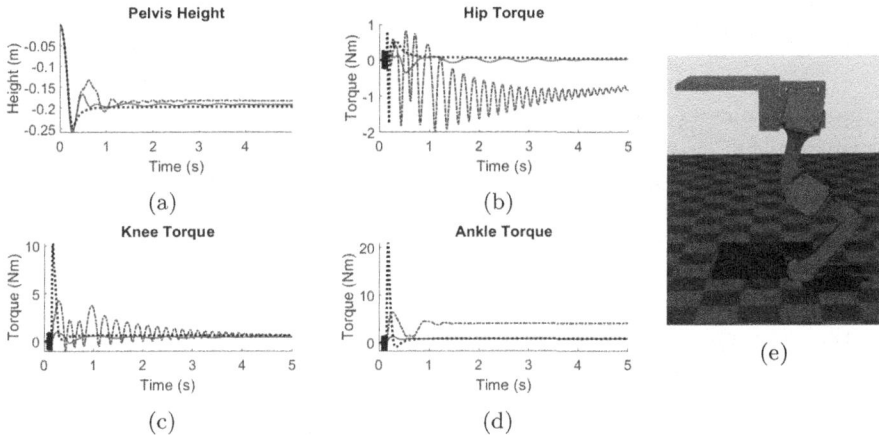

Fig. 6. Simulated leg with joints exhibiting controlled stiffness and damping. **A.** Pelvis height during drop tests. **B–D.** Hip, Knee, and Ankle motor torques during drop tests. **E.** Simulated robot leg in Mujoco [35]. In the simulation, each motor rotates, and the pelvis translates vertically. Three drop tests with varying stiffness and damping: Red solid line: $k = 1$, $c = 0.001$; Blue dashed line: $k = 5$, $c = 0.001$; Black dotted line: $k = 1$, $c = 1$.

4   Conclusions and Further Work

This paper has outlined the design of a robotic hindlimb similar to that of a domestic cat. The hindlimb was designed at 1.75 scale of a normal cat. This was chosen to allow sufficient space to fit the motors while ensuring the increased joint torques do not exceed their capabilities. The initial simulations of the robot performing a drop test show that the motor control code is capable of adapting its stiffness and damping properties. However, the overdamped system results in peak ankle torques of around 20 Nm (Fig. 6d, black dotted line), while the motors peak at 10.4 Nm. Further testing will be done to compare the limits of the stiffness and damping properties and compare the simulated results to the physical robot. A preliminary design of a foot with compliant toes has also been outlined, with the compliant mechanism coming from silicone cast into a 3d printed limb. This will allow the foot to conform to the ground, remaining in contact with the ground throughout the stance phase.

Our future work with the cat robot shall progress in several stages. Upon construction of a complete rear of the cat robot, we will begin to validate an existing neural model of mammalian hindlimb locomotion [8], using data from our partners at Georgia Tech to ensure that the robotic cat's motion is true to that of the cat it is based upon. While validation of the rear of the cat is in progress, research and design efforts will begin for the front of the cat robot. The primary design is the floating scapula to which the rest of the forelimb is anchored. Prior work with cat robots has ignored the floating scapula in favor of a fixed shoulder joint (with one exception [12]), and thus this is a novel area of development. As the mechanics of the robot must reasonably emulate the biomechanics of the cat in order for the robot to be useful in animal-like experimentation, a workable facsimile of the floating scapula is crucial to our goals.

In addition to this continuation of prior work, we have several goals specific to this robot. We aim to explore the impact of various elastic and damping properties on the motion of our robot, with two intended outcomes. First, we aim to determine how different combinations of anatomy and nervous system construction perform. For example, what exactly goes wrong if a robot with the dynamic properties of a cat tries to move like a praying mantis? Secondly, we intend to evaluate the usefulness of passive elements in helping a robot achieve biomimicry in its locomotion. This will aid future roboticists in design decisions, as it will provide insight into interactions between the neural controller and the mechanical system it controls.

In the long term, we aim for the cat robot to be able to walk independently of an external support structure. This will allow us to better replicate prior work in feline biomechanics, as it will increase the range of possible movements achievable by our cat robot. For one such planned experiment, a split-belt treadmill is being built in the lab to capture and verify the ground reaction forces of the robots being tested. The treadmill will record data for speeds up to 1 m per second, and will be able to collect limb data for both left and right limbs simultaneously and independently. Each side of the treadmill will be able to change speed and direction independently of each other [9], which helps with testing inter-limb coordination of the cat robot [11], thus allowing us to simultaneously validate the accuracy of our mechanical design and our controller.

Acknowledgments. We would like to thank the Biomechanics and Motor Control Lab at Georgia Tech for providing access to the data from their work.

References

1. Ache, J., Matheson, T.: Passive joint forces are tuned to limb use in insects and drive movements without motor activity. Curr. Biol. **23**(15), 1418–1426 (2013)
2. Aronhalt, E.R.: Development of a robotic rat hindlimb model and neural controller (2023)
3. Beer, R.D., Quinn, R.D., Chiel, H.J., Ritzmann, R.E.: Biologically inspired approaches to robotics: What can we learn from insects? Commun. ACM **40**(3), 30–38 (1997)
4. Catalano, M.G., et al.: Adaptive feet for quadrupedal walkers. IEEE Trans. Robot. **38**(1), 302–316 (2021)
5. Chatterjee, A., Mo, A., Kiss, B., Gonen, E.C., Badri-Sprowitz, A.: Multi-segmented adaptive feet for versatile legged locomotion in natural terrain. In: Proceedings - IEEE International Conference on Robotics and Automation 2023-May, pp. 1162–1169 (2022)
6. Coulson, A., Lewis, N.: An Atlas of Interpretative Radiographic Anatomy of the Dog and Cat. Wiley (2002)
7. Day, L.M., Jayne, B.C.: Interspecific scaling of the morphology and posture of the limbs during the locomotion of cats (Felidae). J. Exp. Biol. **210**(4), 642–654 (2007)
8. Deng, K., Szczecinski, N.S., Arnold, D., Andrada, E., Fischer, M.S., Quinn, R.D., Hunt, A.J.: Neuromechanical model of rat hindlimb walking with two-layer cpgs. Biomimetics **4**, 21 (2019)
9. Dimiskovski, M., Scheinfield, R., Higgin, D., Krupka, A., Lemay, M.A.: Characterization and validation of a split belt treadmill for measuring hindlimb ground-reaction forces in able-bodied and spinalized felines. J. Neurosci. Methods **278**, 65–75 (2017)
10. Ekeberg, Ö., Pearson, K.: Computer simulation of stepping in the hind legs of the cat: an examination of mechanisms regulating the stance-to-swing transition. J. Neurophysiol. **94**, 4256–4268 (2005)
11. Frigon, A., Hurteau, M.F., Thibaudier, Y., Leblond, H., Telonio, A., Angelo, G.D.: Split-belt walking alters the relationship between locomotor phases and cycle duration across speeds in intact and chronic spinalized adult cats (2013)
12. Fukuhara, A., Gunji, M., Masuda, Y., Tadakuma, K., Ishiguro, A.: Flexible shoulder in quadruped animals and robots guiding science of soft robotics. J. Robot. Mechatron. **34**, 304–309 (2022)
13. Goldsmith, C.A., Szczecinski, N.S., Quinn, R.D.: Neurodynamic modeling of the fruit fly drosophila melanogaster. Bioinspiration Biomimetics **15**, 065003 (2020)
14. Goldsmith, C.A., Zyhowski, W.P., Büschges, A., Zill, S.N., Dinges, G.F., Szczecinski, N.S.: Effects of tarsal morphology on load feedback during stepping of a robotic stick insect (carausius morosus) limb. In: Lecture Notes in Computer Science (Including Subseries Lecture Notes in Artificial Intelligence and Lecture Notes in Bioinformatics), 14157 LNAI, pp. 442–457 (2023)
15. Griffin, C., Choong, W.Y., Teh, W., Buxton, A.J., Bolton, P.S.: Head and cervical spine posture in behaving rats: implications for modeling human conditions involving the head and cervical spine. Anat. Rec. **298**(2), 455–462 (2015)
16. Günther, M., Rockenfeller, R., Weihmann, T., Haeufle, D.F., Götz, T., Schmitt, S.: Rules of nature's formula run: Muscle mechanics during late stance is the key to explaining maximum running speed. J. Theor. Biol. **523**, 110714 (2021)
17. Hauser, S., Eckert, P., Tuleu, A., Ijspeert, A.: Friction and damping of a compliant foot based on granular jamming for legged robots. In: Proceedings of the IEEE RAS

and EMBS International Conference on Biomedical Robotics and Biomechatronics, 2016-July, pp. 1160–1165 (2016)

18. Hooper, S.L.: Body size and the neural control of movement. CURBIO **22**, R318–R322 (2012)

19. Hooper, S.L., Guschlbauer, C., Blümel, M., Rosenbaum, P., Gruhn, M., Akay, T., Büschges, A.: Neural control of unloaded leg posture and of leg swing in stick insect, cockroach, and mouse differs from that in larger animals. J. Neurosci. **29**(13), 4109–4119 (2009)

20. Howell, L., Magleby, S., Olsen, B.: Handbook of Compliant Mechanisms. John Wiley & Sons (2013)

21. Hunt, A., Szczecinski, N., Quinn, R.: Development and training of a neural controller for hind leg walking in a dog robot. Front. Neurorobot. **11**, 18 (2017)

22. Ilton, M., et al.: The principles of cascading power limits in small, fast biological and engineered systems. Science **360**, eaao1082 (2018)

23. More, H.L., Maxwell, D.J.: Scaling of sensorimotor delays in terrestrial mammals. Proc. R. Soc. B. **285**, 20180613 (2018)

24. Liu, Y., Shen, J., Zhang, J., Zhang, X., Zhu, T., Hong, D.: Design and control of a miniature bipedal robot with proprioceptive actuation for dynamic behaviors. In: 2022 International Conference on Robotics and Automation (ICRA), pp. 8547–8553

25. Lyakhovetskii, V.A., Gorskii, O.V., Gerasimenko, Y.P., Musienko, P.E.: Mathematical model of the hindlimbs control during cat locomotion with balance. Rossiiskii Fiziologicheskii Zhurnal Imeni IM Sechenova **101**(2), 200–213 (2015)

26. Mangan, M., et al.: A virtuous cycle between invertebrate and robotics research: perspective on a decade of living machines research (2023)

27. Melo, K., Horvat, T., Ijspeert, A.J.: Minimalist design of a 3-axis passive compliant foot for sprawling posture robots. In: 2019 2nd IEEE International Conference on Soft Robotics (RoboSoft), pp. 788–794. IEEE

28. Misiaszek, J.E.: Control of frontal plane motion of the hindlimbs in the unrestrained walking cat. J. Neurophysiol. **96**(4), 1816–1828 (2006)

29. Prilutsky, B.I., Sirota, M.G., Gregor, R.J., Beloozerova, I.N.: Innovative methodology quantification of motor cortex activity and full-body biomechanics during unconstrained locomotion (2005)

30. Seok, S., Wang, A., Otten, D., Kim, S.: Actuator design for high force proprioceptive control in fast legged locomotion. In: IEEE International Conference on Intelligent Robots and Systems, pp. 1970–1975 (2012)

31. Shen, L., Poppele, R.E.: Kinematic analysis of cat hindlimb stepping. J. Neurophysiol. **74**, (1995)

32. Smooth-On: Dragon skin ^{TM} series. https://www.smooth-on.com/product-line/dragon-skin/

33. Sutton, G.P., Szczecinski, N.S., Quinn, R.D., Chiel, H.J.: Phase shift between joint rotation and actuation reflects dominant forces and predicts muscle activation patterns (2023)

34. Szczecinski, N.S., et al.: Introducing mantisbot: Hexapod robot controlled by a high-fidelity, real-time neural simulation. In: IEEE International Conference on Intelligent Robots and Systems, 2015-December, pp. 3875–3881 (2015)

35. Todorov, E., Erez, T., Tassa, Y.: Mujoco: a physics engine for model-based control. In: IEEE International Conference on Intelligent Robots and Systems, pp. 5026–5033 (2012)

Moving Inward with Front Legs Improves Tripod Gaits for Crab-Like Robot Walking in Sand

Zach Silberstein, Mingyu Pan[✉], Nathan Carmichael,
and Kathryn A. Daltorio

Case Western Reserve University, Cleveland, OH 44106, USA
{zms29,mxp745,nxc258,kam37}@case.edu

Abstract. Locomoting in the surf-zone is a challenge for traditional robots, as they must be able to resist hydrodynamic forces of waves while overcoming the challenges of walking on sand, a granular media. Taking inspiration from live crabs that can navigate the surf zone efficiently, we demonstrate that inward gripping with crab-inspired curved dactyls on a crab-like robot can increase its effective weight underwater, which is the weight of the robot minus the buoyancy force, to better resist wave forces. Gripping can also reduce the cost of transport and allow for more efficient operation in a lab-created surf-zone environment. Six different walking gaits are tested on an 18 degree-of-freedom crab-inspired hexapod robot. The tests are conducted on sand underwater, with and without the presence of waves. Results show that the gait with a smooth swing path combined with front only gripping is on average 50% more energy efficient than the gait with a polygonal swing path with front and rear gripping in still water and 29% more energy efficient in waves.

Keywords: Legged robot · Underwater locomotion · Gait definition.

1 Introduction

During the course of millions of years, crabs have developed traits that make them particularly effective at navigating beach environments both above and underwater. This include different terrestrial and amphibious postures to better withstand hydrodynamics forces [9] and dactyls to increase their underwater weight and prevent them from being dislodged from the sea bed due to waves [3]. Further, despite their small size, crabs are able to seamlessly transition between sandy terrestrial environments and aquatic habitats by preventing excessive dactyl sinkage into sand while resisting hydrodynamic forces [12].

These characteristics motivate researchers to develop crab-like robots for underwater locomotion, sensing, object retrieval, etc. For example, inspired by a Chinese mitten crab, a novel single motor compliant robot leg was developed and a gait for the robot was designed based on the locomotion patterns of live crabs [14]. By analyzing the motion of live crabs, an amphibious robot was developed

N. S. Szczecinski et al. (Eds.): Living Machines 2024, LNAI 14930, pp. 299–314, 2025.
https://doi.org/10.1007/978-3-031-72597-5_21

that could both walk and swim using two swimming legs [2]. Crabs can also utilize their walking legs for object manipulation. To demonstrate this capability, a Klann linkage legged robot was developed to grasp objects weighing up to 2 kg utilizing only 4 Degrees of Freedom [5].

Determining the ideal footpath for a robot has also been explored from various different perspectives. An energy model of the robot was developed and a footpath was created based on a Fourier series with the aim of reducing the energy consumed at each joint [13]. In a different approach, a computationally efficient footpath algorithm was created by analyzing the workspace of a hexapod robot along with its static stability [10]. Further, a contact model had previously been used to create an approach to simulate robot movement on granular media [15]. Each of these methods were successful at determining a footpath for a robot, however none of the above methods considered the challenging operating environment of the surf zone. To combat the difficulties of locomoting in the surf zone, it was demonstrated in our previous work that a crab-inspired dactyl can be used to increase the effective weight of the robot in sand by using the distributed inward gripping (DIG) strategy, where the legs of the robot pull inward on a granular media, applying opposing shear forces inside the media and increasing the total contact force in the normal direction [6]. Here, we define a gait that utilizes the DIG strategy as a gripping gait, while a gait that does not utilize the DIG strategy as a non-gripping gait. For a gripping gait, an extra waypoint or waypoints are added at the end of the swing phase, allowing the dactyl to move inward towards the body during stancing and mimicking the DIG strategy. The gait that implemented DIG strategy was up to 18% faster and 34% more energy efficient than a non-gripping gait while sideways walking on various surfaces [7]. However, when gripping with both front and back legs, there was substantial relative movement between legs on the opposite of the robot body in the sand, leading to loss of energy due to medium deformation.

In this paper, six new gaits are evaluated to determine whether inward gripping enhances a heavier crab-inspired robot's locomotion capabilities and if the walking efficiency of the gait can be further improved. Specifically, the tested robot, Tamatoa, is 2.20 kg heavier than our previous robot Sebastian [6] on which we tested a Non-Gripping Triangle Dactyl Path (TDP) and a Gripping Quadrilateral Dactyl Path (QDP). Then, two new end effector paths that are made of smooth curves, namely Non-Gripping Smooth Path (NS) and Gripping Smooth Path (GS), are created to reduce the effect of undesired jumps in angular velocity during locomotion compared to TDP and QDP. Finally, a Front-only Gripping Smooth Path (FGS) is developed to reduce the effect of tripod interference during locomotion.

All six gaits, including TDP and QDP from previous work, are tested on sand in both still water and lab created wave conditions on an 18 DoF robot: Tamatoa (Fig. 1). The robot's average locomotion speed and Cost of Transport (CoT) are used to compare the gaits' efficiency across all tests. The contribution of this paper is to study the advantages of using smooth curved end effector paths compared to straight line segments paths, and to analyze the advantages of front-only gripping, in both still water and the presence of external hydrodynamic forces.

Fig. 1. Tamatoa, the 18 Degree-of-Freedom (DoF) crab-inspired robot.

2   Platform Development

2.1   Robot Design

The tested robot has six legs, each with three DoF, and are connected to an ABS body where the electronics are stored. Each leg has a hip joint parallel to the x-axis, with the knee and ankle joints parallel to the y-axis (Fig. 2(a)). The design of the hip joint allows for the robot body to tilt at different angles, where the effect of body angle while walking can be explored in future work. The ratio of the length of the distal segment, L_2, to the length of the proximal segment plus the length of the distal segment, $L_1 + L_2$, is 0.63, as that had been found to be the optimal ratio in previous work [3]. The hip joint is geared with a ratio of 1.2:1 to increase torque output and sits on top of an ABS block that also acts as the bushing for the leg axis. The legs (Fig. 2(a)) are primarily made up of 3D printed components made from PLA with 70% infill in addition to 0.635 cm aluminum rods which are selected to reduce weight. The robot weighs 6.56 kg (63.33 N) in air, is negatively buoyant, and has a weight of 11.38 N when fully submerged underwater.

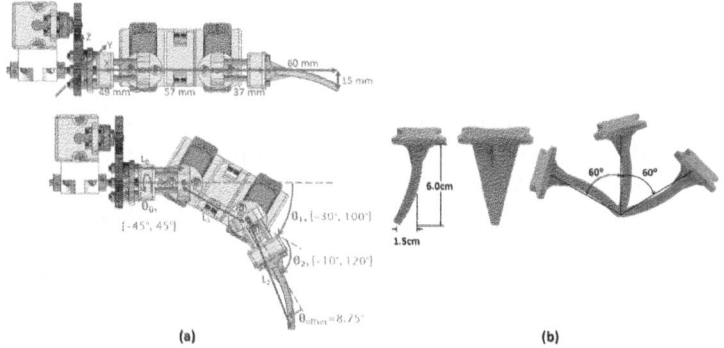

Fig. 2. (a). A render of Tamatoa's leg. The leg contains a hip joint along the x-axis and parallel knee and ankle joints along the y-axis. (b). A dactyl of Tamatoa. The right side image depicts the range of allowed dactyl angles.

2.2 Dactyl Design

In previous work, it was demonstrated that inward gripping with dactyls increases the effective weight of the robot [6]. The dactyls on this robot are designed to have a larger cross-section than those used in [7], which was hypothesized to further increase the effective weight of the robot when gripping. Each dactyl has a length of 6.0 cm and curves inward by 1.5 cm as shown in Fig. 2(b). The dactyls are 3D printed with PLA using 100% infill. The dactyl makes up 62.9% of the L2 segment and 39.7% of the total leg length. These ratios are chosen to balance the additional gripping force of a larger dactyl with the trade-off of also having to raise the end-effector higher up as it sinks more into sand.

2.3 Waterproofing Methods

To seal the body, a 1.27 cm acrylic sheet compresses a 0.635 cm thick rubber sheet onto the top of the ABS body. Eight 7.62 cm long bolts run through the body and are tightened down to compress the rubber sheet which acts as an o-ring and prevents water from entering the body. Six waterproof NPT 1.27 cm cable glands are then filled with silicone and tightened around grouped servo wires.

2.4 Servo Selection

Each leg contains three SAVOX SW2210SG-BE - Waterproof Premium, High Voltage, Brushless, Digital Servo (Torque @ 7.4 V: 3.918 N-m). The servo is IP67 rated (able to operate underwater for up to 30 min at depth of 0.914 m). Each servo is housed inside a 3D printed module that allows for easy connection to other leg parts and can be easily replaced if needed. The servo has a maximum operating range of 130°. Tamatoa's workspace is made with θ_0 ranging from $-45°$ to $45°$, θ_1 ranging from $-30°$ to $100°$, and θ_2 ranging from $-10°$ to $120°$ (Fig. 2(a)).

2.5 Electronics

All electronic components other than the servos are stored inside the waterproofed ABS body. The robot is controlled with a Raspberry Pi Model 4B, powered by a Pisugar 3 Plus (Portable 5000 mAh UPS Lithium Battery Power Module Platform). Commands are sent to the servos via a Mini Maestro 18-Channel USB Servo Controller. The servos are powered by a Zeee Lipo Battery 2S (7.4 V, 50 C, 5200 mAh). An INA260 High or Low Side Voltage, Current, Power Sensor is used to record power data from the servo controller and a BNO055 Absolute Orientation Sensor is used to record the orientation and acceleration of the robot body. The sensors are connected to separate Arduino Nanos via I2C and the Arduinos are connected to the Raspberry Pi over USB.

3 Gait Development

3.1 End-Effector Path Planning

An end-effector path is considered to be a closed-loop path that the end-effector of the robot follows during its gait. The path consists of two phases, a swing phase where the dactyl is off the ground and swings forward, and a stance phase where the dactyl maintains ground-contact and propels the body forward. In this work, the end-effector is considered to be the tip of the dactyl. A sideways walking gait is used in this work as opposed to a forward walking gait, as sideways walking had been previously found to be more energy efficient and resulted in higher locomotion speed [4]. The robot uses the tripod gait due to the gait's ability to maintain balance and stability during walking, turning and stopping, since the center of mass always remains in the triangular base of support [8]. The front left, front right, and rear middle legs form one tripod and complete the swing phase while the rear left, rear right, and front middle legs form the other tripod and stay in contact with the ground and propels the robot forward while stancing.

If an end-effector path is generated, the end-effector is able to follow the path by generating evenly spaced points along the path. At each point, inverse kinematics is used to generate joint angles required for the end-effector to pass through each point. The x, y, and z positions of the end-effector can be calculated with forward kinematics as shown in Eqs. 1–3:

$$x = L_0 + L_1 \cos (\theta_1) + L_2 \cos (\theta_1 + \theta_2 + \theta_{offset}) \tag{1}$$

$$y = \sin (\theta_0)(L_1 \sin (\theta_1) + L_2 \sin (\theta_1 + \theta_2 + \theta_{offset})) \tag{2}$$

$$z = -\cos (\theta_0)(L_1 \sin (\theta_1) + L_2 \sin (\theta_1 + \theta_2 + \theta_{offset})) \tag{3}$$

where L_0, L_1, and L_2 are lengths of the leg segments, θ_0, θ_1, and θ_2 are respective joint angles, and θ_{offset} is the offset angle to account for dactyl curvature as illustrated in Fig. 2(a). Solving the above equations for the joint angles yields Eqs. 4–6:

$$\theta_0 = \text{atan2} \left(\frac{y}{-z} \right) \tag{4}$$

$$\theta_2 = \pm \cos^{-1} \left(\frac{x^2 + y^2 + z^2 - (L_0^2 + L_1^2 + L_2^2) + 2L_0(L_0 - x)}{2L_1 L_2} \right) - \theta_{offset} \tag{5}$$

$$\theta_1 = \cos^{-1} \left(\frac{x - L_0}{\sqrt{(x - L_0)^2 + y^2 + z^2}} \right) - \text{atan2} \left(\frac{L_2 sin(\theta_2 + \theta_{offset})}{L_1 + L_2 cos(\theta_2 + \theta_{offset})} \right) \tag{6}$$

where $\text{atan2} \left(\frac{y}{x} \right)$ is the signed tangent inverse. To ensure optimal leg configurations, only positive values of cos^{-1} in Eq. 5 are used.

For all the tested end-effector paths, the hip angle, θ_0, is set to 0° and therefore all paths are in the x-z plane. It is assumed that the energy consumed by the six hip joints is constant regardless of end-effector path. An additional constraint is applied so that the angle between the ground and the dactyl is never more than 30° as shown in Fig. 2(b). This ensures that the dactyl does not contact the sand at undesirable angles. The workspace resulting from these constraints and the joint limits discussed in Sect. 2.4 are shown in the yellow colored areas of Fig. 3.

To ensure that the only difference between each gait is the swing path, a constant body height of 14.0 cm is set for each gait, since the maximum stride length can be achieved at such height, leading to lower CoT [4]. All of the gripping gaits begin gripping when the end-effector is 3.0 cm vertically above the stance path and grip inward horizontally by 3.0 cm. Additionally, all gaits have a raise of 6.0 cm which ensures the dactyl is entirely removed from the sand during the swing phase. Further, each gait is performed with the same gait period of 2 s. Finally, all gaits share a common stance path. The front legs begin the stance phase at X = 8.9 cm and Z = −14.0 cm and end the stance phase at X = 3.9 cm and Z = −14.0 cm. The rear legs begin the stance phase at X = 3.9 cm and Z = −14.0 cm and end the stance phase at X = 8.9 cm and Z = −14.0 cm.

In [7], the implemented gaits had pauses where the tripod contacting the ground would be stationary while the other tripod completed the plant phase and grip phases. This was done to allow both the front and rear legs to move at the same speed in the world frame while planting and gripping. However, such method forced the center of mass of the robot to maintain stationary during the grip and plant phases and required the legs to have to accelerate the robot from rest during each stance phase. This constant changing of speed was thought to cause an increase in CoT, as seen in humans [11]. In this work, the pause is removed.

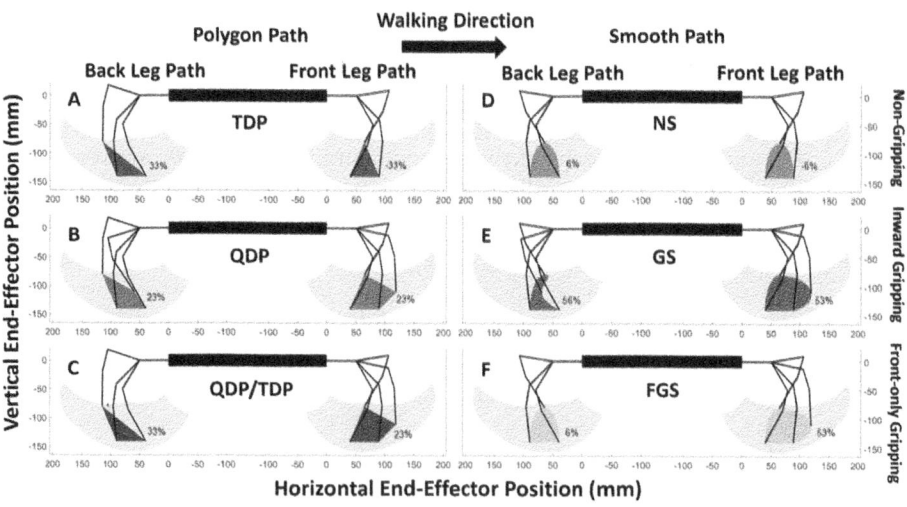

Fig. 3. The six different implemented gaits. The yellow colored area represents the workspace of the robot by applying the dactyl constraint and set hip joint to 0°. (A) The TDP gait. (B) The QDP gait. (C) The QDP/TDP gait. (D) The NS gait. (E) The GS gait. (F) The FGS gait. The percentage labeled on each path is the horizontal distance the end-effector grips inward with 2 cm of dactyl sinkage divided by the hard-ground stance distance. (Color figure online)

3.2   Non-gripping Triangular Dactyl Path (TDP)

The TDP (Fig. 3A) gait used in this work is developed in a similar manner to the TDP and QDP gaits in [7] so that the performance of the newly developed gaits can be compared to previous work. The swing phase of the TDP gait for the front dactyls is created by raising along a straight path from a waypoint at the end of the stance phase to a waypoint at X = 6.4 cm and Z = −8.0 cm, and then planting in a straight line to a waypoint at the beginning of the stance phase to complete the gait cycle. The rear legs start the swing phase by raising along a straight path to X = 11.4 cm and Z = −8.0 cm and then following a straight path to return to the beginning of the stance phase. The rear legs raise backwards so they exit the sand at the same angle as the front legs.

3.3   Gripping Quadrilateral Dactyl Path (QDP)

The QDP gait follows all of the same waypoints as the TDP gait described above but includes an extra waypoint to allow for the legs to grip while walking. For the front legs, this waypoint is located at X = 11.9 and Z = −11.0 cm and for the rear legs the waypoint is located at X = 6.9 cm and Z = −11.0 cm. Both the front and back legs have a horizontal and vertical displacement of 3 cm while gripping.

3.4   Non-gripping Smooth Path (NS)

The motivation to develop the NS gait (Fig. 3D) was so that it can act as a non-gripping baseline to compare to other gaits that grip. Noticeably, the front legs of TDP enter the sand horizontally closer to the body than the beginning of the stance point. This means for the remaining portion of the plant, there will be an undesirable stance like motion in the opposite direction of movement of the body. As a result, an elliptical path is chosen for NS over a parabolic path, since the ellipse allows for less horizontal movement when entering and leaving the sand. The NS gait is made with a waypoint at X = 6.4 cm and Z = −8.0 cm for both the front and back legs. This waypoint is horizontally in the middle of the stance and has a height equal to the raise height. The path is made by tracing out the upper half of an ellipse defined by a minor diameter that is equal to the stance path and a major radius that runs from the center of the stance path to the waypoint. Further, there are no points in the path where the end-effector suddenly changes direction in NS, which means the joint curves also do not have cusps and do required sudden changes in joint velocities.

3.5   Gripping Smooth Path (GS)

Similarly to the QDP gait, the GS gait gripped inward with both front and rear legs while walking to increase the effective weight of the robot, as seen in Fig. 3E, where both legs will grip inward by reaching out further during the end of swing phase compared to Fig. 3D. For the front and rear legs, the GS gait raises along an elliptical path to help minimize horizontal movement while exiting the sand. The planting and gripping portion of the front legs is created by selecting five points to define an ellipse. The ellipse needs to be tangential to the top of the raise ellipse, which means the highest point must be the top of the raise and the ellipse must be symmetric about the vertical axis going through the center of the stance path. Based on these criteria, the first point selected is the waypoint that defines the raise. Since at the end of the gripping phase the path must meet the beginning of the stance phase, the waypoint at the beginning of the stance phase is selected as the second point. Then, due to the need for symmetry, the point at the start of the stance phase is selected as the third point. The fourth point, and its mirror point, determine the "gripness" of the ellipse and are chosen to be the gripping waypoint for QDP and its mirror point so that it has a comparable amount of gripping. The planting and gripping portion of the rear path is created with a Bezier spline with points located at $x = 6.4$ cm and $z = -8.0$ cm, $x = 3.9$ cm and $z = -8.0$ cm, $x = 10.4$ cm and $z = -11.0$ cm, $x = -3.9$ cm and $z = -14.0$ cm. Selecting these points creates a smooth curve that connects to the raise ellipse and has a horizontal and vertical gripping distance consistent with other gripping gaits.

3.6   Front-Only Gripping Paths (QDP/TDP and FGS)

The reason gripping is not implemented for the rear legs is that in the original gripping gaits in [7], when the rear legs grip, they entered the sand prior to horizontally reaching the waypoint at the beginning of the stance phase. This caused a stance-like effect in the opposite direction of the desired motion direction of the body. With constant body velocity, this effect also caused tripod interference and reduced the effectiveness of the stance of the other tripod. To counter this effect, two hybrid gaits are developed in which gripping was only implemented for the front legs and not the rear legs to minimize tripod interference. In one gait, the front legs perform the QDP gait and the rear legs perform the TDP gait (referred to as QDP/TDP, Fig. 3C). In the other gait, the front legs follow the GS path while the rear legs follow the NS path (referred to as FGS, Fig. 3F). With a tripod gait, gripping with only the front legs still results in always having at least one leg that is gripped. Due to the discussed similarities in the rear paths between QDP gait and TDP gait, it is expected that the QDP/TDP gait performs similarly to the QDP gait, although this similarity will show that any improvements from the TDP gait to the QDP gait are caused by the gripping of the front legs.

4   Testing Methods

4.1   Performance Metrics

Tests are performed in both still water with sand and in wave-like conditions with sand to test the effectiveness of each end-effector path. In both still water and wave testings, a camera (GoPro HERO8 Black, 2.7K Resolution, 60 FPS) is fixed over head and records the robot as it walks. The recording is then tracked using a free video analysis and modeling tool Tracker (Version 6.1.5, Brown et al., 2024) to measure the total displacement, d, during each trial. After the displacement is measured, the average speed is calculated with Eq. 7, where N is the number of steps taken by the robot in each trial and T is the gait period. Only displacement along the x-axis of the body is considered and, in turn, the calculated speed is the average speed in the x-direction.

$$v = \frac{d}{NT} \tag{7}$$

A power sensor is used to record the power draw of the servos at 20 Hz for each trial. The robot's CoT is then calculated using Eq. 8 for each trial.

$$COT = \frac{E}{mgd} \tag{8}$$

The energy consumed in the trial, E, is found by numerically integrating the power data for the trial with respect to time using the trapz function of NumPy in Python. Energy consumed by the Raspberry Pi is not considered, as the Pi has its own separate power supply. The mass of the robot, m, is the mass of all components of the robot as listed in Sect. 2.1, not the buoyancy of the robot. Lastly, g is the gravitational constant which is approximated as 9.81 (m/s^2).

4.2   Still Water Experiments

For both still water and wave testings, trials are conducted in a wave tank filled with 20 cm of play sand at the bottom. For still water testing, the water depth is 44.9 cm from the top of the sand layer. This depth completely submerges the robot which cuts off wireless communication. As a result, all commands to the robot are set in advance and then delayed. At the beginning of each trial, the robot is lined up at the same location within the tank and takes four steps with the desired gait before coming to rest to complete a trial. The robot is then moved back to its starting position and pauses for 30 s to allow for any waves created during the moving of the robot to die down before beginning to walk again. After every five trials, the robot is pulled out of the tank and the sand is flattened to ensure any tracks created by the robot will not affect the results. A total of 30 trials are conducted per gait. An example of the robot during a still water experiment is shown on the left of Fig. 4.

4.3   Wave Experiments

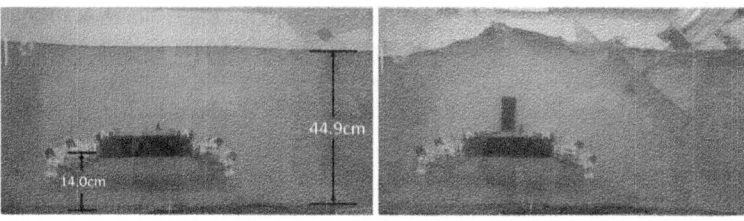

Fig. 4. Tamatoa during a still water trial (left) and a trial with waves (right).

During wave testing, a Styrofoam cuboid (20 cm by 9.5 cm by 3.7 cm) weighing 38.7 g is added to the top of the robot to increase its buoyancy. After attaching the Styrofoam, the robot weighs 0.58 kg when submerged underwater, which is half of its submerged weight without the Styrofoam. Styrofoam is added to increase the relative effect of the waves, emphasizing the importance of stability for each gait. The Styrofoam is lined vertically on top of the robot to increase the cross sectional area where the waves collide with the robot. Waves are generated by an acrylic plate attached to a pneumatic piston striking the water and then retracting as shown in the right of Fig. 4. The piston is pressurized to 689.476 kPa (100PSI) prior to each trial to ensure constant wave magnitudes between trials. The period of waves in the tank is 3.6 s which was previously found in [7]. For wave testing, the water depth is 44.3 cm from the top of the sand layer prior to the waves being generated. Before each trial, the robot is lined up in the same starting position as the still water tests. The waves are generated two seconds before the robot begins to move to ensure there would be waves throughout the trial. The robot then takes three steps with the desired gait and wave generation is stopped exactly as the robot came to rest to ensure the final displacement of the robot is undisturbed by additional waves. Three steps are taken during each trial to ensure the robot operates in the optimal wave region. Five trials are conducted before the robot is pulled out of the water and sand is flattened. Between each trial, a pause of 45 s is added to allow for any waves to come to rest. An example of the robot during an experiment with waves is shown on the right of Fig. 4.

5   Results

5.1   Still Water Results

The results from still water testings are highlighted in Fig. 5 and in Table 1. The results confirm trends from trials performed on a different robot in the previous work, with the average CoT for both TDP and QDP falling within one standard deviation of the results from [7] (32.0 ± 3.5 for TDP and 23.8 ± 2.5 for QDP). Similarly, the QDP gait is both significantly faster and significantly more energy efficient than the TDP gait with P-values of 7.66×10^{-46} and 1.46×10^{-15} respectively.

There is not a significant difference in average speeds between the QDP/TDP gait and the QDP gait (P-value of 0.63) and CoT of the two gaits fall within one standard deviation of each other. This is expected, since the rear paths of the TDP and QDP gaits are very similar. This demonstrates that the improvement from the TDP gait and the QDP gait is due to the addition of gripping in the front, not the back.

Similarly to the results between the TDP and QDP gaits, the GS gait is significantly faster than the NS gait with a P-value of 5.54×10^{-18}. However, this increased speed comes at the expense of increased energy usage, where both NS and GS displays similar CoTs with a P-value of 0.17.

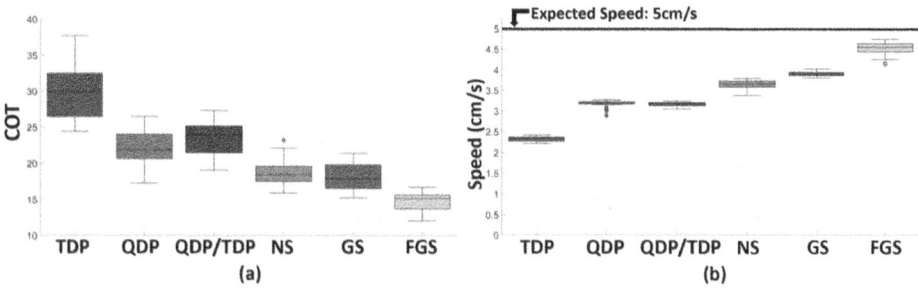

Fig. 5. (a). Cost of Transport (CoT) for each gait for still water testing (n = 30). (b). Speed for each gait for still water testing (n = 30). The expected speed is determined from the stance distance (5 cm) and period of each tripod (1 s).

Unlike the comparison between QDP and QDP/TDP gaits, the FGS gait has both significantly higher average speed and significantly lower CoT compared to the GS gait with P-values of 9.98×10^{-30} and 1.64×10^{-11} respectively. This hybrid gait of the front legs following GS and the rear legs following NS is by far the fastest and most energy efficient. The gait is able to achieve an average speed that is 91% of the desired speed while also having the lowest CoT.

Table 1. The average speed (cm s^{-1}) and CoT (unitless) for each gait during still water testing.

Gait	Average Speed ± SD	COT ± SD
TDP	2.3 ± 0.06	29.8 ± 3.3
QDP	3.2 ± 0.09	22.2 ± 2.1
QDP/TDP	3.2 ± 0.06	23.4 ± 2.3
NS	3.7 ± 0.1	18.7 ± 1.9
GS	3.9 ± 0.06	18.1 ± 1.8
FGS	4.5 ± 0.2	14.7 ± 1.3

As hypothesized, all of the curved end-effector paths outperformed the straight line paths as outlined in Table 2. This is hypothesized due to the joints operating in a smoother manner and not being required to suddenly change angular velocities. However, some of the performance gains may be attributed to variations in the paths. For example, while the front legs of TDP and NS pass through the same three waypoints, they have different angles of extraction and plant, which can also impact the results.

Table 2. The resulting P-Values from still water testings show that the smooth curved gait has a significantly greater average speed and a significantly lower CoT than the gait made with straight line segments.

Curved Gait	Straight Gait	P-Value Speed	P-Value CoT
TDP	NS	6.06×10^{-55}	4.76×10^{-23}
QDP	GS	1.25×10^{-42}	2.41×10^{-11}
QDP/TDP	FGS	1.92×10^{-48}	5.14×10^{-26}

5.2   Wave Results

The results from tests with waves are highlighted in Fig. 6 and in Table 3.

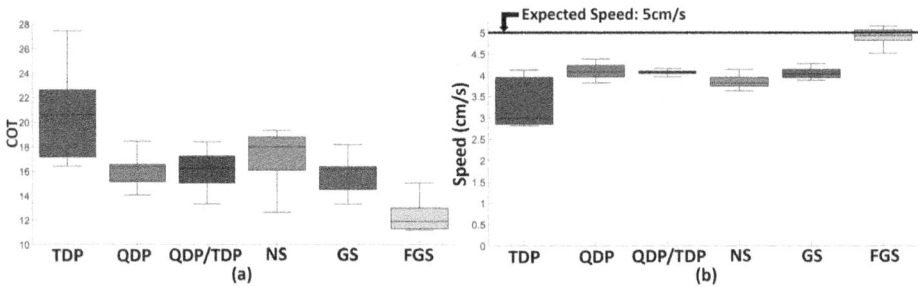

Fig. 6. (a). CoT for each gait for wave testing (n = 15). (b). Speed for each gait for wave testing (n = 15). The expected speed is determined from the stance distance (5 cm) and period of each tripod (1 s).

Upon first glance, it appears that all of the gaits performed better in wave tests than in still water tests. However, this can be attributed to the addition of the Styrofoam. The Styrofoam decreases the effective weight of the robot in water, which results in slightly less energy consumption even with the presence of waves. Further, dactyl sinkage is reduced, allowing for a larger portion of the swing phase to be completed above the sand line. This enables the robot to travel further with higher average speeds compared to trials without waves. For these reasons, comparisons between numerical results from still water testings and wave testings are not made.

The QDP gait is faster and more energy efficient than the TDP gait with P-values of 4.36×10^{-6} and 2.61×10^{-5} respectively [7]. This result demonstrates a clear advantage to gripping inward while walking as suggested in [7]. Again, similarly to still water results, there is not a significant difference between the QDP/TDP and the QDP gaits in terms of average speed and energy efficiency with P-Values of 0.85 and 0.80 respectively. This yet again shows that the performance improvement between TDP and QDP is due to the addition of gripping inward with the front legs.

Table 3. The average speed (cm s^{-1}) and CoT (unitless) for each gait during wave testing (n = 15).

Gait	Average Speed ± SD	COT ± SD
TDP	3.3 ± 0.5	20.3 ± 3.4
QDP	4.1 ± 0.2	16.0 ± 1.1
QDP/TDP	4.1 ± 0.1	16.0 ± 1.4
NS	3.9 ± 0.1	17.1 ± 2.1
GS	4.1 ± 0.1	15.7 ± 1.3
FGS	4.9 ± 0.1	12.3 ± 1.1

The benefit of gripping in waves is further seen in the comparison between non-gripping NS gait and gripping GS gait. The GS gait performs significantly better than the NS gait in terms of average speed and CoT with P-Values of 8.96×10^{-5} and 0.018 respectively. Neglecting gripping with the rear legs in the FGS gait also results in an improvement in walking speed of the robot compared to gripping with both front and rear legs in the GS gait (P-Value of 3.30×10^{-16} for average speed and 1.03×10^{-8} for CoT).

Unlike in still water tests, the curved paths do not unanimously outperform the straight line paths as reflected in Table 4. Here, both the non-gripping and front gripping curved paths (NS and FGS) outperform their straight line counterparts (TDP and QDP/TDP). However, the GS gait (gripping curved path) does not outperform the QDP gait (gripping straight line path).

Table 4. The resulting P-Values from wave testing show that the comparable smooth curve had a significantly greater average speed and a significantly lower CoT than the comparable gait made with straight line segments except for the two gaits that grip, QDP and GS.

Curved Gait	Straight Gait	P-Value Speed	P-Value CoT
TDP	NS	3.49×10^{-4}	0.0021
QDP	GS	0.71	0.31
QDP/TDP	FGS	1.28×10^{-17}	5.45×10^{-9}

5.3 Results Analysis

Several explanations are proposed to clarify the reasons of improvements for different gaits. While efforts are made to make all gaits pass through the same waypoints on the end-effector trajectory, the smooth gaits do not pass through the same raise waypoint for the rear legs as the polygonal gaits. This is done so that the rear legs would raise at the same angle as the front legs regardless of the gait. The largest impact of this difference would be in the effective stance distance of the gait, as illustrated in Fig. 7(a).

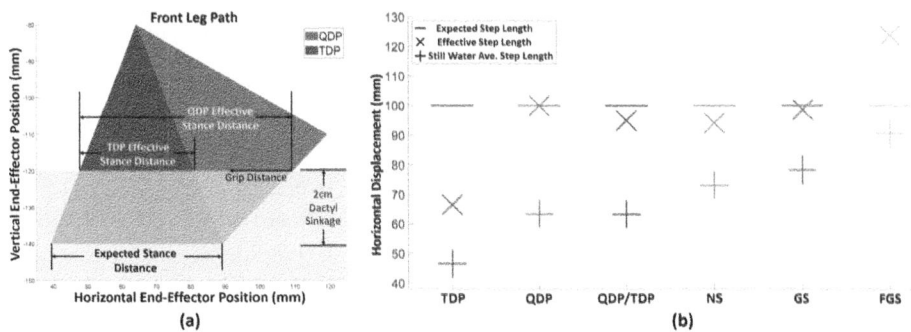

Fig. 7. (a). Expected stance distance vs. effective stance distance between QDP and TDP. (b). The expected step length vs. effective step length vs. still water average step length for all gaits.

In Fig. 7(a), the QDP and TDP gaits have the same expected stance distance. However, the QDP gait has a longer effective stance length, since the tip of the dactyl reaches out further during the swing phase, as seen between the distance comparison between TDP effective stance distance and QDP effective stance distance. Figure 7(b) shows the effective step length with an assumed 2 cm dactyl sinkage and the still water average step length for each gait, both not considering slipping. The expected step length is the displacement expected on a hard substrate in one gait cycle. The effective step length is the swing distance on soft-ground (such as sand) of the rear legs added to the soft-ground swing distance of the front legs with 2 cm of assumed dactyl sinkage. The still water average step length is the average distance the robot travelled in one gait cycle during still water testing. The front paths that grip all have a longer effective stance as it is desired for the dactyl to enter the sand further from the body than the waypoint at the beginning of stance. The paths are designed so the end-effector can then grip in the sand while coming back to the waypoint to begin stance. However, this can lead to a larger horizontal distance travelled above the sand line due to a longer swing length, leading to a longer effective stance distance in addition to gripping as seen in Fig. 7(a). This is desirable, since an increase in stance distance can result in longer stride distance, where an increase in stride distance can lead to higher locomotion speed as seen in species such as the snow crab [1].

6   Conclusions

In this paper, performances of six different end-effector paths of an 18 DoF crab-inspired robot are assessed in still water and wave conditions with sand. The six gaits feature two that grip inward with both legs, two that are not designed to grip, and two that grip with only the front legs. Additionally, three of the swing paths of the gaits are made up of straight line segments and three of the gaits are made up of curved swing paths. Results from testings show that the gait with a smooth swing path and front only gripping is on average 43% faster and 50% more energy efficient than the previously developed QDP gait in still water.

From the results shown in Sect. 5, it can be concluded that gripping gaits (QDP and GS) outperforms their respective non-gripping gait (TDP and NS), highlighting a potential benefit to gripping in sand. While the smooth curved paths outperforms the paths made from line segments in still-water, they perform similar in wave testings, suggesting that gripping in waves is more important than using a smooth curve.

While the results here are improved compared to those in [7], further improvements to the robot's locomotion are still possible. For example, although the effect of relative motion between the front and rear legs is reduced when gripping only with the front legs, there is still a period where both tripods are in sand, causing tripod interference. Further optimization of the waypoints, gait height, location within the workspace, duty factor, and swing path as a whole can still be done. Alternatively, a more optimal end-effector path may be determined by studying the dactyl paths of live crabs in granular media and strategies to combat wave forces may be realized.

References

1. Blickhan, R., Full, R.J.: Locomotion energetics of the ghost crab: II. Mechanics of the centre of mass during walking and running. J. Exp. Biol. **130**(1), 155–174 (1987). https://doi.org/10.1242/jeb.130.1.155
2. Chen, X., Li, J., Hu, S., Han, S., Liu, K., Pan, B., Wang, J., Wang, G., Ma, X.: Study on the design and experimental research on a bionic crab robot with amphibious multi-modal movement. J. Mar. Sci. Eng. **10**(12), 1804 (2022). https://doi.org/10.3390/jmse10121804
3. Chen, Y., et al.: Optimal planar leg geometry in robots and crabs for idealized rocky terrain. Bioinspiration Biomimetics **17**(6), 066009 (2022)
4. Chen, Y., Grezmak, J.E., Graf, N.M., Daltorio, K.A.: Sideways crab-walking is faster and more efficient than forward walking for a hexapod robot. Bioinspiration Biomimetics **17**(4), 046001 (2022)
5. Gong, Y., Behr, A.M., Graf, N.M., Chen, K., Gong, Z., Daltorio, K.A.: A walking claw for tethered object retrieval. J. Mech. Robot. **15**(5), 051014 (2022). https://doi.org/10.1115/1.4055812
6. Graf, N.M., Behr, A.M., Daltorio, K.A.: Dactyls and inward gripping stance for amphibious crab-like robots on sand. Bioinspiration Biomimetics **16**(2), 026021 (2021)

7. Graf, N.M., Grezmak, J.E., Daltorio, K.A.: Get a grip: inward dactyl motions improve efficiency of sideways-walking gait for an amphibious crab-like robot. Bioinspiration Biomimetics **17**(6), 066008 (2022)
8. Herreid, C.F., Full, R.J.: Locomotion of hermit crabs (Coenobita Compressus) on beach and treadmill. J. Exp. Biol. **120**(1), 283–296 (1986). https://doi.org/10.1242/jeb.120.1.283
9. Martinez, M.M.: Running in the surf: hydrodynamics of the shore crab Grapsus tenuicrustatus. J. Exp. Biol. **204**(17), 3097–3112 (2001). https://doi.org/10.1242/jeb.204.17.3097
10. Schmiedeler, J.P., Bradley, N.J., Kennedy, B.: Maximizing walking step length for a near omni-directional hexapod robot. In: International Design Engineering Technical Conferences and Computers and Information in Engineering Conference, vol. Volume 2: 28th Biennial Mechanisms and Robotics Conference, Parts A and B, pp. 1371–1380 (2004). https://doi.org/10.1115/DETC2004-57531
11. Seethapathi, N., Srinivasan, M.: The metabolic cost of changing walking speeds is significant, implies lower optimal speeds for shorter distances, and increases daily energy estimates. Biol. Lett. **11**(9), 20150486 (2015)
12. Taylor, J.R.A.: Aquatic versus terrestrial crab skeletal support: morphology, mechanics, molting and scaling. J. Exp. Biol. **221**(21), jeb185421 (2018)
13. Yang, K., Li, Y., Zhou, L., Rong, X.: Energy efficient foot trajectory of trot motion for hydraulic quadruped robot. Energies **12**(13), 2514 (2019)
14. Zhang, J., Liu, Q., Zhou, J., Song, A.: Crab-inspired compliant leg design method for adaptive locomotion of a multi-legged robot. Bioinspiration Biomimetics **17**(2), 025001 (2022)
15. Zhu, Y., Abdulmajeid, L., Hauser, K.: A data-driven approach for fast simulation of robot locomotion on granular media. In: 2019 International Conference on Robotics and Automation (ICRA), pp. 7653–7659 (2019)

Neural Networks for Computation

Encoding 3D Leg Kinematics Using Spatially-Distributed, Population Coded Network Model

Bohdan Zadokha$^{(\boxtimes)}$ and Nicholas S. Szczecinski ⓘ

West Virginia University, Morgantown, WV 26506, USA
nss00001@mail.wvu.edu

Abstract. Controlling limbs in robotics is a nonlinear, complicated calculation that animals can do without significant effort. In this work we present a dynamical neural model with bioinspired sensory receptive fields which is capable of encoding the forward kinematics of a robotic leg. The model is implemented using the SNS-Toolbox. Synaptic conductance values are tuned using the Functional Subnetwork Approach. No optimization or machine learning is required. To understand how network construction affects encoding accuracy, we systematically varied the sensory neuron receptor functions, the number of sensory neurons, and neuron time constants. We use the root-mean-squared error to check the accuracy of the designed model. Finally, we show that our model with multiple outputs is more efficient than multiple networks with one output each.

Keywords: Dynamical Neural Network · Population Coding · Synthetic Nervous System · Functional Subnetwork Approach

1 Introduction

The control of limbs, whether for an animal or a robot, is a complicated task. For example, to accurately compute the position of the endpoint of the limb (e.g., hand, foot), sensory signals from across the limb must be integrated in a highly nonlinear way [1]. Furthermore, measurements taken along the limb may need to be transformed into the body's or head's frame of reference to be intelligible and useful for control, e.g., targeting placement of a hand or foot [2]. Despite the complexity of such calculations, animals solve problems of limb placement gracefully and without much apparent effort, suggesting that the nervous system has evolved mechanisms for computing (or approximating) such calculations. In this study, we create a dynamical neural model inspired by sensory receptive fields in insect limbs that may perform computations of this type.

In robotics, kinematics problems are solved by formulating vector and matrix equations [1]. For an open chain manipulator (e.g., a leg), the "forward kinematics" are computed by expressing the position and orientation of the end-effector in space as a function of the joint angles. Forward kinematics problems have a unique solution and can be expressed as a cumulative multiplication of transformation matrices [1]. Despite these

N. S. Szczecinski et al. (Eds.): Living Machines 2024, LNAI 14930, pp. 317–332, 2025.
https://doi.org/10.1007/978-3-031-72597-5_22

properties, their computation can be expensive and thus difficult to calculate as part of a real-time robot controller or biomechanical model. This challenge has motivated the utilization of artificial neural networks that reproduce forward kinematic solutions while effectively side-stepping the actual kinematics calculations. Researchers have trained and deployed such networks as part of robot manipulator controllers, enabling real-time control and, thus, the implementation of more sophisticated controllers [3]. Researchers have also used such networks to compute kinematic relationships within biomechanical models, e.g., the length of a muscle as a joint rotates, accelerating simulation and facilitating more rapid model improvement [4]. Such methods represent an advance in computation, but they require a lot of data and time for tuning, and performance cannot be guaranteed. Instead, we seek a model with structural and functional meaning that can be tuned rapidly and directly.

We also seek a model with biological relevance. In insects and other animals, sensory feedback is encoded by "range fractionated" sensory neurons [5–7], in which many neurons respond to the same mechanical state (e.g., joint angle) but with sensitivity to different "ranges". For example, some neurons are only active when the joint is extended; others are active only when the joint is flexed. This is believed to provide redundancy and, therefore resiliency in case of noisy sensory feedback or damaged sensory organs or neurons. We hypothesize that it also has computational advantages by enabling downstream networks to operate like a decoder rather than an analog circuit, which is prone to noise and miscalibration [8].

In this study, we apply tuning methods from our Functional Subnetwork Approach [9] to extend and analyze our previously developed spatially distributed population-coded network model [10]. The present study 1) demonstrates that this method can be applied to accurately encode 3-dimensional forward kinematics problems with no optimization or machine learning; 2) applies this method to compute multiple functions of the inputs using the same network, resulting in efficient computation of many nonlinear functions, simultaneously; and 3) quantifies network accuracy as the number of sensory neurons, their activation functions, and time constants throughout the network are altered. Furthermore, this study implements these models using the SNS-Toolbox [11].

2   Materials and Methods

2.1   Neural and Synaptic Models

The neural network was designed and simulated using the SNS-Toolbox library [11]. Each trial simulates 2 s of neural responses using Forward Euler integration with a timestep of 1 ms. All simulations were performed through JetBrains PyCharm 2022.3.3 (Professional Edition).

All neurons are modeled as leaky integrators whose dynamics follow the equation:

$$C\,{dU}/{dt} = -G(U - E_r) + I_{bias} + I_{syn} + I_{ext}, \tag{1}$$

where C is the membrane capacitance, G is the membrane conductance, U is the compartment's voltage, E_r is the resting potential of the compartment, I_{bias} is the constant bias current, I_{syn} is the synaptic current, and I_{ext} is an external current, for example, the mechanotransductive current in a sensory neuron. In our network, all neurons have $E_r = 0$ and $G = 1$. Setting $E_r = 0$ simply shifts all compartment voltages such that the equilibrium voltage is 0 mV, instead of a physiological resting potential (e.g., $E_r \approx -60$ mV), which complicates tuning and analysis. Setting $G = 1$ effectively normalizes all synaptic conductance values to the leak conductance of that compartment.

Connections between neurons are non-spiking conductance-based chemical synapses, where the conductance is:

$$G_{syn} = G_{max} \cdot \max\big(0, \min\big(1, U_{pre}/R\big)\big), \qquad (2)$$

where G_{max} is the maximum synaptic conductance, U_{pre} is the presynaptic neuron's voltage, and R is the operating range of each neuron's voltage.

Synaptic current has the following dynamics:

$$I_{syn} = G_{syn} \cdot \big(\Delta E_s - U_{post}\big), \qquad (3)$$

where ΔE_s is the reversal potential relative to the postsynaptic rest potential (set to 20 mV for all synapses), and U_{post} is the postsynaptic neuron's voltage.

The maximum synaptic conductance can be related to the functional "gain" of the synapse, that is, $k_{syn} = U_{post}/U_{pre} k_{syn} = U_{post}/U_{pre}$, by the approximation:

$$G_{max} = \frac{k_{syn}R}{\Delta E_s - k_{syn}R}. \qquad (4)$$

The derivation of this expression can be found in [9].

2.2 Network Architecture

For the neural network design, we incorporated and simplified several key features of insect thoracic sensorimotor networks. First, joint angles are encoded by range fractionated sensory neurons that form receptive fields (Fig. 1, yellow and orange circles 1–6) [5–7]. In our model, each sensory neuron has a Gaussian receptive field with a unique mean value (Fig. 2), which is not the most common receptive field in leg joint proprioceptor sensory neurons but can be found [5]. We chose Gaussian receptive fields, which are similar to visual sensory neurons [12, 13], because they facilitate network tuning (see discussion).

The interneuron compartments (Fig. 1, cyan circles 7–15) represent the dendrite of a single nonspiking interneuron (NSI). NSIs are large, branching neurons in insect thoracic sensorimotor networks that integrate sensory feedback from dozens or hundreds of sensory neurons and contribute to adaptive motor output [14–17]. We hypothesize that the way information is integrated may support the calculation of limb kinematics. To simplify the tuning and simulation of our model, compartments are not connected through resistive pathways (see discussion).

Finally, the output neurons (Fig. 1, red, green, and blue circles) represent motor neurons onto which the NSIs synapse. The synaptic connections to them (Fig. 1, red, green, and blue lines) ensure that the output neuron response reflects the quantity of interest in a graded way. Such a scheme could form part of a feedback pathway, in which the motor neurons are excited by sensory pathways and inhibited by other connections that specify the intended leg posture. This network architecture is inspired by motor control network in insects but may be extended to model many different neural structures.

All connections between neurons represent tuned conductance-based excitatory synapses. For a particular angle of θ_2, one of the yellow sensory neurons will be most active. In the same way, for a particular angle of θ_3, one of the orange sensory neurons will be most active. The interneuron compartment that is excited by both these neurons simultaneously will be the most active, so the synapse from that compartment to the output neuron will primarily determine the output neuron's activity level. We tuned each synapse conductance such that the output neuron activity encodes the actual position of the foot.

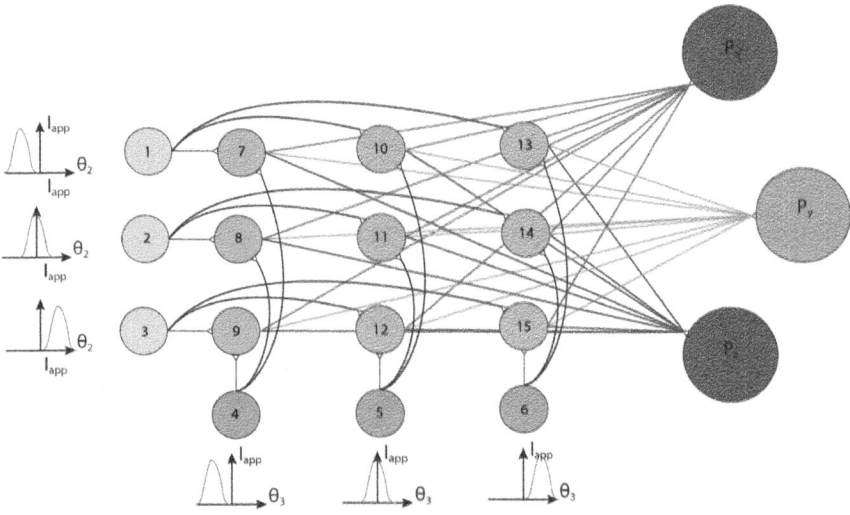

Fig. 1. Example of the designed neural network architecture with 3 sensory neurons per joint. Sensory neurons are represented in yellow and orange, interneuron compartments in cyan, and output neurons for the leg's x-, y-, and z-position are red, green, and blue, respectively. For the synapses between sensory neurons and interneuron compartments, we set Eq. (4)'s gain values for excitatory synapses equal to 1 (black lines). Synapses from interneuron compartments to output neurons were tuned using normalized x-position (red lines), y-position (green lines), and z-position (blue lines) of the foot from the forward kinematics calculation in Eq. (7). All figures are color-coded, please use an online version of the paper for a better experience.

To check the accuracy of the network prediction, we used the root-mean-squared error (RMSE) metric:

$$RMSE = \sqrt{\frac{\sum_{i=1}^{N}(x_i - \bar{x}_i)^2}{N}}, \tag{5}$$

where x_i is the actual time series, $\bar{x}_i$ is the predicted time series, and N is the number of data points.

2.3 Population Coding of an Input

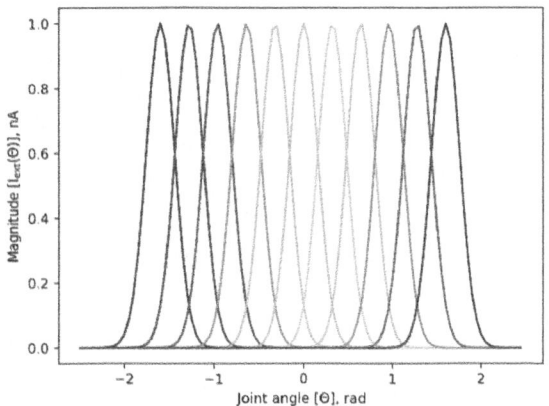

Fig. 2. An example of bell curve sensory encoding is used in the network. Each curve has magnitude A = 1 and width c = 20, but each curve's "mean" value b varies by 0.32 radians from the others. In this way, the activity profile of the neuron signals represents the rotation of the joint.

For every joint, we defined sensory neurons to get an encoded implementation of an input. As an activation function, we used the Gaussian bell curve equation:

$$I_{ext}(\theta) = A \cdot \exp\left(-c \cdot (\theta - b)^2\right), \tag{6}$$

where A is the magnitude, b controls the mean value, and c controls the width of the curve.

2.4 Synaptic Conductance Tuning

To calculate how joint angles map to the position of the end effector, we solved a forward kinematics problem in 3D space with joint angles ranging from -1.6 to 1.6 radians using the product of exponentials formula [1]:

$$T = e^{S_{n-1}\theta_{n-1}}\left(e^{S_n\theta_n}M\right), \tag{7}$$

where T is a 4x4 matrix that represents the position and orientation of the end effector, S is the screw axis matrix, θ is the joint rotation, and M is the position and orientation of the end effector in the "zero configuration", when all joint angles equal 0 (Fig. 3).

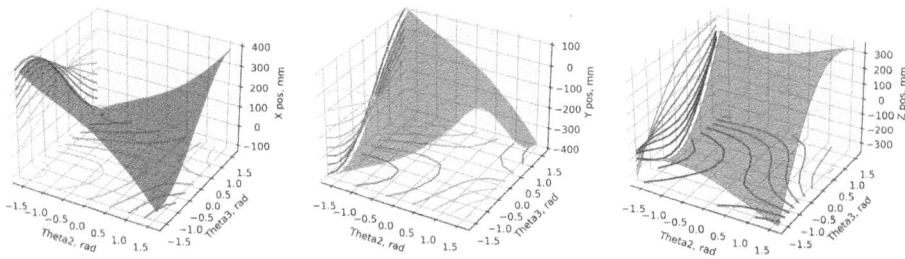

Fig. 3. X-, y-, and z- coordinate position surfaces for θ_2 and θ_3 joint angles

To find all exponential matrices, we used Rodrigues' rotation formula:

$$e^{S\theta} = I + \sin\theta\widehat{[S]} + (1 - \cos\theta)\widehat{[S]}^2, \tag{8}$$

where $\widehat{[S]}$ is a skew-symmetric representation of a screw axis matrix S.

Since every synaptic connection is excitatory, synaptic reversal potential values must be positive. Furthermore, synaptic conductance must always be positive. To comply with these conditions, we normalized all data from the forward kinematics to set gain values for the synapses between interneuron compartments and output neurons:

$$k_{synX} = \frac{P_X - min(P_X)}{max(P_X) - min(P_X)}, \tag{9}$$

where P_X is a calculated x-position. This was repeated for P_y and P_z. Note that no training dataset is required because the parameters are tuned based on the function of the network.

3   Results

To test our approach, we used a robotic leg from the Trossen Robotics PhantomX Hexapod MK-IV (Fig. 4). We used the front left leg, which is rotated 45 degrees about the Z-axis such that rotating either θ_2 or θ_3 changes the X, Y, and Z coordinate of the foot.

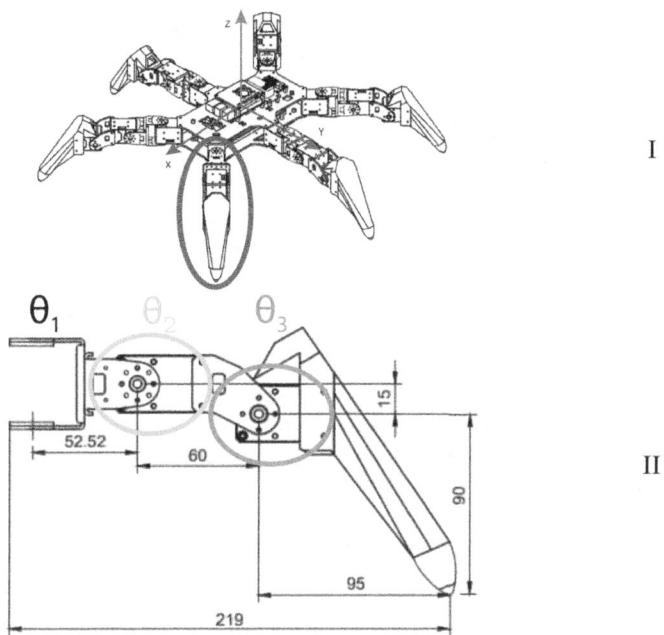

I

II

Fig. 4. The drawing of the PhantomX Hexapod MK-IV with the origin at the center of a robot's body (I) and a leg configuration (II). θ_1 servo was fixed, and only θ_2 and θ_3 were used as inputs to the network. Measurements of the leg were used for the forward kinematics calculation.

The sensory neurons accurately encode the joint angles using the Gaussian activation function (Eq. 6) into neuron voltages (Fig. 5). In this experiment, there are 11 sensory neurons that encode one joint, and each Gaussian "bell curve" function has a parameter value $c = 20$ and magnitude equal to 1. As θ_2 changes, which neuron is most active changes in a corresponding way.

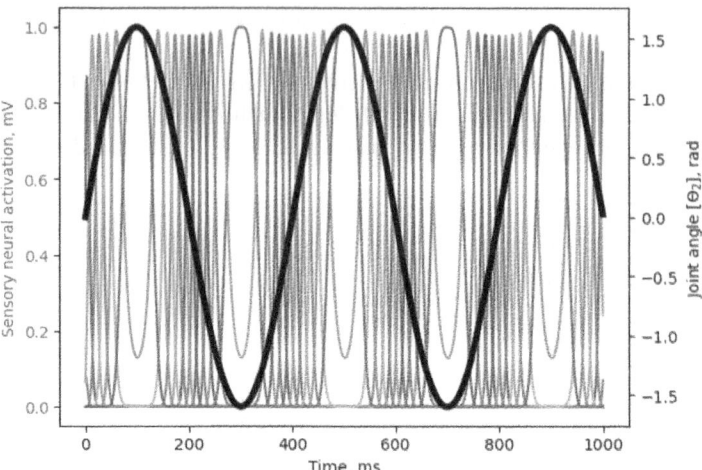

Fig. 5. Bell curve encoded responses (colored lines) of the θ_2 input (black line). Each color represents a sensory neuron response for the specific joint angle.

Each interneuron compartment represents one of the possible combinations of the joint angles for θ_2 and θ_3. It implies that interneuron compartments can be active only if both inputs from θ_2 and θ_3 are active at the same time or if activation of one of those occurs right after another (Fig. 6). The threshold for synaptic activation for each interneuron compartment is 1 mV, which is equal to the magnitude of the Gaussian activation function. Using this threshold, we minimize situations when two or more

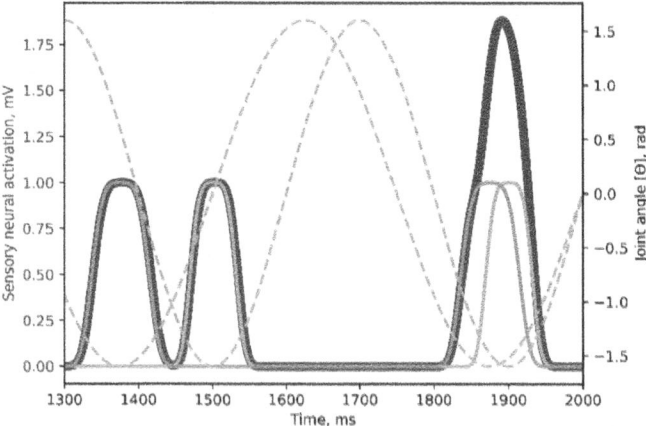

Fig. 6. The interneuron compartment (blue) activation with response to the $\theta_2 = \theta_3 = -1.6$ rad input values (solid yellow and orange lines respectively). Dashed yellow and orange lines represent inputs of θ_2 and θ_3 joint angles.

interneuron compartments are active simultaneously in response to the same sensory inputs.

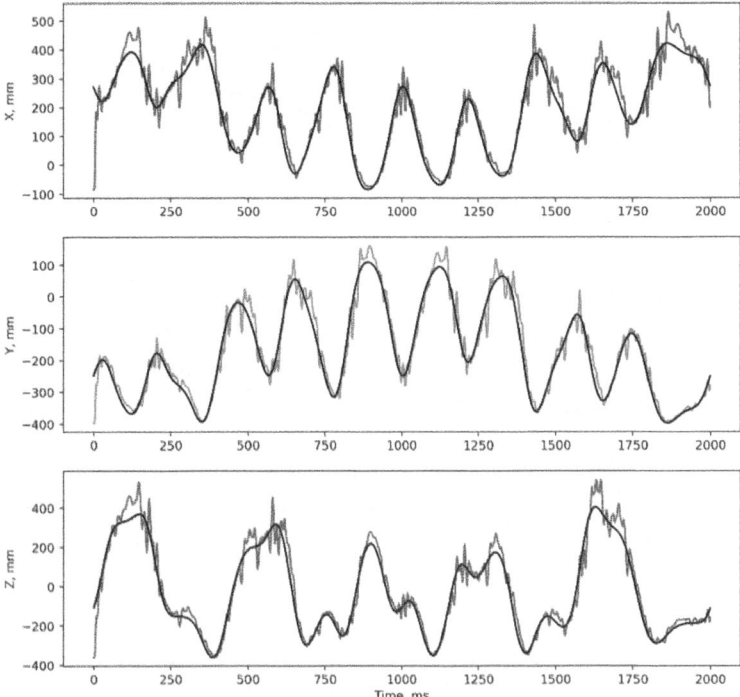

Fig. 7. The network's predicted x-position (red), y-position (green), and z-position (blue) compared to the forward kinematics actual result (black). RMSE for x-, y-, and z-position are 41.76, 31.74, and 51.98 respectively.

By using optimal parameters for the number of sensory neurons per joint and width of the activation function, the network activity tracks P_x, P_y, and P_z for the robot foot (Fig. 7). The neural activity exhibits some fluctuation over time but clearly follows the position of the foot on average. To understand the impact of different network parameters, we tested combinations of bell curve width (c) and the number of sensory neurons per joint (N). We found that for every activation function, there is a specific number of sensory neurons that produces the smallest error (Fig. 8), which we call an "optimal range." For narrower activation functions (higher value of the width parameter c) the RMSE is less sensitive to the number of sensory neurons per joint (N). The best parameters for all x-, y-, and z-positions are $N = 11$ sensory neurons per joint, with the bell curve width $c = 20$ (Fig. 8, black line). We refer to these as the "optimal parameters" throughout the rest of the results section. This model contains 146 neurons/neuron compartments in total (22 sensory neurons, 121 interneuron compartments, and 3 output neurons).

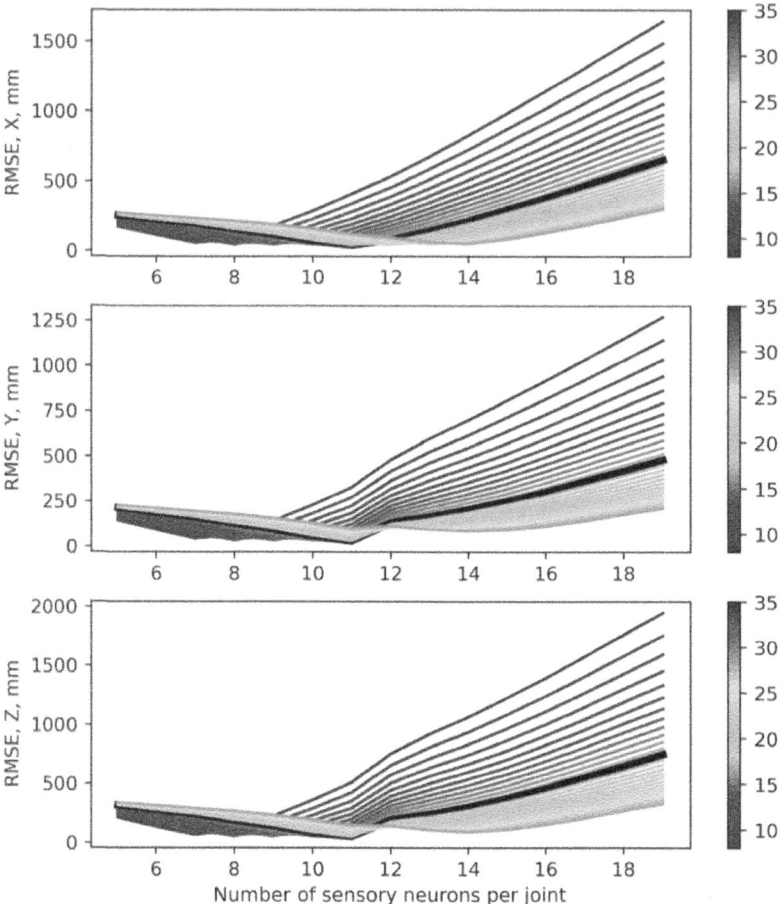

Fig. 8. RMSE of x-, y-, and z-positions for different combinations of bell curve's width (color lines) and number of sensory neurons. Bell curve width (*c*) varies from 8 to 34 (a smaller number of the bell curve width means a wider activation function), and the number of neurons – varies from 5 to 19. Optimal parameter values for the activation function's width are shown in black lines.

Another parameter that affects output is the neuron's membrane capacitance. We calculated RMSE by ranging values from 2 to 40 nF and found that increasing membrane capacitance increases the error, presumably due to increased lag in the response (Fig. 9). Past 40 nF, the RMSE hardly increases.

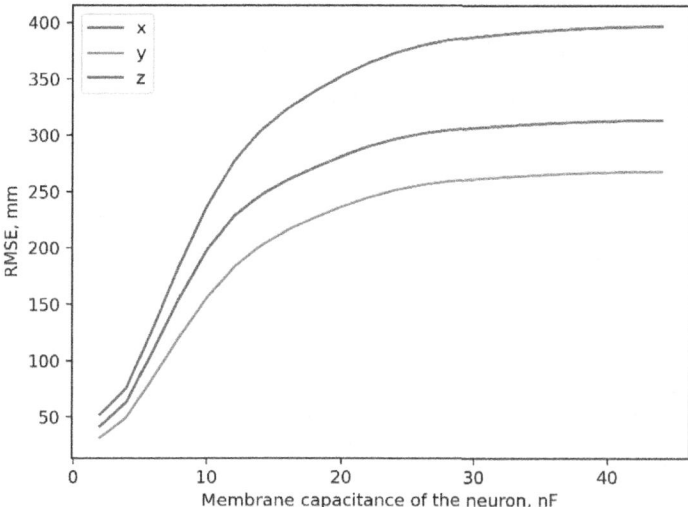

Fig. 9. The RMSE of x-, y-, and z-positions with different values for membrane capacitance of neurons.

To investigate the statistical nature of the network's accuracy, we calculated the difference between the predicted output and the actual calculation at each instant in time and plotted histograms with error distributions (Fig. 10). All three outputs have a bell-curve-like distribution with mean and median values for x-position: -9.4; -10.3, y-position: -7.1; -8.5, and z-position: -15.6; -17.3 respectively. The negative sign indicates peak overshoot (Fig. 7).

In addition, the linear regression slope between actual and predicted signals at each instant in time was found (Fig. 11). This parameter characterizes the correlation between signals: if the slope is equal to 1, it indicates a positive, 1:1 correlation between signals and, thus, accurate network output. Using optimal parameters, slopes for the regression are 1.02, 1.00, and 1.04 for x-, y-, and z-coordinates, respectively. This parameter can also be combined with the RMSE to find optimal network parameters.

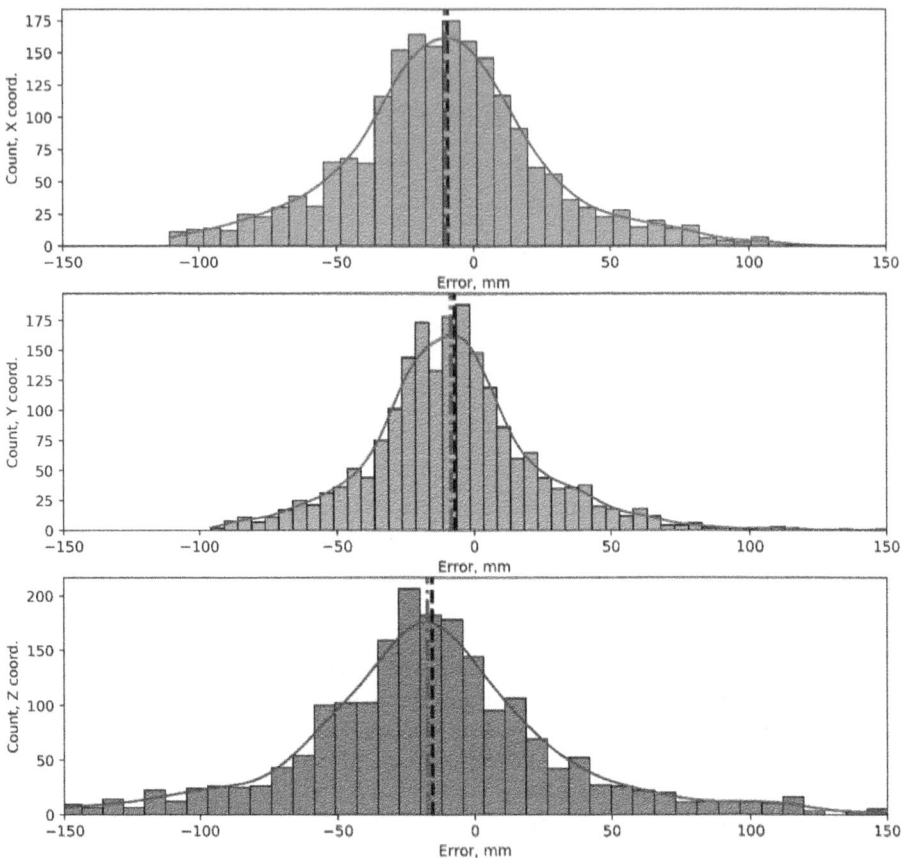

Fig. 10. Error distribution for x- (red), y- (green), and z-coordinate (blue) of the leg. Dashed black lines indicate mean values; dash-dotted magenta lines indicate median

To check the efficiency of the simultaneous multidimensional computation, we compared the running time of the designed network, which has 3 outputs for x-, y-, and z-positions with 3 separate networks that have the same architecture but only 1 output: for x-, y-, and z-positions respectively. Running simulations on the Apple M1 SoC, 3.2 GHz, 7 cores GPU, 16 GB unified memory, we found that the network with 3 output neurons performed calculations on average of 0.6 s for 10 trials, and the 3 networks with one output neuron required 2 s for 10 trials. This suggests that using the same nonspiking compartments to compute multiple quantities would be more efficient than building a separate network for each quantity.

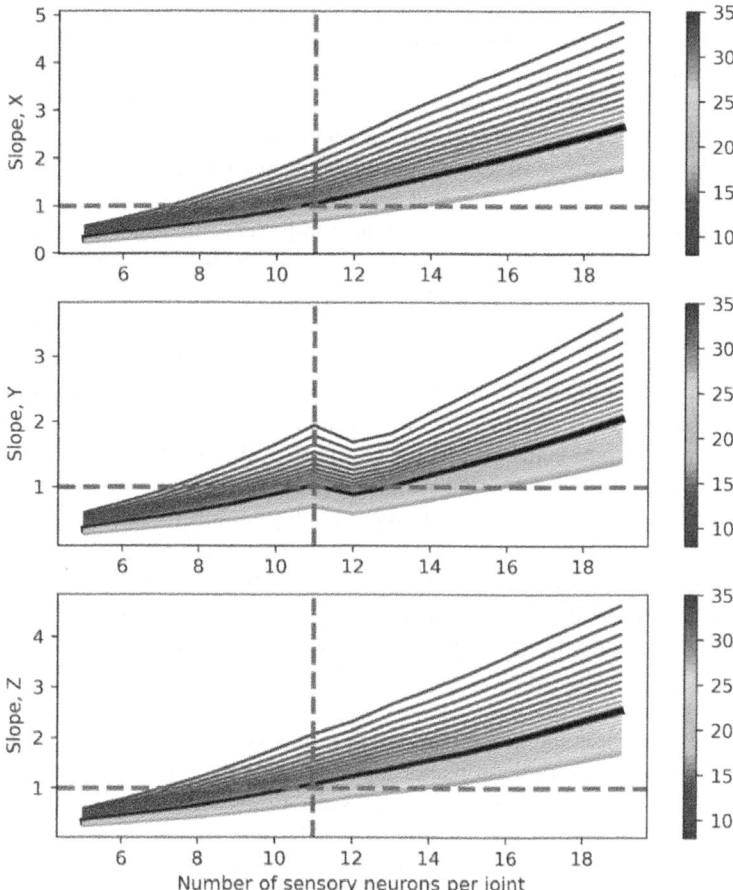

Fig. 11. Slopes of the linear regression between actual and predicted signals for different combinations of activation function's width (color lines) and number of sensory neurons. A dashed horizontal line shows the ideal positive correlation between signals, and a dashed vertical – the number of sensory neurons used in the paper. The black line shows an optimal width parameter.

4 Discussion

We designed a non-spiking neural network using SNS-Toolbox to calculate forward kinematics for the 2 DoF robotic leg in 3D space. Gaussian bell curve was used as an activation function to encode mechanical signals into sensory neuron activation. We used normalized position values from the product of exponentials to tune synaptic connections. No machine learning or optimization was required. By varying the number of sensory neurons and bell curve width, we found parameters that give the best result in forward kinematics computation. We found that the same network could be used to compute multiple functions of the inputs, in this case, separate representations of the x-, y-, and z-coordinate of the robotic leg's foot. We discovered that there is an "optimal range" for the different sets of parameters, but it is unclear why it changes. We suggest that one reason is the overlapping of activation functions. In the designed network, only two neighboring functions may be active at each instant in time. Investigating an optimal range, how it can be found, and its behavior will be useful for future work, such as implementing a designed network into a robot. Since minimum error values were achieved in all three output signals using the same parameters, we think that finding conditions for an optimal range for one activation function will speed up the tunning process for the whole network regardless of the number of inputs and outputs. As a statistical analysis, we calculated a correlation between the predicted and actual signal using linear regression. Alongside RMSE, the slope of the regression may be used in tunning parameters of the network. We compared the running time for the 3-dimensional neural network with that for 3 1-dimensional networks and found that simulation time largely does not depend on a number of outputs once the bulk of the network is constructed. We believe this method can be used in other high-dimensional nonlinear computations, e.g., altering descending commands to change the robot's walking direction [18]. It also does not require large datasets for training which reduces the running time for simulation.

Despite the success of our approach, there are limitations to this study. First, it may be possible to achieve higher accuracy if machine learning methods were used to fine-tune the network we constructed here. Recent work has shown that SNS models are generalized representations of several different artificial neural network models, and has successfully applied backpropagation to tune synaptic weights over time [19]. We anticipate that the synaptic weights we calculated here would greatly accelerate learning more precise values.

Another limitation is the computational complexity of this network. A model with n input states and m sensory neurons per input would require m^n interneuron compartments. This may result in unwieldy networks for limbs with many joints or in cases where many sensory neurons are required for each joint. In the future, we will investigate ways to decrease the number of sensory neurons required. One possibility is that by increasing the width of sensory encoding functions (i.e., decreasing c) or by using different encoding functions (e.g., sigmoids), the network may achieve "hyperacuity" as has been described in other sensory systems (e.g., visual system [12, 13]). Changing the encoding function in this way would require us to adapt the tuning method, but would likely have additional benefits, e.g., the incorporation of resiliency against broken sensors or noisy inputs.

Having demonstrated that our approach works for three different, highly-nonlinear functions, we believe this approach can be applied to other functions, for example, computing Jacobians for transforming sensory data from one reference frame to another. Another example is recent experimental work suggesting that an insect's central brain can transform "vectors" of sensory information to convert egocentric exteroceptive cues into allocentric navigational signals [20]. We may be able to model such a transformation using our approach.

Acknowledgments. This study was funded by NSF EFRI BRAID 2223793 to NSS.

Disclosure of Interests. The authors have no competing interests to declare that are relevant to the content of this article.

References

1. Lynch, K., Park, F.C.: Modern Robotics: Mechanics, Planning, and Control. Cambridge University Press, Cambridge, UK (2017)
2. Burnod, Y., Grandguillaume, P., Otto, I., Ferraina, S., Johnson, P., Caminiti, R.: Visuomotor transformations underlying arm movements toward visual targets: a neural network model of cerebral cortical operations. J. Neurosci. **12**, 1435–1453 (1992). https://doi.org/10.1523/JNE UROSCI.12-04-01435.1992
3. Zubizarreta, A., Larrea, M., Irigoyen, E., Cabanes, I., Portillo, E.: Real time direct kinematic problem computation of the 3PRS robot using neural networks. Neurocomputing **271**, 104–114 (2018). https://doi.org/10.1016/j.neucom.2017.02.098
4. Smirnov, Y., Smirnov, D., Popov, A., Yakovenko, S.: Solving musculoskeletal biomechanics with machine learning. PeerJ Comput. Sci. **7**, e663 (2021). https://doi.org/10.7717/peerj-cs.663
5. Matheson, T.: Range fractionation in the locust metathoracic femoral chordotonal organ. J. Comp. Physiol. A. (1992). https://doi.org/10.1007/BF00191466
6. Mamiya, A., et al.: Biomechanical origins of proprioceptor feature selectivity and topographic maps in the Drosophila leg. Neuron (2023). https://doi.org/10.1016/j.neuron.2023.07.009
7. Delcomyn, F., Nelson, M.E., Cocatre-Zilgien, J.H.: Sense organs of insect legs and the selection of sensors for agile walking robots. Int. J. Robot. Res. **15**, 113–127 (1996). https://doi.org/10.1177/027836499601500201
8. Pouget, A., Dayan, P., Zemel, R.: Information processing with population codes. Nat. Rev. Neurosci. **1**, 125–132 (2000). https://doi.org/10.1038/35039062
9. Szczecinski, N.S., Hunt, A.J., Quinn, R.D.: A functional subnetwork approach to designing synthetic nervous systems that control legged robot locomotion. Front. Neurorobot. (2017). https://doi.org/10.3389/fnbot.2017.00037
10. Guie, C.K., Szczecinski, N.S.: Direct assembly and tuning of dynamical neural networks for kinematics. In: Conference on Biomimetic and Biohybrid Systems, pp. 321–331 (2022). https://doi.org/10.1007/978-3-031-20470-8_32
11. Nourse, W.R.P., Jackson, C., Szczecinski, N.S., Quinn, R.D.: SNS-toolbox: an open source tool for designing synthetic nervous systems and interfacing them with cyber-physical systems. Biomimetics. **8**, 247 (2023). https://doi.org/10.3390/biomimetics8020247
12. Westheimer, G., McKee, S.P.: Integration regions for visual hyperacuity. Vision. Res. **17**, 89–93 (1977). https://doi.org/10.1016/0042-6989(77)90206-1
13. Westheimer, G., McKee, S.P.: Spatial configurations for visual hyperacuity. Vision. Res. **17**, 941–947 (1977). https://doi.org/10.1016/0042-6989(77)90069-4
14. Siegler, M.V.S., Burrows, M.: The morphology of local non-spiking interneurones in the metathoracic ganglion of the locust. J. Comp. Neurol. **183**, 121–147 (1979). https://doi.org/10.1002/cne.901830110
15. Burrows, M., Newland, P.L.: Correlation between the receptive fields of locust interneurons, their dendritic morphology, and the central projections of mechanosensory neurons. J. Comp. Neurol. **329**, 412–426 (1993). https://doi.org/10.1002/cne.903290311
16. Bueschges, A., Kittmann, R., Schmitz, J.: Identified nonspiking interneurons in leg reflexes and during walking in the stick insect. J. Comp. Physiol. A. **174**, 685–700 (1994). https://doi.org/10.1007/BF00192718

17. Gebehart, C., Büschges, A.: Temporal differences between load and movement signal integration in the sensorimotor network of an insect leg. J. Neurophysiol. **126**, 1875–1890 (2021). https://doi.org/10.1152/jn.00399.2021

18. Szczecinski, N.S., Quinn, R.D.: Template for the neural control of directed stepping generalized to all legs of MantisBot. Bioinspir. Biomim. **12**, 045001 (2017). https://doi.org/10.1088/1748-3190/aa6dd9

19. Li, Y., Sukhnandan, R., Gill, J.P., Chiel, H.J., Webster-Wood, V., Quinn, R.D.: A bioinspired synthetic nervous system controller for pick-and-place manipulation. In: 2023 IEEE International Conference on Robotics and Automation (ICRA), pp. 8047–8053. IEEE, London, United Kingdom (2023). https://doi.org/10.1109/ICRA48891.2023.10161198

20. Lyu, C., Abbott, L.F., Maimon, G.: Building an allocentric travelling direction signal via vector computation. Nature **601**, 92–97 (2022). https://doi.org/10.1038/s41586-021-04067-0

Analysis Pipeline for High-Dimensional Neuromechanical Model Improvement

Camila J. Fernandez[1]($\boxtimes$) (ID), Jeffrey M. McManus[4] (ID), Yanjun Li[5] (ID),
Michael J. Bennington[1] (ID), Roger D. Quinn[5] (ID), Hillel J. Chiel[4,6,7] (ID),
and Victoria A. Webster-Wood[1,2,3] (ID)

[1] Department of Mechanical, Carnegie Mellon University, Pittsburgh, PA 15232, USA
{cjfernan,vwebster}@andrew.cmu.edu
[2] Department of Biomedical Engineering, Carnegie Mellon University,
Pittsburgh, PA 15232, USA
[3] McGowan Institute for Regenerative Medicine, Carnegie Mellon University,
Pittsburgh, PA 15232, USA
[4] Department of Biology, Case Western Reserve University,
10900 Euclid Ave, Cleveland, OH 44106, USA
[5] Mechanical Engineering, Case Western Reserve University,
10900 Euclid Ave, Cleveland, OH 44106, USA
[6] Neurosciences, Case Western Reserve University,
10900 Euclid Ave, Cleveland, OH 44106, USA
[7] Biomedical Engineering, Case Western Reserve University,
10900 Euclid Ave, Cleveland, OH 44106, USA

Abstract. To capture and understand animal behavior, engineers and biologists seek to develop biologically accurate neuromechanical models of muscle dynamics and neural control. However, demand-driven enhancement of complex neuromechanics, such as the multifunctional *Aplysia californica* feeding apparatus, can be challenging due to the multidimensional biomechanical and neural models involved. We propose an analysis pipeline that enables reinforcement learning (RL) to classify which aspects of an engineered neuromechanical model can accurately capture animal behavior. As an example, prioritizing where demand-driven enhancement of a biomechanical and neural model is needed, the neural model of a published neuromechanical model of *Aplysia* swallowing during feeding was replaced with an RL controller and their performances were compared and correlated with *in vivo* swallowing behavior. By comparing the performance of the neural model and the learned model to *in vivo* animal behavior, we can pinpoint areas for improvement. The analysis pipeline identified that the neuromechanical model confidently captured force performance with no significant difference from

This work was supported by NSF DBI2015317 as part of the NSF/CIHR/ DFG/FRQ/UKRI-MRC Next Generation Networks for Neuroscience Program, by the NSF Research Fellowship Program under Grant No. DGE1745016, and by internal funding through Carnegie Mellon University. Any opinions, findings, and conclusions or recommendations expressed in this material are those of the authors and do not necessarily reflect the views of the National Science Foundation.

N. S. Szczecinski et al. (Eds.): Living Machines 2024, LNAI 14930, pp. 333–348, 2025.
https://doi.org/10.1007/978-3-031-72597-5_23

animal swallowing force behavior. It most usefully also indicated that the biomechanical model will need to be improved in future iterations to better capture motor neuron activity. Future work should explore the accuracy of the RL-enabled analysis pipeline with a more advanced biomechanical model.

Keywords: reinforcement learning · neuromechanical model · *Aplysia californica*

1   Introduction

Biologically-accurate neuromechanical models of complex animal behavior are valuable tools for engineers and biologists. Engineers and roboticists often use these models to learn how to design robots capable of precise control and robust adaptability witnessed in nature [1–4]. Biologists and neuroscientists can test biological hypotheses using these models to deepen their understanding of what has been observed experimentally and in literature [5–8]. One common model organism for developing these neuromechanical models is the marine mollusk *Aplysia californica*. This animal displays complex multifunctionality in its feeding behaviors despite its relatively small neuromusculature. With this tractable neuromusculature system, *Aplysia* can adjust its feeding behavior between biting, swallowing, and rejecting food (i.e., seaweed) efficiently [9–12]. For example, if *Aplysia* detects that an object it was ingesting is inedible, it can switch from swallowing behavior to rejection behavior. By developing models that represent muscle dynamics and neural control, roboticists and biologists alike can better understand how *Aplysia* is capable of this multifunctionality and how this could be applied to advancing current soft robots [13–15].

When developing models that can represent the multifunctional behavior of *Aplysia's* feeding apparatus, the question of how complex the model should be becomes very important due to the trade-off between low computational cost and high complexity. Therefore, model complexity should be dependent on the application of the model. For example, in robotics, one may want a fast model that is moderately biologically accurate, whereas in neuroscience, one may want a highly accurate model, even if it is computationally slower. Given this trade-off, a model should be as complex as needed for a goal, but no more so. This compromise is at the core of demand-driven complexity [13]. However, in complex neuromechanical models, it can be challenging to identify what aspects of the model need to be refined at any given stage of model development.

In this work, we present a method that leverages reinforcement learning (RL) in an analysis pipeline to identify what aspects of a neuromechanical model of *Aplysia* need to be improved towards better capturing *in vivo* animal behavior. Our approach both identifies which components in the tested model deviate from *in vivo* animal behavior and gives a potential order of priority for which components need improvement.

2   Methods

2.1   Analysis Pipeline

Systematically identifying what aspects of a model to focus on when using demand-driven complexity in neuromechanical modeling is challenging because there are currently few quantitative tools to assess the aspects of these highly complex models that deviate most from the target data. For the approach presented here, we focused on identifying if the biomechanical model, neural model, or both should have priority for future model improvements. Our analysis pipeline begins with the GymSlug Reinforcement Learning Gym [16]. GymSlug is based on a previously published neuromechanical model of *Aplysia* feeding [13] in which the neural circuitry is represented using Boolean operations, and the biomechanics are a simplified quasistatic spring model with 1st order muscle dynamics. The model parameters were hand-tuned simultaneously by experts in *Aplysia* feeding behavior to produce qualitatively similar multifunctional feeding behavior. In GymSlug, the neural model is replaced with an RL controller, which takes the state of the biomechanics as inputs and outputs motor neuron activities. We posit that if the biomechanical model were a perfect representation of the animal biomechanics, given enough training data, then the RL model would converge to a control strategy that highly correlated with the *in vivo* neural signals. We will call the expert hand-tuned neuromechanical model the "Expert" model and the RL policy model the "Trained" model.

To identify areas within the Expert model that may need demand-driven complexity-based improvements, we first ran the GymSlug training program on six randomly-seeded iterations with a training period of 500,000 epoch iterations to match the amount of experimental *in vivo Aplysia* data. This created six individual RL control policies, which were used to generate simulated data for a sequence of four to five swallows each following training.

Following model data generation, all the experimental and predicted animal swallowing data was segmented and normalized. We then calculated the cross-correlation coefficient distribution of fundamental motor and interneural swallowing behavior properties between the Animal data, Expert models, and Trained models. Inter-animal, Animal-to-Expert, and Animal-to-Trained model cross-correlation distributions were compared to determine if the predicted swallowing behavior is highly correlated with *in vivo* swallowing behavior. Using this approach, if the Expert model did not highly correlate with animal data and the learned neural activations of the Trained model resulted in a higher correlation with the animal data than the neural model, improvement for those components in the neural model should be a high priority. If the learned activations are not more highly correlated, then improvements to the biomechanical model should be a priority.

Animal Swallowing Dataset. To test the ability of our analysis pipeline to quantitatively identify discrepancies between animal behavior and neuromechanical models, a diverse dataset of animal behavior and model-predicted behavior is required. The animal data was collected in [9]. Briefly, adult *Aplysia* were placed in a temperature-controlled testing chamber at 14–16°C, and a piece of unbreakable seaweed, composed of two strips of Nori applied on either side of double-sided tape, was hung over this chamber attached to a load cell. Electrodes were implanted in the *Aplysia* to record activity in the I2 muscle, the radular nerve, buccal nerve 2, and buccal nerve 3. For each experiment, 4 to 5 swallow cycles were extracted from the raw data since that is the observed favorable time until the slug begins to behave differently [9]. The dataset from this work consists of six feeding sequences with four to five consecutive swallows from five individual *Aplysia* [9]. Unbreakable seaweed was used to allow swallowing pulling force measurement and recording activity in key motor neurons. This pipeline includes the activation frequency of the I2 muscle as well as the firing frequencies of B8a/b (manipulating the grasper closing I4 muscle), B38 (activating the pinching function in I3), and B6/B9/B3 (controlling the activation of the I3 muscle).

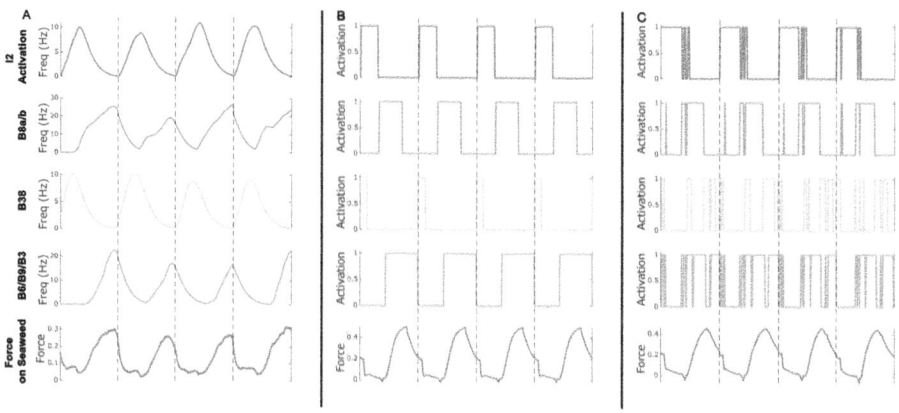

Fig. 1. Example swallowing performance datasets for (A) *Aplysia in vivo* experiments [9], (B) Expert model tuned behavior [13], and Trained model learned behavior [16]. The dashed lines separate consecutive swallowing cycles and were found using the segmentation and normalization methods. The separate swallows were individually used to make cross-correlation comparisons.

Segmentation and Normalization. Since we are interested in how different the models are to the animal data, in other words, how well the models correlate to animal data, we wanted to segment and normalize the animal data, Expert model data, and Trained model data to compare swallows with different phase durations to each other. For the segmentation, we split our time series data based on the onset of B31/32 neuron activation [9]. B31/32 innervates the I2 protractor muscle, rapidly decreasing the force on the seaweed after force peaks during the

retraction stage of the previous swallow [17]. The odontophore is pushed to the
jaw opening, releasing the tension on the seaweed. In the reinforcement learning
model, multiple B31/B32 activity episodes may occur within the same swallow.
Therefore, to distinguish these bursts from the initial onset, a second segmentation criterion was introduced so that the segmentation should only happen
if both an onset of B31/B32 activity and a steep negative slope in the force
data were observed. Following segmentation, each swallow was time-normalized
before subsequent comparisons. For normalization, time was divided by the total
time elapsed in the segment, scaling all swallowing cycles to a normalized time
of one, allowing for direct swallow comparisons. After applying the segmentation and normalization described (Fig. 1), the sample size for the animal swallow
dataset is N = 24, the expert predicted swallow dataset is N = 1, and the trained
predicted swallow dataset is N = 26. Note that the expert dataset is a single
swallow because the neural model activation does not vary with every swallow
cycle, making each swallow in a sequence of swallows exactly the same.

2.2   Statistical Analysis

Animal and Model Performance Correlation. To assess the similarity between two signals, in this case, animal swallowing behavior and model-
predicted swallowing behavior, we conducted a cross-correlation analysis. This
involved shifting the animal data (x) by various lag values (m) and computing
the dot product with the Expert or Trained model data (y). The resulting cross-
correlation coefficients (c) quantify the degree of correlation between the two
signals across different temporal displacements, described by the equation:

$$c = \max(\widehat{R}_{xy}(m - P)), \quad \text{where } m = 1, 2, ..., 2P - 1 \tag{1}$$

where $\widehat{R}_{xy}(m)$ is defined as

$$\widehat{R}_{xy}(m) = \begin{cases} \sum_{n=0}^{P-m-1} x_{(n+m)} y_n^* & m \geq 0 \\ \widehat{R}_{xy}^*(m) & m < 0 \end{cases} \tag{2}$$

where P is the amount of data point in both signals and the asterisk denotes
complex conjugation. We want the max $\widehat{R}_{xy}(m - P)$ because that is the moment
when the lag shift between the two signals results in the highest correlation [18].
This value then has to be normalized to be between $[-1,1]$ so it is normalized as

$$c_{coeff} = \frac{c}{\widehat{R}_{xx}(0)\widehat{R}_{yy}(0)} \tag{3}$$

where Rxx(0) and Ryy(0) refer to the cross-correlation of one signal compared
to itself with zero lag. Cross-correlation coefficients were calculated between
the swallows of a single animal and the swallows of all animals to see how much
Intra- and Inter-animal variation is typical. Additionally, we calculated the cross-
correlation coefficients for all animal swallows to all Expert and Trained model

swallows. Finally, we calculated the cross-correlation coefficients between Expert and Trained models to see how different their simulated swallows are. We will call these five different correlations "Intra-Animal" correlations, "Inter-Animal" correlations, "Animal-to-Expert" correlations, "Animal-to-Trained" correlations, and "Expert-to-Trained" correlations, respectively.

Bootstrapped Confidence Interval. Because our data sets include multiple swallows from each individual (both real and modeled) as well as dependency within our time series data between motor activity and grasping force, statistical comparisons of correlation coefficient distributions were performed using block bootstrapping and confidence intervals. Block bootstrapping is a bootstrapping method used for time series dependence [19] that creates blocks of data with strong dependence and assumes data outside the blocks hold insignificant dependencies. In the case of the swallowing data in this work, we consider a single swallow to be a block and assume that each swallow can be considered sufficiently independent of the next and previous swallow for the purposes of our pipeline. For all comparisons, we applied block bootstrapping and randomly resampled 10,000 times the median difference between the two groups being compared, thereby creating histograms of the bootstrapped differences between the medians of these distributions. Using a 95% confidence interval, the difference between each group is significant if a median difference of 0 does not fall within the confidence interval (i.e., we can reject the null hypothesis) and non-significant if 0 lies within the confidence interval (i.e., we fail to reject the null hypothesis).

We use this bootstrapped confidence interval in three different ways: (1) for animal-to-model correlations (Animal-to-Expert and Animal-to-Trained) relative to the Inter-animal group, (2) for model to RL model correlations (Expert-to-Trained) relative to Inter-animal, and (3) for animal-to-model correlation comparisons (Animal-to-Expert relative to Animal-to-Trained). We will describe these three cases in more detail. (1) If the difference between the animal-to-model and Inter-animal correlations are significant for any given property, we hypothesize that the model did not accurately capture animal swallowing behavior for demand-driven complexity. However, if there is no significant difference, the model can capture animal swallowing behavior, so no improvement is needed for the tested model property. (2) To determine if there is high variability between the Expert and Trained model performance, indicating discrepancies between the tuned neural model's and the RL controller's neural activity and/or swallowing force, we assess whether the difference between Expert-to-Trained and Inter-animal correlations is significant. And lastly, (3) when the confidence interval between Animal-to-Expert and Animal-to-Trained is found, if there is no significant difference, we hypothesize that the biomechanical model should be prioritized since the performance accuracy with different neural models did not change. If the confidence interval does show a significant difference, then there are two possibilities. The neural model should be prioritized if the Animal-to-Trained correlation is higher than the Animal-to-Expert since replacing the neural model with an RL controller increases performance accuracy. Inversely, the biomechanical model should be prioritized if the Animal-to-Expert correlation is higher than the Animal-to-Trained correlation since having the tuned neural model increases performance accuracy. Using these three results, we can confidently pinpoint exactly which components in the neuromechanical model need to be prioritized for demand-driven complexity improvement in future, more advanced iterations.

3   Results and Discussion

After conducting the analysis pipeline on the Expert model for the selected neural activations (i.e., I2 Muscle Activation, B8a/b, B38, and B6/B9/B3) and the resulting force on unbreakable seaweed, we found that force could confidently capture animal-like swallowing behavior, while neural activations could not (Fig. 2). The cross-correlation coefficient distributions were first found for comparisons of Intra- and Inter-animal swallows to serve as a benchmark for the typical variability seen *in vivo*. The cross-correlation coefficient distributions for Intra-animal and Inter-animal comparisons had medians of 0.97 (IQR 0.96–0.98) and of 0.96 (IQR 0.93–0.97), respectively (Fig. 2). As outlined in Sect. 2.1, comparisons were then performed with cross-correlation coefficient distributions of all animal swallows compared to all Expert model swallows (Animal-to-Expert), all animal swallows compared to all Trained model swallows (Animal-to-Trained), and all Expert model swallows compared to all trained model swallows (Expert-to-Trained). The corresponding median and interquartile range were 0.95 (IQR 0.94–0.96), 0.95 (IQR 0.93–0.97), and 0.95 (IQR 0.95–0.96), respectively (Fig. 2). After calculating the bootstrapped confidence intervals of force for both the Expert and Trained models, the null hypothesis failed to be rejected for a confidence level of 95%, ranging from $[-0.0011, 0.0187]$ (Fig. 3A) and $[-0.0014, 0.0121]$ (Fig. 3B), respectively. Given that the expert-tuned model used in this work to test our analysis pipeline was hand-tuned to mimic the force profile from *Aplysia* swallowing data, it is unsurprising that the force time series was not statistically significantly different from that of the animal data.

On the other hand, the analyzed neural activities of both Expert and Trained models failed to accurately capture animal swallowing behavior. The cross-correlation coefficient distribution median and interquartile ranges for all modeled motor neuron activity relative to animal swallows is detailed in Table 1. Compared to the previously discussed force correlations, the correlations found for motor neuron activity are much more variable, with cross-correlation coefficients below 0.9, indicating lower model accuracy. The bootstrapped confidence intervals comparing both the Animal-to-Expert and Animal-to-Trained distributions relative to the Inter-animal distribution rejected the null hypothesis for all neural activities (Fig. 4, Table 2). This indicates that the correlation coefficients varied significantly from the expected distributions across multiple individual animals, and therefore, neither model accurately captures animal-like swallowing

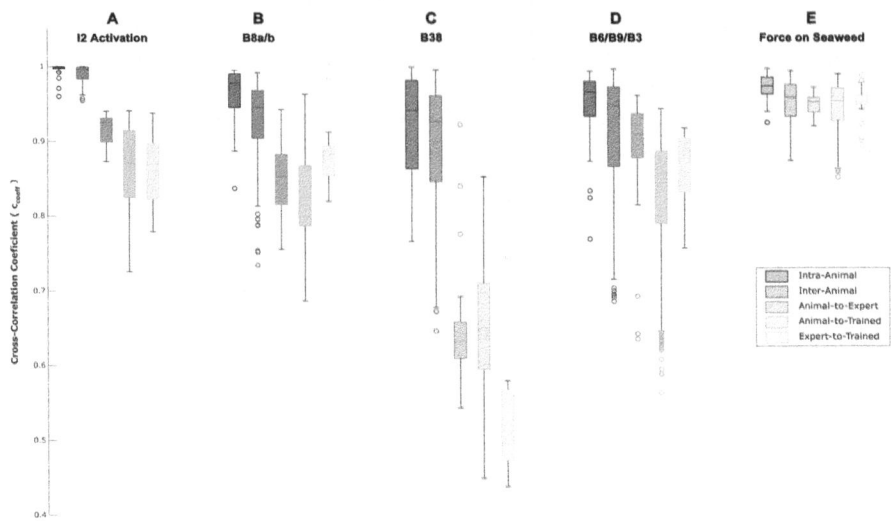

Fig. 2. Cross correlation distributions of animal and model comparisons. Boxes represent the 2nd and 3rd interquartile range with the center line at the median. Whiskers represent the 1st and 4th quartiles. Empty circles are outliers. Animal swallowing comparisons (both Intra-Animal and Inter-Animal) were performed for benchmarking, animal-to-model comparisons (Animal-to-Expert and Animal-to-Trained), and model-to-model comparisons (Expert-to-Trained) were performed as part of the analysis pipeline. Note that the sample size is not the same for the animal swallow dataset (N = 24), expert predicted swallow dataset (N = 1), and trained predicted swallow dataset (N = 26).

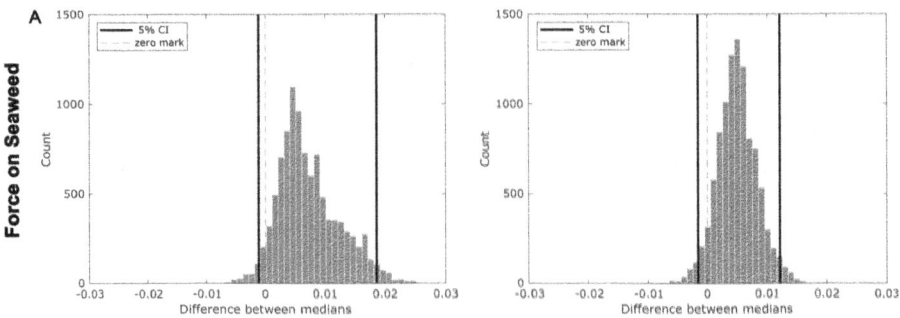

Fig. 3. Bootstrapping confidence intervals for force on seaweed for Animal-to-Expert (A) and Animal-to-Trained (B) relative to the Inter-animal group. Zero was found in both confidence intervals, represented by the red dashed line. Therefore, we fail to reject the null hypothesis. Thus, there is no significant difference between animal swallowing behavior and model-predicted animal behavior. (Color figure online)

Table 1. Median and interquartile range (IQR) of cross-correlation coefficient distributions for internal neural activation properties.

	I2 Activation	B8a/b	B38	B3/B6/B9
	Median	Median	Median	Median
	IQR	IQR	IQR	IQR
Intra-Animal	1.00	0.98	0.94	0.96
	1.00 - 1.00	0.94 - 0.99	0.86 - 0.98	0.93 - 0.98
Inter-Animal	0.99	0.94	0.92	0.95
	0.98 - 1.00	0.90 - 0.97	0.84 - 0.96	0.86 - 0.97
Animal-to-Expert	0.92	0.85	0.63	0.91
	0.90 - 0.93	0.81 - 0.88	0.61 - 0.66	0.88 - 0.93
Animal-to-Trained	0.87	0.82	0.65	0.86
	0.82 - 0.91	0.78 - 0.87	0.59 - 0.71	0.79 - 0.88
Expert-to-Trained	0.87	0.88	0.49	0.89
	0.82 - 0.90	0.85 - 0.89	0.47 - 0.57	0.83 - 0.90

activity for the neurons compared in this work. Alone, this information indicates that model improvements are needed, but we still need to determine specifically what aspects of the model should be targeted for demand-driven complexity improvements.

Table 2. Confidence interval (CI) for Expert and Trained model predictions for internal neural activation properties.

	I2 Activation	B8a/b	B38	B6/9/3
Expert CI	0.0664, 0.0841	0.0716, 0.1197	0.2705, 0.3102	0.0123, 0.0546
Trained CI	0.1207, 0.1295	0.1105, 0.1266	0.2573, 0.2929	0.0816, 0.1009

Comparing the Animal-to-Expert and Animal-to-Trained cross-correlation distribution to each other (Fig. 5), as well as comparing the Expert-to-Trained distribution to the Inter-animal distribution (Fig. 6), gives us insight into which portions of the model, either the neural model or biomechanical model, may need to be prioritized for improvement. For I2 muscle and motor neuron B6/B9/B3 activation, the confidence interval for the median difference between the Animal-to-Expert and Animal-to-Trained correlation distributions rejected the null hypothesis, the intervals being $[-0.0603, -0.0387]$ (Fig. 5A) and $[-0.0785, -0.0359]$ (Fig. 5D), respectively. Even though the Expert and Trained swallows are highly correlated to each other for these two properties (Table 1, Fig. 2A, 2D), there is a significant difference between how well they correlate with the animal swallowing dataset, with the Expert model having a higher correlation to animal swallowing than the Trained model (Fig. 5).

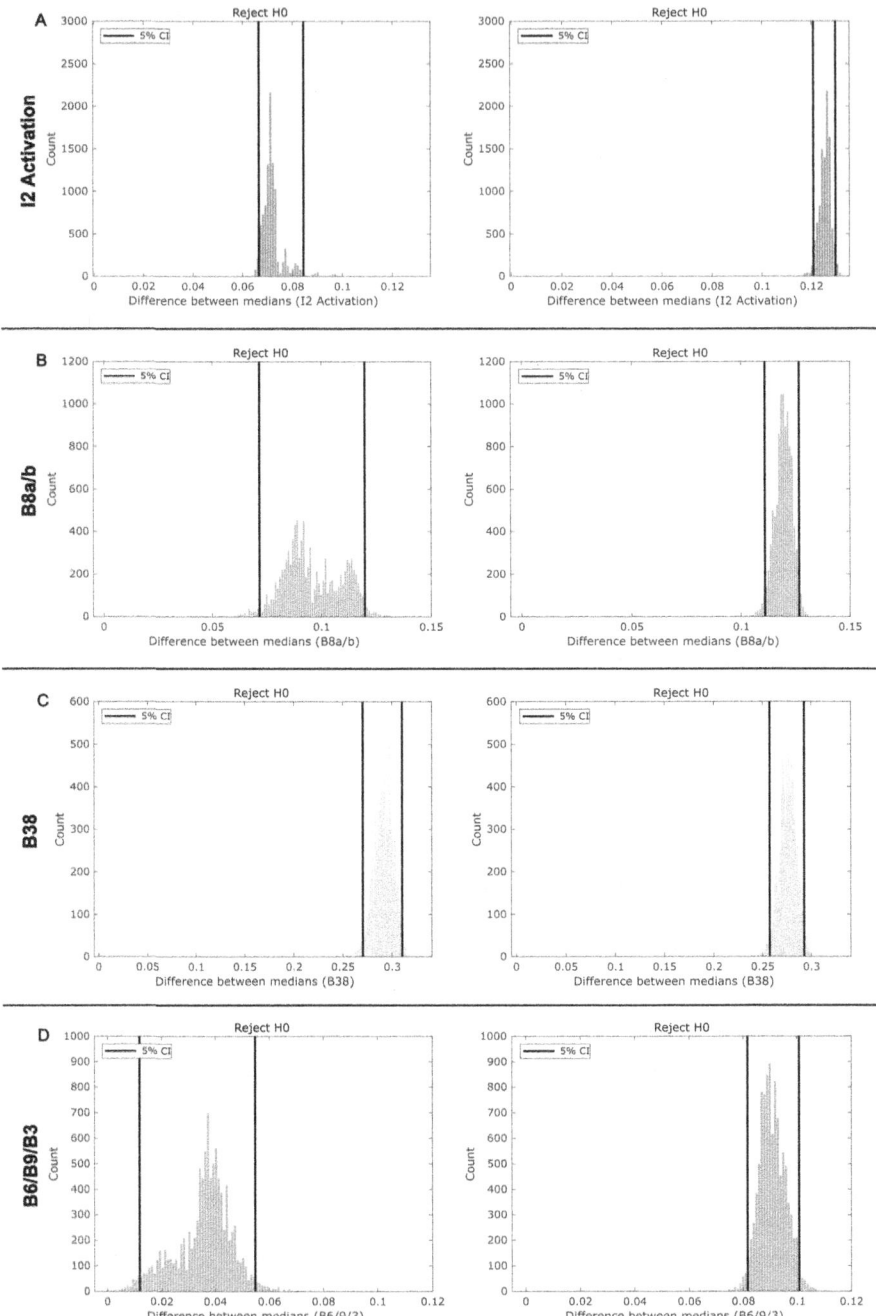

Fig. 4. Bootstrapping confidence intervals for motor neurons. A: I2 muscle activation, B: motor neuron B8a/b, C: motor neuron B38, and D: motor neurons B6/B9/B3 for Animal-to-Expert (left) and Animal-to-Trained (right) relative to the Inter-animal group. (A–D) We reject the null hypothesis for all activation properties since zero was not found inside any of the confidence intervals.

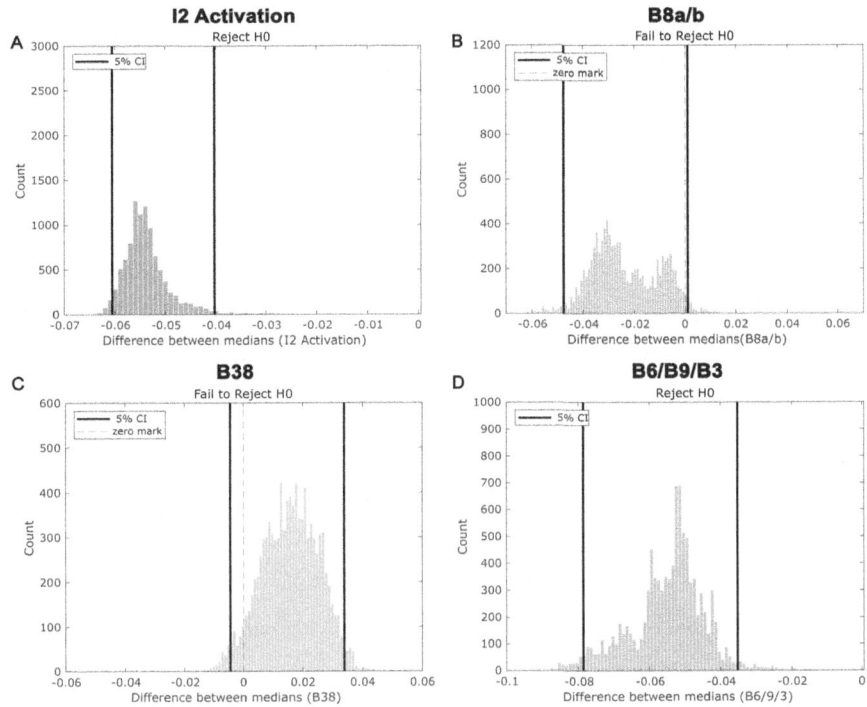

Fig. 5. Bootstrapping confidence intervals for motor neurons to determine which of the two components of the neuromechanical model, the neural or biomechanical model, needs to be prioritized for improvement. A: I2 muscle activation, B: motor neuron B8a/b, C: motor neuron B38, and D: motor neuron B6/B9/B3 for Animal-to-Expert relative to Animal-to-Trained. (A, D) We reject the null hypothesis since zero was not found inside the confidence interval. (B, C) Zero was found inside the confidence intervals, represented by the red dashed line. Therefore, we fail to reject the null hypothesis.

For motor neuron B8a/b, the confidence interval for the median difference between the Animal-to-Expert and Animal-to-Trained correlation distributions failed to reject the null hypothesis, with the confidence interval being $[-0.0482, 0.0012]$ (Fig. 5B). Therefore, there was no significant difference between how well the two models captured *in vivo* B8 activity in swallowing behavior. Based on this analysis, the RL policy did not learn I2, B3/B6/B9, or B8a/b activity that better correlated with animal data than the expert-tuned neuromechanical model. Therefore, future modeling efforts should focus on improving the biomechanical model associated with each of these motor neurons.

Whereas the trends for I2, B3/B6/B9, and B8a/b activity correlations were similar, all correlations of B38 stand out as being substantially lower than those of the other motor neurons. The confidence intervals comparison of the Animal-to-Expert and Animal-to-Trained cross-correlation distributions to that

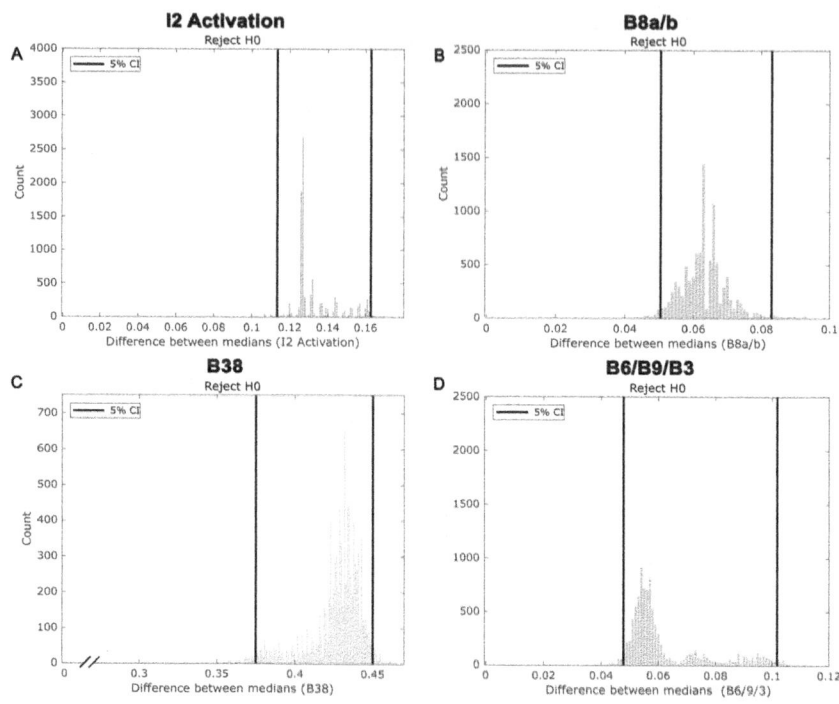

Fig. 6. Bootstrapping confidence intervals for motor neurons' performance correlation. A: I2 muscle activation, B: motor neuron B8a/b, C: motor neuron B38, and D: motor neurons B6/B9/B3 for Expert-to-Trained relative to the Inter-animal group. (A–D) We reject the null hypothesis for all activation properties since zero was not found inside any of the confidence intervals.

Fig. 7. Variability between individual trials of Trained model predicted swallow behavior for B38. The dashed lines separate consecutive swallowing cycles were found using the segmentation and normalization methods. A, B, and C are B38 boolean activation performances during three randomly selected trials, each swallow looking drastically different from consecutive swallows from the same trial and individual swallows from the other trials.

of Inter-animal variability of B38 were significant with [0.2705, 0.3102] and [0.2573, 0.2929], respectively (Fig. 4C). Furthermore, much wider variability was observed in the correlations for the trained B38 activity relative to the Inter-animal group (Table 1). Finally, comparing the Animal-to-Expert and Animal-to-Trained cross-correlation distribution to each other resulted in a confidence interval of [−0.0035, 0.0339] (Fig. 5C), indicating that not only did the models not correlate well with the animal data, they also did not correlate well with the animal data by a similar amount, with no significant difference in their performance accuracy, pointing to priority in improving the biomechanical model. *In vivo*, B38 activity in swallowing begins before I2 activation and then substantially overlaps I2 activation (Fig. 1A) [20]. In the Expert model, B38 activity is much shorter and occurs at the onset of I2 activation (Fig. 1B), whereas in the Trained model, B38 activity is highly variable, and much of the activity often occurs during the retraction phase activation of B6/B9/B3 and B8a/b (Figs. 7, 1C). Thus, the Expert and Trained models both exhibit B38 activity that is very different from the real animal behavior, and the two models are even more different from each other, with an Expert-to-Trained correlation median of 0.49 (IQR 0.47–0.57) and a confidence interval comparing Expert-to-Trained and Inter-animal variability showing a significant difference with [0.3749, 0.4501] (Table 1, Figs. 2C, 6C). Based on these outcomes, future model efforts should revisit both the biomechanics of pinch in the anterior region of I3 and the neural model implementation of B38. In the current biomechanical model, B6/B9/B3 also contribute to the jaw pinch [13,16], whereas the jaw pinch is likely more specifically mediated by B38 in the biomechanics of the real animal. This may make the B38 activation less important in the model implementations and, therefore, more prone to unrealistic variability. Additionally, jaw pinch during the retraction phase could hinder successful behavior by resisting inward seaweed movement; the presence of a large amount of B38 activation in the retraction phase of many Trained model responses suggests the model may not fully capture this.

4   Conclusions

This work presents a pilot study on a reinforcement-learning enabled analysis pipeline that classifies if an engineered neuromechanical model can confidently capture animal behavior, our test case being an existing model of *Aplysia californica* feeding. Using our analysis pipeline, we assessed this model to identify areas for future model refinement. We replaced the neural model with a reinforcement learning neural network and compared the correlation distributions of key motor neurons to those in animal swallowing data. By comparing the model's performance under its own neural control to that under RL-control, we showed that despite the model being able to capture swallowing force, the biomechanical model may not fully capture the complexities of *in vivo* neuromechanics. Furthermore, in comparing the correlations of the neural controller to the RL controller relative to Animal-to-Animal variability, we see that they are markedly different and yet can both generate similar force outputs. This finding may indicate that the biomechanical model does not fully capture the mechanics of the *Aplysia* feeding apparatus, especially concerning motor neuron B38. Another limitation of the model being analyzed in this work is that the Boolean neural model is constrained to be either on or off, whereas real neurons can show much more graded spiking frequencies. The rapid alternation of on/off states in the Boolean model may greatly reduce the correlations, whereas using a more continuous model (e.g., an integrate-and-fire model [21], a synthetic nervous system model [22], or a multi-conductance Hodgkin-Huxley-like model [21]) might show less variation and thus yield better correlations. Finally, the analysis pipeline is limited by the small amount of experimental animal data available. A larger sample size would capture a wider range of possible animal behaviors and yield more precise results.

Future work should compare the results of this analysis pipeline when a more advanced biomechanical model is implemented to determine if this RL-enabled analysis approach has accurately identified areas for improvement. More experimental animal data can also be collected to have a larger sample of *Aplysia* swallowing behavior. Additionally, future tools should supplement this pipeline with an additional RL-enabled analysis wherein the neural model serves as the environment, and the biomechanical model is replaced with an RL policy, thereby further classifying areas for future demand-driven complexity model enhancement.

Acknowledgements. The authors thank Dr. Jeff Gill for sharing the animal data from his 2020 publication [9] for use in these comparisons. We thank the anonymous reviewers for their insightful edits and suggestions.

References

1. Karakasiliotis, K., et al.: From cineradiography to biorobots: an approach for designing robots to emulate and study animal locomotion. J. R. Soc. Interface **13**(119), 20151089 (2016). https://doi.org/10.1098/rsif.2015.1089
2. Ijspeert, A.J.: Biorobotics: using robots to emulate and investigate agile locomotion. Science **346**(6206), 196–203 (2014). https://doi.org/10.1126/science.1254486
3. Ostrowski, J., Burdick, J.W.: The geometric mechanics of undulatory robotic locomotion. Int. J. Robot. Res. **17**(7), 683–701 (1998). https://doi.org/10.1177/027836499801700701
4. Aguilar, J., et al.: A review on locomotion robophysics: the study of movement at the intersection of robotics, soft matter and dynamical systems. Rep. Prog. Phys. **79**(11), 110001 (2016). https://doi.org/10.1088/0034-4885/79/11/110001
5. Sun, X., et al.: A neuromechanical model for Drosophila larval crawling based on physical measurements. BMC Biol. **20**(1), 130 (2022). https://doi.org/10.1186/s12915-022-01336-w
6. Markin, S.N., Klishko, A.N., Shevtsova, N.A., Lemay, M.A., Prilutsky, B.I., Rybak, I.A.: Afferent control of locomotor CPG: insights from a simple neuromechanical model. Ann. N. Y. Acad. Sci. **1198**(1), 21–34 (2010). https://doi.org/10.1111/j.1749-6632.2010.05435.x

7. Sreenivasa, M., Valero-Cuevas, F.J., Tresch, M., Nakamura, Y., Schouten, A.C., Sartori, M.: Editorial: neuromechanics and control of physical behavior: from experimental and computational formulations to bio-inspired technologies. Front. Comput. Neurosci. **13**, (2019). https://doi.org/10.3389/fncom.2019.00013

8. Higuchi, K., Kazawa, T., Sakai, B., Namiki, S., Haupt, S.S., Kanzaki, R.: High performance, large-scale multi-compartment Hodgkin-Huxley simulation of Drosophila's whole-brain neural circuit model. bioRxiv (Cold Spring Harbor Laboratory) (2022). https://doi.org/10.1101/2022.11.01.512969

9. Gill, J.P., Chiel, H.J.: Rapid adaptation to changing mechanical load by ordered recruitment of identified motor neurons. eneuro, pp. ENEURO.0016-20.2020 (2020). https://doi.org/10.1523/eneuro.0016-20.2020

10. Lyttle, D., Gill, J., Shaw, K.M., Thomas, P., Chiel, H.J.: Robustness, flexibility, and sensitivity in a multifunctional motor control model, vol. 111, no. 1, pp. 25–47 (2016). https://doi.org/10.1007/s00422-016-0704-8

11. Shaw, K.M., et al.: The significance of dynamical architecture for adaptive responses to mechanical loads during rhythmic behavior. J. Comput. Neurosci. **38**(1), 25–51 (2014). https://doi.org/10.1007/s10827-014-0519-3

12. Novakovic, V.A., Sutton, G.P., Neustadter, D.M., Beer, R.D., Chiel, H.J.: Mechanical reconfiguration mediates swallowing and rejection in *Aplysia californica*. J. Comp. Physiol. A Neuroethol. Sens. Neural Behav. Physiol. **192**(8), 857–870 (2006). https://doi.org/10.1007/s00359-006-0124-7

13. Webster-Wood, V.A., Gill, J.P., Thomas, P.J., Chiel, H.J.: Control for multifunctionality: bioinspired control based on feeding in *Aplysia californica*. Biol. Cybern. **114**(6), 557–588 (2020). https://doi.org/10.1007/s00422-020-00851-9

14. Li, Y., Sukhnandan, R., Gill, J.P., Chiel, H.J., Webster-Wood, V., Quinn, R.D.: A bioinspired synthetic nervous system controller for pick-and-place manipulation. IEEE Int. Conf. Robot. Autom. (ICRA) **2023**, 8047–8053 (2023). https://doi.org/10.1109/icra48891.2023.10161198

15. Dai, K., et al.: SLUGBOT, an *Aplysia*-inspired robotic grasper for studying control. In: Lecture Notes in Computer Science, pp. 182–194 (2022). https://doi.org/10.1007/978-3-031-20470-8_19

16. Sun, W., Xu, M., Gill, J., Thomas, P., Chiel, H.J., Webster-Wood, V.A.: GymSlug: Deep Reinforcement Learning Toward Bio-inspired Control Based on *Aplysia californica* Feeding, pp. 236–248 (2022). https://doi.org/10.1007/978-3-031-20470-8_24

17. Hurwitz, I., Kupfermann, I., Susswein, A.J.: Different roles of neurons B63 and B34 that are active during the protraction phase of buccal motor programs in *Aplysia californica*. J. Neurophysiol. **78**(3), 1305–1319 (1997). https://doi.org/10.1152/jn.1997.78.3.1305

18. "Cross-correlation - MATLAB xcorr. www.mathworks.com. https://www.mathworks.com/help/matlab/ref/xcorr.html

19. Kreiss, J.P., Paparoditis, E.: Bootstrap methods for dependent data: a review. J. Korean Stat. Soc. **40**(4), 357–378 (2011). https://doi.org/10.1016/j.jkss.2011.08.009

20. McManus, J.M., Lu, H., Cullins, M.J., Chiel, H.J.: Differential activation of an identified motor neuron and neuromodulation provide *Aplysia's* retractor muscle an additional function. J. Neurophysiol. **112**(4), 778–791 (2014). https://doi.org/10.1152/jn.00148.2014

21. Yamazaki, K., Vo-Ho, V.-K., Bulsara, D., Le, N.: Spiking neural networks and their applications: a review. Brain Sci. **12**(7), 863 (2022). https://doi.org/10.3390/brainsci12070863
22. Li, Y., Webster-Wood, V.A., Gill, J.P., Sutton, G.P., Chiel, H.J., Quinn, R.D.: A synthetic nervous system controls a biomechanical model of *Aplysia* feeding. In: Lecture Notes in Computer Science, pp. 354–365 (2022). https://doi.org/10.1007/978-3-031-20470-8_35

Bio-Inspired Neural Networks
for Control

Modulation and Time-History-Dependent Adaptation Improves the Pick-and-Place Control of a Bioinspired Soft Grasper

Yanjun Li[1]([✉]) [ID], Ravesh Sukhnandan[5] [ID], Hillel J. Chiel[2,3,4] [ID],
Victoria A. Webster-Wood[5,6,7] [ID], and Roger D. Quinn[1] [ID]

[1] Department of Mechanical Engineering, Case Western Reserve University,
Cleveland, OH, USA
yxl2259@case.edu
[2] Department of Biology, Case Western Reserve University, Cleveland, OH, USA
[3] Department of Neurosciences, Case Western Reserve University,
Cleveland, OH, USA
[4] Department of Biomedical Engineering, Case Western Reserve University,
Cleveland, OH, USA
[5] Department of Mechanical Engineering, Carnegie Mellon University, Pittsburgh,
PA, USA
[6] Department of Biomedical Engineering, Carnegie Mellon University, Pittsburgh,
PA, USA
[7] McGowan Institute for Regenerative Medicine, Carnegie Mellon University,
Pittsburgh, PA, USA

Abstract. It is widely believed that adaptive peripheral neural control circuits and compliant peripheral biomechanics in biological systems are critical for their control of interactions with the environment. Inspired by the sea slug *Aplysia californica*'s adaptive feeding mechanism, we previously designed a pneumatically actuated soft grasper controlled by Synthetic Nervous Systems for pick and place manipulation. To guarantee the grasping success rate, the controller sends a fixed grasper radius command during grasper closure. However, such a strategy may generate overly high contact force for manipulating soft and fragile objects. To address this problem, we adopted velocity control circuitry to cap the contact force within a force threshold. Furthermore, inspired by the local modulation of *Aplysia* networks and muscles, we incorporated time-history-dependent control into the grasper controller. Such modulatory mechanisms allow the force threshold to adapt according to the external load. We evaluated the adaptive controller's performance in simulation and physical hardware. By comparing it with two baselines, we show the grasper can achieve high success rates for pick-and-place tasks and prevent high contact force when manipulating light objects in a simulation environment. Hardware experiments were also performed to demonstrate that the control network could be transferred to the real-world platform. These results sup-

This work was supported in part by the National Science Foundation (NSF) grant nos. FRR-2138873 and FRR-2138923 and by a GEM fellowship.
Y. Li and R. Sukhnandan—These authors contributed equally to the work.

N. S. Szczecinski et al. (Eds.): Living Machines 2024, LNAI 14930, pp. 351–367, 2025.
https://doi.org/10.1007/978-3-031-72597-5_24

port our hypothesis that soft, morphologically intelligent grasping robots with onboard bioinspired adaptation will improve grasping performance.

Keywords: Soft Robotics · Robotic Manipulation · Synthetic Nervous Systems · *Aplysia* · Neuromodulation.

1   Introduction

Controlling robots to manipulate complex and fragile objects remains an ongoing challenge in robotics. Humans and animals can complete a wide range of manipulation tasks with their soft peripheries. Due to the lack of such compliance, few robots with rigid end effectors and joints can achieve human-level safety and dexterity in manipulation [14, 16, 34]. Many contact-rich tasks, such as harvesting soft, fragile, and irregularly shaped fruits, still rely on humans [15]. Guided by the structure of biological systems, materials with soft properties have appeared with increasing frequency in the design of robots [1, 8, 26]. The compliance allows robots to conform to the objects they interact with, leading to stable contact and evenly distributed contact forces [3]. For example, soft graspers inspired by octopus tentacles and elephants have been developed [2, 9]. However, these continuum robots are characterized by many degrees of freedom, making the state estimation and control computationally complex [4, 31].

Inspired by the adaptive control of soft, many-degree-of-freedom peripheries in the sea slug *Aplysia californica* [17, 32], we previously developed a soft grasper for pick-and-place tasks [27]. The grasper abstractly embodies the morphology and neural control of *Aplysia*'s feeding apparatus. With two layers of cylindrical McKibben actuators, it can conform to and envelop a grasped object. In addition, it can actively tune the contact stiffness by regulating air pressure in the internal cavity of soft jaws. We designed a neural network controller for the grasper and expressed the neural dynamics in the framework of Synthetic Nervous Systems (SNSs), a neural network model previously adopted in modeling the *Aplysia* feeding control circuits [21]. In this prior work, based on position and force sensory feedback, the controller can determine which subtask to complete and generate motor commands to move, open, or close the soft grasper. Force feedback is used to determine whether the object has been grasped or released but not actually leveraged to control the grasping behavior in real time. For robust grasping, the network sends a fixed, pre-determined grasper radius command. This strategy, however, often leads to overly high contact force for picking up lightweight and soft objects. Moreover, it cannot adaptively increase the force applied to pick up heavier objects. In contrast, animals like *Aplysia* can adaptively modify the properties of muscles and joints in response to environmental loading and feedback through neuromodulation [22]. Capturing key features of neuromodulation, such as slow but long-lasting activation enhancement due to repetitive firing of presynaptic neurons, may help to ensure a safer interaction between the grasper and the environment.

In this work, we integrated modulation mechanisms into the SNS controller to implement time-history-dependent contact force adaptation. We modified the

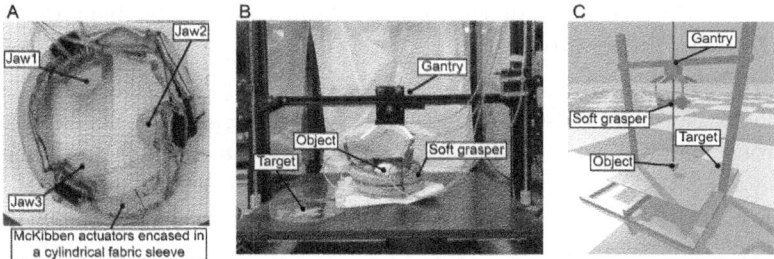

Fig. 1. The hardware and simulation platform for testing the bioinspired soft grasper. (A) Top view of the grasper. (B) The gantry system for pick-and-place manipulation. (C) The simulation model of the system (built in the Pybullet engine).

synaptic connection so that the soft grasper generated a fixed closing speed for grasping and stopped squeezing once the contact force reached a force threshold. This modification allows the grasper to maintain contact force around the force threshold. In addition, we incorporated modulatory synapses to mediate the output of sensory neurons. The modulatory mechanism allows the grasper to temporarily increase the force threshold for the next attempt if the current grasping attempt fails. Our simulation and experimental results suggest that the controller presented here can adaptively regulate the contact force according to the load. Meanwhile, the grasper can achieve higher success rates for grasping objects with various weights when adaptability is enabled. Due to the dynamic range of force capabilities, the integration of the bio-inspired soft grasper and control algorithms can be a plausible candidate for manipulating fragile, slippery, or complex objects, such as harvesting and processing agricultural products.

2   Methods

Bioinspired Soft Grasper and Simulation Environment.   The *Aplysia*-inspired soft grasper and simulation environment were previously described in [27]. Briefly, the grasper abstracted the principles of circumferential contraction of *Aplysia*'s jaw lumen and the ability to sense and tune contact forces found in *Aplysia*'s grasper. Circumferential contraction was achieved through the use of McKibben actuators encased in a cylindrical fabric sleeve (Fig. 1**A**). Three soft jaws, made of Smooth-On Vytaflex 30A whose stiffness could be independently tuned were fixed to the inside of the sheath to provide sensing and tuning of contact forces. When the jaws deformed due to contact, the corresponding increase in pressure was measured by pressure sensors. The soft grasper was connected to a Cartesian gantry robot (Fig. 1**B**) to move the grasper for pick-and-place tasks [20].

To facilitate training of the Synthetic Nervous System (SNS) controller, we developed a model of the grasper robot in PyBullet (Fig. 1**C**). To simulate the radial motion of the jaws with the contraction of the circumferential McKibben actuators, the jaws were placed on linear motor-powered prismatic joints. The soft jaws were represented as rigid bodies with a pressure-dependent contact stiffness [27]. The training of the SNS controller was implemented based on Neural Circuit Policies toolbox for PyTorch [19].

Synthetic Nervous Systems We built the controller for the soft grasper based on Synthetic Nervous Systems (Fig. 2A), a type of neural network model inspired by neurons' biophysical mechanisms for encoding information and conducting computation [30]. In SNSs, signals are typically represented by variables with biophysical meaning, such as membrane potential or neuronal firing rates. Various conductance-based mechanisms can then be incorporated to perform operations on these variables [21,23,29]. Below is a discretized version of equations governing the dynamics of an SNS network with n neurons[1] [27]:

$$y_t = \phi(h_t) \tag{1}$$

$$\hat{\tau}_t = \frac{\tau}{1 + V y_{t-1}} \tag{2}$$

$$z_t = \frac{\Delta}{\hat{\tau}_t + \Delta} \tag{3}$$

$$\hat{h}_t = \frac{b + W y_{t-1}}{1 + V y_{t-1}} \tag{4}$$

$$h_t = (1 - z_t) \odot h_{t-1} + z_t \odot \hat{h}_t \tag{5}$$

where Δ is the time step, t is the sample time. $h_t = [U_1, \cdots, U_n]^\top$ denotes membrane potential of neurons. ϕ in Eq. (1) denotes the activation function[2] relating membrane potential h_t to neurons' normalized firing rates y_t. The time constants $\tau = [\tau_1, \cdots, \tau_n]^\top$ and the bias term $b = [b_1, \cdots, b_n]^\top$ are parameters determining the intrinsic neuronal dynamics, while the other two parameters, the matrix V denoting the input strength of synaptic conductance and the matrix W denoting the product of reversal potential and input strength of synaptic conductance, determine the synaptic dynamics of SNS neurons. Eqs. (2)–(4) describe the relationship between the output variable y_t and three intermediate variables $\hat{\tau}_t$, z_t, and $\hat{h}_t$, which are called the effective time constant vector, update vector, and candidate activation vector in the field of artificial neural networks [13].

Due to their advantages in biological plausibility and computational capability, SNSs have been applied in building neurocircuitry models of animals [5,21,24] and controlling robots [7,10,12,20,27,28]. Designing an SNS controller requires finding appropriate parameter values for τ, b, W, and V. Both analytical methods [29,30] and supervised learning methods [20] have been reported to construct SNSs with desired dynamics for robotic control. In particular, Eqs. (1)–(5) can be viewed as an extension of traditional artificial neural network (ANN) models such as multilayer perceptrons (MLPs) and continuous-time recurrent neural networks [6], meaning that SNSs can be trained as other ANN models using gradient descent methods.

---

[1] In Eqs. (1)–(5), addition, subtraction, and division are performed element-wise. $\odot$ denotes element-wise product, a binary operation that multiplies elements corresponding to the same rows and columns of given matrices.

[2] We selected HardTanh activation function $\phi(h_t) = \min(1, \max(0, h_t))$ ($\min()$ and $\max()$ are the element-wise minimum and maximum, respectively).

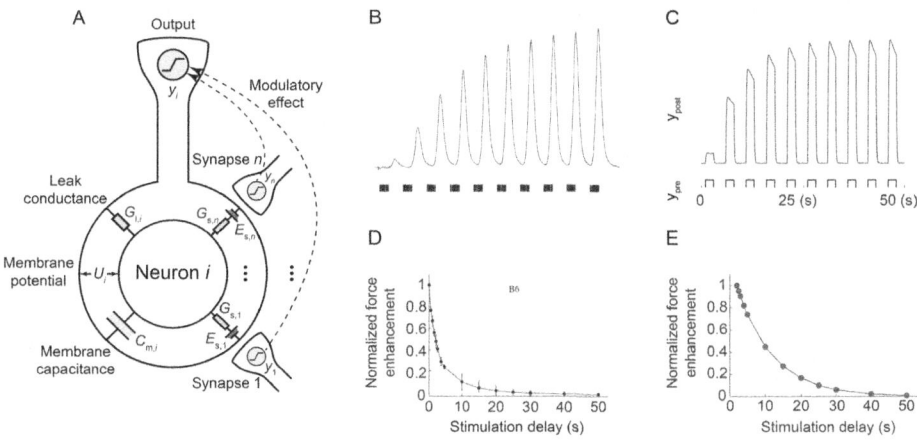

Fig. 2. Synthetic Nervous Systems and the time-history-dependent control mechanism. (A) Schematic of the ith neuron in the SNS network. The membrane capacitance ($C_{m,i}$) and leak conductance ($G_{l,i}$) define the time constant of the neuron. $E_{s,ij}$ and $G_{s,ij}$ denote the reversal potential and input strength of the jth synaptic conductance, respectively. Dashed lines indicate the potential modulatory effects of presynaptic neurons. (B) Repeated firing of B6 enhances the *Aplysia* I3 muscle forces generated by the same neuron during swallowing-like patterns (Fig. 8 in [22] by Hui Lu et al., reproduced under CC BY 4.0). (C) With the time-history-dependent control mechanism, repeated firing of the presynaptic SNS neuron enhances the activity of the postsynaptic SNS neuron generated by the same neuron. (D) Force enhancement decays as the interpattern interval increases in *Aplysia* I3 muscle (Fig. 11 in [22] by Hui Lu et al., reproduced under CC BY 4.0). (E) Activation enhancement decays as the inter-pattern interval increases in SNSs. For (C) and (E), modulation parameters are set to $\tau_m = 1$ s, $t_d = 2$ s, $\beta = 0.1$, $k = 40$, and $\alpha = 1$.

Time History Dependent Control. In this work, we introduced time-history-dependent control into SNSs by augmenting the governing equations. It has been previously demonstrated that time-history-dependent changes in the periphery and neural activity can prepare animal muscles for subsequent actions [22]. For example, repetition of neural activation to the I3 muscle of the sea slug *Aplysia* in biting-like patterns, which would otherwise generate little force, can prepare the muscle to generate higher force during subsequent swallowing-like patterns (Fig. 2B). Incorporating such mechanisms inspired by local modulation into the grasper controller allows the robot to generate robust and adaptive pick-and-place behavior even in the absence of higher-level control. To modulate SNS outputs, we scaled the original activation given by Eq. (1) using the following transformation

$$\boldsymbol{y}_t = (1 + \boldsymbol{k} \odot \boldsymbol{a}_t)^\alpha \odot \phi(\boldsymbol{h}_t) \tag{6}$$

where $\boldsymbol{k}$ is the modulation strength for each neuron. The exponent $\boldsymbol{\alpha} \in \{1, -1\}$ determines whether the modulation amplifies ($\boldsymbol{\alpha} = 1$) or represses $\boldsymbol{\alpha} = -1$ the output. The dynamics of the normalized modulation activity $\boldsymbol{a}_t$ in our model can be expressed as

$$\boldsymbol{u}_t = \widetilde{\boldsymbol{W}} \boldsymbol{y}_{t-t_{\mathrm{d}}} \tag{7}$$

$$\tilde{\boldsymbol{u}}_t = \frac{\boldsymbol{u}_t}{\boldsymbol{\beta} + (1 - \boldsymbol{\beta}) \odot \boldsymbol{u}_t}, \; 0 \leq \beta \leq 1 \tag{8}$$

$$\tilde{\boldsymbol{\tau}}_t = \frac{\tilde{\boldsymbol{u}}_t}{\boldsymbol{u}_t} \odot \boldsymbol{\tau}_{\mathrm{m}} \tag{9}$$

$$\tilde{\boldsymbol{z}}_t = \frac{\varDelta}{\tilde{\boldsymbol{\tau}}_t + \varDelta} \tag{10}$$

$$\boldsymbol{a}_t = (1 - \tilde{\boldsymbol{z}}_t) \odot \boldsymbol{a}_t + \tilde{\boldsymbol{z}}_t \odot \tilde{\boldsymbol{u}}_t \tag{11}$$

Equations (7)–(10) are a discretized version of the pure time delay process $\boldsymbol{u}(t) = \boldsymbol{y}(t - t_{\mathrm{d}}\varDelta)$ and first-order differential equations $\frac{\mathrm{d}\boldsymbol{a}}{\mathrm{d}t} + \frac{1}{\tau_{\mathrm{m}}} \left[\boldsymbol{\beta} + (1 - \boldsymbol{\beta})\boldsymbol{u}(t) \right] \boldsymbol{a}(t) = \frac{1}{\tau_{\mathrm{m}}} \boldsymbol{u}(t)$ [33], where $\widetilde{\boldsymbol{W}}$ is the mask matrix that determines which presynaptic neuron has modulatory effects. Due to the indirect connection between receptors and effectors, the onset of neuromodulatory effects in animals is generally slow [18]. The discrete-time delay, t_{d}, was incorporated here to capture this phenomenon. Another characteristic of neuromodulation is its long-lasting effects. The time course of decay can last many seconds or even minutes (Fig. 2D, [22]). In our model, $\boldsymbol{\beta}$ is the parameter we can use to adjust the rate of decay. Since $0 \leq \boldsymbol{\beta} \leq 1$, the rate constant associated with this first-order dynamics ($\frac{1}{\tilde{\tau}_t}$) linearly increases with increased excitation $\boldsymbol{u}(t)$. Therefore, the time course of decay is slower than the time course of buildup, and the parameter $\boldsymbol{\beta}$ controls the ratio of the time constant for buildup in the full modulation case (i.e., $\boldsymbol{u}(t) = 1$, $\tilde{\boldsymbol{\tau}} = \boldsymbol{\tau}_{\mathrm{m}}$) and the time-constant for decay in the full relaxation case (i.e., $\boldsymbol{u}(t) = 0$, $\tilde{\boldsymbol{\tau}} = \frac{\tau_{\mathrm{m}}}{\beta}$). Figure 2C and 2E demonstrate the activation enhancement and enhancement decay, respectively, of a postsynaptic neuron that is excited by a presynaptic neuron and modulated by the same neuron using the modulation-inspired mechanism. The results suggest the model can qualitatively capture the modulation behavior of muscle forces observed in *Aplysia*.

Control for Pick-and-Place Tasks. Integrating SNSs and time-history-depen-dent control, we designed a soft grasper controller for a basic pick-and-place task (Fig. 3). The task requires the grasper to pick up an object at a prespecified position and then place it in a target position. The pick-and-place controller was taken from our previous work [27], with modifications for the grasper radius commands control and an extension for force threshold modulation. Inspired by neural circuits for *Aplysia* feeding control, the control network has a hierarchical structure and sparse synaptic connections. Neurons in the sensory layer calculate the distance between the grasper, object, and target. Some are also responsible for detecting if contact force is above predefined thresholds. Based on this information, the command neuron layer determines which subtask,

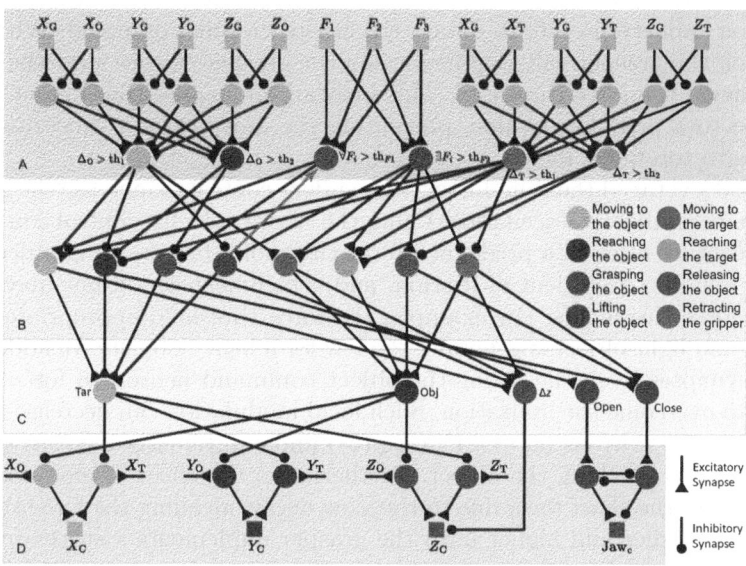

Fig. 3. The SNS controller for the pick-and-place task. (A) Sensory neuron layer. (B) Command neuron layer. (C) Interneuron layer. (D) Motor neuron layer. The sensory layer passes the object position (X_O, Y_O, Z_O), the target position (X_T, Y_T, Z_T), the grasper position (X_G, Y_G, Z_G), and the contact force of three soft jaws (F_1, F_2, F_3) to the network controller. Nodes labeled with the same symbol represent the same sensory neuron. The modulatory synapse is highlighted in red. (Color figure online)

or phase, the grasper should fulfill. Each command neuron in this layer selectively activates neurons in the following interneuron layer, which in turn activates or inhibits motor neurons in the motor neuron layer to implement corresponding motor primitives. Activities of motor neurons encode normalized commands for the grasper position and grasper radius.

We used velocity control to produce the joint radius command for its superiority in contact force regulation. Our previous controller sends a fixed grasper radius command for grasping and moving the object for robust grasp. However, such a strategy would not allow it to adaptively increase the force applied to a heavy object. Moreover, the fixed grasper radius may lead to excessively high contact force when interacting with fragile and soft objects, making them break or deform without returning to their original shape. To address this challenge, the controller presented in this paper adopts velocity control to mediate the opening and closing of the grasper instead of directly generating grasper radius commands. We modified the synaptic connections so that the controller specifies a negative jaw velocity (increasing the grasper closure) when grasping the object and a positive jaw velocity when releasing the object (decreasing the grasper closure). To allow regrasps after potential failures, the controller also specifies a positive jaw velocity in the reaching-the-object phase. For other phases, the velocity commands remain zero. Jaw velocity commands are finally sent to an integration subnetwork [30] to obtain the grasper radius command. With velocity control, the grasper will stop increasing the grasper closure after the contact force achieves the force threshold. This mechanism enables the contact force to stay close to a predefined value, preventing the grasper from squeezing fragile objects with too much force.

We also leveraged the time-history-dependent control to increase the grasping performance in different scenarios. Using the above velocity control can cap the value of contact force to a predefined force threshold, but grasping objects with different weights, coefficient of friction, and attachment conditions may require different force thresholds. For example, the force threshold appropriate to pick up a soft and light object is generally too low for a heavy object. We added modulatory synapses from the lifting-the-object command neuron to force sensory neurons to overcome the limitation. Such local modulation can decrease the gain of force sensory neurons ($\alpha = -1$ in Eq.(6)) and equivalently increase the force threshold when reaching the object. Furthermore, the effect of modulation can accumulate in the short term due to the slow decay, meaning the force threshold will become higher and higher until the grasper implements a successful grasp. With time-history-dependent control, the soft grasper has the ability to adjust the contact force level for various objects.

Validation of Modulation Controller. We first conducted a simulation to demonstrate the effectiveness of the adaptable pick-and-place controller. The task required the soft grasper to pick up a cubic object weighing 500 g from its initial position to a target position in the Pybullet engine. To further evaluate the SNS controller, we tested its performance in simulation scenarios with different ratios of heavy objects and compared its success rate and contact force with two baselines. In the Pybullet environment, we generated 11 groups of objects with the ratio of heavy objects (P_h) varying from 0% to 100%. Each group contains 20 cubic objects, among which $20P_h$ are heavy, and $20(1 - P_h)$ are light. We randomly selected the mass of a heavy object from 500 g to 1000 g and the mass of a light object from 50 g to 300 g. For performance comparison, we consider the following baselines: 1) the SNS controller using the position control for the grasper radius command. This baseline reported in [27] sends a fixed grasper radius command for jaw closure, 2) the SNS controller using the velocity control for the grasper radius command. This baseline is identical to the controller presented in this work, except it does not have modulatory synapses to implement time-history-dependent control. We evaluated how the two baselines and the adaptive SNS controller with time-history-dependent control mechanisms performed on the 11 groups of objects three times. We defined a pick-and-place task as successful if the object was moved to the target position within 15 s. It is possible that the system may get stuck in some phases of the pick-and-place task. Therefore, we set a cut-off time for the manipulation to meet to be considered as successful. In the Pybullet simulation, this time (15 s) allows the grasper to complete the pick-and-place task with at most five attempts to grasp the object. For each simulation, we recorded the maximal contact force generated by the soft grasper and then normalized it with the highest contact force in all experiments. Table 1 lists the main parameters of SNS controllers in simulation.

We also designed hardware experiments to test the effect of modulation on increasing the applied force on subsequent grasps. It should be noted that there was a sim-to-real gap due to the difficulties in modeling the soft contact between the object and the grasper. The heaviest objects the physical soft grasper robot could manipulate were generally lighter than those in the Pybullet simulation. Thus, we performed pick-and-place trials on a 173.4 g object, which was lighter than the object (500 g) we used in the simulation. The modulation gain of the SNS, k, was set to one of two conditions. The first condition, $k = 0$, causes no modulation of the sensory feedback and hence no increase in force on subsequent grasp attempts. The second condition, $k = 29$, results in modulation of the sensory feedback, and hence we expect an increase in grasping force on subsequent grasp attempts. We performed 10 pick-and-place trials for each case. The target object was a 3D printed rectangular prism (cross-section 35 mm × 35 mm, weight 173.4 g). Controls and data were sampled at a rate of 16.7 Hz. The time-history-dependent SNS controller was used with the following parameters. The time constant of the grasper, τ_{grasp}, was set to 5 s. The sensory gain of the SNS, K_{SNS}, was set to 10. The raw pressure values at the jaws were thresholded to prevent false triggering from noise, where the thresholds, $P_{th} \in \mathbf{R}^3$, are $[0.010, 0.020, 0.029]$ psi. The raw pressure readings were scaled by a constant, $K_p = 1750$. Hence, the contact force fed back to the SNS, F_C, is given by the following equation:

$$F_C = max(K_p \cdot (P_C - P_{th}), 0) \tag{12}$$

where $P_C \in \mathbf{R}^3$ is the contact pressures at the jaws, and $max()$ is the element-wise maximum. We determined the values of $k = 29$, $K_{SNS} = 10$, $\tau_{grasp} = 5$ s and $K_p = 1750$ via manual tuning to obtain the desired behavior.

3   Results

Simulation Results. With modulatory mechanisms, the soft grasper controlled by the SNS network can successfully move the 500 g object to the target position (Fig. 4). At t = 4 s, the grasper reached the object position and started its first attempt to grasp. However, the object slipped out of the grasper at t = 5 s due to low force thresholds encoded in the sensory neuron layer. Detecting the loss of contact, the SNS controller switched from the lifting-the-object phase to the reaching phase and performed a regrasp at t = 5.5 s. Synapses from the lifting-the-object command neuron also modulated neurons in the sensory neuron, allowing the encoded force thresholds to increase temporarily. This led to a successful grasp on the second attempt. The soft grasper then lifted the object up and completed the pick-and-place manipulation.

Baseline comparisons suggest that the SNS controller with modulation can adaptively regulate the contact force for objects with different masses (Fig. 5).

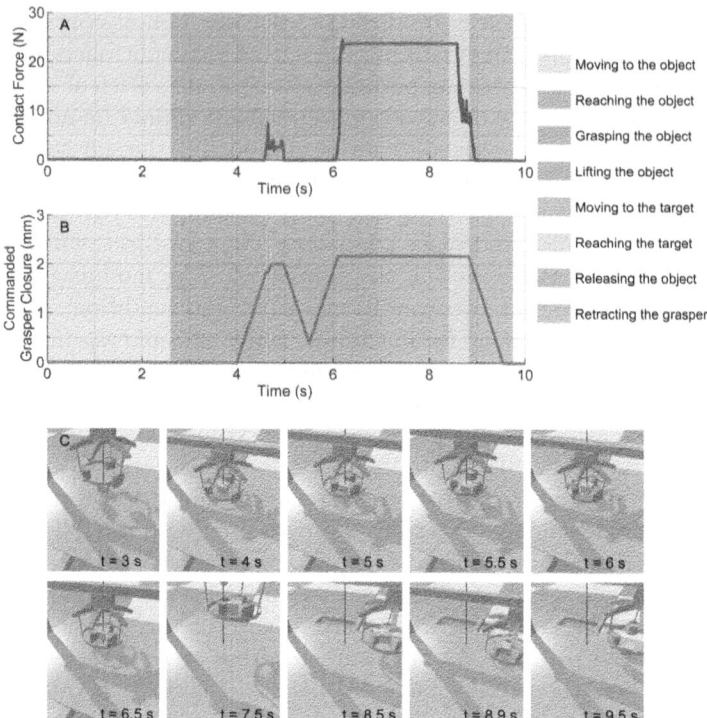

Fig. 4. The soft grasper controlled by the SNS network for pick-and-place manipulation in simulation. The object to pick up was a 500 g cube. Two attempts to grasp the object can be identified according to the contact force curve (A), the commanded grasper closure curve (B), and snapshots of the robot (C). The first attempt to grasp the object (t = 5 s) failed due to the low contact force. The grasper then attempted another grasp (t = 6 s). With the modulatory effect and increased force threshold, the grasper could successfully lift the object and move it to the target position. The colors of shades indicate the phases of the manipulation.

The baseline using position control for jaw closure always sends the highest grasper radius change for grasper closure. This strategy guarantees a high success rate for all groups of objects but may also lead to unnecessary high or even hazardous contact force for manipulating light and delicate objects. On the other hand, the baseline using velocity control for jaw closure can cap the contact force once it approaches a fixed threshold. This mechanism keeps contact forces at a low level for all groups of objects and achieves a high success rate for groups with few heavy objects. However, this baseline achieves a low success rate for groups with a high proportion of heavy objects due to the fixed force threshold. The integration of velocity control and time-history-dependent control alleviates the problem by local modulation. If the current threshold is insufficient to pick up the object, the SNS controller will try to regrasp it and use the

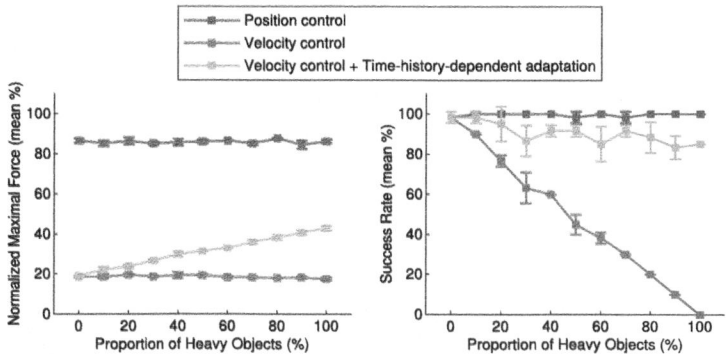

Fig. 5. Performance of the baseline and adaptive control methods for different proportions of heavy objects. Error bars represent standard error of the mean (SEM). Note that velocity control combined with time-history-dependent control results in both a high success rate (right panel) and a lower maximum normalized force (left panel).

modulatory mechanism to increase the threshold. This process repeats until the soft grasper implements a successful grasp. Therefore, as the proportion of heavy objects increases, the adaptive SNS controller can generate higher contact force to maintain a high success rate.

Experimental Results. The SNS with modulation of the force thresholds ($k = 29$) was able to successfully pick up the object 6 out of the 10 trials (Table 1). In contrast, the SNS without modulation ($k = 0$) failed on all 10 attempts. The transition pressure and commanded grasper closure on the 1st attempt for $k = 29$ and $k = 0$ were similar (Fig. 6). At the final attempt, successful grasps with modulation showed a large increase in the commanded grasper closure and, consequently, an increase in the jaw pressure, which can be taken as a proxy for the contact force imparted by the grasped object on the soft grasper (Fig. 6). Without modulation, however, on the final attempt, both the commanded grasper closure and the maximum change in pressure remained close to the values in the initial attempt (Fig. 6), which was insufficient for a successful pick-up.

The increase in success with modulation of the force thresholds (Table 1, Fig. 6) aligns with the simulation results (Fig. 5). However, because of differences in the mechanics of the simulation and the actual soft body mechanics of the real grasper, neither the contact force or grasper closure command behaviors exactly replicate the simulation. These differences also required substantial hand-tuning of the parameters of the SNS controller to obtain the desired behavior of failing on the 1st attempt and getting a successful grasp to complete the pick-and-place motion on subsequent attempts. Future work will further improve the simulation platform to better capture these mechanics and minimize the sim-to-real gap. Furthermore, control schemes like iterative learning control (ILC) that

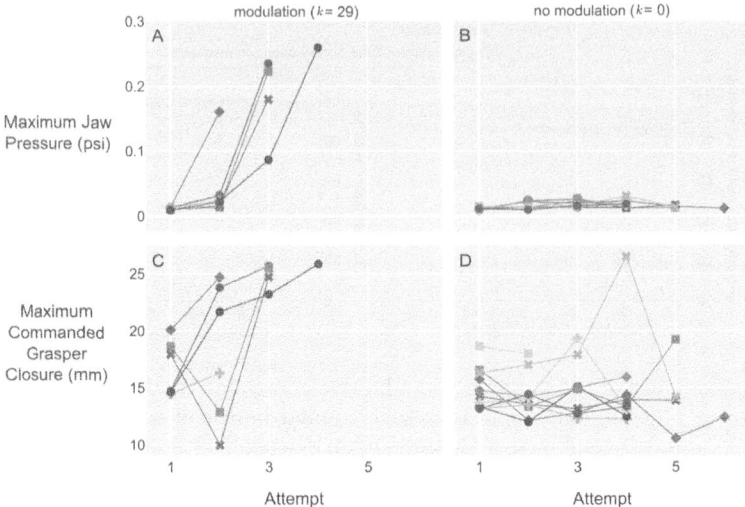

Fig. 6. Maximum jaw pressure experienced by the grasper (top row) and maximum commanded grasper closure (bottom row) for $k = 29$ and $k = 0$ during the lifting-the-object phase. A larger grasper closure indicated that the grasper contracted radially and consequently squeezed the object more. 6 of 10 trials for $k = 29$ were successful (left column). All 10 trials for $k = 0$ were unsuccessful (right column). Successful grasps with $k = 29$ showed increased jaw pressure on subsequent grasp attempts after initial failure on attempt 1 (A). Without modulation, the contact pressure remained consistently small (B). Likewise, when $k = 29$, the final commanded grasp closure for successful grasps was greater than the commanded closure on the initial attempt (C). No such trend was observed when there was no modulation (D). Different color-symbol combinations represent different trials. A comparison of a typical successful and unsuccessful trial with modulation is shown in Fig. 7.(Color figure online)

use rollouts on hardware to optimize control inputs may be used to fine-tune the gains in a more automated way [11, 25].

Though more successful than the case without modulation, grasping failures were still observed. These failures were primarily caused by the inability of the grasper to properly trigger a transition from the lifting-the-object to the reaching-the-object phase because the grasper did not deflate enough during the descent of the re-attempt, and so the jaws made contact with the object (Fig. 7). The grasper would then begin to inflate while stuck on top of the object and would not register a large enough change in contact pressure to trigger the transition from the grasping-the-object phase to the lifting-the-object phase (Fig. 7). This can be remedied in the future by augmenting the soft jaws with other contact sensors distributed spatially around the grasper to detect contact events that are not only localized at the jaws, which are most sensitive to radially directed contact forces. This additional sensory information could help the grasper to reason about such unexpected contact events.

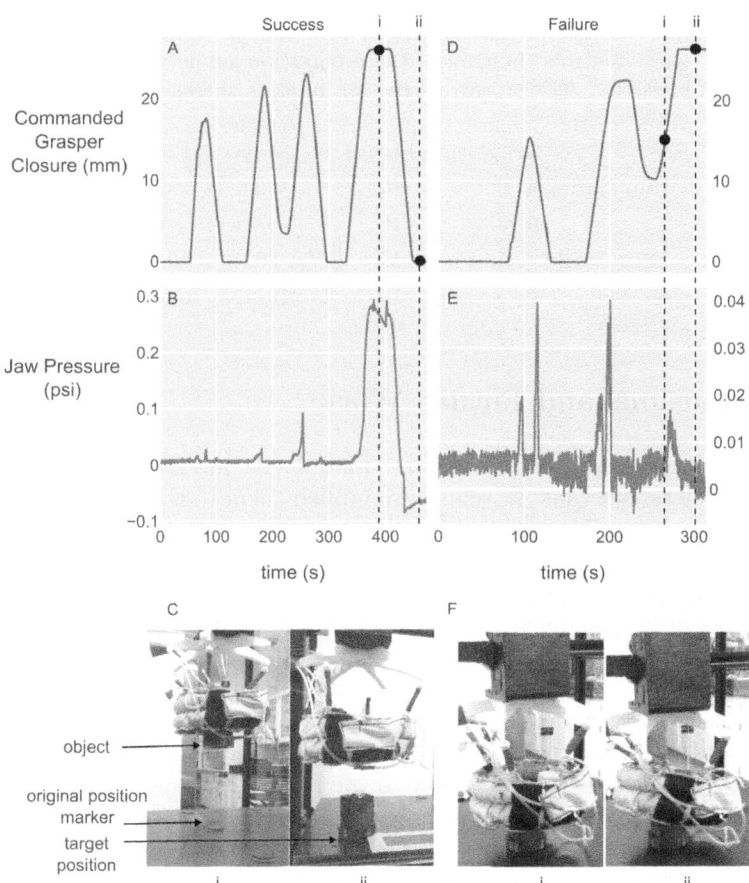

Fig. 7. Comparison of commanded grasper closure and jaw pressure for a successful (left column) and unsuccessful (right column) pick-and-place trial with the SNS modulation of force thresholds ($k = 29$). While the commanded grasper closure shows an increase with subsequent attempts for both successful and unsuccessful grasp (A and D), the jaw pressure at the final attempt is much different (note the different y-axis scales of B and E). In the successful case, the grasper was able to deflate and successfully grasp the object (C, i) and deposit it at the target position (C, ii). In the failure case, the grasper did not fully deflate during the reaching-the-object phase of the reattempt, which caused the jaws to get stuck on top of the object (F, i). The commanded closure increased, but since the object was below the jaws, insufficient contact forces were generated to transition to the lifting-the-object phase (F, ii).

Table 1. Summary of SNS parameters and success rate for pick-and-place experiments in simulation and real-world. Modulation gain $k = 0$ means the modulation mechanism is turned off. τ_{grasp} controls the gain of the integration subnetwork, thus determining the jaw closure velocity. K_{SNS} controls the initial force threshold.

	k	τ_{grasp} (s)	K_{SNS}	K_p	Success Rate (%)
*Simulation	4	3.3	10	–	90.5, $n = 660$
	0	3.3	10	–	48.3, $n = 660$
*Real-world	29	5	10	1750	60, $n = 10$
	0	5	10	1750	0, $n = 10$

4   Conclusions and Future Work

In this work, we incorporated bioinspired modulation mechanisms into the framework of Synthetic Nervous Systems and applied them to the pick-and-place control of a soft grasper. The adaptable SNS controller also used velocity control for jaw closure so that it could exploit the contact force information to regulate the pressure between the grasper and the object. The combination of velocity control and time-history-dependent-control endowed the controller with the capability to adaptively change the force threshold, which is critical for safe interaction with a wide range of objects. Simulation results in the Pybullet environment demonstrated the adaptable SNS controller can achieve high success rates for the pick-and-place tasks while avoiding excessively high contact force. We also successfully transferred the controller to the physical grasper and demonstrated the benefits of using time-history-dependent control.

To reduce the sim-to-real gap, we will focus on improving the fidelity of the simulation to the physical robot. The temporal dynamics of the closure muscles and the soft jaws can be included in the simulation environment in future work. Future work will also explore the tunable stiffness of the soft grasper and the plasticity of the SNS. Due to the usage of soft deformable jaws, our grasper can generate tunable stiffness decoupled from the positional state of the closure muscle. This feature could be critical for safe robot-environment interaction and has drawn much attention in the research of agriculture robots, prostheses, and exoskeletons. In this work, we set the pressure applied to the internal cavity of the jaw to a pre-defined value. Therefore, the advantage of tunable stiffness was not leveraged. Our future work will explore the benefit of real-time stiffness tuning in manipulation tasks. In addition to the local modulation, we aim to integrate short-term and long-term plasticity into SNS networks so that the controller can implement online learning. The plasticity rules will allow the controller to learn appropriate parameters (such as the grasper closing speed and the modulatory gain) from interaction with objects and use its experience of success and failure to improve the control policy over time.

References

1. Bolívar-Nieto, E.A., Thomas, G.C., Rouse, E., Gregg, R.D.: Convex optimization for spring design in series elastic actuators: From theory to practice. In: 2021 IEEE/RSJ International Conference on Intelligent Robots and Systems (IROS), pp. 9327–9332 (2021). https://doi.org/10.1109/IROS51168.2021.9636427

2. Cianchetti, M., Calisti, M., Margheri, L., Kuba, M., Laschi, C.: Bioinspired loco-motion and grasping in water: the soft eight-arm octopus robot. Bioinspiration Biomimetics **10**(3), 035003 (2015). https://doi.org/10.1088/1748-3190/10/3/035003

3. Ciocarlie, M., Miller, A., Allen, P.: Grasp analysis using deformable fingers. In: 2005 IEEE/RSJ International Conference on Intelligent Robots and Systems, pp. 4122–4128 (2005). https://doi.org/10.1109/IROS.2005.1545525

4. Della Santina, C., Duriez, C., Rus, D.: Model-based control of soft robots: a survey of the state of the art and open challenges. IEEE Control Syst. Mag. **43**(3), 30–65 (2023). https://doi.org/10.1109/MCS.2023.3253419

5. Deng, K., Szczecinski, N.S., Arnold, D., Andrada, E., Fischer, M.S., Quinn, R.D., Hunt, A.J.: Neuromechanical model of rat hindlimb walking with two-layer cpgs. Biomimetics **4**(1), (2019). https://doi.org/10.3390/biomimetics4010021

6. Funahashi, K., Nakamura, Y.: Approximation of dynamical systems by continuous time recurrent neural networks. Neural Netw. **6**(6), 801–806 (1993). https://doi.org/10.1016/S0893-6080(05)80125-X

7. Goldsmith, C.A., Szczecinski, N.S., Quinn, R.D.: Neurodynamic modeling of the fruit fly drosophila melanogaster. Bioinspiration Biomimetics **15**(6), 065003 (2020). https://doi.org/10.1088/1748-3190/ab9e52

8. Goncalves, A., Kuppuswamy, N., Beaulieu, A., Uttamchandani, A., Tsui, K.M., Alspach, A.: Punyo-1: Soft tactile-sensing upper-body robot for large object manip-ulation and physical human interaction. In: 2022 IEEE 5th International Confer-ence on Soft Robotics (RoboSoft), pp. 844–851 (2022). https://doi.org/10.1109/RoboSoft54090.2022.9762117

9. Guan, Q., Stella, F., Della Santina, C., Leng, J., Hughes, J.: Trimmed helicoids: an architectured soft structure yielding soft robots with high precision, large workspace, and compliant interactions. npj Robot. **1**(1), 4 (2023). https://doi.org/10.1038/s44182-023-00004-7

10. Hilts, W.W., Szczecinski, N.S., Quinn, R.D., Hunt, A.J.: A dynamic neural network designed using analytical methods produces dynamic control properties similar to an analogous classical controller. IEEE Control Syst. Lett. **3**(2), 320–325 (2019). https://doi.org/10.1109/LCSYS.2018.2871126

11. Hofer, M., Spannagl, L., D'Andrea, R.: Iterative learning control for fast and accu-rate position tracking with an articulated soft robotic arm. In: 2019 IEEE/RSJ International Conference on Intelligent Robots and Systems (IROS), pp. 6602–6607. IEEE, Macau, China (2019). https://doi.org/10.1109/IROS40897.2019.8967636

12. Hunt, A., Szczecinski, N., Quinn, R.: Development and training of a neural con-troller for hind leg walking in a dog robot. Front. Neurorobot. **11**, (2017). https://doi.org/10.3389/fnbot.2017.00018

13. Jordan, I.D., Sokół, P.A., Park, I.M.: Gated recurrent units viewed through the lens of continuous time dynamical systems. Front. Comput. Neurosci. **15**, (2021). https://doi.org/10.3389/fncom.2021.678158

14. Kemp, C.C., Edsinger, A., Torres-Jara, E.: Challenges for robot manipulation in human environments [grand challenges of robotics]. IEEE Robot. Autom. Mag. **14**(1), 20–29 (2007). https://doi.org/10.1109/MRA.2007.339604
15. Khan, A., Martin, P.L., Hardiman, P.: Expanded production of labor-intensive crops increases agricultural employment. Calif. Agric. **58**(1), 35–39 (2004). https://doi.org/10.3733/ca.v058n01p35
16. Kim, Y.J.: Anthropomorphic low-inertia high-stiffness manipulator for high-speed safe interaction. IEEE Trans. Rob. **33**(6), 1358–1374 (2017). https://doi.org/10.1109/TRO.2017.2732354
17. Klein, M., Kandel, E.R.: Mechanism of calcium current modulation underlying presynaptic facilitation and behavioral sensitization in *Aplysia*. Proc. Natl. Acad. Sci. USA **77**(11), 6912–6916 (1980)
18. Koch, C.: Biophysics of Computation: Information Processing in Single Neurons. Oxford University Press (1998). https://doi.org/10.1093/oso/9780195104912.001.0001
19. Lechner, M., Hasani, R., Amini, A., Henzinger, T.A., Rus, D., Grosu, R.: Neural circuit policies enabling auditable autonomy. Nat. Mach. Intell. **2**(10), 642–652 (2020). https://doi.org/10.1038/s42256-020-00237-3
20. Li, Y., Sukhnandan, R., Gill, J.P., Chiel, H.J., Webster-Wood, V., Quinn, R.D.: A bioinspired synthetic nervous system controller for pick-and-place manipulation. In: 2023 IEEE International Conference on Robotics and Automation (ICRA), pp. 8047–8053 (2023). https://doi.org/10.1109/ICRA48891.2023.10161198
21. Li, Y., Webster-Wood, V.A., Gill, J.P., Sutton, G.P., Chiel, H.J., Quinn, R.D.: A synthetic nervous system controls a biomechanical model of *Aplysia* feeding. In: Biomimetic and Biohybrid Systems, pp. 354–365. Springer (2022)
22. Lu, H., McManus, J.M., Cullins, M.J., Chiel, H.J.: Preparing the periphery for a subsequent behavior: motor neuronal activity during biting generates little force but prepares a retractor muscle to generate larger forces during swallowing in *Aplysia*. J. Neurosci. **35**(12), 5051–5066 (2015). https://doi.org/10.1523/JNEUROSCI.0614-14.2015
23. Nourse, W.R.P., Jackson, C., Szczecinski, N.S., Quinn, R.D.: Sns-toolbox: an open source tool for designing synthetic nervous systems and interfacing them with cyber-physical systems. Biomimetics **8**(2), (2023). https://doi.org/10.3390/biomimetics8020247
24. Nourse, W.R.P., Szczecinski, N.S., Quinn, R.D.: A synthetic nervous system for on and off motion detection inspired by the drosophila melanogaster optic lobe. In: Biomimetic and Biohybrid Systems, pp. 364–380. Springer (2023)
25. Patan, K., Patan, M.: Neural-network-based iterative learning control of nonlinear systems. ISA Trans. **98**, 445–453 (2020). https://doi.org/10.1016/j.isatra.2019.08.044
26. Shintake, J., Cacucciolo, V., Floreano, D., Shea, H.: Soft robotic grippers. Adv. Mater. **30**(29), 1707035 (2018)
27. Sukhnandan, R., et al.: Synthetic nervous system control of a bioinspired soft grasper for pick-and-place manipulation. In: Biomimetic and Biohybrid Systems, pp. 300–321. Springer (2023)
28. Szczecinski, N.S., Getsy, A.P., Martin, J.P., Ritzmann, R.E., Quinn, R.D.: Mantisbot is a robotic model of visually guided motion in the praying mantis. Arthropod Struct. Dev. **46**(5), 736–751 (2017)
29. Szczecinski, N.S., Hunt, A.J., Quinn, R.D.: Design process and tools for dynamic neuromechanical models and robot controllers. Biol. Cybern. **111**(1), 105–127 (2017). https://doi.org/10.1007/s00422-017-0711-4

30. Szczecinski, N.S., Hunt, A.J., Quinn, R.D.: A functional subnetwork approach to designing synthetic nervous systems that control legged robot locomotion. Front. Neurorobot. **11**, 37 (2017)
31. Wang, J., Chortos, A.: Control strategies for soft robot systems. Adv. Intell. Syst. **4**(5), 2100165 (2022)
32. Webster-Wood, V.A., Gill, J.P., Thomas, P.J., Chiel, H.J.: Control for multifunctionality: bioinspired control based on feeding in *Aplysia californica*. Biol. Cybern. **114**(6), 557–588 (2020)
33. Zajac, F.: Muscle and tendon: properties, models, scaling, and application to biomechanics and motor control. Critical reviews in biomedical engineering **17**(4), 359-411 (1989), http://europepmc.org/abstract/MED/2676342
34. Zhang, B., Xie, Y., Zhou, J., Wang, K., Zhang, Z.: State-of-the-art robotic grippers, grasping and control strategies, as well as their applications in agricultural robots: a review. Comput. Electron. Agric. **177**, 105694 (2020). https://doi.org/10.1016/j.compag.2020.105694

Sequence Generator Network for Neuromechanical Control of Rat Hindlimbs

Clayton B. Jackson[1]([✉])[iD], William R. P. Nourse[2][iD], and Roger D. Quinn[1][iD]

[1] Department of Mechanical and Aerospace Engineering,
Case Western Reserve University, Cleveland, OH 44106-7222, USA
clayton.jackson@case.edu
[2] Department of Electrical, Computer, and Systems Engineering,
Case Western Reserve University, Cleveland, OH 44106-7222, USA

Abstract. Mammalian locomotion is a complex behavior arising from interaction between neural and biomechanical systems, driven by rhythmic activity originating in the spinal cord. Although it has been extensively studied, the structure of the circuits that produce this behavior remains unknown. One approach to modeling the rhythmic activity is with half-center models, in which there are alternating periods of flexion and extension to coordinate muscle activity. While this approach is sufficient for simple antagonistic muscle pairs, it can be difficult to expand the controller for more complex models with muscle synergies. This work introduces a method of modeling the activity in the spinal cord with a population of neurons exhibiting a continuous cycle of activity, rather than the push-pull of half-centers. To evaluate the effectiveness of this neural model for locomotive behavior, we integrate it with a biomechanical simulation to control the muscle activity in a pair of rat hindlimbs. With this controller, a pair of simulated rat hindlimbs is able to walk on the ground with joint trajectories exhibiting similar features to the animal during locomotion. This model of the spinal cord activity shows promising results on a simple model and demonstrates the ability to be adapted to control more complex biomechanical models with muscle synergies.

Keywords: Pattern Generation · Neuromechanical Simulation · Mammalian Locomotion

1 Introduction

Mammalian locomotion showcases the remarkable adaptability of biological systems. From navigating rugged terrain to scaling tree branches, mammals exhibit a variety of locomotor behaviors. Central to these locomotion abilities is the

This work was supported by NSF DBI 2015317 as part of the NSF/CIHR/DFG/FRQ/ UKRI-MRC Next Generation Networks for Neuroscience Program.

interaction between their neural control mechanisms and biomechanical systems, with the spinal cord playing a crucial role in coordinating their complex movements [10]. Central Pattern Generators (CPG's) in the spinal cord generate rhythmic behavior autonomously and, thus, are a key to vertebrate locomotion behavior [18]. While these circuits have been studied in animals (i.e. salamanders, lamprey, crabs), the structure of locomotion pattern generators remains a mystery [9, 19, 25, 30].

A common approach to modeling the rhythmic activity in the spinal cord is using a half center model [7]. The half center model is based on the principle of escape and release, alternating between periods of flexion and extension. The half centers represent a simplified model of the spinal cord and classifies motor neurons and muscles to be either flexors or extensors. However, locomotion requires the coordination of complex muscle synergies that cannot be simplified to antagonistic pairs [15–17, 36]. Other works have expanded the traditional half center model to include multiple layers of half centers to allow for more complex muscle activation, as well as the ability to control the frequency and amplitude of the motor neuron activity independently [14, 29]. However, these models rely on accurate tuning of parameters and small changes to these parameters may result in significant changes in behavior. Recent studies have shown that optogenetic stimulation to the brain stem of a rat can cause a movement arrest or freezing behavior [6]. Due to the bi-stable nature of the half center models, this sort of stimulation would not result in an immediate ceasing of movement, but rather the animal would continue to move until the neural system reached an equilibrium point. The BSG model behaves similarly but features a greater number of equilibrium points, which may result in a more immediate cessation of movement, offering improved control results.

Another method of modeling the rhythmic activity in the spinal cord can be achieved by taking advantage of population dynamics. A model referred to as the Balanced Sequence Generator (BSG), has been proposed to capture the rotational dynamics observed in the spinal cord during rhythmic movement [24]. Rather than alternating periods of flexion and extention, the BSG provides a continuous cycle of neuron activity which may allow for more complex control of biomechanical models and muscle activations. The BSG is constructed using a pool of randomly connected neurons and is able to change its frequency and amplitude independently. However, the network requires principle component and sensitivity analysis in order to classify its rotational properties and determine which neurons are able to produce these changes when an additional input is applied [24]. As this network represents a low-dimensional trajectory, we can use design principles from Recurrent Neural Networks (RNNs) to design a network similar to the BSG, achieving rotational dynamics with continuous neural activity [5]. With this approach, the network is designed to meet certain criteria rather than analyzed after the fact. Models such as these have been developed, but have yet to be used for the purposes of controlling a biomechanical model [5]. The purpose of this work is to evaluate the effectiveness of such a controller which uses continuous cycles of neuron activity as a CPG for locomotion.

2   Methods

2.1   Modeling

The computational modeling in this work is done through integrating two software packages. We first create a biomechanical model of rat hindlimbs with muscles in the physics simulator Mujoco, which can then be controlled in Python [34]. The neural controller is then designed using SNS-Toolbox, a Python package developed to design and simulate Synthetic Nervous Systems (SNS) [28]. The physics and neural simulations are integrated using a traditional forward Euler method with a time step of 0.1 ms.

Biomechanical Model. The biomechanical model of rat hindlimbs was adapted from previous works which also focused on bio-inspired control schemes [14,22]. The skeleton model used was adapted from a model in OpenSim [12,23,31]. As our model only contains the hindlimbs and pelvis, constraints must be placed such that the model does not immediately fall or tip over. Previous models built in Animatlab2, a neuromechanical simulation software designed by Cofer et. al., placed additional bodies in front of and behind the hindlimbs with a fixed relationship to the pelvis [11,14]. This effectively constrained the model, preventing it from falling to the ground as well as limiting the roll and pitch angles. However, this created additional mass and frictional forces. Rather than placing these additional bodies, the same constraints were achieved in Mujoco by placing hinge and prismatic joints at the pelvis, relative to the ground, with limited ranges (see Fig. 1).

The model of the hindlimbs has also been updated to include passive compliance in the toes of the rat. It has been shown that adding passive compliance in robots can increase stability by allowing the foot to conform to the terrain and increasing the number of contact points [4,8,27]. Based on Alexander (1990), this principle can also be inferred about animals, where the pads on their feet act to reduce the force at impact and conform to the ground [3]. In previous models with rigid feet, the model walked on its toes with a single point of contact on each leg. By adding joints in the toes with stiffness and damping, we can see an increase in the number of contact points between the model and the ground, as shown in Fig. 1. The addition of these passive joints allows the model to conform to the ground and results in a more realistic and stable biomechanical model.

Our model of the rat hindlimbs uses flexor-extensor muscle pairs to control the hip, knee, and ankle joints in the sagittal plane. The muscle attachment points and maximum forces were adapted from the model presented in Deng et al. (2019) and are implemented in Mujoco using a Hill type muscle model [20]. The muscle force generated, as implemented in Mujoco, is a function of the length, velocity, and motor neuron activity [34]:

$$F_M = (F_L(L) \cdot F_v(v) \cdot A(V_{MN}) + F_P(L)) \cdot F_0 \tag{1}$$

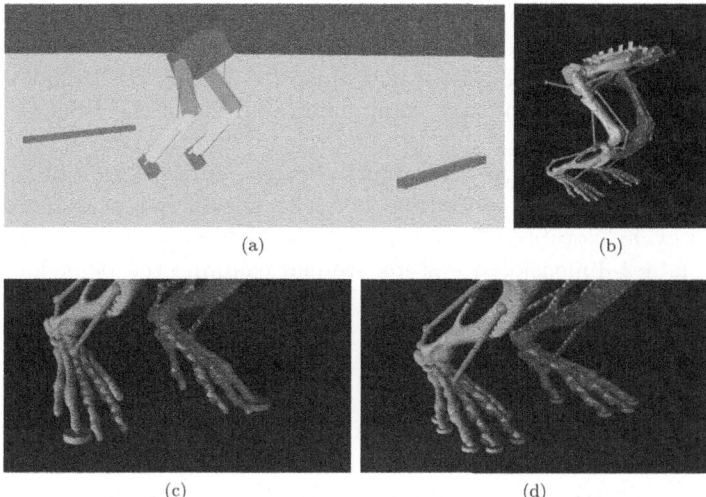

Fig. 1. Biomechanical models of rat hindlimbs. (a) Model in Animatlab2 with additional bodies to prevent falling [14]. (b) Complete model in Mujoco used for this work [23]. (c) Model with rigid toes. (d) Model with passively compliant toes. The orange pucks in (c) and (d) represent the contact points with the ground. (Color figure online)

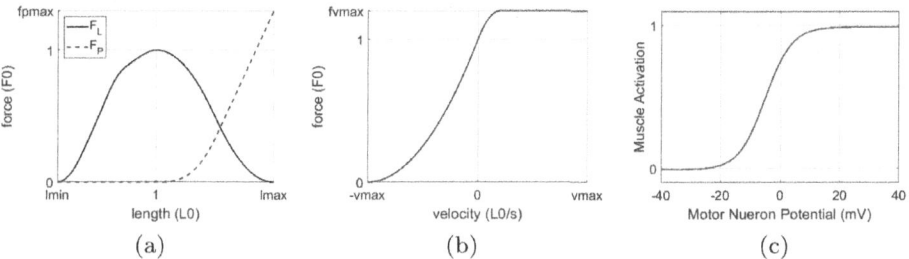

Fig. 2. Muscle model force generation curves. (a) Force-Length and Passive Force curves. *lmin* and *lmax* are computed in the model compiler. (b) Force-Velocity curve. *vmax* is computed in the model compiler [34]. (c) Sigmoidal Curve converting motor neuron activity to muscle activation.

where F_L is the active force as a function of length, F_v is the active force as a function of velocity, L is the length of the muscle, v is the velocity of the muscle, F_0 is the peak active force, F_P is the passive force, and A is a function which converts the potential of the motor neuron, V_{MN}, to a muscle activation between zero and one. Examples of these functions are shown in Fig. 2 [34].

Neural Model. Our objective was to develop a neural model for controlling a biomechanical system. We start by creating a sequence generator which demonstrates continuous cyclic neural activity, inspired by the BSG model proposed by Lindén et al. [24]. A principle component analysis of the BSG showed that the principle components exhibit a limit cycle. While the BSG model relied on random connectivity, our approach aims to design a network that maintains continuous neural activity akin to a BSG but with specific latent dynamics resembling a limit cycle. Notably, the minimum dimensionality of a system to generate oscillations is a 2-dimensional system, we can examine the behavior of a rank two system with the covariance [5]:

$$\sigma = \begin{bmatrix} \sigma_1 & -\sigma_2 \\ \sigma_2 & \sigma_1 \end{bmatrix}. \tag{2}$$

It has been shown that a rank two network with a covariance matrix containing complex eigenvalues indicates an oscillatory behavior [32]. We can apply these principles in designing the connection matrix of a pool of neurons, as was done for RNNs in Beiran et al. Here, we can define a rank two connection matrix, J [5]:

$$J_{ij} = \frac{1}{N} \sum_{r=1}^{2} m_i^{(r)} n_j^{(r)} \tag{3}$$

where N is the number of neurons in the network, $m^{(r)}$ and $n^{(r)}$ are the left and right singular vectors respectfully, and $m^{(r)}$ are also the principle components of the system. The singular vectors are sampled from a single Gaussian distribution with a zero mean and a covariance matrix based upon Eq. 2, $v \sim \mathcal{N}(0, \sigma_{Tot})$ where v are the singular vectors and σ_{Tot} is the covariance matrix [5]:

$$\sigma_{Tot} = \begin{bmatrix} 1 & 0 & \sigma_1 & \sigma_2 \\ 0 & 1 & -\sigma_2 & \sigma_1 \\ \sigma_1 & -\sigma_2 & c & 0 \\ \sigma_2 & \sigma_1 & 0 & c \end{bmatrix}. \tag{4}$$

In this work, we specified the values for the covariance matrix as: $\sigma_1 = 2.25$, $\sigma_2 = 0.25$, and $c = 5.45$.

The resulting connection matrix, J, defines weight based connections. The neural model used in this work, as defined in the Python package SNS-Toolbox [28], is the non-spiking leaky integrator model,

$$C_m \frac{dU}{dt} = -G_m U + I_{app} + \sum_{i=1}^{n} I_{syn_i} \tag{5}$$

where C_m is the membrane capacitance, U is the membrane potential offset by the resting potential ($U = V - E_R$), G_m is the membrane conductance, I_{app} is an applied external current, and I_{syn} is the synaptic current. The synaptic current uses a conductance based model:

$$I_{syn_i} = g_{max_i} \cdot \min\left(\max\left(\frac{U_{pre}}{R}, 0\right), 1\right) \cdot (\Delta E_{syn_i} - U(t)) \tag{6}$$

where g_{max} is the maximum synaptic conductance, U_{pre} is the membrane potential of the pre-synaptic neuron, R is the range of synaptic activity, and ΔE_{syn_i} is the synaptic reversal potential offset by the neural resting potential ($\Delta E_{syn_i} = E_{syn} - E_R$) and describes the function of the synapse. When $\Delta E_{syn_i} < 0$, it indicates an inhibitory synapse. When $\Delta E_{syn_i} > 0$, it indicates an excitatory synapse. The connectivity matrix described in Eq. 3 defines the synapses in terms of weights. To convert this to a conductance based synapse, we define the reversal potentials and maximum synaptic conductance's according to Szczecinski et al. [33].

$$\Delta E_{syn} = \begin{cases} E_{inhibit} & \text{if } J < 0, \\ E_{excite} & \text{if } J \geq 0. \end{cases} \quad (7)$$

$$g_{max} = \frac{JR}{\Delta E_{syn} - JR} \quad (8)$$

The sequence generator is composed of 200 neurons, similar to that of the BSG network proposed by Linden et al. [24]. The activity in the sequence generator defined using Eqs. 2–8 results in continuous neural behavior with the principle components exhibiting a limit cycle, as shown in Fig. 3.

The sequence generator network is then connected to an output level motor circuit consisting of Ia inhibitory neurons, motor neurons, Renshaw cells, and Ia and Ib interneurons to incorporate feedback. Muscle velocity and tension feedback (Ia and Ib, respectfully) are included in the motor circuit. This motor circuit is present in numerous other neural models of locomotive circuitry, typically with an input from pattern generator networks [14, 21, 26, 29]. As the focus of this work is the effectiveness of the sequence generator, the parameters used in the motor circuit model were derived from Deng et al. (2019). Unlike the

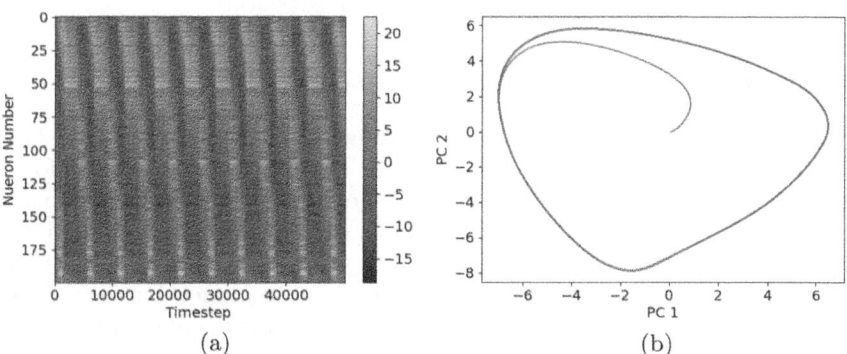

Fig. 3. Sequence Generator Activity. (a) Neuron activity where the color indicates the neuron membrane potential, U, in mV. The x-axis shows the iteration or timestep in the simulation where $dt = 0.1$ ms. (b) Component space showing the rotational behavior of the first two principle components. The principle components are unitless. (Color figure online)

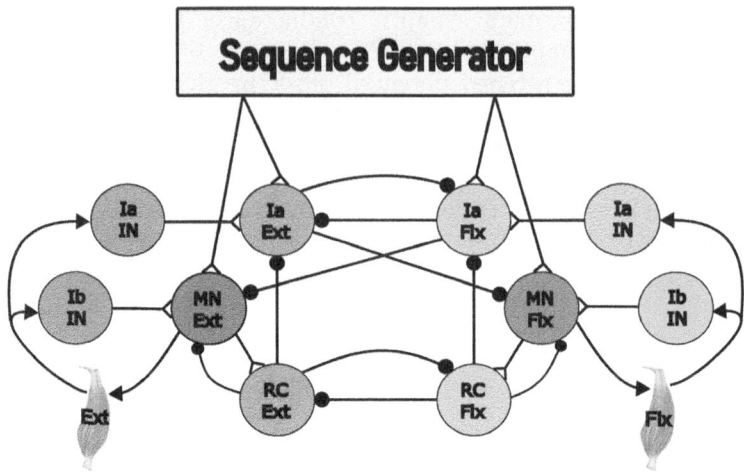

Fig. 4. Motor Circuit receiving input from the sequence generator. The hip, knee, and ankle have separate motor circuits but share the sequence generator. The motor circuit consists of motor neurons (MN), Renshaw cells (RC), Ia and Ib interneurons (IN), and Ia inhibitory neurons. The Ia and Ib interneurons receive velocity and tension feedback, respectively, from the corresponding muscle.

model presented in Deng et al. (2019) type II, length feedback, is not included in the present model. Length feedback was used in previous models as an input to the pattern generator networks [14,29], further analysis of the sequence generator is required to determine how to properly implement length feedback into the network. Figure 4 shows the design of the motor network with input from the sequence generator. Note that the hip, knee, and ankle each have their own motor circuit, but share the sequence generator network.

2.2   Tuning

The tuning process was broken into two stages: the first focusing on how to connect the sequence generator to the motor circuits, and the second focusing on the strength of these connections and the Ia and Ib afferent feedback. In this model, we designate continuous sections of the sequence generator to act as inputs to the flexor and extensor sides of the motor circuits. This stage of tuning dictates the timing of swing and stance in the model. Further tuning of the joint trajectories could be done by tuning the parameters of the motor circuit, however, this has not been done in this work. We first utilized the BFGS non-linear optimization method, as implemented in SciPy [35] to determine which

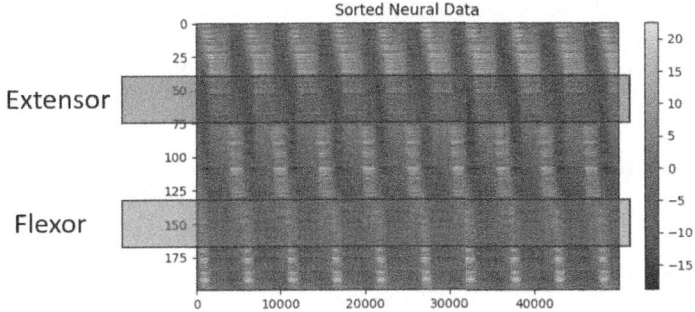

Fig. 5. Designated regions of flexion and extension in the sequence generator. The extensor region (red) and flexor region (blue) are connected to the corresponding sections of the motor circuit. (Color figure online)

regions of the sequence generator to treat as inputs to the flexor and extensor sides of the motor circuits. Examples of these flexor and extensor regions can be seen in Fig. 5. The resulting simulated data of the joint trajectories was compared to animal data of a rat walking on a treadmill, previously collected by Allesandro et al., using a mean square error for single gait trajectories as the loss function. Note that the animal data represents averages over multiple steps, ensuring that the features observed are not artifacts of a single step [2]. The strengths of the synapses from the sequence generator to the motor circuits were fixed during this initial stage in the tuning process and later hand tuned along with the strengths of the Ia and Ib feedback in order to improve and shape the trajectories once the connectivity from the sequence generator was determined.

3   Results

The neural activity shown in Fig. 3 demonstrates the effectiveness of this network design method to produce the rhythmic activity consistent with activity in the spinal cord during locomotive behavior in rats [6]. Integrating these signals with motor circuits consistent with two-layer pattern generator networks [14, 29], we are able to control a simplified model of rat hindlimbs with antagonistic muscle pairs controlling the hip, knee, and ankle joints in the sagittal plane. Neurons 50–98 in the sequence generator were identified as the inputs to the extensor neurons of the motor circuits, while neurons 190–198 were identified as the inputs to the flexor neurons of the motor circuits. The number of the neuron corresponds to the order that it is active in the cycle (see Figs. 3 and 5 for examples). Figure 6

Table 1. Connection strengths from the Sequence Generator (SG) to motor circuits.

Synaptic Connection		Maximum Synaptic Conductance (μS)
Hip Motor Circuit	SG to MN Ext	0.03
	SG to MN Flx	0.1
	SG to Ia Ext	0.025
	SG to Ia Flx	1.5
Knee Motor Circuit	SG to MN Ext	0.3515
	SG to MN Flx	0.5
	SG to Ia Ext	0.09
	SG to Ia Flx	1.0
Ankle Motor Circuit	SG to MN Ext	0.2215
	SG to MN Flx	1.5
	SG to Ia Ext	0.15
	SG to Ia Flx	0.16

shows the joint trajectories generated by the neural and biomechanical models in the simulation, showing similar features between the simulated and animal joint trajectories [2]. Table 1 shows the final strengths of the connections from the sequence generator network to the motor circuits.

4   Discussion

This work has demonstrated the effectiveness of a network designed to produce a continuous cycle of neural activity in controlling a biomechanical model of a pair of rat hindlimbs. While there are noticeable differences in the trajectory for a single gait (see Fig. 6) we are still able to identify key components. Among these components noted in both the animal data and the simulation are: in the hip, we see a slight bump with a change in velocity in early extension; in the knee, leveling off in extension with a distinct peak just prior to flexion; and in the ankle, a dip is observed in the middle of extension, just after touch down.

The joint trajectories could likely be improved through further tuning of the motor network. It has been shown that given a reliable oscillator, the limit cycle can be reshaped with a mapping function [1]. Treating the motor circuit as a mapping function to the muscle activation, this network could be tuned to reshape the input from the sequence generator to better control muscle activation during locomotion. The neural model presented in this work also does not incorporate type II muscle feedback. In other works, which used more traditional half-center oscillators, the type II feedback was used as feedback to the pattern generator networks, helping to control the timing of the transition from flexion to extension and vice versa [14,29]. As the sequence generator presented in this work is constructed as a pool of neurons, it is unclear how to integrate this feedback to achieve a similar impact. Through further analysis of the BSG, Lindén et al. discovered that specific neurons in the network had a more significant impact on the frequency and amplitude of the limit cycle than others. Based on the similar dynamics, it is likely that our network has similar properties, and these neurons would be ideal in integrating the type II feedback. However, further analysis of the sequence generator presented in this work is needed to find such neurons and integrate the feedback.

It should also be noted that the simplified biomechanical model using antagonistic muscle pairs may have also contributed to the differences in joint trajectories shown in Fig. 6. While this simplification is sufficiently able to produce locomotive behavior, it is vastly different than muscle control and coordination of all 38 muscles in the rat hindlimb [36]. We hypothesize that for controlling the more complex model, instead of assigning specific regions for flexion and extension in the sequence generator (see Fig. 5), we can designate small windows of neurons in the sequence generator to connect to motor neurons controlling these muscles, aligning the activity of the sequence generator with muscle activity for each individual muscle. Controlling biomechanical models with these complex muscle synergies is difficult with the half-center model, as not all of the muscles can be classified as flexors or extensors and may be active during both phases. Some half-center models have countered this argument by including additional pattern generators, using the combination of signals to control muscle synergies [13]. However, these additional half-centers add to the complexity of the neural model, leading to the need for further tuning and a more computationally expensive model. To expand the sequence generator model described in

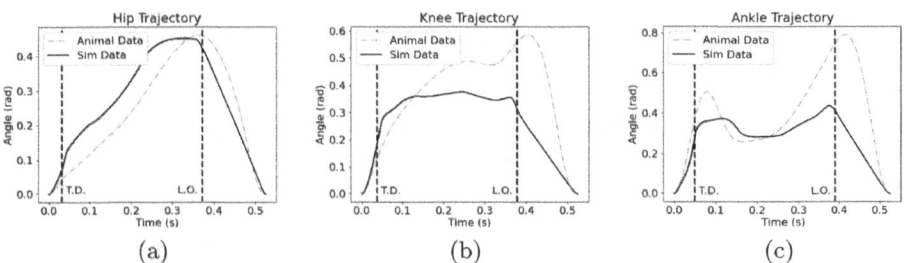

Fig. 6. Joint trajectories for animal and simulated data. The axes were shifted such that both lines start at zero. (a) Hip Joint Trajectory. (b) Knee Joint Trajectory. (c) Ankle Joint Trajectory. T.D. and L.O. indicate touch down and lift off, respectfully, for the simulated data.

this work to more complex muscle synergies, some additional tuning would be required to connect to the additional motor circuits. However, this tuning would be restricted to these lower level circuits, as opposed to the half-center models which require additional tuning to both the lower level circuits and to the additional half-centers involved in driving the rhythmic activity. Future works will expand the biomechanical model to include the full array of muscles in the hindlimb.

5   Conclusion

This study introduces a method of designing a network to model the rhythmic activity in the spinal cord and demonstrates its ability to control a biomechanical model of rat hindlimbs. Through integration with a biomechanical simulation, our neural model successfully controlled antagonistic muscle pairs, resulting in joint trajectories that exhibit similarities to those observed in rats during locomotion. Future work will focus on developing more biologically accurate models and improving joint trajectories. This can be achieved by fine-tuning the motor network and incorporating type II muscle feedback into the sequence generator. Additionally, expanding our biomechanical model to include the full array of muscles in the hindlimb would provide a more comprehensive understanding of how to control muscle synergies during locomotion. It is also important to understand how this model behaves compared to other neural models, future work will explore a comparison of this neural controller to others in the field.

References

1. Ajallooeian, M., Van Den Kieboom, J., Mukovskiy, A., Giese, M.A., Ijspeert, A.J.: A general family of morphed nonlinear phase oscillators with arbitrary limit cycle shape **263**, 41–56 (2013). https://doi.org/10.1016/j.physd.2013.07.016
2. Alessandro, C., Rellinger, B.A., Barroso, F.O., Tresch, M.C.: Adaptation after vastus lateralis denervation in rats demonstrates neural regulation of joint stresses and strains **7**, e38215 (2018). https://doi.org/10.7554/eLife.38215
3. Alexander, R.M.: Three uses for springs in legged locomotion **9**(2), 53–61. https://doi.org/10.1177/027836499000900205
4. Beer, R.D., Quinn, R.D., Chiel, H.J., Ritzmann, R.E.: Biologically inspired approaches to robotics: what can we learn from insects? **40**(3), 30–38 (1997). https://doi.org/10.1145/245108.245118
5. Beiran, M., Dubreuil, A., Valente, A., Mastrogiuseppe, F., Ostojic, S.: Shaping dynamics with multiple populations in low-rank recurrent networks **33**(6), 1572–1615 (2021). https://doi.org/10.1162/neco_a_01381

6. Berg, R., Komi, S., Dmytriyeva, O., Houser, G., Bonfils, M., Kaur, J.: Pedunculopontine-stimulation obstructs hippocampal theta rhythm and halts movement (2024). https://doi.org/10.21203/rs.3.rs-3876253/v1
7. Brown, T.G.: On the nature of the fundamental activity of the nervous centres; together with an analysis of the conditioning of rhythmic activity in progression, and a theory of the evolution of function in the nervous system **48**(1), 18–46 (1914). https://doi.org/10.1113/jphysiol.1914.sp001646
8. Catalano, M.G., Pollayil, M.J., Grioli, G., Valsecchi, G., Kolvenbach, H., Hutter, M., Bicchi, A., Garabini, M.: Adaptive feet for quadrupedal walkers **38**(1), 302–316 (2022). https://doi.org/10.1109/TRO.2021.3088060
9. Chevallier, S., Jan Ijspeert, A., Ryczko, D., Nagy, F., Cabelguen, J.M.: Organisation of the spinal central pattern generators for locomotion in the salamander: biology and modelling **57**(1), 147–161 (2008). https://doi.org/10.1016/j.brainresrev.2007.07.006
10. Chiel, H.J., Beer, R.D.: The brain has a body: adaptive behavior emerges from interactions of nervous system, body and environment **20**(12), 553–557. https://doi.org/10.1016/S0166-2236(97)01149-1
11. Cofer, D., Cymbalyuk, G., Reid, J., Zhu, Y., Heitler, W.J., Edwards, D.H.: Animat-Lab: a 3d graphics environment for neuromechanical simulations **187**(2), 280–288 (2010). https://doi.org/10.1016/j.jneumeth.2010.01.005
12. Delp, S.L., Anderson, F.C., Arnold, A.S., Loan, P., Habib, A., John, C.T., Guendelman, E., Thelen, D.G.: OpenSim: open-source software to create and analyze dynamic simulations of movement **54**(11), 1940–1950. https://doi.org/10.1109/TBME.2007.901024
13. Deng, K., Hunt, A.J., Chiel, H.J., Quinn, R.D.: Biarticular muscles improve the stability of a neuromechanical model of the rat hindlimb. In: Meder, F., Hunt, A., Margheri, L., Mura, A., Mazzolai, B. (eds.) Biomimetic and Biohybrid Systems, pp. 20–37. Springer Nature Switzerland (2023). https://doi.org/10.1007/978-3-031-39504-8_2
14. Deng, K., Szczecinski, N.S., Arnold, D., Andrada, E., Fischer, M.S., Quinn, R.D., Hunt, A.J.: Neuromechanical model of rat hindlimb walking with two-layer CPGs **4**(1), 21 (2019). https://doi.org/10.3390/biomimetics4010021
15. Deng, K., Szczecinski, N.S., Hunt, A.J., Chiel, H.J., Quinn, R.D.: Kinematic and kinetic analysis of a biomechanical model of rat hind limb with biarticular muscles. In: Vouloutsi, V., Mura, A., Tauber, F., Speck, T., Prescott, T.J., Verschure, P.F.M.J. (eds.) Biomimetic and Biohybrid Systems, vol. 12413, pp. 55–67. Springer International Publishing (2020). https://doi.org/10.1007/978-3-030-64313-3_7
16. Grillner, S., Zangger, P.: Locomotor movements generated by deafferented spinal-cord. In: Acta Physiologica Scandinavica, vol. 91, pp. A38–A39. Blackwell Science Ltd PO BOX 88, Osney Mead, Oxford, Oxon, England OX2 0NE (1974)
17. Grillner, S., Zangger, P.: On the central generation of locomotion in the low spinal cat **34**(2) (1979). https://doi.org/10.1007/BF00235671
18. Grillner, S.: Biological pattern generation: the cellular and computational logic of networks in motion **52**(5), 751–766 (2006). https://doi.org/10.1016/j.neuron.2006.11.008

19. Guertin, P.A.: The mammalian central pattern generator for locomotion **62**(1), 45–56 (2009). https://doi.org/10.1016/j.brainresrev.2009.08.002
20. Hill, A.V.: The heat of shortening and the dynamic constants of muscle **126**(843), 136–195 (1938). https://doi.org/10.1098/rspb.1938.0050
21. Ivashko, D., Prilutsky, B., Markin, S., Chapin, J., Rybak, I.: Modeling the spinal cord neural circuitry controlling cat hindlimb movement during locomotion **52–54**, 621–629 (2003). https://doi.org/10.1016/S0925-2312(02)00832-9
22. Jackson, C., Chardon, M., Wang, Y.C., Rudi, J., Tresch, M., Heckman, C.J., Quinn, R.D.: Multimodal parameter inference for a canonical motor microcircuit control-ling rat hindlimb motion. In: Meder, F., Hunt, A., Margheri, L., Mura, A., Mazzo-lai, B. (eds.) Biomimetic and Biohybrid Systems, vol. 14158, pp. 38–51. Springer Nature Switzerland (2023). https://doi.org/10.1007/978-3-031-39504-8_3
23. Johnson, W.L., Jindrich, D.L., Roy, R.R., Reggie Edgerton, V.: A three-dimensional model of the rat hindlimb: musculoskeletal geometry and muscle moment arms **41**(3), 610–619. https://doi.org/10.1016/j.jbiomech.2007.10.004
24. Lindén, H., Petersen, P.C., Vestergaard, M., Berg, R.W.: Movement is governed by rotational neural dynamics in spinal motor networks **610**(7932), 526–531 (2022). https://doi.org/10.1038/s41586-022-05293-w
25. Massarelli, N., Yau, A., Hoffman, K., Kiemel, T., Tytell, E.: Understanding loco-motor rhythm in the lamprey central pattern generator. In: Letzter, G., et al. (eds.) Advances in the Mathematical Sciences, vol. 6, pp. 157–172. Springer International Publishing (2016). https://doi.org/10.1007/978-3-319-34139-2_6
26. McCrea, D.A., Rybak, I.A.: Organization of mammalian locomotor rhythm and pattern generation **57**(1), 134–146 (2008). https://doi.org/10.1016/j.brainresrev.2007.08.006
27. Melo, K., Horvat, T., Ijspeert, A.J.: Minimalist design of a 3-axis passive compliant foot for sprawling posture robots. In: 2019 2nd IEEE International Conference on Soft Robotics (RoboSoft), pp. 788–794. IEEE (2019). https://doi.org/10.1109/ROBOSOFT.2019.8722792
28. Nourse, W.R.P., Jackson, C., Szczecinski, N.S., Quinn, R.D.: SNS-toolbox: an open source tool for designing synthetic nervous systems and interfacing them with cyber-physical systems **8**(2), 247 (2023). https://doi.org/10.3390/biomimetics8020247
29. Rybak, I.A., Stecina, K., Shevtsova, N.A., McCrea, D.A.: Modelling spinal circuitry involved in locomotor pattern generation: insights from the effects of afferent stim-ulation **577**(2), 641–658 (2006). https://doi.org/10.1113/jphysiol.2006.118711
30. Selverston, A.: The stomatogastric ganglion. In: Reference Module in Neuroscience and Biobehavioral Psychology, p. B9780128093245211668. Elsevier (2017). https://doi.org/10.1016/B978-0-12-809324-5.21166-8
31. Seth, A., et al.: OpenSim: Simulating musculoskeletal dynamics and neuromuscular control to study human and animal movement **14**(7), e1006223. https://doi.org/10.1371/journal.pcbi.1006223
32. Strogatz, S.H.: Nonlinear dynamics and chaos: with applications to physics, biology, chemistry, and engineering, pp. 198–212. Westview Press, a member of the Perseus Books Group, second edition edn. (2015), OCLC: ocn842877119
33. Szczecinski, N.S., Hunt, A.J., Quinn, R.D.: A functional subnetwork approach to designing synthetic nervous systems that control legged robot locomotion **11**, 37 (2017). https://doi.org/10.3389/fnbot.2017.00037

34. Todorov, E., Erez, T., Tassa, Y.: Mujoco: A physics engine for model-based control. In: 2012 IEEE/RSJ International Conference on Intelligent Robots and Systems, pp. 5026–5033. IEEE (2012). https://doi.org/10.1109/IROS.2012.6386109
35. Virtanen, P., et al.: SciPy 1.0: fundamental algorithms for scientific computing in python **17**(3), 261–272 (2020). https://doi.org/10.1038/s41592-019-0686-2
36. Young, F., Rode, C., Hunt, A., Quinn, R.: Analyzing moment arm profiles in a full-muscle rat hindlimb model **4**(1), 10 (2019). https://doi.org/10.3390/biomimetics4010010

Multilevel Synthetic Nervous System Control for Legged Locomotion

Ryan Grummer⬤, Clayton B. Jackson$^{(\boxtimes)}$⬤, and Roger D. Quinn⬤

Department of Mechanical and Aerospace Engineering,
Case Western Reserve University, Cleveland, OH 44106, USA
cxj271@case.edu

Abstract. Animals have multiple neurological levels of locomotive control, in vertebrates these can range from the spinal cord and cerebellum to the motor cortex in the upper levels of the brain. The multilevel synthetic nervous system controller presented in this paper was developed to investigate how these systems may be structured. This controller is shown to allow a rat hindlimb to express animal-like behaviors in response to its environment, adjusting its gait and stepping over a perceived obstacle after approaching it. This was achieved by organizing simulated neurons into a higher level controller inspired by the motor cortex. In mammals, the motor cortex influences the behavior of the lower level circuits such as those in the spinal cord, allowing the animal to adapt its environment. The network outlined in this paper shows a proof of concept for a synthetic nervous system with higher level adjustments of a lower level system to adapt legged gaits.

Keywords: Synthetic Nervous System · Controls · Locomotion

1 Introduction

Complex locomotive behaviors are necessary for animals to survive in the wide range of environments that they must traverse throughout their lives. They may need to climb up slopes, step over obstacles, speed up or slow down their walking or perform countless other behaviors that are slight variations on common locomotion. In order to plan and execute these behaviors higher processes must adjust and direct lower level controllers. In the mammalian brain, the cerebral cortex is responsible for a wide variety of high level functions, such as reasoning, decision making, and memory [3,5,14,25]. Contained within the cerebral cortex is the motor cortex, an area highly correlated with motor control and actions [31]. It has been shown that the motor cortex is capable of influencing many lower level neural systems, from more primitive regions like the cerebellum and brain stem, to motor neurons that interface with the muscles in the body [7,15,16,24]. This influence allows animals to adjust their habitual behaviors in

This work was supported by NSF DBI 2015317 as part of the NSF/CIHR/DFG/FRQ/UKRI-MRC Next Generation Networks for Neuroscience Program

N. S. Szczecinski et al. (Eds.): Living Machines 2024, LNAI 14930, pp. 382–396, 2025.
https://doi.org/10.1007/978-3-031-72597-5_26

response to stimuli [8,19]. The motor cortex is essential for skilled locomotion, as significant impairments to complex locomotive abilities appear in rats with damage to this region [10]. In this paper, a multilevel synthetic nervous system was developed to investigate how a higher level system might influence a lower level system to control legged movements. Synthetic nervous systems (SNS's) are networks of dynamic, mathematically modeled, and simulated neurons connected to mimic neural structures and behaviors in animals [28]. It follows that stacked SNS structures would also likely gain the greater capabilities of stacked neural structures in animals.

The concept of having multiple subsections of a synthetic nervous system network has existed in a number of previous networks, although their purposes were different. For example, the locomotive network developed by Deng et al. [6], was constructed as a multilayered CPG network. In that case the two layers of the network allowed for separate control of the gait frequency and amplitude, while also resulting in a more robust controller in response to perturbations [6]. This separate control was essential for the development of the stepping network described in this paper. However, both layers of pattern generators acted at the "spinal cord" level, working together to produce basic locomotion. Other works have looked at incorporating supraspinal signals, but generally focus on the effect of these signals to transition between a walk, trot, and gallop [4,22].

The cockroach synthetic nervous system controller developed by Rubeo et al. [20] shares more similarities in complex locomotive behavior, although its function still appears as that of a lower process. This cockroach SNS uses an upper level controller to organize its various legs (each with their own intermediate and lower level controllers), directing its legs to allow for standing and stable walking behaviors in multiple directions. Additionally there are sub-networks to make other adjustments such as body height control and freezing the tarsus in the stance position. However, these behaviors do not have the same sort of planning, working memory and response capabilities displayed in the rat stepping network described in this paper. This makes the Rubeo et al. [20] cockroach higher level controller more in line with an intermediate neurological stage in an animal central nervous system.

Multilevel control systems have been previously developed for robots and are clearly outlined in Brooks et al. [1]. Repurposing of lower level systems is used to manifest the more complex desired behaviors of the higher level controllers. This enabled the robot to avoid obstacles and even pathfind to achieve movement goals. While the controller presented in this paper is designed to step over obstacles rather than steer around them, the controllers share similar core structures. The key difference being that the network presented in this paper uses a more biomimetic controller, an SNS, on a more biomimetic "robot", a rat hindlimb. This allows our network to offer a better look into how biological systems may operate, compared to previous multilevel controllers that aimed to make a more capable robot with little interest in what solving these problems might suggest about biology.

We believe layering multiple levels of SNS controllers will allow the hindlimb to express more advanced locomotive behaviors and enable the model to adapt its gait to its environment, while still maintaining a high level of biological feasibility. The network presented in this paper was created as a conceptual demonstration with this overall goal in mind.

2   Methods

2.1   Models

The modeling in this work made use of separate neural and physics modeling platforms, integrating them with a forward Euler method using a time step of 0.075 ms. The biomechanical model was generated in Mujoco, a physics engine designed to simulate biomechanics which can be controlled in Python [29]. The neural controller was designed in SNS-Toolbox, a package in Python developed to design and simulate SNS's [18].

The biomechanical model of the rat hindlimbs used in this work was adapted from previous works in biomechanics [6,11]. The skeleton model has been adapted from Johnson et al. [12], while the muscle attachment points were derived from Deng et al. (2019) [6]. Mujoco implements a Hill type muscle model, where the force generated can be found using the equation [29]:

$$F_M = \Big(F_L(L) \cdot F_v(v) \cdot A(V_{MN}) + F_P(L) \Big) \cdot F_0 \tag{1}$$

where F_L is the active force as a function of length, L , F_v is the active force as a function of velocity, v, F_0 is the peak active force, F_P is the passive force, and A is the muscle activation as a function of the corresponding motor neuron potential, V_{MN}. In this work, we use a sigmoid muscle activation function which was derived from Deng et al. (2019) [6]. Default muscle parameters were used in the biomechanical model, meaning that Mujoco computes the muscle properties when compiling the model. Examples of these functions, as implemented in Mujoco, along with the rat hindlimbs model are shown in Fig. 1 [29].

The neural model used in this work, as implemented by SNS-Toolbox [18], is the non-spiking leaky integrator model. The neural dynamics are represented by the equation:

$$C\frac{dV}{dt} = -I_{leak} + I_{app} + \sum_{i=1}^{n} I_{syn_i} \tag{2}$$

where C is the membrane capacitance, V is the membrane potential, I_{leak} is the membrane leak current, I_{app} is an applied current, and I_{syn_i} are the synaptic currents. The leak current, which is a function of the membrane conductance, G, the neurons resting potential, E_R, and the membrane potential, is given by the equation:

$$I_{leak} = G \cdot (V(t) - E_R). \tag{3}$$

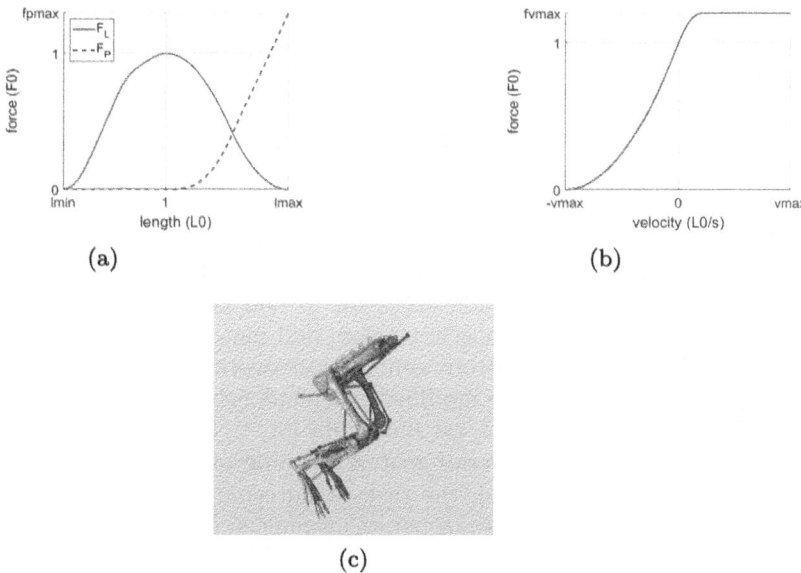

Fig. 1. Rat Hindlimb and Muscle Models in Mujoco. (a) Force-Length and passive force curves. (b) Force-Velocity curve. In (a) and (b) *lmin*, *lmax*, and *vmax* are computed in the compiler [29]. (c) Rat Hindlimb model in Mujoco. The red lines represent the muscles. (Color figure online)

The synaptic currents are modeled as conductance-based synapses with a piece-wise function:

$$I_{syn_i} = g_{max_i} \cdot \min \left(\max \left(\frac{V_{pre} - E_{lo_i}}{E_{hi_i} - E_{lo_i}}, 0 \right), 1 \right) \cdot (E_{syn_i} - V(t)) \qquad (4)$$

where g_{max} is the maximum synaptic conductance, V_{pre} is the membrane potential of the pre-synaptic neuron, E_{hi_i} and E_{lo_i} are saturation and threshold parameters, respectively, and E_{syn_i} are the synaptic reversal potentials.

2.2   Network Design

The multilevel SNS presented in this paper was designed with the goal of having a system that can receive stimulus corresponding to a perceived obstacle in its path and be able to step over it. This stimulus will be of varying magnitude, which corresponds to the height of the obstacle, and will be applied one second before the system reaches its perceived obstacle. There is no real obstacle in the simulation; rather, a stimulus is used to mimic visual input. This causes the system to behave as if an obstacle were present, adjusting its gait to step over the imaginary obstruction during the swing phase. Thus, the addition of this higher level system will allow the SNS to show more complex behaviors like planning (in adjusting its gait cycle) and memory (in remembering that it will need to take a step when it reaches the obstacle). The lower level system used as a base is the two-layer central pattern generator (CPG) SNS for a rat hindlimb was adapted from Deng et al. [6], and other models [17,21,23,26,27]. The network is composed of two layers of pattern generator networks modeled as half-center oscillators: the rhythm generator (RG) and the pattern formation (PF) layer. The RG controls the overall timing for the leg, while the PF layer manages specific joint movements (one PF layer for the hip and one for the knee and ankle). The PF networks then connect to motor circuits, which consist of motor neurons, type Ia inhibitory neurons, Renshaw cells, and interneurons for afferent feedback. In this model, we include types Ia, Ib and type II feedback, which corresponds to muscle velocity, muscle tension, and muscle length, respectively. The use of multiple layers of pattern generator networks allows the system to have its frequency and amplitude modified independently, which is essential for modifying the walking cycle of the rat hindlimbs [6].

In order to accomplish the overall goal of stepping over an obstacle of arbitrary size and time of occurrence, the tasks of altering the gait and stepping over the obstacle were split into two separate systems: a stepping network and a gait network. The stepping (or bump) network would have the tasks of storing the magnitude of the stimulus, counting the number of steps to take until the obstacle will be reached and making the lower level system take a larger step when it is reached based on the magnitude of the stimulus. The gait network would be responsible for deciding how to alter the gait based on when the stimulus was applied, as well as storing this information and providing adjustment to the lower level gait accordingly. This allows the rat to reach the obstacle at the proper point in its walking cycle to step over it. Before making either of these networks however, a basic form of memory would be needed to store information (how much to change the gait, how big of a step to take, etc.) until the obstacle is reached. For this purpose, the memory module, shown in Fig. 2a, was developed.

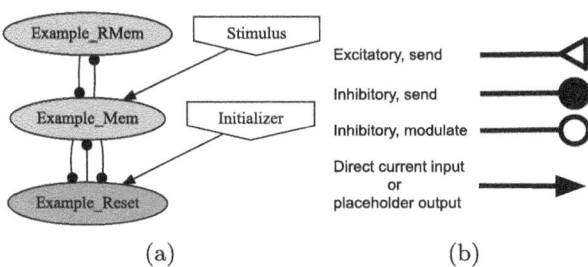

(a)   (b)

Fig. 2. (a) Full memory module. The colored ovals represent neurons while the white pentagons represent inputs to the network. (b) Synapse legend

This memory module features a pair of neurons combined as an integrator (Example RMem and Example Mem) [28]. The main memory, Example Mem, is by default being inhibited to its minimum by the reset neuron, Example Reset.

As a result, the reverse memory neuron, Example RMem, is pushed to its maximum. The memory neuron has two inhibitory synapses going to the reset neuron, one of which inhibits the reset neuron when the memory neuron is below its natural minimum to ensure that the reset neuron does not continue attempting to push the memory neuron lower below its natural minimum. This synapse decreases the downtime of the memory network after excessive stimulus is applied to the reset neuron. The other inhibitory synapse is only used in some of the memory modules, depending on application. It is a "hold value" synapse that keeps the reset neuron from bringing the memory neuron down to its minimum whenever the memory neuron is storing a value over a certain threshold. Meaning that the reset neuron requires an external stimulus to actually begin resetting the memory neuron, while instances without the "hold value" synapse will automatically begin resetting unless the reset neuron is being externally inhibited. Additionally, the reset neuron requires an initialization excitatory stimulus when the network is booted up in order to get the system into its proper default state.

With this groundwork in place, the stepping network (shown in Fig. 3a) was constructed around two memory modules, one to retain the magnitude of the stimulus and one to count the number of steps the hindlimb has taken so the hindlimb will take its step at the proper moment after the proper delay. The stimulus is applied to the bump memory neuron, which then holds that value while also inhibiting the reset neuron for the step counting memory module, allowing it to start counting the number of steps based on the type II hip flexion neuron (as hip motion was found to give the most reliable indication of position in the gait cycle). After the correct number of steps have been counted, the Mag Stop neuron is inhibited at the start of the swing phase of the gait. This in turn allows the Mag Boost neuron to apply stimulation to the motor neurons, leading to an increase in step size. After the system takes its larger step, it is reset by the combination of Mag Boost neuron activity and the type II hip extension neuron detecting that the leg has reached the end of its swing phase. As the activity of the type II hip neuron corresponds with the length of the hip extensor muscle, the neuron is most active at the end of swing, when this muscle is longest during the gait cycle. This implementation of stimulation from a higher level directly to the motor neurons is based on the corticospinal tract, which in humans and many larger mammals allows the motor cortex to directly control motor neurons [2, 13, 15]. The corticospinal tract does not reach quite that low into the system in rats [30], however this was determined to be an acceptable compromise in biological accuracy. This network is meant to be a proof-of-concept for a multilevel structure. It should be noted that applying negative stimulus to the bump memory reset neuron at the same time as the stimulus to bump memory neuron greatly improved the reliability of the network and was done for all tests. Without this, the network occasionally failed to latch onto the stimulus when the bump memory reset neuron was being excited by the type II hip extension neuron.

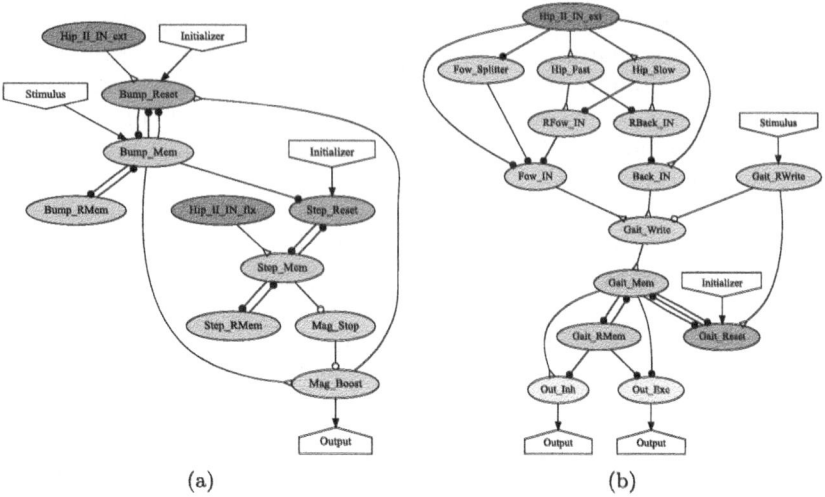

(a)   (b)

Fig. 3. Higher level networks. (a) Stepping network. (b) Gait adjustment network. See Fig. 2b for the synaptic legend.

The gait network (pictured in Fig. 3b) uses a single memory module that stores a signal proportional to the point in the gait cycle when the stimulus was initially applied. However, this system is more complex than the stepping network due to the mapping function necessary to change the pseudo-sine wave of hip swings into a useful representation of different points in the gait cycle. The set of neurons between the Hip II IN ext neuron and Gait Write neuron does this mapping. As the position value increases, the value of Fow IN decreases while that of Back IN increases. The velocity value (derived via a derivative network of the hip position [28]) chooses which of the Fow/Back IN neurons feeds into Gait Write. This creates a linear ramp mapping position in the gait cycle to output current, lowest at the start of the swing phase and highest at the end of the stance phase. The Fow Splitter Neuron splits the stance phase part of the ramp to high and low sections to recenter the ramp about the middle of the swing phase of the gait. Gait Write constantly receives this mapping but only reaches enough voltage to actually write to the gait memory neuron when the Gait RWrite neuron is suppressed by the stimulus. In the gait network the stimulus is negative current of the same value as the stimulus to the stepping network. This stored position of the initial stimulus in the gait cycle is fed into the Out Inh and Out Exc neurons to inhibit and excite the rhythm generator CPG of the lower level network, thus slowing down and speeding up the pace of the gait, respectively. Missing from Fig. 2 is that the Mag Boost neuron in the stepping network excites the Gait Reset neuron, resetting the gait network as soon as the hindlimb takes its larger step so that the pace of the hindlimb walk is only altered for the relevant time period. A diagram of the full network, with both higher level and lower level systems implemented, is pictured in Fig. 4.

Some crucial behaviors can only be implemented due to the combination of the two networks. Most importantly, the system sees four peaks of hip extension (and thus four steps) when stimulus is applied during the latter half of the stance phase of its gait but only three steps otherwise. This is because that timing of stimulus application requires the gait be sped up the most to reach the perceived obstacle during the swing phase. Speeding up the gait decreases the size of the stride, thus decreasing the magnitude of the type II hip neuron wave. This decreases the stimulus to the step counter on each step just enough so that at very fast walking speeds the counter must count four steps instead of three to activate the magnitude boost neuron.

3   Results

When combined, these higher level controllers in the network allowed the hindlimb to respond to an external stimulus (perception of an incoming obstacle), adjust its gait and step over the perceived obstacle. This is shown in Fig. 5a, where the right foot of the model is noticeably higher than the model without the stimulus representing an obstacle (Fig. 5b. Although the network succeeded in its overall goals, it was unable to adjust its gait for some scenarios and could not effectively alter the height of the step as intended. Plots of the knee joint angle results of various stimulus scenarios are shown in Fig. 6.

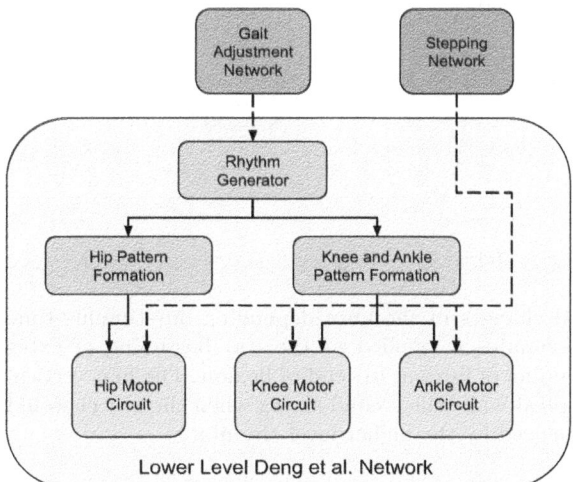

Fig. 4. Full multilevel network. Dashed lines indicate connections only activated due to the external stimulus.

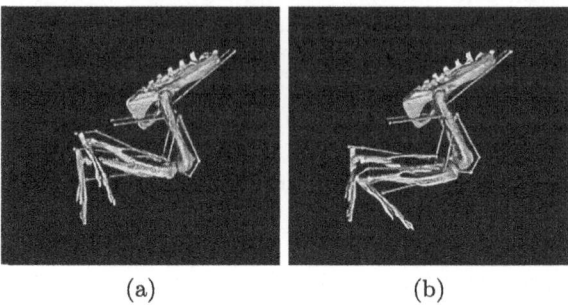

Fig. 5. Simulation of rat walking with adjusted gaits comparison. (a) Model stepping over an obstacle. (b) Model with normal gait. It can be seen that the right foot in (a) is lifted higher during the swing phase, simulating the behavior of the animal stepping over an object.

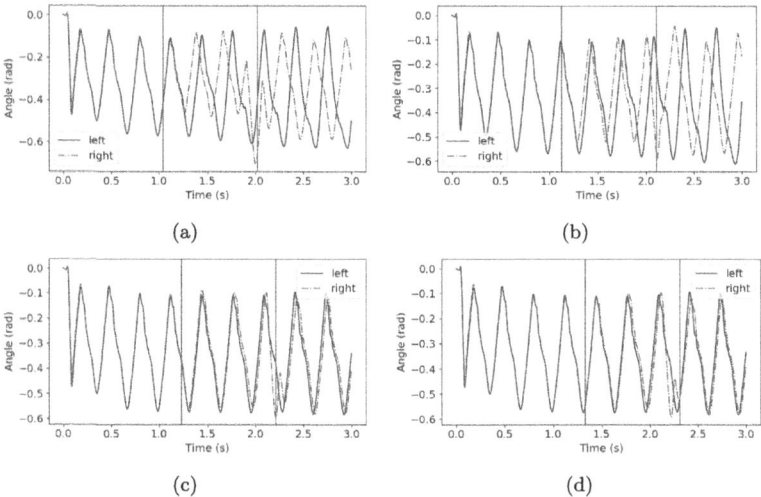

Fig. 6. Gait speed changes in the knee depending on stimulus time, shown by knee joint angle. The stimulus is applied at the: (a) beginning of extension, (b) end of extension (c) beginning of flexion, (d) end of flexion. The first vertical line shows when the stimulus is applied while the second shows when the object would be reached. The left leg is not influenced by the higher level circuits.

As seen, the network is capable of altering the gait from large speed increases (up to $\approx 20\%$ faster) to small speed decreases ($\approx 5\%$ slower). These successes are seen as the step (represented as a dip in the knee joint angle) occurs at the second vertical line in Fig. 6. However, large speed decreases fail to manifest in the system, as seen in Fig. 6d. The higher level controller is able to hold the proper signal to accomplish this, as shown in Fig. 7, by the output neurons of the gait network. However, this signal is not able to decrease the speed of the rhythm generator below a certain amount.

Figure 6a also shows the property of the large speed increase region to take four steps rather than the three that are needed for the other regions. A comparison between the stepping network for a four step and three step case are shown in Fig. 8. This difference arises from the slightly smaller range of hip angles covered by the rat walking when it has a faster gait, which has been

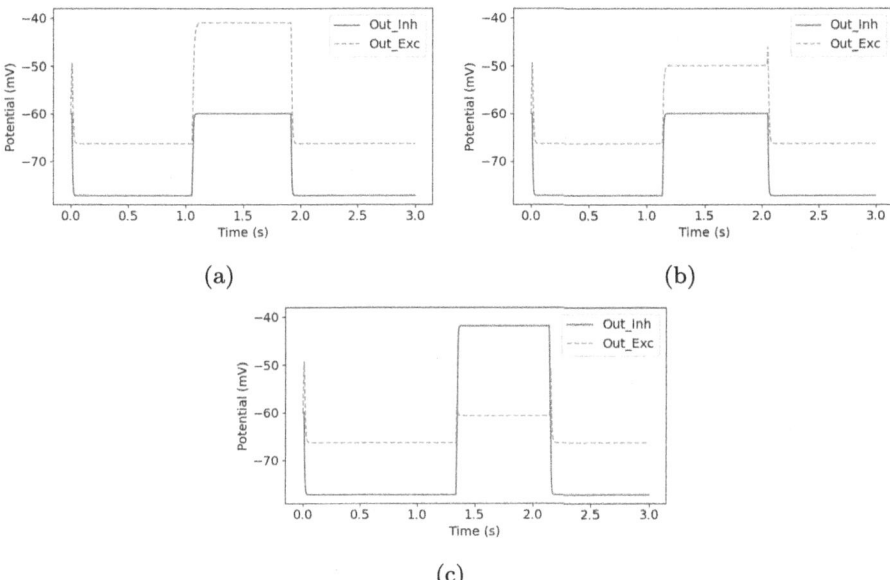

Fig. 7. Gait network response with stimulus applied at the: (a) beginning of extension, (b) end of extension, (c) beginning of flexion. (a) Results in a large speed increase. (b) Results in a small speed increase. (c) Results in a large speed decrease.

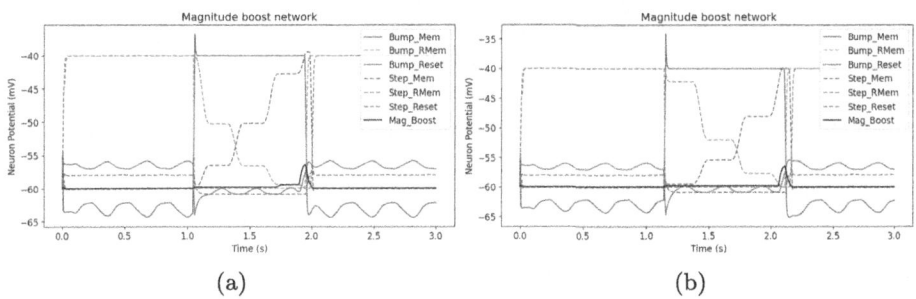

Fig. 8. Demonstration of the network's ability to count different numbers of steps based on when the obstacle will be reached. (a) Large speed increase results in counting 4 steps. (b) Slight speed increase results in counting 3 steps.

tuned such that the transfer between three and four step activation happens at the correct initialization point in the gait cycle. However this system does have a breakdown, as shown in Fig. 9, when attempting to vary the magnitude of the input stimulus as originally intended.

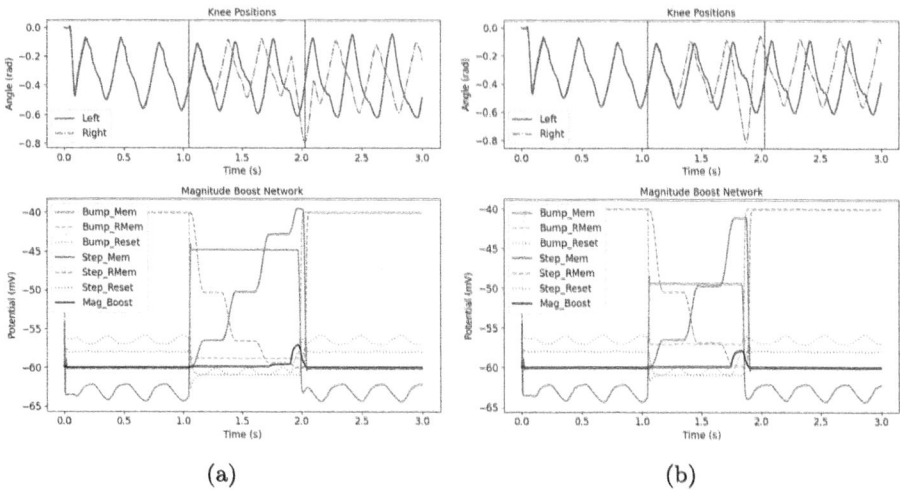

Fig. 9. Effect of varying stimulus on network result. (a) 14 nA stimulus. (b) 12 nA stimulus.

While the four step activation can be maintained down to 14 nA of stimulation (all previous results were run at 17 nA of stimulation), past this the relationship begins to break down. This means the hindlimb may take its step slightly before it reaches the perceived obstacle. This is because the decreasing stimulus changes the way the gait network responds, leading to a slower gait than should be used. Thus, a three step activation rather than a four step activation. Additionally, when stimulation to the gait network is kept constant the changing response of the minimum knee angle (and thus step size) is highly inconsistent with the goals. This often results in larger minimum knee angles (and thus larger steps) even though the value stored in bump memory is lower. This effect can be seen by comparing the knee angle graph in Figs. 9a (14 nA stimulus) and 6a (17 nA stimulus). The code used to develop this SNS is openly available at https://github.com/RGrummer/Step-Multilevel-SNS.

4   Discussion

4.1   Future Network Improvements

While the synthetic nervous system presented in this paper acts as a proof of concept for multilevel synthetic nervous system controls, it failed to achieve some of the goals of this work. Interestingly, the gait network is unable to manifest large decreases in speed of the rhythm generators of the lower level network. The reason the system fails in this regard is that the rhythm generator for the lower level system has feedback from the type II hip neurons. These forcibly flip the CPG when they reach a certain hip joint angle. For increasing the gait frequency (and thus shortening the stride) this has no effect as the rhythm generator will flip on its own before reaching that threshold. However, when decreasing the frequency (and thus increasing in stride) the hip feedback dominates the system. In order to manage this, the outputs from the gait network should influence the hip feedback rather than the CPG itself. To solve this problem, one may choose to have the outputs of the gait network influence the type II hip neurons directly, although this would require separate type II hip neurons for the higher level networks and other parts of the system that depend on those neurons. Alternatively, interneurons could be placed between the type II hip neurons and the rhythm generator to act as a buffer adjusted by the gait network. While this has the disadvantage of requiring modification of the lower level network to allow it to work, it would be more realistic than adjusting the type II hip neurons themselves and having multiples of those same sensors.

Another issue found in this work was the inability to adjust the step size of the biomechanical model based on the magnitude of the stimulus to the gait adjustment network, which represented an obstacle. Fixing the issues with the stimulus altering the gait network response could be fixed with something as simple as having a single unified stimulus neuron which receives the stimulus and distributes it everywhere else. Having different synapses for the different networks would allow the signal going to the gait network to remain relatively constant in magnitude, despite variations in input to the stimulus neuron, while the signal to the stepping network would reflect these differences more accurately. The greater problem of the failure to adjust step size, however, is localized within the gait network. Due to the way in which the magnitude boost neuron resets the system, a smaller magnitude boost neuron voltage (intended to result in a smaller step) will last longer than a larger voltage. This leads to a larger step because the smaller signal to the motor neurons persists for a longer duration than it would otherwise. Fixing this problem would require a redesign of the reset method for the stepping network. Using an intermediate spiking neuron and synapse between the Hip II IN ext neuron and the Bump Reset neuron may help with this issue. Currently the reset voltage slowly ramps up to the threshold to reset the system. This process is based on a simple non-spiking synapse from the type II hip extensor neuron, making the response more susceptible to varying stimulation from the magnitude boost neuron. However, the complex relationship between the various memory modules, their resets, and the magnitude boost neuron makes any sort of response difficult to guarantee.

This network is successful as a proof-of-concept for how higher-level networks may influence motor activity. While this multilevel structure is manifested in biology as a consequence of progressive evolution, it provides an easy and flexible method to manifest complex, dynamic behaviors, especially when compared to making a purpose built system. Further, this multilevel approach allows more accurate investigation of biology through the design and testing of synthetic nervous systems, as it has an inherently biomimetic structure. Biologically informed synthetic nervous system design can give a strong understanding of why things manifest in nature as they do. Their designs can provide hypotheses for how currently indecipherable systems may operate in the very animals the system is trying to emulate.

Given the wide variety of behaviors animals express in response to their ever changing environments, it is no surprise that there are a plethora of network goals that could be researched further. Rodent forelimbs provide interesting avenues of research as well. Mice have been shown to use a multilevel cortico-cerebellar loop to enhance reaching behaviors with greater accuracy and success rates [9]. This sort of loop uses the spinal cord for base communications with the muscles, the motor cortex for generating the overall movement and feedback from the cerebellum to fine tune the movement. Thus, such a network would likely be more complex than the one developed in this paper.

Acknowledgments. A special thanks is given to Dr. Britton Sauerbrei for inspiring the concept of this network through his own work.

Disclosure of Interests. The author has no competing interests to declare that are relevant to the content of this article.

References

1. Brooks, R.: A robust layered control system for a mobile robot. IEEE J. Robot. Autom. **2**(1), 14–23 (1986). https://doi.org/10.1109/JRA.1986.1087032
2. Canty, A.J., Murphy, M.: Molecular mechanisms of axon guidance in the developing corticospinal tract. Prog. Neurobiol. **85**(2), 214–235 (2008). https://doi.org/10.1016/j.pneurobio.2008.02.001
3. Cerebral cortex: What it is, function & location (2022). https://my.clevelandclinic.org/health/articles/23073-cerebral-cortex
4. Danner, S.M., Shevtsova, N.A., Frigon, A., Rybak, I.A.: Computational modeling of spinal circuits controlling limb coordination and gaits in quadrupeds. eLife **6**, e31050 (2017). https://doi.org/10.7554/eLife.31050
5. deCharms, R.C., Zador, A.: Neural representation and the cortical code. Annu. Rev. Neurosci. **23**(1), 613–647 (2000). https://doi.org/10.1146/annurev.neuro.23.1.613
6. Deng, K., Szczecinski, N.S., Arnold, D., Andrada, E., Fischer, M.S., Quinn, R.D., Hunt, A.J.: Neuromechanical model of rat hindlimb walking with two-layer cpgs. Biomimetics **4**(1), (2019). https://doi.org/10.3390/biomimetics4010021
7. Donoghue, J.P., Sanes, J.N.: Motor areas of the cerebral cortex. J. Clin. Neurophysiol. Off. Publ. Am. Electroencephalographic Soc. **11**(4), 382–396 (1994)
8. Fogassi, L., Luppino, G.: Motor functions of the parietal lobe. Curr. Opin. Neurobiol. **15**(6), 626–631 (2005). https://doi.org/10.1016/j.conb.2005.10.015
9. Guo, J.Z., et al.: Disrupting cortico-cerebellar communication impairs dexterity. eLife **10**, e65906 (2021). https://doi.org/10.7554/eLife.65906

10. Hicks, S.P., D'Amato, C.J.: Motor-sensory cortex-corticospinal system and developing locomotion and placing in rats. Am. J. Anat. **143**(1), 1–42 (1975)

11. Jackson, C., Chardon, M., Wang, Y.C., Rudi, J., Tresch, M., Heckman, C.J., Quinn, R.D.: Multimodal parameter inference for a canonical motor microcircuit controlling rat hindlimb motion. In: Meder, F., Hunt, A., Margheri, L., Mura, A., Mazzolai, B. (eds.) Biomimetic and Biohybrid Systems, pp. 38–51. Springer Nature Switzerland (2023). https://doi.org/10.1007/978-3-031-39504-8_3

12. Johnson, W.L., Jindrich, D.L., Roy, R.R., Reggie Edgerton, V.: A three-dimensional model of the rat hindlimb: musculoskeletal geometry and muscle moment arms. J. Biomech. **41**(3), 610–619 (2008). https://doi.org/10.1016/j.jbiomech.2007.10.004

13. Koontz, D.W.: Corticospinal/corticobulbar tracts. In: Aminoff, M.J., Daroff, R.B. (eds.) Encyclopedia of the Neurological Sciences (Second Edition), pp. 879–880. Academic Press (2014). https://doi.org/10.1016/B978-0-12-385157-4.01140-4

14. Loeb, C., Poggio, G.F.: Neural Substrates of Memory, Affective Functions, and Conscious Experience, Advances in Anatomy, Embryology and Cell Biology, vol. 166. Springer Berlin Heidelberg (2002). https://doi.org/10.1007/978-3-642-59432-8

15. Lopes, G., Nogueira, J., Dimitriadis, G., Menendez, J.A., Paton, J.J., Kampff, A.R.: A robust role for motor cortex. Front. Neurosci. **17** (2023). https://doi.org/10.3389/fnins.2023.971980

16. Matelli, M., Luppino, G., Geyer, S., Zilles, K.: MOTOR CORTEX. In: The Human Nervous System, pp. 973–996. Elsevier (2004). https://doi.org/10.1016/B978-012547626-3/50027-2

17. McCrea, D.A., Rybak, I.A.: Organization of mammalian locomotor rhythm and pattern generation. Brain Res. Rev. **57**(1), 134–146 (2008). https://doi.org/10.1016/j.brainresrev.2007.08.006

18. Nourse, W.R.P., Jackson, C., Szczecinski, N.S., Quinn, R.D.: SNS-toolbox: an open source tool for designing synthetic nervous systems and interfacing them with cyber-physical systems. Biomimetics **8**(2), 247 (2023). https://doi.org/10.3390/biomimetics8020247

19. Rizzolatti, G., Luppino, G.: The cortical motor system. Neuron **31**(6), 889–901 (2001). https://doi.org/10.1016/S0896-6273(01)00423-8

20. Rubeo, S., Szczecinski, N., Quinn, R.: A synthetic nervous system controls a simulated cockroach. Appl. Sci. **8**(1) (2018). https://doi.org/10.3390/app8010006

21. Rybak, I.A., Shevtsova, N.A., Lafreniere-Roula, M., McCrea, D.A.: Modelling spinal circuitry involved in locomotor pattern generation: insights from deletions during fictive locomotion. J. Physiol. **577**(2), 617–639 (2006). https://doi.org/10.1113/jphysiol.2006.118703

22. Rybak, I.A., Shevtsova, N.A., Markin, S.N., Prilutsky, B.I., Frigon, A.: Operation regimes of spinal circuits controlling locomotion and role of supraspinal drives and sensory feedback (2024). https://doi.org/10.1101/2024.03.21.586122

23. Rybak, I.A., Stecina, K., Shevtsova, N.A., McCrea, D.A.: Modelling spinal circuitry involved in locomotor pattern generation: insights from the effects of afferent stimulation. J. Physiol. **577**(2), 641–658 (2006). https://doi.org/10.1113/jphysiol.2006.118711

24. Sanes, J.N.: Primary motor cortex. In: Weiner, I.B., Craighead, W.E. (eds.) The Corsini Encyclopedia of Psychology, pp. 1–2. Wiley, 1 edn. (2010). https://doi.org/10.1002/9780470479216.corpsy0707

25. Schröder, H., Moser, N., Huggenberger, S.: The mouse cerebral cortex. In: Schröder, H., Moser, N., Huggenberger, S. (eds.) Neuroanatomy of the Mouse: An Introduction, pp. 231–265. Springer International Publishing (2020). https://doi.org/10.1007/978-3-030-19898-5_10
26. Shevtsova, N.A., Hamade, K., Chakrabarty, S., Markin, S.N., Prilutsky, B.I., Rybak, I.A.: Modeling the Organization of Spinal Cord Neural Circuits Controlling Two-Joint Muscles, pp. 121–162. Springer New York, New York, NY (2016). https://doi.org/10.1007/978-1-4939-3267-2_5
27. Shevtsova, N.A., Rybak, I.A.: Organization of flexor-extensor interactions in the mammalian spinal cord: insights from computational modelling. J. Physiol. **594**(21), 6117–6131 (2016)
28. Szczecinski, N.S., Hunt, A.J., Quinn, R.D.: A functional subnetwork approach to designing synthetic nervous systems that control legged robot locomotion. Front. Neurorobot. **11**, (2017). https://doi.org/10.3389/fnbot.2017.00037
29. Todorov, E., Erez, T., Tassa, Y.: Mujoco: A physics engine for model-based control. In: 2012 IEEE/RSJ International Conference on Intelligent Robots and Systems, pp. 5026–5033. IEEE (2012). https://doi.org/10.1109/IROS.2012.6386109
30. Vahlsing, H.L., Feringa, E.R.: A ventral uncrossed corticospinal tract in the rat. Exp. Neurol. **70**(2), 282–287 (1980). https://doi.org/10.1016/0014-4886(80)90027-8
31. Yip, D.W., Lui, F.: Physiology, Motor Cortical. StatPearls Publishing, Treasure Island (FL) (2024)

Biohybrid Systems

Biocompatibility of Asiga Dental Resins Using a Low-Cost Printer for Biohybrid Actuator Applications

Ashlee S. Liao[1](✉)(iD), Kevin Dai[1](iD), Bhavya Chopra[1](iD), Saul Schaffer[1](iD),
Rebekah Adams[1](iD), Ji Min Seok[1](iD), Alaeddin Burak Irez[1,2,3](iD),
Yongjie Jessica Zhang[1,2](iD), and Victoria A. Webster-Wood[1,2,4](iD)

[1] Department of Mechanical Engineering, Carnegie Mellon University, Pittsburgh,
PA 15217, USA
{ashleel,kdai,bchopra,sschaffe,raadams,
jseok2,airez,jessicaz,vwebster}@andrew.cmu.edu
[2] Department of Biomedical Engineering, Carnegie Mellon University, Pittsburgh,
PA 15217, USA
[3] Department of Mechanical Engineering, Faculty of Mechanical Engineering,
Istanbul Technical University (ITU), Istanbul, Turkey
[4] McGowan Institute for Regenerative Medicine, University of Pittsburgh 4200 Fifth
Ave, Pittsburgh, PA 15260, USA
http://engineering.cmu.edu/borg,
https://www.meche.engineering.cmu.edu/faculty/zhang-computational-
bio-modeling-lab.html

Abstract. Biohybrid actuators and robots require the integration of
biological materials with synthetic materials. Synthetic materials provide structural support and attachment points for biological materials.
One technique for fabricating these synthetic support structures is 3D
printing. Although some 3D-printable resins have been designed to be
biocompatible, the process for assessing biocompatibility is not reported
consistently. Furthermore, the ISO 10993-1 standard emphasizes that
biocompatibility must be evaluated based on specific use cases. Therefore, for biohybrid actuator applications, two commercial Asiga dental
resins, DentaGUIDE and DentaGUM, were printed using a low-cost,
LCD resin printer (Phrozen Sonic Mini 8K) and analyzed for their biocompatibility with C2C12, a muscle cell line commonly used in biohybrid
actuators. C2C12 cells were cultured in direct contact with resin samples
for 72 h, and their viability was examined using ethidium homodimer-1
and calcein acetoxymethyl ester (calcein AM), fluorescent dyes that mark
dead and live cells, respectively. The ratio of calcein AM to ethidium
homodimer 1 (CalAM:EthD-1) fluorescence was significantly larger for
cultures exposed to the autoclaved ($4,941 \pm 1,122$) or ethanol-sterilized
($3,783 \pm 683$) DentaGUIDE samples as compared to the ratio for cultures exposed to polydimethylsiloxane (PDMS) (autoclaved: $1,940\pm989$,
ethanol-sterilized: 345 ± 446). The CalAM:EthD-1 ratio measured in cultures exposed to DentaGUM (autoclaved: 43.67 ± 9.38, ethanol-sterilized:
101.7 ± 86.0) was significantly lower than the ratio found for autoclaved

N. S. Szczecinski et al. (Eds.): Living Machines 2024, LNAI 14930, pp. 399–412, 2025.
https://doi.org/10.1007/978-3-031-72597-5_27

PDMS. This analysis suggested that DentaGUIDE has little to no impact on the health of C2C12, but DentaGUM negatively impacted the culture. Therefore, DentaGUIDE could be a suitable rigid material choice for bio-hybrid actuators.

Keywords: Resin 3D Printing · Biocompatibility · Biohybrid

1 Introduction

Naturally occurring biological actuators, such as muscle tissue, demonstrate several qualities that are difficult to achieve in artificial robotic actuation [34]. Biological tissues are naturally compliant, biodegradable, capable of self-healing, and are found in nature at a wide range of size scales [30]. To integrate these inherent biological qualities with robotic systems, biohybrid actuators combine living and synthetic materials. Synthetic materials, such as polydimethylsiloxane (PDMS), can be used to support muscle cells and tissues [11]. However, current biohybrid actuators do not have comparable performance with that of natural muscle [30].

One potential method to improve the performance of biohybrid muscle actuators is to incorporate synthetic substrates for supporting muscle maturation [30]. For example, scaffolds with micropatterns can help promote myoblast differentiation and myotube assembly in 2D cultures [14,29]. In addition, larger cantilever beams have been used to form 3D muscle constructs to mimic densely packed tissues [6,27,32]. Scaffolds can also be fabricated using soft lithography [14,29,32], which utilizes planar silicon wafers etched with patterns. However, using these planar silicon wafers makes fabricating more complex 3D structures beyond pillars or planar patterns challenging. Furthermore, etching patterns into the silicon wafer requires photolithographic techniques that need specialized equipment and clean rooms, which can reduce the accessibility of such methods.

For more complex 3D scaffold designs, resin-based 3D printing could be a viable, easily accessible method while maintaining high resolution (e.g., Formlabs Form 3+ series [8], Asiga MAX X27 [3], Phrozen Sonic Mini 8K [26]). Within the resin-printing industry, several resins, such as select Asiga [2] and Formlabs [9] dental resins, have been developed to be biocompatible. For engineered muscle strips, both custom [27] and commercial [6] resins have been explored. However, these specialized resins are commonly optimized for specific printers, such as the Asiga MAX series [3] or Formlabs Form 3B+ [7]. The starting cost of these commercial printers starts at several thousand USD (Table 1), which may limit the accessibility to such equipment. In contrast, the cost of consumer resin printers, such as the Phrozen Sonic Mini series, is commonly a few hundred USD (Table 1). However, printers from different manufacturers may use different technologies (Table 1, "Printer Type"). Thus, for fabricating using low-cost printers, the printing conditions must be optimized for each resin and printer. Additionally, due to differences in fabrication procedures, the biocompatibility of samples printed on an alternate printer must be reevaluated.

Table 1. Printing resolutions and costs of current resin printers on the market. For the printer types, the following acronyms are used: LCD - Liquid-Crystal Display; SLA - Stereolithography; DLP - Digital Light Processing. Note: for the Formlabs Form 3+, the resolution was determined as the laser spot size (the reported XY resolution).

Manufacturer	Printer	Printer Type	Resolution (μm)	Cost (USD, April 2024)	Ref.
Phrozen	Sonic Mini 8K	LCD	22	$485	[26]
Formlabs	Form 3B+	SLA	85(25)	$4,429	[7,8]
Asiga	MAX X27	DLP	27	$9,990	[3,5]

Not only would changing the printer necessitate a reevaluation of biocompatibility, the characterization of biocompatible resins has differed among different laboratories [12] and is often not clearly reported by manufacturers, even with the use of various certifications, such as CE marking or the International Organization for Standardization's (ISO) 10993 series of standards [13]. Furthermore, the ISO 10993-1:2018 standard specifies that biocompatibility tests should be designed and used for specific material usages [16]. As such, commercial resins that have been reported for biocompatibility to be used in medical devices should be reassessed for their applicability to biohybrid systems.

This work investigated two commercially available resins for their applicability to biohybrid actuators: Asiga [2] DentaGUIDE and DentaGUM. Asiga DentaGuide, which is used for fabricating surgical guides, is advertised to be biocompatible (CE Class I) and autoclavable [2], which are necessary qualities for usage with biological materials in biohybrid devices. DentaGUM is a flexible resin designed to mimic the gingiva, which might provide a suitable environmental stiffness for myocyte differentiation. There were no sterilization recommendations by the manufacturer for DentaGUM. Both materials' biocompatibility was evaluated in direct contact with C2C12, a common immortalized mouse myoblast cell line used for biohybrid actuators. A direct contact assessment was selected to mimic culture conditions in a biohybrid actuator since biological and synthetic materials must be well integrated.

2 Methods

DentaGUIDE and DentaGUM (Asiga, Ann Arbor, MI, USA) were evaluated for their biocompatibility for use in biohybrid devices. Samples of each resin were printed on a Phrozen Sonic Mini 8K resin printer (Phrozen Tech Co., LTD., Hsinchu, Taiwan), which is a low-cost (<$1,000) LCD resin 3D printer (Table 1). These samples were designed to be cylinders with a 2 mm diameter, which produces a flat face that would occupy at least 10% of the surface area of a well in a 96-well plate, as recommended by ISO 10993:5:2009 [15]. These samples were sterilized by a 70% ethanol soak or by autoclaving, two common techniques used for sterilization before being introduced into an ongoing C2C12 culture to assess biocompatibility. Six samples were used for each resin per sterilization technique.

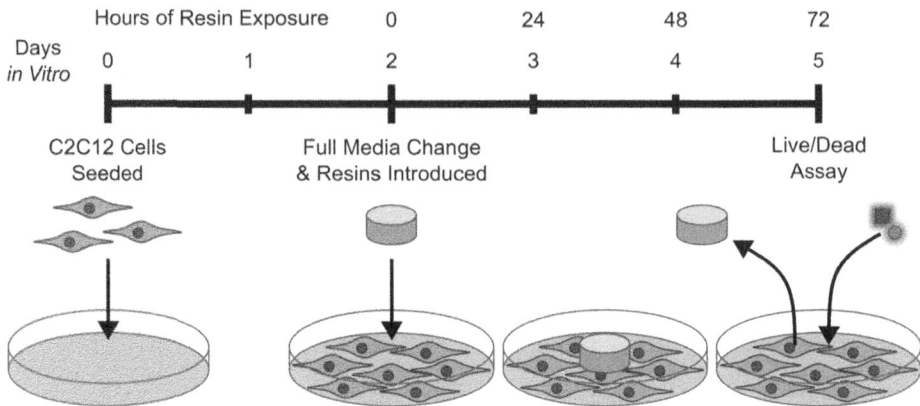

Fig. 1. Cells were seeded and cultured for 2 days before the introduction of a resin sample. After 72 h of incubation with the resin sample, a live/dead assay was used to evaluate biocompatibility.

2.1 Fabrication of Samples

The resins were printed on a Phrozen Sonic Mini 8K resin printer (Phrozen Tech Co., LTD., Hsinchu, Taiwan). Immediately after printing, they were washed in isopropanol for 5 min in an ultrasonic bath. This wash was repeated once in a second container of isopropanol. Following these washes, the samples were placed in a Phrozen Curing Station (Phrozen Tech Co., LTD., Hsinchu, Taiwan) with a 30-minute fan period and subsequent 15-minute cure period. Afterward, the samples were flipped over for a second 15-minute cure period.

For the negative controls, PDMS (SYLGARD 184; Dow Corning, Midland, MI, USA) samples were used. The samples were fabricated using a 10:1 base-to-curing-agent (w/w) ratio. A 2 mm biopsy punch was used to cut the PDMS samples.

2.2 Sample Sterilization

After the sample preparation, the samples were sterilized using one of two methods: soaking in 70% ethanol or autoclaving. For the ethanol soak, the samples were submerged in 70% ethanol for 1 h, after which they were washed three times in sterile, phosphate-buffered saline (PBS) (10-010-049; Gibco ThermoFisher, Waltham, MA, USA). They were then dried in ambient conditions in a biosafety cabinet (1300 Series A2, Model 1377; ThermoFisher, Waltham, MA, USA) with a single 1-hour ultraviolet light cycle. For the autoclave (ADV-PRO; Consolidated Sterilizer Systems, Billerica, MA, USA) procedure, the samples were subjected to a gravity cycle for 45 min at 121 °C, followed by a drying period of 15 min.

2.3   Cell Culture

Cryopreserved C2C12 cells were thawed and plated into a black-walled 96-well plate (655087; Greiner Bio-One, Kremsmünster, Austria) at their 9th passage at a density of 2,100 cells/well ($\approx$6,200 cells/cm^2). For the entire period, the cells were cultured in a growth medium composed of 1% L-glutamine (200 mM, 25030081; Gibco ThermoFisher, Waltham, MA, USA), 1% penicillin-streptomycin (10,000 U/mL, 15140122; Gibco ThermoFisher, Waltham, MA, USA)), and 10% fetal bovine serum (A5256801; Gibco ThermoFisher, Waltham, MA, USA) in high glucose Dulbecco's Minimum Essential Medium (11965126; Gibco ThermoFisher, Waltham, MA, USA). For the duration of the culture, the cells were in an incubator that maintained 37 °C and 5% CO$_2$ conditions. The cells were cultured for two days and exhibited an average of 20–30% confluency before a complete medium change and the addition of resin samples (Fig. 1). After 72 h of incubation with the resin samples, a viability/cytotoxicity assay was conducted (Sect. 2.4, Fig. 1).

Six replicates were performed per resin and sterilization method. In addition, six replicates were performed for the PDMS negative control samples per sterilization method. Lastly, 12 wells were not exposed to any resin samples. Of these wells, 6 were blanks in which they were expected to contain a healthy, living population of cells. The remaining six wells were the positive, dead-cell controls and exposed to cold 70% ethanol for 15 min just prior to the viability/cytotoxicity assay.

2.4   Cytotoxicity Analysis

To test for biocompatibility, a viability/cytotoxicity assay (L3224; Invitrogen ThermoFisher, Waltham, MA, USA) was conducted using ethidium homodimer-1 to stain dead cells and calcein acetoxymethyl ester (calcein AM) to stain live cells as per the manufacturer's protocol [25]. Before staining, the resin and PDMS samples were carefully removed from the wells using sterile forceps. Afterward, the medium was removed from all wells. Then, the wells were washed three times with PBS. After removing PBS from the final wash, 100 µL of PBS was added to each well.

For staining the cells, 100 µL of 2 µM calcein AM and 4 µM ethidium homodimer-1 were added to each well that originally contained either a resin or PDMS sample, resulting in a final concentration of 1 µM calcein AM and 2 µM ethidium homodimer-1. As controls, for the wells that did not have any sample exposure (the live-cell blanks and dead-cell positive controls), only 100 µL of 2 µM calcein AM was added to half of the wells, resulting in a final concentration of 1 µM, as per manufacturer's protocol [25]. For the remaining half, 100 µL of 4 µM ethidium homodimer-1 was added, resulting in a final concentration of 2 µM. These wells were separately stained to ensure the expected fluorescence from each dye. All wells were incubated at room temperature for 30–60 min before their fluorescence intensities were measured using a plate reader (Synergy H1; Agilent BioTek, Santa Clara, CA, USA). Since the fluorescence intensities are linearly proportional to the number of cells [25], the relative fluorescence units measured by the plate reader were used instead of cell count.

The cultures were imaged using brightfield and epifluorescence in an inverted microscope (Revolution; Echo Bico, San Diego, CA, USA) with a 10X objective lens. The brightfield camera used a 5 MP CMOS color camera, whereas the fluorescence camera used a 5 MP CMOS mono camera. FITC and Texas Red LED light cubes were used to visualize the calcein-AM and ethidium homodimer-1, respectively.

2.5   Statistics

The fluorescence intensity data collected from the plate reader was statistically analyzed using Minitab 2023 (v 21.4.2; Minitab, LLC, State College, PA, USA). The data was first assessed for normality using the Anderson-Darling test [21] and for equal variances using the Bartlett test [22]. Based on the results from this initial analysis, a balanced analysis of variance (ANOVA) [20] with a significance level of 0.05 and a post-hoc pairwise Bonferroni multiple comparison test between groups [23] was used for analyzing the data.

3   Results and Discussion

Based on the brightfield microscopy images, cultures exposed to DentaGUIDE and PDMS exhibited similar morphology as the live cell (blank) controls with >90% confluency (Fig. 2A–H). The C2C12 cell layer also grew close to the DentaGUIDE samples, but qualitatively, there appeared to be less growth near the autoclaved DentaGUIDE samples (Fig. 2E, G). Additionally, cultures exposed to DentaGUM exhibited a much lower density (<10% confluency) with a rounded cell morphology, with very few cells found near the DentaGUM samples (Fig. 2I–L).

After the PBS washing and application of the calcein AM and ethidium homodimer-1 stains to quantify the viability, fewer cells were found remaining in the wells exposed to DentaGUM (Fig. 3G,J) than before these steps (Fig. 2I–L). Before the wash and dye application, several cells exhibited a rounded morphology, which indicates that these cells were likely dying and beginning to detach from the culture surface. As such, a number of these dead or dying cells could be aspirated during the PBS wash steps prior to the dye loading. Although this reduction is most clearly observed for cultures exhibiting mostly rounded cell morphology, such as the DentaGUM exposed cultures, this could reduce the ethidium homodimer-1 fluorescence intensities reported by the plate reader for all of the cultures.

Unlike the rounded cells, the live, healthy cells were expected to remain attached to the culture surface during the PBS wash steps. However, the empty regions and highly dense regions observed in the culture for the blank (live cells with no resin or PDMS exposure) control indicated that the cells began

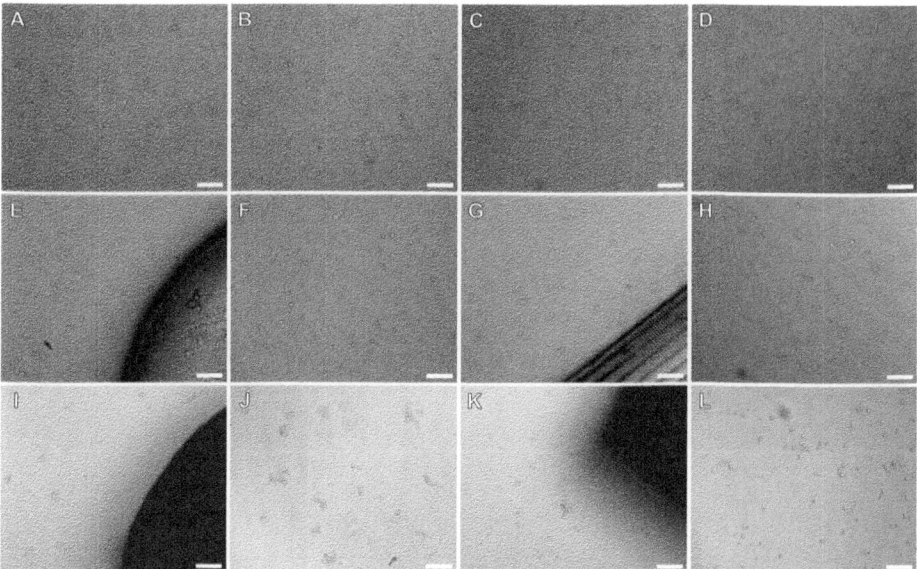

Fig. 2. Brightfield images of C2C12 cultures prior to loading calcein AM and ethidium homodimer-1. The top row illustrates the controls: (**A**) blank (live cell), (**B**) positive control (live cell at the time of imaging, just prior to exposure to ethanol for a dead cell control), (**C**) negative control (ethanol-sterilized PDMS), (**D**) negative control (autoclaved PDMS). The middle row illustrates cultures exposed to DentaGUIDE, that was (**E-F**) ethanol-sterilized and (**G-H**) autoclaved. The bottom row illustrates cultures exposed to DentaGUM, that was (**I-J**) ethanol-sterilized and (**K-L**) autoclaved. For (**E**), (**G**), (**I**), and (**K**), a portion of the resin sample was included in the image. Samples of PDMS could not be imaged with the cells since the PDMS tended to float in the culture medium. The scale bar in each subfigure represents 100 μm.

to detach from the surface after the PBS washes and dye application (Fig. 3A-B). This was also observed in the cultures exposed to PDMS and DentaGUIDE (Fig. 3E-F, H–I). This phenomenon was not as clearly observed in the cultures exposed to DentaGUM (Fig. 3G,J) since there was initially very little healthy cell attachment prior to the PBS wash steps and dye loading (Fig. 2I–K). However, the several DentaGUM cells tagged with the fluorescent dyes still exhibited a more rounded morphology, similar to the blank cultures.

Since PBS is non-toxic and isotonic, the wash steps were not expected to affect the cellular morphology or surface attachment. Therefore, the detachment of the cell layer could be attributed to the use of calcein AM, since calcein AM may be toxic to some cell lines [28]. Furthermore, since this was conducted as an endpoint assay and the fluorescence readings were done shortly after the dye application, the dye's impacts on long-term cell health would not affect the results in this study. Since the dyes are applied after the PBS washes, any affected live cells should remain in the wells and not affect the calcein AM fluo-

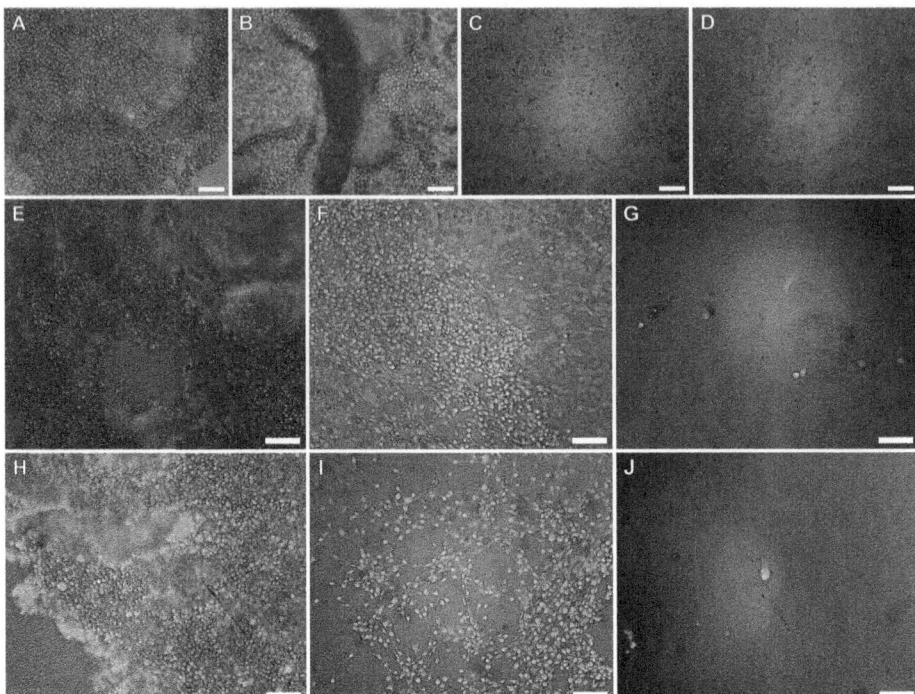

Fig. 3. Calcein AM (green) and ethidium homodimer-1 (red) fluorescent images over-laid images taken with transmitted light. Top row: blank (live cell) control (**A-B**) and the positive (dead cell) control (**C-D**). Cultures in (**A**) and (**C**) were loaded only with calcein AM. Middle row: cultures with ethanol-sterilized samples: (**E**) PDMS (negative control), (**F**) DentaGUIDE, (**G**) DentaGUM. Bottom row: cultures with autoclaved samples: (**H**) PDMS (negative control), (**I**) DentaGUIDE, (**J**) DentaGUM. Cultures in (**B**) and (**D**) were loaded only with ethidium homodimer-1. The remaining cultures were loaded with a combination of calcein AM and ethidium homodimer-1. The scale bar in each subfigure represents 100 μm. (Color figure online)

rescence intensities captured by the plate reader. Therefore, instead of comparing the individual fluorescence intensities of each dye, the ratio of the fluorescence intensities of calcein AM and ethidium homodimer-1 (CalAM:EthD-1) was used for the quantitative assessment of biocompatibility (Fig. 4).

The CalAM:EthD-1 responses for all groups exhibited normal distributions ($p > 0.05$), except ethanol-sterilized DentaGUM and PDMS ($p \leq 0.05$). Since a majority of the groups were normal, the Bartlett method was selected for the test for equal variances, in which the groups were determined to not have equal variances ($p = 0.000$). Based on these results, a balanced ANOVA was determined to be the appropriate statistical analysis since it is not sensitive to unequal variances if there are only fixed factors and equal sample sizes [22].

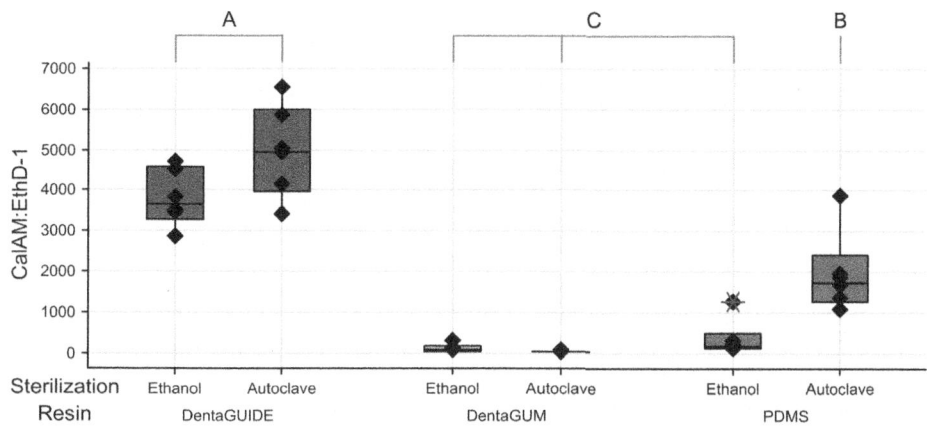

Fig. 4. Box plots of the CalAM:EthD-1 responses for each sterilization and resin condition. The first and third quartiles are represented by the bottom and top lines of each box, respectively. The minimum and maximum, excluding outliers, are represented by the whiskers extending from the interquartile range boxes. The median is represented by the middle line of each box. The black diamonds (♦) are the individual data points. Outliers are marked by a red asterisk (∗). The grouping results from the Bonferroni pairwise comparisons (Table 3 are also denoted in the boxplots in which conditions that do not share a letter are significantly different. (Color figure online)

The balanced ANOVA indicated significant associations between CalAM: EthD-1 and the resin type, sterilization mode, and the interaction effect between the resin type and sterilization mode ($p < 0.05$, Table 2). This is indicative that the means are not equal and that the effects of the resin and sterilization mode should be considered together.

Since the ANOVA indicated significant differences based on the sterilization method and the resin type, a post-hoc Bonferroni pairwise comparison was conducted to identify which groups were significantly different (Table 3, Fig. 4). The autoclaved and ethanol-sterilized DentaGUIDE samples demonstrated sig-

Table 2. Balanced ANOVA of CalAM:EthD-1 results. The Source lists the factors (Sterilization and Resin) and interactions between the factors (Sterilization*Resin) considered. DF: degrees of freedom per source; SS: adjusted sum of squares. MS: adjusted mean squares; F: ANOVA test statistic; p is the probability value.

Source	DF	SS	MS	F	p
Sterilization	1	7,266,940	7,266,940	14.99	0.001
Resin	2	119,621,488	59,810,744	123.39	0.000
Sterilization*Resin	2	4,403,350	2,201,675	4.54	0.019
Error	30	14,542,365	484,745		
Total	35	145,834,143			

nificantly larger CalAM:EthD-1 means than the means of the PDMS samples, which suggests that DentaGUIDE has little impact on cell viability. In addition, the DentaGUM CalAM:EthD-1 means were significantly lower than the means from the autoclaved PDMS samples, which suggests that DentaGUM negatively impacts the health of the culture. Both the DentaGUIDE and DentaGUM conclusions are in alignment with the morphology observed prior to the introduction of the dyes (Fig. 2).

In addition to considering different resin types for biohybrid devices, sterilization techniques are also important in tissue engineering [4]. For example, PDMS slightly swells after ethanol immersion [18], but the mechanical properties are altered after steam autoclaving [19,24]. Therefore, an appropriate sterilization technique must be selected based on desired bioactuator functions. In this study, when investigating the impacts on sterilization techniques in conjunction with the resin type, there was not a significant difference between the responses to ethanol-sterilized DentaGUIDE and autoclaved DentaGUIDE (Table 3, Fig. 4). This indicates either technique is acceptable for sterilizing DentaGUIDE, but additional studies should be conducted to investigate any impacts of sterilization on the mechanical properties of DentaGUIDE. Although the cellular responses to sterilization techniques on DentaGUIDE were not significantly different, there was an unexpected, significant difference between the responses to ethanol-sterilized PDMS and autoclaved PDMS (Table 3, Fig. 4) since both techniques are commonly used for sterilizing PDMS [19,24]. This might suggest that the impacts of ethanol exposure on PDMS, such as swelling [18], could impact the C2C12 culture, but additional study is needed to explore this.

Furthermore, since PDMS is known to be a biocompatible, inert elastomer [24], the lower CalAM:EthD-1 means, as compared to those of DentaGUIDE, were also unexpected (Table 3, Fig. 4). The lower PDMS means could potentially be attributed to the resin removal process prior to the washing and dye loading procedures. PDMS samples tended to float in the culture medium, which caused their removal via forceps to be more challenging than the DentaGUIDE samples that rested at the bottom of the wells. In turn, this could have caused the PDMS samples to move more during the removal process and act as a cell scraper. Any cells detached from the culture surface during the resin removal process will likely be aspirated during the wash steps before the loading of the dye. Therefore, the removal of these cells could reduce the CalAM:EthD-1 response of PDMS. In future work, elution studies, an indirect biocompatibility test using sample extracts, can be performed to verify this theory (ISO 10993-5 [15] and ISO 10993-12 [17]). However, using only sample extracts will not adequately mimic biohybrid use cases since it would only test for the impacts of potential leachants. Since the biological materials will be physically integrated with the synthetic materials, direct contact testing more closely represents the environment living cells will experience in a biohybrid system.

In addition to exploring elution studies to complement direct testing, the use of additional cell viability assessments could further the understanding of the impacts of the resin on C2C12. Calcein AM specifically tags for intracel-

Table 3. Post-hoc Bonferroni pairwise comparison between factors for each type of source: sterilization, resin, and combination of the sterilization and resin. For each source, means with a different letter are significantly different (i.e., factors that are assigned to "A" are significantly different from factors assigned to "B" within the same source).

Factor		N	Mean ± Standard Deviation	Grouping		
Sterilization						
Autoclave		18	2,308 ± 2,228	A		
Ethanol		18	1,410 ± 1,786		B	
Resin						
DentaGUIDE		12	4,362 ± 1,072	A		
PDMS		12	1,143 ± 1,108		B	
DentaGUM		12	72.7 ± 65.8			C
Sterilization	**Resin**					
Autoclave	DentaGUIDE	6	4,941 ± 1,122	A		
Ethanol	DentaGUIDE	6	3,783 ± 683	A		
Autoclave	PDMS	6	1,940 ± 989		B	
Ethanol	PDMS	6	345 ± 446			C
Ethanol	DentaGUM	6	101.7 ± 86.0			C
Autoclave	DentaGUM	6	43.67 ± 9.38			C

lular esterase activity, which is typically present in living cells, while ethidium homodimer-1 binds to nucleic acids, but can only pass through damaged plasma membranes that are typical of dead cells [25]. In addition, there was a noticeable impact on the cellular morphology with the use of calcein AM and ethidium homodimer. Another cell viability assay, such as measuring the extracellular concentration of lactate dehydrogenase (LDH) which is only released when with the loss of plasma membrane integrity [1], could be explored. Furthermore, calcein AM/homodimer-1 assays and LDH assays can be suitable for assessing cell viability in 3D tissues [10]. However, the use of LDH, calcein AM, and ethidium homodimer will not inform if the resins have impacts on other aspects of cellular activity. To investigate this, other cell viability assays, such as tetrazolium-based assays (*e.g.* 3-(4,5-dimethylthiazol-2-yl)-2,5-diphenyltetrazolium bromide (MTT) tetrazolium reduction assays) for metabolism [31] or 5-ethynyl-2'-deoxyuridine (EdU) for proliferation [33], could complement the calcein AM and ethidium homodimer-1 results in this study. In addition to studying the effects on metabolism and proliferation, this study can be extended to investigate the impacts on C2C12 differentiation, which is crucial for the maturation of contractile myotubes necessary for functional biohybrid actuators [30]. The use of these additional assays as well as the same calcein AM/ethidium homodimer-1 viability assay in a 3D culture can further validate DentaGUIDE's applicability to future biohybrid actuators.

4   Conclusion

In biohybrid actuators, synthetic material components are used to support living materials, such as muscle. For fabricating these supportive, synthetic structures, 3D printing is one avenue that can be used for producing complex structures. However, the biocompatibility assessment of resins is not clearly reported by manufacturers. Furthermore, the assessment cannot be generalized and must be designed for specific use cases. Therefore, for the use in biohybrid actuator fabrication, the biocompatibility of two commercial resins, Asiga DentaGUIDE and DentaGUM, was evaluated. Cultures of C2C12, a common muscle cell line used in biohybrid actuators, were exposed to DentaGUIDE and DentaGUM samples for 72 h. Based on the observed morphology and a viability/cytotoxicity assay, DentaGUIDE was found to have minimal impact on the culture health, whereas DentaGUM negatively impacted the culture. Therefore, DentaGUIDE is likely suitable as a rigid supporting structure for biohybrid actuators, but more soft, elastomeric materials need to be explored.

Acknowledgments. This material is based upon work supported by the National Science Foundation (NSF). ASL and SS were supported by the Graduate Research Fellowship Program under Grant No. DGE1745016. This work was also supported by the NSF Faculty Early Career Development Program under Grant No. ECCS-2044785. Any opinions, findings, and conclusions or recommendations expressed in this material are those of the author(s) and do not necessarily reflect the views of the NSF. This research was also sponsored by the Army Research Office and was accomplished under Cooperative Agreement Number W911NF-23-2-0138. The views and conclusions contained in this document are those of the authors and should not be interpreted as representing the official policies, either expressed or implied, of the Army Research Office or the U.S. Government. The U.S. Government is authorized to reproduce and distribute reprints for Government purposes notwithstanding any copyright notation herein. KD was also supported by the Innovation Commercialization Fellowship from Carnegie Mellon University (CMU). ABI gratefully acknowledges financial support for this publication by the Fulbright Post Doctoral Program, which is sponsored by the U.S. Department of State and Turkish Fulbright Commission. For ASL, funding to attend this conference was partially provided by the CMU Graduate Student Association (GSA)/Provost Conference Funding.

References

1. Allen, M., Millett, P., Dawes, E., Rushton, N.: Lactate dehydrogenase activity as a rapid and sensitive test for the quantification of cell numbers in vitro. Clin. Mater. **16**(4), 189–194 (1994). https://doi.org/10.1016/0267-6605(94)90116-3
2. Asiga: Materials Dental - Asiga (2024). https://www.asiga.com/materials-dental/
3. Asiga: Max X - Asiga (2024). https://www.asiga.com/max-x/
4. Dai, Z., Ronholm, J., Tian, Y., Sethi, B., Cao, X.: Sterilization techniques for biodegradable scaffolds in tissue engineering applications. J. Tissue Eng. **7**, 204173141664881 (2016). https://doi.org/10.1177/2041731416648810
5. DELRAY Systems: Asiga MAX X (2019). https://www.3d-printer.com/products/asiga-max-x/163943000017772029

6. Finkel, S., et al.: FRESH^{TM} 3D bioprinted cardiac tissue, a bioengineered platform for in vitro pharmacology. APL Bioeng. **7**(4), 046113 (2023). https://doi.org/10.1063/5.0163363
7. Formlabs: Form 3B+ (2024). https://formlabs.com/3d-printers/form-3b/
8. Formlabs: Formlabs Stereolithography 3D Printers Tech Specs (2024). https://formlabs.com/3d-printers/form-3/tech-specs/
9. Formlabs Dental: Materials (2024). https://dental.formlabs.com/store/materials/?Biocompatible=5457
10. Gantenbein-Ritter, B., Potier, E., Zeiter, S., Van Der Werf, M., Sprecher, C.M., Ito, K.: Accuracy of three techniques to determine cell viability in 3D tissues or scaffolds. Tissue Eng. Part C Methods **14**(4), 353–358 (2008). https://doi.org/10.1089/ten.tec.2008.0313
11. Gao, L., et al.: Recent progress in engineering functional biohybrid robots actuated by living cells. Acta Biomater. **121**, 29–40 (2021). https://doi.org/10.1016/j.actbio.2020.12.002
12. Gruber, S., Nickel, A.: Toxic or not toxic? The specifications of the standard ISO 10993–5 are not explicit enough to yield comparable results in the cytotoxicity assessment of an identical medical device. Front. Med. Technol. **5**, 1195529 (2023). https://doi.org/10.3389/fmedt.2023.1195529
13. Guttridge, C., Shannon, A., O'Sullivan, A., O'Sullivan, K.J., O'Sullivan, L.W.: Biocompatible 3D printing resins for medical applications: A review of marketed intended use, biocompatibility certification, and post-processing guidance. Annals 3D Printed Med. **5**, 100044 (2022). https://doi.org/10.1016/j.stlm.2021.100044
14. Huang, N.F., et al.: Myotube assembly on nanofibrous and micropatterned polymers. Nano Lett. **6**(3), 537–542 (2006). https://doi.org/10.1021/nl060060o
15. International Organization for Standardization: ISO 10993-5:2009: Biological evaluation of medical devices Part 5: Tests for in vitro cytotoxicity (2009). https://www.iso.org/standard/36406.html
16. International Organization for Standardization: ISO 10993-1:2018: Biological evaluation of medical devices Part 1: Evaluation and testing within a risk management process (2018). https://www.iso.org/standard/68936.html
17. International Organization for Standardization: ISO 10993-12:2021: Biological evaluation of medical devices Part 12: Sample preparation and reference materials (2021). https://www.iso.org/standard/75769.html
18. Lee, J.N., Park, C., Whitesides, G.M.: Solvent compatibility of poly(dimethylsiloxane)-based microfluidic devices. Anal. Chem. **75**(23), 6544–6554 (2003). https://doi.org/10.1021/ac0346712
19. Mata, A., Fleischman, A.J., Roy, S.: Characterization of polydimethylsiloxane (PDMS) properties for biomedical micro/nanosystems. Biomed. Microdev. **7**(4), 281–293 (2005). https://doi.org/10.1007/s10544-005-6070-2
20. Minitab Support: Methods and formulas for Balanced ANOVA (2024). https://support.minitab.com/en-us/minitab/help-and-how-to/statistical-modeling/anova/how-to/balanced-anova/methods-and-formulas/methods-and-formulas/
21. Minitab Support: Methods and formulas for Graphical Summary (2024). https://support.minitab.com/en-us/minitab/help-and-how-to/statistics/basic-statistics/how-to/graphical-summary/methods-and-formulas/methods-and-formulas/
22. Minitab Support: Understanding test for equal variances (2024). https://support.minitab.com/en-us/minitab/help-and-how-to/statistical-modeling/anova/supporting-topics/basics/understanding-test-for-equal-variances/

23. Minitab Support: What is the Bonferroni method? (2024). https://support. minitab.com/en-us/minitab/help-and-how-to/statistical-modeling/anova/ supporting-topics/multiple-comparisons/what-is-the-bonferroni-method/
24. Miranda, I., Souza, A., Sousa, P., Ribeiro, J., Castanheira, E.M.S., Lima, R., Minas, G.: Properties and applications of PDMS for biomedical engineering: a review. J. Funct. Biomater. **13**(1), 2 (2021). https://doi.org/10.3390/jfb13010002
25. Molecular Probes: LIVE/DEAD ® Viability/Cytotoxicity Kit *for mammalian cells* (2005). https://assets.thermofisher.com/TFS-Assets%2FLSG%2Fmanuals %2Fmp03224.pdf
26. Phrozen: Phrozen Sonic Mini 8K Resin 3D Printer. https://phrozen3d.com/ products/sonic-mini-8k
27. Raman, R., Cvetkovic, C., Bashir, R.: A modular approach to the design, fabrication, and characterization of muscle-powered biological machines. Nat. Protoc. **12**(3), 519–533 (2017). https://doi.org/10.1038/nprot.2016.185
28. Ramirez, C.N., Antczak, C., Djaballah, H.: Cell viability assessment: toward content-rich platforms. Expert Opin. Drug Discov. **5**(3), 223–233 (2010). https:// doi.org/10.1517/17460441003596685
29. Ricotti, L., Fujie, T., Vazão, H., Ciofani, G., Marotta, R., Brescia, R., Filippeschi, C., Corradini, I., Matteoli, M., Mattoli, V., Ferreira, L., Menciassi, A.: Boron nitride nanotube-mediated stimulation of cell co-culture on micro-engineered hydrogels. PLoS One **8**(8), e71707 (2013). https://doi.org/10.1371/journal.pone. 0071707
30. Ricotti, L., et al.: Biohybrid actuators for robotics: a review of devices actuated by living cells. Science Robotics **2**(12), eaaq0495 (2017). https://doi.org/10.1126/ scirobotics.aaq0495
31. Riss, T.L., et al.: Cell Viability Assays. In: Markossian, S., et al. (eds.) Assay Guidance Manual. Eli Lilly & Company and the National Center for Advancing Translational Sciences, Bethesda (MD) (2004). http://www.ncbi.nlm.nih.gov/ books/NBK144065/
32. Sakar, M.S., et al.: Formation and optogenetic control of engineered 3D skeletal muscle bioactuators. Lab Chip **12**(23), 4976 (2012). https://doi.org/10.1039/ c2lc40338b
33. Salic, A., Mitchison, T.J.: A chemical method for fast and sensitive detection of DNA synthesis in vivo. Proc. Natl. Acad. Sci. **105**(7), 2415–2420 (2008). https:// doi.org/10.1073/pnas.0712168105
34. Webster-Wood, V.A., Akkus, O., Gurkan, U.A., Chiel, H.J., Quinn, R.D.: Organismal engineering: toward a robotic taxonomic key for devices using organic materials. Sci. Robot. **2**(12), eaap9281 (2017). https://doi.org/10.1126/scirobotics. aap9281

Speed-Independent Wall Distance Estimation Along a Given Trajectory of a Biohybrid Fly-Robot-Interface

Jiaqi V. Huang$^{(\boxtimes)}$ ⓘ and Holger G. Krapp ⓘ

Imperial College London, London SW7 2AZ, UK
j.huang09@imperial.ac.uk

Abstract. Collision avoidance in flying insects is mostly based on visual motion cues such as retinal image expansion or the relative magnitude of retinal image shifts. In earlier studies, we found that the activity of an identified visual interneuron (H1-cell) in a fly mounted on a bio-hybrid fly robot interface (FRI) was modulated by the robot's turning radius and the distance to the walls of an experimental arena. To characterise the neural mechanisms underlying visual distance estimation we set up a virtual reality environment (FlyVR) that enabled us to reproduce the input to the motion vision pathway experienced by flies on the FRI and record the H1-cell activity without modulations by other sensory modalities. After establishing a qualitative alignment of the results obtained on the FRI and our FlyVR system, we now address the outstanding question of whether the distance-dependent modulation of the H1-cell activity depends on the velocity of the FRI. Our results suggest that at a fixed turning radius within the range tested the robot velocity hardly affects the H1-cell spike rate. The functional significance of this surprising result is discussed as well as further analysis steps to elucidate the neural computations involved.

Keywords: H1-cell · virtual reality · distance estimation · blowfly

1 Introduction

There are two types of motion-sensitive interneurons in the insect visual system responding to translational ego-motion, which are potentially useful for collision avoidance: the looming cells [1–3], and wide-field cells [4–8]. Looming cells are specialised neurons responding selectively to approaching objects, that cause expanding retinal image shifts, generated by object movement towards the observer. These cells are crucial for the detection of looming stimuli, which are often associated with impending threats or potential collisions. Looming cells play a vital role in the insect's visual ecology, contributing to the organism's ability to react to objects in its environment, supporting collision-free navigation and predator avoidance. However, wide-field cells in the insect visual system are neurons with large receptive fields that cover an extended area of the visual field. These cells are characterised by their ability to integrate visual motion information across their receptive field, allowing them to detect and respond to large-scale features

N. S. Szczecinski et al. (Eds.): Living Machines 2024, LNAI 14930, pp. 413–427, 2025.
https://doi.org/10.1007/978-3-031-72597-5_28

and movements in the environment. Wide-field interneurons are normally used for optic-flow-based self-motion estimation for flight and gaze control. They receive input from elementary movement detectors (EMDs) [9, 10] which is not true for looming-sensitive interneurons (LGMD) in locust. In Drosophila, however, looming-sensitive neurons may receive input from directional-selective elements [3], which is also true for descending neurons involved in triggering the landing response in houseflies [11]. They play a crucial role in various visual behaviours, including navigation, and guidance where the distance to visual structures in the environment triggers appropriate behavioural responses.

The retinal slip speed is an important parameter for looming-sensitive cells, which have been characterised in many insects, such as: locust LGMD [1, 2] and Drosophila LPLC2 [3, 12]. The ratio l/v, where l is the half-size of an approaching object and v is its constant approach velocity [13], defines the instantaneous object size and its expansion velocity [13]. This ratio helps to determine the degree of threat or urgency associated with the approaching object, which is crucial for the animal's behavioural responses such as evasive manoeuvres or defensive actions.

Blowflies have been observed navigating through narrow corridors along an oscillatory forward trajectory at a frequency of 6 Hz [14], effectively avoiding collisions with the walls. Motion vision is crucial for this agile manoeuvring. Previous research suggested that blowflies may exploit the response properties of direction-selective interneurons, specifically the HSE-cell [15], to gauge distance during inertia-induced sideslip following a rapid body saccade. Blowflies employ approximately 60 optic flow processing wide-field neurons located in the lobula plate, the posterior region of the fly's fourth visual neuropil and are called Lobula Plate Tangential Cells (LPTCs) [6–8].

The H1-cell, known for its function as a matched filter for optic flow to distinguish between translation and rotation, was utilised in a bio-hybrid fly robotic interface (FRI) to navigate and avoid collisions with the experimental arena's walls [16, 17]. The FRI is mobile experimental system that has been developed to study multisensory integration under closed-loop conditions. On this 2-wheeled robotic platform, the spiking activity of the H1-cell was recorded, processed and employed to estimate the distance to the wall of an experimental arena, triggering collision avoidance manoeuvres whenever the activity (e.g. spike rate) surpassed a predefined threshold [17]. Notably, the closer the FRI approached the wall, the higher the spike rate increased. Due to the cell's preferred directions, a pure forward translation would entirely inhibit spiking in the H1-cell, that is why an oscillatory trajectory is required where increased and decreased spike rates are alternating [7, 18], such as the FRI trajectory that was set to follow an oscillatory path, alternating between turning towards and away from the wall, respectively (Fig. 1).

Systematic experiments, both in open- and closed-loop, revealed that smaller turning radii of the FRI led to a broader dynamic range where the H1-cell spike rate was inversely proportional to wall distance (Fig. 4D) [17, 19]. However, interpreting these observations was not straightforward considering the response properties of EMDs. For instance, as turning radii increased, the dynamic range of the H1-cell decreased and became independent of wall distance, with the largest turning radii even resulting in an inverted response (Fig. 4D).

Previous studies suggested that the complex dependence of the H1-cell response on FRI turning radius and wall distance could be explained by the cell's receptive field organization in conjunction with the optic flow generated during the oscillatory FRI trajectory [20, 21]. Model simulations indicated that the oscillations induced optic flow vectors in parts of the H1-cell receptive field aligned with the cell's motion preferences, thus enhancing the spike rate. However, in other parts of the H1-cell receptive field, optic flow vectors were pointing in the opposite direction, inhibiting the cell's response [20]. The ratio of between excitation and inhibition at various turning radii and wall distances dynamically changed along the FRI's oscillatory trajectory.

Despite providing insight into the dependence of H1-cell responses on turning radius and wall distance, experimental data obtained with the FRI failed to identify and characterise the underlying processing at a mechanistic level.

To systematically investigate the neuronal processing of visual motion leading to distance-dependent responses, we established a virtual reality environment for flies (FlyVR) [21]. FlyVR stimulates the eye of a stationary fly positioned in front of high-speed computer monitors while recording the neural responses of the H1-cell. Ultimately, this system will grant full control and knowledge of relevant visual and kinematic input parameters, facilitating the design of specific stimuli to analyse the cell's integration properties. The ultimate objective of this project is to gain a mechanistic understanding of the emergence of distance-dependent responses of the H1-cell.

Virtual reality systems have been used in fly electrophysiological experiments before, by using LED panels, front projection, or back projection techniques [22–24]. In this study, we introduce the FlyVR2 (Fly Virtual Reality dual-screen system), an updated version of the FlyVR, and present the findings from our open-loop experiments. These results are compared with previously collected data obtained using the FRI system. Furthermore, we analyse the results, particularly focusing on the velocity-independent, distance-dependent H1-responses for different turning radii, wall distances and robot speeds. Additionally, we outline future steps aimed at identifying neural processing strategies for obtaining distance estimates using elementary movement detectors.

2   Methods

2.1   FlyVR2 Setup

Hardware components of the FlyVR2 include two high-speed (240 fps, 1080p) computer gaming monitors (Model: UG25I, 24.5-inch, Z-edge, Zero Edge Technology LLC, U.S.). The computer was equipped with Intel Core i9-11900KF (@ 3.5 GHz), Nvidia GeForce RTX 4070 (12 GB VRAM) and 32 GB RAM. The brightness of the monitor was set to low (white: 34.28 cd/m2, black: 0.02 cd/ m2, Michelson contrast = (34.28–0.02)/(34.28 + 0.02) = 99.88%) to avoid saturating the photodiode. The computer was streaming visual stimuli at maximum frame rate to the computer screens with compatible G-sync (i.e. vertical synchronisation). The stimuli were programmed in a 3D game engine (Godot, version 4.1.1) for rendering 3840 × 1080p outputs on two screens (1920 × 1080p), simultaneously.

The FlyVR2 video output was composed of a wall with a vertical black-and-white grating pattern on the left-hand side and a black fabric-patterned (distribution of pixels' grayscale [out of 255] $= 36 \pm 14$ [as $\mu \pm \sigma$]) global background in the virtual arena. Two virtual cameras were moving in an alternating forward quarter circular arc trajectory along the virtual wall, with turning radius and wall distance as controlled parameters, to approximate the experimental conditions used by Huang and Krapp [19] in earlier FRI studies (Fig. 1). The mean distances from the oscillatory forward trajectory to the patterned wall were 10, 15, 20, 25, 30 cm, and the virtual cameras were moving at turning radii of 5, 10, 15, 20, 25 cm.

To replicate the FRI kinematics utilised by Huang and Krapp [19], we opted for a virtual FRI with a wheel-to-wheel distance of 10 cm, yielding a robot radius $R_r = 5$ cm. We established the maximum speed of the robot's wheels. The parameters of the experiment, as outlined in Table 1, were determined using the equation:

$$\omega = \frac{V_{low}}{R_t - R_r} = \frac{V_{robot}}{R_t} = \frac{V_{high}}{R_t + R_r}, \tag{1}$$

where R_r represents the robot's radius, R_t denotes the turning radius, and V_{robot} signifies the ground speed of the virtual FRI robot as it travels along an oscillatory quarter circular arc trajectory. V_{high} represents the speed of the centre of the robot wheel (with the higher velocity) moving in parallel to the ground. V_{low} indicates the lower speed of the robot wheel. Additionally, ω represents the angular velocity of the robot as it moves around the turning centre of the quarter circular arc trajectory (Fig. 1).

Table 1. Values of turning radii and velocities in the FlyVR2

V_{high} (cm/s)	R_t (cm)	V_{low} (cm/s)	V_{robot} (cm/s)	ω (rad/s)
15	5	0	7.5	1.5
15	10	5	10	1
15	15	7.5	11.25	0.75
15	20	9	12	0.6
15	25	10	12.5	0.5
30	5	0	15	3
30	10	10	20	2
30	15	15	22.5	1.5
30	20	18	24	1.2
30	25	20	25	1
45	5	0	22.5	4.5
45	10	15	30	3
45	15	22.5	33.75	2.25
45	20	27	36	1.8
45	25	30	37.5	1.5

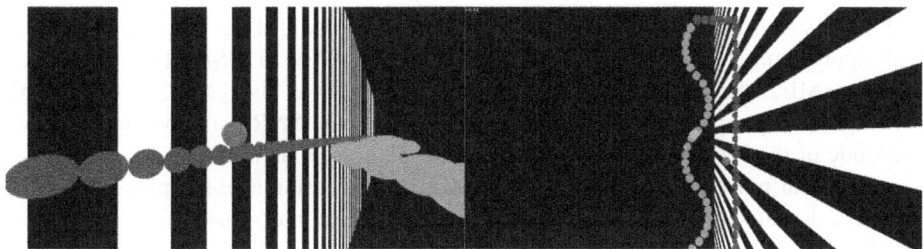

Fig. 1. The trajectory of the virtual FRI (green dot) in the FlyVR2 virtual arena (**Left**: horizontal view, **Right**: top-down view). The view in the left screen was the virtual camera on the FRI shooting from the cyan dot towards the red dot on the right screen. The FRI was moving along the green path. The lateral field of view (FOV) was covering ~120°. The green dots give consecutive positions of the FRI in the virtual arena, indicate the turning radius (Rt) and the difference between corresponding green and blue dots give the distance to the virtual wall (Dw), respectively. The red dot marks the centre of the sectional quarter circular arc trajectory. (Note: The image here was showing the relative scale in virtual space, a video for the final calibration of the FlyVR2 stimulus can be found at: https://youtu.be/uOra8ITj04Q)

Given five different turning radii, five wall distances and three velocities, there were 75 parameter combinations. The responses of the H1-cell to each of those 75 parameter combinations were logged over 17 s. The overall recording time was ~75 * 17/60 = 21.25 min for one animal. Our results are based on experiments in 5 different animals.

2.2 Fly Preparation

The fly preparation was the same as the previous series of experiments [16, 17, 19–21, 25, 26]. As a brief description: we conducted experiments using blowflies, *Calliphora vicina*, which were bred in an insect breeding chamber maintained at a temperature of 20–25 °C and relative humidity of 50–60%, subjected to a 12:12-h light:dark cycle. Female blowflies aged between 4 to 11 days were selected for the experiments. Before mounting the fly onto a specialised fly holder, the legs and proboscis were removed, and any open wounds as well as the wing hinges were covered with beeswax. The deep pseudopupil method [27] was used to align the eye equator with the horizontal plane. Next, the animal's head was affixed to the fly holder by beeswax, and the thorax was gently pushed down and waxed to the holder, leaving a gap between the back of the head and the thorax for inserting the recording electrode. The cuticle on the back of the head was cut open to access the visual neuropil, and air sacs, fat, and muscle tissue were removed to expose the lobula plate. Ringer solution was applied to the opening in the head capsule as needed to prevent tissue desiccation (for the recipe of the Ringer solution, see e.g., [28]). Dissection was operated under optical magnification using a 75 × –500 × stereo microscope (OPMI 1-F, Zeiss©).

Responses of H1-cell were recorded extracellularly using sharp tungsten electrodes (with approximately 3 MΩ impedance, product code: UEWSHGSE3N1M, FHC Inc., Bowdoin, ME, USA). The signal-to-noise ratio (SNR) was always $\geq$ 2:1 when commencing the experimental protocol. The definition of the SNR was dividing the peak amplitude of the H1-cell spikes by the largest peak amplitude in the background noise (e.g. electrical noise and spikes from other cells). The instantaneous spike rate of the cell was calculated based on the inverse of the inter-spike intervals (ISIs).

2.3   Electrophysiological Recording

Before the recordings, the blowflies were placed in front of the centre of two orthogonally positioned computer screens, and perpendicular to both screens (see Fig. 2) for around 30 min. After the visual stimulus alignment, the distance to the left screen was 12.5 cm, while the distance to the frontal screen was 28 cm. A 2-mm thick black cart board was placed in between the screens, aligning from the fly to the screen bezel, to avoid screen reflections. Due to the announced 16:9 screen ratio, the FOV (field of view) for the left screen was set as 90° (elevation angle), while the frontal screen was set as 60° (elevation angle). The left screen FOV ensured the average screen pixel resolution ($90°/1080 = 0.083°$), while the frontal screen FOV ensured the resolution of ($60°/1080 = 0.055°$). This pixel resolution was approximately two orders of magnitude more precise than the smallest inter-ommatidial angle of a fly, which is 1.1° [29], adjusting with the spatial sampling basis of neighbouring inputs to the motion detection circuits.

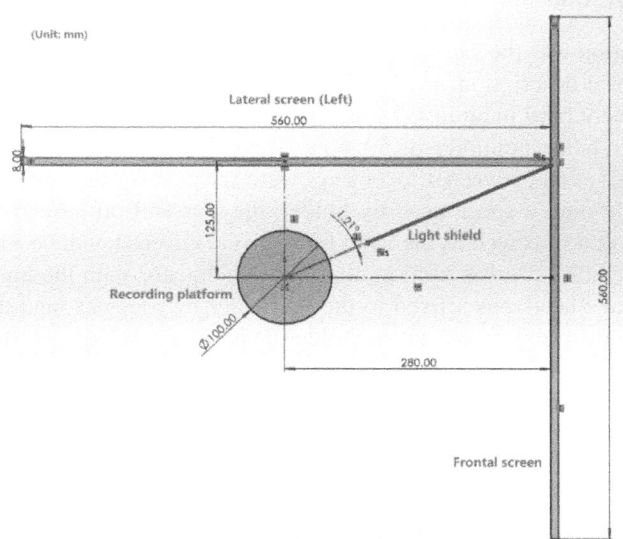

Fig. 2. Arrangement of the recording platform in front of two orthogonal high-speed monitors. An A4-sized black cardboard light shield was positioned in between the monitors, aligned from the monitor bezel to the insect, to minimise its visibility to the retina.

We used a data acquisition board (NIDAQ USB-6009, National Instruments Co., U.S.) to record two analog input channels at a sampling frequency of 20 kHz: (i) the extracellular H1-cell response and (ii) the output of a photodiode attached to the computer screen, providing a sync signal. The signal of the photodiode was activated when the virtual robot was making a turn towards the virtual wall and deactivated during the rest of the oscillatory circular trajectory movement (see Fig. 1).

A video demonstrating a test run of an experiment using the FlyVR2 system can be viewed at: https://youtu.be/aXqZy2OxZc8.

3 Results

To assess the suitability of the FlyVR2 system for systematically investigating the neural mechanisms involved in distance estimation, we conducted experiments recording the responses of the H1-cell under conditions that mimic previous FRI experiments. This entailed selecting turning radii and wall distances according to the methods outlined in the Methods section (i.e. Table 1), followed by analysing the recorded H1-cell activities within time windows comparable between the two datasets.

Figure 3 depicts an illustration of the raw data and initial analysis outcomes obtained using the FlyVR2 system with a turning radius of 5 cm and a wall distance of 15 cm (the mean trajectory distance from the wall) in the virtual environment. During the projection of the visual stimulus onto the less sensitive portion of the caudo-lateral receptive field of the cells, the H1-cell spike rate increased. As the virtual robot turned away from the wall, the spike rate was entirely inhibited. To facilitate a comparison between the FlyVR2 data and the FRI robot data, the neural response was selected from the rising edge of the sync signal of the stimulus until the falling edge of the sync signal, making it comparable to the robotic trajectory in the FRI setup (see Fig. 1). The sync signal was provided by thresholding the photodiode signal at 4.75 V. Voltage thresholds were used in the spike detection. However additional Butterworth filters were applied to reject noise (Krapp Lab unpublished).

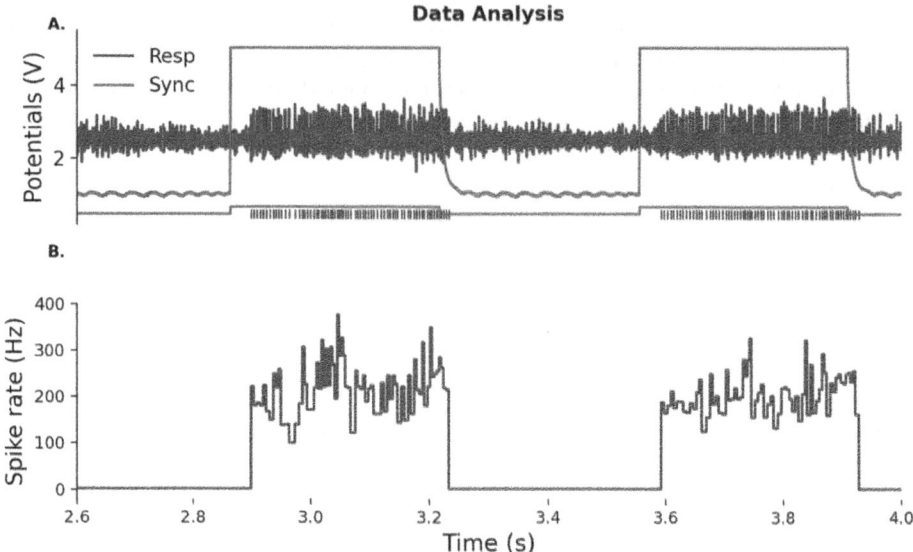

Fig. 3. Example recording trace and spike rate estimation of the H1-cell activity obtained using the FlyVR2 system. (The parameters of the example data: angular velocity = 4.5 rad/s, Rt = 5 cm and Dw = 15 cm) (**A**) The extracellularly recorded raw signals (blue: H1 response, red: photodiode signal as synchronisation) plotted as a function of time. The sync indicates the time period during which the fly's body was turning towards the patterned wall when moving along an oscillatory trajectory in the FlyVR2 environment. (**B**) The instantaneous spike rates (blue) of the H1-cell under FlyVR2 stimulation. (Stimulus parameters: Rt = 5 cm, Dw = 15 cm, Vh = 45 cm/s)

The average spike rates of the H1-cells were investigated at various turning radii (Rt) and wall distances (Dw) in five flies (N = 5). To aggregate data across experiments conducted in different animals for each combination of parameters, we calculated the mean spike rates and the standard error of the mean (SEM) observed during the stimulus intervals. These results are compared with those obtained at different velocities (e.g. Vh = 15, 30, 45 cm/s) in the same system in Fig. 4.

From the results obtained using the FlyVR2 system, it is evident that the turning radius (Rt) has a similar effect on the H1-cell wall-distance-dependence as found in previous FRI studies [19]. Particularly, at smaller wall distances (e.g., Dw = 10 cm), the modulations of the H1-cell responses on the FlyVR2 (Fig. 4) mirrored the trends observed on the robot platform [19]. In essence, the spike rates demonstrated distance-related modulation at wall distances < 20 cm. However, this modulation became small when the wall distance exceeded 20 cm, with all spike rates converging to closely similar values regardless of the turning radii, for instance, Dw = 20, 25, 30 cm.

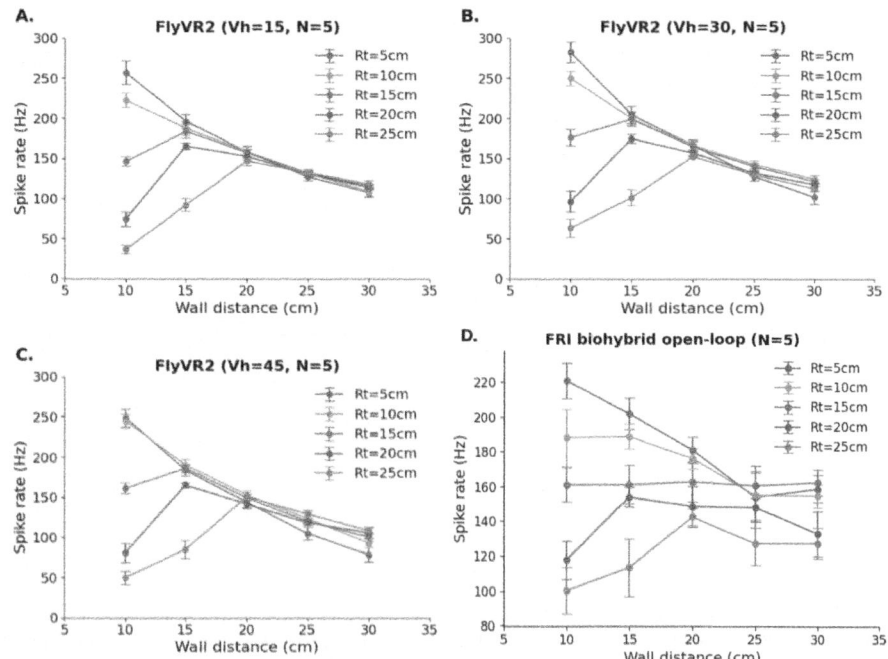

Fig. 4. Average H1-cell spike rate as a function of wall distance for different turning radii (*Rt*) **(A)** Data obtained with the FlyVR2 system under open-loop conditions, Vh = 15 cm/s (N = 5). **(B)** Vh = 30 cm/s (N = 5). **(C)** Vh = 45 cm/s (N = 5). **(D)** Data obtained with the FRI system under open-loop conditions (N = 5. Note: the maximum values of the spike rate axes may differ, modified from [19]). (Note: Error bars represent SEM.)

By focusing on Dw = 10 cm, where the distance dependency was maximised, we plotted the H1-responses and compared the instantaneous spike rates at different turning radii (e.g. Rt = 5, 15, 25 cm) with different robot velocities (Fig. 5). The instantaneous spike rates (such as those shown in Fig. 3) were selected based on their related photodiode signals (without neural delays) and averaged among multiple repetitions. The averaged instantaneous spike rates were binned into 6 sections along the quarter circular arc trajectory, 90°/6 = 15° per bin. The mean and SEM of each bin were then computed from 5 insects.

For the small arc trajectories (Rt = 5) the instantaneous spike rates rose to around 250 Hz (Fig. 5A). Along the medium arc trajectories (Rt = 15), the spike rates rose to around 180 Hz (Fig. 5B), and for the large arc trajectories (Rt = 25) the spike rates fluctuated around 50 Hz (Fig. 5C).

The one-way ANOVA test was applied in each Rt group (Fig. 5D), after applying Shapiro-Wilk test as the data's normality test. Except for the test between the data "Vh30Rt25" and "Vh15Rt25", there was no statistically significant difference in all data groups.

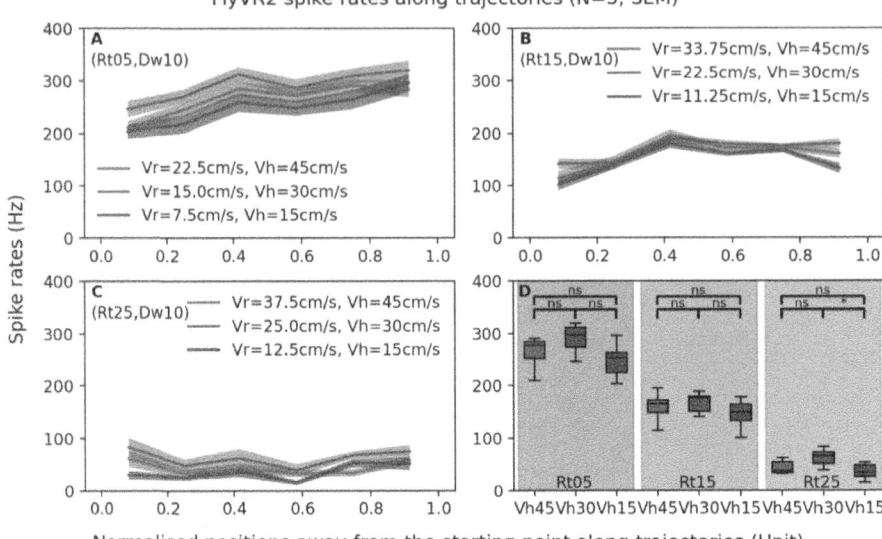

Fig. 5. Instantaneous spike rates of H1-cell at normalised positions from the starting point to the end point of the arc trajectories, which the FRI was turning towards the wall. (Vr = robot velocity) **(A)** The spike rates were recorded on an (Rt05) trajectory with three robot velocities. **(B)** on an Rt15 trajectory, **(C)** on an Rt25 trajectory. (The error bars of the spike rates were the SEM, N = 5) **(D)** the one-way ANOVA test for each Rt group. ("ns" for p-value > 0.05, "*" for p-value > 0.01)

4   Discussion

4.1   The FRI Speed Does not Affect the Instantaneous Spike Rates Along a Trajectory of Fixed Turning Radius

The instantaneous H1-responses were not dependent on the FRI speed along a trajectory of a constant turning radius (Fig. 5). The H1-cell integrates spatially local EMD outputs that were analysing visual motion across a large fraction of the visual field along azimuth and elevation.

The parameters Rt and Dw determine the shape of the arc trajectory and its location relative to the wall, respectively. These two parameters also determine the retinal image shift at each location along the arc trajectory.

The H1-cell receives input from EMDs which are known to produce signals that are dependent on temporal frequency, TF, which is the ratio between the angular velocity (ω) and the spatial wavelength (λ) of the visual grating in a bell-shaped function [25, 30, 31]. It remains to be studied what the neural mechanisms are that explain the distance dependence of the H1-cell's spike rate irrespective of the FRI speed along a trajectory of a given turning radius.

A possible explanation could be that the ratio of excitatory and inhibitory inputs to the H1-cell, although dependent on the (ratio of FRI translation and rotation) is hardly affected by FRI speed along its oscillatory trajectories.

4.2 Advances of the FlyVR2 for Studying the Distance Dependence of H1-Cell Responses

Compared to the initial version, the design of the FlyVR2 system has been improved: (1). The dual-screen setup covers a larger fraction of the fly's visual field, (2). The Godot game engine simplified the programming, easily constructing oscillatory trajectories, and (3). Risk-free reconfigurability.

Instead of using only one 360 Hz lateral screen on the FlyVR system, the FlyVR2 system used two 240 Hz screens, enabling not only stimulation of the fly's lateral visual field but also its frontal visual field. The H1-cell is a wide-field motion-sensitive interneuron, with a receptive field that covers an azimuthal range from $-15°$ to more than $135°$ [7]. The fly's frontal compound eyes contain a higher number of ommatidia, providing higher spatial resolution [29]. By adding a screen in the frontal visual field of the insect, the FlyVR2 more closely approximates the visual environment in which the FRI operates.

Compared to OpenGL programming, the Godot game engine simplified the programming massively. There was a user-friendly interface that provided a high level of flexibility when recreating the experimental environment of the FRI in virtual reality. Another advantage was the simpler validation of the preprogrammed oscillatory quarter circular arc trajectory, and the setup of the cameras (e.g. the FOVs of the frontal camera and the left camera). The oscillatory forward trajectory was recreated by the parameters used in the FRI [19], which provides both the preferred directional and the null directional optic flows to the H1-cell. It was different from the circular trajectory used on the mono-screen FlyVR system, which did not contain the phase of a global null-directional optic flow to inhibit the H1-cell [21].

Finally, the risk-free reconfigurability of the parameters of the FlyVR2 allows us to quickly test the neural responses against a particular robot parameter, e.g. the robotic speed, without worrying about the inconsistency of the friction between the wheels and floor (e.g. grease and dust on the wheels), the power fluctuation of the onboard battery, nor the health condition of the recorded cells, through the modification of the parameter (e.g. frequently plug/unplug the USB programming cable on FRI, creating massive vibration to the nearby electrophysiology platform, which could deteriorate the signal-to-noise ratio of the recording. In the worst case, damages the cell).

4.3 The Advantages of a Nearby Speed-Independent Distance-Related H1-Cell Spike Rate

The H1-cell responses were hardly affected by different robot speeds along a given trajectory in the VR experiments. The results shown in Fig. 4 obtained with the FlyVR2 suggest that all the distance-dependant H1-responses were similar across different Vh parameters, at each given trajectory.

The distance-dependent spike rates of the H1-cell were only used in active sensing when an ego-motion was involved. For example: a fly is switching Rt in between 5 cm and 25 cm, during a flight. The delta of the Rt could result in different delta of spike rates, depending on Dw. If the Dw is large (e.g. Dw > 20 cm), $\Delta Rt = 25 - 5 = 20$ cm, producing nearly 0 $\Delta Fspk$ (delta spike rates). However, if the Dw is small (e.g. Dw = 10 cm), $\Delta Rt = 20$ cm, produces more than 200 Hz $\Delta Fspk$. (Fig. 5).

4.4 Future Experiments

There are future investigations for the H1-cell and the opto-motor pathway. (1). The velocity of the fly, (2). The field of view, (3). The modelling of the H1-cell, and (4). The descending neural pathway.

In our experiments, we used a moderate velocity range of 0.5 to 4.5 rad/s. The velocity tuning of the H1-cell showed that the cut-off frequency of the angular velocity was around 1000°/s (=17.44 rad/s) in a lab environment [32]. This means that, if the angular velocity reaches 17.44 (rad/s), the gain of the H1-responses might attenuate to zero. Interestingly, this cutoff frequency of the angular velocity matches the 6 Hz oscillations of freely flying blowflies described by Kern et al. [14], where the angular velocity would be roughly $6*\pi = 18.84$ (rad/s). In the future, the higher velocities could be tested in the fly virtual reality system, to see the boundary of the H1-cell responses, e.g. at a saccade with 3g acceleration [33].

The FlyVR2 system showed its merit in characterising cellular outputs with its precision. A future FlyVR4 could be built to complete the FlyVR2 system, which contains 4x portrait 240 Hz monitors around the insect, providing panoramic visual stimulus, using identical FOV setup in the game engine, to avoid the distortion from the mismatching FOVs, for both open-loop and closed-loop experiments. In addition, it could enable us to dig deeper. For example, to model an array of EMDs that receive an input according to the optic flow calculations and see how Rt and Dw affect the results. Then we will be able to identify the transformation of the input into the output and any discrepancies between model predictions and experimental results.

A detailed model of the H1-cell could be investigated. It could be a two-step process: (1) compute the optic flow input as a function of the FRI kinematics. (2) Use the computed optic flow to parameterise the pattern motion across the different parts of the eye, calculate the outputs of the EMDs, and integrate the outputs in a way similar to the neural integration of inputs on the dendrites of LPTCs. A model that is specified/parameterised based on experimental and theoretical studies would be extremely helpful, e.g. for developing future FRI, or automobiles.

In the long term, descending neurons with receptive field properties similar to those of the H1-cell [34] could be studied, to test whether they integrate wingbeat signals from the thoracic ganglion, or gated by the ascending neurons.

5 Conclusion

In our study of the responses of H1-cells in the FlyVR2 system, we found that the distance-dependent H1-responses were only mildly affected by the insect's velocities on a given trajectory. The turning radius, on the other hand, had a strong effect on how the cell's spiking activity reflected the distances to objects in the fly's visual environment.

Further investigations, informed by modelling its directional motion vision system, will be necessary to unravel the neural mechanisms governing visual distance estimation in blowflies, and potentially other animal model systems. The results may inspire the design of novel energy-efficient sensors complementing traditional reflection-based optical devices for distance estimation in robotic systems.

Acknowledgments. This work was supported by US AFOSR/EOARD grant [FA8655-22-1-7030] (HGK).

References

1. Gabbiani, F., Krapp, H.G., Koch, C., Laurent, G.: Multiplicative computation in a visual neuron sensitive to looming. Nature **420**, 320–324 (2002). https://doi.org/10.1038/nature 01190

2. Simmons, P.J., Rind, F.C.: Orthopteran DCMD neuron: a reevaluation of responses to moving objects. II. Critical cues for detecting approaching objects. J. Neurophysiol. (1992). https://doi.org/10.1152/jn.1992.68.5.1667

3. Klapoetke, N.C., et al.: Ultra-selective looming detection from radial motion opponency. Nature **551**, 237–241 (2017). https://doi.org/10.1038/nature24626

4. Wicklein, M., Strausfeld, N.J.: Organization and significance of neurons that detect change of visual depth in the hawk moth Manduca sexta. J. Comp. Neurol. **424**, 356–376 (2000). https://doi.org/10.1002/1096-9861(20000821)424:2%3c356::AID-CNE12%3e3.0.CO;2-T

5. Longden, K.D., Wicklein, M., Hardcastle, B.J., Huston, S.J., Krapp, H.G.: Spike burst coding of translatory optic flow and depth from motion in the fly visual system. Curr. Biol. **27**, 3225-3236.e3 (2017). https://doi.org/10.1016/j.cub.2017.09.044

6. Hausen, K.: Motion sensitive interneurons in the optomotor system of the fly. Biol. Cybern. **46**, 67–79 (1982). https://doi.org/10.1007/BF00335352

7. Krapp, H.G., Hengstenberg, R., Egelhaaf, M.: Binocular contributions to optic flow processing in the fly visual system. J. Neurophysiol. **85**, 724–734 (2001)

8. Krapp, H.G., Hengstenberg, B., Hengstenberg, R.: Dendritic structure and receptive-field organization of optic flow processing interneurons in the fly. J. Neurophysiol. **79**, 1902–1917 (1998)

9. Hassenstein, B., Reichardt, W.: Systemtheoretische Analyse der Zeit-, Reihenfolgen- und Vorzeichenauswertung bei der Bewegungsperzeption des Rüsselkäfers Chlorophanus. Zeitschrift für Naturforschung B. **11**, 513–524 (1956). https://doi.org/10.1515/znb-1956-9-1004

10. Egelhaaf, M., Borst, A.: Movement detection in arthropods. Rev. Oculomot. Res. **5**, 53–77 (1993)

11. Borst, A.: How Do Flies Land? Bioscience **40**, 292–299 (1990). https://doi.org/10.2307/131 1266

12. Zhao, J., Xi, S., Li, Y., Guo, A., Wu, Z.: A fly inspired solution to looming detection for collision avoidance. iScience **26**, 106337 (2023). https://doi.org/10.1016/j.isci.2023.106337

13. Gabbiani, F., Krapp, H.G., Laurent, G.: Computation of object approach by a wide-field. Motion-Sensitive Neuron. J. Neurosci. **19**, 1122–1141 (1999). https://doi.org/10.1523/JNE UROSCI.19-03-01122.1999

14. Kern, R., Boeddeker, N., Dittmar, L., Egelhaaf, M.: Blowfly flight characteristics are shaped by environmental features and controlled by optic flow information. J. Exp. Biol. **215**, 2501–2514 (2012). https://doi.org/10.1242/jeb.061713

15. Kern, R., van Hateren, J.H., Michaelis, C., Lindemann, J.P., Egelhaaf, M.: Function of a fly motion-sensitive neuron matches eye movements during free flight. PLoS Biol. **3**, e171 (2005). https://doi.org/10.1371/journal.pbio.0030171

16. Huang, J.V., Wei, Y., Krapp, H.G.: Active collision free closed-loop control of a biohybrid fly-robot interface. In: Vouloutsi, V., et al. (eds.) Biomimetic and Biohybrid Systems, pp. 213–222. Springer International Publishing (2018)

17. Huang, J.V., Wei, Y., Krapp, H.G.: A biohybrid fly-robot interface system that performs active collision avoidance. Bioinspir. Biomim. **14**, 065001 (2019). https://doi.org/10.1088/1748-3190/ab3b23

18. Huang, J.V., Krapp, H.G.: A predictive model for closed-loop collision avoidance in a fly-robotic interface. In: Duff, A., Lepora, N.F., Mura, A., Prescott, T.J., Verschure, P.F.M.J. (eds.) Biomimetic and Biohybrid Systems, pp. 130–141. Springer International Publishing (2014). https://doi.org/10.1007/978-3-319-09435-9_12

19. Huang, J.V., Krapp, H.G.: Neuronal distance estimation by a fly-robot interface. In: Biomimetic and Biohybrid Systems, pp. 204–215. Springer, Cham (2017). https://doi.org/10.1007/978-3-319-63537-8_18

20. Huang, J.V., Wang, Y., Krapp, H.G.: Wall following in a semi-closed-loop fly-robotic interface. In: Biomimetic and Biohybrid Systems, pp. 85–96. Springer, Cham (2016). https://doi.org/10.1007/978-3-319-42417-0_9

21. Huang, J.V., Krapp, H.G.: Fly H1-cell distance estimation in a monocular virtual reality environment. In: Meder, F., Hunt, A., Margheri, L., Mura, A., Mazzolai, B. (eds.) Biomimetic and Biohybrid Systems. pp. 325–337. Springer Nature Switzerland, Cham (2023). https://doi.org/10.1007/978-3-031-38857-6_24

22. Isaacson, M., et al.: A high-speed, modular display system for diverse neuroscience applications (2022). https://doi.org/10.1101/2022.08.02.502550

23. Prech, S., Groschner, L.N., Borst, A.: An open platform for visual stimulation of insects. PLoS ONE **19**, e0301999 (2024). https://doi.org/10.1371/journal.pone.0301999

24. Williamson, W.R., Peek, M.Y., Breads, P., Coop, B., Card, G.M.: Tools for Rapid High-Resolution Behavioral Phenotyping of Automatically Isolated *Drosophila*. Cell Rep. **25**, 1636-1649.e5 (2018). https://doi.org/10.1016/j.celrep.2018.10.048

25. Huang, J.V., Krapp, H.G.: Miniaturized electrophysiology platform for fly-robot interface to study multisensory integration. In: Lepora, N.F., Mura, A., Krapp, H.G., Verschure, P.F.M.J., Prescott, T.J. (eds.) Biomimetic and Biohybrid Systems, pp. 119–130. Springer Berlin Heidelberg (2013). https://doi.org/10.1007/978-3-642-39802-5_11

26. Huang, J.V., Krapp, H.G.: Closed-loop control in an autonomous bio-hybrid robot system based on binocular neuronal input. In: Wilson, S.P., Verschure, P.F.M.J., Mura, A., and Prescott, T.J. (eds.) Biomimetic and Biohybrid Systems. pp. 164–174. Springer International Publishing (2015). https://doi.org/10.1007/978-3-319-22979-9_17

27. Franceschini, N.: Pupil and Pseudopupil in the Compound Eye of Drosophila. In: Wehner, R. (ed.) Information Processing in the Visual Systems of Anthropods, pp. 75–82. Springer, Berlin Heidelberg (1972)

28. Karmeier, K., Tabor, R., Egelhaaf, M., Krapp, H.G.: Early visual experience and the receptive-field organization of optic flow processing interneurons in the fly motion pathway. Vis. Neurosci. **18**, 1–8 (2001)

29. Petrowitz, R., Dahmen, H., Egelhaaf, M., Krapp, H.G.: Arrangement of optical axes and spatial resolution in the compound eye of the female blowfly Calliphora. J. Comp. Physiol. A **186**, 737–746 (2000). https://doi.org/10.1007/s003590000127

30. O'Carroll, D.C., Bidweii, N.J., Laughlin, S.B., Warrant, E.J.: Insect motion detectors matched to visual ecology. Nature **382**, 63–66 (1996). https://doi.org/10.1038/382063a0

31. Longden, K.D., Krapp, H.G.: State-dependent performance of optic-flow processing interneurons. J. Neurophysiol. **102**, 3606–3618 (2009). https://doi.org/10.1152/jn.00395.2009

32. Lewen, G.D., Bialek, W., de Ruyter van Steveninck, R.R.: Neural coding of naturalistic motion stimuli. Network **12**, 317–329 (2001).

33. Bomphrey, R.J., Walker, S.M., Taylor, G.K.: The typical flight performance of blowflies: measuring the normal performance envelope of calliphora vicina using a novel corner-cube arena. PLoS ONE **4**, e7852 (2009). https://doi.org/10.1371/journal.pone.0007852
34. Huston, S.J., Krapp, H.G.: Visuomotor transformation in the fly gaze stabilization system. PLoS Biol. **6**, e173 (2008). https://doi.org/10.1371/journal.pbio.0060173

Larva in the Loop, Utilizing Zebrafish Larvae to Control Robots in Real Time via Optokinetic Response Feedback

John Jutoy$^{(\boxtimes)}$ and Erica Jung

Department of Mechanical and Industrial Engineering, University of Illinois at Chicago, Chicago, Il 60607, USA
jjutoy2@uic.edu

Abstract. The optokinetic response (OKR) in Zebrafish (*Danio Rerio*) had been characterized for its robust response to visual stimuli. Expanding on these works, we developed a novel closed loop control schema to drive a robot utilizing the OKR of Zebrafish larvae. Our system keeps a larva's body constrained via a novel agarose mold holder that allows for eye movement and vision. The larva is then put under a microscope camera and processed through computer vision in order to track its eyes through ellipse fitting. Relative eye angle data is then parsed through an algorithm and used to send movement signals to a robot on a lined track. Simultaneously, the robot returns its relative position with respect to the line and converts that information into an OKR stimulation animation which is displayed on an LCD screen in the ventral plane of the larva, thus closing the loop. Through this work we show the capability of larvae OKR to keep a robot on a linear track after an initial oblique entrance to the line. This work displays the potential of our system and how it can pave way to a Zebrafish Brain-Machine Interface.

Keywords: Zebrafish Larvae · Optokinetic Response · Feedback Control

1 Introduction

To understand and perhaps control the human brain, it is key to have tools that could monitor and elicit responses in the brain. Although great strides have been made in mapping and interfacing with the human brain, there is merit to studying organisms with less complex brain systems such as *C. Elegans*, *Drosophila*, and *Danio Rerio* [1]. Animal brain models can help in understanding neuropathobiology [2], improving brain mapping [3], or developing better methodologies for bio-machine interfaces, all of which we hope to address with our system and its future iterations.

N. S. Szczecinski et al. (Eds.): Living Machines 2024, LNAI 14930, pp. 428–436, 2025.
https://doi.org/10.1007/978-3-031-72597-5_29

Zebrafish larvae in particular are ideal model organisms due to their fast reproduction rate, external development, and translucency [4] . In particular, Zebrafish larvae translucency combined with genetic engineering tools and optics (optogenetics), allow for non-invasive neural activity measurement and stimulation [5]. The work presented here describes the progress towards a neural monitoring and elicitation system for Zebrafish larvae.

Thus far, we have been able to develop a visual stimulation system that works in conjunction with a larvae holder. We display the capabilities of the developed Zebrafish Machine Interface which utilizes optokinetic response in both open and closed loop manner. We discuss how the work presented is a stepping stone towards our goal of a Zebrafish Brain-Machine Interface.

1.1 Optokinetic Response

To validate our system, we aimed to reproduce what has been widely done with Zebrafish Larvae which is to demonstrate its optokinetic response through visual stimulation [6]. The Optokinetic response (OKR) is one of the gaze stabilization mechanism which moves the eye such that a feature of interest is kept in focus.

The Zebrafish larvae OKR has been used for visual screening of mutants due to its robust and reliable response [6] and has been used to quantify Zebrafish visual acuity [7]. Work presented here capitalizes on this robust response by introducing it in a closed feedback system. We posit that the OKR response of the Zebrafish can maintain a set-point with proper parameter tuning of OKR stimulation.

1.2 Novel Larvae Fixation

Consistent and accurate eye tracking requires larva head fixation without obstructing eye movement or vision. Agarose embedding [6,8] became the standard in Zebrafish larvae fixation due to its transparency and non-toxic attributes. Although agarose embedding has became the standard, it is generally a time consuming process. We introduce in this work a novel and more efficient method for larvae fixation inspired by Copper et. al [10].

2 Methods

A modular approach was taken to develop the Zebrafish Machine Interface so that modules can be easily added or improved in future work. Brief descriptions are provided for individual modules along with the larvae care methodologies.

The open-loop system, OKR visual stimulation, and eye tracking were used in conjunction to verify that the system could properly elicit OKR in larvae.

The closed-loop system is simply the open-loop system with the addition of the robot car module.

2.1   Larvae Fixation

A resin 3D printed positive mold was created with features of a Zebrafish larva as seen in Fig. 1c. The dimensions were such that it would constrict larva movement while having enough space for eye movement.

Creation of the device consisted of heating up agarose gel into its liquid form and placing it into a petri dish with the positive mold. The agarose solidifies into a translucent gel in which the positive mold can be carefully removed. Negative space left by the positive mold is then filled with a larva through a hair loop device [9].

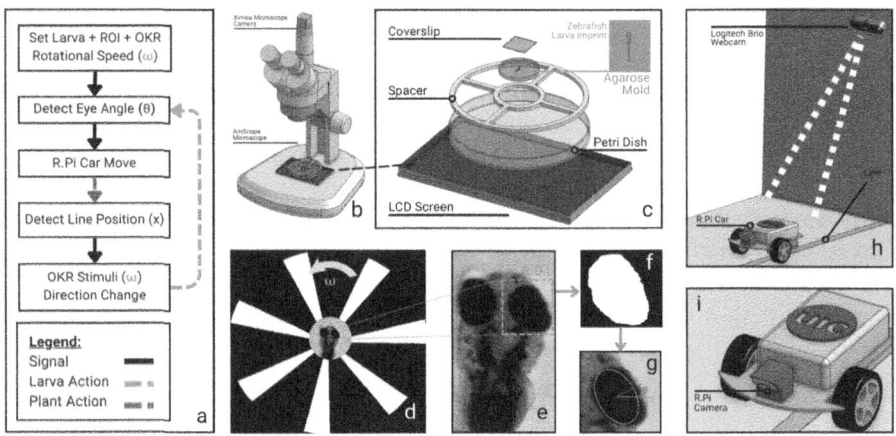

Fig. 1. System Setup of Zebrafish Machine Interface including system flow chart, renderings of hardware components, and image processing of eye angle. (a) System logic flowchart with key parameters (ω = constant angular speed of stimuli animation, θ = minor axis angle of fitted ellipse on larva eye with respect to positive horizontal axis, x = distance between center of R.Pi camera and center of yellow line) highlighted and colored. (b) Rendering of Zebrafish system (c) Closeup of Zebrafish larva holder. (d) Animation of rotating black and white arcs at constant angular speed ω provided by LCD screen to elicit optokinetic response. (e) Zoomed in image of greyscale larva video frame along with region of interest (R.O.I.) highlighted. (f) R.O.I. passed through Gaussian filter to isolate larva eye. (g) Ellipse fitted to (f) overlayed into (e) to extract θ. (h) Rendering of R.Pi system. (i) Zoomed in rendering of R.Pi car to display the horizontal distance between camera and line. (Color figure online)

2.2   OKR Visual Stimulation

A module in the system software was created to provide a rotating grating animation using the OpenCV python library. Several parameters can be easily modified by the system including grating rotation speed ω, number of gratings, grating arc length, and grating radius. Sufficient contrast for the eye tracking module was provided by including a blank white circle directly under the fish.

The parameters chosen for testing were identified manually based on visual inspection of OKR from the larvae. These parameters were found to be: 5 gratings, 50% grating spacing (ie: half of the grating is black and half is white).

2.3   Eye Tracking

The fish eye tracking module converts images from the microscope camera video stream into eye angles of the Zebrafish eye of interest. Using the openCV library of python, raw images are converted to grey scale, blurred, then thresholded to a value found suitable for isolation of the Zebrafish eye. Contouring is done on the isolated eye and an ellipse is then fitted to it. The major axis of the ellipse is then used as the angle of the eye.

2.4   Robot Car

A raspberry pi car with two wheeled motors in the front and a free moving wheel in the back was chosen as the vehicle for the Zebrafish to control. The modified chassis was made to accommodate a raspberry pi camera. Communication to the raspberry pi car from the main workstation was done through the Paramiko library.

The robot car was tracked through a Logitech Brio webcam and procesed through OpenCV to extract its estimated position.

2.5   Zebrafish Larvae

Larvae were bred from wild-type adult in a dedicated fish room, temperature controlled to 26 °C, with a 14-h light and 10-h darkness cycle. Larvae are harvested and kept in the fish room until 4–5 days post fertilization (dpf) from which they are brought to the testing facility a day prior for experiments. Larvae are kept in an incubation chamber set at 27 °C outside of experimental trials.

3   Results

3.1   Verification of Optokinetic Response

To verify that OKR is displayed by Zebrafish larvae, a simple test with a duration of 140 s was created to analyze eye response to the developed OKR stimuli. The first and last 10 s of the test hides the individual arc features of the stimuli to serve as a baseline of no response and is referred to as $\omega = 0$. The stimuli are displayed at $\omega = 5, 15, 30, 45, 60°/s$ in 20 s time intervals between 20–120 respectively. Within each 20 s time bin, a direction switch is made.

Analysis of eye movement direction agreement was done in (Fig. 3) and total eye angle response (Fig. 4) in order to display that the OKR response was related to the visual stimuli of the system.

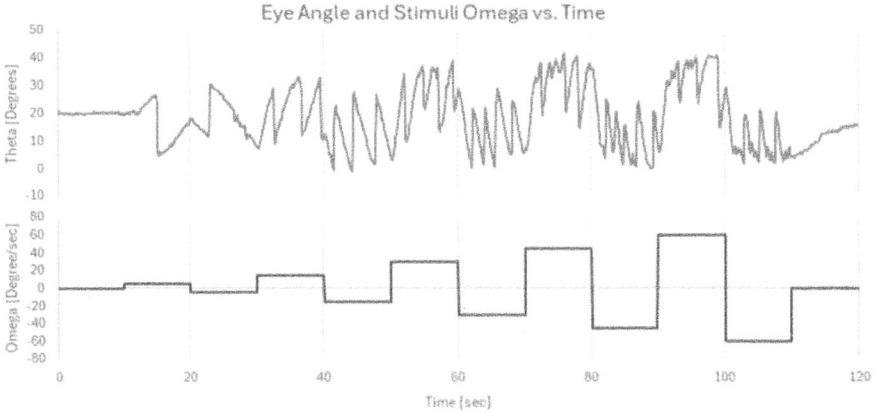

Fig. 2. Right eye angle response for a single Zebrafish larva at varying direction and ω as seen in Fig. 1-d. Eye angles are in terms of degrees while ω are in terms of degrees/sec. Note that eye angle slope direction agree with stimuli ω direction within times that the stimuli was given: 20–120 s.

3.2   Larvae in the Loop Line Following

Once optokinetic response was identified in a fish, trials were conducted to see if the larvae can maintain a robot car within a line at different ω as seen in Fig. 5. A representative set of trials from a single larva driver can be seen in Fig. 6. Each trial consisted of starting the robot car facing the yellow line at a slight random oblique angle. The car was tracked and driven by the larvae for a duration of 45 s.

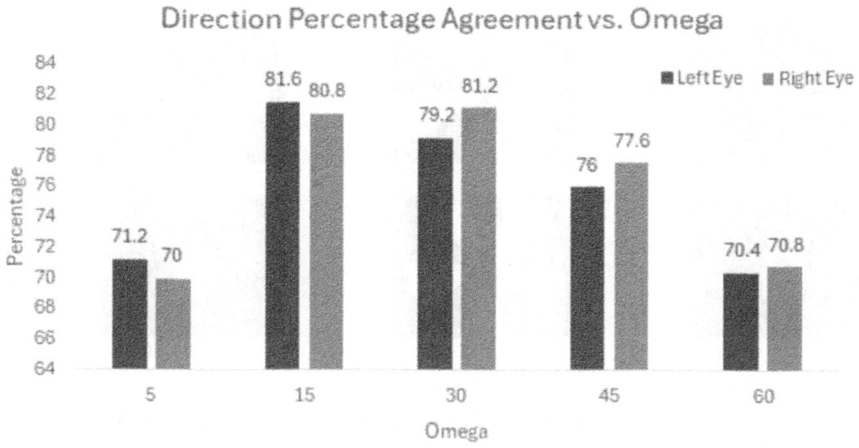

Direction Percentage Agreement vs. Omega

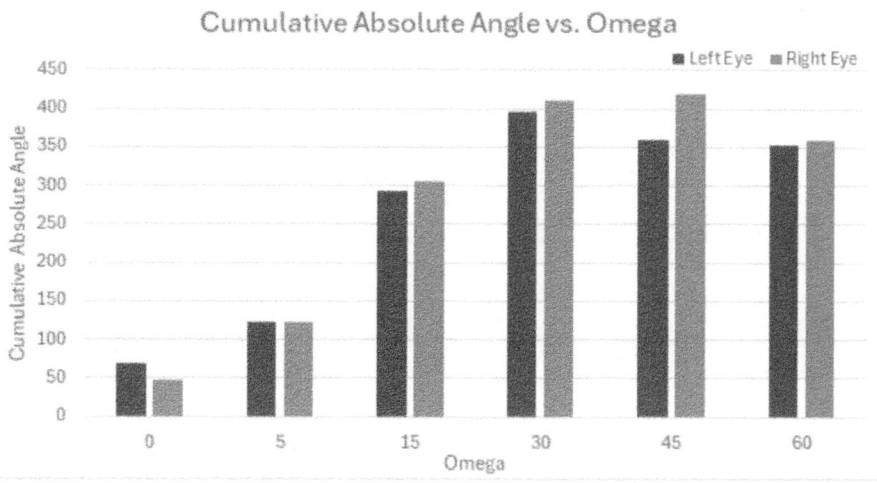

Fig. 3. Left and right eye agreement response for a single Zebrafish larva at varying direction and ω. Eye agreement percentage represents the percentage of time that the eye is rotating at the same direction as the stimuli. Note that this should not be 100% as larvae eye can't rotate 360°

Cumulative Absolute Angle vs. Omega

Fig. 4. Absolute cumulative eye angle of left and right eye compared to stimuli speed ω was done to display that larvae response is due to our visual stimuli system. $\omega = 0$ represents no visual stimuli present.

Fig. 5. Larvae in the loop line following real time view. A larvae with its left eye being tracked superimposed on top of the visual stimuli its receiving (left) and the robot car being controlled by the Zebrafish larva (right). The change in left eye angle is checked with a threshold in order to send a move signal (left if $|\theta| <$ threshold, right if $|\theta| >$ threshold, and forward if within threshold) A camera in front of the robot car sends the location of where it last saw the yellow line to the visual stimuli system adjusting direction/display respectively in order to direct the larva's eye to back to the direction of the yellow line. Note that ω is kept constant throughout the driving trial. (Color figure online)

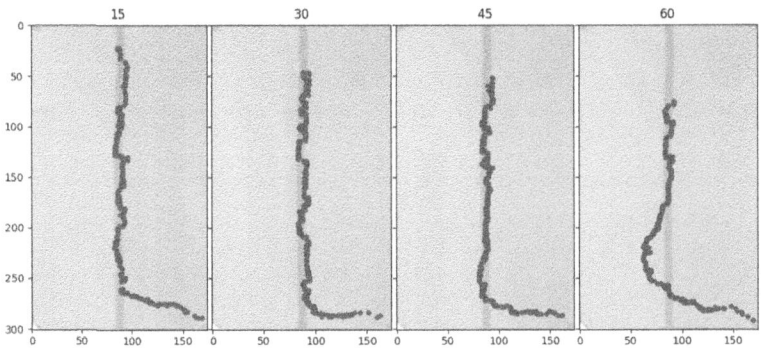

Fig. 6. Pathway traces of the Zebrafish driven car at different ω. The top number on the plots represents ω in degrees/sec and each plot represents a trial with a duration of 45 s. Axis are in terms of pixels. The robot car is started initially at the bottom right

4   Discussion

4.1   Novel Larvae Fixation Method

The larvae fixation method introduced in this work succeeded in keeping larvae in place to run cumulative visual experiments up to several minutes long. Visual experiments can elicit startle responses, which were observed in some trials, still our device was able to keep the larvae fixed and within the region of interest. For the use case in this paper, this device made trials significantly more efficient as minor decoupling of a larvae and the device can be tolerated but may be inappropriate for other cases where slight movements are not tolerable.

4.2 Mechanism of Visual Stimuli

The mechanism behind optokinetic stimuli projected from below the larvae was not a focus of this project. We posit that it may be due to the fish responding to the visual stimuli below it as in optomotor response setups. Alternatively, it may be due to the refraction of light across various interface mediums that are causing a frontal-lateral projection to the larvae. It may also be a combination of the two mentioned theories. Regardless, optokinetic response is clearly present from the projection of the stimuli below the larvae as seen in Fig. 2 as the eye angle response agrees with the stimuli direction and is sporadic or not present when the stimuli is either not displayed or paused.

4.3 Movement Thresholds

Individual larvae display variation in OKR sensitivity. As such, the movement threshold utilized for an OKR sensitive larva was not sufficient for a larva with less OKR sensitivity. Future work should identify this threshold and compare the driving of larvae with varying OKR sensitivity. Variation in OKR sensitivity may be due to the below ventral projection of visual stimuli as discussed above. Another explanation may be due to slight misalignment's between larva, fixation device, and microscope. Since there is a range of tolerances depending on larvae size and hydration of the agarose, slight dorsal misalignment's were noticed in some trials. However, there is also possibility that these OKR sensitivities observed through this system may be an aspect of the Zebrafish larvae not investigated before.

4.4 Future Work

We emphasize that the work presented here is a fundamental step towards developing a Zebrafish Brain-Machine Interface. In order to map the brain of an organism through high throughput inputs, we require a way to simultaneously stimulate and record the larvae. In addition to this, we have to keep the larvae in place without interfering with the input stimuli and output responses. Although the current output responses we utilize in this work are not explicitly neural signals, we demonstrate the potential of our system to visually stimulate the larvae which we aim to map to neural activity.

Further characterization besides ω will be explored in the future. Visual parameters such as the spacing between gratings, number of gratings, and distance of gratings from the larvae may affect the response. As mentioned in the OKR section of methodology, the visual parameters were tuned manually based on reactivity of the specific larvae. Whether there exists relationships between these parameters and the larvae will be analyzed in detail in a future paper.

Work is planned to further explore the novel larvae fixation method described in this short paper. Although the overarching concept was provided, in depth discussion was not included here as current work is ongoing to characterize fixation parameters.

5   Conclusion

This work displays that Zebrafish larvae can be utilized as controllers to simple systems like line following robots. Further experimentation is required to elucidate system relationships, however, with coarse parameter settings (i.e. arbitrary setting of thresholds) promising results can be gained. Furthermore, we briefly showcased our novel, fast, and efficient technique for fixing a larvae in place with the trade-off that startled larvae may get slightly misaligned.

Acknowledgement. This work was supported by the National Science Foundation [Neuron-to-Neuron Interface: Optically Connected Neurons Between the Brains of Two Zebrafish. Grant#: 2309589].

Disclosure of Interests. The authors have no competing interests to declare that are relevant to the content of this article.

References

1. Stewart, A.M., Kalueff, A.V.: Developing better and more valid animal models of brain disorders. Behav. Brain Res. **276**, 28–31 (2015)
2. Razali, K., et al.: The promise of the Zebrafish model for Parkinson's disease: today's science and tomorrow's treatment. Front. Genet. **12**, (2021)
3. Randlett, O., et al.: Whole-brain activity mapping onto a zebrafish brain atlas. Nat. Methods **12**(11), 1039–1046 (2015)
4. Best, J.D., Alderton, W.K.: Zebrafish: an in vivo model for the study of neurological diseases. Neuropsychiatr. Dis. Treat. **4**(3), 567–576 (2008)
5. Simmich, J., Staykov, E., Scott, E.: Chapter 8 - Zebrafish as an appealing model for optogenetic studies. In: Knöpfel, T., Boyden, E.S. (eds.) Progress in Brain Research in Optogenetics: Tools for Controlling and Monitoring Neuronal Activity, vol. 196, pp. 145–162. Elsevier (2012)
6. Brockerhoff, S.E., et al.: A behavioral screen for isolating zebrafish mutants with visual system defects. Proc. Natl. Acad. Sci. **92**, 10545–10549 (1995)
7. Cameron, D.J., et al.: The optokinetic response as a quantitative measure of visual acuity in Zebrafish. J. Vis. Exp. **80**, 50832 (2013)
8. Huang, M.Y.-Y., Neuhauss, S.: The optokinetic response in zebrafish and its applications. Front. Biosci. **13**, 1899–916 (2008)
9. Benard, E., et al.: Infection of zebrafish embryos with intracellular bacterial pathogens. J. Vis. Exp. 61, (2012)
10. Copper, J.E., et al.: Comparative analysis of fixation and embedding techniques for optimized histological preparation of zebrafish. Comp. Biochem. Physiol. C Toxicol. Pharmacol. **208**, 38–46 (2018)
11. Rodwell, V., et al.: Zebrafish optokinetic reflex: minimal reporting guidelines and recommendations. Biology (Basel) **13**, 4 (2023)

Biomechanics

Passive Stability of Stance is Determined by the Relationship Between Natural Frequency and Walking Frequency

Shane Riddle[1]($\boxtimes$)(ID), Gregory Sutton[2](ID), Victoria A. Webster-Wood[3](ID),
Hillel J. Chiel[4](ID), and Roger D. Quinn[1](ID)

[1] Department of Mechanical and Aerospace Engineering, Case Western Reserve
University, Cleveland, OH 44106, USA
shane.riddle@case.edu
[2] School of Life Sciences, University of Lincoln (UK), LN6, 7TS, UK
[3] Department of Mechanical Engineering, Carnegie Mellon University, Pittsburgh,
PA 15213, USA
[4] Department of Biology, Case Western Reserve University,
Cleveland, OH 44106, USA

Abstract. The passive dynamics of stance can explain why large animals, like horses and humans, require neuromuscular activity to maintain stance whereas smaller animals like cockroaches do not [20]. The dynamic properties that govern an animal's movement, like inertia, stiffness, and damping, are dictated by its size, scaling with its length [28]. The natural frequency of an animal's limb in stance can be predicted using its stiffness to inertia ratio, which scales inversely with length. We theorize that the passive mechanics of smaller animal limbs, with higher resonant frequencies than walking cycle frequencies, restore limb position quickly enough that neuromuscular intervention is not needed to correct perturbations during stance. Larger animals, however, require muscle activation since their mechanics depend more on inertia and are less dominated by viscoelastic effects, leading to a lower natural frequency.

Keywords: Scaling · Stance · Passive Stability · Resonant Frequency.

1 Introduction

Regardless of size, the movements of all legged animals are governed by the same forces: inertia, gravity, stiffness, and damping. Scale, however, affects which of these influences locomotion dynamics the most. Recent studies suggest that locomotion behaviors can be split into three categories (kinetic, viscous, and quasi-static) based on limb length and walking cycle period [28]. Sutton et al. state that the differences in each behavior manifest in the phase shift between

This work was supported by NSF DBI 2015317 as part of the NSF/CIHR/DFG/FRQ/UKRI-MRC Next Generation Networks for Neuroscience Program a joint's actuation and its displacement. A joint's rotational position (θ) can be described using a sinusoid while its velocity ($\dot{\theta}$) and acceleration ($\ddot{\theta}$) are the first and second time derivatives of its position. Each time derivative of a sinusoid shifts behavior 90° further out of phase. This means the actuation of a viscous system, largely dominated by velocity-dependent effects like damping, is 90° out of phase from joint motion. Similarly, a kinetic system, dominated by acceleration effects like inertia, is 180° out of phase. How do we categorize animals into these three regions?

An animal's size is the biggest contributing factor to its dynamic behavior. Because of the square-cube law, the mass of a given animal scales in accordance with its length cubed. At the same time, the linear stiffness and damping of an animal's joint muscles scale proportionally to its length [28]. This means the ratio of damping and stiffness to inertia is high for smaller animals and low for larger animals. As a consequence, the limbs of small creatures, like insects, are largely dominated by viscous and elastic forces, whereas the limbs of larger creatures like humans and horses are dominated by kinetic forces. The ratio of stiffness to inertia determines the natural frequency (Eq. (1)).

$$\omega_{\mathrm{n}} = \sqrt{\frac{k}{m}} \qquad (1)$$

Given how mass (m) and stiffness (k) scale with size, the natural frequency (ω_{n}) will be higher for smaller animals and lower for larger animals.

When a non-periodic perturbation is applied to a passive dynamic system, it oscillates at its natural frequency. Animals, however, are not passive systems since they are capable of generating torques about their joints using their muscles. Many investigators have studied how animal locomotion and stance stability are affected by perturbations *in vivo* and in simulation [2,5,23,26,29,30]. A prevalent focus of these studies is how the nervous system controls the muscles to perform corrective actions accounting for perturbations. Bingham et al., for example, discuss that while a wider stance is commonly accepted as more stable for humans, this is actually due to the mechanical advantage wider stances offer neuromuscular control for torque generation as opposed to inherent mechanical stability [2]. On the other end of the spectrum, Jindrich et al. have shown that insects, like cockroaches, are passively stable; they do not need any neuromuscular interference to remain standing [20].

In this paper, we explore the interplay between animal size and passive stability in stance. We theorize that the need for corrective neuromuscular interference depends on the difference between an animal system's natural frequency and the frequency of its locomotion cycle. From literature, it is known that walking cycle frequency tends to scale inversely with animal size [3,10,11,15,16,18,19,34] and we have established that the same is true for animal natural frequencies while in stance. In particular, we expect walking frequencies to scale with $\frac{1}{\mathrm{length}^{0.35}}$, per Hooper 2012 [17], while resonant frequencies should scale with $\frac{1}{\mathrm{length}}$ per Eq. (1) and Sutton et al. 2023 [28]. The different scaling coefficients for these two values mean that animals of different sizes have different relationships between resonant frequency and walking frequency.

We believe that the point at which natural frequency is overtaken by walking cycle frequency is when neuromuscular intervention is required to stabilize the system: the passive mechanics of the limb will restore limb position at the limb's natural resonant frequency, and if this frequency is very high, as it is in small insects, the speed of this reaction can be sufficiently fast that the nervous system will have no need to add additional torque. This would explain why larger animals require muscle activation to remain standing while smaller insects can do so passively [20]. Unlike cockroaches and fruit flies, kinetic force dominated animals on the scale of horses and humans have such low stiffness and damping compared to their mass that they cannot recover passively within one period of their walking cycle. This means they are liable to become unstable and potentially fall over during the walking cycle when perturbed unless they use their muscles to provide active stabilization.

2   Methods

To test this theory, we first constructed a mathematical inverted pendulum model of a leg in stance. We then used this to guide our modification of the 4-bar mechanism presented by Bingham et al., which mimics the standing position of a human [2]. This model is scalable so that we can import the mass and length of an animal to obtain an isometrically scaled human stance analog for that animal's size.

2.1   Inverted Pendulum

One of the simplest ways to represent the dynamics of a leg in stance is with an inverted pendulum spring-mass-damper system with the point of ground contact fixed via a pin joint. The general equation of motion for a rotational system, such as this, can be expressed as:

$$T = J\ddot{\theta} + c\dot{\theta} + k\theta \tag{2}$$

where J is inertia, c is rotational damping, and k is rotational stiffness. This study is interested in the leg's passive response when a perturbation is experienced during the stance phase. To this end, we considered the response of the inverted pendulum for an impulse of magnitude A applied at the hip, which can be modeled using the following textbook solution [24], which is based on impulse-momentum:

$$\theta(t) = \frac{A}{\sqrt{kJ}\sqrt{1 - \left(\frac{c}{2J\omega_n}\right)^2}} e^{\left(\frac{-ct}{2J}\right)} \sin\left(\omega_n \sqrt{1 - \left(\frac{c}{2J\omega_n}\right)^2} t\right) \tag{3}$$

The hip was chosen to replicate the force application site of the Stanford Bump'em system, a perturbation apparatus used to analyze human locomotion stability [29].

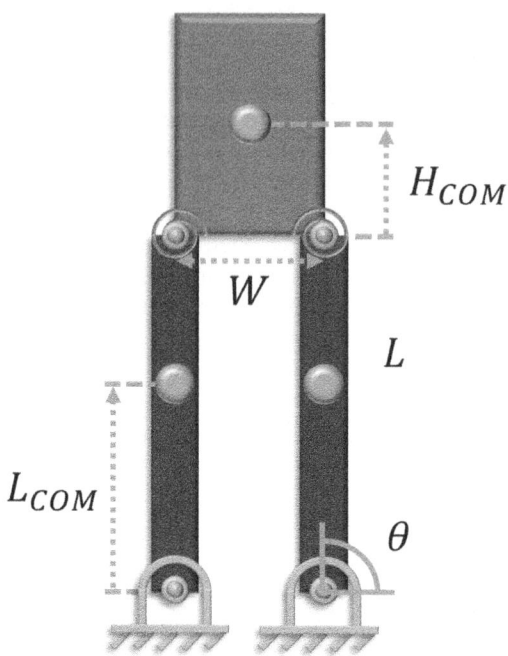

Fig. 1. The 4-bar model, modified from Bingham et al. 2011 [2]. The center of mass for each linkage is denoted by a gray circle and the hip torsion spring and dampers are denoted by the green spirals at the top of each leg. (Colour figure online)

2.2   Modified 4-Bar Model

While useful for analyzing the general motion of a leg, the inverted pendulum relies on the stiffness and damping of a joint between the leg and the ground, a joint that, anatomically speaking, does not exist. To create a more accurate stance model, we developed a dynamic model in Simscape, a Simulink (MAT-LAB) add-on package, similar to the 4-bar model presented in Bingham et al. 2011 [2]. The 4-bar consists of two pin joints at the ankles fixed to the ground and two pin joints at the hips with a leg link running from ankle to hip on each side and a torso link spanning the hip joints (Fig. 1).

The Bingham model implemented motors at the hip joints to study the effects of neuromuscular hip torque feedback on balance. We replaced these with torsional springs and dampers to emulate the passive dynamic properties of a hip joint. The stiffness and damping parameters were tuned in accordance with Sutton et al. [28], where rotational stiffness and damping for each hip can be calculated using leg length as:

$$k_{\mathrm{r}} = \frac{n}{2} k_0 s^2 L^3 \tag{4}$$

$$c_{\mathrm{r}} = \frac{n}{2} c_0 s^2 L^3 \tag{5}$$

where k_0 ($12 \cdot 10^3 \frac{N}{m^2}$, [18, 27]) and c_0 ($1.31 \cdot 10^3 \frac{Ns}{m^2}$, [7, 13, 27, 31, 35]) are empirically determined proportionality constants and s ($10^{-1.5}$, [6, 9, 12, 32]) is a unitless lever arm coefficient [28]. To allow this model to approximate stance for 6-legged insects, 4-legged mammals, and 2-legged humans, we lump the joint and leg properties of ipsilateral limbs. This means that each leg of the model actually represents half the number of legs (n) of the given animal. For a human with two legs, each hip model only contains one leg's worth of stiffness ($\frac{n}{2} = 1$), but for a fruit fly with six legs, each hip model has three legs worth of stiffness ($\frac{n}{2} = 3$). This simplification was made so that the effect of scale for the range of models tested could be explored using a single, approximate model.

Mass, inertia, and center of mass (COM) parameters were kept roughly the same as the Bingham model except for the distribution of mass between the legs (m_{leg}) and the trunk (m_{trunk}). The portion of the mass in all of the legs combined was changed from 32% of the total body mass to 25%, that of a rat [33]. Larger animals have a greater proportion of their mass in their legs compared to smaller species, like insects. To accommodate this, and generalize the model for the variety of animals analyzed, the rat mass distribution was used as it lies in the middle of the length scale of the species included in this study. The equations for all of the model parameters can be found in Table 1. Importantly, all of these parameters can be calculated with just two properties: effective leg length (L) and total body mass (m_{tot}). Both of these are somewhat commonly reported data points, allowing us to test this model for a wide variety of animals.

Table 1. The calculations for the parameters of the 4-bar model, using only body mass (m_{tot}) and leg length (L).

Model Parameter	Calculation
Leg Length [m]	L - From Literature
Total Body Mass [kg]	m_{tot} - From Literature
Total Body Length [m]	$L_{\text{tot}} = \frac{L}{0.530}$
Leg Mass [kg]	$m_{\text{leg}} = 0.125 * m_{\text{tot}}$
Leg Inertia about COM [kg m^2]	$I_{\text{leg}} = 0.030 * m_{\text{tot}} * L_{\text{tot}}$
Leg COM from ankle [m]	$L_{\text{COM}} = 0.293 * L_{\text{tot}}$
Trunk Mass [kg]	$m_{\text{trunk}} = 0.75 * m_{\text{tot}}$
Trunk Inertia about COM [kg m^2]	$I_{\text{leg}} = 0.020 * m_{\text{tot}} * L_{\text{tot}}$
Trunk COM from hip [m]	$H_{\text{COM}} = 0.108 * L_{\text{tot}}$
Hip Width [m]	$W = 0.134 * L_{\text{tot}}$

As for the perturbation, a linear force impulse was applied at the left hip of the 4-bar linkage to emulate the Stanford Bump'em, which applies sudden perturbation to subjects about the hip [29]. An impulse can be expressed in units of Force $\cdot$ time, which can be expanded to mass $\cdot$ acceleration $\cdot$ time, which has units of $\frac{\text{length}^4}{\text{time}}$. To accommodate this, the magnitude of the pulse was scaled with L^4. As the Bump'em can apply up to 200 N of force for a human, the scaled force magnitude for other species was calculated as follows:

$$F_{\text{impulse}} = 200(\frac{L}{L_{\text{human}}})^4\text{N} \tag{6}$$

Since the leg length of an average human is roughly 1 m this reduces to $200L^4\text{N}$, where L is the animal leg length given in meters.

2.3   Animal Data

Animal masses and leg lengths were gathered from the literature and compiled in Table 2. The test animals included: horse, human, cat, rat, mouse, cockroach, and fruit fly. These cover leg lengths from 5 mm to 1.5 m, a range of 4 orders of magnitude. A table containing the walking cycle period of each animal was found in the supplementary documentation of Sutton et al. 2023 [28]. These values were converted to walking cycle frequency, with units $[\frac{\text{rad}}{\text{s}}]$, via the relationship $\omega = \frac{2\pi}{T}$ and recompiled into Table 2 here.

Table 2. The masses, lengths, and walking cycle frequencies gathered from the literature for the species of interest in this paper.

Species	Leg Length [m]	Body Mass [kg]	Walking Frequency $[\frac{\text{rad}}{\text{s}}]$	Refs
Horse	$1.5 \cdot 10^0$	$5.0 \cdot 10^2$	$7.1 \cdot 10^0$	[16, 18]
Human	$1.0 \cdot 10^0$	$7.0 \cdot 10^1$	$1.3 \cdot 10^1$	[2, 11]
Cat	$2.5 \cdot 10^{-1}$	$4.5 \cdot 10^0$	$2.5 \cdot 10^1$	[1, 10]
Rat	$5.0 \cdot 10^{-2}$	$5.0 \cdot 10^{-1}$	$3.1 \cdot 10^1$	[8, 19]
Mouse	$2.0 \cdot 10^{-2}$	$2.6 \cdot 10^{-2}$	$6.3 \cdot 10^1$	[4, 15]
Cockroach	$8.0 \cdot 10^{-3}$	$1.0 \cdot 10^{-3}$	$1.4 \cdot 10^2$	[3, 20]
Fruit Fly	$5.0 \cdot 10^{-4}$	$1.0 \cdot 10^{-7}$	$1.3 \cdot 10^2$	[25, 34]

3   Results

To find the natural frequency (ω_n) of the 4-bar system for each animal, the perturbation simulation was run with each set of parameters neglecting damping terms. The position of the torso center of mass was recorded at each timestep and the peak-to-peak times of the resulting oscillations were calculated, giving us the period of oscillation (T) for the system. This was then converted into natural frequency, with units $[\frac{\text{rad}}{\text{s}}]$, the same way the walking frequencies were calculated. These frequencies, along with the walking cycle frequencies, were plotted against leg length in Fig. 2. This shows that the natural frequency scales inversely with animal leg length.

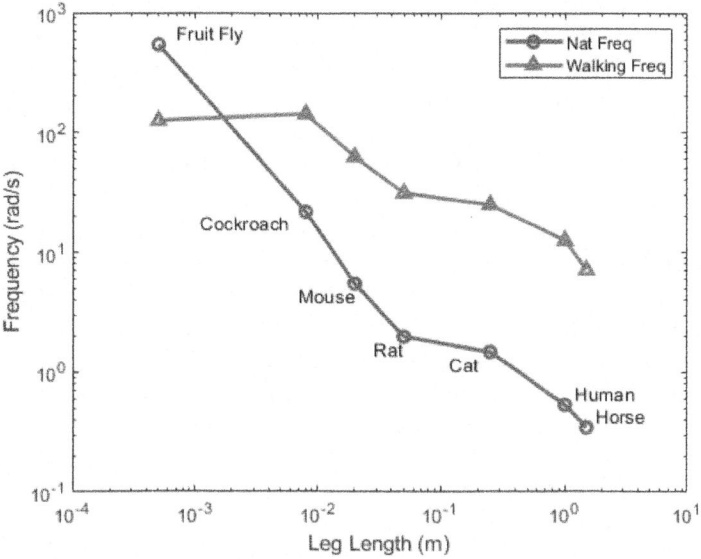

Fig. 2. The natural frequencies of the 4-bar model (blue) and walking cycle frequencies from literature (orange), as they scale with animal mass and leg length. (Colour figure online)

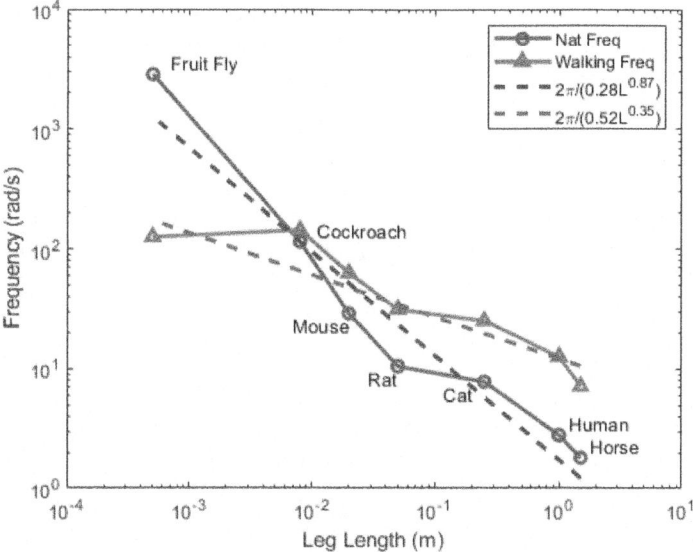

Fig. 3. Corrected natural frequencies of the 4-bar model (blue) and walking cycle frequencies (orange). Relation between walking frequency and length from Hooper 2012 [17] (red dashed line), and the linear regression of our data (blue dashed line) are also plotted. (Colour figure online)

From these results, it is apparent that the natural frequencies gathered from the model are smaller than the walking cycle frequencies for every animal, except for the fruit fly. This was unexpected given that we know, at the very least, that cockroaches possess passively stable stances [20]. To understand this discrepancy, we compared the stiffness of our model cockroach to that of a live cockroach. Jindrich et al. found the linear stiffness of a cockroach to be 16 $\frac{N}{m}$ [20] while our model parameters calculate a torsional stiffness of $5.1 \cdot 10^{-4} \frac{Nm}{rad}$ for a single hip joint. We know from Sutton et al. that linear stiffness scales with L while rotational stiffness scales with L^3, so we divide our rotational stiffness by L^2 ($L = 8$ mm), giving us an equivalent linear stiffness of 0.29 $\frac{N}{m}$ per modeled hip, or 0.58 $\frac{N}{m}$ total. This means our 4-bar model may underestimate hip joint stiffness for the cockroach by a factor of 28.

To assess if this underestimation is responsible for the discrepancy between natural and walking frequency, we scaled all of our hip stiffnesses by a factor of 28 and re-ran the simulations. The results in Fig. 3 show that the lines now cross as expected, with the cockroach having a higher natural frequency than walking cycle frequency with the inflection point near the mouse scale (10^{-2} m). Also plotted in Fig. 3 is the trendline corresponding to walking frequency as a function of length, presented in Hooper 2012 [17]. Hooper states that the walking frequency of an animal scales with $\frac{1}{L^{0.35}}$, which agrees with the frequencies we found in the literature. While all animals are capable of a range of walking speeds, we considered only the maximum walking speeds reported in the literature for this analysis, as these closely aligned with the Hooper trendline. To estimate how our model's natural frequencies scaled with leg length, we performed a linear regression on the log-scaled data. This gave us Eq. (7) with a fraction of variance explained of $R^2 = 0.95$.

$$\omega_\mathrm{n} = \frac{2\pi}{0.28L^{0.87}} \tag{7}$$

Equation (7) suggests that the natural frequency of our model scales with $\frac{1}{L^{0.87}}$. This deviates from the $\frac{1}{L}$ scaling we predicted based on Eq. (1) and Sutton et al. 2023 [28].

4   Discussion

To understand why the resonant frequency of our model does not scale as predicted, we consider the equation for the natural frequency of a rotational system:

$$\omega_\mathrm{n} = \sqrt{\frac{k_\mathrm{r}}{J}} \tag{8}$$

where torsional stiffness k_r and inertia J are expected to scale with L^3 and L^5 respectively [28]. We deduced that if the natural frequency was not scaling as expected, it was because at least one of these model properties was not scaling as expected. To test this, we reintroduced damping to the model and ran the simulations again. This time, we used a constant force, scaled with L^4 as before, applied at the same location as the impulse, and recorded the steady state angular displacement of the system from rest with respect to the ankle $\Delta\theta$. The equation for the moment generated by a torsion spring is:

$$M = k_{\mathrm{r}} \cdot \Delta\theta \tag{9}$$

so, to find the stiffness of the whole model k_{r} we took the applied force multiplied by the leg length squared, to calculate the applied moment M, and divided by the recorded $\Delta\theta$. We then ran a linear regression on the log-scaled stiffnesses and found that the measured k_{r} scales with $L^{2.9}$, which is reasonably close to the expected L^3 scaling.

With stiffness scaling as expected, the discrepancy must lie in the inertia. Breaking J down further, we see it is not actually an independent variable, but rather it is proportional to mass $\cdot$ length^2. Since leg length is the variable by which we scale our model, it did not make sense to run a linear regression on this parameter. The body masses, however, were empirically determined, not calculated with L. We ran a linear regression on the log-scaled body masses and found that the values from the literature scaled with $L^{2.64}$, rather than L^3, meaning the total inertia of the model scales with $L^{4.64}$. Substituting this scaling and our findings from the stiffness regression into Eq. (8), we find a natural frequency that scales with $\frac{1}{L^{0.87}}$, exactly what we see from the original linear regression run on the measured natural frequencies of the model. This confirms that our model scaling unexpectedly is due to the true mass of the species we tested scaling with $L^{2.64}$, not L^3.

What might account for the scaling difference? The notion that mass scales with length cubed was originally derived under the assumption that animals are roughly cylindrical in shape [14,22], which works well for larger animals. However, smaller animals tend to take on a much more crouched posture, which would affect the distribution of body mass and leg geometry [21]. This very different posture could affect the mass-to-leg length relationship and consequently lead it to deviate from the isometric L^3 scaling.

Frequency scaling aside, our model, before correction, may also underestimate stiffness by a factor of 28. There may be multiple reasons for this, but two primary causes are likely our model's inability to account for significant anatomical differences between species and musculature differences between the joints in a given leg. The 4-bar mechanism is modeled after a human standing with feet hip-width apart and isometrically scaled to the size of each animal. This means we do not account for changes in stance width, body center of mass location, or species-specific mass distributions, among other factors. It makes sense that stiffness for our cockroach-scaled model would be underestimated since cockroaches have a splayed-out stance, which should theoretically be more stable than the hip-width leg stance modeled. Additionally, we considered only rotational hip stiffnesses that apply torques linearly proportional to the angular displacement. However, passive forces in biological muscles exhibit large transient effects and viscoelasticity, which may need to be reflected in future model interactions. Finally, joint stiffness data reported in literature and used in this work, typically comes from the knee joint, which for many species has less musculature than the hip joint. Cross sections of a cockroach coxa and femur, provided by Sasha Zill (personal communication), show there is roughly seven times more cross-sectional area in the muscles controlling the hip than the knee. Since joint stiffness is correlated to muscle size, this would further explain why our model underestimates stiffness. These findings highlight the importance of considering stance configuration, posture, biological material properties, and leg joint anatomy in future modeling efforts.

5   Conclusions and Future Work

In this work, we explored the relationship between an animal's natural frequency during stance and its passive stability. We theorized that when a creature's undamped natural frequency is larger than its walking cycle frequency, it has a passively stable stance. As a consequence, in response to perturbations, large animals, such as humans, require nervous system activity to remain stable [2], whereas small animals, such as cockroaches, maintain stability without additional neural activity [20]. Our initial model implementation, assuming mass scaled with L^3 and isometrically scaling the human-inspired four-bar mechanism, resulted in deviations from this prediction. However, further analysis found that this approach underestimated hip stiffness compared to reported values in the literature. Correcting this underestimation and re-running the simulations produced results supporting this claim. With the correction, when scaled for both cockroaches and fruit flies, the model exhibits higher natural frequencies than walking frequencies, while the opposite is true for larger animals like horses and humans. This supports the theory that, in small animals, the passive mechanics of the joint are fast enough to dampen perturbation without the aid of neuromuscular feedback.

While this is a promising result, there are still a few issues with this model that require further investigation. As stated previously, we needed to increase the stiffness of the hip joints by a factor of 28 to get the model stiffness for a cockroach to agree with the stiffness found in the literature [20]. However, we have not yet investigated whether this factor should be constant across all species. It is also possible that the stiffness multiplier may not be so large if we change the model to account for preferred stance widths and limb postures. Wider stances would naturally manifest a greater overall stiffness for the 4-bar mechanism, giving the cockroach model a stiffness closer to that found in the literature. As this is an ongoing project, both of these issues will be explored in future work

Acknowledgements. We would like to thank Dr. Alexander Hunt and Dr. Nicholas Szorcinski for their assistance with simulation troubleshooting and lending us their expertise on legged locomotion behavior for a large variety of animals. We would also like to thank Dr. Sasha Zill for sharing cross sections of a cockroach leg, which we used to verify the difference in musculature and stiffness for the knee and hip joints.

References

1. Audet, J., et al.: Control of forelimb and hindlimb movements and their coordination during quadrupedal locomotion across speeds in adult spinal cats. J. Neurotrauma **39**(15–16), 1113–1131 (2022). https://doi.org/10.1089/neu.2022.0042
2. Bingham, J.T., Choi, J.T., Ting, L.H.: Stability in a frontal plane model of balance requires coupled changes to postural configuration and neural feedback control. J. Neurophysiol. **106**(1), 437–448 (2011). https://doi.org/10.1152/jn.00010.2011
3. Delcomyn, F.: The locomotion of the cockroach Periplaneta Americana. J. Exp. Biol. **54**(2), 443–452 (1971). https://doi.org/10.1242/jeb.54.2.443
4. Demertzis, N., et al.: Effect of olive oil phenolics on lipidemic profile and oxidative stress in mice. Elyns Group - Journal of Food, Nutrition and Dietetics (2018)
5. Deng, K., Szczecinski, N., Arnold, D., Andrada, E., Fischer, M., Quinn, R., Hunt, A.J.: Neuromechanical model of rat hindlimb walking with two-layer cpgs. Biomimetics **4**(1), (2019). https://doi.org/10.3390/biomimetics4010021
6. Full, R., Ahn, A.: Static forces and moments generated in the insect leg: comparison of a three-dimensional musculo-skeletal computer model with experimental measurements. J. Exp. Biol. **198**, 1285–98 (1995). https://doi.org/10.1242/jeb.198.6.1285
7. Garcia, M., Kuo, A., Peattie, A.M., Wang, P., Full, R.: Damping and size: insights and biological inspiration (2000)
8. Ghasemi, A., Jeddi, S., Kashfi, K.: The laboratory rat: age and body weight matter. EXCLI J **20**, 1431–1445 (2021). https://doi.org/10.17179/excli2021-4072
9. Greene, E.C.: Anatomy of the rat. Trans. Am. Philos. Soc. **27**, iii–370 (1935). https://doi.org/10.2307/1005513
10. Grillner, S.: Locomotion in vertebrates: central mechanisms and reflex interaction. Physiol. Rev. **55**(2), 247–304 (1975). https://doi.org/10.1152/physrev.1975.55.2.247
11. Grillner, S., Halbertsma, J., Nilsson, J., Thorstensson, A.: The adaptation to speed in human locomotion. Brain Res. **165**(1), 177–82 (1979). https://doi.org/10.1016/0006-8993(79)90059-3
12. Guschlbauer, C., Scharstein, H., Buschges, A.: The extensor tibiae muscle of the stick insect: biomechanical properties of an insect walking leg muscle. J. Exp. Biol. **210**(6), 1092–1108 (2007). https://doi.org/10.1242/jeb.02729
13. Hajian, A.Z., Howe, R.D.: Identification of the mechanical impedance at the human finger tip. J. Biomech. Eng. **119**(1), 109–114 (1997). https://doi.org/10.1115/1.2796052
14. Hemmingsen, A.: Energy metabolism as related to body size and respiratory surface, and its evolution. Rep. Steno Meml. Hosp. **13**, 1–110 (1960)
15. Herbin, M., Hackert, R., Gasc, J.P., Renous, S.: Gait parameters of treadmill versus overground locomotion in mouse. Behav. Brain Res. **181**, 173–9 (2007). https://doi.org/10.1016/j.bbr.2007.04.001
16. Hildebrand, M.: Motions of the running cheetah and horse. J. Mammal. **40**(4), 481–495 (1959). https://doi.org/10.2307/1376265

17. Hooper, S.L.: Body size and the neural control of movement. Curr. Biol. **22**(9), R318–R322 (2012). https://doi.org/10.1016/j.cub.2012.02.048

18. Hooper, S.L., Guschlbauer, C., Blümel, M., Rosenbaum, P., Gruhn, M., Akay, T., Büschges, A.: Neural control of unloaded leg posture and of leg swing in stick insect, cockroach, and mouse differs from that in larger animals. J. Neurosci. **29**(13), 4109–19 (2009). https://doi.org/10.1523/JNEUROSCI.5510-08.2009

19. Hruska, R.E., Kennedy, S., Silbergeld, E.K.: Quantitative aspects of normal locomotion in rats. Life Sci. **25**(2), 171–179 (1979). https://doi.org/10.1016/0024-3205(79)90389-8

20. Jindrich, D.L., Full, R.J.: Dynamic stabilization of rapid hexapedal locomotion. J. Exp. Biol. **205**(18), 2803–2823 (2002). https://doi.org/10.1242/jeb.205.18.2803

21. JR, U.: Constraints on muscle performance provide a novel explanation for the scaling of posture in terrestrial animals. Biol Lett **9**(4), (2013). https://doi.org/10.1098/rsbl.2013.0414

22. McMahon, T.: Size and shape in biology. Science **179**(4079), 1201–1204 (1973). https://doi.org/10.1126/science.179.4079.1201

23. Merlet, A.N., et al.: Sensory perturbations from hindlimb cutaneous afferents generate coordinated functional responses in all four limbs during locomotion in intact cats. eNeuro **9**(6), (2022). https://doi.org/10.1523/ENEURO.0178-22.2022

24. Rao, S.: Mechanical Vibrations. No. v. 978, nos. 0-212813 in Mechanical Vibrations. Prentice Hall (2011). https://books.google.com/books?id=TOpBswEACAAJ

25. Smith, W., Thomas, J., Liu, J., Li, T., Moran, T.: From fat fruitfly to human obesity. Physiol. Behav. **136**, 15–21 (2014). https://doi.org/10.1016/j.physbeh.2014.01.017

26. Stark, H., Fischer, M.S., Hunt, A., Young, F., Quinn, R., Andrada, E.: A three-dimensional musculoskeletal model of the dog. Sci. Rep. **11**(1), (2021). https://doi.org/10.1038/s41598-021-90058-0

27. Stein, R., Zehr, E., Lebiedowska, M., Popović, D., Scheiner, A., Chizeck, H.: Estimating mechanical parameters of leg segments in individuals with and without physical disabilities. IEEE Trans. Rehabil. Eng. **3**, 201–11 (1996). https://doi.org/10.1109/86.536776

28. Sutton, G.P., Szczecinski, N.S., Quinn, R.D., Chiel, H.J.: Phase shift between joint rotation and actuation reflects dominant forces and predicts muscle activation patterns. PNAS Nexus **2**(10), pgad298 (2023). https://doi.org/10.1093/pnasnexus/pgad298

29. Tan, G.R., Raitor, M., Collins, S.H.: Bump'em: an open-source, bump-emulation system for studying human balance and gait. In: 2020 IEEE International Conference on Robotics and Automation (ICRA), pp. 9093–9099 (2020). https://doi.org/10.1109/ICRA40945.2020.9197105

30. Vasudevan, E.V.L., Hamzey, R.J., Kirk, E.M.: Using a split-belt treadmill to evaluate generalization of human locomotor adaptation. J. Vis. Exp. (126), (2017). https://doi.org/10.3791/55424

31. Weiss, P., Hunter, I., Kearney, R.: Human ankle joint stiffness over the full range of muscle activation levels. J. Biomech. **4**, 539–44 (1988). https://doi.org/10.1016/0021-9290(88)90217-5

32. Williams, S.B., Wilson, A.M., Rhodes, L., Andrews, J., Payne, R.C.: Functional anatomy and muscle moment arms of the pelvic limb of an elite sprinting athlete: the racing greyhound (canis familiaris). J. Anat. **213**(4), 361–372 (2008). https://doi.org/10.1111/j.1469-7580.2008.00961.x

33. Witte, H., Biltzinger, J., Hackert, R., Schilling, N., Schmidt, M., Reich, C., Fischer, M.S.: Torque patterns of the limbs of small therian mammals during locomotion on flat ground. J. Exp. Biol. **205**(9), 1339–1353 (2002). https://doi.org/10.1242/jeb.205.9.1339
34. Wosnitza, A., Bockemühl, T., Dübbert, M., Scholz, H., Büschges, A.: Inter-leg coordination in the control of walking speed in Drosophila. J. Exp. Biol. **216**(3), 480–491 (2013). https://doi.org/10.1242/jeb.078139
35. Zakotnik, J., Matheson, T., Dürr, V.: Co-contraction and passive forces facilitate load compensation of aimed limb movements. J. Neurosci. **26**(19), 4995–5007 (2006). https://doi.org/10.1523/JNEUROSCI.0161-06.2006

A Method to Characterize Rat Hindlimb Mechanics Using Dynamic Perturbations

Zhong Wang[1] , Sam Tran[1], Gil Serrancolí[2] , and Matthew C. Tresch[3,4,5]( )

[1] Department of Neuroscience, Northwestern University, Chicago, IL 60611, USA
[2] Department of Mechanical Engineering, Universitat Politècnica de Catalunya, Barcelona, Spain
[3] Department of Biomedical Engineering, Northwestern University, Evanston, IL, USA
m-tresch@northwestern.edu
[4] Department of Physical Medicine and Rehabilitation, Northwestern University, Chicago, IL, USA
[5] Shirley Ryan AbilityLab, Chicago, IL, USA

Abstract. Biomechanical properties, including elasticity, viscosity, and inertia, determine the forces necessary to produce movements. Understanding motor control strategies used by small animals requires knowledge of these properties and their relative importance in motor control. This study established a technique to dynamically perturb the rat hindlimb to determine hindlimb mechanics across a range of configurations. We used a linear motor with high acceleration and precise position servo control to implement fast transient perturbations. A force/torque transducer was mounted on the motor to record force and torque responses from six degrees of freedom during perturbation. A two-camera motion capture system was set up to reconstruct the 3D hindlimb kinematics. A deeply anesthetized animal was placed on a platform, and the hind paw was attached to the transducer. The limb was translated by the motor through a pseudorandom binary sequence of rapid movements with small displacements (2mm). We then fit a second-order linear model to parameterize the elasticity, viscosity, inertia, and background forces of the perturbed system. We obtained mechanical parameters from 197 hindlimb configurations in 3 rats measured across their workspace. The linear model captured $R^2 = 0.93 \pm 0.02$, 0.95 ± 0.01, and 0.93 ± 0.02 of the dynamic responses from three rats. Parameter values were consistent across repeated trials, demonstrating the reliability of the estimation process. Similarly, analysis of joint kinematics also showed minimal kinematic redundancy of limb joint angles across repeated perturbations. These preliminary results show that this dynamic perturbation platform can reliably characterize the mechanical properties of rat hindlimbs. The hindlimb characteristics measured with these procedures will be critical to understanding the control strategies during locomotion and other behaviors.

Keywords: Limb Mechanics · Limb Configuration · Locomotion

© The Author(s), under exclusive license to Springer Nature Switzerland AG 2025
N. S. Szczecinski et al. (Eds.): Living Machines 2024, LNAI 14930, pp. 452–459, 2025.
https://doi.org/10.1007/978-3-031-72597-5_31

1   Introduction

Understanding the control strategies responsible for complex behavior is one of the fundamental endeavors of many fields, such as neuroscience, robotics, and artificial intelligence. The control strategies used by organisms are adapted to and constrained by the mechanics of the body [1]. The major mechanical forces dominating movement control include inertial, elastic, and viscous forces [2]. For animals such as rats, all three types of forces might play a significant role during behavior, but their relative importance is unclear, as is how they might vary across the range of limb configurations or in different behavioral conditions.

The passive properties of the limb are important for real-world control. Viscoelastic properties of biological systems can maximize kinetic power and enhance movements over motor-driven systems alone [3]. The passive mechanics of the joints are also critical for resisting hyperextension and maintaining joint stability [4]. However, we lack accurate measurements of those passive components for small animals such as rats.

To estimate these mechanical parameters, we established a perturbation platform to evaluate the dynamic responses of rat hindlimbs. We apply small perturbations with minimal disturbance to the limb configuration to obtain stable estimates of limb parameters. The velocity and the acceleration of the perturbations are high enough to excite high-frequency mechanical components such as viscosity and inertia. A second-order linear model was fit to the measured motion and forces of the perturbation to find mechanical parameters.

2   Methodology

2.1   Instrumentation and Surgical Procedures

Perturbation Motor. This platform consists of a body support platform, a linear motor mounted with a compact force and torque transducer, and a two-camera system for motion capture (Fig. 1). We used a 3-phase synchronous brushless motor stage (MKS Instruments, Inc.) which can perform translations with high acceleration and velocity capacity. The maximum acceleration and velocity can reach $20000 \, mm/s^2$ and $500 \, mm/s$. This motor also had a travel range of 200 mm to accommodate a range of configurations. It was driven by a programmable controller that could perform prescribed perturbation sequences. The motor controller exploited a customizable PIDFF (proportion, integral, derivative and feedforward) controller to minimize the following error between the setpoint and actual position.

Force and Torque Transducer. A compact force transducer (mini40, 20 N and 1 Nm range, ATI Industrial Automation) with six degrees of freedom was mounted on the motor stage to measure the interaction forces and torques of the hindlimb during perturbations. An interface plate was mounted on top of the transducer to attach to the animal foot securely with epoxy.

Motion Capture. Two cameras were positioned to estimate 3D limb configurations. We used monochrome industrial cameras with CMOS image sensors of 1.58M effective pixels and a 5-megapixel lens with a focal length of 6mm (The Imaging Source). We

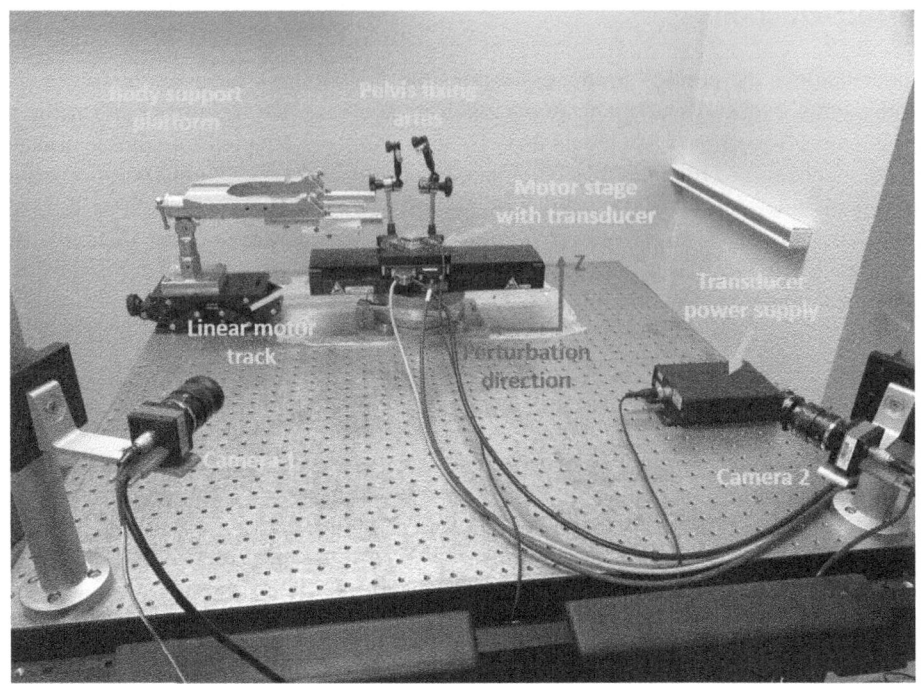

Fig. 1. An overview of the dynamic perturbation platform

captured the hindlimb kinematics with a resolution of 1024×768 pixels at 200 frames per second (FPS).

Animal Surgery Procedures. All animal procedures were approved by the Animal Care Committee of Northwestern University. Female Sprague-Dawley rats (250–350 g) were anesthetized with 3% isoflurane with oxygen supply during the surgery and the perturbation experiments. The body temperature was maintained at 36.5 °C using a warming pad and regularly monitored. The depth of the anesthesia was regularly evaluated by pinch reflex. The animal was first implanted with two orthopedic pins into the rostral and caudal ends of the right pelvis. The animal was then transferred to the body support platform, and the two pins were clamped with fixation arms to hold its right pelvis in position while its left limb was perturbed. The left forefoot was attached to the transducer and the motor stage. The following joint landmarks were labeled to be tracked in videos for kinematics and configurations: pelvis top and bottom, hip, knee, ankle, metatarsal, and toe. After the experiments, the animals were euthanized using Euthasol® (Pentobabital Sodium 390 mg/ml & Phenytoin Sodium 50mg/ml).

Perturbation Protocol. In this study, the passive limb mechanics were characterized without reflexive or active control. The left limb was perturbed, while the right limb was immobilized. To minimally perturb the limb, we used a perturbation magnitude of 2 mm ($\pm$ 1 mm from a neutral position). These fast perturbations are necessary to activate the high-frequency mechanical components such as viscosity and inertia [5].

A pseudorandom binary sequence of forward and backward translations perturbed the hindlimb at one configuration for 40 translations. The limb was then moved by the motor to a new configuration and the sequence repeated. To minimize hysteresis due to stress-relaxation of passive properties, we waited at least 60 s after moving to a new limb position before applying the perturbation sequence.

2.2 Data Acquisition

Data Collection and Synchronization. The kinematics (displacement, velocity, acceleration) of the perturbations were collected from the built-in motor controller interface. The force and torque were transformed from the strain gauge signals and collected using MATLAB. Motion, force, and torque data were synchronized by analog signals and collected at 10000 Hz. Cameras were triggered and synchronized by the analog signals from the motor controller.

Kinematics Analyses. We used the markerless motion capture pipeline DeepLabCut (DLC) to track the body markers on the hindlimb during perturbations [6]. The trained DLC neural network estimated the 2D coordinates for all videos taken by each camera. In addition to the markers on the hindlimb, we also labeled three reference points on the interface plate in order to measure the coordinates of the transducer origin. 2D coordinates from two synchronized cameras were input into the Anipose toolkit to estimate 3D poses [7]. From those triangulated 3D coordinates, we calculated the joint angles of hip, knee and ankle at each time point.

2.3 Model Fitting and Parameter Estimation

We used synchronized displacement and interaction force during pseudorandom binary perturbations to quantify the mechanical parameters. Both signals were fourth-order Butterworth low-pass filtered at 50 Hz.

We fit second-order linear models to parameterize the mechanics. The linear model was as follows:

$$F = m\ddot{x} + c\dot{x} + kx + F_{BG}$$

F stands for force. m, c, k are the identified system inertia, viscosity and elasticity, x is the displacement, and $\dot{x}$, $\ddot{x}$ are its first and second derivatives velocity and acceleration. F_{BG} is the system background force. We used R^2 to evaluate the quality of model fits.

To evaluate model reliability, we quantified the percent of variation between the parameter estimates from repeated trials.

To estimate the interface mechanical properties, we used the perturbation data without the animal attached to parameterize the interface properties (elasticity, viscosity, and inertia) using the linear model. This model captured the variance of the observed force responses (R^2 of 0.9988 ± 0.0004) very well and was dominated by inertia, as expected. Using these parameters, we predicted the forces due to the interface during perturbations with the animal attached and subtracted them from all observed forces in order to obtain the forces specifically due to the animal. We then fitted the displacement and animal-specific force (Fig. 2) using the linear model to parameterize rat hindlimb dynamics.

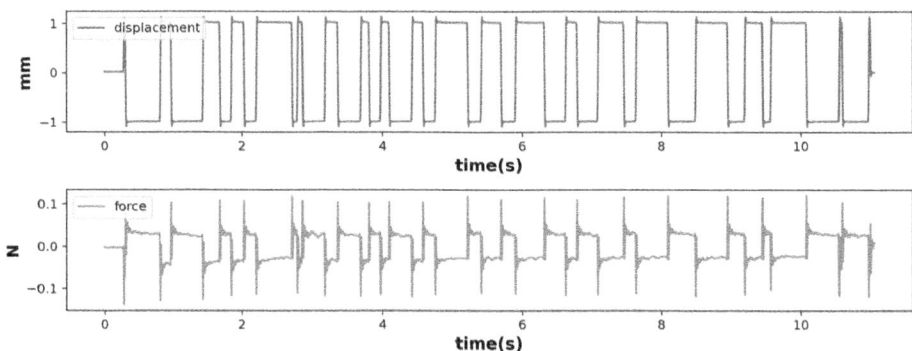

Fig. 2. Displacement and animal-specific force during hindlimb perturbation

3   Results

3.1   Model Fitness and Reliability

To evaluate our experimental setup for estimating rat hindlimb dynamics, we performed perturbations in a total of 197 limb configurations from three rats. A representative trial illustrates that the modeled force captured key features of the measured animal force, especially during the transients (Fig. 3 left). The model score distributions are also shown in Fig. 3. The mean $\pm$ standard deviation of the R^2 scores from all three animals are: Rat1 0.92 ± 0.02; Rat2 0.95 ± 0.01; Rat3 0.93 ± 0.02.

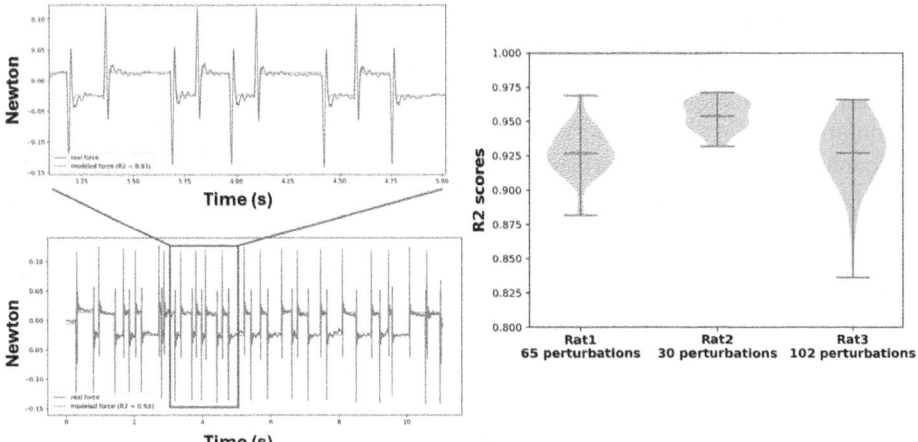

Fig. 3. Comparison between real force and fitted force with one perturbation with $R^2 = 0.93$ (left); Model R^2 scores distributions from three rats (right).

We found that estimates of elasticity, viscosity and inertia were consistent across repeated perturbations. To quantify the differences between repeated measures, we calculated the percentage of variation between the parameters estimated between the two repeated measurements (Fig. 4). Elasticity: $5.4 \pm 3.2\%$; Viscosity: $4.4 \pm 3.4\%$; Inertia: $2.5 \pm 0.8\%$. The variations of each property across repetitions were usually below 10%, indicating the model can generate relatively repeatable system estimates.

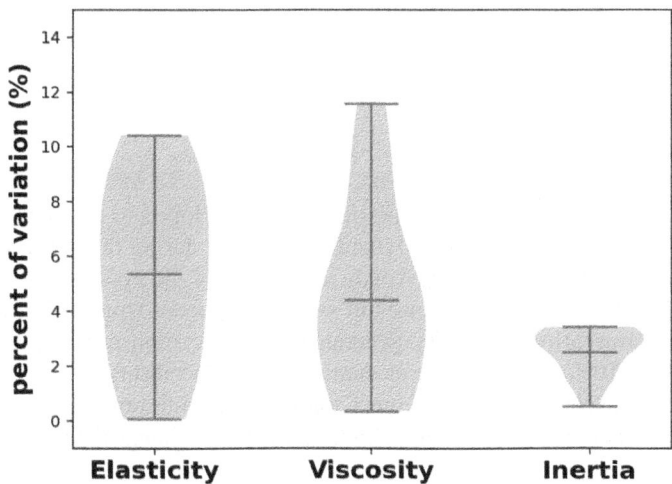

Fig. 4. The percent of variation of all parameters between repeated measures

3.2   Consistency of Limb Configurations Before Perturbations

One issue in these experiments is that, in order to permit free movement of the limb without reaching joint singularities during perturbations, it was necessary to allow internal motion of limb joint angles. As a consequence, there was the potential for variations in limb configuration across perturbation trials, which might lead to poor estimates of limb mechanics. For this purpose, we compared the limb configurations between repeated trials before each perturbation around the same initial configuration (Fig. 5 left), and calculated the joint angle differences between trials across 15 configurations (Fig. 5 right). The between-trial differences in hip angles were $0.46 \pm 0.36°$; knee angles were $0.45 \pm 0.23°$; and ankle angles were $0.32 \pm 0.15°$, suggesting that there were minimal between-trial variations in joint configurations due to kinematic redundancy.

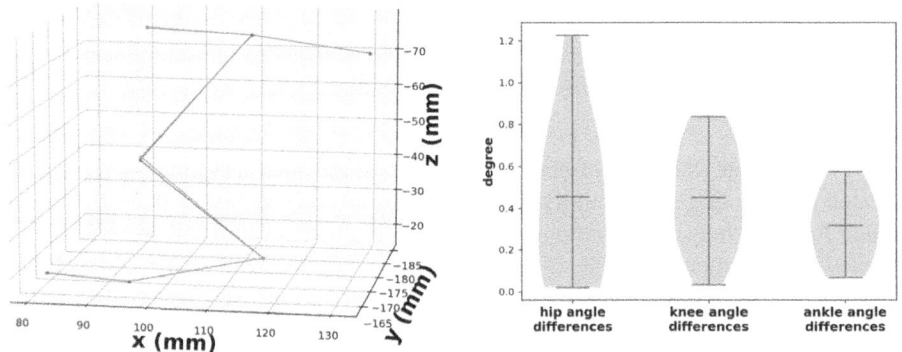

Fig. 5. Configuration comparison between two repeated trials (left). The joint angle differences between repeated trials across configurations.

4   Discussion

In this study, a dynamic perturbation platform was developed to estimate the mechanical properties of rat hindlimbs. The dynamic responses during fast perturbations were used to characterize the elasticity, viscosity and inertia of the system. The model could account for above 90% of the variances in system responses from 197 configurations, and repeated perturbations typically generated similar system parameters with variations of less than 10%. These measures demonstrated the validity and reliability of this technique for measuring the hindlimb mechanics across configurations. In the future, we plan to use this technique to systematically investigate the changes in hindlimb mechanics across the range of configurations used by the animal during different behaviors, such as locomotion. Further, the data obtained from these measurements can be used to evaluate the contribution of passive mechanics to the responses observed during similar perturbations applied to behaving animals. Finally, these parameter estimates and measured data can be used to determine parameters in a detailed musculoskeletal model of the rat hindlimb, choosing muscle model parameters to best match the measured data.

Taken together, these basic measurements of passive rat hindlimb mechanics, along with the platform for performing precise limb perturbations, provide useful information for investigating and interpreting neuromechanical control strategies.

Acknowledgments. We want to acknowledge the generous funding from NSF 2015317 NeuroNex: Communication, Coordination, and Control in Neuromechanical Systems (C3NS) project.

Disclosure of Interests. The authors have no competing interests to declare that are relevant to the content of this article.

References

1. Hogan, N.: Impedance control: an approach to manipulation: part ii—implementation. J Dyn Syst Meas Control. **107**, 8–16 (1985)
2. Sutton, G.P., Szczecinski, N.S., Quinn, R.D., Chiel, H.J.: Phase shift between joint rotation and actuation reflects dominant forces and predicts muscle activation patterns. PNAS Nexus **2** (2023)
3. Ilton, M., et al.: The principles of cascading power limits in small, fast biological and engineered systems. Science **360**, eaao1082 (2018)
4. Villamar, Z., Perreault, E.J., Ludvig, D.: Frontal plane ankle stiffness increases with axial load independent of muscle activity. J. Biomech. **143**, 111282 (2022)
5. Kearney, R.E., Hunter, I.W.: System identification of human joint dynamics. Crit. Rev. Biomed. Eng. **18**, 55–87 (1990)
6. Nath, T., Mathis, A., Chen, A.C., et al.: Using DeepLabCut for 3D markerless pose estimation across species and behaviors. Nat. Protoc. **14**, 2152–2176 (2019)
7. Karashchuk, P., et al.: Anipose: a toolkit for robust markerless 3D pose estimation. Cell Rep. **36**, 109730 (2021)

Author Index

N. S. Szczecinski et al. (Eds.): Living Machines 2024, LNAI 14930, pp. 461–462, 2025.
https://doi.org/10.1007/978-3-031-72597-5

GPSR Compliance

The European Union's (EU) General Product Safety Regulation (GPSR) is a set of rules that requires consumer products to be safe and our obligations to ensure this.

If you have any concerns about our products, you can contact us on ProductSafety@springernature.com

In case Publisher is established outside the EU, the EU authorized representative is:

Springer Nature Customer Service Center GmbH
Europaplatz 3
69115 Heidelberg, Germany

The manufacturer's authorised representative in the EU is Springer
Nature Customer Service Centre GmbH, Europaplatz 3, 69115 Heidelberg,
Germany. If you have any concerns regarding our products, please
contact ProductSafety@springernature.com

Printed and bound by CPI Group (UK) Ltd, Croydon, CR0 4YY

24/04/2026

02096357-0004